THE SECONDARY SCHOOL CURRICULUM

EXPLORATION SERIES IN EDUCATION

Under the Advisory Editorship

of

JOHN GUY FOWLKES

The Secondary School Curriculum

EDWARD A. KRUG

School of Education
University of Wisconsin

HARPER & BROTHERS, PUBLISHERS, NEW YORK

CONTENTS

v

meaning ?]

For many years official secondary school curricula, established by state educational agencies and local boards of education, were devoted practically exclusively to subject matter or content specifications. Stimulated no little by the publication of the *Cardinal Principles of Secondary Education,* the curricular functions of the secondary school have been identified under a wide variety of terms such as curricular objectives, goals, desirable outcomes, aims, learning experiences and/or activities, and so forth. It seems apparent that during the days in which the function of the secondary curriculum was defined in terms of content, it was assumed that application of the content would be made by individuals in terms of real life situations. It also seems that, without desirable attention being given in the schools to specific application of content, this assumption was somewhat fallacious. On the other hand, an exclusive or major emphasis on matter symbolized by life adjustment, challenges to education, and curriculum for contemporary living, to the neglect of the basic content of such areas as mathematics, social studies, and science seems equally, if not even more, undesirable than an emphasis which neglects the daily application of the curriculum.

Many stimulating and valuable volumes have appeared during recent years on the secondary school curriculum. However, careful examination of them leads to the question whether many if not most have stressed a particular point of view, form of organization, or what some call the process of curriculum development as opposed to the subject matter aspects of the matter involved. This book is a scholarly, balanced, and enlightening treatment of both the philosophical and content foundations of what has been, is, and should be offered in the high schools of the United States.

The first four chapters present historical background and an overview of the secondary school program of the past and the present. Chapters 5 through 8 deal with the relationship of the high school and the college, and the organization of the curricular offerings of the high school. Chapters 9 through 20, present a remarkable, thorough, and able treatment of the following specific content fields: English, foreign languages (classical and modern), mathematics, social studies, natural sciences, visual fine arts, industrial arts, physical education, music, business education, homemaking, agriculture. Chapter 21, "The Curriculum Beyond the Classroom Studies," deals with non-classroom activities. The concluding chapter, "Present and Future Possibilities," presents a summary of the entire volume in addition to the imaginative thinking of the author concerning things to come in the American high school.

As students of our secondary institutions know, the author is unusually qualified for the task he has so brilliantly performed. Edward A. Krug is held in high esteem both within and outside the field of professional education and has served as classroom teacher, curriculum consultant in local secondary schools, director of a state curriculum revision program, and for many years, Professor of Education with his attention directed toward courses on secondary school curricula. This treatment of the secondary school curriculum will be of considerable interest and wide benefit to all those concerned with the improvement of our secondary schools.

JOHN GUY FOWLKES

PREFACE

Secondary schooling forms part of one continuous program which begins in the kindergarten or primary grades and for some students extends through the college or graduate school. It is, however, a distinctive part of this program, as are also those periods of schooling which precede and follow it. Each period of schooling deserves separate treatment with regard to the substance and organization of what is taught and learned. This book deals with the content and organization of the instructional program from Grade 7 through Grade 12, and the relationship of this program to the periods of elementary and higher schooling.

Examination of the content and organization of the high school curriculum involves both the classroom studies and the non-classroom services and activities. The classroom studies are identified by 12 major fields of instruction. While it is true that 12 fields do not automatically combine to make a high school program, it is equally true that the curriculum of the high school taken as a whole reflects what these fields are and do. One of the exciting challenges before us is that of incorporating into the high school curriculum the advances in knowledge taking place in our own time. This demands historical perspective, particularly that furnished by the ways in which these fields have developed in our high school programs. It also demands specific consideration of issues in the revision of content field by field. These matters are treated in Chapters 9 through 20.

Concern with the instructional fields does not preclude the possibility of organizing a portion of the classroom studies along lines represented by core classes. Few students of the high school curriculum have ever advocated that core entirely replace organization of the classroom studies by fields or subjects. Nevertheless, core is a different approach to the organization of classroom studies; the issues involved in this approach are important ones and are accordingly examined in Chapter 8.

The procedures of planning and working with the curriculum are for the most part common to all levels of schooling and therefore are not included in this book. Similarly, since this is not a book on methods of teaching, the chapters on the instructional fields do not for the most part deal with methods in the sense of devices for putting across the subject matter. Consideration of method is included in some cases, however, when the way of teaching affects and is affected by objectives other than those of transmitting content as such. This is the case, for example, with laboratory work in the natural sciences, since the use of laboratory method is related directly to the objective of scientific thinking, regardless of what that objective is taken to mean. The major concerns dealt with in the series of chapters on the instructional fields, however, are those of choice and organization of content.

Current developments in the wider use of communication media such as television and in the redefinition of teachers' schedules and responsibilities will be welcomed by all with a generous vision of the future of secondary schooling. Significant developments affecting the instructional staff are described in the booklet, *Images of the Future,* by J. Lloyd Trump, Director, Commission on the Experimental Study of the Utilization of the Staff in the Secondary School of the National Association of Secondary-School Principals. Teachers will be able to accomplish more in the way of effective instruction and at the same time will be freed from many of the frustrating demands on time and energy that have hampered them in the past. Detailed aspects of these developments, however, belong properly to such fields as methods of teaching and school administration and are not included in this book. They do not affect what we should teach in high school, although they undoubtedly mean that we may aim high rather than low with regard to the quantity and quality of the subject matter appropriate to our high school programs.

Some of the data in Chapter 5 on the college-preparatory function were drawn from a study made possible by a grant-in-aid that Professor Clifford S. Liddle and I received from the Graduate School of the University of Wisconsin. Dean Lindley J. Stiles of the University of Wisconsin School of Education arranged our teaching schedules to facilitate work on this project and provided sympathetic criticism and counsel throughout its development. The report was published by the University of Wisconsin School of Education in 1959 under the title, *The College-Preparatory Function in Wisconsin High Schools,* by Edward A. Krug, Clifford S. Liddle, Russell Mosely, and Daniel S. Parkinson.

For critical reading and specific suggestions on portions of the manuscript, I am most grateful to Professors Walter Bjoraker, Merle Borrowman, Julia Dalrymple, Robert Francis, Russell Hosler, Laura Johnson, Frederick Logan, Milton Pella, Robert Petzold, Burr Phillips, John Rothney, John Searles, and Henry Van Engen, all of the University of Wisconsin, and to Professor Delbert Oberteuffer of the Ohio State University and Professor Roy Roberts of the University of Arkansas. I have received substantial help from students over a period of years in Education 141, the course in secondary school curriculum at the University of Wisconsin, and from teachers and administrators of the Nicolet High School, Milwaukee County, Wisconsin, and the Waukesha, Wisconsin, High School, where I enjoyed the opportunity of participating in field activities in curriculum planning while working on this book.

For inspiration, guidance, and criticism going far beyond the usual activities of a series editor, I am, as I have been on previous writings, deeply in debt, professionally and personally, to Professor John Guy Fowlkes of the University of Wisconsin School of Education.

EDWARD A. KRUG

THE SECONDARY SCHOOL CURRICULUM

CHAPTER 1

....

The High School in the United States

The people of the United States have committed themselves to three major ideals of secondary schooling. One is that high schools should be free, with no tuition payments required of those who attend. A second is that high schools should be popular, with programs reflecting the desires and needs of people in local communities. The third is the most striking of all—that high schools should be universal in the sense of accepting practically all youth who can be persuaded to come. In combination these three ideals have made our high school a unique phenomenon in the history of education.

Nevertheless, our high schools once again have become the occasion of controversy and criticism. The very uniqueness of the high school in the United States tends to suggest questions and possible doubts. We are not entirely at ease with innovations that seem to challenge so much past wisdom and experience. This uneasiness has in part been stimulated by increased awareness of what goes on in the rest of the world. We hear reports about secondary schools that appear to teach much more much better than we think ours do. It is difficult not to wonder whether we or the rest of mankind are out of step.

The fact is too that we have lived with the high school long enough to have some of the attraction and romance of newness rubbed off. While it is true that the past half century represents only a small portion of history, it is also true that human beings live their own lives slowly and get exaggerated impressions of contemporary time periods. People are no longer astonished to see half or more of the youth of a community going to high school. We now find ourselves different from other societies without the driving force that motivated those who took part in creating the differences.

In addition, the high school no longer commands the awe that once led to uncritical acceptance of its claims. Many people have been to high school and can speak freely and vigorously about the way it works. This is consistent with our American conviction that schools belong to the people. But it does not make for tranquillity in the field of education. Professional educators and the general public have not yet found ways to sit down and think together about schools, especially about high schools. What we call public participation remains, so far as the high school is concerned, to many professional educators merely an aspect of public relations and to many members of the general public an opportunity to express views without engaging in study.

Also involved is the possible relationship between universal secondary education and what is sometimes referred to as the high school's custodial function. The high school looks like a cold storage locker to keep youth off the general labor market. This may account in part for the apparent listlessness and lack of enthusiasm displayed by many high school students in the face of opportunities which we think should serve as inspiration to effort and achievement. Such a situation is admittedly unacceptable and gives rise to dissatisfactions and uncomfortable stirrings of conscience.

Closely related to and in part an outgrowth of the foregoing difficulties are the disagreements about graduation and the high school diploma. In the past high school graduation symbolized the satisfactory completion of a body of intellectual requirements, represented by the accumulation of units of credit, many of them in specifically designated subjects. To the general public a high school graduate was a reasonably literate person with a good general education in history, mathematics, science, literature, and probably a foreign language. Today, according to the critics, a high school diploma may testify to nothing but the fact that its holder has spent four years in high school. While the credit requirements for high school graduation have not been changed in quantity, they do not in practice mean what they once did. The student has more freedom in selecting units to make up the total necessary for graduation. This may result in the selection of fewer academic subjects. Whether the non-academic subjects are in fact intellectually less demanding than others is still open to debate; nevertheless many people think they are. When mathematics is required for graduation, it may often be taken as general mathematics rather than in the algebra-geometry sequence. Many schools provide sections for low-ability students in English and social studies, the subjects most frequently listed as graduation constants. These tendencies have made it possible for many students to obtain diplomas who at one time would have been unable to do so. Along with this, schools have developed better records, which make it possible to transmit accurate information about individual students to colleges and prospective employers. But in many high schools the diploma itself no longer symbolizes any fixed level or area of accomplishment.

Disagreements about the diploma reflect differing interpretations of the broad ideal of universal secondary schooling. To some this means the opportunity to go to high school regardless of social or economic circumstances. To others it means not only this, but also the right to stay in and to complete high school regardless of intellectual or academic abilities. According to the latter point of view, no young person with good intentions and reasonable industry who is above the mentally retarded level should be denied his chance to go to high school simply because he cannot learn certain specified subjects. Likewise, once he has this right to stay in high school, there seems no reason why after four years of attendance he should be marked off from his fellows and sent packing without the graduation diploma. Obviously, this point of view does not command general acceptance among school people or other members of the general public. Moreover, the disagreement on this point is one that particularly affects the high school. Most people accept without question a very flexible administration of whatever symbol is used for the completion of elementary schooling. Similarly, most people agree that a college diploma should mean definite intellectual accomplishment. But people are by no means agreed where the diploma of the high school is concerned.

Closely allied to the questions about the meaning of the diploma is the sharp increase in discussion about the academically gifted student. This is undoubtedly in part a correction of previous lack of balance and as such is not too remarkable. But it probably reflects something more as well: namely, our fear of being left behind in an advancing world civilization. Nor is this fear solely one of military conquest by other nations. We are anxious to maintain our position in scientific and cultural matters on a peacetime basis as well. To do this means cherishing and nurturing those gifted and creative individuals who make the difference between first-rate and second-rate culture. Logically, there is no reason why high schools cannot do this as well as provide education for others. Nevertheless, it appears to some that the adjustment of the high school to young people of all levels of abilities sets up an environment within which the gifted individual is neglected or lost.

Another source of controversy is the tendency to multiply the activities and functions of the secondary school. The popular character of the high school has led many to regard it not only as a service institution, but as one with service responsibilities to many divergent interests and problems in community and national life. As a result the high school finds itself charged with responsibilities in such matters as delinquency prevention, vocational training, health and safety, conservation, intergroup relations, and the like. Many of the activities carried on in these connections are desirable and worthy; the need is not for an indiscriminate rejection of such responsibilities, but rather for some rational bases for deciding whether given responsibilities are desirable or not. From a practical standpoint, the present situation is rich in possibilities for controversy. People tend to champion their own interests and to criticize those of others. An individual may feel strongly that the high school is trying to do too much and yet strongly join with his like-minded fellows in promoting just one more activity, naturally the most important one, to which the high school should devote its attention.

To say the high school is trying to do too much or too many things implies some notion of what the high school should properly be doing. By its very nature, secondary education has not enjoyed a clear-cut role unique to the ages of its students. The period of secondary schooling lies between two other periods, each of which seems to have something specific to accomplish. This uncertainty about secondary schooling to begin with, coupled with the challenges implied by free, universal, and popular secondary schooling, serves as a constant temptation to create something to fill what looks like a vacuum. Our controversies on this point reflect our efforts as a people to achieve agreements on what this in-between institution should really do.[1]

To all these possible sources of uncertainty about our high schools must be added the matter of cost. Several trends come together to make this a critical point in the development of high schools, probably throughout the rest of this century. One is the increase in population of high school age.[2] To continue even our present degree of universal secondary schooling will demand many more teachers and a great deal of new building. This alone may suggest to many the possible desirability of more selective secondary education. Second are the attempts to raise the standards and the salaries of the teaching profession itself, both of which will be easier to accomplish if we are not at the same time greatly expanding the size of the teaching force. Established teachers may doubt the wisdom of sacrificing their own opportunities for economic and professional improvement in order to maintain our present degree of universal secondary schooling. Third, while schooling is largely the financial responsibility of states and local communities, we have larger and larger fractions of income

[1] This is not unique to American society. "One of the main defects in our system of secondary education has been that it lacks a clear definition of its objectives and scope. It has generally been treated as a mere continuation of primary education or only as a preparation for higher education in colleges and universities." Humayum Kabir, *Education in New India,* Harper & Brothers, 1955, pp. 42–43.

[2] Estimates of enrollments run to 12,000,000 in 1965, about double the number for the early 1950's. Educational Policies Commission, *Manpower and Education,* The National Education Association, 1956, pp. 65–66.

drawn off by national taxation. If this tendency continues, local communities and states will find it difficult to take on an expansion of secondary schools.

THE CURRICULUM—OUR CENTRAL CONCERN

The central concern in the foregoing questions is, of course, the curriculum. On this there is general agreement. The most enthusiastic advocate of universal secondary schooling admits that his point of view makes sense only to the extent that the curriculum of a universal high school makes sense. If the only kind of curriculum that can be offered under universal secondary schooling is a nonsense curriculum, then universal secondary schooling is nonsense, and the fact had better be admitted. The same consideration applies to the curriculum of a selective high school. It also must stand the test of inquiry and criticism.

A curriculum consists of the means used to achieve or carry out given purposes of schooling. There are many such means that might be used. One who proposes a curriculum must decide what to include and what to leave out. Substantial consensus exists on two points: (1) that organized classroom instruction is a necessary part of the curriculum, and (2) that a desirable curriculum includes more than organized classroom instruction alone. On the second point, most people would agree on extraclass activities and on counseling services. Some would add more controversial items, such as school-and-community service projects, school-related work experience, and school camps.

Discussion of the curriculum proceeds on at least three levels: (1) that of the high school in the United States, taken as a general proposition; (2) that of particular schools in particular communities; and (3) that of individual learners. None of these can stand by itself; all three are necessary.

The first of these levels, the general or national one, is necessary for any comprehensive examination of the meaning of high schools in any type of society. Decisions made about particular school programs will inevitably reflect national trends, issues, and points of view. Citizens in every community read articles in national magazines. Important as the idea of the "American high school curriculum" is in discussion, however, it does not exist as uniform and concrete reality. This is particularly true in our country, since we do not establish curriculums in a national ministry or department of education. Furthermore, although education is a function of the various states, we do not even have state-wide uniform patterns in the high school curriculum.

It is in particular schools and communities that the working decisions are made. Here the means are defined in detail. Itemization of the classroom studies includes not only the naming of courses, but also specification of the content and teaching procedures. A similar inventory can be made of extraclass activities. Moreover, those responsible for the curriculum in a given school make subjective interpretations concerning the relative importance of various aspects of the program. But it is unwise to restrict the discussion to the local level. While a high school should serve the community, it never serves an isolated one, nor should its program be built exclusively on local needs.

The third level recognizes the primacy of the individual student. Not all the resources of a given school are applied to every student, nor is any one of them applied in exactly the same way to all students. Each student receives and develops for himself an individualized selection of the various instructional means used in the school. He interacts with these instructional means in a manner unique and personal to himself. This interweaving of the external and objective means of instruction on one hand and the student's individual and internal response to it forms a learning experience. It is through this experience rather than from the external means alone that the student learns. Every student has a curriculum entirely his own, not identical with that of any other student. From this point of view, a given high school has not one curriculum, but hundreds of curriculums. This is a fact, not a quibble. When people talk about the high school curriculum, they are usually talking about the curriculums of their own children or of other young people with whom they are acquainted.

This third and deepest level of discussion taken by itself, however, does not provide a convenient or usable mechanism for the study of the high school curriculum. It would take a substantial volume to record the curriculum of any one student, even if the learning experiences could be identified and described. Curriculum study would break down into an incalculable number of case studies.

All three levels, therefore, are essential to the curriculum discussion. A writer in a national magazine may, for example, call for more study of foreign languages. A given school must decide what foreign languages to offer, for how long, and to which students. A student who takes a foreign language will have his own unique interaction with it to form his own learning experience. Any citizen may encounter the discussion at all three levels. He may read and react to the article in the national magazine. As a member of the high school P.T.A., school board, or study council he may join others in considering whether two, three, or four years of French should be offered. He may view with pride, alarm, or indifference what the study of French is or is not doing to and for his own children in high school at the time.

THE MANY-SIDED ENTERPRISE OF CURRICULUM-MAKING

The shaping of the high school curriculum involves many people and agencies. Some of these, such as state legislatures and school boards, function as official controls. Others are purely unofficial, though not necessarily less important. Members of the teaching profession as well as other citizens work through these official and unofficial agencies and groups.

Our national government exercises only limited functions so far as official controls are concerned. Apart from its work in administering the schools of the territories and the Armed Forces abroad and in regulating specific programs based in part on federal funds, the national government's role is that of offering advice and stimulation.[3] The Office of Education in the Department of Health, Education, and Welfare publishes journals, bulletins, and reports; at times it may engage actively in fostering study and discussion of an idea or proposal as it did, for example, in connection with the movement for life-adjustment education.

[3] Decisions of federal courts, of course, may have considerable influence on conditions within which schools carry on their work.

State-wide agencies of official control include legislatures and departments of public instruction. Legislatures frequently make specific requirements of courses to be included in the high school program, but rarely try to define the curriculum as a whole. State departments are charged with the responsibility for enforcing constitutional and legislative provisions. In addition they influence the curriculum through sponsoring or participating in state-wide programs of curriculum study, through issuing recommended courses of study and other curriculum bulletins, and through the supervisory visits of staff members to local schools.

In a city school system or in a reorganized rural district, the professional leadership group works under the direction of the board of education. Such a group includes the superintendent, the building principals, members of the central office staff, and those classroom teachers on system-wide curriculum committees. In a rural area the local leadership group consists of the county superintendent, county supervising teachers, and county curriculum committees. Working with and through these leadership groups both officially and unofficially are classroom teachers, the general public, and the students. Classroom teachers select what they will try to teach; students decide what they will try to learn. Members of the general public participate through P.T.A.'s, citizens' councils, letters to the editor, and a variety of other formal and informal means. Beyond these we have teachers' professional organizations, accrediting associations, textbook authors and publishers, and college teachers both inside and outside departments of education, plus an array of political, religious, economic, civic, and philanthropic organizations on local, state, and national levels.

In spite of decentralized authority and the sometimes confusing participation of many agencies and groups, United States schools are surprisingly alike in many ways. The extent to which our people have moved freely about the country accounts for this in part, as does also the rapid transmission of ideas through books, newspapers, magazines, radio, television, and films. But these similarities among our high schools reflect something more, namely a body of widely shared beliefs, not only about schools, but also about the rights and responsibilities of individuals and the nature of our society itself. The significance of these beliefs or values is in no way diminished by the difficulties of expressing them in words.

Such common values and beliefs have not on the other hand prevented the making of changes in our high schools and in their curricula. These changes do not necessarily mean, as some have suggested, that the beliefs and values are changing. What looks like a change in values may in many cases be only a change in manners and customs. It is more likely that changes in the curriculum represent new applications of traditional values to changing conditions. As times change, there are differences of opinion about changes that might be made in schools. Such differences of opinion require study of what the traditional beliefs are, thereby providing more explicit bases for resolving current and future issues. We have not repudiated our traditional value of equality of opportunity, but are defining it more fully in relation to questions we face about programs for academically gifted students. Change then does take place, but adherence to common values and a common effort to understand what these values mean tend to make our changes fairly uniform over the country as a whole.

This process of making changes in our schools has taken place many times, in fact almost continuously, throughout our past. Some mistakes have been made, for it is not always easy to tell what changes are consistent with our values even when these values are taken into account. But the process of debate and inquiry has provided opportunity for correcting mistakes. The record of this process defines the United States high school, and it is from our past differences of opinion that the United States high school has emerged and is still emerging. We are still examining our high schools and deciding what to retain, what to drop, and what to add, or perhaps deciding whether or not we seek some new and comprehensive design of what we want our high schools to be. Our traditional values will probably be more clearly defined, but they will serve, as they have in the past, to unify the efforts of school boards, teachers, state departments, state legislatures, textbook writers, parent-teacher associations, and the other groups who study, discuss, and make the high school program.

Bibliography

American Association of School Administrators, Thirty-Sixth Yearbook, *The High School in a Changing World,* The Association, 1958, chap. 1.

Bereday, George Z. F., and Lauwerys, Joseph A. (eds.), *The Secondary School Curriculum,* The Yearbook of Education, 1958, prepared under the auspices of the University of London Institute of Education and Teachers College, Columbia University, World Book Company, 1958, sect. III (pp. 286–365).

Bereday, George Z. F., and Volpicelli, Luigi, *Public Education in America: A New Interpretation of Purpose and Practice,* Harper & Brothers, 1958.

Chase, Francis S., and Anderson, Harold A. (eds.), *The High School in a New Era,* The University of Chicago Press, 1958, pt. 1 (pp. 3–48).

Halverson, Paul M. (ed.), *Frontiers of Secondary Education I,* Syracuse University Press, 1956, and *Frontiers of Secondary Education II,* Syracuse University Press, 1957.

Hollinshead, Byron S., "Is European Education Better?" *The Educational Record,* April, 1958, pp. 89–96.

Korol, Alexander G., *Soviet Education for Science and Technology,* published jointly by The Technology Press of Massachusetts Institute of Technology and John Wiley & Sons, Inc., Chapman & Hall, Ltd., 1958, chaps. 1–4.

Krug, Edward A.; Babcock, Chester D.; Fowlkes, John Guy; and James, H. T., *Administering Curriculum Planning,* Harper & Brothers, 1956, chaps. 1–6.

Richmond, W. Kenneth, *Education in the U.S.A.: A Comparative Study,* Alvin Redman, Ltd., London, 1956.

Romine, Stephen, *Building the High School Curriculum,* The Ronald Press Company, 1954, chaps. 1, 2.

Saylor, J. Galen, and Alexander, William M., *Curriculum Planning for Better Teaching and Learning,* Rinehart & Company, Inc., 1954, chaps. 1, 16.

CHAPTER 2

··

Origins and Development of Our High Schools

Secondary education is a comparatively modern term, one which probably did not come into extensive use until the nineteenth century. Nevertheless, it is customary to refer to many schools of the past as secondary schools, since these schools can be compared and contrasted with high schools of today. Among those that provide such useful historical perspective are the Latin grammar schools of western Europe in the late Middle Ages.

These schools, like our own high schools, prepared some of their students for advanced study in universities and some for immediate careers that did not require university training.[1] The Latin used was medieval Latin, different in some respects from the written language of classical literature, but nonetheless a strong and flexible tool for scholarly discourse and everyday affairs. Objectives of

[1] "The social conditions which led in so many instances to the development of universities out of cathedral schools, as in Paris, or out of private schools, as at Bologna, stimulated the activities of existing grammar schools and led to the development not only of new schools but of whole new classes of schools. Some local preparation had to be given the thousands of youth who were frequenting the seats of professional learning, and besides the preparatory function, the local schools were serving a clientele for whom the ability to read and write clerk's Latin was a sure passport to business opportunity. For it must not be forgotten that during this period all important documents such as business accounts, wills, international business correspondence, town records, and deeds were written in Latin. For the most part the humbler civil and ecclesiastical servants could get all the learning that was necessary for the successful conduct of their duties in the grammar school, and certainly the great mass of attorneys, reeves, acolytes, sacristans, etc., never set foot inside a university classroom." Edward H. Reisner, *Historical Foundations of Modern Education,* The Macmillan Company, 1927, pp. 341–342.

these schools were practical and down-to-earth and, if we are to judge from the performances of some of their students, achieved to an almost unbelievable degree. For the leading scholars and often the statesmen of that day, some of whom had known no Latin before attending school, were able not only to read and write the language with ease, but to conduct vigorous and sometimes acrimonious debates in it. Undoubtedly many struggled with this curriculum in vain, but the major figures of European history at the time testify to the effectiveness of instruction in these schools.

Then came the intellectual revolt known as "humanism," one major objective of which was to recover the literary treasures of the ancient world and to equip people with the ability to read, write, and speak the Latin and Greek of classical times. It was, in part, a movement of curricular reform and one in which the grammar schools were directly involved. Educational innovators, the progressives of their day, fought running battles with traditionalists to change not only the language of instruction, but the books that determined the instructional content. Over a period of a century and a half the contest went gradually to the innovators, with victory well established by the middle of the sixteenth century. The new grammar schools emerged, often in the same buildings and with the same foundations or grants as the old, with classical Latin and to a lesser extent classical Greek as the main if not the only items in the classroom studies.

During the latter part of this intellectual uprising occurred the series of events known as the Reformation or the Protestant revolt. But the spread of classical or humanistic studies transcended lines of both religious and national differences. The new grammar school in diverse forms and with varying degrees of emphasis on strictly religious materials became standard equipment in the countries of western Europe, including England, where there was no conflict on this point between Puritans and other Anglicans.[2] The nonconformist academy was still in the future, not to come into being until after the Anglican restoration of 1660.

---

[2] England in 1600 had 360 grammar schools, or one for every 13,000 people. A. L. Rowse, *The England of Elizabeth: The Structure of Society,* The Macmillan Company, 1951, p. 496.

THE COLONIAL GRAMMAR SCHOOL

It was practically inevitable that the first English emigrants to the new world, if concerned about education at all, would seek to establish grammar schools. The Anglican settlers in Virginia in fact planned specifically to do so and even raised funds for this purpose. But Indian massacres in 1622 and the collapse of the Virginia company in 1624 squelched these hopeful plans.[3] Later in the century, the College of William and Mary got under way, not as an institution of "higher" learning in its first years, but as a Latin grammar school.[4]

The Puritans of Massachusetts Bay Colony, however, did succeed in starting the Boston Latin Grammar School in 1635. There was nothing uniquely Puritan in this action; as educated men, many of whom had university degrees, the Puritans founded the kind of school that educated men in western Europe took for granted. Soon other communities in Massachusetts Bay Colony followed the Boston example. Grammar schools appeared in other New England colonies as well as in the middle and southern groups. Secondary education in the new world was under way.

These colonial grammar schools demand examination from the standpoint of their possible contributions to present-day assumptions about secondary education. The tuition picture is somewhat confused; at least there were some provisions for free schooling for those not in a position to pay. They were certainly popular in the sense that community initiative seemed to have much to do with their founding, at least in the earliest days. But they were not universal, nor were they intended to be. Latin grammar schools were attended by only a minority of the male population, with the lines drawn partly in terms of social class, partly in terms of academic ability, and partly in terms of family and individual motivation. Not all boys from the upper classes necessarily went to grammar school; nor was enrollment limited to those from such classes.

[3] Elmer Ellsworth Brown, *The Making of Our Middle Schools,* Longmans, Green, and Company, 1905 ed., p. 34.
[4] *Ibid.,* p. 50.

The stated purposes of the grammar schools in the Massachusetts Law of 1647 indicate a more exclusive concentration on preparation for college than had apparently been the case in Europe.[5] This high degree of awareness of the college-preparatory function is one of the bequests of the Latin grammar school to the subsequent development of secondary education in our country. Whether or not it has been a happy bequest has been the object of much discussion. Without doubt, preparation for advanced schooling must in any culture be one of the essential functions of a secondary school. The unfortunate effect has been to create a sort of perpetual embarrassment about the presence in the high school of those who are not going to college, leading to the dualism of the college-preparatory and the non-college-preparatory courses. This dualism often carries with it the unhappy implication that traditional academic subjects are of value only for college-preparatory purposes and that the non-college-bound student should either be spared or protected from them.

But the founders of the Latin grammar schools had more in mind than the mechanics of getting students into college. The purpose of grammar school and of the college itself was to develop a leadership group educated in the classics and in religion.

The college and the grammar school, then, were parts of one educational system, though not bound together in one system of administration. In both alike the ideal of education was an ideal of public service. They were established to train up young men "for the service of God, in church and commonwealth." And the form of public serv-

---

[5] The law of 1647 ordered "that where any town shall increase to the number of 100 families or householders, they shall set up a grammar school, the master thereof being able to instruct youth so far as they may be fitted for the university." *Records of the Governor and Company of the Massachusetts Bay in New England,* November 11, 1647, p. 203, quoted in Alexander Inglis, *Principles of Secondary Education,* Houghton Mifflin Company, 1918, p. 166.

This does not necessarily mean that all or even most of those who completed the Latin Grammar School went to college. "We do not know what proportion of New England grammar-school graduates entered the college. I would guess less than half; for down to 1690, the college classes were so small as to allow for only one or at the most two students, on an average, from each of the existing New England grammar schools." Samuel Eliot Morison, *The Puritan Pronaos: Studies in the Intellectual Life of New England in the Seventeenth Century,* New York University Press, 1936, p. 87.

ice which was uppermost in the minds of their founders was the Christian ministry. Even preparation for the other learned professions and for political life might be left to take care of itself, but it was felt essential that a body of educated ministers should be trained up for the public offices of religion. We shall not understand our educational development if we fail to see that modern systems of education, like much else in our modern civilization, are deeply rooted in the religious life of two and three centuries ago.[6]

This connection between religion and education was not, of course, invented by the Puritan colonists. But it was through them that it was first effectively transferred to the colonial scene. It was fostered not only in secondary and higher education, but in the "lower" schools as well, at which level, according to the law of 1647, the objective was to teach people to read the scriptures in English. The idea was to establish a common base of religious literacy in the whole population, plus that of guaranteeing enlightened leadership on the part of the few who could go straight to the ancient languages. This connection between religion and education, in spite of church-state separation, has never been completely lost in American life. It has been transformed in part at least to a connection between school instruction and morality; the tendency to couple spiritual with moral values in recent discussions suggests that the concern may go beyond that of morality alone.

One other element has been transmitted to us by the Latin grammar school, a deep and abiding respect for the sources of our western culture in classical antiquity. True, this is sometimes narrowly identified with the mechanics of the Latin language. At its best, however, it has always been concerned with the substance as well as the forms of our intellectual and moral heritage, both Christian and non-Christian.

As time went on, both in Europe and in this country, Latin grammar schools, as often happens with educational institutions, tended to lose sight of the purposes which had stirred their founders. In Europe, the schools reverted in part to the more practical objectives of the Latin schools of the late Middle Ages, although

[6] Brown, *op. cit.*, p. 57.

they held to the classical Latin usage that had been revived during the early humanistic period.[7] Then as the practical need for Latin began to diminish, instruction centered more than ever on mechanics and forms. When Latin was later attacked by modernists of various persuasions, its proponents could fall back on nothing better than the theory of formal discipline, an idea that can neither be proved nor disproved.

[7] "But the humanism of the schools in England, as in Italy and Germany, soon degenerated into the narrower and more formal sort. The purpose of humanistic education became not so much a real training in literature as a practical command of Latin as the means of culture in all ages. The Roman and Greek literatures were treated not so much as ends in themselves as storehouses of adequate and eloquent expression that was needed by all. The legal, medical, and clerical professions all required a ready acquaintance with Latin, and it was a necessity in travel and international communication. The educators of the times did not belittle the literary aspect, but felt that an understanding of the authors would be limited to the intellectual genius, whereas Latin conversation, and an adaptation of classical terms and phrases to the communication of ideas, was perfectly feasible for all.

"Accordingly, the training of the grammar schools in the later sixteenth and the seventeenth centuries became one of dictionaries, grammars, and phrase books. . . . The methods became, therefore, largely *memoriter* and passive, although some exercise of judgment and taste was required of the pupils in making the proper selections, and in analyzing paragraphs, sentences, phrases, and words." Frank P. Graves, *A History of Education during the Middle Ages and the Transition to Modern Times,* The Macmillan Company, 1914, p. 171.

"The task of teaching and learning two highly inflected languages of which the syntax is extremely intricate was enough in itself to take up most of the energies and time of the school. The result was that the humanistic school tended to teach the rules of grammar, to apply them in written and oral composition, and to construe authors, while the exalted aim of opening up the riches of classical culture and applying them in the education of the younger generation to a considerable extent went by the board. At their worst the school exercises became a dreary and exacting drill on word forms, constructions, and literary artifices, and even at its best the humanistic school must have been a severe test upon the interest and the capacity of all but the more gifted pupils." Reisner, *op. cit.,* p. 485.

"As long as the secondary schools of the Renaissance and Reformation periods studied the humanities, later called the 'classics,' in order to enter into a richer appreciation of goodness and beauty, they prospered mightily. But when these schools began to find their principal model of beauty in one author, Cicero, they began to show signs of formalism and decline. Furthermore, when they began to content themselves with the mere command of the Latin and Greek tongues or even with just a command of the grammar, their sun was beginning to set. As long as grammar held to its Roman connotation of including the liberal arts, the Latin grammar school of England and America had vitality. But when this school undertook little more than a narrow study of the word forms and constructions of grammar, its sun was already well before the horizon.

"It should occasion no surprise that formalism and decay overtook the Humanistic secondary school." John S. Brubacher, *A History of the Problems of Education,* McGraw-Hill Book Company, Inc., 1947, pp. 424–425.

So it was too that the Latin grammar schools of the American colonies became poor imitations of their former selves, although there were undoubtedly notable exceptions among teachers who continued to exemplify the older humanistic objectives. For the students who were responsive to them, the authors studied still communicated much in the way of historical, philosophical, and religious content.

It is doubtful, moreover, that the tendency to concentrate increasingly on the forms rather than the substance of humanism can validly be identified as the reason why the grammar schools declined in America. Their European counterparts were at least as formal as those in the new world, but maintained their monopoly on secondary education well into the nineteenth century and have continued as healthy competitors with other kinds of schools to the present day. We do know, however, that the Latin grammar schools in our country declined, that it became increasingly difficult to maintain them in the eighteenth century, and that in the nineteenth they virtually disappeared.

Although the Latin grammar school did contribute to the broad traditions of schooling in our country, its role in the development of what we now call secondary education is by no means clear. We think today of a secondary school as one that presents general education to students approximately between 12 and 18 years of age. But the Latin grammar school served students who were much younger than this, and its studies were highly specialized, being devoted almost entirely to the mastery of foreign tongues. To find general studies taught to students between 12 and 20 years of age in the colonial period, we must turn instead to the colleges.

On the other hand, if we think of a secondary school as one which a student normally completes before going to college, even though many of its students do not go to college at all, the Latin grammar school was a secondary school and in that sense a predecessor of the high school. Even this distinction between secondary and higher education became blurred as more colleges were founded, and overlapping of functions persisted to a marked degree well into the nineteenth century. Many of the students listed in college enrollments were actually in preparatory departments. As the academies and high schools began offering subjects which previously had been taught only in the colleges, it became difficult to tell from catalogues where secondary education left off and higher education began. In fact, it is difficult to tell this in some instructional fields even today.

THE ACADEMY

The academy also had European antecedents. With the restoration of Charles II and Anglicanism in 1660, the English counterparts of the American Puritans found themselves outside the church and state in their own country. Grammar schools and universities were closed to them. They were not allowed to set up schools of their own. Lax enforcement of the laws, however, made it possible for nonconformists to establish some schools, and modification of the laws themselves in 1689 opened the way to the development of these schools on an above-board basis. Such schools became known as "academies," probably after Milton's use of the term in his treatise, *Of Education,* written in 1643. The term was borrowed from Plato's ancient academy of Athens and reflected the enthusiasm of Milton and other humanists for the classical tradition.

Neither Milton in his treatise, however, nor the nonconformist academy masters of the later seventeenth century confined their curriculum to the study of the classical languages. Milton had set forth an ambitious program including not only Latin and Greek, but modern languages, mathematics, science, music, and physical education. His program was in fact so ambitious and comprehensive that probably no school in the history of time, past, present, or future, could offer it. Certainly it was not reproduced in detail by the actual academies that developed in the latter part of the seventeenth century. But these schools did begin to add other studies to those of Latin and Greek.[8] Of particular interest is the fact that these schools began to pay attention not only to the form

[8] See J. W. Ashley Smith, *The Birth of Modern Education,* Independent Press, Ltd., London, 1954, for a recent account of the English dissenting academies.

but to the subject matter of education and were doing this at a time when the humanistic schools were beginning to defend their programs not on the basis of the content, but on that of form.

Word of these new kinds of schools spread to the American colonies. An academy master, Charles Morton, emigrated to Massachusetts in 1685. One of the students at Morton's school was Daniel Defoe of *Robinson Crusoe* fame, who in 1699 wrote *Essay on Projects* in which he suggested various kinds of specialized academies. This essay was later read by Benjamin Franklin and may have contributed to him the term and some of the ideas for the Philadelphia academy. At any rate, Franklin, who had first written on the academy in 1743, was able to secure enough funds to open such a school eight years later.

Franklin himself had little enthusiasm for the program of the humanistic school. He was interested in the content of education; furthermore, he was preoccupied by the idea of content useful for the civic and occupational careers of the rising middle classes in the colonies. His proposal included not only the science and mathematics of the English academies, but also practical studies in agriculture, commerce, industry, and mechanics.[9] One suggestion he made was a novel one for the time: namely, that specific attention be given to the study of history. His attitude toward the study of Latin and Greek is not clear. According to one writer, "Franklin would gladly have made this academy an English school pure and simple. But he yielded to men of wealth and learning whose cooperation was needed, and included both ancient and modern

---

[9] Schools in Philadelphia had earlier anticipated these kinds of subjects, as well as others. "Because of its commercial prosperity and increasing population, Philadelphia early developed a variety of private schools, especially schools stressing utilitarian subjects. A youth could find a school in Philadelphia where he could learn mathematics, bookkeeping, navigation, surveying, and the rudiments of natural science. One of the most popular of the private teachers was Andrew Lamb, who escaped hanging in London by being sold in Philadelphia as a transported convict. He set up a school in 1733, and his skill as an instrument worker made him an especially authoritative teacher of navigation as well as other useful subjects. Many of the private schools ran at night for the benefit of apprentices and workers. For women and girls there were schools where they could learn needlework, plain sewing, and various handicrafts." Louis B. Wright, *The Cultural Life of the American Colonies 1607–1763,* The New America Nation Series edited by Henry Steele Commager and Richard B. Morris, Harper & Brothers, 1957, p. 109.

languages."[10] The academy opened with three divisions, the Latin, the English, and the mathematical, with a fourth division, the philosophical, added later. In practice, however, the academy emphasized the Latin studies, and Franklin later expressed dissatisfaction with the program.

Later the academy invaded New England itself, the original home of the Latin grammar school in the colonies. In 1778 several members of the Phillips family opened an academy at Andover, Massachusetts; five years later they opened another at Exeter, New Hampshire. The objectives stated for the academy at Andover deal with several matters of considerable interest to us today. ". . . it is again declared, that the *first* and *principal* object of this Institution is the promotion of true PIETY and VIRTUE; the *second,* instruction in the English, Latin, and Greek Languages, together with Writing, Arithmetic, Music, and the Art of Speaking; the *third,* practical Geometry, Logic, and Geography; and the *fourth,* such other of the liberal Arts and Sciences or Languages as opportunity and ability may hereafter admit, and as the TRUSTEES shall direct."[11] Note that so far as subject matter is concerned these objectives go far beyond the scope of the Latin grammar school. Since they were set forth by men who were among the intellectual leaders of their society, we catch from them some indication of which way the wind was blowing. Also of interest is the fact that the founders of this academy placed the moral objective first and the more strictly intellectual or academic objectives second, third, and fourth. In so doing, they were making explicit what probably had been implicit in the assumptions of the Latin grammar school as well. Controversialists of the present who argue vehemently the relative priorities of intellectual and other kinds of objectives will do well to ponder this statement from one of the most respectable and allegedly traditional secondary schools in our country. Those who contend that the secondary school has no business with other than strictly intellectual objectives may at least question the extent to which they have so-called tradition on their side. On the other hand, those who are identified with the disparagement of academic

---

[10] Brown, *op. cit.,* p. 181.
[11] Cited *ibid.,* p. 195.

disciplines may well note that the first objective is quickly followed by those which spell out at least the broad categories of subject matter to be learned.

The two academies of the Phillips family seemed to set the fashion. During the following six or seven decades academies prospered and Latin grammar schools declined. Some of the Latin grammar schools became academies. The academy movement spread to many states, including the new frontier states beyond the mountains. By 1850 there were about six thousand such schools in existence, probably with marked variations in endowments, faculties, buildings, and student bodies.

Perhaps the most important characteristic of the academies was that they were popular institutions, although they were neither free nor universal. "The academies were the popular institutions of the day in more senses than one."[12] They were accessible to people in thousands of American communities and were responsive to popular interests and demands. One great barrier to popular and universal secondary education was broken down when academies were started for girls as well as boys. Furthermore, while academies did prepare some students for college, they also served many whose plans did not include college attendance.[13] Their curricula included many new subjects, some of which were probably regarded with skepticism by the adherents of the Latin grammar schools.[14] Al-

[12] *Ibid.*, p. 247.

[13] "The earlier academies were not bound up with the college system in the same way as the grammar schools: they were not primarily 'fitting schools.' They were, instead, institutions of an independent sort, taking pupils who had already acquired the elements of an English education, and carrying them forward to some, rather indefinite, rounding out of their studies.

"The constitutions of the Philadelphia academy and of the two schools founded by the Phillips family set forth the purposes of those several institutions, but make no such mention of preparation for college as is contained in the New England laws providing for grammar schools, or in official documents relating to the grammar schools of Maryland and Virginia. We even find the interests of the academies sometimes set over against those of the colleges, as in New York and Maryland, the two institutions being regarded as belonging to diverse educational systems. The colleges were for the higher, and particularly the professional, classes. The academies were the colleges of the people. So the matter stood in the controversies of the time." *Ibid.*, p. 230.

[14] It may be doubted that the curriculum of the Latin grammar school was subject-centered at all in the modern sense. There was really only one subject, Latin, so handled that it looks in some ways like an integrated curriculum around the single theme of language study. The separate classes were organized around books, not subjects.

though some of these were strictly practical and vocational in character, the new subjects for the most part were aimed at completeness or wholeness of liberal education. Some of these were subjects previously taught only in colleges. They reflected not only the expansion of knowledge which had taken place in the seventeenth and eighteenth centuries, but the hunger for this knowledge on the part of many people who for the first time in history had some leisure and opportunity for study. The colleges also were responsive to this new spirit and added to the usual subjects acceptable for entrance purposes a body of new subjects, including geography, English grammar, algebra, geometry, and ancient history.[15]

Of course the academies charged tuition fees. In this they may have differed from the town grammar schools of New England, although the situation on this point respecting the grammar schools is not clear. Evidently the fees were no great barriers to attendance; otherwise, six thousand academies could not have survived for long.

An interesting British comment on the academies made in 1819 bears somewhat negative testimony regarding their intellectual character. Perhaps it illustrates a perennial tendency to regard popular education as something substandard in quality.

The Americans take a strange delight in high-sounding names, and often satisfy themselves for the want of the thing, by the assumption of the name. These academies are not always exclusively classical schools; some are partly appropriated to education for the counter and the counting-room; and so far as this object goes, there is no striking defect in them; it not being a very difficult matter to teach a lad to count his fingers and take care of his dollars. But in all that relates to classic learning, they are totally deficient: there is not one, from Maine to Georgia, which has yet sent forth a single first-rate scholar; no, not one since the settlement of the country, equal even to the most ordinary of the thirty or forty, which come out every year from Schule Pforta, and Meissen. . . .[16]

If indeed American secondary education is collapsing, the start of the collapse may be traced back a century and a half!

Academies are still with us, but they no longer have the popular

15 Brown, *op. cit.,* pp. 231–232.
16 From *Blackwood's Magazine,* cited *ibid.,* p. 246.

connotation associated with them in the first half of the nineteenth century. To some they suggest social snobbery. Others find in them, as well as in private or independent schools in general, the last refuge of the higher standards allegedly repudiated by the public high school.

DEVELOPMENT OF THE PUBLIC HIGH SCHOOL

The occasion for the eventual shift in role of the academy was probably the development of the public high school, beginning with the establishment in 1821 of the Boston English Classical School, renamed three years later as the English High School. Just what the town committee had in mind when it took this step has long been a matter for interesting speculation. From the text of the subcommittee report it appears that the members thought of it as a logical and necessary extension upward of the English grammar schools, the name applied to their elementary schools. It appears too that what they had in mind was an academy-like institution conducted under public auspices and at public expense.[17] From their proposed curriculum we infer that they did not intend it as a competitor of the Latin grammar school, for no classical languages whatsoever were included. Instead we find provisions for English literature and composition, mathematics through trigonometry, history, philosophy, science, and the vocational subjects of navigation and surveying. What they proposed then was really a publicly supported academy with the classical department left out. The term

[17] "The mode of education now adopted, and the branches of knowledge that are taught at our English grammar schools, are not sufficiently extensive nor otherwise calculated to bring the powers of the mind into operation nor to qualify a youth to fill usefully and respectably many of these stations, both public and private, in which he may be placed. A parent who wishes to give a child an education that shall fit him for active life, and shall serve as a foundation for eminence in his profession, whether Mercantile or Mechanical, is under the necessity of giving him a different education from any which our public schools can now furnish. Hence, many children are separated from their parents and sent to private academies in this vicinity, to acquire that instruction which cannot be obtained at the public seminaries. Thus, many parents, who contribute largely to the support of these institutions, are subjected to heavy expense for the same object, in other towns." Cited *ibid.*, pp. 299–300.

Josiah Quincy, mayor of Boston 1823–1828, referred to the new school as relieving parents "from the necessity of incurring the expense incident to private academies." *Ibid.*, p. 304.

high school itself was not original, having been used previously for a secondary school in Edinburgh, Scotland, as well as for two eighteenth-century classical secondary schools in Pennsylvania. None of these high schools, however, corresponded in their characteristics to the one established in Boston.

Apparently the action taken in Boston was consistent with aspirations and ideas in Massachusetts generally, for a state law was passed in 1827 requiring every community of 500 families or householders to establish an English high school. This law set forth curricular requirements, including orthography, reading, writing, English grammar, geography, arithmetic, good behavior, the history of the United States, bookkeeping by single entry, geometry, surveying, and algebra.[18] But the law did not stop there. It went on to require communities of 4,000 inhabitants to maintain high schools to which were added the Latin and Greek languages, history, rhetoric, and logic.[19] This in effect merged the programs of the Latin grammar schools with those of the newer high schools. Some of the early Massachusetts high schools were created by adding the newer subjects to the existing Latin grammar schools.

Although the original Boston high school had been set up with an English curriculum only, many later high schools were organized on the basis of English and classical departments, a division also used in many of the academies, thereby encouraging the dualism of preparation for college and preparation for life that still haunts our discussions of secondary education. This combination did not of course create the dualism, for it had already existed; but it helped perpetuate it. The dualism, furthermore, lives with us in somewhat different form. Latin is no longer the key item in college preparation. For the older notion of "Latin vs. English," we have substituted that of "academic vs. practical studies."

Except in New England, the high school idea was not widely heralded as the dawn of a new day in secondary education. Two high schools, one for boys and one for girls, were started in New

---

[18] Laws of Massachusetts, January Session, 1827, chap. CXLIII, cited in Emit Duncan Grizzell, *Origin and Development of the New England High School Before 1865*, The Macmillan Company, 1923, pp. 86–87.
[19] *Ibid.*

York City in the 1820's under the auspices of a private group called the High-School Society. Philadelphia, Baltimore, and Charleston followed with high schools of their own in the latter 1830's.[20] The movement grew, but it grew very slowly. In 1851, according to one report,[21] there were high schools in only 80 cities. Possibly many schools came into existence as upward extensions of the common grades, a year or two at a time, and were omitted from the records. It is clear, however, that the movement progressed by no means as rapidly as had that of the academy and that as late as the 1860's academies far outnumbered high schools.

In most states, high schools were established by local communities without specific legislative mandate. Controversies were set off by those who objected to such uses of public funds. Sometimes these controversies jelled into specific legal issues taken to the courts. And it was one such case that led to a landmark in the history of United States secondary education, the Kalamazoo decision of 1872. The plaintiffs in this case sought "A judicial determination of the right of school authorities . . . to levy taxes upon the general public for the support of what in this state are known as high schools, and to make free by such taxation the instruction of children in other languages than the English."[22] In this context the languages referred to primarily were Latin and Greek, and what the plaintiffs had in mind was the right of the high school to offer college preparation at public expense. It was this broader issue that the court emphasized in its decision.

The more general question which the record presents we shall endeavor to state in our own language, but so as to make it stand out distinctly as a naked question of law, disconnected from all considerations of policy or expediency, in which light alone we are at liberty to consider it. It is, as we understand it, that there is no authority in this state to make the high schools free by taxation levied on the people at large. The argument is that while there may be no constitutional provision expressly prohibiting such taxation, the general course of legislation in the state and the general understanding of the people

---

[20] Brown, *op. cit.*, pp. 311–312.
[21] Cited *ibid.*, p. 313.
[22] *30 Michigan 69*, cited *ibid.*, p. 356.

have been such as to require us to regard the instruction in the classics and in the living modern languages in these schools as in the nature not of practical and therefore necessary instruction for the benefit of the people at large, but rather as accomplishments for the few, to be sought after in the main by those best able to pay for them, and to be paid for by those who seek them, and not by general tax. And not only has this been the general state policy, but this higher learning of itself, when supplied by the state, is so far a matter of private concern to those who receive it that the courts ought to declare it incompetent to supply it wholly at the public expense. This is in substance, as we understand it, the position of the complainants in this suit.

When this doctrine was broached to us, we must confess to no little surprise that the legislation and policy of our state were appealed to against the right of the state to furnish a liberal education to the youth of the state in schools brought within the reach of all classes. We supposed it had always been understood in this state that education, not merely in the rudiments, but in an enlarged sense, was regarded as an important practical advantage to be supplied at their option to rich and poor alike, and not as something pertaining merely to culture and accomplishment to be brought as such within the reach of those whose accumulated wealth enabled them to pay for it. As this, however, is now so seriously disputed, it may be necessary, perhaps, to take a brief survey of the legislation and general course, not only of the state, but of the antecedent territory, on the subject.[23]

The decision then goes on to include a historical account of provisions for schools in Michigan, going back to 1817,[24] leading toward the court's conclusion.

If these facts do not demonstrate clearly and conclusively a state policy, beginning in 1817 and continuing until after the adoption of the present constitution, in the direction of free schools in which education, and at their option the elements of a classical education, might be brought within the reach of all the children of the state, then, as it seems to us, nothing can demonstrate it. . . . We content ourselves with the statement that neither in our state policy, in our constitution, or in our laws, do we find the primary school districts restricted in the branches of knowledge which their officers may cause to be taught, or the grade of instruction that may be given, if their voters consent

[23] *Ibid.,* pp. 357–358.
[24] *Ibid.,* p. 358.

in regular form to bear the expense and raise the taxes for the purpose.[25]

This decision confirmed free and popular secondary education, but it did more than that. Commenting on the constitution of 1850 in the historical review, the court makes the following interpretation. "The instrument submitted by the convention to the people and adopted by them provided for the establishment of free schools in every school district for at least three months in each year, and for the university. By the aid of these we have every reason to believe the people expected a complete collegiate education might be obtained. . . . The inference seems irresistible that the people expected the tendency towards the establishment of high schools in the primary-school districts would continue until every locality capable of supporting one was supplied."[26] Notice the wording, "high schools in the primary school districts." In these primary school districts, the high school was an upward extension of the elementary school, not a parallel institution overlapping part of the preadolescent years. The court then was identifying classical education as a legitimate function for public high schools of the *common* school system.[27] It implied the familiar "ladder" of the American school system: elementary school, high school, and college, as contrasted with the systems of Europe. While considerable advance had been made in elementary schooling in European countries during the nineteenth century, these elementary (folk) schools were regarded as terminal institutions and not continuous with the secondary schools. The distinction between elementary and secondary education in Europe became more and more one of social class. In making it possible for the "primary school districts" to establish secondary schools which might include "the elements of a classical education," the Michigan court avoided and by impli-

[25] Cited *ibid.*, p. 359.
[26] *Ibid.*

[27] "Moreover, having legalized classical education at public expense, the court had closed one more door on the opportunity for a dual system to develop; for not only useful and practical studies, but cultural, college-preparatory studies as well were now the just province of the secondary school." R. Freeman Butts and Lawrence A. Cremin, *A History of Education in American Culture*, Henry Holt and Company, 1953, p. 419.

cation rejected such a distinction. In so doing, it undoubtedly reflected a substantial body of public opinion at that time.

The high school movement continued to prosper during the remaining decades of the nineteenth century. Of this development the Kalamazoo decision was probably more a reflection than a cause, although the removal of technical difficulties and controversies probably encouraged school districts to go ahead with their plans for high schools, not only in Michigan, but in other states as well. State laws specifically encouraged the establishment of high schools by local districts. Wisconsin, for example, in 1875 provided "for the maintenance of high schools by towns, incorporated villages, cities, or school districts containing incorporated villages or two-department graded schools within their limits."[28] State financial aids for high schools began to appear.

By 1889–1890 there were 2,526 public high schools reporting to the United States Commissioner of Education. In that biennium only 1,632 private high schools, academies, and seminaries were reported.[29] So far as numbers were concerned, the public high school had overtaken and passed the private academy. This did not mean that "universalization" was taking place. The total number of students in both public and private high schools reported in 1889–1890 came to 297,894, of which 202,963 were in public high schools.[30]

High schools of the closing decade of the nineteenth century were much like high schools of the present in being coeducational, free from tuition charges, and fairly available to youth in villages and cities, although the absence of school buses made them somewhat less available to rural youth. But they enrolled only a small fraction of youth of high school age. To this extent they were selective. Whether the selection was intellectual, economic, or both is a question that has attracted much interest and speculation. Present-day teachers, especially at the end of a hard day, are sometimes inclined to look wistfully back to this period as a golden age,

[28] *Ibid.,* p. 364.
[29] *Report of the Commissioner of Education for the Year 1899–1900,* Government Printing Office, vol. 2, 1901, chap. 39, p. 2120.
[30] *Ibid.*

characterized by students who were intellectually able, highly motivated, and easily managed. This may be an expression of a human tendency to regard the past as more lovely and serene than the present. On the other hand, some high schools in the latter part of the nineteenth century did give entrance examinations, a practice aimed presumably at some kind of academic or intellectual selection.[31] And it is probably true that elementary school graduation was in itself more difficult to achieve than later came to be the case.

The high school of 1890 was, of course, highly aware of its college-preparatory function. Several modifications, however, had begun to develop with regard to the question of college admission requirements. Various plans for high school accreditation were making it possible for students to enter many colleges without examinations. Colleges were modifying their entrance requirements in a direction away from classical and toward modern studies.

College-bound students, however, constituted a minority group in the high schools of 1890, just as they do today. According to the U.S. Commissioner of Education's report, only 14.83 percent of the total number of public and private high school students in 1890–1891 were listed as preparing for college.[32] Nevertheless 39.8 percent of all students were taking Latin.[33] To some modern educators this might represent a high degree of inconsistency; what it probably meant to the educators of 1890 was that so-called college-preparatory subjects provided a good education for all students who could learn them whether they were going to college or not. The question of Latin versus something else is not the important point here; it is rather that of drawing a hard distinction between preparation for college and preparation for life on the basis of subject choices.

By 1890 the curriculum in the classroom studies had come to

---

[31] One local history, for example, reports on this point as follows. "The high rate of mortality on these examinations was illustrated by the fact that of 120 desiring entry into high school in 1873, only eighty-four managed to pass the test." Clinton F. Karstaedt (ed.), *Oshkosh: One Hundred Years a City 1853–1893*, Oshkosh, Wisconsin, Centennial, Inc., 1953.

[32] Cited in Brown, *op. cit.*, p. 472.

[33] *Ibid.*

include a great variety of subjects, including those which many today call academic, although this term disguises the struggle that had been necessary to establish some of these as academically respectable. The Committee on Secondary School Studies (Committee of Ten) of the National Education Association appointed in 1892 grouped most of these subjects in nine major areas: Latin; Greek; English; other modern languages; mathematics; physics, astronomy, and chemistry; natural history (biology, including botany, zoology, and physiology); history (civil government and political economy); and geography (physical geography, geology, and meteorology).[34]

This then in rough outline was the high school of 1890, in the period which some might regard as the lull before the storm. The following decades were to witness: (1) the increase in numbers of high school students; (2) the rise of the junior high school movement; and (3) the attempt to define more explicitly the educational functions and objectives of high schools.

EXPANSION OF THE PUBLIC HIGH SCHOOL

Expansion in numbers was already under way by the close of the nineteenth century. Twice as many students were in secondary schools in 1900 as ten years before. By 1914–1915, however, the total number reached 1,484,028, nearly five times that of 1889–1890. Furthermore, only 155,044 or about one tenth of the total were students in private schools and academies.[35] Of course the population had increased too since 1889–1890, but not at the same rate. In 1890, secondary school students formed about one half of 1 percent of the population;[36] by 1914–1915, they formed 1½ percent.[37] But further increases were yet to come. The numbers of students in Grades 9 through 12 in public high schools moved from 1,851,965 in 1920 to 4,135,171 in 1930 and then to

[34] National Education Association, *Report of the Committee of Ten on Secondary School Studies,* The Association, 1894, pp. 8–11.
[35] *Report of the United States Commissioner of Education* (1916), vol. 2, p. 449, cited in Alexander Inglis, *Principles of Secondary Education,* Houghton Mifflin Company, 1918, p. 119.
[36] Obtained by dividing 200,000 students by 63,000,000 population.
[37] Inglis, *op. cit.,* p. 118. Figure given as one in 70.

5,926,722 in 1938.[38] A declining population base in the adolescent years reduced this total to 5,417,122 in 1946, but by 1952 it had increased again, this time to 5,695,514.[39] A total of 6,262,–975 students in 1953–1954 established a new high, and in 1956–1957 enrollments stopped just short of 7,000,000 with a figure of 6,963,000.[40] It should be kept in mind that all these figures are for the last four high school years and do not include seventh-grade and eighth-grade students in junior high schools.[41]

No other society in history had engaged upon the task of taking the majority of its adolescents out of full-time gainful employment and putting them in school. In part this tendency was a reflection of economic prosperity in the United States, based on abundant natural resources and a full development of the possibilities of productive energy and mechanical improvements in trade, industry, agriculture, and transportation. The services of youth on the labor market could be released without damage to industrial or agricultural output. Perhaps the increase in enrollments was motivated by the educational demands of a complex, industrialized society such as ours had become by the end of the nineteenth century. But increasing enrollments in high schools were based on more than economics. They were testimony also to assumptions (1) that more schooling meant better opportunity for the individual and (2) that every individual should have the fullest possible opportunity. And these assumptions went back at least as far as the

[38] "Statistics of Public Secondary Day Schools, 1951–1952," *Biennial Survey of Education in the United States, 1950–1952,* Federal Security Agency, Office of Education, 1954, table A, p. 6.

[39] *Ibid.*

[40] Cited in Educational Policies Commission, *The Contemporary Challenge to Education,* National Education Association, 1958, Appendix A, p. 25.

[41] Although the increase in numbers is often given as a reason for the marked decline of relative enrollments in some academic subjects, there was no such decline during the early period of expansion. The high school population doubled between 1890 and 1900, but the percentage of students in public high schools taking Latin increased from 34.69 to 50.61 in the same period. Similarly, the percentage taking algebra increased from 45.4 to 56.29 and that taking geometry went from 21.33 to 27.39. Since 1910, percentage enrollments in Latin and mathematics have declined, but it is difficult to establish this as a result of the universalizing of high school attendance. *Report of the Commissioner of Education for the Year 1899–1900,* Government Printing Office, 1901, vol. 2, chap. 39, p. 2123.

resolutions of the committee that had recommended the founding of the Boston English School back in 1821. *Technological*

THE JUNIOR HIGH SCHOOL

Much attention was directed after 1890 to the organization of the educational ladder, with particular emphasis on the location of the seventh and eighth grades. Various educational leaders had become dissatisfied with the 8–4 arrangement, which they felt unduly prolonged the period of schooling for those who planned on college and professional school. Recommendations of national committees stimulated the development of the junior high school, and by 1920 they were 883 in existence.[42] The original idea of saving two years in the students' programs was lost in the process; most of the reorganization plans simply transferred the seventh and eighth grades to the secondary school, thereby lengthening the secondary period to six years without saving any time. In many reorganized systems, the ninth grade was attached to the seventh and eighth to produce the familiar 6–3–3 pattern.

Although the time-saving argument disappeared, proponents of the movement later claimed other values for junior high schools. They contended that the junior high provided a better transition between elementary schooling and that of the later high school years. As developed in practice, however, the new organization simply moved the breaking point down two years; since the new junior high schools became highly departmentalized in character, no gradual transition took place. Departmentalization in the seventh and eighth grades grew out of the practice of using these years for a variety of exploratory courses designed to help the student sample a number of subjects, particularly along prevocational lines. This created the need for the specialized teacher, and departmentalization followed in natural sequence. When specialization and departmentalization later became unpopular, junior high school curriculum leaders promoted the development of larger

[42] "Statistical Survey of Education 1919–20," *Biennial Survey of Education in the United States*, U.S. Bureau of Education Bulletin 1923, No. 16, p. 32, cited in William T. Gruhn and Harl R. Douglass, *The Modern Junior High School*, The Ronald Press Company, 1947, p. 39.

time blocks under one teacher.[43] This development, although a reversal of one of the early features of junior high, has seemed more consistent with the early claims for it as a transitional school.

In summarizing the junior high school situation up to 1947, Gruhn and Douglass identify three early claims that had not been realized: the acceleration of students or economy of time, the earlier introduction of high school studies, and the introduction of vocational or semivocational courses. "In all three cases, however, there seems to have been a considerable shift in the point of view of educators regarding the desirability of these claims. Apparently this change in point of view, rather than weakness on the part of the reorganized schools, has discouraged the realization of these claims."[44]

In spite of various back trackings with regard to purposes, the movement for reorganization has gone steadily ahead, producing not only the 6–3–3 plan, but also others such as the 6–4–2, 6–2–4, the 6–6, and the 6–4–4. By 1952, of the 23,746 high schools then in existence, 13,578 (about 57 percent of the total) were of the reorganized type.[45] These reorganized schools furthermore enrolled 74.8 percent of the students,[46] an increase from 61.5 percent in 1946.[47] One result of all this is to give us two undefined and ambiguous periods in the educational ladder. The seventh and eighth grades may be either elementary or secondary, depending on the school system; Grades 13 and 14 may be either secondary or higher. One inconvenient aspect of this is confusion in terminology and statistics. When a given writer or speaker talks about the secondary curriculum, he must define the grades he is talking about or leave his audience in the dark. There are now so many reorganized schools, however, that it is a matter of practical necessity to include Grades 7 and 8 in curricular discussions dealing with

[43] See Leonard V. Koos, *Junior High School Trends,* Harper & Brothers, 1955, chap. 5, "Retreat from Departmentalization."

[44] Gruhn and Douglass, *op. cit.,* p. 83.

[45] "Statistics of Public Secondary Day Schools, 1951–1952," *Biennial Survey 1950–1952, op. cit.,* table I, p. 23.

[46] *Ibid.,* table J, p. 23.

[47] *Ibid.*

the secondary school, and the term secondary curriculum is so used in this book.

THE 1918 STATEMENT OF CARDINAL PRINCIPLES

The same period of ferment that produced rising enrollments and the junior high school also witnessed growing interest in the defining of the functions or objectives of secondary education. Such interest may have been stimulated in part by rising enrollments, since many felt that the college-preparatory function was no longer applicable to the "newer" types of students, although it should also be recalled that only about 15 percent of the students in 1890 had been in college-preparatory programs. Perhaps it was stimulated also by the rise of specialized high schools in large cities, for there were many who saw in these commercial, technical, and industrial schools the danger of losing sight of liberal education.

In 1911, a committee of the National Education Association on the articulation of high school and college "set forth briefly its conception of the field and function of secondary education and urged the modification of college entrance requirements in order that the secondary school might adapt its work to the varying needs of its pupils without closing to them the possibility of continued education in higher institutions."[48] This report led to the creation of the Commission on Reorganization of Secondary Education which in 1918 produced its report on the Cardinal Principles, listing seven major objectives, namely health, command of fundamental processes, worthy home-membership, vocation, civic education, worthy use of leisure, and ethical character. These constituted, in the minds of the commission, the platform of the secondary school. Also of considerable interest is the general orientation of the committee as expressed in the following statement: "Education in the United States should be guided by a clear conception of the

[48] Commission on the Reorganization of Secondary Education, National Education Association, *Cardinal Principles of Secondary Education,* Bulletin 1918, No. 35, Department of the Interior Bureau of Education, U.S. Government Printing Office, 1937, p. 5.

meaning of democracy. It is the ideal of democracy that the individual and society may find fulfillment each in the other. Democracy sanctions neither the exploitation of the individual by society, nor the disregard of the interests of society by the individual."[49]

The Cardinal Principles undoubtedly reflected the practical, utilitarian temper of the people of the United States at the opening of the twentieth century. Those who deplore what they consider to be anti-intellectualism would undoubtedly feel that the most important objectives had been left out. For even the objective of command of fundamental processes is strictly utilitarian and viewed from the standpoint of tools, such as "reading, writing, arithmetical computations, and the elements of oral and written expression."[50] There is no mention of intellectual competence or training in the classical sense. It would be unfair to suggest that the Commission was anti-intellectual; but it is also probable that the Cardinal Principles would not satisfy those who feel that intellectual training must be identified explicitly as the sole or the most important objective of secondary education.

Dynamic slogans of one generation tend to become worn-out clichés to the next. So it happened with the Cardinal Principles. They have been committed to memory and reproduced on objective tests by thousands of teachers in their professional study programs. By many they have been considered stodgy and conservative. Yet more recent attempts to redefine the objectives of secondary education have not departed far from the 1918 statement.

Stated simply, the contribution of the Commission on the Reorganization of Secondary Education was to redefine the role of the secondary school. To the extent that in so doing the Commission was able to grasp certain new and highly significant and intellectual forces in American life, its redefinition became a lever for needed change and reform. The effects of the *Cardinal Principles* have been legion. Indeed, it does not seem amiss to argue that most of the important

[49] *Ibid.,* p. 9.
[50] *Ibid.,* p. 11.

and influential movements in the field since 1918 have simply been footnotes to the classic itself.[51]

The increase in enrollments in high schools of the 1920's and 1930's coupled with the new directions for secondary education implied by the Cardinal Principles brought about a critical examination of the so-called traditional program. High schools became increasingly restive under what they considered to be the restrictions of college entrance requirements. This restiveness led to the Eighth-Year Study of the 1930's in which 30 selected high schools were permitted to send their graduates to college regardless of their patterns of studies provided the schools recommended them as qualified for college study. Encouraged by this opportunity, the 30 schools, plus a great many others, turned with interest to various curricular innovations with the major emphasis centering on the core.

Probably the most dramatic response to what some saw as the challenge of the Cardinal Principles came in the middle and late 1940's in the form known as life-adjustment education. The impetus to this movement came from the Prosser resolution, quoted in part below, at a conference on "Vocational Education in the Years Ahead" in Washington, June, 1945.

It is the belief of this conference that, with the aid of this report in final form, the vocational school of a community will be able better to prepare twenty per cent of its youth of secondary school age for entrance upon desirable skilled occupations; and that the high school will continue to prepare twenty per cent of its students for entrance to college. We do not believe that the remaining 60 per cent of our youth of secondary school age will receive the life adjustment training they need and to which they are entitled as American citizens —unless and until the administrators of public schools with the assistance of the vocational education leaders formulate a similar program for this group.

We therefore request the U.S. Commissioner of Education and the Assistant Commissioner for Vocational Education to call at some early

[51] Lawrence A. Cremin, "The Revolution in American Secondary Education, 1893–1918," *Teachers College Record*, March, 1955, p. 307.

date a conference or a series of regional conferences between an equal number of representatives of general and of vocational education— to consider this problem and to take such initial steps as may be found advisable for its solution.[52]

The term "life-adjustment education" caught on and was soon widely and vigorously discussed throughout the country not only in school journals, but in general magazines and the public press. Acting on the request in the resolution, the U.S. Office of Education arranged a series of regional conferences throughout the country. What evolved was not a new curriculum, in the sense of a different sequence of courses, but a renewed effort to relate secondary education to the problems and concerns of everyday living with respect to such matters as occupations, leisure time, citizenship, family living, and the like. This was seen furthermore as a desirable effort not only for the 60 percenters, but for all high school youth. In general the movement might be regarded as an attempt to realize more completely the Cardinal Principles stated back in 1918.

Unfortunately, many people including friends and critics drew rather fantastic conclusions about the enterprise. The critics accused the life-adjustment educators first of planning a separate curriculum for one group in the high school population and later, with the shift in discussion from the 60 percent to all youth, of seeking to dilute the entire high school program. With this the criticisms grew into the discussions of the 1950's about intellectual competence as an objective of secondary education. By the middle and late 1950's, the term "life-adjustment education" gradually disappeared as a favored term. In this it probably suffered nothing more than the fate of all slogans.

KINDS AND SIZES OF HIGH SCHOOLS

Differentiated educations for youth of varying interests, goals, and abilities brings up—and has repeatedly brought up—still another question, whether high schools should be comprehensive

---

[52] Cited in *Conference on Life Adjustment Education,* Sacramento, California, September 30—October 1, 1946, p. 1. Also in J. Dan Hull, "Progress in Life Adjustment Education," *Educational Leadership,* March, 1950, p. 361.

or specialized.[53] This is a somewhat cloudy subject, in which definitions are difficult to pin down. The earliest high schools in our
country included some vocational subjects, particularly in the
business fields, and were, in effect, comprehensive high schools.
With the great drive toward vocational education after 1905,
some of our larger metropolitan communities built specialized
high schools to house vocational programs plus those academic
subjects related to general education. This left the academic high
schools just as specialized as the vocational ones. During the
1920's and 1930's, however, the technical high schools and high
schools of commerce lost favor, and much was said about the
desirability of comprehensive high schools again. Smaller communities with vocational subjects in their single high schools had,
of course, been practicing comprehensiveness all along. More
recently the climate has shifted again, at least in large metropolitan
communities, and the question confronts us anew. Resolution of
this in large cities depends in part on the resolution of issues
related to the vocational objective of the secondary school. But it
does not depend on this alone, since proposals have been made for
special high schools for the gifted, whether in vocational programs
or not.

In many parts of the country, however, the question has been
not how to get high schools large enough for specialized purposes,
but how to get them large enough to offer good general programs.
Thirty percent of our high schools (including reorganized or
junior high types) in 1952 enrolled less than 100 students each,
55.4 percent enrolled less than 200 each, while 68.4 percent
enrolled less than 300 each.[54] Many students of secondary education
have been disturbed about the small high schools, particularly
those under 300 enrollment. A high school should maintain at
least one teacher in each of the 12 or so major fields of instruction.
If we use a ratio of one teacher to every 25 students, which provides
a reasonable cost basis, it follows that about 300 students are

[53] For treatment and examination of this question see Franklin J. Keller, *The Double-Purpose High School*, Harper & Brothers, 1953, and *The Comprehensive High School*, Harper & Brothers, 1955.

[54] "Statistics of Public Secondary Day Schools, 1951–1952," *Biennial Survey 1950–1952, op. cit.*, table D, p. 14.

needed to provide one teacher in each field. One could, of course, maintain 12 teachers for 50, 100, or 200 students, but the per-student cost would shoot far above the normal or usual standards of sound public support. In addition, schools of 300 or more are in a better position to provide adequate libraries, equipment, and instructional materials. The Conant report goes farther than the usual 300 figure and recommends that high schools be large enough to have at least 100 students in the graduating class.[55] This would mean 400 students in a four-year high school if there were no dropouts.

Concern about minimum enrollments does not deny the excellent work done in some small high schools; it recognizes that such achievement takes place under handicaps. Neither should we overlook the driving idealism that has created these schools. Many of them were built in the era before modern transportation made the consolidated high school a possibility. Under the conditions from 1870 to 1910 or so, they were the only way of providing any opportunities for secondary schooling. Had they not been built, we would have fallen far short of our professions. But such limitations no longer exist, and in fact have not existed since 1920. One of the less spectacular but equally important movements in secondary education since the 1920's, therefore, has been that of reorganizing school districts and rebuilding high schools so as to approach the 300 enrollment figure.

Perhaps an equally important concern since the 1920's has been to keep metropolitan high schools from getting too large. The great expansion of the 1920's resulted in some high schools of almost monstrous size—10,000 students and above. School boards in such areas, however, kept working on this matter and, aided in part by some population shifts and the slight enrollment decline of the 1940's, managed to reduce the number of such excessively large schools. In 1952 there were only five public day high schools with above 5,000 enrollment as contrasted with 27 in 1930,[56] and four

[55] James Bryant Conant, *The American High School Today,* McGraw-Hill Book Company, Inc., 1959, pp. 37–38.
[56] "Statistics of Public Secondary Day Schools, 1951–1952," *Biennial Survey 1950–1952, op. cit.,* p. 17.

of these were in the Brooklyn area of the New York City school system.[57]

As enrollments increase again, the problem of large enrollments in high schools will reappear, not only in metropolitan communities but in other cities as well. It will be possible to put more students into the existing buildings, at least up to a point, not only by increasing class size, but by the use of staggered shifts. We may hope this will not be the case. It is true, of course, that a large school with enough teachers and good counseling services may provide better individual attention than a small one with too few teachers and with inadequate counseling. So far as curriculum planning is concerned, however, it is desirable to have faculties of not more than 40 or so members, since this is probably the maximum number that can meet and effectively discuss and study the school program as a whole.

The most tangible problem of secondary schooling for the next several decades will be that of housing the students. There is some danger that buildings, enrollments, and budgets will tend to overshadow consideration of what the school is for and what it teaches. Such danger is minimized, however, by two important facts: (1) buildings, enrollments, and budgets can really never be adequately understood or dealt with apart from the curriculum; (2) the people of the United States have long been and are at present supremely concerned about curricular matters and will in all probability continue to be so concerned. The nature of these concerns has directed our past history of secondary schooling and will be the major consideration in determining its future as well.

Bibliography

Association for Supervision and Curriculum Development, 1956 Yearbook, *What Shall the High Schools Teach?* The Association, 1956, chap. 1.

Brown, Elmer Ellsworth, *The Making of Our Middle Schools,* Longmans, Green and Company, 1905.

Brubacher, John S., *A History of the Problems of Education,* McGraw-Hill Book Company, Inc., 1947, chap. 14.

---

[57] *Ibid.,* table F, p. 18.

Butts, R. Freeman, and Cremin, Lawrence A., *A History of Education in American Culture,* Henry Holt and Company, 1953.

Commission on the Reorganization of Secondary Education, National Education Association, *Cardinal Principles of Secondary Education,* Bulletin 1918, No. 35, Department of the Interior, Bureau of Education, U.S. Government Printing Office, 1937.

Franzen, Carl G. T., *Foundations of Secondary Education,* Harper & Brothers, 1955, chaps. 2–5.

Grizzell, Emit Duncan, *Origin and Development of the New England High School Before 1865,* The Macmillan Company, 1923.

Gruhn, William T. and Douglass, Harl R., *The Modern Junior High School,* The Ronald Press Company, 1947, chaps. 1 and 2.

Kandel, I. L., *History of Secondary Education,* Houghton Mifflin Company, 1930.

Koos, Leonard V., *Junior High School Trends,* Harper & Brothers, 1955.

Latimer, John Francis, *What's Happened to Our High Schools?* Public Affairs Press, 1958, chaps. 1–3.

Morison, Samuel Eliot, *The Puritan Pronaos: Studies in the Intellectual Life of New England in the Seventeenth Century,* New York University Press, 1936.

National Education Association, *Report of the Committee of Ten on Secondary School Studies,* The Association, 1894.

Smith, J. W. Ashley, *The Birth of Modern Education,* Independent Press, Ltd., 1954.

Stout, John Elbert, *The Development of High-School Curricula in the North Central States from 1860 to 1918,* The University of Chicago, 1921.

....

CHAPTER 3

High School Students

The growth of the high school in the United States reveals our commitment to the idea that it is the right and duty of all normal youth to be in school. Rightly or wrongly, we have sought to adapt high school to youth rather than the other way around. Our high schools reflect what adults consider to be the capacities, characteristics, and needs of youth. Since the nature of youth is rather complicated, teachers and parents have devoted a great deal of study to the matter; and psychologists, sociologists, and philosophers, both amateur and professional, have supplied a vast body of literature to aid such study.

Any study or discussion of youth or young people involves the terms "adolescent" and "adolescence." They come from a Latin verb meaning to grow or to grow up. Taken as such, they are neutral terms with no special emotional significance. Few words remain entirely neutral, however, and such has been the case with these. So profound is the mystery of growth and so mixed are the feelings of adults in relation to it that these terms carry more than the usual degree of emotional impact. Unfortunately, some of this impact is negative, and the term "adolescent" has come in part to signify callowness in personality and behavior. It is particularly important for those who concern themselves about high schools to avoid the overwrought emotional folklore often associated with discussions of adolescence; but it is equally important to avoid the severe coldness of scientific detachment.

Generalizations and conclusions about adolescence present several kinds of difficulties. One is that adolescents share many of their characteristics with people of other age levels. To label certain behavior patterns typically or uniquely adolescent is risky business, for the chances are that they may be simply characteristics of humanity at large. The second difficulty is the familiar one that all generalizations about human behavior obscure important individual differences; the average or typical adolescent is a myth. A third point to be kept in mind is the variability of human behavior in a given individual under differing circumstances and conditions. Fourth, biological and cultural factors interweave to produce the specific tasks and problems to which the adolescents themselves must respond. This makes it difficult to identify adolescent behavior patterns outside the confines of specific environments. The study of adolescence, therefore, presents no easy answers, but it does provide materials that direct our attention to important questions about the high school curriculum.

PHYSICAL AND MENTAL GROWTH

The facts of physical change have bewildered and amazed every generation of parents throughout history. We get used to the steady growth of our children during the early elementary grades. Then growth begins to take place not only more rapidly, but in different ways. Yesterday's children vanish forever to be replaced in a few swift years, from the standpoint of the adult's time perception, by young men and women physically ready for adulthood.

Students of adolescence have catalogued these facts of physical and physiological change with great care and in prolific detail. In some departments of the high school program, such as physical education, teachers need a great deal of such technical information. Only the most important and outstanding features, however, need concern us here. Among these are the range and scope of what adolescent psychologists call the "growth spurt."

Usually between the age of eight years and twelve years among girls and between nine years and thirteen years among boys there commences a sequence of changes in velocity of increase in height, body breadth, and body depth, in heart size, lung capacity, muscular strength, and other structures and functions. This particular sequence of changes in the velocity of physical growth is unlike anything which has occurred before and unlike anything which comes afterward. The sequence lasts for from four and one-half to seven and one-half years and is completed somewhere between the ages of fifteen and eighteen years in girls; between seventeen and twenty years in boys.[1]

This growth spurt begins early for some children and is often apparent in the upper elementary grades. It is in the seventh, eighth, and ninth grades, however, that most children have their most rapid growth.

Rapidity of growth sets the stage for physical awkwardness, a feature of adolescence that although overstressed in popular literature is one of considerable importance.

Adolescent awkwardness is so common that few individuals are fortunate enough to escape it. The cause of awkwardness may be traced to muscle growth. During childhood, growth is moderate and relatively uniform, so that the child acquires control of his body and has fairly good coordination. With the sudden rapid growth of bones and muscles at puberty, the bones bear a new ratio to one another. Furthermore, the muscles are elongated and pulled into new patterns. The result is an upset in the built-in motor achievements acquired during childhood. This necessitates the learning of new controls and new coordinations.[2]

This may have much to do with physical restlessness of high school students, especially in Grades 7 and 8. It poses specific problems for the physical education curriculum and for certain aspects of the junior high school extraclass activities program, such as parties and dances.

Along with the physical growth spurt come those physiological changes leading to puberty, "that time in the life cycle when the reproductive organs attain functional maturity and the individual is potentially capable of reproducing his kind."[3] Of particular im-

[1] Herbert R. Stolz and Lois Meek Stolz, "Adolescent Problems Related to Somatic Variations," National Society for the Study of Education, Fifty-third Yearbook, pt. 1, *Adolescence,* University of Chicago Press, 1944, p. 81.

[2] Elizabeth B. Hurlock, *Adolescent Development,* McGraw-Hill Book Company, Inc., 1955, p. 58.

[3] John E. Horrocks, *The Psychology of Adolescence,* Houghton Mifflin Company, 1951, p. 311.

portance to the adolescent are the secondary sex characteristics, such as changes in body proportions, voice, and distribution of hair. There is some apparent confusion in the literature on the timing of pubescence, owing to the use of varying criteria. One writer summarizes the situation as follows. "At the present time it is generally accepted that the average age for pubescence is 13.5 years for girls and 14.5 years for boys. Approximately 50 per cent of all girls mature between 12.5 and 14.5 years and 50 per cent of all boys between 14 and 15.5 years."[4] For about half the students, then, these changes will appear somewhere through the seventh, eighth, and ninth grades.

The most important fact of all in relation to physical and physiological change is the wide range of individual differences, especially through the junior high school years. Children who reach these stages at or about the average times will experience only the usual concerns that accompany them. But those who develop much ahead of or behind schedule often suffer in their own minds from the fact of being different and sometimes wonder whether or not they are normal. Fortunately, these differences are usually leveled off by the time physical growth is completed.

Physical and physiological changes provide the objective setting for any consideration of adolescence. In some cultures, these changes serve as the identifying symbols of adulthood. Young people are even formally initiated into the adult society through some objective ceremony. In our society, however, rapid physical growth does not automatically lead to adult status.

There is no sudden spurt of mental growth corresponding to the physical. "Mental ability grows rapidly during childhood and begins to decelerate in adolescence."[5] But although the rate slows down, mental growth does continue in the early adolescent years. "Intelligence or mental ability increases with age throughout childhood and well into adolescence. There is some disagreement as to the exact year at which mental growth reaches its peak, but the consensus is that it is sometime in the late teens or early twenties

[4] Hurlock, *op. cit.,* p. 23.
[5] Horrocks, *op. cit.,* p. 226.

with only small additions occurring after the sixteenth year."[6] The same writer, however, goes on to caution us that "Curves of mental growth, as reported in the literature, are usually composites of many individual curves and tend to conceal the wide individual differences characteristic of mental growth."[7]

In considering the high school program, we are concerned not only with the growth but with the distribution of mental ability. The field of intelligence testing has become extremely complex and controversial; few writers commit themselves as definitely to conclusions on this matter as was once the case. In particular, the familiar symbol of the intelligence quotient[8] or the IQ has been vigorously challenged and defended and is subject to many qualifications in its interpretation and meaning. Perhaps the only safe conclusion is that "Many studies have shown that mental ability varies greatly in any group of pupils in any grade or age in the adolescent period."[9] Nevertheless various studies in the past have indicated about one tenth of the children as having intelligence quotients have 120, about one fourth above 110, and about three fourths above 90, with about half of the total distribution located between 90 and 110.[10] It is likely that a high school population especially in the junior high school grades would show a distribution not too different from that for school-age children generally, at least down to the 70 IQ level. Seventh-grade and eighth-grade children might easily show a range in mental age from 10 to 20.

Ability to do high school work depends also on reading, a skill that is highly related to general intelligence as measured by verbal tests. Here again we face a tremendous range of individual differ-

---

[6] *Ibid.*, p. 245.

[7] *Ibid.*

[8] An intelligence quotient is the ratio of mental age as measured on tests to chronological age, multiplied by one hundred. A ten-year old child with a mental age of ten would have an IQ of 100, one with a mental age of seven would have an IQ of 70, and one with a mental age of 12 would have an IQ of 120.

[9] David Segel, *Intellectual Abilities in the Adolescent Period: Their Growth and Development,* Office of Education, Federal Security Agency, Bulletin 1948, No. 6, p. 5.

[10] These fractions are approximate figures based on a summary made and presented by Sidney L. Pressey and Francis P. Robinson, *Psychology and the New Education,* Harper & Brothers, 1944, table 6, p. 89.

ences. A study of 7,380 eighth-grade graduates of St. Louis elementary schools showed that 968 were reading at the eleventh-grade level or above, while 1,163 were reading at the fifth-grade level or below.[11] Such extensive variation in mental ability and reading level presents an inescapable reality confronting every high school teacher, administrator, guidance worker, and curriculum consultant. It is by no means certain that this situation is any more pronounced today than it was in the golden age of the 1890's or early 1900's to which we often longingly refer. Although comparable IQ and reading scores are not available for those periods, there was a good deal of informal writing which testified to substantial differences among students in the ability to do their work.

Whether or not intelligence quotients may be raised has long been debated among psychologists. This question depends in part on the degree of confidence we have in the validity and accuracy of intelligence tests themselves. Some students of testing have suggested the possibility that our current tests may have greater validity for students from the middle and upper than for those from the lower socioeconomic levels. Tests containing concepts and vocabulary more familiar to the lower socioeconomic groups, therefore, might yield different results. We must remember, however, that the term "intelligence" as used in psychology and education means primarily the ability to handle school work, which is not always the same meaning attached to the term in everyday speech. Since it is true that school work makes use of the same concepts as appear in our current intelligence tests, changing these tests would not change the nature or the range of the individual differences confronting the teacher. It is also true that many students from the lower socioeconomic levels do score high on our current intelligence tests, a fact that casts some doubt on the criticism of such tests as suitable only for middle-class and upper-class students.

[11] William Kottmeyer, "Improving Reading Instruction in the St. Louis Schools," *Elementary School Journal,* September, 1944, pp. 33–38, cited by Paul A. Witty, "Current Role and Effectiveness of Reading among Youth," National Society for the Study of Education, Forty-seventh Yearbook, pt. 2, *Reading in the High School and College,* University of Chicago Press, 1948, pp. 15–16.

SOCIAL AND MORAL CHARACTERISTICS

The social characteristics of adolescence are also of great importance to the educator, regardless of his point of view on the relative importance of intellectual and social adjustment objectives. Even the most severe advocate of intellectual development realizes that the attainment of this goal by individual students is often fostered or hampered by degrees of social acceptance or adjustment. Moreover, the term "adjustment" does not necessarily imply passive or blind conformity to the group. It means rather the achievement of satisfactory social relationships without abandoning individuality or personal standards. Such adjustment is a necessity to everyone but a hermit, and it is a rather complex and critical matter to young people traversing the long pathway from childhood to adulthood. Boys and girls who achieve such adjustment easily are able to devote more of their emotional and mental effort to intellectual achievement in school work than is true of those who have difficulties. In any case, a high school is a complicated social institution, and the pattern of its social life will inevitably affect favorably or unfavorably the achievement of curricular objectives, even though these be defined strictly in intellectual terms.

Again we must be on guard against the tendency to exaggerate or overemphasize the allegedly unique characteristics of adolescent social life. Basically, the social aspirations of adolescents are no different from those of other people. They want belongingness, participation, and recognition or status, accompanied by that reasonable assurance of stability which we call security.

The adolescent of course does face problems in his social life. According to Horrocks, an initial problem is presented by the fact that the bases for acceptance in adolescence differ from those in childhood.

One of the most difficult social changes in adolescence is the need of exchanging a passive for an active social role. As a child, the individual's physical presence was usually enough to insure inclusion in a play group, a schoolroom group, or some other children's gathering. The whole matter of group participation was transitory at best, since most child groups gather without any great degree of premeditation, unless it is on the part of a supervising adult; the groups are loosely knit without enduring intra-group alliances. On the other hand, if the adolescent wishes to be included in a group, he usually finds it necessary to do something so that his acceptance will be continued. In a social sense the child group is natural and not critical. It accepts what is there. The adolescent group tends to be hypercritical, snobbish, and highly artificial. Physical presence does not equal acceptance. With good reason, the adolescent has to worry about what others think.[12]

Along with these changes in ways of gaining acceptance comes increased desire on the part of the adolescent for participation in group activities, especially those initiated and managed by other adolescents. This is a characteristic of adolescence which, like the physical growth spurt, never ceases to astonish and sometimes dismay the adult world. The reason for it, according to Ausubel, is largely that the adult society offers young people little opportunity for status in its own activities.

The reasons for this intense preoccupation with social experience are apparent. It is true, of course, that group activity is facilitated by the adolescent's greater mobility and newly won emancipation from the home. Group activity also provides an opportunity for gratifying newly acquired heterosexual needs and interests. Much more important, however, is the adolescent's increasing concern with acquiring primary status as an independent entity. And since there can be no status apart from a system of relationships to a constituted social unit, adolescent peer groups are "formed spontaneously to serve the function of a social institution, to secure a status and a social identity for youngsters not genuinely provided with such an identity by society at large." Denied membership in the adult community that dispenses status roles in the central stratum of social interaction, he must create a substitute albeit peripheral status-giving instrumentality of his own.[13]

If the foregoing statement is correct, the adolescent finds it a matter of critical necessity to be accepted by his own kind. Further-

[12] Horrocks, *op. cit.*, p. 89.

[13] David P. Ausubel, *Theory and Problems of Adolescent Development,* Grune & Stratton, 1954, pp. 342–343. Quoted material within the quotation from M. Sherif and H. Cantril, *The Psychology of Ego-Involvements,* John Wiley & Sons, Inc., 1947.

more, as pointed out by Horrocks, he must do something more than just be around in order to gain this acceptance. It is little wonder, then, that he will seek well-grooved and standardized patterns of behavior that carry assurance of acceptance. He must do something, but he must do what is approved by other adolescents and do it along approved lines. He must conform. Ausubel sees the conformity of adolescents as growing both from the needs of the group and from that of the adolescents themselves.

Apart from the structural needs of the peer groups, various developmental characteristics of adolescents make them prone to overvalue the importance of conformity. First, any person with marginal status is excessively sensitive to the threat of forfeiting what little status he enjoys as a result of incurring the disapproval of those on whom he is dependent. To allay the anxiety from the threat of disapproval he conforms more than is objectively necessary to retain group acceptance or to avoid censure and reprisal. Thus, many perfectly *safe* opportunities for the expression of individuality are lost.

Second, as pointed out, adolescents are partly *motivated* to perceive age-mates as deviants, non-conformists, and out-groupers because by so doing they can enhance the value of their own conformity and in-group status. The larger the number of persons who can be perceived as *outside* the charmed circle, the more individuals they can perceive as inferior to themselves, the greater their own self-esteem becomes by comparison, and the more status value their in-group membership acquires.[14]

Groups in which adolescents seek acceptance include cliques, crowds, and gangs, which are given varying technical definitions in the literature. These are the groups which adolescents set up for themselves. In addition, many take active part in groups set up by adults, through school activities and through churches and community organizations. Adolescents face a wide variety of patterns to which they may or may not conform, some of which are certainly more acceptable than others to parents, teachers, and other members of adult society.

Unless group standards and requirements violate morality or decency, the efforts of the adolescent to adapt himself may have

[14] *Ibid.,* p. 355.

some informal educative value. Every individual must do a certain amount of conforming. Danger lies in that excessive conformity which leads to the abandonment of individual conscience and standards. As pointed out by Ausubel, however, it is the person with "marginal status" who is "excessively sensitive to the threat of forfeiting what little status he enjoys."[15] It may be necessary for an individual to conform in many non-essential aspects of living to gain the confidence necessary to express and maintain individuality in those which are essential. Paradoxically, conformity may be for the adolescent, as well as for the adult, the road to individuality.

Individual differences enter the picture on this matter of acceptance, as they do on most human characteristics. Much has been made of racial, ethnic, and socioeconomic factors in the acceptance and rejection patterns of adolescent groups. But the problem of the individual with marginal status is not usually a matter of race, ethnic membership, or socioeconomic level. Students from so-called minority groups form their own cliques and crowds. Furthermore, there are young people from the majority culture who do not gain acceptance. The plight of the young person who comes from the "right side of the tracks" and still remains an isolate is especially severe.

The most important factor, then, is probably the individual adolescent himself. This does not mean there is something intrinsically wrong with the rejected adolescent, only that there is something wrong with him so far as the appraisals of other adolescents are concerned. Possibilities of such "wrongness" include personal appearance, dress, voice, conformity to the culturally accepted stereotypes of masculine or feminine behavior, interests, skills in social activities such as games and dancing, and a host of others. Numerous studies have identified such possibilities, but it still remains a secret the adult world does not successfully penetrate. The adolescent world understands and applies its own criteria, but individual adolescents themselves do not find it easy to put them into words.

So far as the non-accepted adolescent is concerned, the social

[15] *Ibid.*

program of the school may provide some training in social skills. On the other hand it may be of little or no help.

Apparently school dances, for example, as commonly conducted, present a number of serious obstacles to social adjustment and this appears truer of younger than of older children. Large numbers of adolescents who have not attained a feeling of security in meeting social situations will tend to avoid them, and the physical presence of a social facility does not mean that it will serve its adjustment function unless a specific program is carried out to help those who cannot or will not participate. This does not mean that a school dance serves no one. Many adolescents get great social benefits from such a dance. It is simply an indication that there are also many who fail to receive social benefits for a number of different reasons, and it is those people who need and should receive help.[16]

The acceptance-rejection patterns of groups initiated by adolescents affect in various ways the success or adequacy of groups and activities sponsored by adults. Sometimes a clique will enter enthusiastically into school activities to such an extent that it appears to dominate them. Under such circumstances, the isolates or near-isolates feel they are not wanted and so miss whatever educational opportunities those activities may offer. Or it may happen that the social stars look disdainfully on school activities. The prestige of the activities declines or collapses, although this does not usually happen in the case of interscholastic athletics. Again, this does not imply that the clique or crowd groupings necessarily reflect ethnic or socioeconomic distinctions in the community. When they do, however, the problems and difficulties of the extraclass activities program are compounded.

Socioeconomic distinctions among adolescents usually reflect those in the community itself. Whether or not such distinctions constitute a class system, as suggested by numerous community studies,[17] is a complex question that has been vigorously debated in the literature. The impact of social class on the school-and-com-

[16] Horrocks, *op. cit.,* p. 183.
[17] See W. Lloyd Warner, *American Life: Dream and Reality,* University of Chicago Press, 1953, for a summary of community studies on the social class question.

munity life of adolescents has been intensively studied by Hollingshead, who concludes that "there is a functional relationship between the class position of an adolescent's family and his social behavior in the community."[18] Communities differ, and it is desirable for a high school faculty to understand as accurately as possible what its own situation really is. The presence or absence of socioeconomic factors and distinctions may have important bearings on the extraclass activities and the general social life and program of the school.

Regardless of such possibilities, however, each adolescent is still an individual who, in spite of conformity patterns, makes many choices for himself in terms of his moral values and standards. Teen-age morality has always been a matter of intense concern on the part of adults. In part this reflects the conviction of each succeeding generation of adults that "young people are going to the dogs." This conviction is reinforced in contemporary society by popular fiction, radio and television dramas, newspaper headlines and stories, and movies, all of which make generous use of adolescent stereotypes. Occasional articles from the opposite standpoint appear in popular magazines testifying to faith in today's adolescents, comparing them favorably with those of yesterday. Those who view with alarm and those who point with pride can find numerous examples of real adolescents to support their cases. Relatively few youth get into serious trouble,[19] and the pointers with pride cite the more impressive quantitative evidence of the overwhelming majority who do not. Juvenile crime is, of course, a serious and tragic problem not to be dismissed or ignored. But its presence should not be allowed to distort the general state of affairs with regard to adolescent character and morality.

[18] August B. Hollingshead, *Elmtown's Youth,* John Wiley & Sons, Inc., 1949, p. 441.

[19] "It is all too easy to conclude that the youth of today is thundering downhill on a bobsled and that no good can come of it. But that would be an alarmist's view, irrational and completely unjustified by the facts. Even though statisticians estimate that 1,250,000 of our teenagers this year will become involved in trouble, this is only about one-eighteenth of the population between ten and seventeen years of age. And only one-third of this total, some 435,000 or less, will become involved in actions so serious that they actually will be brought into court." Robert C. Hendrickson with Fred J. Cook, *Youth in Danger,* Harcourt, Brace and Company, 1956, pp. 4–5.

Adolescent psychologists have conducted hundreds of studies dealing with character and moral behavior. These show the wide range of individual differences to be expected. But the usual cautions about broad generalizations apply with greater force to this aspect of adolescent development than to any other. They apply with such force that the reader is tempted to despair of the possibility of any stable conclusions at all. Some observations, however, are reasonably valid at least for many or most adolescents. They are not spectacular observations, but they are important.

General agreement prevails among psychologists that adolescence is a time of moral earnestness and purpose. "Most of these young people seem to be eager to respond to moral values. Even those who rebel against their environment seem to cherish an inward ideal of desirable conduct."[20] Adolescents do not fling aside the moral precepts learned in childhood, even though they may seek reasons for such precepts. "Essentially, however, there is less rejection of old moral values than a change in the basis on which they are accepted. The basic moral values of our culture are inculcated in the early years and show little variability in degree of acceptance from childhood to adult life. However, adolescents are more likely to give their own than conventional reasons for disapproving of such practices as lying and stealing, and place equity in interpersonal relationships above such considerations as fear of 'getting caught.' "[21]

Behavior choices can be complicated matters for adolescents. Some of the time the adult world appears to demand unquestioning obedience, while at other times it puts the stress on independent judgment. And adults often are inconsistent in their own behavior toward one another. The adolescent therefore seeks general guidelines that will clarify the confusions and contradictions he encounters in his daily affairs. "Growth in cognitive capacity alone accounts for several significant changes in character organization during adolescence. For one thing, moral concepts, like all other

---

[20] Robert J. Havighurst and Hilda Taba (in collaboration with the Committee on Human Development, the University of Chicago), *Adolescent Character and Personality,* John Wiley & Sons, Inc., 1949, p. 96.

[21] Ausubel, *op. cit.,* p. 248.

concepts, become more abstract. This enables moral behavior to acquire greater generality and consistency from situation to situation, since abstraction presupposes the identification of essential common elements."[22] Moral development then becomes in part a matter of reflective thinking. But growth in reflective thinking in relation to difficult moral choices does not come suddenly. "The ability to apply moral beliefs to an increasing range of conflicting life situations is quite undeveloped at the age of sixteen. These subjects see the more obvious lines of action but seem at a loss whenever a subtle weighing of values is called for."[23] The school seeks to develop the general skill known as application of principles; in this connection it can help young people "to study moral problems and to apply moral principles to a wide variety of situations."[24]

To do this, adolescents need principles to apply. It is sometimes contended that adolescents tend to move from moral absolutism to moral relativism. Much depends on the meanings attached to these terms. If moral absolutism means a prescribed code of behavior applied without discrimination and judgment, the generalization may have some validity. But this is a straw-man definition that confuses absolute principles with rigid prescription. Moral absolutism more appropriately means adherence to principles independent of cultural variations and group opinions, even though they require judgment in their application. In this sense the adolescent's search for broader and more abstract concepts may even represent a firmer adherence to stable moral values.

There is, however, some possible relationship between moral relativism and social conformity, if the conformity is carried to the point of sacrificing individual conscience and moral convictions to gain group acceptance. We know how strong the desire for group acceptance may be on the part of adolescents. The general tendency to group conformity in adult life may encourage adolescents to over-conformity in behavior and outlook. It is the socially insecure adolescent, however, who is most likely to become overdependent

---

[22] *Ibid.*, p. 249.
[23] Havighurst and Taba, *op. cit.*, p. 95.
[24] *Ibid.*, p. 194.

on others and to be tempted to overconforming behavior in an effort to gain approval.

Adolescents are no different from people at other age levels with regard to doing things they know are wrong. "Studies of cheating in the junior and senior high schools as well as in colleges suggest that about one-third of the students cheat, and under specific circumstances the number may be as high as two-thirds."[25] This is the age-old dilemma of moral knowledge and moral action. It may be due to an absence of stable moral principles, but it may also reflect the intellectual difficulties involved in making application of these principles. Another possible source of such conflict is emotional disturbance within the individual himself. "Good emotional adjustment is, therefore, an important prerequisite for desirable character development in adolescence."[26] Moral behavior interrelates understanding, skill, and emotion. This does not mean that wrong actions are to be condoned, but that the adolescent be helped through home, school, and church to develop those aspects of his personality which lead to right actions.

While moral principles do not necessarily depend on religious belief, practically every form of religious belief places much stress on moral behavior. Numerous studies have been made of religious development in adolescence. "Studies seem to indicate that adolescence does not bring with it particularly great changes in religious beliefs and attitudes; the longer a child has retained his beliefs the less likely he is to change."[27] Ausubel similarly points out that "Just as adolescence brings no great upheaval in moral structure, it effects no revolution in religious belief or activity. Contrary to widespread opinion there is no rampant repudiation of religion during adolescence."[28] Neither do recent writers on adolescent psychology note any special tendency to strong emotional crises of the kind associated with religious conversion. There does seem to be a period of what is called "religious awakening," defined as "an increased interest in religion which leads to a reconstruction of re-

[25] Hurlock, *op. cit.*, p. 327.
[26] Havighurst and Taba, *op. cit.*, p. 96.
[27] Horrocks, *op. cit.*, p. 549.
[28] Ausubel, *op. cit.*, p. 268.

ligious beliefs and attitudes."[29] This seems to reflect intellectual development rather than emotional crisis and is supposed to occur usually at about a mental age of 12.[30] For the majority of adolescents, it is a gradual process rather than a sudden occurrence, at least as they report it themselves.[31]

Adolescent development then takes place along a number of important lines: physical, intellectual, social, and moral. Some of these occur more rapidly and suddenly than others. The adolescent goes through a rather long and complex learning process in which the desired symbols of adult status are identified and acquired. From the various aspects of this learning process flow the needs and tasks, as well as many of the interests, of students in our high schools.

INTERESTS, NEEDS, AND TASKS

A number of members of the adult world have suffered from guilty consciences over the alleged "imposition" of the school curriculum on children, in particular that of the high school curriculum on adolescents. The past 50 years or so have consequently witnessed numerous attempts to base the curriculum not on the preconceived adult notions of the intellectual heritage, but on some factors more intrinsic to the actual lives and problems of youth.

The earliest efforts were those based on the identification of adolescent interests. Investigators have surveyed such interest patterns and in some cases have attempted to draw conclusions from them for the curriculum. From such studies it is clear that adolescents take considerable interest in their social activities, particularly those that promote boy-girl relationships, in sports and games, in their personal and vocational futures, in grooming and appearance, in reading, and in mass media of entertainment such as movies,

---

[29] Hurlock, *op. cit.*, p. 292.

[30] *Ibid.*, p. 293. Citation of L. S. Hollingsworth, "The Adolescent Child," in C. Murchison, *A Handbook of Child Psychology*, Clark University Press, pp. 882–908. Slightly higher ages reported by B. W. Allport, J. M. Gillespie, and J. Young, "The Religion of the Postwar College Student," *Journal of Psychology*, 25:3–33, cited *ibid.*

[31] *Ibid.*, p. 295. This is also based on citation from Allport. See Note 30.

television, and radio. These interest patterns broadly parallel at least some of the major elements in the curriculum. The high school program, for example, requires a lot of reading, and adolescents clearly like to read. Some of their reading interests match the selections used in high school literature programs while others do not.[32] There is of course much difference of opinion about the extent to which the literature program should be revised in the direction of such interests.

It may be that the question of interest is more acute at the secondary than at the elementary level. Jersild and Tasch comment specifically on the apparent difference in enthusiasm for school between young children and adolescents.

As the average child moves up through the grades he seems to become less eager about things that distinctly belong to school and scholarliness, more inclined to complain, more interested in the things that go along with school rather than with work in the classroom. He becomes relatively more interested in recess periods than in class periods. He mentions play and sports more often. There is a greater hiatus between his wishes and what the school offers. This is particularly marked, as we have seen, in connection with his wishes for self-improvement and for vocational competence, on the one hand, and his recognition of what the school offers to further his aspirations.

The older child reveals in various ways that the school program has less vitality for him, compared with its interest for him in the earlier grades. He says this in mentioning his likes and interests. He also actively complains about school in describing what he dislikes. The

[32] Many studies have been made of children's and adolescents' reading interests. One of the most recent and most comprehensive is that of George W. Norvell, *The Reading Interests of Young People*, D. C. Heath and Company, 1950. According to this study adolescents accept some of the "classics," but not others. "Certain observations may be made with respect to the classics. The generation-long opposition by certain leading English teachers to such widely used classics as Burke's 'On Conciliation,' 'L'Allegro,' 'Il Penseroso,' *As You Like It, The Vicar of Wakefield,* Webster's 'Bunker Hill Oration,' *The Odyssey,* and Macaulay's *Life of Johnson* are borne out by students' reactions. On the other hand, some of the classics have met the test by fire: *Macbeth, Hamlet, Silas Marner, David Copperfield, Treasure Island,* 'Old Ironsides,' 'The Barefoot Boy,' 'Paul Revere's Ride,' 'The Deacon's Masterpiece,' 'A Dissertation upon Roast Pig.'

"It is not necessary, then, for the teacher to throw overboard all classic literature to meet the interests of young people. However, in view of the high standing both artistically and in children's favor of many modern selections, the use of a large proportion of modern literature seems justified." *Ibid.,* p. 86.

high school youth more often than the younger child expresses dislike of his teachers, of the school program, of discipline, of rules and regulations, and of the physical appointments of the school.[33]

Why this should be so is not clear. Perhaps adolescents identify the school with the childhood status they are trying to leave behind them. Jersild and Tasch explore a number of possible explanations, including the one that the curriculum is based on the interests of adults rather than on those of adolescents.

It appears that high school pupils often fail to see the meaning or values of many subjects when each is served in a separate academic bundle, as though it had an intrinsic value of its own. To throw light on this problem would require more study and experimentation than the present investigation provides. However, the fact that many children of high school age do not seem to get from their course of study what the school apparently intends that they should get, suggests that the course of study as a whole and individual projects within the course are planned more from the point of view of the interests and tastes of adults in the school and in the community at large than from the point of view of what would best promote curiosity and interest in children. At the high school level, a great deal of what is taught is couched in terms of the finished logic of the scholar rather than in terms suited to the psychology of the learner.[34]

Nevertheless few educators would claim that interests should provide the major basis for the school program. Interests do have strong motivational force, however, and current interests of youth might be used as leads to more formal studies. Certain patterns of interests tend to appear at various ages; these patterns sometimes provide valuable clues to grade-level designation of certain subjects, topics, or literature selections. These rather modest claims for the use of interests in the curriculum probably came to represent the views of the great majority of educators.

But this did not mean that adult qualms of conscience about im-

[33] Arthur T. Jersild and Ruth J. Tasch in collaboration with committees of teachers of the public schools of Springfield, Missouri, *Children's Interests and What They Suggest for Education,* Bureau of Publications, Teachers College, Columbia University, 1949, pp. 41–42.

[34] *Ibid.,* p. 45.

position were soothed. If interests did not provide the basis for the curriculum, some other approach to the question might. The term "needs" sprang into the literature and was welcomed by many as at least a partial solution. Needs implied something far more substantial than the passing whims or fancies suggested by interests. The appeal of the term proved to be tremendous, so much so that one investigator in 1942 wrote as follows, "If there is one point upon which most educators today appear to be in agreement it is that educational programs, particularly those of the secondary school, should be founded upon the needs of the children concerned."[35] The same writer then goes on to point out, "But in regard to just what it is that the children or youth need, in regard to the implications of their needs, and in regard to the place of needs in determining such programs, there is far from general agreement."[36]

One of the issues has been whether or not needs should be interpreted as the "felt needs" of youth. From one point of view it can be argued that young people should know their own needs better than anyone else, from another that the adult world is in a better position to know what adolescents need. These of course represent extreme responses to the question. Most people who accept the needs idea try to work out some combination of approaches.

It is possible to study felt or expressed needs by going directly to the adolescents themselves. Doane, for example, presented students with descriptions of 19 kinds of school courses, from which they were to choose 5 they would like to take. The courses included some on personal adjustment problems, some on social problems, and others that "represented other subject fields or other common areas of interest."[37] In addition he asked the students to check specific items or topics from a 159-point list. Such areas as vocational choice and placement, getting along with people, relationships with the opposite sex, and health ranked high in the students' choices. Religion, government, history, and current prob-

---

[35] Donald C. Doane, *The Needs of Youth: An Evaluation for Curriculum Purposes,* Teachers College, Columbia University Contributions to Education, No. 848, Bureau of Publications, 1942, p. 1.

[36] *Ibid.*

[37] *Ibid.,* p. 115.

lems ranked relatively low. Doane noted some implications from this for a shift in the "focus" of the high school curriculum. "This shift should be away from a focus upon purely adult concerns and subject matter for its own sake toward a focus upon youth's own concerns—themselves as individuals and as members of society, their problems of adjustment to their vocational future, to their fellow youth, and to their emerging adult status."[38] Doane did not, however, accept the extreme interpretation that the curriculum should include only those items which rank high in student choice.

The low value placed by pupils on a topic in a study such as this does not mean, however, that the goals sought by such a topic should be excluded if they are otherwise justified, but rather that if they are deemed worth while they must be sought through the concerns immediately vital to the youth under consideration. If only one-fifth of the respondents indicated interest in a topic, that fifth is of importance. Investigation of the sources of such interest may lead to suggestions for its further cultivation and for stimulating interest on the part of others.[39]

Difficulties in estimating the capacity of youth to interpret their own needs led to much dissatisfaction with the felt-needs idea. The point of view developed that adults might have a share in the identification of adolescent needs. In this more comprehensive approach, student expressions were by no means rejected, but they were considered in the light of other data, such as employment trends, requirements of citizenship, and general social conditions.

In the context of this more comprehensive approach, the needs idea picked up considerable momentum. The continuing force of the idea was demonstrated by the appearance in 1953 of a yearbook of the National Society for the Study of Education entitled *Adapting the Secondary-School Program to the Needs of Youth.* In the opening article of this yearbook, Brink identified three other "conflicts and uncertainties as to the meaning of the term:"[40] (1) the relationship between the immediate needs of youth and

---

[38] *Ibid.,* p. 119.

[39] *Ibid.*

[40] William G. Brink, "Introduction: The Youth-Need Motives in Secondary Education," National Society for the Study of Education, Fifty-second Yearbook, pt. 1, *Adapting the Secondary-School Program to the Needs of Youth,* The University of Chicago Press, 1953, p. 3.

those which refer more to the future demands of adult life; (2) the relationship of the personal needs of youth to the broader needs of society;[41] and (3) the relative usefulness of general and specific statements of needs. The yearbook committee took moderate and balanced positions on all three questions. On the first, it rejected "the assumption of an antithesis between present and future needs."[42] On the second, it took the position that personal needs and needs of society are "reciprocal in nature."[43] On the third, it recognized "that although such general statements of needs may serve a useful purpose, it is only when they are defined closely enough to indicate the specific types of knowledge, ability, skill, appreciation, and behavior to be developed that they can be of greatest value to teachers in selecting and organizing instructional materials."[44]

Lists of general needs are probably not intended to serve as anything more than categories or headings under which more specific needs may be classified. Such lists, however, do indicate the points of view of those who prepare and endorse them and the impact which the needs idea might make on the high school curriculum if it were widely followed. Low presents examples of a number of such classifications.[45] Many of these are stated along the lines of social functions or common human activities, as, for example, the following.

Protecting life and health
Living in and improving the home
Conserving and improving material conditions
Co-operating in social and civic action
Getting a living
Securing an education
Expressing religious impulses
Engaging in recreation.[46]

[41] This is not the same issue as that of felt needs. The adult world might adopt the personal-needs position and still feel that it is in a better position to identify these than adolescents themselves are.

[42] Brink, op. cit., p. 3.

[43] Ibid., p. 4.

[44] Ibid., pp. 4–5.

[45] Camilla M. Low, "Determining the Needs of Youth," chap. 2, National Society for the Study of Education, op. cit., pp. 30–40.

[46] Ibid., p. 34. Cited from O. I. Frederick and L. J. Farquear, "Areas of Human Activity," Journal of Educational Research, May, 1937, pp. 672–679. This list was derived by Frederick and Farquear from 30 such lists.

Such lists as these give a rather severely functional appearance and seem to leave little place for the intellectual and cultural heritage as such. This appearance is probably deceptive, for each of the social functions would demand considerable use of subject matter from the traditional academic disciplines. As Low points out, "If each of the social functions were exhaustively analyzed, the resulting curriculum would certainly not be lacking in content."[47]

Once identified, needs may serve as bases for objectives, or may even replace objectives as usually stated and serve as independent criteria for decisions on curricular organization, content, and teaching procedures. There are varying interpretations of what needs may or may not imply for curricular organization. Some advocates of the needs idea happen also to be advocates of core classes in the high school program. Core classes do provide one kind of organization for carrying out the needs approach, but it does not follow that one who adopts the needs approach of necessity adopts the core curriculum along with it. So far as many students of curriculum are concerned, the traditional subject organization also provides a framework for helping students learn to meet their needs.

Neither does the needs idea necessarily suggest all the connotations of life-adjustment education. Some of the critics who fear anti-intellectualism in the schools might wish for more explicit recognition of the need for intellectual competence or reflective thinking and problem-solving processes in carrying out the social functions or common activities. Advocates of the needs idea do not contend that the school meets needs directly, except perhaps in unusual circumstances. The emphasis is always on the school as an educative agency engaged in the process of teaching students how to meet their own needs individually and at times in association with their fellow citizens. Neither do most advocates of the needs idea claim that the school should teach youth how to meet any and all needs. Some selection is always implied, even though differences of opinion exist on how broad or restricted such selection should be.

Nevertheless, the needs approach has contributed somewhat to the current confusions about the secondary school program. Very

[47] *Ibid.,* p. 35.

few, if any, of the statements on needs explicitly call for a high school curriculum based exclusively on such matters as personality development, going on dates, how to be popular, and the like. But people derive their impressions not so much from explicit statements as from overall emotional impact. As is true of other movements in education, the needs approach has suffered from slogans and clichés. To many people, modern secondary education implies a "curriculum based on students' needs," which in turn seems to imply a curriculum based on triviality. For, although educators do not confine their thinking to felt needs, they have not always made this point clear in public discussion.

The more recent interpretation of needs as developmental tasks gives promise of resolving some of the difficulties and of providing a workable basis for recognizing adolescent development in the high school program. This term was developed in the middle 1930's and it has since come into extensive use. Havighurst, who has done much of the writing in this field, points out as follows how he came to use the term. "Because I had seen so much misunderstanding result from the use of the equivocal term 'needs' as a central concept in such discussions, I was determined to try out the term 'developmental task' instead."[48] Just what then is a developmental task? "A developmental task is a task which arises at or about a certain period in the life of the individual, successful achievement of which leads to his happiness and to success with later tasks, while failure leads to unhappiness in the individual, disapproval by the society, and difficulty with later tasks."[49] Such tasks may be described for any growth level from infancy to old age. The growth-level designations are in part arbitrary ones, but they correspond pretty well to those assumed in common sense and popular speech. Obviously one of the most important levels is that of adolescence. Defined in these terms, the developmental tasks idea seems to dispose of the old difficulty about felt needs, for it takes into account not only the wishes and feelings of the individual, but the responsibilities individuals assume in relation to

[48] Robert J. Havighurst, *Developmental Tasks and Education,* Longmans, Green, and Company, 1950, p. 2.
[49] *Ibid.,* p. 6.

others. "Thus developmental tasks may arise from physical maturation, from the pressure of cultural processes upon the individual, from the desires, aspirations and values of the emerging personality, and they arise in most cases from combinations of these factors acting together."[50] In addition, developmental tasks help resolve the long-standing dilemma of present versus future needs. While the task is one that confronts the individual at a particular time, the carrying out of the task is in part at least preparatory to the meeting of tasks in the future. Some tasks furthermore "recur over a long period of time, in varying and closely related aspects."[51]

The following list is representative of those that have been prepared on the developmental tasks of adolescence.

1. Accepting one's physique and accepting a masculine or feminine sex role.
2. New relations with age-mates of both sexes.
3. Emotional independence of parents and other adults.
4. Achieving assurance of economic independence.
5. Selecting and preparing for an occupation.
6. Developing intellectual skills and concepts necessary for civic competence.
7. Desiring and achieving socially responsible behavior.
8. Preparing for marriage and family life.
9. Building conscious values in harmony with an adequate scientific world-picture.[52]

Most if not all of the tasks in this list bear some relationship to society's definition of adulthood and to adolescents' attempts to fit themselves into that definition. Adolescents undoubtedly recognize and accept some of these tasks more than others.

Since these tasks are in part culturally imposed, they again raise the question of conformity and its relation to group standards of moral behavior. There is always such danger, at least in uncritical conformity, but it does not necessarily follow from the developmental tasks idea as such. For the tasks defined here do not conflict with stable moral values or criteria. The individual still has to

---

[50] *Ibid.,* p. 8.
[51] *Ibid.,* p. 28.
[52] Taken from headings, *ibid.,* pp. 30–55.

make the choices about ways in which he seeks to carry out the tasks. There are moral and immoral occupations, as well as moral and immoral ways of achieving economic independence. Nothing in these tasks implies need for or approval of immoral choices. Again we may observe that the temptation to take immoral short-cuts will be relatively greater for those who feel they have little chance of carrying out the tasks any other way. This does not mean that individuals who are failing in these tasks necessarily make such immoral choices or that successful individuals never make them. Human behavior is too unaccountable for such a neat dis-tinction. But it is true that the unsuccessful individual is under stronger emotional pressure to accept questionable means of gain-ing social approval in some quarters.

The developmental tasks idea is a challenging one for education at any level. It does not follow, however, that these tasks constitute the entire basis for a school program. If the idea is so regarded, it will probably follow into oblivion other and similar "grand de-signs" and universal answers. But its implications cannot be over-looked. Havighurst suggests two important possibilities, one in "discovering and stating the purposes of education in the schools," the other "the timing of educational efforts."[53] Whether or not they help us discover objectives in the everyday sense of finding some previously unknown is debatable. They do, however, provide im-portant criteria for judging the worth of various objectives and for resolving some of the controversial issues about what our schools should do. The strength of the "selecting and preparing for an occupation"[54] task provides argument for the vocational objective. And if there are really any modern educationists who disregard the intellectual objective as charged by the critics, they would have to find some way of getting around the task of "developing intel-lectual skills and concepts necessary for civic competence."[55]

Havighurst's other suggestion has to do with the timing of educa-tional efforts, a most important matter from the standpoints of motivation and of effective placement of materials and topics

[53] *Ibid.,* p. 8.
[54] *Ibid.,* p. 41.
[55] *Ibid.,* p. 45.

throughout the school grades. Examination of the tasks of childhood as contrasted with those of adolescence may throw much light on important differences between elementary and secondary schooling. So far as levels within secondary curriculum are concerned, however, most present statements do not differentiate the tasks of early from those of later adolescence. Further inquiry along these lines should yield helpful information relevant to needed distinctions between junior and senior high school curricula. It is possible, for example, that some of the materials and topics in junior high school general mathematics, such as insurance and investments, are more relevant to the tasks of older than of younger students.

In addition the tasks may throw light on some of the intermediary steps in the achievement of broad objectives. Many people, for example, agree that mental health is an important goal but are uncertain about the means of dealing with it in the school. This uncertainty has led sometimes to unwise choices, such as direct teaching of units and courses on mental health problems. The best approach of the school to the mental health objective may be an indirect one, through helping youth achieve their developmental tasks. For it is through the meeting of these tasks that people develop the self-acceptance, confidence, and inner assurance needed for healthy personalities. There is no suggestion in this of "soft pedagogy," for such qualities as self-acceptance and inner assurance include the essential element of critical self-appraisal based on realistic awareness of one's assets and liabilities. It is not necessary for an adolescent to succeed at everything, but to have the opportunity of succeeding at some important things. Unmitigated and continuous success based on avoidance of new challenges is fully as defective a basis for mental health as unmitigated and continuous failure.

Just as the mental health function neither demands nor justifies a "course," neither do the various developmental tasks imply setting up courses specifically identified in those terms. Much of what the high school can do to help youth meet these tasks is informal, although not necessarily incidental, and may be accomplished through the subject matter of various courses, as well as in features of the school program beyond the classroom studies. Nor does it mean always taking large blocks of time in the established subjects for new units, unless these units are intrinsic to the objectives and subject matter of the course. In some junior high school physical education classes, for example, time is taken for study of variations in growth during the early adolescent period. This subject matter is relevant to the first task in Havighurst's list, but it is also relevant to physical education. The same is true of the study of occupational trends in social studies. English, on the other hand, has been the victim of much of the tendency to insert irrelevant units, often based on the questionable assumption that there is no intrinsic content in the field itself. This tendency should be carefully watched and checked. Even here, however, there may be legitimate opportunities. If, as is the case in some schools, a specific block of time is taken in eleventh-grade or twelfth-grade English to develop research skills and the writing of term papers, some students at least may select and develop topics in vocational exploration. And literature is often relevant to personal-social problems even though not organized in problem units.

At all times, curriculum workers need to apply good judgment and common sense on these matters. There may have been schools which, as the critics charged, devoted units in social studies to such matters as dating. A very literal interpretation of task No. 2 in Havighurst's list might seem to justify such a unit, but common sense and a sense of humor might make one pause and reflect before putting it in. Group study of such topics may even be harmful and embarrassing to many students. We can probably do more to help young people on such matters through sympathetic and judicious individual counseling and through an extraclass program of social activities that fosters wholesome boy-girl relationships than by setting up a unit for group study.

ADOLESCENCE AND THE DROPOUT PROBLEM

Concern about students who drop out of high school usually reflects some degree of commitment to the proposition that all "normal" youth belong in high school and should remain for the "normal" period through the twelfth grade. The term "normal" is one with generous dimensions. It obviously starts at the highest intelligence levels and ranges downward to the lower end of the distribution to include those often called low-ability students. At this lower end, it includes at least those who can be accommodated in a high school with provisions for ability grouping, remedial reading classes, and the like, but not those who require unusual or special arrangements. Somewhere a level is reached at which most individuals cannot be readily accommodated in a high school without a specialized program. It is important, however, that decisions affecting those near this level be made on individual rather than group bases, since motivation, effort, previous opportunities for schooling, and other intangibles also play their parts in school achievement.

Those who favor "selective" schooling may be concerned about dropouts among students in the higher intelligence ranges, but are probably not concerned about dropouts in general. In fact, we sometimes hear arguments for excluding lower-ability students from high school. Advocates of "selective" secondary schooling do not necessarily use the IQ alone as a basis for selection; neither do they necessarily agree among themselves on the criteria they would use or the degree of rigor to which they would apply them. It is easy to conclude that incapable students should be excluded from high school, but it is not easy to gain acceptance of specific policies for identifying who the incapable are.

Even the most ardent advocate of universal secondary schooling, on the other hand, may become discouraged about the indifference allegedly shown by many adolescents to their educational opportunities. Perhaps those who do not want to go to high school should be allowed to drop out without misgivings on the part of the adult world. The Danish folk school movement has in part reflected the assumption that young adults show more interest in academic and cultural studies than is true of adolescents. Many young people in Denmark have gone from folk school to apprenticeship and then have returned enthusiastically to school later on.

Adult education undoubtedly is a field well worth developing, and there has been rising interest along these lines in our country since World War II. Most of us feel, however, that adult education should continue rather than replace high school education. The assumption we make is that the high school not only serves as an equalizer in the quest for occupational and social mobility, but that it is a good arrangement for helping young people to grow up, that is, to meet the challenges of society during the long period between childhood and adulthood that exists in most modern societies. It is perhaps inevitable that some adolescents will regard the high school as part of the adult conspiracy to keep them in childhood status as long as possible. But this reaction is part of what we might call a calculated risk. We may need to do some things in the high school curriculum to reduce or mitigate this impression on the part of adolescents; but we do not let it shake our conviction that the high school is a good place for young people to be during the adolescent years. It is this assumption that probably accounts more than anything else for our preoccupation with student needs and tasks: that is, for a curriculum more specifically related to the growing-up process itself.

Growing up is a civilizing process that includes intellectual and moral as well as physical and social maturity. Item Number 6 in Havighurst's list, which refers to intellectual skills and concepts for civic competence, is not just a string of fine words, but refers to something real and important in any valid notion of maturity. The same is true of item Number 9, which deals with the building of values. Democracy is a complex scheme of human relationships that calls for as much intellectual and moral maturity on the part of everyone as can possibly be achieved and for the transmission of as much culture to every individual as possible. It is desirable for every student to stay in high school for a full term so he can learn as much history, literature, science, and the like as is possible for him, even though this means tremendous variations in achievement from one student to the next. The student may grumble about these things while in high school, but it is our national conviction that he and society will be the better for it in the long run.

In view of these assumptions, every student who drops out of high school before graduation represents a real and substantial loss. How much of this loss do we have? Distribution of enrollments by grades provides one way of examining the matter. In 1952, the percentages of the total high school population for the upper four years (Grades 9 to 12) ran respectively 30.7, 27.1, 23.0, and 19.2 from the first year to the fourth. These figures may be contrasted with those of 1920, in which 40.1 percent of the students were in the first year and only 14.1 percent in the fourth.[56] But there is a more precise way of looking at the question. This is to use as a base of comparison not the total high school population, but the population of entering ninth-grade classes, as in Table 1, which shows, for example, that the twelfth-grade class of 1951–1952 was only two thirds the size of the ninth-grade class that had entered in 1948–1949. One third had dropped out somewhere along the way.

An interesting phenomenon of American secondary education is the tendency of girls both to enter and to stay in high schools to a greater extent than boys, although the difference is not as great as in the past. Girls made up 51.1 percent of the students in the last four years of high school during the school year 1951–1952 and 52.6 percent of the graduating class of 1950–1951.[57] Back in 1920, however, girls made up 56 per cent of the enrollment and 61 percent of the graduates.[58] G. Stanley Hall, writing of a still earlier period, points out an even more pronounced tendency along these lines, along with an interesting comment on course selection.

In the high schools of this country the girls conspicuously outnumber the boys. This disparity is increasing, and it is rare indeed to find a class in which the sexes are equal. From 1890 to 1897 the number of boys in the public schools of this country averaged about forty-one per cent; this proportion has changed but little, and does not vary greatly in different parts of the country as a whole. The proportion of boys decreases very rapidly during the course. Girls predominate especially in English, Latin, algebra, and French classes, so much so that in a few places sentiment decrees it good form to avoid some of these as "sissy" courses.[59]

[56] "Statistical Summary of Education 1951–1952," *Biennial Survey of Education in the United States 1950–1952,* Office of Education, Department of Health, Education, and Welfare, 1955, table B, p. 7.

[57] *Ibid.,* p. 9.

[58] *Ibid.*

[59] G. Stanley Hall, *Adolescence,* D. Appleton and Company, 1914 edition, vol. 2, p. 505.

TABLE 1. Retention Rates, Ninth Grade Through High School Graduation

High School Year	1936–1937	1937–1938	1938–1939	1939–1940	1940–1941	1941–1942	1942–1943	1943–1944	1944–1945	1945–1946	1946–1947	1947–1948	1948–1949
I	1000	1000	1000	1000	1000	1000	1000	1000	1000	1000	1000	1000	1000
II	845	868	885	891	838	837	822	862	892	885	884	901	882
III	725	751	760	721	660	640	668	707	725	736	748	761	766
IV	649	618	638	573	506	527	558	609	649	652	660	674	648
Graduates	570	583	582	540	469	490	526	577	616	618	625	623	616
Year of high school graduations	1940	1941	1942	1943	1944	1945	1946	1947	1948	1949	1950	1951	1952

These retention rates are approximate only. They are based on enrollments in public schools in Grades 9 through 12 in successive years and on the number of public high school graduates.

SOURCE: "Statistical Summary of Education 1951–1952," *Biennial Survey of Education in the United States 1950–1952*, Office of Education, Department of Health, Education, and Welfare, 1955, table 14, p. 21.

This is in distinct contrast to the situation in Europe where people have regarded secondary education as predominantly a masculine enterprise. It has led to the oft-repeated question, "Where are the boys?" and has brought about an emphasis in dropout discussions of the situation as it affects boys rather than girls.

The fact is, however, that far too many students of both sexes drop out of high school: too many, that is, in terms of our assumptions about the value of high school education. Many studies have been made to find out why, but findings are far from conclusive.

When early school-leavers have been questioned concerning their reasons for dropping out of school, their answers have been most often classified under low family incomes, failures in school, poor health, lack of interest in school, and lack of parental interest in education. Youth who drop out of school may not be completely aware of their reasons or they may be anxious to conceal them. Hence, whenever possible, investigations should be conducted by skilled interviewers rather than through questionnaires which are delivered by mail.

In general the studies of drop-outs indicate that this very large group, most of whom leave school soon after the law for compulsory attendance permits them to leave, includes a considerable number whose needs are not being met either by the school or by other institutions in the community.[60]

It should be kept in mind that such factors as academic success, intelligence, and economic status are general factors only. Some high-ability students drop out, while some low-ability students stay. Some students from even the lowest socioeconomic levels go on to finish high school and even continue in college. The decision to leave high school, when the choice is a free one on the student's part, is always an individual and personal decision, affected by the unique complex of factors that inpinge on that particular individual. Two students, for example, may be equally bored by the curriculum and equally capable of mastering it. If one of the students comes from a home where the parents place high value on high school graduation, that student will likely stay in school. If the

---

[60] J. Dan Hull and Howard Cummings, "Discovering the Extent to which Youth Needs Are Being Met," chap. 4, National Society for the Study of Education, *op. cit.*, pp. 69–70.

other comes from a home where formal education is not highly valued, that student will likely drop out. Similarly, one student from a low-income group who likes schoolwork, does well in it, and sees it as a route to occupational mobility will stay in school, while another from the same group who dislikes school and is not doing very well academically will probably not stay.

But there may yet be something more in the picture than any of the factors previously mentioned, and that is the extent to which the student feels that he is gaining adult status. Many students probably have moments when they resent high school as a symbol of childhood, but those who achieve reasonable success with their developmental tasks can feel they are making progress. The student who feels he is getting nowhere, however, may easily conclude that the real way to gain recognition as an adult is to get out of school and go to work. This is a possibility worth exploring at any rate. Since boys usually feel the pressure for adult status more than girls, this factor may account for the greater tendency of boys to drop out of school. If such a factor as this does operate, there is particular need for high school activities that tend to identify adolescents more specifically with the adult community. One such activity is that of school-related work experience. Another is the use of projects in which youth work side by side with adults in studying community problems and rendering needed community service.

The argument suggested in the foregoing paragraph may or may not be the answer to the dropout question. So far no conclusive answer has been achieved, and we continue to witness from one decade to the next the substantial losses in students between ninth and twelfth grades. To the extent that our national assumptions about universal secondary education are valid, these are serious losses indeed. And the argument from developmental tasks suggest that these assumptions possess considerable validity.

COEDUCATION IN THE ADOLESCENT YEARS

The older European cultures have tended for the most part to maintain separate secondary schools for boys and girls. In part this reflects the conviction that intellectual studies are most effectively conducted without the distractions of boy-girl relationships. It may also reflect the viewpoint that educational objectives for girls are different from those for boys and demand different curricula. The traditional academic disciplines have been regarded in these cultures largely as masculine prerogatives. Those who would not put the case in such terms feel at any rate that a somewhat different kind of secondary education may be more relevant to woman's role in homemaking and motherhood, enough so to warrant separate schools at some levels.[61]

Most Americans, however, have long felt that coeducation is the better arrangement. This is probably to some extent a reflection of financial reality. We believe girls should have equal opportunities with boys for secondary education. There is disagreement as to whether this might be better handled through separate or combined schools, but there is little doubt that the financial costs of separate schools would be excessive, particularly in small communities. But this does not tell the whole story. If we wanted universal non-coeducational secondary education, we would undoubtedly find a way of paying for it.

What coeducation most probably represents is a feeling that it is good education for wholesome and desirable boy-girl relationships, as well as for ideals of partnership and mutual respect in marriage and family life. Coeducation means that boys and girls work together in classrooms, in school plays, in getting out the school paper, and like activities in which they learn to understand and appraise one another on bases other than sexual attraction alone. It is doubtful that this could be achieved as well by restricting boy-girl relationships to out-of-school life. Coeducation seems to function as a curricular means with reference to developmental tasks Nos. 2 and 8 in Havighurst's list, those dealing with age-mate relationships and preparation for marriage and family life.

It does not mean that the question is closed beyond possible adaptation and modification. It may be that coeducation is better at some levels than at others. The more rapid physical and social

---

[61] Hall, *op. cit.*, chap. 17. Hall went so far as to suggest that "While girls may be trained with boys, coeducation should cease at the dawn of adolescence at least for a season." *Ibid.*, p. 635.

development of girls in early adolescence, for example, might warrant separation in Grades 7, 8, and 9. At least this possibility seems worthy of further study and exploration. Another possibility is that coeducation may be better for some aspects of the school program than for others. The values claimed for coeducation might be equally well served by having boys and girls in the same school, but not in the same sections of the classroom studies. This permits their working together in the extraclass activities and other features of the social life of the school. It might make possible more concentrated attention on the classroom studies. While this implies a sharper distinction between classroom studies and extraclass activities than most students of secondary education would like to accept, it is also worthy of further study. Coeducation in a general sense seems right and good to us, but we do not need to regard our present arrangements along these lines as final answers. This is especially true in view of the fact that reputable students of human development usually disclaim having any final answers on the nature of adolescence itself.

ADOLESCENCE AND THE JUNIOR HIGH SCHOOL

The movement for reorganization of secondary education along the lines of the junior high school has grown steadily for many years. One argument for it is that elementary schooling is not appropriate for the early adolescent. The Committee on College Entrance Requirements in 1899 claimed, "The seventh grade, rather than the ninth, is the natural turning-point in the pupil's life, as the age of adolescence demands new methods and wiser direction."[62] In the period following 1900, this argument did not appear to any great extent, and the case for the junior high school was based on other grounds. In more recent years, however, the nature of early adolescence has again become an important consideration. In many community discussions and controversies, teachers and parents tend to state their convictions both for and against junior high schools on the grounds of their interpretations of early adolescence.

What then does our present knowledge imply? Mental develop-

[62] National Education Association, *Report of the Committee on College Entrance Requirements,* July, 1899, The Association, University of Chicago Press, 1899, p. 31.

ment seems to take place gradually and uniformly over the whole period of childhood and adolescence. This provides little basis for a sharp break between the sixth and the seventh grades so far as the organization of studies is concerned. On the other hand, early adolescence is a distinct period of rapid change so far as physical growth and social development are concerned. It presents new and complex social tasks that can probably be met more effectively in a separate school than in one made up largely of younger children. When junior high schools are available, sixth graders usually show much eagerness to leave their elementary buildings and "move up." Many seventh graders resent the multiple-period or block schedule on the grounds that it reminds them too much of what they have left behind. This strong motivation for going to the junior high school may in part at least be culturally determined. But it is not irrelevant to the students' developmental tasks since these also contain cultural factors.

There remains, however, the other end of the question, namely, whether the junior high should be administratively and physically separated from the tenth, eleventh, and twelfth grades. This is the issue of the 6–3–3, 6–2–4, or 6–4–2 organization versus the 6–6.[53] Parents are inclined to deplore the tendency of the early adolescents to grow up too fast by imitating the social patterns of later adolescence. Although the developmental tasks of early adolescence have more in common with those of later adolescence than they have with late childhood, there are some important differences

[53] Gruhn and Tompkins point out that six-year high schools are largely adjustments to given sets of financial and administrative conditions. "The chief argument for the 6-year school is that it gives some of the advantages of the junior high school to pupils in communities that otherwise could not afford them. Pupils in Grades 7 and 8 have available many facilities that in small communities would be limited to the high school, such as the industrial-arts shops, homemaking, music, and arts and crafts rooms." William T. Gruhn and Ellsworth Tompkins, "What's the Best Combination?" *N.E.A. Journal*, November, 1956, p. 498. They see advantages for the separate junior and senior high schools. "Especially for the junior high-school group, the separate junior and senior high schools have decided advantages. In the 6-year school, the early adolescents are often treated as little more than second-class citizens, with the preference given to the upper-grade pupils with regard to building facilities, extracurriculum activities, leadership positions, and sometimes teachers." *Ibid.*, p. 498. They insist none the less that the 6-year high school *"can"* be organized and administered to provide adequately for the educational needs and interests of the early adolescent." *Ibid.*

in ways of meeting them. Providing for these differences implies more than administrative separation of junior and senior high in the same building unit. It probably means separate buildings. Whether this calls for a 6–3–3 or 6–4–2 is not clear. This question demands more precise differentiation of growth characteristics than can be inferred from our present knowledge of adolescence. Some of the data, however, indicate that completion of physical growth comes between the ages of 15 and 18 years for girls and 17 and 20 for boys.[64] From this standpoint, the junior high or intermediate unit may well be extended for a year beyond the ninth grade, as is done in a 6–4–2 organization.

Any generalizations along these lines are bound to encounter the stubborn facts of differences in rates of growth between boys and girls, as well as individual differences in both groups. There has been much speculation about ways of meeting these through unconventional grouping arrangements at the junior high school level. Some of these include grouping younger girls with older boys. Mental development, however, does not correspond to the differences in physical and social acceleration. Perhaps separating boys and girls in the classroom studies but not in the social life of the school may be particularly relevant to the junior high school level. This would eliminate the difficulties arising from disparity in social development from the classroom and yet leave room for desirable social relationships between younger girls and older boys in other kinds of school activities. All this is admittedly speculative, but at any rate no adequate answer to the question has yet been achieved for the junior high school years.

Bibliography

Ausubel, David P., *Theory and Problems of Adolescent Development,* Grune & Stratton, 1954.

Crow, Lester D., and Crow, Alice, *Adolescent Development and Adjustment,* McGraw-Hill Book Company, Inc., 1956.

Doane, Donald C., *The Needs of Youth: An Evaluation for Curriculum Purposes,* Teachers College, Columbia University, Contributions to Education, No. 848, Bureau of Publications, 1942.

[64] Stolz and Stolz, *op. cit.,* p. 81.

Gordon, C. Wayne, *The Social System of the High School: A Study in the Sociology of Adolescence,* The Free Press, Glencoe, Illinois, 1957.

Hall, G. Stanley, *Adolescence,* D. Appleton and Company, 1914.

Havighurst, Robert J., *Developmental Tasks and Education,* Longmans, Green and Company, 1950.

Havighurst, Robert J., and Taba, Hilda (in collaboration with the Committee on Human Development, the University of Chicago), *Adolescent Character and Personality,* John Wiley & Sons, Inc., 1949.

Hollingshead, August B., *Elmtown's Youth,* John Wiley & Sons, Inc., 1949.

Horrocks, John E., *The Psychology of Adolescence,* Houghton Mifflin Company, 1951.

Hurlock, Elizabeth B., *Adolescent Development,* McGraw-Hill Book Company, Inc., 1955.

Jersild, Arthur, *The Psychology of Adolescence,* The Macmillan Company, 1957.

Jersild, Arthur T., and Tasch, Ruth J. (in collaboration with committees of teachers of the public schools of Springfield, Missouri), *Children's Interests and What They Suggest for Education,* Bureau of Publications, Teachers College, Columbia University, 1949.

Merry, Frieda Kiefer, and Merry, Ralph Vickers, *The First Two Decades of Life,* (2d ed.), Harper & Brothers, 1958.

National Society for the Study of Education, Forty-third Yearbook, pt. 1, *Adolescence,* The Society, 1944.

National Society for the Study of Education, Fifty-second Yearbook, pt. 1, *Adapting the Secondary-School Program to the Needs of Youth,* The Society, 1953.

Norvell, George W., *The Reading Interests of Young People,* D. C. Heath and Company, 1950.

Remmers, H. H., and Radler, D. H., *The American Teenager,* The Bobbs-Merrill Company, Inc., 1957.

Segel, David, *Intellectual Abilities in the Adolescent Period: Their Growth and Development,* Bulletin 1948, No. 6, Federal Security Agency, Office of Education, 1948.

...

CHAPTER 4

What High Schools Are For

Schools exist for a fundamental purpose so taken for granted that it is often unstated and sometimes forgotten. This is the transmission of culture to the young. In a general and inclusive sense, the term "culture" refers to the whole way of life of a society. A relatively simple society transmits its culture without schools at all. Schools appear as the culture of a society becomes complex.[1] Even in such a society, much of the culture is transmitted through the informal processes of everyday living; most, if not all, such societies employ schools to transmit the knowledge, values, and skills on which other desirable aspects of their cultures are based and which do not lend themselves well to more informal transmission.

Consequently, the term "culture" is used here not in the general

[1] This need for schools is well developed as follows by Dewey: "But as civilization advances, the gap between the capacities of the young and the concerns of adults widens. Learning by direct sharing in the pursuits of grown-ups becomes increasingly difficult except in the case of the less advanced occupations. Much of what adults do is so remote in space and in meaning that playful imitation is less adequate to reproduce its spirit. Ability to share effectively in adult activities thus depends upon a prior training given with this end in view. Intentional agencies—schools—and explicit material—studies—are devised. The task of teaching certain things is delegated to a special group of persons.

"Without such formal education, it is not possible to transmit all the resources and achievements of a complex society. It also opens a way to a kind of experience which would not be accessible to the young, if they were left to pick up their training in informal association with others, since books and the symbols of knowledge are mastered." John Dewey, *Democracy and Education,* The Macmillan Company, 1916, p. 9.

sense, but to mean the accumulated knowledge, wisdom, values, and skills needed to preserve and to advance the material and the non-material aspects of civilized life. On these matters no society stands alone, but is interdependent with other societies past and present. Each civilized community selects from and contributes to this intellectual and moral heritage and endeavors through its schools to insure continuity from one generation to the next. And it is through schooling that individuals acquire this heritage for their personal development and use.

In a ladder system of schooling such as ours, each level has a somewhat distinctive function in cultural transmission although there is, of course, overlapping from one level to the next. The elementary school equips children with the basic tools of literacy in the vernacular tongue and in addition begins the process of communicating knowledge and values in such subjects as history, the natural sciences, and the arts. The secondary school continues the development of the vernacular language skills, but is primarily responsible for transmitting a body of knowledge which defines the general studies. Some of this knowledge is transmitted to all in the constants or required subjects; other portions are selectively used in relation to the abilities and interests of individual students. At one time, the secondary school confined itself to developing literacy in a foreign tongue and left the general studies to the college. Today, the college or university, while it still includes some general studies, assumes the function of transmitting highly specialized aspects of the culture for highly specialized purposes. When the college continues the transmission of the general studies, as in freshman and sophomore years, it sometimes repeats material the high school has already presumably taught.

These considerations suggest one distinctive function for free, popular, and universal secondary schooling, namely the transmission to as many people as possible of more culture in the form of general studies than can be transmitted solely through the elementary schools. This function reflects, as the beginnings of schools once reflected, the accumulation of culture itself. The development of this idea of secondary schooling in the American academy and in the high school paralleled the great nineteenth-century expansion in many fields of human knowledge and skill. What is sometimes called the explosion of knowledge in our own time accentuates rather than diminishes the function of cultural transmission. It is more important than ever before to provide for organized, orderly, and systematic transmission through some agency such as the school, particularly the high school. The task of selection has become more difficult, but not less important.

Nevertheless, cultural transmission is not the only general function of the high school; neither does it in itself resolve all questions of purposes or objectives. Culture is transmitted not for its own sake, but for the development of individuals. It is necessary, therefore, to consider human activities, relationships, and aspirations and to identify the kinds of personal-social development most relevant to the process of schooling. Furthermore, the high school transmits culture to people in the period of transition between childhood and adulthood; it cannot ignore the personal-social characteristics and needs of adolescents. A second or parallel function of the high school then is that of fostering individual development of adolescents in various aspects of living. Identification of objectives dealing with these aspects of living becomes necessary to relate the transmitted culture to those it is designed to serve. Such objectives, however, do not necessarily imply corresponding units or courses as such in the program of studies.

Even those who accept the necessity of further defining objectives along these lines do not agree on the aspects of living to be included. It is around such matters as intellectual competence, health, use of leisure time, and family living that our disagreements and controversies have evolved. Obviously there are many points of agreement as well. The identification of agreements as well as disagreements becomes, therefore, a matter of first-level importance in any study of the high school curriculum.

Such identification is subject to certain qualifications. The first is the presence of many publics in American life, some of which are based on regional differences, while others reflect differences in ethnic backgrounds, occupational status, socioeconomic level, and religious affiliation. As noted in Chapter 1, we also have a body of common assumptions and values. These do not guarantee, however, that specific expressions of educational objectives will coincide from one group to the next, and possible variations must be taken into account.

A second qualification is that formal statements of educational objectives drawn up by professional educators may or may not reflect the convictions of the educators' fellow citizens. This difficulty is mitigated by the fact that school and society in American culture interact to a considerable degree. We do not have educators in an intellectual vacuum. Professional educators help perform the useful service of giving special attention and study to school problems; but these same educators are also part of the general public. Verbal statements of objectives such as the Cardinal Principles, although prepared by professional educators, do not necessarily conflict with the public mind as a whole, even when written in pedagese, and disagreements about objectives do not necessarily imply that professional educators are in conflict with their fellow citizens. When disagreements occur, we are likely to find professional educators disagreeing among themselves, just as do members of other occupations. Objectives of secondary education in our country may be regarded as the objectives of the general citizenry in which professional educators are included.

This is not to say that objectives merely reflect majority opinion at given times and places. They are related to independent criteria drawn from common intellectual and ethical traditions, both in our culture and that of the Western world generally. Professional educators and their fellow citizens alike grow up in this common intellectual and moral environment, a further indication that the dualism which seeks to identify controls either in the school or in the society is inherently a false and misleading one.

A third qualification is that agreement on a list of objectives does not necessarily imply agreement on the relative importance of the objectives included. Some objectives appear to be more the business of the school than others. Parents are expected to provide the foundations of moral behavior and character in their children; what the school does in this area is often regarded as supplementary. On such matters as vocational preparation, vigorous disagreements are likely to occur between those who would assign high schools the primary roles and those who would assign them no roles at all.

Several observations may be kept in mind on this matter of relative importance. Schools have no monopoly on any educational objective whatsoever. They provide only part of anyone's education; the question is which part. Furthermore, we cannot put the relative importance in quantitative terms. To say that the school has 95 percent responsibility for intellectual development and 5 percent for social development would be a rhetorical rather than a mathematical expression. We may, however, assign priorities in the sense of identifying some objectives as being more important than others. This is possible in general terms only and may demand modification so far as particular children and youth are concerned. The significance of priorities depends in part on the use of objectives as criteria or bases for curricular decisions. There may be some decisions in which one objective conflicts with others. The assigning of top priority to any objective, intellectual competence, for example, means that it prevails over others in such cases of conflict. It does not mean that we spend so many hours a day fostering intellectual development and then turn to other objectives if we have a few minutes left over. Priority is not a quantitative matter, but an ordering of values.

Desirable perspective on the whole question of objectives may be fostered by remembering that education should never be reduced to a mere instrument for the achievement of ends external to itself. One of the most explicit reminders on this point comes from Dewey.

For it is assumed that the aim of education is to enable individuals to continue their education—or that the object and reward of learning is continued capacity for growth. . . . In our search for aims in education, we are concerned, therefore, with finding an end outside of the educative process to which education is subordinate. Our whole conception forbids. We are rather concerned with the contrast which exists when aims belong within the process in which they operate and when they are set up from without.[2]

[2] Dewey, *op. cit.*, p. 117.

A more contemporary expression somewhat along the same lines puts the matter as follows.

> One of the most conspicuous things about American writing and speaking on education is a strange and pervasive reluctance—even when the writers and speakers are teachers and scholars—to admit that enjoyment of the life of the mind is a legitimate and important consummation in itself, at least as valid among the ends of life as the enjoyment, say, of sports, sex, or liquor. Education is justified apologetically as a useful instrument in attaining *other* ends: it is good for business or professional careers; it is good because it makes good citizens; it is good because it fosters something called 'democratic living'; it is good for the arts of government; it is good for machine technology. Rarely, however, does anyone presume to say that it is good for man.[3]

It is not always easy, however, to distinguish between education for its own sake and education for something else. Much depends on the spirit in which given objectives are interpreted. Nevertheless, the caution is a good one. Excessive concern about what learning is good for may in the end destroy the love of learning itself.

With these considerations in mind, we turn to some broad categories frequently referred to not only in writing but in everyday discussion of the high school curriculum: (1) intellectual development; (2) moral or character development; (3) citizenship; (4) physical health; (5) mental or emotional health; (6) enjoyment of living; (7) family living; and (8) preparation for jobs. Some of these, particularly physical health, mental health, enjoyment of living, and family living, are at times grouped together as "personal-social development," a term that also includes connotations related to personality, getting along with people, and the like. This is useful and convenient shorthand. Strictly speaking, however, intellectual development, moral development, citizenship, and preparation for jobs are also personal and social matters.

INTELLECTUAL DEVELOPMENT

Much criticism of high schools today centers on the alleged abandonment of this objective. This body of criticism proceeds

---

[3] Richard Hofstadter and C. DeWitt Hardy, *The Development and Scope of Higher Education in the United States,* Columbia University Press, 1952, pt. 1, "The Development of Higher Education in America," by Richard Hofstadter, p. 104.

from a serious point of view, one which demands examination, not dismissal. To say this is not necessarily to endorse the stereotype of so-called academic traditionalism. Neither does critical review of the criticisms necessarily commit one to the opposite stereotype of so-called life-adjustment education.

Criticisms of alleged anti-intellectualism in education should not be narrowly identified with controversies about the three R's. Of course intellectual development includes language competence. But schools can teach reading and other tools of literacy without being in the slightest degree committed to the development of higher intellectual skills and processes. Some nations have openly used their elementary or folk schools in this very way. Critics of anti-intellectualism then may be critical of school achievement in the three R's, but they are talking about something broader and deeper than the foundations of literacy.

It also needs to be made clear that the critics of anti-intellectualism do not necessarily want to limit the high school population to the so-called academic or college preparatory student. Their point of view is rather that all normal United States youth deserve an education grounded in the academic disciplines or intellectual studies.[4] As we confront the possibility of greatly increased high school enrollments, some American citizens may urge limitation of numbers as a means of holding down costs. They may draw upon some of the arguments raised by the critics of anti-intellectualism as support for such contentions. But critics of anti-intellectualism for the most part have advanced no such suggestions.

The revolt against anti-intellectualism is, however, closely related to an earlier revolt against narrow utilitarianism.[5] Some of

---

[4] "I believe there are universal values in education that are good for everyone, whether he intends to become a butcher or a banker, a minister or a motorman, a professor or a plumber. The average student should not be treated as a second-class citizen of the educational world who can be thrown a few devitalized crumbs and then shoved into a variety of nonacademic courses devoid of real content." Mortimer Smith, *The Diminished Mind,* Henry Regnery Company, 1954, p. 8.

[5] For example, "People motivated by a narrow utilitarianism do not really desire education. They are quite content with a vulgar substitute—if it pays. Education does not transform them; they tend to transform it after their own likeness. That many are seeking 'education' from such motives is evident. One has only to study the advertising pages of the popular magazines to note the kind of appeal that is made to induce the ambitious to enroll in certain correspondence schools. The prospective student is given the promise that if he will subscribe for certain courses he may some

the critics write from both points of view. Neither of these two groups insists on the intellectual objective as the only task worthy of educational effort. They are inclined rather to regard other objectives as supplementary and subordinate. Moral or character education is often accorded high status, with a strong case being made for a close integration of this objective with that of intellectual development.[6] But it is the intellectual objective that they feel to be most seriously threatened by current school practice.

Anti-intellectualism is a term that has grown in use and popularity over the past several decades.[7] What it stands for is no new thing in human history. It means distrust of, hostility to, or skepticism about the use of human reason and rational processes, reflecting sometimes a gloomy view of human abilities, sometimes open contempt for human personality. The first of these bases for anti-intellectualism is one employed by frustrated intellectuals themselves, the second by those who would assault human freedom and dignity in any form. If then there are anti-intellectual tendencies in our schools, they should not be taken lightly, for they would have serious consequences in our society as well.

---

day sit in the boss's chair, and associate with the big men at the top who do real things." Everett Dean Martin, *The Meaning of a Liberal Education,* W. W. Norton & Company, 1926, p. 12.

[6] Mark Van Doren decries an exclusive preoccupation with character development in education and states, "The conscious business of education is with the intellect." Mark Van Doren, *Liberal Education,* Books, Inc., distributed by Henry Holt and Company, 1943, p. 62. He goes on, however, to warn against the separation of character from intellect. "The danger in separating character from intellect and asking it to operate alone is that men will then be licensed to handle moral ideas as though they were not ideas. . . . So it would appear that any radical disjunction of moral education and intellectual education is perilous. Character is both intellectual and moral." *Ibid.,* p. 63.

Mortimer Smith similarly includes the moral objective. "I would grant a lot of ancillary functions, but I think the *primary* function of the school *is to transmit the intellectual and cultural heritage and knowledge of the race, and in the process to teach young people to think, and to buttress moral values.*" *Op. cit.,* p. 6.

[7] Hutchins, for example, in 1943 referred to anti-intellectualism as one of four cults of modern life, the others being skepticism, presentism, and scientism. "Finally, we have the cult of anti-intellectualism, which has some oddly assorted members. They range from Hitler, who thinks with his red corpuscles, through the members of the three other cults, to men of good will, who, since they are men of good will, are at the opposite pole to Hitler, but can give no rational justification for being there." Robert M. Hutchins, *Education for Freedom,* Louisiana State University Press, 1943, pp. 34–35.

But is the charge of anti-intellectualism in the schools a true one? The critics are sincere in this charge. If wrong, they are mistaken, not malicious. Mistakes grow out of misunderstanding. In any use of language, the possibilities of misunderstanding are tremendous. The critics themselves often contend that their own positions have been misunderstood.

The charges of anti-intellectualism are usually made on the following grounds: (1) that professional educationists have disparaged the intellectual objective in statements of what schools are for, sometimes by direct omission and sometimes by attaching greater value to so-called non-intellectual objectives; (2) that the curriculum has been watered down and made less difficult, thereby depriving students of intellectual challenge and discipline; and (3) that professional educationists have unjustly categorized many students as incapable of profiting from intellectual study.

It is true that educationists for the most part have not used the specific terms "intellectual development" or "intellectual competence" to any great extent in their formulations of objectives. These terms do not appear as such in the Cardinal Principles, in the Imperative Needs of Youth, or in the platform of Life-Adjustment Education. In all these, including that of Life-Adjustment Education,[8] however, there is either direct or indirect reference to such matters as critical or reflective thinking, problem solving, and scientific method.

But, the criticisms run, the professional educationist, although giving lip service to reflective thinking in some form, tends to drown even this version of intellectual development in a flood of other objectives, such as mental and physical health, personal adjustment, family living, and the like, which if admitted at all should be regarded as supplementary and subordinate. One must grant that writing in the field of curriculum for the most part contains more examples of these everyday-living or life-adjustment objectives than of those more explicitly intellectual in character. This does not necessarily imply disparagement of the intellectual objective. It may well be that the professional educationists felt

---

[8] See the statement of major points of Life Adjustment Education as proposed by the Life Adjustment Education Commission, cited in Harl Douglass (ed.), *Education for Life Adjustment,* The Ronald Press Company, 1950, p. 10.

this to be so widely assumed that it needed no explicit identification as such. They may have felt it necessary to concentrate on objectives that were apparently being neglected without feeling the need to testify on behalf of those well established. Most men who are happily married do not go about protesting that they love their wives; they know they do and assume others know it too. They would be astonished to find their reticence on the subject interpreted as a sign of infidelity.

Culture in the United States in the twentieth century at least has displayed a strong utilitarian bent with a tendency to demand that education justify itself in practical results. It would be unusual if this tendency did not appear in the writings of some professional educationists, perhaps in exaggerated form. But utilitarianism, even when narrow and mistaken, is not necessarily anti-intellectual. In periods dominated by utilitarianism, educational objectives are more likely to express the results hoped for in everyday living than the intellectual processes on which these results are based. The Cardinal Principles, for example, are strongly utilitarian in character; so was the period in which they were written.

We need also to remember that teachers have been assured by several generations of experts in the field of intelligence testing that intellectual differences among students are innate and not subject to modification by training or education. With such a point of view presented by an impressive body of intellectuals, teachers may well have concluded that it was futile to include intellectual development as an objective of schooling. Fortunately, they have not arrived at such a conclusion. Our teachers have realized that while schooling may not be able to lift an individual above his maximum intelligence level, it has much to do with bringing him to intellectual productivity at that level. Most of us do not think at the level on which we are capable of thinking. Intellectual development in the sense of coming close to that level has never been renounced as an objective of schooling, even though it may not always be made explicit in formal terms.

Intelligence testing was probably not the only long-term development in educational psychology that may have discouraged explicit recognition of intellectual development as an objective of schooling. Another was the controversy about various theories of transfer of training. One of these theories, that of identical or similar elements, cast a great deal of doubt on the possibilities of any generalized outcomes. This encouraged the statement of very specific objectives, which had to be sought directly through particular activities and materials. The older theory of formal discipline was cast aside and with it even the possibility of mental discipline as a generalized characteristic. Not all educationists accepted this conclusion even at the time of its greatest popularity. Probably most students of curriculum today accept the theory of generalization, which occupies a position between the extremes of formal discipline on one hand and identical or similar elements on the other and admits generalized intellectual skills such as reflective thinking or problem solving.[9]

The second basis advanced for the charge of anti-intellectualism is that modern educationists have watered down the curriculum. Many educationists, as well as other people, have felt that reflective thinking may be developed in the study of *any* problem of concern to the individual—for example, a problem of teen-age dating. The so-called traditionalist puts higher value on those problems and concerns which have been systematically organized and treated in the fields of human inquiry symbolized by the established academic subjects. He feels that today's schools include subject matter that is both too easy for intellectual challenge and too trivial for serious consideration. To study life-adjustment problems constitutes, according to this point of view, dilution of the curriculum and a move in an anti-intellectual direction.

It is unrewarding to make a case either way in terms of the difficulties of various subject matters. There is much difficult subject matter that would not be enthusiastically advanced by anyone as appropriate for school use. The working of Chinese puzzles is probably more difficult than the study of history. Obviously the critics would not suggest Chinese puzzles in the curriculum. Fur-

---

[9] See Charles Hubbard Judd, *Psychology of Secondary Education*, Ginn and Company, 1927, pp. 441–442.

For an excellent recent overview of the history of the transfer problem and its related controversies, see Walter B. Kolesnik, *Mental Discipline in Modern Education*, The University of Wisconsin Press, 1958.

thermore, there are individual differences on such things. Some students find "hard" subjects easier than "easy" subjects. The futility of the difficulty criterion is illustrated by Huxley's famous satire on this way of organizing and teaching palaeontology.

It is wonderful how close a parallel to classical training could be made out of that palaeontology to which I refer. In the first place I could get up an osteological primer so arid, so pedantic in its terminology, so altogether distasteful to the youthful mind, as to beat the recent famous production of the headmasters out of the field in all these excellences. Next, I could exercise my boys upon easy fossils, and bring out all their powers of memory and all their ingenuity in the application of my osteo-grammatical rules to the interpretation, or construing, of these fragments. To those who had reached the higher classes, I might supply odd bones to be built up into animals, giving great honor and reward to him who succeeded in fabricating monsters most entirely in accordance with the rules. That would answer to verse-making and essay-writing in the dead languages.[10]

But the critics seek to make their case for the academic disciplines as over and against life-adjustment problems not only on the grounds of difficulty, but on those of importance. They make much of the apparent triviality of some of the life-adjustment materials and of the superior importance of the established disciplines. This is both attack and defense. As an attack on the newer materials it is open to question. It is at least uncharitable to write off as trivial the immediate problems and concerns of students. Furthermore, some of the academic disciplines established today were once considered rather dubious themselves. It seems wiser to reserve judgment concerning the alleged triviality of the so-called newer courses and materials.

On the other hand, the school's general role in the transmission of culture does provide a basis for defending the established disciplines if and when they need such defense. Our students should develop reflective thinking not only on immediate and current matters, but on those perennial problems which extend our en-

[10] Thomas H. Huxley, *Science and Education: Essays,* "A Liberal Education; and Where to Find It." D. Appleton and Company, 1897, pp. 98–99. (Date of essay, 1868.)

vironment in time as well as space. There is a place for both the traditional academic disciplines and the so-called newer subjects. There is no place for trivialities, whether traditional or new. These matters are so well understood and accepted by the people of the United States, including most professional educationists, that we may assume a permanent place for the subject matters of the traditional academic fields in the secondary curriculum.

Some of the critics, however, fear that the "modern" educator divides the school population into sheep and goats, with the intellectual objectives and the traditional curriculum deëmphasized or even eliminated for the latter.[11] Possible grounds for this fear are not new, but go back at least as far as the first years of the twentieth century. As more and more youth of high school age came to high school, teachers became increasingly aware of individual differences in abilities, interests, and cultural backgrounds among their students. Much attention was given to the possibility of handling these differences through differentiated curricula. In the middle 1940's, however, preliminary statements from those associated with life-adjustment education referred to the "60 percenters," students in our schools who were presumably served neither by the traditional program (in this case labeled college preparatory) nor by technical vocational training, and who should receive life-adjustment education.[12] This original position was later

[11] "When the schoolman of today implies that education is only for an intellectual elite and attempts to water it down, or practically eliminate it, on the assumption that most people aren't up to it—when he does this, he is dooming the vast majority to intellectual and cultural subservience. The irony of the situation is that this is done by those who often talk as if they were the only legitimate guardians of the sacred flame of democracy." Mortimer Smith, *op. cit.,* p. 8.

[12] "Apparently the fantastic conclusion has been reached that sixty per cent of American youth is incapable of being either prepared for college or trained in vocational skills and that therefore a sort of gigantic program of social services must be devised for these backward ones in which the attempt will be made to adjust them to the stresses of society through a curriculum that will be concerned largely with such personal matters as how to be well groomed, what to talk about on a date, what to do with leisure time, and how to shop for the groceries. This is done in the name of democracy but one may well ask if it isn't a perverted sense of democracy which implies that second best is sufficient for the great average. Or have we reached the point of complete collapse of values, where there is no best and no second best, where the ideal is undifferentiated *doing* rather than *reflective* being?" Mortimer Smith (ed.), *The Public Schools in Crisis: Some Critical Essays,* Henry Regnery Company, 1956, "Introduction" by Mortimer Smith, p. 6.

modified to include the remaining 40 percent of the students as well. Extension of life-adjustment education to all students was a point which could hardly be expected to satisfy the liberal critics.[13] It did, however, strike out the possible implication that we had on our hands a large number of students who constituted a group apart from others.

Teachers and administrators on the firing line in our high schools nevertheless realize that students do differ in the extent to which they can study and learn traditional academic materials. Handling five classes a day in a typical high school is a grinding task, made no easier by the presence of some students who neither can nor will respond to much of what adults consider important. To the teacher on the job, the intellectual critic may seem to dwell in ivory towers far removed from actual conditions. We must not, however, give way to defeatism, which could lead to the setting up of selective high school admission in conflict with our aspirations for universal secondary education. Nor do most of the critics themselves want this to happen. We may at least hope that the improvement of teaching methods, the development of new media of communication, the strengthening of necessary literacy skills, and the enrichment of instructional materials will make it possible to reach many more students with our intellectual heritage than we think possible today. From this it does not follow that all students should receive identical educations. The fact of individual differences cannot be denied. What is important is to be sure that we deal with individual differences, not with differences of students thrown arbitrarily into groups.

In conclusion, it does not appear that the schools have deliberately and consciously fostered anti-intellectualism either in their objectives or in the curriculum. At the same time, the preoccupation of professional educationists with what they consider to be new needs and some very real and difficult problems in the schools may account for not placing the explicit and positive emphasis on in-

[13] Mortimer Smith offers the following comment on the modification of the original Life-Adjustment position. "There's a noble ideal to aim at—mediocrity, or worse, for all. Instead of trying to reduce the ranks of the sixty per cent, let's be democratic and bring the other forty per cent down to the same level." *The Diminished Mind, op. cit.,* p. 46.

tellectual development in a form acceptable to the critics. Much of the controversial literature leaves the impression that the professional educationists and the critics are actually in closer agreement than appears to be the case on the surface. The controversy has nonetheless been a healthy and stimulating one. It has redirected attention to one of our most important objectives and has brought about a desirable reappraisal of some specific school practices. The criticism has served also to underscore convictions from which the majority of the people of the United States, including professional educationists, have never departed, namely that schooling should foster something known as intellectual development, mental discipline, or more simply the ability to think.

MORAL DEVELOPMENT

The home is regarded as the primary agency of moral development. For those parents who profess religious belief, churches play an important part. A widespread conviction has existed in American culture that schools also should do something along these lines, even though their role may be regarded as supplementary. This conviction has a long and honorable ancestry in educational theory and practice. Writers on education have long been preoccupied with the possibilities of schooling as a means of developing moral behavior. In our culture this was reinforced by the strong moral emphasis of the New England Puritans, as well as by other religious groups among the early settlers. Throughout the nineteenth century these convictions were symbolized by the extensive use of moral content in school readers. In the present century we have had one large-scale study of character education, while extensive discussion of moral and spiritual values has occupied a great share of our attention in more recent years.

This concern for character education or moral and spiritual values, moreover, is shared by people with otherwise divergent views on many important educational and philosophical issues. So-called progressives have testified to this concern fully as much as have so-called traditionalists. Equally concerned are those who hold conservative religious views and those who profess no religious views at all. Inevitably the sharing of a common platform on a matter such as this by people with otherwise divergent viewpoints leads to considerable difference of opinion both on what is meant and how it should be accomplished. It is a matter rich in paradox. Everyone admits ignorance, yet speaks with authority. Few admit knowing how to do it, yet everyone knows how it should be done. The net result has been not merely a certain amount of disagreement, but a rather substantial amount of confusion and indecision among professional educators and the general public.

MORAL PRINCIPLES AS ABSOLUTE OR RELATIVE

Some of the controversy revolves around the question of moral absolutes, that is, moral principles independent of cultural variations. In the relativist view, there are no such independent principles; right and wrong are culturally determined. Our American tradition for the most part has been one of moral absolutes. The Declaration of Independence fairly rings with them. Throughout the nineteenth century the existence of absolute right and wrong continued to be assumed. People disagreed about the sources of these principles. Some took them from traditional Christian teaching, while others who accepted little that was specifically Christian derived theirs from the natural law. They disagreed about the content of these values. But disagree as they might about the sources and the content, Americans have generally held to a standard of rightness and wrongness that transcends purely temporal or cultural considerations.[14]

On the other hand, relativism appears strong not only in academic circles, but in much popular speech and writing. Just how widely or deeply held these relativistic views may be in present-day American thinking is a matter of conjecture. One writer, Robin Williams, Jr., tends to feel that adherence to absolute moral principles is still characteristically American.[15] It is

[14] Ralph Henry Gabriel, *The Course of American Democratic Thought,* The Ronald Press Company, 1940, pp. 14–15.

[15] "Authoritative observers from De Tocqueville, through Bryce, Siegfried and others, down to such recent studies as those of Vernon L. Parrington, Margaret Mead, Gunnar Myrdal, and Harold Laski, have agreed on at least one point: Americans tend to 'see the world in moral terms.' They do not mean mere conformity to the detailed prescriptions of a particular code, but rather to a systematic moral orientation by which conduct is *judged.* It is asserted that the quasi-mythical figure, the 'typical

undoubtedly true that many people who repeat relativistic slogans tend to take an absolute position when confronted by specific situations and problems. But it seems to be the case also that the general propositions of moral relativism are regarded in many quarters as symbols of open-mindedness, liberalism, or advanced thought. As such, they enter into the discussion of moral objectives in education.

The origins of relativism in our society are also a matter of conjecture. Among those who deplore it, some blame the whole affair on Dewey and the pragmatists. If this has any truth in it at all, one might ascribe it to the folklore of Deweyism rather than to the writings of Dewey himself.[16] Probably a more substantial factor in relativistic thinking has been the popularization of anthropologic studies showing variations in customs, beliefs, and ideals among peoples of differing cultural settings. The great impetus in this direction came from William Graham Sumner's *Folkways,* published in 1906. While Sumner undoubtedly was much impressed by these variations, he also closes his book with a stern warning against some of the conclusions that might be drawn from them: "The antagonism between a virtue policy and a success policy is a constant ethical problem. The Renaissance in Italy shows that although moral traditions may be narrow and mistaken, any morality is better than moral anarchy. Moral traditions are guides which no one can afford to neglect. They are in the mores and they are lost in every great revolution of the mores. Then the men are morally lost."[17]

Disagreements exist not only on the extent and origins, but also on the possible consequences of relativism. According to some, relativism is the straight road to moral degeneration and national

---

American,' thinks in terms of right or wrong, good or bad, ethical or unethical. This attitude goes beyond purely traditional or customary criteria of behavior—to test conduct against some systematic ethical principles." Robin Williams, Jr., *American Society: A Sociological Interpretation,* Alfred A. Knopf, 1951, pp. 396–397.

[16] In his *American Pragmatism and Education,* Henry Holt and Company, 1956, John L. Childs points out that while Dewey considered "institutional forms" as subject to change, the values for judging change have considerable stability. "The kind of values which we have just described persist, however, and they provide the perduring moral standards by which proposals for meeting these changing life conditions are evaluated." P. 135.

[17] William Graham Sumner, *Folkways,* Ginn and Company, 1906, p. 653.

collapse. To others, it is the road to national progress and advance. The views of any given individual will depend on his own philosophical and religious orientation. A working basis of agreement for school purposes may be found, however, in the following considerations.

1. There is a definite practical danger in extreme relativistic positions. It is the danger of blind and uncritical conformity to the standards of the social group. The extent of the danger depends on the nature, quality, and extent of the social group looked to as a source. For adolescents this is a real and not a conjectural problem. Our culture has placed so much stress on acceptance and adjustment that individuals may be tempted to seek these at the cost of other values. To the adolescent the strongest motivation is acceptance by the peer or age group. Standards of conduct vary from one peer group to another. An adolescent confronted by these will have little to guide him in his decisions without some stable values, which lie outside the group itself.

2. Cultural agreements tend to have the force of absolutes when they are sought in the wider culture and in terms of some historical perspective. If there are such things as values unique to a given culture, these are usually held with considerable conviction and provide a more suitable basis for individual decisions than the narrow standards of peer or clique groups. To this the objection may be raised that a body of values quite unacceptable to us was strongly held in Nazi Germany. The Nazi values, however, failed to meet the test of historical perspective, for they constituted a rejection of more widely held values in Western culture over a long period of time. Our present American value system on the other hand, even if considered as relative to our own culture, may be legitimately viewed as fully consistent with historical traditions drawn from a wider source.[18] Such values should provide a common meeting ground for absolutists and relativists.

3. Absolutism does not necessarily imply a detailed code of behavior prohibitions. The fear of such mechanistic formulations

[18] "The central themes of morality in America have undoubtedly had a common base and unified direction, derived from Judaic-Christian ethics." Williams, *op. cit.*, p. 398.

has possibly been one of the factors in the growth of relativism. Absolute values, however, constitute criteria for judgment and decision-making in relation to particular circumstances. They must always be used with discrimination, common sense, and intellectual skill. That this has been so regarded in the Judaic-Christian tradition is testified to by the great attention given to the field of moral theology, that is, the application of general rules to particular cases.

MORALITY AND RELIGION

The relationship between morality and religion is difficult to define in precise terms. Some who profess no religion at all in the formal sense exhibit much concern about morality. Likewise there have been some religions with little concern for morality as usually understood. Furthermore, studies that have attempted to identify relationships between formal religious education and moral behavior have been inconclusive, largely because of the presence of variables difficult to control.

Such difficulties as the foregoing, however, do not diminish or detract from the fact that throughout human experience, religion and morality have been closely and inescapably interwoven. In practical terms, the two areas are always associated in some way with each other. Whether or not the relationship is causal is perhaps beyond determination, but the relationship itself is a fact. And it is a fact that adds further confusion to the problem of moral education in the public schools of a society seeking to avoid church-state relationships.

During the early period of public schools in the United States this seemed to present little or no problem. The Christian moral system in specifically Protestant or even Puritan form was taken for granted, even though a smaller percentage of people belonged to churches than is the case today. Nothing more was needed than to detach the moral system from the theological differences among Protestant groups and go ahead with the teaching of it. To a limited extent the broad theological base could even be assumed and on occasion taught along with the ethical system. In some cases the base was specifically provided for by legislation prescribing Bible reading and the use of prayers in public schools. As time went on, however, the public included larger percentages of Roman Catholic Christians. While this presented no problem so far as general Christian morality was concerned, it did present one with regard to specific interpretations of the theological base. With Jews, the problem of the theological base became more accentuated, even though the broad platform of Judaic-Christian morality was one shared in common. The effect of this was not so much to change the pattern of legislation, for some of the Bible reading and prayer laws still remain on the books, but to reduce the degree of confidence with which schools and teachers could present without inhibitions matters formerly taken for granted. Teachers came to feel the obligation to offer a neutral appearance so far as religion was concerned. The discussion of historical periods such as the sixteenth century was regarded as touchy; it was considered prudent to stay as far away from religion as possible. This does not mean that the schools have ceased to teach moral behavior or that our schools have become Godless. But it has left us with the dilemma of how to proceed.

Whether or not we can proceed on the basis of a common morality independent of religious assumptions seems to be the heart of the dilemma. At first glance, it should be possible to identify the common elements of Judaic-Christian morality and to present these as our cultural heritage. To this approach, however, two contrasting objections have been raised, one that this is watered-down religion acceptable neither to religious groups nor to the so-called secularists. The other objection is that something more than common morality is needed, namely a common set of spiritual values. It is this feeling which probably accounts for the tendency in recent literature to stress moral *and* spiritual values.

In response to the first of the foregoing objections it may be urged that Judaic-Christian morality does not constitute a religion except possibly in the broadest and most informal sense of the word. It certainly is not a church and so does not bring up the church-state relationship. Since it is a common heritage of western culture, there would be no violation of anyone's religious freedom involved in its use in schools. Nor on the other hand is it a weak or anemic system; it includes some of the most vigorous and positive values held by our people. Its systematic and brutal violations in totalitarian states have shocked and dismayed us throughout our history.

In response to the second objection, it may be urged that moral values, although difficult to put into words, can be more objectively defined than those values called spiritual. The difficulty is that as spiritual values become explicitly defined, they take on more and more the appearance of specifically religious beliefs. It is here then, rather than in the common moral system, that the danger presents itself both of watering down religion in the attempt to find common denominators and of introducing religious teaching into the public school program.

These problems will not be easily resolved in public education in the United States, and they are not reducible to formulas. The problem is partly one of labels. Americans seem to be substantially agreed on fundamental moral principles. Disagreements on whether these principles are secular or religious do not seem to affect agreement on their nature and importance. Those who hold religious beliefs that go beyond the moral system may well doubt whether the moral system can stand up by itself. To this doubt history gives conflicting answers. Whether or not it can be done in our society is a question that can be answered only through experience; whether or not this is the choice before us depends on the job churches and families do in specifically religious instruction. Much depends also on the way this or any other body of moral content is actually handled in classroom instruction and on what people mean when they say it is a job of the schools to teach morality.

MIDDLE-CLASS VALUES AND MORALITY

The terms "middle," "upper," and "lower" class have long been used in literature and in popular speech. More recently sociologists have attempted to define these terms precisely and to study the phenomena related to them in United States communities. These studies have set off a vigorous train of discussion, particularly among those concerned with schools. One aspect centers on the extent to which the middle classes hold a distinctively different value system from other Americans and whether these moral values may legitimately be taught in the schools. According to one point of view, much conflict may result in schools when middle-class teachers seek to impose their notions of conduct on children from other classes, particularly the lower.

What kinds of moral behavior then are alleged to be middle class? This question usually evokes a listing somewhat as follows: individual advancement and success, hard work, thrift, paying one's own way, personal trustworthiness in business and financial matters, neatness, and dependability. Failure, laziness, spendthrift-ness, dependence on others, cheating, untidiness, and undependa-bility become by contrast, according to this viewpoint, a list of specifically middle-class sins. That Americans do value the virtues and disapprove of the defects here listed may be taken for granted, but that these ways of looking at conduct are uniquely or specifically the convictions of any one segment of American culture does not necessarily follow.

For one thing, it seems to be the tendency of most Americans to identify themselves with the middle class, even though they may not be classified as such in community studies. Who then is imposing whose values on whom? Our teachers would probably be called to account if they did not exemplify such behavior and demand it from their students. They would probably be called just as severely to account in so-called lower-class neighborhoods as in others.

It may well be that these values do represent the everyday work-ing moral principles of the American people, as contrasted with the broader aspects of the Judaic-Christian tradition, such as the importance and dignity of the individual. This is not to say that the working principles are in conflict with the broader principles; perhaps they represent the broader principles translated into the language of everyday human relationships. It may be doubted that even those who criticize the schools for teaching them would long be happy or comfortable if such values disappeared from our cul-ture; they like most Americans would prefer to have dealings with dependable, honest, hardworking people rather than with their conjectural opposites.

Sometimes the criticism is made that the middle-class values are stern or harsh, that they place so high a premium on success as to bear down with undue rigor on those who cannot attain it. To counteract this possibility we need to remember that any good quality of behavior may when distorted or exaggerated become something less desirable. Success may become success at any price, thrift degenerate into miserliness, and even neatness turn into a psychological obsession. Common sense has always recognized these possibilities. Americans have never applauded success when it has been gained through cruelty or dishonesty. The many humanitarian movements in our history testify to the American disposition to aid all who are victims of cruelty, injustice, or disaster. So-called middle-class values are highly interrelated; they must be looked at in their entirety rather than piece by piece.

Again, as in the case of those broader values associated with the Judaic-Christian ethic, the relevance of these middle-class values to the work of the public schools depends on what is meant by teaching moral behavior and how it is done. The fact that these values in the minds of many carry a middle-class label should not frighten educators into a repudiation of them.

THE MEANS AND MATERIALS OF MORAL EDUCATION

What then does it mean to *teach* morality? Much discussion of this question has centered on the role of verbal indoctrination in moral precepts. This is in great part a straw-man discussion, since few people advocate such indoctrination as the exclusive or even major approach to moral education.

Moral education demands a threefold approach so far as means and materials are concerned. One is that of providing or transmitting information: the knowledge of moral or ethical principles as guides to conduct. A second is that of providing an environment in which these principles are exemplified. The third is to develop the intellectual ability to relate ethical principles to specific situations calling for decisions.

The first approach, that of transmitting ethical knowledge, is the one that comes closest to verbalization and is further exposed to the danger of becoming what is known in the language of stereotypes as moralizing. It is nevertheless a necessary approach, for without it moral instruction lacks substance and subject matter. The most valid subject matter for this purpose is the Judaic-Christian moral system in historical terms. Use of history in this connection helps prevent the oversimplification that leads to stereotypes and formulas. Recognition of the historical fact that this ethical system has not always been practiced and has at times had to struggle for its existence helps to guard against moralizing and sentimentality. It has, of course, always been apparent that knowledge does not guarantee behavior. But knowledge provides the basis for behavior and is indispensable in any objective intellectual approach to the problem. In a society where good citizenship is closely related to morality, the widespread sharing of this knowledge provides the criteria for the making not only of individual but of broad political and social decisions.

But since knowledge alone does not guarantee behavior, something more is needed. This is where environment—family, church, school, and community—comes in. It is along these lines that the school, with its insistence on neatness, accuracy, punctuality, and effort, has done an effective job of teaching the so-called middle-class values. Schools can also provide an environment to exemplify some of the broader aspects of Judaic-Christian morality, particularly the dignity and importance of the human individual. One way in which many teachers have done this is through practices which respect, build upon, and in some cases adapt instruction to individual differences. This is not always easy to accomplish in situations where teachers are overloaded and is one point that must be kept in mind as we face the problem of rising enrollments and teacher shortages.

The third thing needed is individual student growth in the reflective thinking skills. Moral decisions are applications of principles to specific circumstances and situations. General development in reflective thinking, it is hoped, will transfer to this area. Just how far teachers should go in explicit teaching along this line is difficult to determine. Unless this process is carried on with great skill and judgment, it may become mechanical routine. Such techniques as paper-and-pencil tests of the applications-of-principles variety developed in the Eight-Year Study when used as a basis for discussion and analysis give promise of usefulness in this connection.

When all this is done, there is still no guarantee that desirable behavior will result, but it is inconceivable that we should ever surrender the moral objective in schooling. It deserves the best skill and judgment teachers can bring to it. And schools do not work alone; families, churches, and community agencies are dedicated to the same end.

THE MORAL OBJECTIVE IN SECONDARY SCHOOLING

But what, it may be asked, does the moral objective have to do with the work of the high school? For to many, the high school should be concerned primarily with intellectual development and the mastery of difficult knowledge and skills. Such things as moral instruction are associated with the care and nurture of very young children, not with the adolescent on the verge of adulthood. This point of view is expressed as follows by Bertrand Russell.

The building up of character, which has been our theme hitherto, should be mainly a matter for the earlier years. If rightly conducted, it ought to be nearly complete by the age of six. I do not mean that a character cannot be spoilt after that age; there is no age at which untoward circumstances or environment will not do harm. What I mean is that, after the age of six, a boy or girl who has been given the right early training ought to have habits and desires which will lead in the right direction if a certain care is taken with the environment. A school composed of boys and girls rightly brought up during their first six years will constitute a good environment, given a modicum of good sense in the authorities; it ought not to be necessary to give much time or thought to moral questions, such further virtues as are required ought to result naturally from purely intellectual training. I do not mean to assert this pedantically as an absolute rule, but as a principle guiding school authorities as regards the matters upon which they ought to lay emphasis. I am convinced that, if children up to the age of six have been properly handled, it is best that the school authorities should lay stress upon purely intellectual progress, and should rely upon this to produce the further development of character which is still desirable.[19]

But it is precisely because the secondary school deals with intellectual development on an advanced level that it is concerned with the moral objective. The use of the higher mental processes in dealing with moral issues and problems is an absolute necessity if we are to avoid the dangers of mechanical formulas and of sentimental moralizing. On these grounds alone one may argue that moral education should be carried beyond the elementary school. This is not to say that young children are incapable of reflective thinking. We know that they do very good reflective thinking on problems appropriate to their level of development. There remain, however, both a difference in mental development between childhood and adolescence and a difference in the degree of complexity of problems faced at those levels.

If, as has been contended, the study of history serves as a vehicle for the transmission of moral traditions and agreements, there is even further necessity for continuing moral education into the secondary school. Elementary schooling is not likely with many students to put across more than the skeleton outlines of history. Secondary schooling can do something more. It can provide the basis for thoughtful and reflective uses of past human experience. This does not mean teaching history with a moral, but on the other hand it does mean teaching history as something more than facts and dates. It requires sober consideration of the ways in which people in the past faced and resolved or were sometimes overwhelmed by their moral dilemmas.

A third reason for extending moral education into the secondary school is that adolescents do show deep concern about moral issues and problems. One need not subscribe to the storm-and-stress theory of adolescence to recognize this transition period between childhood and adulthood as one presenting the individual with a number of difficult decisions, many with definite moral aspects.

[19] Bertrand Russell, *Education and the Good Life,* Boni & Liveright, 1926, pp. 239–240.

Probably we have in the past tended to identify moral education more with the admonishing of very young children than with the intellectual development of adolescents. Yet our tradition is not devoid of the latter, as may be seen in the document in which Samuel and John Phillips endowed Andover Academy in 1778. This statement is of considerable interest, for in it "the promotion of true piety and virtue" is regarded not merely as one, but as "the *first* and *principal* object" of the school being established.[20]

CITIZENSHIP

The association of education with citizenship is taken for granted by most people of the United States. It dates back to the War of Independence and the period of national organization immediately following. Our founding fathers were convinced that popular sovereignty, or government of the people, could not be taken for granted, but that its successful operation depended on popular education in the skills and understandings of citizenship.

These convictions were translated into practice over a period of time. During the first half of the nineteenth century the American dream of free, popular elementary schooling took hold and was shaped into reality in most of our states. And it was in the following decades that we began developing the idea of free and popular schooling at the secondary level also. This is not to say that concern about citizenship caused the expansion of schooling. As schools were multiplied, however, the theme of education for citizenship was continuously reinforced. Strong, new motivation in this direction took place when large-scale immigration from Europe developed toward the end of the century. Nor has this feeling about education for citizenship diminished in our own time. When people are asked what schools are for, one of their answers at least is likely to be, "to make good citizens."

Good citizenship is a broad term and is interpreted in various ways. There has always been general agreement, however, on its important aspects. Most people, for example, regard a good citizen as a well-informed citizen, one who possesses knowledge about

[20] Elmer Ellsworth Brown, *The Making of Our Middle Schools*, Longmans, Green and Company, 1903, p. 195.

the structures, processes, and functions of government. Most would also agree that good citizenship includes loyalty to one's country, such as might be developed through study of our history and institutions. We also tend to believe that a good citizen is a freedom-loving person who will exert effort on behalf of his freedoms, but who will do so in the context of social responsibility.

This fusion of freedom and responsibility is probably one of the major features of the American way of citizenship. Both have appeared prominently in the American tradition. In his *Talks on Pedagogics* (1891), Francis W. Parker gave expression to the freedom aspect as follows.

The goal of humanity is freedom. Freedom comprehends the aim and direction of progress and the personal education of man. Liberty is the right of all men, but freedom is an individual acquirement through search for God's laws and obedience to them. The possession of freedom includes every possible good to the possessor—happiness, citizenship, personal development, and ethical action. The highest personal right a community can accord to an individual is the liberty and the means to become free. Liberty is accorded by laws, written and unwritten, which restrict the way of freedom entirely to personal effort, which place nothing between the individual and freedom but the inherent limitations of personality. The means of acquiring freedom may be summed up in one word—education. True education is the presentation of the conditions necessary for the evolution of personality into freedom. Democracy is the only form of government under which the methods of freedom can be fostered. The great central principle of democracy is mutual responsibility. Democracy in its essence gives to each individual the liberty of becoming free; raises no artificial barriers, political or social, between him and his goal. This is the ideal of democracy.[21]

Notice, however, that although the foregoing statement puts the stress on freedom, it does not neglect responsibility and self-discipline.

The other side of the freedom-responsibility relationship puts emphasis on the need for order and stability. During the 1830's and 1840's, the school's role in maintaining social stability re-

[21] Francis W. Parker, *Talks on Pedagogics,* Published for the Progressive Education Association by the John Day Company, 1937, pp. 317–318.

ceived much comment.[22] It should be kept in mind that this was a period in which several outbreaks of mob violence took place in this country and in which many people still remembered the French Revolution. Among those who felt strongly on this point was Horace Mann, who wrote as follows. "Had the obligations of the future citizen been sedulously inculcated upon all the children of the Republic, would the patriot have had to mourn over so many instances where the voter, not being able to accomplish his purpose by voting, has proceeded to accomplish it by violence; where, agreeing with his fellow-citizens to use the machinery of the ballot, he makes a tacit reservation, that, if that machinery does not move according to his pleasure, he will wrest or break it?"[23] Such expressions do not imply compliance with injustice. What is stressed is the need for peaceful and orderly means of expression and protest, rather than resort to violence. Assumed too is a setting characterized by the free ballot and by freedom of expression and thought. The free citizen of a free nation needs self-discipline to obey the laws made by his own representatives. An important element in good citizenship is willingness to obey laws and to use lawful processes in changing the laws themselves.

From this fusion of freedom and responsibility has evolved our point of view on social change, and on the function of school instruction in the process. We distrust social change by formula or blueprint. We tend to view it as something that grows out of specific solutions to specific problems and needs. It is empirical and inductive in character. Such a view of social change obviously calls for individual citizens skilled in the discussion processes required for interchange of opinion and in the problem-solving processes of reflective thinking. Under these circumstances, it becomes the job of the school not to build new social orders or to lead in reconstruction, but to equip children, youth, and adults with the skills needed for the practical job of working out their own solutions. While these processes function at the state and national levels as

---

[22] See Merle Curti, *Social Ideas of American Educators,* Charles Scribner's Sons, 1935, pp. 79–87, for examples from writings of this period.

[23] Horace Mann, Report for 1848, *Life and Works,* vol. 3, p. 696, cited by Curti, *op. cit.,* p. 129.

well as at that of the local community, it is in the local community that most citizens exercise direct participation. The ideal of a good citizen in our culture includes, therefore, in addition to the points previously stated, this quality of direct participation in solving problems close to home. A good citizen is one who stirs himself to devote time and energy to his local and neighborhood responsibilities. This tradition has come down to us from the New England town meeting and continues to function at least in terms of what the ideal should be. Our strong feelings about political corruption in local affairs are based not only on the facts of such corruption itself, but on the implications that the local citizens generally have failed to assume and exercise their responsibilities and freedoms.

But it is not enough that citizens be skilled in the problem-solving processes. The worthwhileness of a given feasible solution must be tested against some independent moral criteria. Good citizenship in our tradition has for this reason always had substantial ethical content as well. The good citizen knows right from wrong and can apply this knowledge in his decisions. Our citizenship objective is then closely related to another major category—that of ethical character.

We may therefore define a good citizen in our national tradition as one who: (1) is informed and literate on the structure, processes, and functions of government; (2) is loyal to our country; (3) understands and applies the ever-delicate balance between individual freedom and social stability; (4) applies himself intelligently to the solution of civic problems, with special emphasis on the local level; and (5) who carries on these tasks in relation to a clearly defined standard of ethical behavior. That this ideal is not always reached in our everyday lives in no way negates its force or vitality in our thinking.

The school then assumes its share of responsibility for developing these qualities in individuals. Does this responsibility, however, call for the extension of schooling to the secondary levels for large numbers of people? Cannot these functions be accomplished through the eight years of elementary schooling under the 8–4 plan? Our answer has been yes to the first, no to the second question. This may in part reflect the desire to justify the universalizing of the secondary school. It can also be legitimately interpreted as a response to the increasing complexities of civic and social life, complexities which do not lend themselves to study and treatment at the younger age levels.

The understanding of history, for example, is seen as increasingly important in the understanding of present social, political, and economic problems. Elementary schooling can give only the foundations of such historical understanding; even the years of the secondary school are short enough if not too short for the task. But the secondary school brings the individual closer to adult life itself, where it is hoped that he will continue his study and reading. In addition, we have recognized that the interpreting of controversial writing on social problems calls for more subtle reading skills than can be developed in most young children. Then too it has been increasingly felt that book study of citizenship problems should be supplemented by some direct participation through community-service projects, many of which are complex enough to be more appropriate for youth of high school age than for children.

The fact that we do not always accomplish these things in secondary schooling does not eliminate the need for them, if such a need exists. That it does exist is a conviction widely shared in American life today. It is upon this conviction that we rest in part our desire to make the secondary school a truly universal rather than a selective institution. This is testified to not only by the way in which we look to the school to accomplish these values, but also by the way we tend to blame the school, especially the high school, when we encounter evidence that everyday citizenship in practice does not quite match our ideals. True, we have in our midst some skeptics who doubt not only that the school succeeds in doing these things, but that they can be done at all. This contemporary cynicism, however, has not received general or even widespread support.

PHYSICAL HEALTH

There is little dispute about the individual and social importance of physical health. It is widely held that schools should do something about it. Physical education, which many people tend to identify with the health objective, is next to English the most universally required subject in United States high schools.

Much force has been given to this objective by fears that youth in the United States is becoming soft and perhaps unequal to its responsibilities in national defense. For this reason the physical-fitness aspect of health has been given special prominence in high school programs, with more emphasis than was once the case on strength, agility, endurance, and specific skills.

But there is more to health than physical fitness alone. Even powerful athletes may be laid low by disease or by their own personal health habits and attitudes. Many people were astonished by the fact that thousands of young Americans were rejected for military service, especially in the light of assumptions that had been made about our high standards of nutrition, disease prevention, and medical care.

The problem is at least partly one of education, that is of the development of understandings and skills related to health problems and needs. The school's function in health, therefore, is broader than those activities implied by the term "physical fitness." This broader aspect of health education can be dealt with in part by the physical education department, but it also requires specific attention and specifically pointed subject matter in other fields as well, particularly the natural sciences, home making, and social studies.

MENTAL OR EMOTIONAL HEALTH

This is a controversial objective. Much of the controversy centers about what acceptance of such an objective might mean in school practice. One way to approach this question is to state what is not meant, at least by the majority of those who see mental or emotional health[24] as a legitimate objective for the schools.

[24] The following may be taken as a good characterization of mental health. "Here it should be made clear that the ideal of healthy personality is not that of a 'perfect' person who has no problems or feelings or who is perfectly 'adjusted.' Rather the conception of healthy personality, as we today may tentatively state it, is of a person who recognizes the life tasks and problems that living in a social order and in a symbolic cultural world presents to every person, but who meets them with self-confidence, courage, and the ability to conduct his interpersonal relationships with generosity and dignity, responding with feelings that are appropriate to his stage of

Mental health in the school most assuredly does not mean that teachers become psychiatrists, amateur or otherwise. Teachers do not diagnose and do not treat mental disease. Occasionally, it is true, a teacher may feel that specialized help is necessary for a student and through legitimate channels refers the matter to those who are competent to provide such help. But this is occasional only. It is what any teacher would do no matter what objectives the school might profess.

Neither does the mental health function imply the teaching of abnormal psychology. Teachers do not teach students how to diagnose and treat themselves. Some work may be done in some courses to help students understand themselves and the role of emotion in everyday living. But this is done on a positive and constructive basis and does not include the study of abnormalities or aberrations. Moreover, it is not clear that any direct teaching of such materials in the classroom is a good way of dealing with the mental health objective.

The school's role in mental health is to be interpreted rather as the establishing and maintaining of a school environment consistent with good emotional development. Mental health is something which the individual builds for himself over a considerable period of time. It is based on a reasonable degree of success in gaining belongingness, participation, and status or recognition. Along with this is needed some sense of security—the feeling that there is a reasonable chance of keeping and building on what has been gained. Every environment is important for the individual. The first and most important environment in this connection is of course the home. A good home environment provides the child with substantial resources for meeting life's problems. But no environment —not even the home—stands alone in this matter. The child leaves the home in part at the age of six and spends much of his time in school and community. These environments must be equally good. Otherwise the effects of a fine home background in mental health may be undone. It should be recognized that oppor-

---

development." Lawrence K. Frank, "The Promotion of Mental Health," *The Annals of the American Academy of Political and Social Science,* vol. 286, March, 1953, p. 169.

tunities for belongingness, participation, and status are no guarantee against mental disease, particularly of an organic character. When other things are equal, however, individuals who make reasonable achievement along these lines are likely to secure good mental and emotional health.

An environment favorable to mental and emotional health is not a soft environment, nor is it one in which students are protected from reality. It is one rather that presents many opportunities for participation and for response both to achievement and failure. Richness and variety of activities in the school program help every student find opportunity for participation, achievement, and recognition. Individual differences are respected and built upon, but nobody is given a false picture of his own achievements and abilities. Possibilities for helping students gain opportunities for belongingness, participation, and status exist in all phases of the school program: classroom studies, extraclass activities, school and community service projects, and school-related work experience. Awareness of the mental health function contributes to the effective use of these possibilities.

The importance of a good school environment for mental health is usually granted so far as the early grades of the elementary school are concerned. Many people express considerable concern, and properly so, about the immediate emotional adjustment of the child starting school. Opinions on adolescence, however, are mixed. According to the storm-and-stress school of thought that held sway in nineteenth-century romanticism, adolescence is a period of violent and spectacular emotional crises. The fact is, however, that adolescents are like other people in their emotional lives, but differ from those of other age levels in facing more contradictory demands from the culture. It is a commonplace but nevertheless true observation that people sometimes expect adolescents to behave like children and at other times like adults. These conflicting demands do create for the adolescent a somewhat specialized set of problems, defined in part as developmental tasks. The rules for gaining belongingness, participation, and status are, therefore, mixed and confusing. It is this reason and not any innate storm and stress in the makeup of adolescents that makes the mental health objective important at the high school level.

Nor do we need to regard the mental health objective as one in conflict with or even irrelevant to intellectual or academic standards. True, some geniuses have made outstanding artistic and intellectual contributions in spite of poor mental health. Whether or not good mental health would have interfered with their achievements we do not know. But most people probably do better work intellectually when relatively free from emotional conflict or disturbance. Concern for mental health should promote rather than retard the attainment of academic excellence in the secondary school, or indeed on any level of schooling.

ENJOYMENT OF LIVING

Every person does something with his life that goes beyond earning a livelihood, preserving health, or exercising the responsibilities of citizenship, although he may enjoy any or all of these activities. Just what he does with it represents a combination of his opportunities and his personal tastes. These personal tastes may be modified or developed through schooling, but they remain unique to the individual nonetheless. Any school that takes this objective seriously, therefore, provides a wide variety of instructional resources, including music, literature, the graphic arts, athletics, and the industrial arts. Any high school subject may contribute to the enrichment or enjoyment of living for some students. It is particularly important for every teacher to enjoy his subject so that students may catch this enjoyment from him.

The individual need not, in fact dare not, rest content with passive enjoyment. More is needed, and that more is some form of striving for creative expression along aesthetic lines. This includes expression not only in the fields of art, music, and literature, but in many other aspects of human living. The development of creativity is relevant not only to the classroom studies, but also to the extra-class activities. If this urge to expression is fostered in the educational process, each individual will continue to develop it in those areas uniquely his own. Apparently the high school curriculum has not effectively fostered such expression or, at least, has not offset other forces working against it.

High school pupils have a not inconsiderable collection of information, even though it is spotty and not very well organized. If there is a lack, it is easily remedied, given a real need for further information. More disturbing are shortages in skills and procedures. Most disturbing is the fact that for many of the pupils the hardening of the intellectual arteries has already set in; i.e., the disposition to create new forms and to perceive new forms is beginning to die. The tendency to stereotyped speech, dress, and attitudes is beginning to congeal. This is puzzling on two counts: (a) as children these pupils probably manifested remarkable flexibility of thought, and (b) adolescence is admittedly a period of the liveliest curiosity, speculation, and experimentation.[25]

The need for creativity is not, of course, confined to times or periods of leisure. On the other hand, all enjoyment, whether on or off the job, demands something in the way of creativity.

The importance of this objective to the individual is accentuated by current social trends. Industrial and technical progress have given us more leisure time than enjoyed by most people in the past. The future promises even more. Here lies the opportunity of the school to help make this leisure a blessing rather than a curse. But schools need to keep two cautions in mind. One is that the best cultural standards need neither be cheapened nor debased. Every student is entitled to the opportunity at least of responding to the cultural resources which have in previous ages been the possession of the leisured few. The other caution is that no individual should have patterns of leisure-time use forced upon him. We have had horrible examples of "strength through joy" before us in our time, and such writers as George Orwell have provided pictures of the dreary uniformity of enjoyment that may develop in the future if the social aspect of this matter is ever allowed to suppress the individual. For one of the supreme rights of the individual

[25] Harry S. Broudy, "The Neglect of Aesthetics as an Educational Resource," *Progressive Education,* November, 1950, p. 39.

is to enjoy himself in his own way as long as he does not harm or interfere with others.

FAMILY LIVING

By the time a student gets to high school, he has already been living in a family for 12 or 13 years. He has also probably had several units on home and family in his progress through the elementary grades. What, if anything, remains to be done at the high school level? Perhaps this is one of the functions which the high school in a period of withdrawal from untenable ground might be in a good position to drop. We need to examine this possibility from the standpoint of three kinds of possible activities: (1) instruction in such matters as foods, clothing, family finance, and home mechanics; (2) instruction in the area of family relationships; and (3) sex education.

The first of these is relatively non-controversial. In our practical way of looking at things, such instruction is not only permissible but highly desirable. Furthermore, there is enough good subject matter for advanced study in connection with such topics to warrant placement at the high school as well as at the elementary level. Some of this instruction may even have more meaning and make more sense to the adolescent than to the younger child.

The second area, that of human relationships in the family, occupies somewhat middle ground. So far as the instruction is aimed specifically at the adolescent's future responsibilities, there seems to be much public support and demand. Practically no discussion of divorce and separation goes by without the observation that the schools should educate young people for permanent and stable marriage. Extraclass activities and the social life of the school are seen by many as contributing to the kinds of human relationships needed in good family life. But there is another side to such instruction, namely the study of the adolescent's current responsibilities in family relationships. Schooling probably should help children and youth to be good members of their families. At the elementary level much of this is done without much difficulty, since the matter of parent-child relationships for younger children seems clearly established. But adolescents differ from younger children, and relationships with their parents become more complex. There is less agreement to go by. Guidance along these lines demands a skilled and understanding teacher, one who realizes sympathetically the needs not only of the adolescents, but those of his parents as well. The situation varies from one community to the next; there are no easy generalizations available.

Sex education is still another matter. This term means many different things to different people. No matter what it is taken to mean, however, it is always controversial. Practically every community has articulate proponents of sex education as well as those who react against it strongly as an item in the school curriculum. Consensus just does not exist on this point even within given communities. Sometimes working agreements are achieved for limited instruction along the lines of carefully defined objectives.

It is probably safe to say that family living is regarded by most people as something less than a primary function of the secondary school. In any case, whatever the school does along these lines is supplementary to the education carried on by families, churches, and community agencies. Some of the school's possible activities under this general heading, however, are enthusiastically received by most parents and other members of the general public. This is particularly true of the more tangible aspects of homemaking, such as foods, clothing, and home mechanics.

OCCUPATIONAL COMPETENCE

This objective applies to all high school students, not just to those in so-called non-college-preparatory courses. Many college-bound students are pointing toward professional schools in their higher education; even those who plan to take the general or liberal arts course are usually hopeful of finding some kind of market for what they learn. The stereotyped notion of the occupational objective as applicable to terminal students only has always been a fiction. Its survival in the present serves as a confusing element in discussions about secondary schools.

The vocational objective furthermore need not necessarily be identified with specific vocational training and is never to be exclusively identified with preparation for the industrial or mechanical trades. Both of these are essential parts of the curriculum for some students, but they do not even begin to define the range of activities related to the occupational objective in the secondary school. Misunderstandings of these points have led to two conflicting criticisms of the secondary school: one that the school is too academic and therefore by implication unrelated to the practical needs of its students, the other that it has been corrupted by narrow vocationalism or materialism. The first group of critics assumes that any education is academic unless preoccupied with imparting the skills and techniques of a particular trade; the second group assumes no education is academic or intellectual unless it is completely detached from the materialistic considerations of earning a living.

For the most part the people of the United States seem convinced that earning a living is an important part not only of our private but also of our public welfare and that preparation for it should in some way be part of the business of our secondary schools. Earning a living is regarded not only as a means of providing for life's necessities; it is seen as an important element in individual self-realization or fulfillment. The major emphasis in this objective, as in others, is on benefit to the individual. But public benefit has been given increasing emphasis in recent writing and discussion. The requirements of a complex technology and the shortages existing in scientific as well as other professions have tended to make us acutely conscious of what is known as the manpower problem. These considerations have reinforced previously existing convictions that the development of occupational competence is a legitimate function of the public schools.

Occupational competence as an objective in the secondary school may be broken down into the following specific functions or objectives: (1) to provide vocational guidance for all students; (2) to help every student develop skills and understandings relevant to success in many occupational fields; (3) to help every student develop the personal qualities generally needed in work relationships; (4) to provide some students with essential preparation for advanced professional study; and (5) to provide to some students under some circumstances specific training in the skills and techniques of particular occupations.

VOCATIONAL GUIDANCE FOR ALL STUDENTS

The term "guidance" arouses conflicting emotions. It is sufficient for the present purpose to state that guidance is aimed at helping the individual to understand himself and to make intelligent decisions on the basis of this understanding. Vocational guidance seeks to develop the individual's understanding of his interests and capacities in relation to work and employment. It involves both individual counseling and group instruction. Since choices of courses and programs are related to vocational choice, this aspect of guidance is never separated from the broader area of educational guidance.

Much of the skepticism about vocational guidance rests on antipathy to testing. The use of vocational aptitude and interest tests seems to suggest the manipulation of the individual. On the other hand, some people place far too much faith in such tests and tend in spite of all protests from guidance specialists to regard them as absolute verdicts. Tests are nothing more than tools by means of which the counselor helps the individual to gain a better understanding of what interests him and what he can do. They are never used in isolation from other relevant clues along the same lines. Properly used and interpreted, they are among the most important means in the school to aid individual fulfillment.

Group instruction in various classroom studies can provide accurate information about job trends and opportunities. Much of this can be done in social studies classes. Another function of group instruction is to develop understanding and appreciation of some of the techniques used in individual counseling, such as tests. Some of this may need to be repeated in the individual counseling itself, but classroom teaching can lay the groundwork.

Much energy has been expended on the issue of the appropriate age or grade levels for vocational guidance. So far as individual counseling is concerned, this depends on the individual student. Some are ready for such help in the junior high school, while others seem to need it late in senior high or even in college. There is no special virtue in being ready earlier or later. Group instruction must, of course, have definite placement in a curriculum sequence on a basis sufficiently flexible to permit and encourage classroom teachers to make adaptations to particular groups. Some of it begins in the elementary school social studies units on such matters as communication, transportation, and marketing. The community living course in ninth grade often includes the study of occupational trends in particular localities. American history both in the eighth and eleventh grades provides opportunities for such study in national terms. The twelfth-grade senior problems course may include a study of the meaning and limitations of tests.

Other aspects of the school's program may also contribute to the student's understanding of his interests and capacities. Extraclass activities such as dramatics, journalism, athletics, and various kinds of school clubs provide clues in a number of directions. Jobs in community service projects or in paid part-time employment, whether school-coördinated or not, serve as further avenues of self-appraisal and understanding. These all underline the fact that vocational guidance is something much broader and more comprehensive than the stereotyped picture of an allegedly omniscient counselor making pronouncements to a student across a desk.

GENERAL SKILLS AND UNDERSTANDINGS

Much of what is taught in school may be defined as vocational education in a broad sense. English is probably the broadest vocational subject of all, for the ability to read, write, and speak accurately is an asset in practically all human occupations. Another broadly vocational subject is mathematics, although the mathematically illiterate seem to have a wider range of occupational choice than is possible for those who have difficulty with ordinary language. Nevertheless there are many jobs in which some degree of mathematical competence is an absolute requisite. Modern languages offer similar occupational advantages, although the range of jobs to which this applies is smaller than is the case with English and mathematics. All three fields, furthermore—English, mathematics, and modern languages—are useful assets to those who enter military service.

Other classroom studies, such as industrial arts and business education, may seem to be and often are more directly vocational in nature. Yet in many schools these subjects are offered on a general education basis. As such they make contributions to occupational competence on the same general basis as do English and mathematics. Some understanding and skill in the use of tools are useful in about half the kinds of jobs available. Nor are these all production jobs; many of them are distinctly in the service classification. In like manner, skills in bookkeeping, typing, and shorthand tend to have occupational value for many who are not accountants or secretaries.

PERSONAL QUALITIES FOR OCCUPATIONAL SUCCESS

Such personal qualities as punctuality, neatness, dependability, initiative, and industry are assets in most jobs. Teachers have devoted much effort both to exemplifying these qualities in their own work and in expecting evidences of them in students. Parents hope their children will develop such qualities; employers demand them. When children do not show these characteristics, the school is criticized whether it is to blame or not. Much of the reaction against the stereotype or caricature that people call progressive education probably grew out of fears that schools were developing laziness, undependability, and the like.

Schools in the United States have long been conscious of the need to develop general character traits such as the foregoing. More recently, however, a good deal of attention has been centered on a complex body of behavior qualities symbolized by the oft-repeated phrase, getting along with people. There are two good reasons for this. One is that human relationships enter into practically every kind of job. Studies indicate that even in highly skilled production jobs people are judged not only in terms of their technical skills, but in terms of their ability to work with others. There are workers who constantly shift jobs because on each one there is something wrong with the boss or the worker on the next bench. The other reason is that more and more of our jobs today are in the category known as service jobs, in which the worker deals not only with the boss and his fellow employes, but with the public.

Many of these jobs depend more on skills in human relationships than on anything else.

Getting along with people, however, is an outgrowth not of success formulas but of healthy personality generally. What is needed is neither the caricature of the go-getter or the hearty extrovert, nor the hypocritical adapting to others of a Uriah Heep. It is rather the poise that comes from self-respect and respecting others. As such it comprehends the whole range of objectives included in self-realization.

PREPARATION FOR ADVANCED PROFESSIONAL STUDY

So-called academic subjects provide not only general skills and understandings for life work, but specific preparation for advanced professional study in higher institutions. There is nothing new in this. Latin was once a prerequisite to professional study in law, medicine, and theology. Not even the Latin Grammar School escaped this taint of vocationalism. The most conspicuous examples today are science and mathematics as preparatory to advanced study for engineering, scientific research work, and other technical fields. Moreover, it is for alleged shortcomings in these areas that high schools today are severely criticized. With the increased demand for professional workers in these technical fields, the high school is not likely to find itself relieved of this particular vocational function.

SPECIFIC JOB TRAINING IN THE SECONDARY SCHOOL

Enthusiasm for specific job training has fluctuated throughout educational history in the United States. The major period of enthusiasm occurred between 1905 and 1920, during which a sharp distinction was often drawn between preparation for college and preparation for work. Specialized trade and technical high schools developed in our large cities. The Smith-Hughes Act of 1917 gave the movement not only semiofficial endorsement, but the tangible advantage of federal financial aid. Since 1920 the movement has maintained itself fairly well where previously established. Enthusiasm for further expansion, however, has declined, although in some quarters there are signs of revival. In fact, there are not a few secondary educators today who doubt whether such job training should be offered at all and who would prefer that the fields of agriculture, home economics, business education, and industrial arts be reorganized entirely as general education.

No blanket recommendations are possible. The issues must be met and resolved through specific decisions in local communities. In some places a school may offer a good vocational program without any specific job training whatsoever. But for other communities, specific job training is entirely appropriate and necessary.

The question is always a most difficult one to resolve. One of the facts that must be kept in mind is the nature of the local and regional job market. It seems obvious that a community with little industry and few openings for skilled mechanics should think twice before putting specialized shop programs into the high school curriculum. The facts of geographical mobility in our country, however, tend to disturb that easy conclusion. A non-industrial community also must decide whether it wants to stay that way or try to develop itself along industrial lines.

Another consideration is the availability of job-training programs carried on by industries and trade unions. It seems undesirable for schools to duplicate functions already performed by such agencies. The training programs of industry, however, are usually limited to semiskilled jobs that can be learned in a relatively short time. While trade union apprenticeship programs are aimed more at highly skilled work, it is often difficult for more than a few students to become apprentices. Schools, therefore, may need to supplement industrial and apprenticeship training programs. Desirable arrangements have been developed in some communities for coöperative programs in which trade unions, industries, and high schools participate, each agency contributing the kind of training for which it is best equipped and fitted.

Local decisions may also be affected by the presence or absence of schools offering job training on a post-high school basis. Wisconsin, for example, has developed a system of vocational schools in the larger cities. While these schools have come to serve in part as continuation schools for dropouts, the main portion of their program is aimed at high school graduates. In other states, many communities have local junior colleges that offer a variety of specialized programs in the skilled trades and in so-called semi-professional employment.

The nature of the high school student body must also be taken into account. Some schools have installed job training programs only to discover that they had relatively few students who wanted or could qualify for them. Such programs demand students who (1) are willing to devote a substantial portion of their high school program to specialized courses and (2) have the ability to do the work. A specific job-training program is usually no place for the low-ability student, and teachers in such programs have long deplored the tendency to use their courses as dumping grounds.

Whether or not the contemplated program offers broad possibilities of educational transfer serves as an additional criterion in decision-making. As mentioned previously, skills learned in business education may be used in a wide variety of jobs. Those who possess them are not limited to secretarial or bookkeeping work. Home economics, even when thought of in vocational terms, provides the student not only with marketable skills for paid employment, but with general skills and understandings for everyday living. Vocational shop courses provide training in specific areas that should transfer to others requiring mechanical skill and understanding. Vocational agriculture is another field rich in significance for general education.

After the local school board has considered all these matters, it must turn to the question of costs. Even with federal aids, job-training programs are expensive, usually requiring heavy outlay in space, equipment, and staff. If the need exists, however, effort should be made to work out the financial problems involved. The cost question, moreover, should not enter into the preliminary analysis of the need for such training. It is too easy to give up at the outset by concluding that the program costs too much. Conversely, the availability of funds should not in itself dictate a conclusion to go ahead with the program. The need, therefore, should be studied first, with the cost problem coming in only if the need exists.

IS THE HIGH SCHOOL TRYING TO DO TOO MUCH?

Every one of the objectives examined in this chapter can be supported to some extent both by our traditional national beliefs and by contemporary circumstances and conditions. But can the high school really do all these things effectively? If some are included, do not others have to be left out? How can the time, energy, and resources of teachers, students, and communities be adequately budgeted for such a task? This is a basic question that has to be answered in specific and detailed terms and as such is one of our major concerns throughout the rest of this book. At this point, however, several general observations may be made.

For one thing, these objectives are highly interrelated. Intellectual development, for example, enters all the others. Moral character depends to a large extent on the ability of the individual to relate basic criteria to choices of behavior, essentially a process of reflective thinking. Good citizenship is intelligent and informed citizenship.

Second, it is the cultural transmission function of the school rather than any of the aspects-of-living objectives that should determine the form and organization of the classroom studies. The statement of an objective such as mental health does not imply the creation of a course aimed specifically at that objective. Neither, one might add, does the statement of an objective such as intellectual competence. In some cases, an objective and a course may legitimately coincide, as is the case with the objective of family living and the instructional field of homemaking or home economics. But homemaking is an instructional field because it is an important part of culture, not because it coincides with one of the aspect-of-living objectives. The curriculum of the classroom studies is cluttered and jammed; this cannot be ascribed to the existence of the aspects-of-living objectives, but rather to their use as primary determinants of the classroom studies. As supplementary bases for resolving specific questions about what might or might not be included in various courses, they can be very helpful indeed, provided they are regarded as supplementary. Assignment of priorities among these kinds of objectives as supplementary bases will vary from one instructional field to the next. Some will be more important than others in history, but not necessarily in science, or the other way round. In addition, these kinds of objectives are useful in resolving questions about other parts of the curriculum, such as the extraclass activities.

Third, the use of curricular means outside the classroom will vary greatly from one student to another and from time to time throughout his school career. Several hours a day in school-related work experience may be desirable for student A in the 11th grade. This does not mean that every student in the 11th grade will spend several hours a day in work experience; it does not even mean that student A will do so in Grade 12. The fact, then, that a school offers a wide variety of out-of-class opportunities in the curriculum does not mean that too much student time is being spent in them. Neither does a small number of different activities suggest that students are not spending too much time. The number of activities is not necessarily in direct proportion to the amount of student time devoted to them.

Fourth, whatever the school does might conceivably be done by other agencies and in many cases is already being done. People could get along without schools at all, but not very well. There are some matters on which it could get along less well than others, which is another way of saying that some functions or objectives are more important than others. The organized, orderly, and systematic transmission of culture is one function that many societies have felt could be more readily handled by schools than by other agencies, especially as culture accumulates and becomes more complex. So far as the aspects-of-living objectives are concerned, schools are in a unique position to deal with such matters as intellectual development. But even on cultural transmission and intellectual development, schools have no monopoly. Furthermore, the importance of an objective for the school is not necessarily indicated by the extent to which other agencies deal with it. Mental health, for example, may be affected by practically everything one does in life, but this does not make it any less important a basis for the making of decisions in school practice. It would obviously be futile for the school to try to do everything about every aspect of living. It is also futile to seek purposes for the school with which other agencies of society are not concerned.

We may assume, then, that high schools are devoted both to the transmission of culture and to the fostering of various objectives related to aspects of living. Variations in degree of importance among the objectives represented by these aspects of living are in part related to individual differences, but not to differences among students taken as groups. The objective of intellectual development, for example, is just as important for the so-called terminal as for the college-preparatory group. Similarly, the job or career objective is just as important for the college-preparatory group as for those not going to college.

Bibliography

Bereday, George Z. F., and Lauwerys, Joseph A. (eds.), *The Secondary School Curriculum,* The Yearbook of Education, 1958, prepared under the auspices of the University of London Institute of Education and Teachers College, Columbia University, World Book Company, 1958, pp. 127–280.

Berkson, I. B., *The Ideal and the Community: A Philosophy of Education,* Harper & Brothers, 1958.

Bestor, Arthur E., Jr., *Educational Wastelands,* University of Illinois Press, 1953.

Brinton, Crane, *Ideas and Men: The Story of Western Thought,* Prentice-Hall, Inc., 1950.

Broudy, Harry S., "The Neglect of Aesthetics as an Educational Resource," *Progressive Education,* November, 1950, pp. 37–40.

Commission on the Reorganization of Secondary Education, National Education Association, *Cardinal Principles of Secondary Education,* Department of the Interior, Bureau of Education, Bulletin 1918, No. 35, U.S. Government Printing Office, 1937.

Curti, Merle, *American Paradox: The Conflict of Thought and Action,* Rutgers University Press, 1956.

Douglass, Harl (ed.), *Education for Life Adjustment,* The Ronald Press Company, 1950.

French, Will, and Associates, *Behavioral Goals of General Education in High School,* Russell Sage Foundation, 1957.

Hutchins, Robert M., *Education for Freedom,* Louisiana State University Press, 1943.

Kolesnik, Walter, *Mental Discipline in Modern Education,* The University of Wisconsin Press, 1958.

Martin, Everett Dean, *The Meaning of a Liberal Education,* W. W. Norton & Company, 1926.

National Society for the Study of Education, Fifty-fourth Yearbook, pt. 2, *Mental Health in Modern Education,* The Society, 1955.

Russell, Bertrand, *Education and the Good Life,* Boni & Liveright, 1926.

Smith, Mortimer, *The Diminished Mind,* Henry Regnery Company, 1954.

Smith, Mortimer (ed.), *The Public Schools in Crisis: Some Critical Essays,* Henry Regnery Company, 1956.

Van Doren, Mark, *Liberal Education,* Books, Inc., distributed by Henry Holt and Company, 1943.

....

CHAPTER 5

The High School and the College

All secondary schooling, in fact schooling at any level, is preparation for further learning and study. So far as the high school graduate is concerned, further study may take place in a college or university, it may be pursued through the informal agencies of adult education, or it may be a private venture of his own as a leisure-time activity. Obviously, college is only one of several routes, but it happens to be the one that provides the most tangible and organized opportunities. Colleges as well as secondary schools have developed in response to various needs and circumstances. The relationships between them reflect a variety of social and intellectual currents not only in the wider context of western culture, but in our specific United States background as well.

The Boston Latin Grammar School prepared students for a particular college—Harvard. Since the curricula both of secondary and higher education, however, were defined largely by the classical languages, there was no implication of conflict or domination. As other colonial grammar schools were established, particularly in New England, they accepted the responsibility of equipping students for advanced work at Harvard and other colleges.

Franklin's original idea for his academy, on the other hand, was that of providing a scientific, practical education in English for the middle classes of colonial society.[1] As the school developed, how-

---

[1] Some "practical" studies had begun to appear in the Latin grammar schools in the eighteenth century. "The new studies so admitted were of a commercial and mathematical sort: arithmetic and merchants' accounts; geometry, navigation, and

ever, it was divided into English and classical departments, with the function of the classical department identified strictly as college preparation. Here was the seed of distinction between college-preparatory and non-college-preparatory programs, a seed now grown into a flourishing plant that has long outlived the emphasis on classical studies themselves. This distinction between the English and the classical departments appeared and was maintained in the numerous academies established in subsequent years.

Although Franklin's hopes for a non-college-preparatory school devoted to modern studies had miscarried, a new start was made in this direction in the Boston English High School of the 1820's. In fact, the founders of this school were so explicit about their intentions and revealed these to such an extent in the first program of studies that the principal of the Latin Grammar School objected to the original name by which the school was called, namely, the English Classical School.[2] But the high schools founded in other cities were no more successful in maintaining these original intentions than Franklin had been with the academy. Classical studies and programs were added and with them the college-preparatory function.[3] This was inevitable and in the light of all our democratic conceptions legitimate and right. Had the high school closed to the people the road to advanced studies it could not have become a popular institution.[4] Less fortunate was the tendency of the high

surveying; and some closely related subjects. . . . Of course such studies, previous to the middle of the eighteenth century, had no connection with preparation for college. They represented the intrusion of a different view of the function of the school. They smacked of trade. The notion that they might have some sort of educational value in and of themselves, was not then abroad." Elmer Ellsworth Brown, *The Making of Our Middle Schools,* Longmans, Green, and Company, 1903, p. 134.

[2] Brown, *op. cit.,* p. 308.

[3] "The period of the forties was one of expansion of both the work of the high schools already established and of new high schools throughout New England. The beginnings of the movement in Connecticut, Vermont, and Rhode Island are found in this decade. The most prominent change in the course of instruction was the differentiation of curricula. The aim of the high school had expanded to include both the preparation for college and the provision of higher English instruction. . . . The main change since 1827 was the inclusion of the languages and this was due to the merging of the English and Latin schools and the development of separate departments or curricula." Emit Duncan Grizzell, *Origin and Development of the High School in New England before 1865,* The Macmillan Company, 1923, pp. 288–289.

[4] "But the high schools gravitated toward the colleges, as the academies had done before them. None of the many protests raised against this movement could check it

schools to follow the academies in the use of such terms as "classical course" and "English course," thereby maintaining the distinctions between preparation for college and so-called preparation for life. The introduction of Latin studies in the English High School was entirely appropriate; their introduction on the grounds of the college-preparatory function is to be regretted.

The colleges, however, began to place some of the newer subjects taught in academies and high schools on the lists of those required or accepted for entrance. "In 1800 there were only three subjects required for admission to any college in the United States —Latin, Greek, and arithmetic. Between 1800 and 1870 eight new subjects found a place among admission requirements—geography, English grammar, algebra, geometry, ancient history, physical geography, English composition, and United States history. In other words, in less than seventy years eight new entrance subjects were introduced, whereas during the century and a half prior to 1800 the only addition of any consequence was elementary arithmetic."[5] This trend may be viewed as liberal in the sense of fostering a more inclusive program of studies. The classical department no longer had a monopoly on college preparation, and for a time the rigid distinction between Latin and other studies in terms of the college-preparatory function appeared to be breaking down.

Further expansion took place after 1870. "Since 1870 the new subjects that have been added to the list of college admission requirements are English literature, French, and German, and physical and natural science."[6] Not every college, of course, required the entire range of subjects.[7] This presented to high schools the task of preparing students not for a common set of requirements, but for those that varied from one college to the next, a state of affairs

---

for any length of time. It was, in fact, a thoroughly American movement. It answered to that broad, American logic which maintained that since any youth might rise to the highest offices, every youth should have the opportunity offered to him of rising to the highest education." Brown, *op. cit.*, p. 373.

[5] Edwin Cornelius Broome, *A Historical and Critical Discussion of College Admission Requirements,* Columbia University Contributions of Philosophy, Psychology and Education, vol. 11, Nos. 3–4, The Macmillan Company, April, 1903, p. 46.

[6] *Ibid.,* p. 61.

[7] *Ibid.,* p. 62.

that could not easily be resolved by a uniform or standard college-preparatory curriculum. No easy solution to this problem has yet been found.

Liberalization took the form not only of recognizing the newer subjects, but also of providing more flexibility in the entrance patterns themselves. This was accomplished in part by the creation of college programs with somewhat more flexible entrance requirements leading to the degrees of Bachelor of Science and Bachelor of Philosophy.[8] Next, some of the colleges began setting up admission requirements in groups of preparatory subjects, with various choices within the groups, thereby introducing more flexibility in admissions to all degree programs, although the patterns were not necessarily identical from one program to the next.[9] The so-called elective system introduced still more flexibility, and in 1891, Stanford University went over to it almost completely, with English as the only prescribed subject.[10] By this time the picture of entrance requirements confronting the high school principal must have been one of general chaos, matched by similar chaos in the high school curriculum itself. For the high schools had been busily engaged not only in expanding their offerings, but in finding about every possible way of organizing and naming their subjects.[11]

THE ERA OF THE COMMITTEE OF TEN

The desire to achieve some uniformity and standardization of college entrance requirements, not only in naming the courses but in defining them, led in 1892 to the NEA Committee of Ten. It

[8] *Ibid.*, pp. 75–88.
[9] *Ibid.*, pp. 88–100.
[10] *Ibid.*, p. 101.
[11] The growth of these curricula had been phenomenal, but the resulting pattern was so diversified that many people began to feel the need for some uniformity and standardization. This need was probably felt acutely by college admissions officers who had to figure out the high school transcripts and come to some conclusions about what the applicant had studied. Courses varied not only in content but in length. One of the characteristics of high school programs, for example, was the presence of numerous "short courses" covering specialized interests and activities. Brown reports on his teaching experience in one high school in which the course of study was "three years in length and included twenty-four subjects, all required" and in which the senior-year subjects were "natural philosophy, zoology, civic government, essays, astronomy, physiology, universal history, mental philosophy, and chemistry, the most of them for one-third of the year each." Brown, *op. cit.*, p. 417.

is noteworthy that this was a committee set up not by an association of colleges, but by the National Educational Association representing teachers and administrators at all levels.[12] As the first step in its work, the committee surveyed course offerings in "forty leading secondary schools of the United States" and found nearly 40 different subjects, many of which "were taught for such short periods that little training could be derived from them." It reported that "Even for the older subjects, like Latin and algebra, there appeared to be a wide diversity of practice with regard to the time allotted to them."[13] Next, the committee set up conference groups or subcommittees in the following nine areas: Latin; Greek; English; other modern languages; mathematics; physics, astronomy, and chemistry; natural history; history, civil government, and political economy; and geography.[14] A common list of 11 questions guided the work of these subcommittees. These questions provided for a detailed examination of the curricular practices in each field.

One of the key questions ran as follows: "Should the subject be treated differently for pupils who are going to college, for those who are going to a scientific school, and for those who, presumably, are going to neither?"[15] The nine subcommittees were unanimous in answering this question with a blunt "No." The overall committee agreed with the "No" answer. In so doing, it opened itself to the charge of neglecting individual differences. This does not necessarily follow. Possibly the committee was bearing witness against the dualism of college-preparatory and non-college-preparatory courses. The motive, however, was probably to clear up the confusion that characterized many high school programs at the time. "The principle laid down by the Conferences will, if logically

[12] The committee itself was made up of five college administrators, three secondary school administrators, one college teacher, and the U.S. Commissioner of Education. The chairman was Charles W. Eliot, President of Harvard. National Educational Association, *Report of the Committee of Ten on Secondary School Studies with the Reports of the Conferences Arranged by the Committee,* American Book Company, for the Association, 1894, p. 4.

[13] *Ibid.*, pp. 4–5.
[14] *Ibid.*, p. 5.
[15] *Ibid.*, p. 6.

carried out, make a great simplification in secondary school programmes."[16]

It is clear that the committee by no means interpreted the function of the high school to be entirely or even mainly that of preparing students for college.

The secondary schools of the United States, taken as a whole, do
not exist for the purpose of preparing boys and girls for colleges. Only
an insignificant percentage of the graduates of these schools go to colleges or scientific schools. Their main function is to prepare for the
duties of life that small proportion of all the children in the country—
a proportion small in number, but very important to the welfare of
the nation—who show themselves able to profit by an education prolonged to the eighteenth year, and whose parents are able to support
them while they remain so long at school. . . . The preparation of a
few pupils for college or scientific school should in the ordinary secondary school be the incidental, and not the principal object.[17]

The term "small in number" may seem to indicate a preference
on the committee's part for restricted secondary education, but it
was more likely an expression of the situation as it existed at the
time. Members of the committee evidently did not anticipate the
movement toward universal secondary education as it developed
in the following decades.

On the general question of college-entrance requirements, the
committee recommended that colleges take high school graduates
without close prescription of subjects. They recognized the difficulties in this recommendation under conditions prevailing at
the time, but felt that the projected reforms from their subcommittees would make it possible.

A college might say,—We will accept for admission any groups of
studies taken from the secondary school programme, provided that
the sum of the studies in each of the four years amounts to sixteen,
or eighteen, or twenty periods a week,—as may be thought best,—
and provided, further than in each year at least four of the subjects
presented shall have been pursued at least three periods a week, and

[16] *Ibid.*, p. 17.
[17] *Ibid.*, pp. 50–51.

that at least three of the subjects shall have been pursued three years or more. For the purposes of this reckoning, natural history, geography, meteorology, and astronomy might be grouped together as one subject. Every youth who entered college would have spent four years in studying a few subjects thoroughly; and, on the theory that all the subjects are to be considered equivalent in educational rank for purposes of admission to college, it would make no difference what subjects he had chosen from the programme—he would have had four years of strong and effective mental training.[18]

The committee did suggest, however, some patterns within which choices might be made. These were the classical, Latin-scientific, modern languages, and English; and the committee offered its opinion "that the satisfactory completion of any one of the four years' courses of study embodied in the foregoing programmes should admit to corresponding courses in colleges and scientific schools."[19] Since two of the four tracks required no Latin, this recommendation broke with the older tradition that college preparation should always include some study of the classical languages. It repudiated the distinction between college-preparatory and non-college-preparatory programs fostered by the earlier division of high schools into classical and English departments. What the committee presented then was not the standardization of college-entrance requirements, but a new way of thinking about them, one which perhaps reflected the development of elective systems in the colleges themselves.[20] Preparation for college, as regarded by the Committee of Ten, was something no different from a valid definition of a good high school education in and of its own right.

The Committee of Ten led to other committees; in fact from this time on, one committee led to another. In 1895 one of the speakers at the Denver meeting of the NEA Secondary Education

[18] *Ibid.,* pp. 52–53.

[19] *Ibid.,* p. 53.

[20] Charles W. Eliot, considered the chief spokesman for the elective system, however, might not necessarily have welcomed its application to the matter of college entrance requirements. "It is noteworthy that Eliot's conception of the elective system assumed a wide preparation on the part of the student coming to college from the preparatory school." Richard Hofstadter and C. DeWitt Hardy, *The Development and Scope of Higher Education in the United States,* Columbia University Press, 1952, p. 49, footnote 31.

Department presented a paper entitled "What action ought to be taken by universities and secondary schools to promote the introduction of the programs recommended by the committee of ten?"[21] The action turned out to be the creation of the Committee on College-Entrance Requirements. The temper of the committee, and perhaps of the times, is indicated in the following quotation from one of its preliminary reports.

One after another the old idols are broken. The giants that stood in the path and said to every student, "Let him who enters here" leave all behind but Latin, Greek, and mathematics, are growing limp and lifeless. Requirements for admission are being leveled up; wide options are to be allowed; the element of value in preparation is to be a time element; Harvard, Cornell, Vassar, University of Michigan, University of Chicago, and Leland Stanford, Jr., are unfurling their banners of freedom. There is already a path blazed thru the thicket and jungle of conservatism and tradition, and before the twentieth century dawns in its glory there will be a broad highway thru which a pupil may walk unfettered, amid attractive associations, from the kindergarten to a degree at the end of the postgraduate course of the university, and still will the people of the future be able to say, "There were giants in those days."[22]

As might be expected from the commitment in the foregoing quotation, the Committee on College-Entrance Requirements recommended "That the principle of election be recognized in secondary schools."[23] It added, however, that "it does not believe in unlimited election, but especially emphasizes the importance of a certain number of constants in all secondary schools and in all requirements for admission to college."[24] Here the committee approached what the high schools were looking for: some standardization of requirements to simplify their own problems in guiding and preparing students. It pointed out, furthermore, that its recommended constants were to be "regarded as suggestive rather than unalterable."[25]

[21] National Educational Association, *Report of Committee on College Entrance Requirements,* The Association, University of Chicago Press, 1899, p. 5.
[22] *Ibid.,* p. 11.
[23] *Ibid.,* p. 27.
[24] *Ibid.,* p. 32.
[25] *Ibid.,* p. 33.

Few colleges, few committees, few boards of education will dissent from the proposition that every pupil should have at least one year of history, one year of some science taught by laboratory methods, and two years of English, including composition and literature; some will argue that there are those who cannot master geometry, and yet, if one has the scholarship which will warrant the expenditure of four years in college, he will have the ability to assimilate algebra and geometry to the extent of two full years of work. The question of foreign languages is a mooted one, and yet most intelligent people will agree that one foreign language—and that, too, pursued four years—or two, each followed two years, is valuable, if for no other purpose than to give the pupil an enlarged and a more appreciative idea of our incomparable English. These constants are submitted, therefore, as important for every secondary school.[26]

Note how this statement continues the general proposition of the Committee of Ten, namely that a high school curriculum good in itself was also good for college-preparatory purposes.

This recommendation set a pattern of high school graduation and college-entrance requirements. As time went on, the four years of foreign language were reduced to two years, while English was increased from two years to three. With these modifications, it is a pattern similar to the entrance requirements of many colleges today. But, even as modified, it no longer survives as a pattern of constants for high school graduation.

So stood the matter at the close of the century. The elective system was endorsed, but not in the extreme sense. Five fields of instruction assumed the major roles in college preparation: English, mathematics, history, science, and foreign languages. Latin was no longer an absolute requirement. Unfortunately, so far as the high school principal or counselor was concerned, not all colleges adopted these patterns in all particulars. He faced and still faces numerous exceptions. But at least his task had been simplified to some extent.

Meanwhile a parallel development had been taking place on another matter, that of determining whether or not students were adequately prepared in the subjects they presented for admission.

[26] *Ibid.*

Dissatisfaction with the traditional method of entrance examinations led to a search for other ways of assuring colleges that applicants for entrance have adequate preparation for college work. One way has been that of high school accreditation, under which graduates of the accredited high schools are admitted to college without examination, provided they meet other admission criteria.[27] Accreditation activities have been carried on by universities, by state boards, and by regional associations of colleges and secondary schools. In 1901, for example, the North Central Association of Colleges and Secondary Schools established a Commission on Accredited Schools. Over the years, such associations have done much to stimulate curriculum study and the improvement of school facilities and faculty preparation. Although purely unofficial in character, they have on several occasions proved to be powerful allies of local citizens seeking school improvement.

Not all colleges were convinced that accreditation systems could replace entrance examinations. Even these colleges, however, recognized some of the defects and problems in the examination system as traditionally administered, particularly the problem faced by high schools trying to prepare students for examinations at many different colleges. This recognition led to the college board system initiated in 1900 by the Association of Colleges and

[27] "The problem as it presented itself to those who laid the general interests of education to heart was this: How might a more vital relationship be established between the secondary schools and the colleges, with a view of conserving the highest educational efficiency of both institutions? One of the earliest and most notable attempts at its solution is the so-called accrediting system, introduced by the University of Michigan in 1871. Under this arrangement, a university admits to its freshman class without examination, such graduates of approved secondary schools as are especially recommended for that purpose by the principals of those schools. The system has met with great favor and has widespread application. The United States Commissioner of Education reported in 1896 that there were then 42 state universities and agricultural and mechanical colleges, and about 150 other institutions in which it had been adopted. (*Rept. Comr. Ed.,* 1894–1895, II., pp. 1171–1188.)

"It depends upon a purely voluntary agreement between the secondary schools and the higher institutions. The college or university satisfies itself that the secondary school applying for such recognition is properly taught. Usually a committee of the faculty is sent to inspect the school, and the school agrees to submit itself to such inspection. Commonly, too, students admitted on school credentials are understood to be on probation during the first term of the college course. It is the school rather than the individual that is examined; and the inquiry relates chiefly to the vitality, intelligence, and general effectiveness of the instruction." Brown, *op. cit.,* pp. 373–374.

Preparatory Schools of the Middle States and Maryland,[28] under which examinations are administered by a single board or association for a group of member colleges. The College Entrance Examination Board has since become a national institution and the "college boards" a major event in the lives of high school faculties that send students to the member colleges. At one time this system affected mainly those students entering schools in the eastern region of our country. More recently, however, there has been an upswing of sentiment in their favor, with the 1957–1958 list of member institutions including 184 colleges and universities in all regions. The possible danger of encouraging "teaching for examinations" has been mitigated to a large extent by the nature of the examinations themselves and by the care and thoughtfulness that have gone into their preparation.

The major features of college preparation, then, were set at the beginning of this century. Included were the identification of the subject requirements for college entrance and the twin developments of accrediting associations and college entrance examination boards. Next came the Carnegie unit. This represented a further attempt to standardize the basis for college admission and did so by providing a measuring stick for quantities of work. The unit was suggested in the first and second reports of the Carnegie Foundation for the Advancement of Teaching in 1906–1907. By 1916 the definition assumed the shape it has held substantially ever since. " 'A unit represents a year's study in any subject in a secondary school, constituting approximately a quarter of a full year's work.' This assumes that the length of the school year is from thirty-six to forty weeks, that a period is from forty to sixty minutes in length, and that the study is pursued for four or five periods a week; but under ordinary circumstances a satisfactory year's work in any subject cannot be accomplished in less than one hundred and twenty

[28] "The first examination under this arrangement was held the week beginning June 17, 1901. The questions had been sent out to various centres, at which those taking the examination might assemble. The examination accordingly took place simultaneously at sixty-seven points in the United States, and two in Europe, and was taken by a total of 973 candidates. Over forty colleges and universities, many of them outside of the territory directly represented by the examination board, declared their willingness to accept the board's examinations as satisfactory substitutes for their own, in the topics covered, and three institutions in the city of New York took the further step of dispensing with their own separate examinations." *Ibid.,* p. 389.

sixty-minute hours, or their equivalent."[29] A good deal of energy has been spent in criticism of the Carnegie unit, but it is difficult to identify precisely what the evil effects have been. It is simply a unit of measurement and as such not different from pounds, quarts, yards, feet, or bushels. True, it provides no index of content or quality, but neither as such does a quart measure. Other means must be used for description. It has probably discouraged the proliferation of short courses which characterized the high school program before the 1890's, for which it may deserve our gratitude rather than blame. The breakdown of whole units into half and quarter units, however, testifies that it has not been wholly successful along these lines.

Closely following the Carnegie unit came the appointment of a new committee entitled, The Committee on the Articulation of High School and College. In its 1911 report this committee "urged the modification of college entrance requirements in order that the secondary school might adapt its work to the varying needs of its pupils without closing to them the possibility of continued education in higher institutions."[30] Its specific recommendations had more effect on high school graduation requirements than on those for college entrance; for example, the possibility of substituting additional units in social science and natural science for either mathematics or foreign language and reducing language requirements from four to two years.[31] High schools apparently accepted the recommendations, while most colleges did not. Without intending to do so, this committee set in motion a return to the distinction that had applied throughout the nineteenth century between college-preparatory and non-college-preparatory programs, a distinction explicitly rejected by the Committee of Ten.

THE DEBATE OVER COLLEGE DOMINATION

From the Committee on Articulation of High School and College evolved the Commission on the Reorganization of Secondary Education, which published its report on the Cardinal Principles in

[29] Bureau of Education Bulletin (1916), no. 20, quoted by Alexander Inglis, *Principles of Secondary Education,* Houghton Mifflin Company, 1918, pp. 316–317.

[30] Clarence D. Kingsley in the preface to *Cardinal Principles of Secondary Education,* Department of the Interior, Bureau of Education, Bulletin 1918, no. 35, p. 5.

[31] Inglis, *op. cit.,* p. 323.

1918. This Commission took a long step in the direction of universalizing the high school by holding "that education should be so recognized that every normal boy and girl will be encouraged to remain in school to the age of 18, on full time if possible, otherwise on part time."[32] The Commission also commented on college-entrance requirements as follows.

In view of the important role of secondary education in achieving the objectives essential in American life, it follows that higher institutions of learning are not justified in maintaining entrance requirements and examinations of a character that handicap the secondary school in discharging its proper functions in a democracy. . . . The tradition that a particular type of education, and that exclusively nonvocational in character, is the only acceptable preparation for advanced education, either liberal or vocational, must therefore give way to a scientific evaluation of all types of secondary education as preparation for advanced study.[33]

This meant that not even the specified constants recommended by the preceding committees should be regarded as binding on all students. It meant further that the flexibility held up as the ideal should apply to all students whether college bound or not. In taking this position, the 1918 Commission held just as firmly as had the Committee of Ten to the conviction that good high school education was good preparation for college as well.

The idea that college-entrance requirements exercise a cramping or restricting influence on the development of high school curricula was by no means new,[34] but it gained widespread acceptance in the

[32] *Cardinal Principles of Secondary Education, op. cit.,* p. 30.

[33] *Ibid.,* pp. 19–20.

[34] On one point, that of Greek as an admission requirement, the high schools were able to dominate the colleges. "The opening campaign between the high schools and colleges was won by the high schools. With an unrealistic perception of the origin, nature, and problems of the high schools, the colleges demanded that they teach Greek because it was an entrance requirement. While the high schools rather willingly taught Latin, they were outspoken in their refusal to include Greek. To a considerable extent this victory was achieved by circumstances rather than valor. . . . Then, too, the colleges were desperately in need of students. Repeatedly they called for the establishment of preparatory schools with a program that would conform to college requirements. Perceiving the improbability of such schools being established, they tried vainly to induce the high schools to teach Greek. While they resented the refusal of the high schools to do so, they reluctantly discovered, without too much delay, that Greek was after all a college subject and made various adjustments for

decades following the 1918 report. It probably represented a response on the part of high school educators to the demand that they develop curricula in the light of the Cardinal Principles. Even when the emphasis shifted from the Cardinal Principles to other considerations, such as the needs of youth, the impression of college domination as the major barrier to curricular progress still remained. If only the high schools were freed from college domination, so the impression ran, they would show the world what good secondary education could be.

The Eight-Year Study of the 1930's, sponsored by the Progressive Education Association, was set up to give some high schools their chance. The Association was not necessarily interested in the Cardinal Principles, but it felt that what high schools needed was more venturesome creativity and the willingness to pioneer. Its Commission on the Relation of School and College of the Association accordingly effected an agreement between a number of colleges on one hand and 30 selected secondary schools on the other. Under the terms of the agreement, the colleges would accept from the selected schools any graduate recommended by his faculty regardless of the subjects he had pursued throughout high school years.

Here, then, was an open invitation to a group of selected schools to experiment freely without the burden of meeting specified college entrance requirements. It is little wonder that the selected schools were soon popularly known as the "thirty unshackled schools." Interest centered on two important aspects of the study: (1) the kinds of experimental programs developed[35] and (2) the extent to which graduates of the 30 schools would or would not be able to hold their own in college studies, if they went to college. It was the second aspect that promised to register impact on college-entrance requirements and the college-preparatory function of the high schools.

The research staffs of the Progressive Education Association

taking care of those students who could be induced to study it without having had any previous preparation." Edgar B. Wesley, *NEA: The First Hundred Years*, Harper & Brothers, 1957, p. 71.

[35] See Progressive Education Association Commission on the Relation between School and College, *Thirty Schools Tell Their Story*, Harper & Brothers, 1943.

gathered many data on the performance of the selected graduates in the colleges. Each graduate was paired with an opposite number from a high school not in the agreement. Great care was exercised to match the students as closely as possible in important characteristics that might affect the outcome.

So far as academic achievement was concerned, the graduates of the 30 schools did as well as their matchees from "conventional schools."

Comparable data on matched pairs have been given on absolute achievement, achievement in relation to scholastic aptitude, performance on placement tests, probationary actions, academic honors, and graduation. In terms of each of these indexes it is clear that the S students have, as a group, been at least as successful as their more conventionally trained matchees. In many of the areas small margins of superiority obtain. The large majority of these small differences favor the S group. A series of small differences obviously increases the statistical probability of a true difference between groups. The importance of each of these small margins, however, will depend largely on the reader's point of view.[36]

Furthermore, the 30 schools graduates did "somewhat better than their comparees" on such points as "good habits of work, a passion for weighing evidence, and an insatiable intellectual curiosity."[37] In addition, they were "at least as successful in extra curriculum activities as were comparable students from other schools."[38]

Among the 30 schools, however, were considerable variations in the degree of departure from "traditional" programs. The investigators, therefore, made additional studies of students from schools judged to be "the most experimental" and those judged to be "the least experimental." "The graduates from the most experimental schools are characterized not only by consistently higher academic averages and more academic honors but also by a clear-cut superiority in the intellectual intangibles of curiosity and drive,

[36] Dean Chamberlin, Enid Chamberlin, Neal E. Drought, and William E. Scott, *Did They Succeed in College?* Harper & Brothers, 1942, p. 41.
[37] *Ibid.,* p. 63.
[38] *Ibid.,* p. 93.

willingness and ability to think logically and objectively, and an active and vital interest in the world about them. . . . The students from the least experimental schools are, on the other hand, seldom indistinguishable from their matchees."[39] From this one might be tempted to infer that the most experimental schools had evolved some approach to college preparation superior in quality to those previously existing and that henceforth college preparation should be conducted along those lines. This extreme position was not taken. Commentators tended to confine themselves to the more modest position that there might be many good roads to college preparation. One of them, Max McConn, put the case in the following direct terms.

Can boys and girls be at least equally well prepared through a considerable variety of widely different programs devised by competent secondary-school teachers? The answer is, *Yes—because it has been done,* in a number of cases sufficient to provide ample statistical validity.

From now on if any individual dogmatically asserts that the traditional program is essential for college success, he can be politely assured that he is talking nonsense, which has been *proved* to be nonsense, and can be counseled to consult the evidence before conversing further on this topic.[40]

Nonsense or not, many colleges have continued for the most part to operate on the basis of so-called traditional programs. In a national survey made in 1949, "approximately 60 per cent of the colleges reported that a fixed pattern of subject matter requirements is in effect."[41] This pattern apparently differs only in detail from the recommendations of the 1899 report for the Committee on College Entrance Requirements. "In general, then, the pattern of requirements remains a great deal the same as it has been for years past, with the usual requirements being three units of English, two of mathematics, two of foreign languages, one of social studies,

[39] *Ibid.,* pp. 173–174.
[40] *Ibid.,* preface, pp. xxi–xxii.
[41] Arthur E. Traxler and Agatha Townsend (eds.), *Improving Transition from School to College,* A Study of Admission by the Committee on School and College Relations of the Educational Records Bureau, Harper & Brothers, 1953, p. 66.

and one of science."[42] Still this does leave presumably 40 percent of the colleges that do not make fixed requirements.[43]

One of the interesting departures from so-called traditional bases has been that of the Michigan College Agreement. This program had its origins in the Michigan Secondary School Curriculum Study, under which 55 high schools could send their graduates to Michigan colleges and universities "without reference to the pattern of subjects pursued for the years 1940 through 1950."[44] In the fall of 1946 a new agreement was made under the auspices of the Michigan College Association and the Michigan Secondary School Association. High schools entering this agreement committed themselves to the maintenance or development of adequate guidance, evaluation, and curriculum procedures. It was recognized, of course, that blanket admission to a particular institution could not guarantee admission to any or all programs within that institution. The proposal, therefore, urged secondary schools "to make available such basic courses as provide a necessary preparation for entering technical, industrial, or professional curricula" and recommended "that colleges provide accelerated programs for preparation for specialized college curricula for those graduates who are unable to secure such preparatory training in high schools."[45] Even the most liberal agreements apparently cannot avoid the realities of specific prerequisites for specific programs, and the life of the high school counselor must necessarily remain a complex one. It is perhaps this factor of complexity and diversity rather than tradition as such which accounts for the feelings of

[42] *Ibid.*, p. 70.

[43] "Only a little more than a third of the teachers colleges said that they have a fixed pattern of requirements for entrance, whereas two-thirds of the liberal arts colleges and three-fourths of the technical colleges made this reply. As in other aspects of the study, the colleges in the Northwest seem to be somewhat more liberal in their entrance practices than those in the other regions. Exactly half the colleges in the Northwest said that they have no fixed pattern of entrance requirements, in contrast to less than a third in the East and the South. The colleges in the North Central region are also somewhat more liberal in their entrance requirements than those in the East and South, but less so than the colleges in the Northwest." *Ibid.*, p. 66.

[44] Roland C. Faunce, "A Functional Program for Michigan Youth," *Educational Leadership*, March, 1949, p. 382.

[45] *Ibid.*

high school staffs that they are restricted by college entrance requirements.

Freedom for the high school to pursue its own destiny, which was probably the major object of the Eight-Year Study, remains a somewhat elusive will-o'-the-wisp. It is elusive because it is undefined. High schools have some freedom as things stand. On the other hand this freedom is neither unrestricted nor absolute in character. Whether or not the high schools themselves want such freedom is not clear. It is, of course, perfectly obvious that high school administrators, counselors, and teachers welcome clarity and simplicity in college-entrance requirements, but these are not the same as freedom.

In an attempt to gauge at least in part how high schools feel about such matters, the Committee on School and College Relations of the Educational Records Bureau made a survey of practice in 1950, based on returns from 1101 public and 250 independent secondary schools. They found among other things that "Most of the high schools have a fixed pattern of requirements for college preparation. In fact, the percentage of secondary schools reporting a fixed curriculum for college preparatory pupils was greater than the percentage of colleges reporting a similar requirement."[46] With regard to English requirements, for example, "It is noteworthy that, while 62 percent of the colleges said that they are willing to accept three units of English and only about 32 percent ask for four units, 62 percent of the high schools indicated that they require their college preparatory students to take four years of English. . . ."[47] Such practices may not, however, actually indicate how much freedom the high schools want, but how much they believe can be safely exercised under given conditions. That the committee recognizes this state of affairs is clearly indicated in the following quotation from its report.

Many secondary schools feel that making sure their pupils are properly prepared means a curriculum that would satisfy the most conservative college entrance requirements. *If they are sending their*

[46] Traxler and Townsend, *op. cit.*, p. 68.
[47] *Ibid.*, p. 71.

graduates on to many different colleges, schools can hardly take the position that, because some of the colleges have liberalized their entrance requirements, they will make their own prescriptions less rigid. They could do this only if their instruction were entirely on an individual basis and if pupils never changed their minds about the colleges to which they would apply. Consequently, if a small number of influential colleges hold rigidly to a fixed and extensive pattern of subject matter requirements, this practice will tend to lead to the maintenance of conservative programs in numerous high schools.[48]

Nevertheless, "A clear-cut, broad generalization emerging from the committee's study is that, on the whole, high school administrators apparently have no greater eagerness for change in requirements for college preparation than the colleges themselves have."[49] On the other hand, "About 80 percent of the high schools said that college requirements were either seriously or moderately restrictive."[50]

So the picture remains a confused one. What it may mean is that high school staffs would like more freedom, but not enough to push vigorously for its attainment. The Committee suggests several reasons "why high schools are lukewarm toward proposals for easing college entrance requirements."[51] One is that "in many schools, ranging from small rural high schools to the largest high schools in the country, the college preparatory group is a small minority of the pupil population."[52] A second reason suggested is "that it is much easier for busy school personnel to accept control from above than it is to work for greater freedom and then to use that freedom wisely."[53] A third possibility, stated by the Committee, "is to be found in the basic attitudes of high school administrators and teachers in America. Contrary to much that has appeared in the public press, they are naturally conservative. They like things as they are. They believe in teaching fundamentals, and, mistaken

[48] *Ibid.,* p. 72.
[49] *Ibid.,* pp. 77–78.
[50] *Ibid.,* p. 82.
[51] *Ibid.,* pp. 77–78.
[52] *Ibid.*
[53] *Ibid.,* p. 79.

or not, they have a conviction that adherence to the traditional pattern of requirements is best."[54]

In addition, the possibility exists that high school people do not feel that the problem of so-called "college domination" is as crucial as suggested in educational literature, or at least not sufficiently so to warrant placing it high on a list of other tasks in secondary education to which attention must be given. Another point that has never been clear is just what experimental changes high schools would introduce if the alleged incubus of college requirements were removed. The "unshackled" schools in the Eight Year Study, for example, developed stimulating and challenging curricular ventures. Just how much these were made possible by the "unshackling" would be difficult to say. Perhaps they could have been carried on anyway. All this tends to suggest at least the possibility that the effect of college-entrance requirements on high school programs has been largely in the realm of symbolism. This is not to deny reality to such effect, for, as we know, symbols have been powerful motivators of human behavior throughout all human history. Even though the 30 schools could have experimented without "unshackling," they probably would have felt less free to do so.

It is difficult to tell which way the colleges are moving on this matter of specifying subjects for admission. The following statement made for the Commission on Liberal Education of the Association of American Colleges indicates the possibility that recommendations may become more specific rather than less so.

The Commission recommends that each member college re-examine its entrance requirements, its course standards and its degree requirements to the end that the quality of education may be enhanced. With respect to entrance requirements the Commission believes that a general stiffening of standards will be in the interests of all—the student, the school, the college and the nation. It therefore recommends to member colleges certain minimal entrance requirements: four years of English, with emphasis upon grammar and composition, two years of a foreign language, two years of mathematics, and one year of a labo-

[54] *Ibid.,* pp. 79–80.

ratory science at the junior or senior year level. This is at best a temporary program. As a more adequate goal, to be attained as rapidly as possible, the Commission recommends four years of English, four years of one foreign language, or two years each of two, four years of mathematics, and two years of laboratory sciences. In addition each student should be grounded in history and geography. Such familiarity with basic facts and tools would enable the college to raise the standards of its own courses and to achieve further mastery by its students of the tools and skills which are the liberal arts, as well as those which constitute more specialized techniques. The Commission's recommendation represents no desire to dictate to secondary schools but rather an effort to help them in clarifying essentials, a task which they have already begun. Cooperative effort and time will be required to approach the common goals, particularly in the case of smaller schools and colleges.[55]

The Commission also recommended the creation of a new Commission on Coöperation with Secondary Schools to deal with admission requirements and other matters. It should be kept in mind that the proposals in the foregoing quotation are recommendations only and are not binding on the member colleges of the Association.

On the other hand, recent college bulletins continue to stress the fact that patterns of subjects for admission constitute only one of several admission criteria. Other criteria usually include the standing of the applicant in his graduation class, references on character and personality, and recommendations of the high school principal. The extent to which the required or recommended subjects are followed rigidly in relation to the other criteria varies from one college to the next. It is possible that an increase in the number of formally specified subjects for admission may be accompanied by greater flexibility in their interpretation and application to the individual student. This does not, of course, mitigate the problem for the high school or affect the contention of high school faculties that their curricula are governed by patterns of college admission.

The most tangible consequence in our high schools of the whole situation on entrance requirements is the so-called college-prepara-

[55] Richard D. Weigle, "Commission on Liberal Education," *Association of American Colleges Bulletin,* March, 1958, pp. 150–154, reprint pp. 2–3.

tory course, which includes not only the graduation constants applicable to all students, but also such subjects as algebra, geometry, advanced laboratory science, foreign language, and a fourth year of English. These additional subjects presumably enable the student who takes them to meet the entrance requirements of most colleges. It does not guarantee that he will meet the requirements of the particular college he wants to attend. And since there are many colleges that do not require these subjects for entrance, a college-bound student does not necessarily have to be in the college-preparatory course or track at all. It is a short-cut counseling device applicable to most students planning to enter most colleges, but it does not eliminate the need for individual counseling.[56]

The degree to which the college-preparatory course exists as a specifically identified sequence varies from one high school to the next. Some high schools label it as such and print the list of requirements in the school handbook and other materials furnished to parents and students. Other high schools identify it less specifically and list certain subjects as recommended for those who plan to attend college. Some high schools avoid the designation altogether in their printed materials. Even in such schools, however, the terms may be used unofficially by teachers, students, and parents.

Unfortunately, all this tends to leave the impression that college-preparatory subjects—those associated with the college-preparatory course—are in the school program mainly for college-preparatory students. Larger percentages of college-preparatory students take such subjects than is true of non-college-preparatory students. Some may suggest that the college-preparatory group includes larger numbers of students qualified to take the college-preparatory subjects on the basis of academic ability. But there are

[56] The Conant report recommends that track classifications be abandoned and that each student's program be made on an individual basis. James Bryant Conant, *The American High School Today*, McGraw-Hill Book Company, Inc., 1959, pp. 46–47. Along with this, the report suggests that counselors recommend four years of mathematics, three years of science, four years of a foreign language to academically talented students in addition to the English and social studies requirement. *Ibid.*, p. 57. The academically talented students are defined as the top 15 or 20 percent on a national basis. The important point here is that these subjects are recommended for academically talented students, not for college-preparatory or college-bound students as a general group.

also many such qualified students among those in the non-college-preparatory group.[57] Some of these qualified non-college-preparatory students do take these subjects, but many do not, as is indicated in Table 2.

TABLE 2. Subjects Taken by College-Preparatory
and Non-College-Preparatory Students

	College-Preparatory Students, N = 1,703				Non-College-Preparatory Students, N = 2,568			
	Upper Half N = 1,230		Lower Half N = 473		Upper Half N = 967		Lower Half N = 1,601	
	Number	Percent	Number	Percent	Number	Percent	Number	Percent
Algebra	1,222	99.3	447	94.5	797	82.4	910	56.8
Plane Geometry	1,153	93.7	364	77.0	492	50.9	391	24.4
Chemistry	944	76.7	278	58.8	407	42.1	399	24.9
Physics	633	51.5	159	33.6	296	30.6	251	15.7
Foreign Languages	851	69.2	233	49.3	294	30.4	252	15.7

Numbers and percentages of public and private college-preparatory and non-college-preparatory students in the upper and lower halves of their graduating classes on the Henmon-Nelson Test of Mental Ability who had taken the indicated subjects at some time during their high school careers. (N = 4,271 Wisconsin seniors in the spring of 1957.)

SOURCE: Edward A. Krug, Clifford S. Liddle, Russell C. Mosely, and Daniel Parkinson, *The College-Preparatory Function in Wisconsin High Schools,* University of Wisconsin School of Education, 1959, table 26, p. 58.

Whether or not such subjects as algebra, geometry, foreign languages, and the physical sciences are relevant to the needs of non-

[57] In a survey made of Wisconsin public and private high school seniors in the spring of 1957, 37.6 percent of the students who said they had not taken a college-preparatory course were ranked in the upper halves of their classes on the Henmon-Nelson Test of Mental Ability. Of those who said they had taken a college-preparatory course, 72.2 percent were ranked in the upper halves of their classes. These data are based on responses made by 4,271 seniors who answered the question about the college-preparatory course on whom Henmon-Nelson percentile ranks were available, and who were part of a group of 5,675 seniors constituting a one-sixth sample of approximately 95 percent of public and private high school seniors in the state, of whom approximately one seventh were in private schools. There were in addition 642 seniors on whom Henmon-Nelson percentile ranks were available, but who did not answer the question about the college-preparatory course. Edward A. Krug, Clifford S. Liddle, Russell C. Mosely, and Daniel Parkinson, *The College-Preparatory Function in Wisconsin High Schools,* University of Wisconsin School of Education, 1959, table 20, p. 56.

college-preparatory students is a point on which opinions differ. If they are not, then in what sense are they relevant to the needs of college-bound students who do not plan to major in these fields? One possible answer is that these subjects meet the need of college-bound students to get into college. This demotes the college-preparatory subjects to the level of admission tickets, a conclusion most of us would not be willing to accept.

The notion of a college-preparatory course presents the high school with a dilemma not easy to resolve, namely, that of identifying or justifying the general-education value of the so-called college-preparatory subjects. This is probably the most unfortunate consequence of the whole idea of prescribing subjects for college admission. It does not mean, however, that the colleges have forced this dilemma on the high schools. On the contrary, our history strongly suggests that the high schools have coöperated with the colleges both in creating and maintaining the dilemma, and this with the best of intentions on the part of both groups.

As more high school students prepare for college, particularly as more high-ability students are urged to go to college and can do so regardless of the financial circumstances of their families, we shall probably see a general increase in enrollments in the college-preparatory subjects. This will not in itself resolve the philosophical dilemma of the intrinsic worth of the so-called college-preparatory subjects. From the practical standpoint, however, it will seem that the dilemma has ceased to exist.

CURRENT DEVELOPMENTS AND FUTURE POSSIBILITIES

It would be impossible today for any national body to state with any degree of justification, as did the Committee of Ten in its 1894 report, that "The secondary schools of the United States, taken as a whole, do not exist for the purpose of preparing boys and girls for colleges."[58] This is precisely one of the major reasons, although by no means the only one, for which our high schools do exist, and this to a greater degree than at any time in the American past. As one writer has commented, "It is hardly necessary to say that we in America today are living in the midst of the most remarkable

[58] *Report of the Committee of Ten,* p. 51.

extension of college education to the general population ever seen in the history of the world."[59] While we are probably not moving toward universal college education, the current expansion of the colleges parallels in many ways the expansion of the high school itself during the first decades of this century.[60]

The people of the United States face a major decision: whether or not they wish this expansion to continue, which means, in the long run, whether or not they will want to pay for it. This decision is before us regardless of the balance that might take place between expansion of publicly supported colleges and independent colleges. In either case, the money must come from somewhere. We can reasonably expect that the facilities will be increased.[61] Whether they will be increased enough to provide places for all high school graduates who want to attend is another question. If not, colleges will have only one line of action open to them, to become more selective in their admission and retention policies than ever before. Here, indeed, may be the golden opportunity for the college

[59] Samuel A. Stouffer, "Social Forces that Produce the 'Great Sorting,' " in College Entrance Examination Board, *College Admissions: The Great Sorting,* the Board, 1955, p. 1.

[60] In 1957, The President's Committee on Education Beyond the High School wrote, "It should be remembered that college enrollments have already doubled since 1940 even though the college-age population is smaller and admission standards have been tightened in many institutions." *Second Report,* July, 1957, p. 10. It also predicted that enrollments would again double themselves, "at least 6 million by 1970 compared to 3 million now." *Ibid.,* p. 3.

[61] Several authorities have expressed confidence along this line. For example, "By careful planning and action based on clear vision, I am confident we shall be able to make adequate preparation for the added millions of youth now coming through our elementary and secondary schools in order that they may be given the same high-quality educational opportunities it was our good fortune to enjoy." Ronald B. Thompson, "The Need for Expanded Facilities," *The Strength to Meet Our National Need* (Charles G. Dobbins ed.), American Council on Education, 1956, pp. 97–98.

Another expresses confidence in terms of the long-range relationship between educational and economic expansion in our country. "The central fact which emerges from this analysis is that there is a deep-rooted interaction between the educational system as a whole and the economy as a whole which has made it possible for our economy to expand by literally forcing the expansion of our educational system.

"However, the two expansions, while basically related, are not necessarily in phase. It is to this point that we can look for the explanation of the attention given to higher education during the last decade. The reason is that higher education is now the only remaining segment of our educational system in which there yet remains any real room for expansion, which is perhaps another way of saying that higher education has gotten out of phase with the expansion of the economy." Frank H. Bowles, "Higher Education and American Society." *Ibid.,* p. 12.

to dominate the high school, although it is unlikely that colleges will wish to do so. College people will be too busy processing floods of applications to want to dominate everybody. But select they must, unless facilities are expanded to provide places for all who want to come, and each progressive step in the refinement of admission procedures will impose additional responsibilities on the high school program.[62]

The desire on the part of colleges to select the best qualified students from the enormous number of applications probably explains the recent increase in membership of the College Entrance Examination Board. Where there were 50 member colleges in 1945, there were 184 in 1957.[63] This is an important development, but it need not be a frightening one. The Board does not want high school education distorted into a cram session for examinations.[64] Its objective is to develop tests which will reflect the normal acquisitions of a good high school education. Another fact to keep in mind is that the board does not set entrance requirements for the colleges. It administers both a general scholastic aptitude test and a series of subject achievement tests. Some colleges require the aptitude test only. No candidate may take tests in more than three subjects. Not only do the colleges set their own requirements, but also their own ways of interpreting and using the test

---

[62] Increased selectivity is a real possibility even with the expansion in facilities. "Since these previous papers will have made clear that there will be a growing supply of high school graduates, and that there will be a need for these graduates if we are to meet the requirements of our economy and of our society, I take it that it is my function to emphasize the point that higher educational institutions are called upon to perform a service that they cannot perform unless they receive a *larger* supply of *better qualified* students. It seems to me then, that Topic IV is meant to emphasize *Quality* since, as far as quantity is concerned, we shall in all likelihood be faced with the embarrassment of riches." Edward B. Rooney, S.J., "Higher Education's Consequent Need for a Larger Supply of Qualified Students." *Ibid.*, pp. 62–63.

[63] The 1945 figure is based on a count made in William A. Neilson (ed.), *Annual Handbook 1945, Terms of Admission to the Colleges of the College Entrance Examination Board,* Ginn and Company, 1945. The 1957 figure is based on a count made in College Entrance Examination Board, *The College Handbook, 1957–1958.*

[64] "No special preparation should be necessary. The tests are designed to be taken in stride and to minimize the effect of cramming or last-minute study. However, candidates taking tests in specialized subjects, such as mathematics, biology, or chemistry, may find it helpful to review material covered in previous courses if they have not had a course in the subject shortly before taking the test." College Entrance Examination Board, *College Board Tests: Bulletin of Information 1955–1956,* p. 3.

results. "The scores are used by colleges as only one measure of the student's ability and academic preparation. Admissions officers also consider school grades, rank in class, recommendations, interviews, and other indications of the candidate's readiness for college. Each college makes up its own mind about each candidate for admission."[65]

Nevertheless, this development presents many high schools with a new responsibility, that of preparing large numbers of students for examinations administered by an agency outside the high school itself. How to discharge this responsibility without distorting other aspects of the educational program may well become one of the major curricular issues of the next several decades. If this issue can be resolved satisfactorily, the College Board examinations may even prove to be an asset to good curriculum planning, for a good test is never inconsistent with a good course.

The recent upsurge of public interest in scholarship programs, both national and local, is another matter that will affect the high school's activities in college preparation. Scholarship awards traditionally have been based on two factors, ability and need. The major purpose has been to help able students attend college who would otherwise be unable to do so. They have been designed neither for the needy indifferent student nor for the able student with well-to-do parents. The first of these conditions is still held to, but on the second considerable modification seems to be taking place. Increasingly, able students from all economic levels seek scholarships as symbols of academic distinction. In part this reflects the failure of schools to provide adequate recognition for students with good academic records. The scholarship perhaps fills a vacuum. And the development of national scholarship programs, such as the National Merit Awards and those of major industries, with sliding scales adjusted to the student's economic need, has further intensified the prestige aspects. The use of such sliding scales, of course, helps to resolve the long-standing dilemma of providing recognition for outstanding students who may not need the financial aid.

With such a view of scholarships, communities are likely to

[65] *Ibid.*

judge their high schools not only on college-preparatory effectiveness in general, but on the success of graduates in winning scholarships. High schools will compete with one another and compare their respective records on scholarship acquisition. All of this will become a most important item in the school's public relations program.

In a second large western city the faculty member in charge of the scholarship program in one high school each year constructs a huge thermometer in the main lobby. On this thermometer in red is registered in dollars the total amount of scholarship awards garnered by students of the high school's graduating class. The fact that this high school is located in one of the more prosperous sections of the city, and the fact that the high school leads all others in the city in the value of scholarship awards accumulated seems to me to be an anachronism. In a third western city all of us have thrown the majority of our scholarship awards into the high school drawing from the wealthiest district of the city, to the virtual neglect of other schools. The chief counselor at that school boasts of his success, and leads his students to expect assistance as their right. It seems to me there is little difference between this and the bidding for outstanding football players in high schools.[66]

Public interest in scholarships and the tendency of able students to seek them independent of the need factor are all to the good in that they foster recognition of academic achievement and healthy competition along intellectual lines of endeavor. Sliding scales can help to keep the prestige aspect separate from the need aspect. Top-level students who need financial aid will get it no matter how the programs are devised. In the interest of the individual and of the national welfare, however, we should remember the needy boy or girl who is not at the very top academically, but is still a well-qualified student.

An important current development that has not come as dramatically to national attention as others is the growth and expansion of the junior or community college, in itself a relatively old institution that originated over a half-century ago.

---

[66] Rixford B. Snyder, "Recruiting," College Entrance Examination Board, *College Admissions,* The Board, 1954, p. 131.

The first public junior college which is still in existence was founded at Joliet, Illinois, in 1902. Since that date, this new educational agency has multiplied and spread until it currently numbers 598, of which 338 are public institutions and 260 are private. At the close of its first half-century, the number of junior colleges is 40 per cent of the number of four-year colleges and universities in America, institutions which have a history of more than three hundred years.

The junior college is presently in a period of especially rapid growth and expansion. From the last prewar year, 1940–41, to 1953–54, junior college enrollment has more than doubled, the increase being from 267,406 to 622,864.[67]

Particularly striking has been the development of the city publicly supported junior college enrolling thousands of full-time and part-time students from the local community. This may take some of the physical pressure off the traditional four-year college or university and relieve to some extent the need in those institutions for extremely rigid admission and retention policies. Admission policies can be worked out within local school systems with the transition from twelfth grade to thirteenth grade not necessarily more marked or critical than that from ninth to tenth in a 6–3–3 system. This presents, of course, the unwelcome possibility that the junior college may become the dumping ground for those students who cannot meet the admission requirements of other colleges.

The junior college has been and will continue to be a school with a double purpose. On one hand it provides terminal vocational education for students planning only two years beyond twelfth grade, while on the other it provides the usual program of the first two college years for students who wish to transfer to the four-year college.

In each of the twenty-one states surveyed for this chapter of the yearbook, at least 50 per cent of the students declare at entrance that their purpose in attending the public junior college is to prepare for advanced standing in four-year colleges and universities. In most states the percentage runs higher: about 66 per cent in Arizona, California, and Illinois, for example, and about 77 per cent in Colorado, Michigan,

[67] B. Lamar Johnson, "Purpose and Plan of the Yearbook," National Society for the Study of Education, Fifty-fifth Yearbook, pt. 1, *The Public Junior College*, The Society, 1956, p. 5.

Mississippi, and Texas. In some individual junior colleges, it runs as high as 90 per cent. While the aim of many students is not always realistic, the opportunity to prepare for transfer to senior institutions remains the largest single motivating force for their entering the junior college at all.[68]

The effect of this is to shift somewhat the responsibility of preparing students for admission to the traditional college from the senior high school to the junior college itself. Preparing high school students for the local junior college is not quite the same as college preparation in general. The impact of such developments depends partly on geographical location of particular high schools. It is felt much more in metropolitan areas and in those states with heavy concentrations of population. Junior colleges in small cities are not able to afford the range and breadth of programs possible in metropolitan centers. In sparsely settled regions, junior colleges are too far away from many students to be of much help in offsetting the cost of moving away from home. Under these conditions, the traditional four-year colleges and universities face admission and selection problems on two levels: the usual one at the beginning of the freshman year plus the additional one at the beginning of the third or junior year.

The first and most important need in relation to all these developments is to strengthen and expand guidance services. One of the many important responsibilities of high school counselors is to help students think carefully about their post-high school plans for employment or continued study or both and to make wise choices in the light of those plans. The nature of this responsibility will vary from one student to another. Students who know they are going to college and know where they are going need help in selecting subjects to meet the requirements of particular institutions and programs. Those who are not immediately planning for college might be encouraged to elect a reasonable number of "academic" subjects. There will also be some college-bound students who might be encouraged not to take algebra and geometry and to select those colleges and college programs which do not require these for entrance. Such students are not necessarily poor

[68] Grace V. Bird, "Preparation for Advanced Study." *Ibid.,* pp. 79–80.

students generally and will make good college material in respectable academic fields other than mathematics.

In short, the counselor must be aware of a broad range of individual differences growing out of a number of factors and circumstances: differences in students, in colleges, and in programs within colleges. To do his job, the counselor needs fewer students and more time. Whether the counselor should be a guidance specialist or a general classroom teacher is an important question, but not necessarily relevant to this aspect of counseling. In either case, the person who does the counseling needs circumstances and conditions under which the job can be done. Such circumstances prevail neither for the guidance specialist who has "full time" for allegedly counseling 500 students nor for the classroom teacher who carries an advisory group of 30 students in addition to a teaching load of five or more classes. Of course no counseling system, no matter how well staffed or supported, will be able to protect the student who makes a drastic change in his plans during the second semester of the senior year. But good counseling should do much to reduce the number of such occurrences.

A second potential improvement in helping students make the transition from secondary to higher education is the reduction of undesirable overlapping between the subject matter of the upper high school and the lower college years. Overlapping exists not only in general, but even among colleges and preparatory schools which have common interests and work closely together. A committee of faculty members from Andover, Exeter, Lawrenceville, Harvard, Princeton, and Yale noted such overlapping between preparatory school and college courses in their own institutions.

A student may waste his time in a number of ways. The most obvious is to do much the same thing twice. This happens, our inquiries show, in many fields. It happens most conspicuously in history, English, and the sciences. A few figures may press the point. All but a very small fraction of the students in the three schools take American history; it is usually a substantial course in the 12th grade. Yet one out of three graduates of these schools who were members of the class of 1951 at the universities took the basic, or introductory course in American history in college. The evidence of repeated reading and duplicated material is overwhelming. In English, where it is normal for boys to study literature in both the 12th and 13th grades, we found a striking similarity between the 12th grade course in all three schools and the standard freshman English course at two of the universities.

The most striking evidence of sheer repetition is in the sciences. Of our 344 students, 209 took physics, chemistry, or biology in college. Of this number, almost half took in college the beginner's course in the same science they had taken in school. Furthermore, the great majority of the prospective concentrators in engineering or the physical sciences spent *four years,* two in school and two in college, completing elementary physics and elementary chemistry; they repeated *both* subjects. Yet when we compared the grades of these repeaters with those of boys taking physics or chemistry in college for the first time, we found that the repeaters had only a negligible advantage.

It may be argued either that this repetition shows the failure of the school, or that the school and college courses are so differently taught as to be two separate educational experiences. We find, in the cases we have noted, that this is wishful thinking. The students involved did the same work twice, if not all the way through, at least to a plainly unprofitable extent.[69]

It is important for all high schools and colleges to guard against undesirable overlapping. The broad responsibility, however, as stated by the committee members in the study cited, "is to integrate the work of the school and college in the area of general education."[70] One approach to this objective and the one most stressed in recent years is to provide opportunity for advanced placement or college credit for work taken in high school. Such credit is used either to reduce the degree requirements in the college for such students or to replace designated prerequisites in the college for certain college courses.

The advanced standing program, however, is subject to limitations. For one thing, the development of such courses is much more likely to occur in large high schools than in small ones. In the second place, such opportunities are suitable only for students in the upper intelligence levels who can meet the necessarily

[69] A Committee Report by members of the faculties of Andover, Exeter, Lawrenceville, Harvard, Princeton, and Yale, *General Education in School and College,* Harvard University Press, 1952, pp. 12–13.

[70] *Ibid.,* p. 8.

rigorous requirements. The need for better integration of high school and college work is perhaps just as great for the average good student as for the highly gifted. One possible answer is the reorganization of general education courses in the colleges themselves. Such programs as the Integrated Liberal Studies at the University of Wisconsin are organized along somewhat broader lines than the traditional freshman and sophomore program. While some of the material may overlap that studied in high school, it is reorganized to bring out the relationships among the various fields.

Another possible answer is to encourage some college-preparatory students to take certain courses in college rather than in the high school. This would free such students to take more so-called non-college-preparatory work, particularly to enrich their high school programs with courses in art, music, and industrial arts. Such a step would not necessarily reduce enrollments in the advanced language, science, or mathematics programs, for at the same time we should encourage more of our non-college-bound students to elect courses in those areas. This implies a reversal of our traditional attitudes about course selections by college-bound and non-college-bound students. Undoubtedly there are limits to the extent of such a possible reversal. In part at least, though, it is reasonable to assume that the study of advanced academic subjects is more critical for the terminal student whose future opportunities are conjectural than for the college-bound student who is likely to have them.

A fourth possibility is to achieve a tighter definition of general education requirements for high school graduation and to have colleges build their courses on this foundation. This is an elusive bird, which has been pursued at least since the Committee of Ten. The great range of individual differences among students at both levels operates against the guarantee of uniform standards by the high school and the uncritical acceptance of high school performance on the other. The reluctance of the college to assume common definitions and standards from a great variety of high schools is an understandable one, even with the development of more rigorous entrance requirements and the use of entrance tests.

In the long run, however, the most important responsibility of the high school in connection with college preparation is not to furnish students with tickets of admission, but with the understandings and skills needed to do advanced intellectual work consistent with the best college practices and standards. Many a high school graduate has found to his sorrow that it is one thing to get into college and another to do the quality of work required for staying in. The reason is to be found partly in the differences between high school and college teaching practices. High school teachers are more likely to give daily assignments with frequent checkups through recitations or tests. College teachers allegedly give long-term reading assignments in a variety of books, expect the students to choose and develop topics for individual research papers, use class periods for presenting additional material in lecture form, and give only several examinations during a semester. The need for more complex reading and study skills at the college level has been known for a long time. It is brought out with renewed vigor and emphasis in the following excerpts from a study of the scholastic problems of college freshmen.

Students with greater insight into the complexities of the task of reading realize that while merely "getting through" the extensive college reading assignment is a major problem for the slow reader, the more important need is for flexibility in reading skills: knowing where skimming is indicated, where careful reading and re-reading is required, how to seek evidence to solve a problem, how to compare and criticize sources. Some students appreciate more vividly than others the differences between the short written assignments common in school and the sustained effort needed to organize a term paper.[71]

Length of assignment and reading load is only part of the change from high school to college work. There is a change in complexity as well. Reading must be not only more extensive but more selective. Information given in one reference source must be checked, criticized, and perhaps rejected because of information given in another. The task of evaluation, in other words, assumes major significance.[72]

[71] Agatha Townsend (for the Committee on School and College Relations of the Educational Records Bureau), *College Freshmen Speak Out,* Harper & Brothers, 1956, p. 28.
[72] *Ibid.,* p. 31.

In this evidence that college work differs both in quantity and in kind from high school tasks there is an important comment on the general complaint that study methods which were previously effective are no longer bringing results.[73]

Some might contend that long-term projects, wide reading assignments, and the development of critical reading are undesirable at the high school level and that colleges should take the responsibility for more gradual induction of their students into these complex activities. On the other hand, it can be maintained that the reading and study skills called for are important not only for the college-bound student but for the terminal student. If complete responsibility for the development of such skills were assigned to the college, large numbers of our high school graduates would not have the opportunity to learn them, at least in school. From a general-education standpoint alone, high schools need to begin developing such skills early in the program and particularly to adapt their teaching procedures along these lines in the eleventh and twelfth grades. Many high school teachers have been doing so for a long time. The experience of college freshmen, however, indicates there are still not enough. Here we have perhaps another example of the fact that good general education and good college preparation become much the same thing.

To take another kind of example, one skill of immense benefit to the college student is that of personal typing. Again, this skill is one that could be useful for many students not going to college. The tendency in our high schools, however, has been to regard typewriting as a vocational subject for students in the business education track. Ability to type is of course no automatic guarantee of college success, but it is a most helpful asset to the college student as well as to people in many other occupations.

There remains yet another possibly important factor in college success, that of emotional and personal development. One college medical director writes as follows from his own experience and that of other observers.

These observations, whether made by psychiatrists, psychologists, or counselors have been remarkably similar. They may be summarized in

[73] *Ibid.*, p. 32.

a very general way by the statement that failure in college, leaving out the obvious instances of low intelligence, is not due to lack of ability so much as it is due to some internal conflict or external hindrance which prevents the student from applying himself to his work. To put it another way, a large percentage of those who fail in college are capable of success, but do not succeed because of the way they feel about things, their suspicion, hostility, confusion, resentment, or rebellion.[74]

To many the foregoing will appear to be a far-fetched conclusion. Everyone in college work can call up examples of emotionally disturbed students who nonetheless did good or superior academic work. But since there is no ceiling on intellectual achievement, one can speculate about how much better even those students might have done had they been less handicapped by emotional disturbance. Definitive research is indeed lacking on this whole matter, but in its absence such informed observations as reported by Dr. Farnsworth in the foregoing quotation should not lightly be ignored. Dr. Farnsworth, however, cautions us against extreme interpretations. "This does not mean necessarily that such persons should be denied admission to college. It does mean that careful individual attention is needed to see whether such persons have the possibility or probability of success."[75] So far as the high school is concerned, we may observe that concern for the development of healthy personality need not be regarded as inconsistent with or irrelevant to the objectives of academic or intellectual development. For some students the high school's efforts in the controversial area of personal-social development may be a most important part of college preparation: that is, preparation for the academic as well as the social demands of college life.

Bibliography

A Committee Report by members of the faculties of Andover, Exeter, Lawrenceville, Harvard, Princeton, and Yale, *General Education in School and College,* Harvard University Press, 1952.

[74] Dana L. Farnsworth, "Some Non-Academic Causes of Success and Failure in College Students," College Entrance Examination Board, *College Admissions: The Great Sorting,* The Board, 1955, p. 72.
[75] *Ibid.*

Aikin, Wilford, *The Story of the Eight-Year Study,* Harper & Brothers, 1942.

American Council on Education, *The Strength to Meet Our National Need,* Charles C. Dobbins (ed.), The Council, 1956.

Association for Supervision and Curriculum Development, "Curriculum Planning for the Surging College Enrollment," *Educational Leadership,* November, 1957. (Entire issue.)

Berdie, Ralph F. (with chapters by Wilber L. Layton and Ben Willerman), *After High School—What?* University of Minnesota Press, 1954.

Broome, Edwin Cornelius, *A Historical and Critical Discussion of College Admission Requirements,* Columbia University Contributions to Philosophy, Psychology and Education, vol. xi, Nos. 3–4, The Macmillan Company, April, 1903.

Brubacher, John S., and Rudy, Willis, *Higher Education in Transition,* Harper & Brothers, 1958, chap. 12.

Chamberlin, Dean, Chamberlin, Enid, Drought, Neal E., and Scott, William E., *Did They Succeed in College?* Harper & Brothers, 1942.

College Entrance Examination Board, *College Admissions,* 1954, and *College Admissions: The Great Sorting,* 1955.

Faunce, Roland C., "A Functional Program for Michigan Youth," *Educational Leadership,* March, 1949, pp. 381–384.

Fuess, Claude M., *The College Board: Its First Fifty Years,* Columbia University Press, 1950.

Hillway, Tyrus, *The American Two-Year College,* Harper & Brothers, 1958.

Iffert, Robert E., *Retention and Withdrawal of College Students,* U.S. Office of Education, Department of Health, Education, and Welfare, Bulletin 1958, no. 1.

Krug, Edward A., Liddle, Clifford S., Mosely, Russell C., and Parkinson, Daniel, *The College-Preparatory Function in Wisconsin High Schools,* School of Education, University of Wisconsin, 1959.

National Association of Secondary-School Principals, "Advanced Placement Programs in Secondary Schools," *The Bulletin of the National Association of Secondary-School Principals,* December, 1958. (Entire issue.)

National Educational Association, *Report of the Committee of Ten on Secondary School Studies with the Reports of the Conference Arranged by the Committee,* American Book Company, for the Association, 1894.

National Educational Association, *Report of Committee on College Entrance Requirements,* The Association, University of Chicago Press, 1899.

National Society for the Study of Education, Fifty-fifth Yearbook, pt. 1, *The Public Junior College,* The Society, 1956.

Progressive Education Association Commission on the Relation Between School and College, *Thirty Schools Tell Their Story,* Harper & Brothers, 1943.

Tompkins, Ellsworth, and Gaumnitz, Walter H., *The Carnegie Unit: Its Origin, Status, and Trends,* U.S. Office of Education, Department of Health, Education, and Welfare, Bulletin 1954, no. 7.

Townsend, Agatha (for the Committee on School and College Relations of the Educational Records Bureau), *College Freshmen Speak Out,* Harper & Brothers, 1956.

Traxler, Arthur E., and Townsend, Agatha (eds.), *Improving Transition from School to College,* A Study of College Admission by the Committee on School and College Relations of the Educational Records Bureau, Harper & Brothers, 1953.

Weigle, Richard D., "Commission on Liberal Education," *Association of American Colleges Bulletin,* March, 1958, pp. 150–154.

....

CHAPTER 6

The Shape of the High School Program: Requirements and Standards

_____

Every high school program has a distinctive shape, wrought by the educational resources available, the relative importance of these resources, and the ways they are used for the benefit of students. The educational resources of the usual high school include classroom studies, extraclass student activities, and guidance or counseling services. Variations from school to school often reflect variations in size and financial means. Large high schools tend to offer broader and more varied patterns of subjects, greater diversity and specialization in extraclass activities, and more specific and formalized guidance or counseling arrangements than are usually found in small ones. A few high schools, regardless of size, use such supplementary resources as school-related work experience and community-service projects.

The distinctive and unique program of a high school (no two high schools are exactly alike) is in itself shaped to and by the students, who come to it with varying degrees of willingness and enthusiasm and with widely varying capacities and interests. There are, as far as our everyday speech goes, average students, below-average students, and above-average or superior students. General provisions are usually aimed at the norm of the average student. Yet we must admit that such terms as average, below average, and superior are nothing more than a convenient, necessary, and misleading kind of shorthand. The average student, with his fellows the below average and the superior, is a myth. Every student is an exceptional individual with his own bewildering mixtures and arrangements of merits and demerits, handicaps and gifts. The dilemma of organized schooling is that while no school is set up for a single student, its program must be shaped, so far as human ingenuity permits, to every single student as though he were the only one in attendance. It is a dilemma that precludes the possibility of easy answers as to what the shape and substance of the high school program ought to be. Teachers and all others concerned with high schools are thereby denied the comforts of extreme and uncompromising positions. We are led into compromises and adjustments that sometimes appear inconsistent or absurd, especially on such matters as requirements, constants, standards, and graduation.

The process of resolving the dilemma is the daily one of specific decision-making in the local high school. It is the process by which the high school program is shaped and is continuously in the shaping. We make our decisions in the light of our ideals of free, popular, and universal secondary education; of the nature of high school students; and of the agreements concerning educational objectives and functions as far as these agreements can be identified. But there is one thing more that governs our daily decisions and the shaping of the local high school program. This is the traditional general shape of the high school program as it has come down to us from high school programs of the past and as it confronts us in the present. Even those who might wish to shatter the traditional program and design secondary education anew are motivated in part by the familiar shape they would reject. The traditional program consists of traditional answers to the dilemma of organized schooling in relation to the individual student. But the practical task is not that of rejecting these traditional answers for some new and grand design. It is rather that of adapting them through critical inquiry to the demands of the present and future.

Our dilemma contains several parts. Should high school education be defined in terms of quantity? If so, how much? What kinds of studies should be required of which students? To what standards of accomplishment should students be held? How should their work be judged and marked? What meanings should be attached to the symbol of high school graduation? What adaptations if any should be made in the educational interests of superior students?

The answer to the first of the foregoing questions has been "no" in theory, "yes" in practice. High school education takes four years. The 8–4 organization is older than either the junior high school or the Carnegie unit system. So although we have had fifty years of persuasion that secondary education includes the seventh and eighth grades, we do not, even in 6–3–3 systems, usually start counting units until Grade 9. The Carnegie unit system has not determined the four-year span; it has been fitted into it. Students usually take four solid or major units at a time, each representing an academic year's work for so many clock hours a week. Four units each year for four years yield 16 units, the standard formula. Students do take additional fractional units in physical education and sometimes in band, orchestra, or chorus. The usual practice, however, is to put these outside the 16-unit boundaries.

There have always, however, been exceptions in the system, and more are beginning to appear. Some schools count physical education as a quarter-unit toward graduation each year, thereby reducing the total of major or solid units to 15. A few students with high grade-point averages have been permitted to take five solids at a time rather than four. These may end up with more than 16 units or they may confront the world with the accomplished fact of having accumulated 16 units in less than four years. Units earned in summer school produce the same effects. A more recent tendency in some quarters has been to challenge the four-subject-at-a-time idea and to move toward five subjects at a time, with less distinction between major and fractional subjects and with more than 16 units for graduation. Florida, for example, has gone to 20 units as a state requirement, followed closely by California and Oregon with 19.[1] A study of 106 city systems, 100,000 or over, made in 1954, showed 26 of the 69 responding to have requirements of more than 16 units.[2]

---

[1] Grace S. Wright, *High School Graduation Requirements Established by State Departments of Education,* U.S. Department of Health, Education, and Welfare, Office of Education, Circular No. 455, September, 1955, pp. 4, 5, 11.

[2] Department of Research, Statistics, and Information, Cincinnati Public Schools, *High School Graduation Requirements in Cities of 100,000 or Over,* January, 1954, p. 3. (Mimeo.)

Nobody has the answer to the question of how many subjects should be taken at a time by students in general. Conceivably the familiar load of four major subjects could be modified upwards or downwards in many cases. With students of average or above average academic ability, we probably should not only permit but encourage more students to take five subjects.[3] Regulations on the taking of fifth subjects in some schools are restrictive and might well be liberalized. Encouragement could be provided on the basis of individual counseling. Raising the graduation requirements from 16 to 20 units of course would force all students to take five subjects. Another possibility is to raise the requirements not to twenty, but to 17 or 18 units. This would leave more student choice as to the timing of his five-unit semesters or years throughout his four-year program. Some would require all superior students to take five subjects each year in high school. It is not clear that such general or overall policies do anything that could not be done as well or better through individual counseling and the liberalizing of present regulations on the taking of five subjects.

Units toward graduation are ordinarily granted only in the classroom studies. Extraclass activities, school-related work experience, and community-service projects have been regarded as supplementary. This is a desirable state of affairs so far as most students are concerned. Classroom studies are and should be the main business of the high school. For some students at some levels of their education, however, this practice might well be modified, as in fact it has been in a few school systems, by granting units for school-related work experience.[4] We have spent much energy trying to keep low-ability students in school by inventing classroom studies suited to their capacities. Beyond this, we have under a mistaken idea of vocational education seriously threatened standards

---

[3] High school students in other countries sometimes take seven or eight academic subjects at a time, some of them only twice or three times a week as in the college. Similar practices in American schools of the latter nineteenth century led to the chaos deplored by the Committee of Ten in its 1893 report. We have tended since to shy away from this kind of flexibility. A limited amount of experimentation along these lines might be in order provided we could discipline ourselves against multiplying subjects without end.

[4] It is not necessary to grant credit to accomplish this. A school might simply reduce the number of required graduation units in individual cases. This makes it possible to avoid unnecessary academic bookkeeping.

in vocational courses by using them for low-ability students. A better program for some students might be just two classroom studies plus greater use of work-experience opportunities and other school-community activities.[5] Such modifications would not necessarily lower, but could even raise standards, by making it possible for the student to do better work in fewer subjects. This is not to be regarded, however, as a wholesome approach for groups of students, but rather as an adaptation that might be made under appropriate circumstances to shape programs to individuals.

GRADUATION CONSTANTS AND VARIABLES

The next question is that of constants, those subjects required of all students in a school, and variables, those required of students in particular tracks or programs. During the nineteenth century, a number of such tracks had evolved as the major determiners of what students had to take. Students could choose tracks, but they had relatively little room for electives within the tracks. In 1899 the Committee on College Entrance Requirements recommended "that the principle of election be recognized in secondary schools."[6] They pointed out also that they did "not believe in unlimited election"[7] and went on to recommend the following constants: one year of history; one year of laboratory science; two years of English; one year each of algebra and geometry; and four years of foreign language. Presumably this left room for some electives along with specified track variables.

It is sometimes assumed that standards have been lowered in recent years by reducing the number of such constants. This is not necessarily the case, although accurate information covering local variations and year-to-year fluctuations from one high school to the next is lacking. The four-year language requirement recommended by the 1899 committee has disappeared from most high schools, but it has been partly offset, quantitatively at least, by

---

[5] Work experience is not presented here as something peculiarly appropriate for low-ability students. It offers challenging possibilities also for the gifted, but not as a subtraction from the classroom studies.

[6] National Education Association, *Report of Committee on College Entrance Requirements,* The Association, 1899, p. 27.

[7] *Ibid.,* p. 32.

an increase in the English requirement from two years to three. The algebra-and-geometry requirement has been reduced in many schools to one year of mathematics, which may be met by general mathematics instead of algebra. Again, this is offset by an increase in social studies from one year to two. Hovet summarizes the situation today as follows. "Anyone bold enough to hazard a national 'norm' with respect to units of required subjects would present a picture about as follows: English, 3 units; social studies, 2 units; mathematics, 1 unit; science, 1 unit; health, 1 unit. This adds up to 8 required Carnegie units of the 16 usually required for graduation from high school."[8] With regard to the health requirement, Hovet comments, "Statutory requirements and enrollments in the area of health-physical education have increased steadily over the past thirty years, although practice varies in including credit among the 16 Carnegie units required for high school graduation."[9] The requirements have gone down from the ten recommended in 1899 to the seven or eight usually required today. But this is far from a completely or even an extremely elective system.[10]

The extent and nature of student freedom, however, are revealed not only by the graduation constants, but by the variables. A school may state its requirements as three years of English, meaning that these are the only ones common to a variety of curricula or tracks. Each curriculum or track then bristles with its own requirements. The student in the college-preparatory track faces additional requirements in foreign languages, science, and mathe-

[8] Kenneth Hovet, "What Are the High Schools Teaching?" Association for Supervision and Curriculum Development, 1956 Yearbook, *What Shall the High Schools Teach?* The Association, 1956, p. 72.

[9] *Ibid.*

[10] Although local autonomy governs many aspects of educational practice in the United States, local high schools are not always entirely free in this matter of graduation requirements. Some states set minimum requirements to which local high schools may add, but from which they are not free to subtract. Examination of state requirements throws some light on the amount and kinds of variability which operate in the general pattern previously stated. A survey made by the U.S. Office of Education in 1955 showed that our states varied from five which made no requirements of subject units at all to one which required 12, two which required 11, and four which required ten. The state that requires 12 units places four of them in health and physical education. These are minimum requirements. Local schools may set them higher. Wright, *op. cit.,* p. 1.

matics, while one in the business track faces them in typewriting, stenography, or bookkeeping, office practice, and the like. So far as the student is concerned he is in about the same situation as one in the 1890's. He is free to choose tracks.[11] This is not an unusual state of affairs in our high schools and indicates a greater tendency to prescription than is ordinarily assumed.

On the other hand, some schools provide much flexibility and choice in the meeting of the specified constants. The student is required to take English, but has a choice of specialized classes in creative writing, speech and dramatics, history of literature, or journalism. This is often found in the eleventh and twelfth grade levels. Is English then a requirement or an elective? One might argue the point either way.

What then is desirable? For many years following the 1890's, opinion tended to favor the elective system. These expressions, it should be noted, were voiced not only by professional educationists, but by many educators in the academic disciplines. The elective system was identified with liberalism and reform, constants with conservatism and reaction. As previously noted, however, high schools did retain a substantial number of constants. Perhaps practitioners expected opinion to swing around in their direction again, and they have not been disappointed. In recent years expressions of educators—not only academic disciplinarians but professional educationists as well—have become much more friendly to the idea of common studies. The notion of constants has in fact been most earnestly promoted by one group of professional educationists, the advocates of common learnings or core classes.

Constants depend on certain assumptions about the nature of general education. This latter term is rather hard to define. Henry lists the following, for example, as "types" of general education: (1) subjects required of all pupils; (2) a reduction of each subject field to manageable size; (3) a general course for "average" pupils; (4) well-roundedness or versatility; (5) general method; (6) common product or common outcomes; (7) the atmosphere

---

[11] A modification of the track plan, sometimes used in connection with it, is the requirement of majors and minors under which a student presents a minimum number of units in each of two or three different fields of study.

or tone of a school; (8) the improvement of the present living of pupils; (9) the essential heritage; (10) the common experience of participating in schooling.[12] Concern for constants then proceeds on the assumption that general education can in part at least be legitimately defined in terms of common classes or courses, whether in the traditional subject organization or in the core. This is accepted here as a legitimate assumption. It does not deny the possible contributions of other ways of considering general education or the value of other curricular means, such as extraclass activities and school-related work experience.

The idea of required subjects is repugnant to many people since it suggests compulsions or restraints. On the other hand it can be argued that constants in the curriculum are not only consistent with but necessary in order to realize equality of educational opportunity. In this sense the situation is analogous to compulsory education itself, which can be viewed on one hand as restraint and on the other as safeguarding the rights of youth to attend school. Unless we are prepared to reject adult wisdom completely, it seems reasonable to assume that not only compulsory education but some required studies serve to fulfill the promise of universal secondary education. This does not mean that the requirements should be applied without exception. The possibility should always exist of waiving any requirement in individual cases for good reasons. In some instances this might be done with superior students who can demonstrate their knowledge of the course by examination. In others it might be done with and for students with obvious handicaps, intellectual, physical, or emotional. Admittedly these may be rare instances, but the system should be flexible enough to admit them. It is better to admit such flexibility in the application of a constant than it is to make some subjects entirely elective for all students.

Of course the main difficulty is that we can so easily see reasons for constants in every field of study. Certainly in an age of increasing leisure, we should help students enrich their lives through the

[12] George H. Henry, "Foundations of General Education in the High School," Association for Supervision and Curriculum Development, 1956 Yearbook, *What Shall the High Schools Teach?* The Association, 1956, pp. 142–161.

graphic, industrial, and musical arts. Living in a world shrunk by modern transportation and communication requires knowledge of the histories and civilizations of peoples beyond our own boundaries. Foreign languages provide pathways to the riches of literature and the understanding of other peoples. Science and mathematics in our age of complex technology are necessary both for individual and social reasons. Such arguments would eliminate electives entirely. The whole program would consist of constants. Since this is out of the question, choices must be made.

Some subjects, foreign languages for example, although possibly not appropriate as graduation constants, should be elected by more students than is now the case. This can be accomplished through individual counseling, not in the sense of pressure but by pointing out educational values students may not otherwise take into account. Modification or elimination of the track system might individualize to a much greater extent that portion of the student's program outside the constants. The track system is a series of short cuts in the guidance process and tends in the long run to limit student choice as much if not more than the constants themselves. It also tends to identify some subjects as peculiar to a college-preparatory track when they may have much value for terminal students. With the track system out of the way, students and counselors are in a better position to relate choices to abilities and interests. Admittedly, this places more responsibility on the counseling system, but not more than such a system should be equipped to assume. It can be done, and there are high schools which have done so, in which neither faculty nor student body thinks in terms of tracks at all. The major-minor system is less restrictive, but probably unnecessary in a school with adequate counseling provisions.

High schools should and will continue to require certain subjects of all students. Determining the specific listing is left to local communities within the frameworks set by their respective states. Examination and study of the instructional fields by local teachers and other citizens help provide the bases for the making of such decisions. General recommendations made by individual observers or groups on a national basis are worthy of consideration by, and should be of help to, local groups. The Conant report, for example, recommends four years of English, three or four years of social studies including two years of history, one year of mathematics, and one year of science in the four years of Grades 9 through 12.[13]

This writer's suggestions and the reasons for them are dealt with in the series of chapters (9 through 20) devoted to the instructional fields. The setting assumed is that of a six-year secondary program from Grade 7 through 12, in which some students might take five units each year for a total of 30 units and in which the average or normal program would be five units each year in Grades 7 and 8 plus four units each year in Grades 9 through 12 for a total of 26 units, exclusive of required physical education. These suggestions are as follows: (1) five units (years) of English; (2) four and one-half units of social studies; (3) two units of natural science; (4) three units of mathematics; (5) one unit of music; (6) one unit of the visual fine arts; and (7) one unit of combined industrial arts and homemaking for boys and girls, or one unit of industrial arts for boys and one unit of homemaking for girls. With possible new developments in science and mathematics curricula, increased requirements in those fields may be desirable.

The foregoing requirements come to 17½ units, exclusive of required physical education. Ten of them might be taken in Grades 7 and 8; namely, two units of English, two of mathematics, two of social studies, one of science, one of art, one of music, and one of industrial arts–home economics. Those pertaining especially to the four-year program from Grades 9 through 12 are three units of English, two and one-half of social studies, one of science, and one of mathematics, amounting to 7½ units in the average or conventional 16-unit program. In any consideration of constants, it should be remembered that there are students with exceptional circumstances for whom the program should be modified.

GRADUATION STANDARDS

Review of constants and variables leads directly to the question of standards. Some students cannot do good work in some required subjects no matter how hard they try. This may arise from general

[13] James Bryant Conant, *The American High School Today*, McGraw-Hill Book Company, Inc., 1959, p. 47.

lack of ability or in exceptional cases from blind spots in particular fields. Hovet states the dilemma as follows.

Schools have employed several procedures in adapting their programs to this influx of youth. Requirements have been met by teaching students differently in the curriculum programs variously labeled "academic," "vocational," "commercial," or "general." Students have been "grouped homogeneously" in high and low classes so that different standards of evaluation of achievement may be applied. Stress has been placed upon and provision has been made for "remedial work" in the required subjects especially. Promotion policies have recognized "growth" and "social maturity" when students have experienced difficulty in meeting achievement standards. Prescription sometimes is cut to a minimum and students are permitted to elect those courses in which they have some hope of success.

The classroom teacher is the person first responsible in the case of any given pupil for answering the question, What is a requirement and when is it "met"? In difficult cases involving promotion policy, the teacher may confer with the guidance counselor, with the school counselor, with the school psychologist, with a committee of teachers, with parents, and with the school principal. Answers as to what is best will vary with personnel, with subjects, with schools, and with states. In spite of the great amount of back-breaking work that has been done to "adjust the school to the pupil, his needs, his interests, and his abilities," more such adjustment is on the way; and the limits to which the school should go in its program of adjustment are not yet in sight.[14]

The problem may not necessarily be one brought about by an "influx of youth." High schools of yesteryear also had their low-ability students and probably about the same percentage of them in the total student body as is true today. Even if the percentage of low-ability students to the total is no greater than in the past, however, the total number of such students is much greater. No school administrator and no teaching staff can remain unaware of their presence. Some response must be made to the difficulties thereby presented. The response must take into account the following factors: the retention, modification, or abolition of the constants; the desirability of keeping and graduating students who have difficulty

[14] Hovet, *op. cit.*, pp. 73–74.

meeting standards; the nature of the marking system; and the desirability of making not only the study, but the passing of the constants a condition for graduation. There are at least the following possible kinds of responses.

1. One response is to reduce the number of constants or to abolish them entirely. This one is referred to by Hovet in his comment that "Prescription sometimes is cut to a minimum and students are permitted to elect those courses in which they have some hope of success."[15] In this approach the school could presumably use a marking system based on defined standards of achievement in each subject.

2. A second response is to keep a substantial number of constants, to make the passing of these a condition of graduation, and to base marks on defined standards of achievement. This system would increase the numbers of dropouts and reduce the numbers of graduates. It would still be universal secondary education, but only in the sense of equality of opportunity defined along specified lines. Those who do not wish to surrender either the constants or the ideal of universal secondary education as now understood and practiced must proceed to other possibilities.

3. One way is to abandon the idea that marks stand for defined levels of achievement and to attach other kinds of meanings to conventional symbols. This practice is of extremely doubtful value. While the school may attach unconventional meanings to the conventional symbols, the tendency on the part of all concerned is to continue thinking in terms of the usual or conventional meanings. The result is confusion, and the marking system no longer communicates anything. Nevertheless, this approach has been used in various ways and to varying degrees. A school that proceeds along these lines can keep the constants, require that they be passed, and still graduate all or nearly all the students who stay through the twelfth grade. One way of adjusting the marks is referred to by Hovet in his comment that "Students have been 'grouped homogeneously' in high and low classes so that different standards of evaluation of achievement may be applied."[16] One

[15] *Ibid.*, p. 73.
[16] *Ibid.*

might, for example, in three English classes sectioned for ability grouping, set a different standard to be achieved in each class. Or one might let the standard in each class be set by the class average or norm. At any rate students in low-ability sections are marked in terms of a standard set for them, determined either by the teacher's judgment of what an appropriate standard for the class might be or by the distribution of achievement within the class itself. It is possible under an extreme application of this system for a student in a low-ability section to get an A for work that would bring a C or a D to a student in a high-ability section. To guard against this awkward possibility, schools often place ceilings on marks in low-ability classes. A teacher who feels that a student in a low-ability class has earned a grade above the ceiling is supposed to recommend the student for possible transfer to another group.

Another way of adjusting marks is to include factors other than academic achievement, such as effort, character, deportment, and attitudes. This is not a new practice. Some teachers have done it under marking systems based on absolute achievement standards. It is after all a hard thing to fail a conscientious, well-mannered student who has put forth considerable effort, but who cannot master the skills of a particular course, although he has made some progress. Few teachers enjoy it.[17] So far as this is a matter between the teacher and his academic conscience, we have always had a certain amount of this kind of adjustment. What is relatively new is the acknowledgment that such adjustments are made.[18]

[17] There is little to enjoy in any part of marking. "Few people know how much time and energy teachers spend in preparing and correcting tests and in computing and recording grades, but only teachers know how unpleasant these chores can be. Sensitive people are naturally hesitant to sit in judgment on fellow mortals, even though they be younger. This reluctance to rate others is heightened when one loses faith in the importance of the criteria, in the validity of the procedures that are used for rating, or in the contribution that these procedures make to improving the quality of the education our students receive." Harry N. Rivlin, *Teaching Adolescents in Secondary Schools,* Appleton-Century-Crofts, Inc., 1948, p. 448.

[18] The difficulties presented by these adaptations are recognized and stated in the following quotations.

"The term grade should not reflect the teacher's opinion of the student's character or of his potentialities. The mathematics student whose demonstrated ability entitles him to the final grade of A should not have his final grade lowered to a B because he regularly was tardy in turning in homework assignments or because the teacher thinks the student is so conceited that a lower grade may have therapeutic value. Similarly,

Still another kind of adjustment involves the idea that marks should represent not absolute achievement, but growth or progress in achievement in relation to the student's ability. Attempts to evaluate student achievement in these terms, however, are usually more satisfactory in the conference approach than in the giving of grades on report cards. Some systems nonetheless have set up report cards and marking systems along these lines, with each mark representing a combination of achievement and effort in terms of student progress. This requires complicated explanations sometimes printed on the report card itself. It also can lead to the awkward situation in which a student with low achievement may get a higher mark, as usually understood, than one with higher achievement.

4. This response retains the constants and a marking system based on defined standards of achievement in each subject, but grants graduation credit in required subjects to those students who in the judgement of their teachers have made honest efforts even though their work falls below the defined standard.[19] Standards

---

another mathematics student whose demonstrated ability entitles him to a C should not have his final grade raised to a B because the teacher knows how conscientious the student is and how faithful he is in doing every assignment made in class. There should be some other provision on the students' permanent record card for the teachers' comments on personality traits and scholastic habits that may be better bases for guidance than are the term grades, but these comments should be separated from the grades themselves.

"Unless the term grades are restricted to measures of achievement, they cannot be readily interpreted by anybody other than the teacher who has submitted the grade. How can you interpret the grade of B in Plane Geometry if you do not know whether it means that the student is brilliant in mathematics but conceited, or that he is little better than mediocre in his mastery of the subject but is a very conscientious and personable young man?" *Ibid.*, p. 447.

"Many teachers will object to leaving out of consideration such factors as the pupils' attitude, effort, conduct in class, and various personality traits. These are certainly important and should be taken into account in some way. But if only one mark is given, it should be a mark in scholarship, and not a hodgepodge of miscellaneous items. A second mark, in *citizenship,* including most of the above items, has been added by many schools, with a considerable amount of success. It is better still, no doubt, to provide a separate mark or rating to indicate growth in each characteristic or trait deemed important by the school." C. C. Ross, *Measurement in Today's Schools,* 2d ed., Prentice-Hall, Inc., 1947, p. 405.

[19] This system is used only in modified form. A student who fails a required course may take another one in the same instructional field instead of repeating the failed course. Or the adjustment is made in the total number of units required for graduation. For example, the school may require 16½ units to be taken, but only 14½ to be

are defined by the faculty members in the various instructional fields as has traditionally been the case. Ability grouping may be used, but the meanings of the various marks are the same for low, middle, and high sections, with such adaptations as may be necessary because of different amounts or kinds of subject matter included. The benefits of ability grouping to the student are viewed as those of adapting instructional procedures rather than standards. One argument in favor of this response is that it can maintain accuracy and clear communication in the marking system. It does not close the door on the graduation possibilities of a student who has made a sincere effort to do the work. The student has in such cases worked up to capacity and has learned more about an important field of study than if he had not taken the subject at all. Difficulties, however, are that failure implies to many people some moral deficiency and that the recording of a failing mark stands as a kind of condemnation of the student. Low achievement on the part of a student who has made a conscientious effort, however, should be viewed objectively in intellectual rather than in moral terms. From this standpoint it might be advisable to use the numbers 1, 2, 3, 4, and 5 rather than the letter marks A, B, C, D, and F. The use of the F symbol tends to mean failure, since the letter E would serve as well and be more consistent with the other letters. In some schools the letter E was used for conditions, but this practice is rarely followed today.

5. In this response the report card is replaced by the teacher-parent-student conference. The conference makes possible the discussion of the student's achievement in relation to his ability and effort in a manner that is practically impossible to achieve through report card symbols. Attention may be directed not only to the student's achievement, but to his progress and growth. In the light of these considerations, the teacher makes recommendations as to whether or not the student's work merits graduation credit. Records may be kept of the student's achievement on standardized tests.

passed. It may require three years of English, but permit the student to submit four, one of which has been failed.

Another device used in a few schools is to give a D— mark to a student who has worked up to capacity, but still below some minimum standard of achievement. A course with a D— grade may be used for graduation credit.

These and other data may be sent to colleges or prospective employers.

The conference system is used in many elementary schools, often as a supplement to the report card. It is not soft pedagogy. Full and sufficient attention can be directed to areas of study in which students need to improve. The major requirement, however, is that the teacher have a chance to know the student. This is possible in the self-contained elementary school classroom where the teacher works with 30 to 40 children. High school teachers usually have five classes of 30 each, or a total of 150 different students. It is practically impossible for the teacher to know so many students well enough to hold conferences that mean anything; in fact, it is practically impossible even to schedule and hold conferences. The conference system can be effectively used in high schools only when scheduling arrangements cut down the number of different groups and the number of students with whom the teacher works.

Each of the foregoing responses has its peculiar difficulties. Response Number 1 tends to eliminate the constants, while response Number 2 tends to eliminate students. In response Number 3 the marking system confuses all concerned. In response Number 4 the school seems to be contradicting itself by failing some students and still permitting them to be graduated without making up or repeating the failures. The difficulties in response Number 5 are mainly administrative, since a valid case can be made for the conference system on intrinsic grounds. On the whole, if the administrative difficulties can be overcome, response 5 appears to provide the most satisfactory solution. When this is not the case, our best possibilities lie in response 4, since this makes it possible to base marks on achievement without denying low-ability students the opportunity of graduation.

In addition there is a criticism that might be leveled at responses 3, 4, and 5: namely, that they lower graduation standards. The validity of this criticism depends on what we want the high school diploma to represent and accomplish. It is probably fair to state that the various adjustments introduced by high schools in response to student differences have brought about a diploma that communicates practically nothing about student achievement. It is a certificate of attendance and reasonably good character. This has been brought about largely through the use of response Number 3, but it would be equally true under 4 and 5. It is an inevitable state of affairs under our assumptions that the vast majority of youth should attend high school and complete the program through the twelfth grade. But it need not be regarded as a ruinous state of affairs. We have other ways of providing information about students to college officials, prospective employers, and the like.

Let it be noted that colleges felt compelled to administer their own entrance examinations even in the days of strict graduation policies. No diploma, taken by itself, regardless of the standards used in granting or withholding it, tells us anything about the various strengths and weaknesses of a given student, both of which are important points for the prospective employer and the college admissions officer. It is possible, of course, to put additional information on the diploma. Special designations such as "graduated with distinction" and "graduated with highest distinction" provide desirable recognition for a few students. One may also record the rank in class of every graduating student, but this does not provide specific information about achievement in given subjects. Employers who hire typists want to know what the student achieved in typewriting. Admissions officers in engineering schools want to know about specific achievement in mathematics and science. Such information could, of course, be provided by printing the entire transcript of courses and marks on each diploma. This is unnecessary, since transcripts may be sent directly by the school to prospective employers and colleges.

The Conant report recommends giving each student a "durable record of the courses studied in four years and the grades obtained," this to be, however, a document separate from the diploma."[20] In addition, the report suggests the possibility of placing a seal or notation on the diplomas of students who make an honors average in the sequence of courses recommended for academically talented students.[21] The report recommends against the use of rank in

[20] Conant, *op. cit.,* p. 50.
[21] *Ibid.,* p. 67.

class since "in many schools the desire to rank high has led bright students to elect easy courses in order to obtain high grades."[22] These recommendations of the Conant report are worthy of study; if any special recognition symbol is placed on the diploma, it is better to have it represent the achievement of the student in relation to a defined standard than in relation to other students. Eliminating rank-in-class designation would resolve a number of practical difficulties. Whether or not the seal of recognition should be confined to students in a particular sequence of studies is another matter. Achievement based on a defined standard might well be recognized in any valid program of studies.

A school with an adequate testing and record system can supply valuable information which supplements that provided by marks. Standardized achievement tests based on national norms are now available in practically all instructional fields. Aptitude tests are also available, although these need to be interpreted with some reserve and caution. Vocational interest scores supply valuable information. But we are not confined to tests. Teachers' judgments about students on such important matters as work habits, responsibility, and initiative can be summarized by counselors and under appropriate conditions made available to colleges and employers.

It is possible to use differentiated diplomas in connection with the adjusted marking system or in response Number 4. One kind is given to the student whose work comes up to a given expectation level, the other to the student who falls below it. One is standard, the other (in the minds of the student and the public) substandard. One document is sometimes called a diploma, the other a certificate. It is doubtful that much is gained by these practices so far as communication about the individual student is concerned.

We might, of course, do away entirely with the diploma, as well as with the other ceremonies of high school graduation. This would probably be a mistake. High school graduation is an important point in the life of the adolescent and of his parents. Symbolically, it is important to the same degree that going to high school is in itself important. After the music and the speeches of

[22] *Ibid.*, p. 66.

graduation day (or night) have died away, the diploma remains as the tangible symbol of all that high school has meant. It is a scrap of paper only to the cynic who has lost most of his human sentiment and compassion.

SHAPING THE PROGRAM
TO ACADEMICALLY GIFTED STUDENTS

The shape of the high school program should fit not only the low-ability student and the so-called average, but also those who are gifted or superior. This may include modifying graduation requirements, as well as other adaptations in the school program. Gifted students, however, pose no obvious problems, except for the few who become disciplinary cases through boredom or lack of work. But although the situation of the gifted student is less obvious, it is no less real or important. The people of the United States came to a sudden realization of this around 1950, since which time the gifted have become a national concern discussed with much vigor not only in educational journals, but in general magazines and daily newspapers. We have before us now a number of plans, approaches, and systems, most of which are based on ideas expressed long before the present popular interest developed.

There is, however, no typical gifted student, any more than there is a typical low-ability or average student. Gifts may be academic, artistic, mechanical, social, and athletic. Nor is any one of these necessarily all of one piece. Academic gifts may be mathematical, scientific, historical, literary, and the like. Some individuals are consistently gifted, average, or below average in many lines of endeavor. Others may be gifted in some respects, average in others, and in still others, possibly below average. Our commitment to individuality means fostering the development of many kinds of gifts or talents. Nevertheless, it is academic superiority, both general and special, which is most likely to be overlooked since it lacks the spectacular qualities that bring other kinds of gifts to public attention. It is all the more important, therefore, that we direct our attention particularly to the student whose gifts and interests run along academic or intellectual lines.

Identification of the academically gifted is not so easy as it looks.[23] Let us assume that it can be done and consider the question of what should be done for, by, and about the gifted student once he is identified. Varying approaches to the education of the gifted have been not only widely discussed in the literature, but used in a number of school systems, singly and in combination.

1. One approach which has gone through cycles of popularity and rejection is that of acceleration. The accelerated student may be graduated and sent to college ahead of the usual age for college entrance. One way to accomplish this is by permitting the gifted student to take five or more subjects each semester, possibly supplemented by summer school attendance. Another way is to have the high school waive its graduation requirements and the college its entrance requirements. This has been done in several experimental programs. The ever-recurring question of course is whether or not younger students are ready for college in terms of social and physical development. And the ever-recurring answer is that it depends on the individual student. Much depends also on the availability of colleges near the students' homes. A community with a good junior college as part of the school system, or with a regular four-year college or university close at hand, can probably go much farther along these lines than one without such conveniently located resources. For the most part, however, the tend-

[23] If a single measure such as the IQ is used, there still remains the question of the cutoff point. Shall the gifted be defined as the top 5 percent, 10 percent, 15 percent, or what? But the use of a single measure is in itself open to question. "The most common error in identification is based on the assumption that mental organization is a simple unitary thing and that IQ or some other single measure is about as perfect an index of ability as can be obtained. There is ample evidence that the mental organization is highly complex and that single measure tests are apt to conceal important differences. As rapidly as tests or devices are developed to assess different types of aptitudes, they should be used. The potential theoretical physicist and the potential distinguished historian may differ in important ways which can be detected early, and it is unfortunate if, by using a single measure, we tend to pick a person who will be only the average physicist or historian." John M. Stalnaker, "Methods of Identification—The Complexity of the Problem," in *The Identification and Education of the Academically Talented Student in the American Secondary School*, The Conference Report, National Education Association, February, 1958, pp. 24–25. Stalnaker goes on to the following conclusion. "The task of properly identifying all of these academically talented students who, given the chance, will become the educated, trained thinkers of tomorrow is no small one. It can be done, however, and we are on our way to doing it now." *Ibid.*, pp. 26–27.

ency has been to seek ways of accelerating the education of the gifted student in high school itself.

2. The gifted may be placed by themselves in separate high schools. These high schools may be specialized in the sense that they provide programs aimed at certain kinds of gifts or talents. The Bronx High School of Science in New York City is a specialized high school for the gifted. It provides a full academic program, but encourages specialization or majoring in the sciences. Specialized high schools may emphasize areas other than the traditional academic disciplines. One high school in the New York City system is devoted to vocational training in the dramatic arts. A vocational high school then can be a specialized high school for the gifted in that particular field. On the other hand, separate high schools for the gifted may be comprehensive in the sense of providing a wide variety of courses and programs. These are possible in fairly large cities, whereas the specialized schools for the gifted are possible only in the largest metropolitan centers. Either kind is open to the objection that many students must spend time traveling long distances to other parts of the city rather than attending high schools closer to home. On the other hand, this is probably no more time than is spent by many rural students on school buses. Separate schools are also criticized on grounds of being undemocratic. This depends on what a given person regards as democratic criteria and how he interprets separate high schools in relation to them. Possibilities of controversy along this line are endless. This much is clear. Setting up a separate high school for superior students will not in itself produce better education for those students unless the programs and practices of the school are developed accordingly. It is possible to use these programs and practices in high schools that include not only the gifted, but other kinds of students, except for vocational programs of a highly specialized kind, such as the dramatic arts. These demand separate schools. Not even large metropolitan centers can provide such a specialized program in every school.

3. The gifted may be kept in conventional high schools, but placed in separate sections of the required courses and those elective courses open to all students. Traditional ability grouping

usually sets up three levels, high, middle, and low. The high groups include not only the very superior student, but those who may be only slightly above average. It is also possible to arrange the grouping to produce sections made up entirely of the highest level students. Ability grouping has of course long been a controversial matter argued along lines similar to those concerning separate high schools.[24] Whether or not ability grouping provides better education for the gifted depends on what is actually done in the special sections. The expectation is that gifted students will not only cover additional materials in the subject but also penetrate into the deeper meanings of the content usually covered. Teachers will make greater use of long-term assignments, special projects, and supplementary reading than is possible with other students.

4. Gifted students may be required or strongly urged to take a particular sequence of courses. The Conant report recommends

[24] Much depends on the system of ability grouping used. Under one system, students are placed in groups that stay together throughout the entire school day, with the bases for identification being intelligence or reading tests, or both. This is open to criticism on two grounds: (1) it accentuates the awareness of the grouping on the part of the students; (2) it disregards individual differences in ability from one subject to the next. A different system of ability grouping is one that groups by subjects. This is more complicated to handle administratively, but it is more defensible.

In his summary of the discussions at the National Conference on the Identification and Education of the Academically Talented Student in the American Secondary School, Conant reported much agreement on this point as far as it concerns the superior student. "There was a strong sentiment in all the working groups for arranging classes so that a pupil of high ability in a given subject—English, for example—will study this subject together with other students of comparable ability. The same would be true in the social studies and in mathematics, foreign language, and science if these subjects are elected by many pupils of less ability than those we are here considering. That this is a highly important conclusion goes without saying.

"Such organization of instruction should not be confused, of course, with a mechanical separation of all pupils with an IQ above an arbitrary value into a fixed curriculum as a block. The sentiment against any such arrangement appeared to be as strong as the sentiment for a grouping according to ability subject by subject." James B. Conant, "Conference Summary." *Ibid.*, pp. 137–138.

The same point of view is expressed in another recent report. "In courses in which there is a wide spread of student ability—in English and other courses required of all students—there should be sections arranged according to aptitude *in that subject*. It is important to note that a student might be in a fast-learning group in mathematics, in a second group for history, a third group in French. This is a very different thing from arbitrarily separating all students with intelligence scores above a certain figure and placing them in a separate curriculum as a block." Rockefeller Brothers Fund America at Mid-Century Series, *The Pursuit of Excellence: Education and the Future of America,* Panel Report V of the Special Studies Project, Doubleday & Company, Inc., 1958, p. 31.

that the academically talented students, defined as the top 15 percent nationally, take four years of mathematics, three years of science, four years of one foreign language, and the generally required courses in English and social studies.[25] This would be accomplished through individual counseling rather than formal prescription, thereby making it possible to take individual differences into account. An approach of this kind could be used in a comprehensive high school and does not require special schools for the gifted.

5. Instruction for the gifted may be enriched in regular classes. The attempt here is to do many of the same kinds of things more conveniently done in special sections. To some extent this calls for grouping within a class along lines used in many elementary schools. Again, the elementary teacher under the self-contained classroom system has 30 to 40 students; the high school teacher usually has 150. A high school teacher attempting to enrich the program for the gifted in unselected groups is seriously handicapped.

6. Advanced courses going beyond the scope of the usual high school studies may be developed for superior students. Students taking such courses may on the basis of examination be granted advanced placement or credit at the college level.[26] Rearrangement of the entire sequence of courses for gifted students is sometimes desirable in a given instructional field. Superior students in mathematics do not, for example, ordinarily need five semesters to do the work represented by algebra, plane geometry, and intermediate algebra. Time saved at these beginning levels provides opportunities for studying analytic geometry and possibly differential calculus

[25] Conant, *The American High School Today, op. cit.*, p. 57.

[26] The major effort along these lines of recent years is the Advanced Placement Program of the College Entrance Examination Board. "During the school year 1956–57, 2,100 pupils from 212 schools took approximately 4,200 advanced-placement examinations; 95 of these 212 schools were generally classified as comprehensive high schools." Lloyd S. Michael and other contributors, "Secondary-School Programs," National Society for the Study of Education, Fifty-Seventh Yearbook, pt. 2, *Education for the Gifted*, The Society, 1958, p. 266. Sometimes arrangements are made by individual colleges. The University of Buffalo has had such a program in effect since 1932. Malcolm S. MacLean and Robert B. Carlson, "College and University Programs for the Gifted." *Ibid.*, pp. 321–322.

in the senior year. Such modifications may be made not only in mathematics, but also in other fields.

7. The gifted student may be excused from some of the required subjects on the basis of examinations, thereby permitting him to spend more time in his field of special interest. Suppose, for example, that a gifted student with a special interest in science is so advanced in English at the end of the tenth grade that he can pass a twelfth-grade attainment examination. Why then, it may be argued, should he spend two more years in required English? If excused from this requirement, he would have more time for science, or possibly for other subjects he might otherwise not take. The same opportunity, of course, should be available to the student with a special interest in English who can meet his science requirement on an examination basis.

8. Independent study arrangements may be set up either in connection with regular classes or in place of some of them. If the student is registered in a class (either required or elective), he may be released from regular class attendance to work on reading or laboratory projects under the direction of the teacher. Or the student may register directly for independent study under the direction of a teacher without relation to a scheduled class. Independent study, either in connection with a class or as a separate registration, demands careful supervision by teachers; adequate provisions must be made in the loads of teachers who assume such responsibilities.

9. Educational opportunities for the gifted may be extended through appropriate use of other curricular resources, such as extraclass activities, community-service projects, and school-related work experience. Student clubs related to the instructional fields are stock items in the traditional extraclass activities program and have long offered stimulation and guidance for gifted students. Members of the community with special talents and experience are sometimes available to help sponsor the clubs and to work with students on projects. This has the additional value of engaging gifted adolescents in worthwhile activities with adults. Another medium for this is the community-service project. Gathering, treating, and interpreting information from community surveys provide

challenging activities for gifted students with adult supervision. Selected work-experience opportunities, designed particularly for the gifted student, not only contribute to academic learning, but help supplement the vocational guidance facilities of the school.

It is likely that acceleration will remain an isolated phenomenon in the school systems of our country. High schools for the gifted in special fields are possible only in the largest metropolitan centers; even comprehensive high schools for the gifted demand good-sized populations in small geographic areas. Most communities will probably continue to provide for the gifted in comprehensive high schools serving student bodies with wide ranges of ability. Within these we shall find varying points of view concerning ability grouping, but it is unlikely that many schools will go beyond the conventional ability grouping of the three-level type. Exceptionally gifted students will for the most part take their constants in classes with students in the top third of the ability distribution. The most promising frontiers then lie in the latter four of the approaches stated in the foregoing paragraphs: the development of special advanced courses with the possibility of college credit; exemption of superior students from required subjects on the basis of achievement examinations; independent study arrangements; and a creative use of extraclass activities, community-service projects, and school-related work experience. In small high schools, special advanced courses will have very small enrollments. This will require a good deal of sympathetic understanding on the part of administrators, school boards, and the public of the importance of such provisions. Even so, there is a minimum school enrollment below which such provisions can hardly be made; independent study, however, is always a possibility.

There are other features of high schools that should be generously developed for the benefit of all students, but are particularly critical in the education of the gifted. One of these is the school library. No matter what special provisions might or might not be made, the gifted student with encouragement can find his own way to better education provided he is plentifully supplied with the most important of all resources, books. The need will of course vary from community to community, depending on the quality of public library services available, but no school can abdicate its responsibility completely to the public library. Another important feature consists of science laboratories and equipment. Careful selection is of course mandatory in smaller schools. Of much importance also is the provision of art and music resources: recordings, films, musical instruments, and art materials. Naturally, these things are difficult to provide in very small high schools, all of which underscores the importance of school district reorganization, supplemented by county-wide or regional services.

The situations of both gifted and low-ability students have one thing in common. Both demand that the shape of the high school program be flexible and adaptable rather than rigid and unyielding in character and application. The same thing is true, however, when we consider the mythical average student. Every student, gifted, average, or below average, is a unique individual who deserves an individual fit. This means that traditions, even important traditions, will often need modification where the individual student is concerned. Specific traditions, however, can be safely modified or disregarded only in the light of criteria that reflect the broader traditions of secondary education in our culture. Valid modifications can be made only by those who have sympathetically understood and participated in the broader traditions, particularly as those are reflected in a generous and humane conception of what our high schools are for. To adapt the general shape of the high school program to the individual student we must first have a general shape to adapt. Adaptations cannot be made from chaos.

Bibliography

Abraham, Willard, *Common Sense About Gifted Children,* Harper & Brothers, 1958.

Association for Supervision and Curriculum Development, 1956 Yearbook, *What Shall the High School Teach?* The Association, 1956, chaps. 3, 5.

Chase, Francis S., and Anderson, Harold A. (eds.), *The High School in a New Era,* The University of Chicago Press, 1958, pp. 362–388.

Conant, James B., *The American High School Today,* McGraw-Hill Book Company, Inc., 1959.

Conant, James B. (chairman of the conference), *The Identification and Education of the Academically Talented Student in the American Secondary School,* The Conference Report, National Education Association, February, 1958.

Cutts, Norma E., and Moseley, Nicholas, *Teaching the Bright and Gifted,* Prentice-Hall, Inc., 1957.

De Haan, Robert F., and Havighurst, Robert J., *Educating Gifted Children,* University of Chicago Press, 1957.

National Society for the Study of Education, Fifty-seventh Yearbook, pt. 2, *Education for the Gifted,* The Society, 1958.

Nickel, Kenneth E., "Better Education for Nonacademic Pupils," *The North Central Association Quarterly,* April, 1957, pp. 355–384.

Rickover, H. G., *Education and Freedom,* E. P. Dutton and Company, Inc., 1959.

Tyler, Leona E., *The Psychology of Human Differences,* Appleton-Century-Crofts, Inc., 1956.

Witty, Paul (ed.), *The Gifted Child,* The American Association for Gifted Children, D. C. Heath and Company, 1951.

Wrightstone, J. Wayne, *Class Organization for Instruction, What Research Says to the Teacher,* No. 13, Department of Classroom Teachers and the American Educational Research Association of the National Education Association, May, 1957.

CHAPTER 7

The Subject Organization of the Classroom Studies

A group of students meeting with a teacher on a regular schedule for lectures, recitations, discussions, and other activities provides the most familiar symbol of schooling. It is an almost universal feature of schools of all times and places. There have been exceptions. Oxford and Cambridge, for example, have relied heavily at times on a combination of independent study and individual conferences, supplemented by occasional lectures at which attendance was voluntary. In the high schools of our country, however, classroom studies[1] have been and are the most widely used single means in the curriculum. They give to any high school program its distinctive outline or shape.

Just how the materials of the classroom studies should be arranged and organized for use remains the key question in curriculum planning. In our time, subject organization[2] is the most familiar. It has enjoyed predominance in most periods of educational history, but has declined in others, at least at the secondary level. The term "subject" is easy to understand, but difficult to define. It may refer to a particular course, such as algebra, or to a family of courses, such as mathematics. And a single subject of course, such as physics, may be subdivided into specialized courses at advanced

[1] A classroom of course may be a shop, a gymnasium, or an open field, that is, anywhere a class meets. It does not need the traditional "four walls."
[2] Not subject-matter organization as it is sometimes called.

levels of instruction and study. Let us say that a subject is a body of subject matter, facts, generalizations, ideas, processes, or skills, selected and organized for instructional purposes in relation to some aspect of human activity and experience. Families of subjects such as mathematics, the natural sciences, social studies, and the like are more conveniently referred to as instructional fields, although the distinction between subjects and instructional fields is not a rigid one to be maintained at any or all times.

Given pieces or collections of subject matter may appear in many different subjects. Any piece of subject matter, or any subject, may appear trivial or significant to various observers, depending on the criteria used in making such judgments. Since there are many aspects of human activity and experience, there are many possible subjects and instructional fields. Subjects have appeared, disappeared, and reappeared, depending on what people in various ages and societies have considered worth teaching in school. Those who agree on the subject organization may not and in fact have not agreed either on the specific selection of materials or on the packages in which the materials should be wrapped.

The subject organization as we know it today contains many modern innovations. Much of what we consider traditional dates no farther back than the nineteenth century. Its origins in western society, however, are customarily traced to the Greeks and to the Greek passion for creating, organizing, and explaining human knowledge and skill.

There is no period of equal length in all the centuries of Western history before the eighteenth which has been so vigorously creative as the one under consideration, and there is no period of equal length, without any exception, which created more of those cultural elements which live on in the life of our contemporary society. It is a great period because it staged the first crisis of rational enlightenment which the Western world experienced. It is great from the standpoint of its production of literary forms and masterpieces of literary art. It is great for its cultivation of the fine arts. It is great as the maturing period of our traditional Western philosophy of life. And for the student of education it is specifically important as the period during which were created, for the first time, and as a totally new resource of human cultivation, the materials of secondary and higher education.[3]

Greek education included a variety of literary, mathematical, philosophical, and scientific studies, plus music and athletics. Taken over by the Romans with some selection and modification, these were shaken down into two major categories, the *trivium* (grammar, rhetoric, and logic) and the *quadrivium* (arithmetic, geometry, astronomy, and music), which come to us through the latter Graeco-Roman period as the seven liberal arts. These fixed the definition of the subject organization in the early medieval period.

This canon of the proper studies, which was adopted by the monastic and other mediaeval schools, is of so much importance as to demand a detailed account both of its origin and its content. It was a gradual evolution from Graeco-Roman days, but became the especial topic for many treatises during the fifth and sixth centuries. The discrimination of these liberal studies may be said to have begun with *Plato,* whose scheme of education included two groups of subjects—the lower, consisting of gymnastics, musical practice, and letters, and the higher, made up of arithmetic, geometry, musical theory, and astronomy. These "liberal" subjects, during the later days of Greece and the Roman Republic, gradually combined with the "practical" studies of the sophists,—rhetoric and dialectic, and, after various changes, the pagan course settled down about the beginning of the Christian era into grammar (or literature), rhetoric, and dialectic, arithmetic, geometry, music, and astronomy. It is known, for example, that when the Roman *Varro* (116–27 B.C.) wrote upon the Hellenized school curriculum, he included all seven, although he added also medicine and architecture.[4]

The mood of the later middle ages, however, became intensely practical. In the universities, for example, the three major fields were theology, medicine, and law, and these were primarily vocational in character and aim. It is not clear to what extent the seven liberal arts prevailed as strictly categorized subjects even in

[3] Edward H. Reisner, *Historical Foundations of Modern Education,* The Macmillan Company, 1927, pp. 42–43.
[4] Frank P. Graves, *A History of Education During the Middle Ages and the Transition to Modern Times,* The Macmillan Company, 1914, p. 15.

the preparatory or grammar schools. Latin grammar, of course, was a major item, not only for university preparation but for vocational success and occupational mobility in many kinds of jobs. For students in northern European countries, this meant gaining ease and familiarity in the use of a strange tongue, by no means an easy task. The accomplishment of it left somewhat less time and energy for the beauties of literature and the philosophical overtones of language use. The Latin, furthermore, was that of the middle ages, not of classical literature. With the coming of the humanistic renaissance of the fifteenth and sixteenth centuries, the classical Latin was reëstablished, as was the study of classical Greek. The curricular struggle ended in the victory of the humanists, but the humanistic secondary school became even more language-centered. Mathematics survived, but more or less as a poor relation, somewhat like an extracurricular activity.[5] The other "liberal arts" were absorbed by language study or ceased to exist. The "trivium" outlasted the "quadrivium," but even grammar, logic, and rhetoric were not necessarily organized as subjects. Classroom studies were organized with courses centered on the study of particular authors or books. The contents of these books were integrated around the single thread of language study. If this was subject organization at all, it was an extreme variant of it, not the multisubject organization we know today.

In spite of seventeenth- and eighteenth-century developments in modern science, the secondary curriculum remained for the most part centered in language studies, into which of course the vernacular was not admitted. The only major exceptions in the English-speaking world were the nonconformist academies. It was not until the nineteenth century that the gates burst and the subjects came once more into their own, although with names that differed from the old seven liberal arts. Among these were English, history, modern languages, and the physical and biological sciences. Each of these had to fight its way into the secondary curriculum against considerable resistance. Even recently some have considered the grammar and literature of one's mother tongue as not worthy

[5] Even in the early nineteenth century mathematics and a few other subjects were listed as "extras."

of study in school, particularly in the secondary school or college.[6]

The nineteenth century witnessed also the introduction of those instructional fields characterized as non-academic, such as industrial arts, business, agriculture, the fine arts, physical education, and home economics, the latter under the now obsolete name of domestic science. In the present century all these have become standard equipment in many high schools. This acceptance has completed the broad outline of the classroom studies as we know them in secondary schools today.

Development of courses within subject organization nevertheless goes on continuously. This does not necessarily mean new subjects in the sense of additions. Much curriculum effort has centered on the attempt to find broader patterns combining two or more subjects. These courses are often known as broad fields.[7] Sometimes they are referred to as the broad fields organization. This is not, however, a different way of organizing classroom studies, for broad fields are based on categories of knowledge and skill. They are part of the subject organization and in fact are usually regarded as subjects after the newness wears off.[8]

[6] "Why, then, is it that 'courses in English' should hold so large a place in the newest type of institutional organization? They do so for a very simple reason. Under the conditions that we have been describing, great masses of ineducable people come into our institutions. They must be kept there, and must nominally be kept busy with something or other as *pro forma* justification for keeping them. Therefore something has to be found for them that they can do, and this is a hard matter because they can do almost nothing. One thing they can do, albeit after a very poor fashion, is to read; that is to say, they can make their way more or less uncertainly down a printed page; and therefore 'courses in English' have come into their present extraordinary vogue." Albert Jay Mock, *The Theory of Education in the United States,* the Page-Barbour lectures for 1931 at the University of Virginia, Harcourt Brace and Company, 1932, pp. 86–87.

[7] Broad fields courses should not be confused with the families of courses known as "instructional fields." Within an instructional field, each course may be taught separately. Mathematics, for example, is an instructional field housing algebra, arithmetic, geometry, and the like. A broad fields course is one made from existing subjects taken from one or more instructional field families. Sometimes a broad fields course carries the title of the instructional field, for example, general mathematics. The terminology is tricky: Social Studies II in a high school schedule may be a broad fields course, or on the other hand it may be simply the schedule designation for the subject of world history.

[8] Various ways of interpreting the broad fields are found in educational writing. With reference to elementary curriculum, Herrick, Goodlad, Eberman, and Estvan regard subjects and broad fields in the same context. "Both subject and broad field forms of curriculum organization are based on the same kind of curriculum thinking.

Such broad fields courses usually reflect the conviction that the subjects as traditionally constituted are too narrowly drawn. As usually developed, they grow out of the application of two approaches: correlation and fusion. The term "correlation" refers to attempts to draw subjects closer together by establishing their connections and relationships. Fusion refers to the creation of a new category in which the combined subjects lose their separate identities. Correlation may be roughly compared to a physical mixture, such as that of sand and sugar; fusion to a chemical compound, such as water, whose properties are not the same as those of its elements.

A familiar example of correlation in high school is the interrelating of history and literature. There are at least five possible administrative arrangements.

1. The teachers plan the work together, but do not necessarily have the same students. Each teacher, however, uses some material from the other teacher's field.

2. The teachers plan their work together and have the same group of students, but not at the same time. Section A may have literature the first period with the English teacher and history the second with the history teacher.

3. The teachers have separate classes on a criss-cross schedule that permits combining the groups on occasion. Take two groups A and B, and two teachers X and Y. Group A has English with teacher X during the first period, while group B has history with teacher Y at the same time. In the second period, group A has teacher Y in history and group B has teacher X in English. When desired, groups A and B may meet with both teachers, X and Y, for the two periods, possibly for films or a field trip.

Differences between these two subject-oriented approaches are determined on the extent to which broader areas of subject matter are considered." Virgil E. Herrick, John L. Goodlad, Frank J. Estvan, and Paul W. Eberman, *The Elementary School,* Prentice-Hall, Inc., 1956, p. 134. Smith, Stanley, and Shores treat the correlated curriculum and broad fields curriculum as "modifications of the subject curriculum." B. Othanel Smith, William O. Stanley, and J. Harlan Shores, *Fundamentals of Curriculum Development,* revised, World Book Company, 1957, pp. 252–262. Hopkins places broad fields between the end points of a continuum ranging from subject curriculum to what he calls experience curriculum, with some broad fields being closer to subjects and others to the experience designation. L. Thomas Hopkins, *Interaction: The Democratic Process,* D. C. Heath and Company, 1941, pp. 18–19 and chap. 2.

4. Two teachers meet with the class for two periods and co-operate not only in the planning but in the teaching. This is obviously an expensive arrangement and not likely to be widely used.

5. One teacher, with competence in both fields, teaches the class for both periods.[9]

The example of history and literature is that of a broad field achieved through correlating not only two subjects, but two instructional fields. Correlation may also be attempted between two subjects in the same instructional field: for example, geography and history. Courses of this kind are sometimes found in junior high schools; physics and chemistry may be combined to form a "physical science" course in senior high school. Twelfth-grade courses called "problems of democracy" and the long-established tenth-grade biology are examples of broad fields on a single-period basis. English as we know it today represents the combination of previously taught separate subjects of composition, literature, and grammar.[10]

Some of the broad fields courses in the foregoing paragraph have been developed around the fusion rather than the correlation principle. It is necessary to examine the particular subject matter in such a course to identify the possible motivations of the curriculum workers who developed it. Biology, for example, may consist of separate units in zoology and botany with attempts to draw interrelationships, or it may be developed around principles of life and growth that presumably cut across or apply to both plant and animal life. Similarly, the twelfth-grade American problems course may consist of separate units on government, sociology, and economics, or it may be organized around problems or topics that demand the use of political, social, or economic data and principles. The line of distinction between correlation and fusion is often a thin one. One reason for this may be that the fusion principle is

[9] This does not mean that every two-period or three-period class is an example of correlation. Such an arrangement may be used within a strict subject framework for the purpose of reducing the number of different students the teacher works with in the school day. Or it may be used with those reorganizations of classroom studies that go beyond modifying the subjects.

[10] Correlation does not of course depend on the setting up of broad fields. Every good teacher "correlates," that is, he relates the subject matter of his own course to that of other courses.

easier to name than to apply. The idea of creating new courses from pieces of old ones without having the pieces stick out is a fascinating one intellectually. Practically, it is difficult to keep the pieces from showing.

Whether broad fields courses are set up on the correlation or fusion principles, however, they remain basically in subject organization. They are really subjects organized on broader bases than those we have come to think of as traditional. When they are new, we think of them as different, but when we get used to them we think of them as subjects. Few people today think of English, biology, or American problems as broad fields. Scheduling arrangements and course titles have something to do with the ways they are regarded. Those which settle down into single periods are more likely to be thought of as subjects; those which occupy double periods as broad fields. Those with titles suggestive of the previously existing subjects, such as biology, seem more in the context of subject organization; those with unfamiliar titles, such as "social living,"[11] carry broad field connotations.

Somewhat more dramatic efforts in the broad fields have been made in college-level survey courses, particularly in the freshman and sophomore years. They appear under such titles as Man in Society, Man and the Physical Universe, and the like. Such courses reflect a desire to get away from fragmentation, which is often more apparent in the two-day and three-day a week college schedule than it is in the high school. They possibly also grow out of a desire for a fresh organization of some materials students may have encountered in high school courses. Possibly the college is the more appropriate place for such broad surveys in that some previous knowledge of the materials may be assumed.

CRITICISMS OF THE SUBJECT ORGANIZATION

A number of writers on curriculum have summarized, catalogued, and reported both the major criticisms directed against subject organization and the arguments set forth on its behalf.[12]

---

[11] A popular title for combined English and social studies courses in the 1930's and 40's.

[12] For reports on and discussions of many of these criticisms see, for example, the following; these writers do not necessarily agree with the criticisms. Hopkins, *op. cit.,*

The criticisms break into two groups, one of which centers on the practical consequences of subject organization, the other on its inherent characteristics. They appear overwhelming at first glance, and one is tempted to wonder how the subject organization has managed to survive with all these alleged inadequacies.

Some of the "practical consequence" criticisms tend to center on ways subjects have been misused. The accumulated evils of inflexible, inhumane, and inconsequential teaching have been ascribed to the subject organization. As Featherstone points out, however, "Teaching a subject need not be a mere matter of expounding what has already been learned. Learning a subject need not be a mere matter of absorption, an undergoing of verbal bombardment, or a spongelike soaking up of knowledge for mere possession. The means of education need not become the end."[13] The dangers of excessive "verbalism" were recognized, for example, by Thomas Huxley in the following passage.

I remember, in my youth, there were detestable books which ought to have been burned by the hands of the common hangman, for they contained questions and answers to be learned by heart, of this sort, "What is a horse? The horse is termed *Equus caballus;* belongs to the class Mammalia; order, Pachydermata; family, Solidungula." Was any human being wiser for learning that magic formula? Was he not more foolish, inasmuch as he was deluded into taking words for knowledge? It is that kind of teaching that one wants to get rid of, and banished out of science. Make it as little as you like, but unless that which is taught is based on actual observation and familiarity with facts, it is better left alone.[14]

Notice what Huxley "wants to get rid of." It is "that kind of teaching." He wants it "banished out of science." But he does not propose banishing either the subject of science or the subject organization itself.

---

p. 50; William B. Featherstone, *A Functional Curriculum for Youth,* American Book Co., 1950, pp. 93–112; Smith, Stanley, Shores, *op. cit.,* pp. 244–249; Harold Alberty, *Reorganizing the High School Curriculum,* The Macmillan Company, 1953 (rev.), pp. 134–137; J. Galen Saylor and William M. Alexander, *Curriculum Planning for Better Teaching and Learning,* Rinehart & Company, Inc., 1954, pp. 257–264.

[13] Featherstone, *op. cit.,* p. 112.

[14] Thomas H. Huxley, *Science and Education: Essays,* "On Science and Art in Relation to Education," D. Appleton and Company, 1897, p. 170.

There is one "practical consequence" criticism, however, that reflects not poor teaching but certain practices in curriculum planning and school administration. It is the overlapping of subject matter from one subject or field to another. We should remember that high school departments were once urged to develop subject matter related to as many school objectives as possible. Many a department has conscientiously sought to include something for most of or all the Cardinal Principles, the Ten Imperative Needs of Youth, and the like.[15] This practically guarantees that some materials will turn up in several subjects or fields. Not all such overlapping is necessarily undesirable, but enough of it has been to arouse periodic concern. It can be corrected within the subject organization itself. Such corrections are difficult to bring about, however, when the administrative policies of the school encourage excessive departmental isolation. Curriculum councils with representatives from all departments can do much to offset departmental isolation and to provide means for avoiding waste and undesirable overlapping.

Another curricular difficulty associated with the subject organization is the proliferation of seemingly trivial subjects. The first impulse of those with a pet idea is usually to create a new subject or course. There has been much less of this kind of thing than is ordinarily assumed, and the impulse often comes from interest groups in the general public rather than from teachers. Nevertheless the subject organization does invite this tendency. Of course the critical issue is not as much the proliferation of subjects as the alleged triviality of the material. If the material is really trivial, the application of relevant criteria should help to keep it out of the program. If it is worthwhile, there is no reason why it might not appear as a new subject.

One way to handle important new material is to introduce it into already existing subjects. This should be done only when the material is appropriate to its proposed subject home and only when

---

[15] The full range of objectives for secondary schooling can appropriately serve as criteria for making decisions in any subject. Some of these decisions are those of method, some of content. When objectives are so used, they often provide bases for eliminating materials. What causes the difficulty is the tendency to move deductively from objectives to decisions, rather than inductively from decisions to objectives.

it does not displace other desirable material already in the subject. A good example is driver education. Many schools have tried to incorporate it into English, Civics, and other existing courses. It becomes increasingly apparent that the materials of driver education not only do not belong in those courses, but that they push out materials that do belong there. The more recent tendency is to teach it as a subject by itself.[16]

Probably the most important practical dilemma of the subject organization and one less easily dealt with has been the expansion of human knowledge. As Featherstone says, "It is difficult, if not impossible, through the medium of any reasonable number of ordinary subjects to provide a curriculum of adequate scope and breadth."[17] He recognizes that "certainly not all subjects would have to be taken at one and the same time."[18] Nevertheless, "the number of subjects which any pupil must take in order to have a curriculum of even moderate coverage is fairly large. It is certainly a great deal larger than the conventional 15 or 16 units required for graduation from a conventional high school."[19] The movement toward 20 or so units in the four-year program has been designed in part to meet this difficulty, but the wisdom of requiring this of all students has not yet been demonstrated. Some students should take more than four subjects, while others probably should take only two or three. The important question is whether or not it is necessary for all students to take all desirable subjects. Selection cannot be avoided. Furthermore, the classroom studies, no matter how organized, need not bear the responsibility for all the relevant functions of secondary schooling. There are other means in the curriculum. What may be needed is the identification of those functions for which the classroom studies are particularly designed. Clarification on this point may help in the selection of the con-

---

[16] Many regard this course as trivial. This writer believes the subject matter of driver education meets the test of appropriateness when examined in the light of relevant criteria. It does not follow, however, that driver education should be carried on in the formal classroom program with credit. It can be handled as an activity outside the classroom studies.

[17] Featherstone, *op. cit.*, p. 107.

[18] *Ibid.*

[19] *Ibid.*, pp. 107–108.

stants—those subjects which should be studied by all youth. This is no easy task. It is, however, no more difficult than the task of (1) teaching many more subjects to all students or (2) that of developing an organization of the classroom studies which will contain all the essential subject matter now represented by the complete battery of existing subjects.

In addition to criticisms based on "practical consequences" of "related abuses," there are those which purportedly refer to inherent characteristics of the subject organization. One appearing in many of the reported lists is that subject organization represents the finished products of adults rather than the problems, needs, interests, or motivations of children and youth. The question becomes one of "logical" as against "psychological" organization. Dewey explores this matter in his essay on *The Child and the Curriculum* (1902).[20] After recognizing what he calls "apparent deviations and differences between child and curriculum," he proceeds as follows:

What, then, is the problem? It is just to get rid of the prejudicial notion that there is some gap in kind (as distinct from degree) between the child's experience and the various forms of subject-matter that make up the course of study. From the side of the child, it is a question of seeing how his experience already contains within itself elements—facts and truths—of just the same sort as those entering into the formulated study; and, what is of more importance, of how it contains within itself the attitudes, the motives, and the interests which have operated in developing and organizing the subject-matter to the plane it now occupies. From the side of the studies, it is a question of interpreting them as outgrowths of forces operating in the child's life, and of discovering

[20] John Dewey, *The Child and the Curriculum,* University of Chicago Press, 1902, reprinted in the Phoenix Books Series, *The Child and the Curriculum and The School and Society,* University of Chicago Press, p. 11. Dewey is cited here not as an authority with the final word on the matter, but as one whose analysis on this matter is still about the clearest in educational writing. The fact that it is Dewey who makes it is beside the point. Actually, he seems in some later writings to draw a sharper distinction between logical and psychological, curriculum and child, than he does in the work cited here. See, for example, *Democracy and Education,* The Macmillan Company, 1916, pp. 214–216, and *Experience and Education,* The Macmillan Company, 1938, pp. 86–112. Even in these later writings, however, he puts the emphasis on the interrelationships of these two aspects and on the fact that neither one nor the other should be ignored or neglected.

the steps that intervene between the child's present experience and their richer maturity.

Abandon the notion of subject-matter as something fixed and ready-made in itself, outside the child's experience; cease thinking of the child's experience as also something hard and fast; see it as something fluent, embryonic, vital; and we realize that the child and the curriculum are simply two limits which define a single process. Just as two points define a straight line, so the present standpoint of the child and the facts and truths of studies define instruction. It is continuous reconstruction, moving from the child's present experience out into that represented by the organized bodies of truth that we call studies.

On the face of it, the various studies, arithmetic, geography, language, botany, etc., are themselves experience—they are that of the race. They embody the cumulative outcome of the efforts, the strivings, and the successes of the human race generation after generation. They present this, not as a mere accumulation, not a miscellaneous heap of separate bits of experience, but in some organized and systematized way—that is, as reflectively formulated.

Hence, the facts and truths that enter into the child's present experience and those contained in the subject-matter of studies are the initial and final terms of one reality. To oppose one to the other is to oppose the infancy and maturity of the same growing life; it is to set the moving tendency and the final result of the same process over against each other; it is to hold that the nature and the destiny of the child war with each other.[21]

Much of the criticism of subject organization as psychologically defective turns out to be reiteration of alleged defects in methods of teaching. It becomes another kind of "practical consequence" criticism rather than one based on the inherent characteristics of subjects.

There is, however, one frequently stated criticism truly based on the inherent characteristics of subjects, namely that the subject organization cuts the unity of knowledge or of life itself into separate pieces. This criticism may be answered along the lines expressed here by Featherstone.

But is life all of one piece? Certainly it should be all of one plan with clarity of central purpose and consistency of action from day to

[21] John Dewey, *The Child and the Curriculum,* pp. 11–12.

day and from year to year. In fact, such purposefulness and consistency are the earmarks of a stable, mature, well-integrated personality. But a thing can be all of one plan and still not be all of one piece. A house may consist of numerous rooms housing fairly distinct kinds of life activities but having a great many common characteristics harmoniously related to comfortable, gracious efficient home living. Not even the most modern architects have insisted on turning the house into a single room equipped with furnishings equally well adapted to all and sundry kinds of activities.

Such an analogy can be overdrawn, of course; for life is a growing thing, not a static inert thing like a house. However, to draw another analogy, a tree is a growing thing with a life purpose to survive until full realization of its potential capacities. Its stem is not its tap root, its bark is not its heart, nor are its leaves its seeds. Each part has its own form and its own organic imperatives. All parts contribute harmoniously to the life of the tree.[22]

Undesirable fragmentation can be corrected by developing subjects along broad rather than narrow lines. Overzealous crossbreeding of subjects and fields, however, produces difficulties too. The broad generalizations that govern the relationships among subjects seem obvious to the mature scholar who has worked his way through the separate parts. Whether they are obvious without the parts is another question. Such generalizations provide bases for selection of teaching materials, but do not necessarily determine appropriate ways of organizing them for teaching and learning purposes. The need for differentiation and specialization exists even for the advanced student. There are levels, however, at which broader or more comprehensive patterns may be introduced. Identification of these levels is in part at least a matter to be worked out in each instructional field.

The case against the subject organization cannot then be regarded as conclusive. Most of the criticisms deal with surface characteristics not necessarily inherent in it as a way of organizing classroom studies. Some of the negative features could conceivably occur in other forms of organization. Even the fact that a subject deals with only a part of human knowledge may not necessarily

[22] Featherstone, *op. cit.,* p. 104.

be a defect. But the conclusion that subject organization is not as bad as critics make out does not on the other hand establish it as desirable. There may be nothing against it; possibly there is nothing for it.

ARGUMENTS FOR THE SUBJECT ORGANIZATION

Many writers have also summarized and reported the claimed advantages and strengths of subject organization.[23] Some of the advantages cited are like the criticisms in that they deal with surface features or consequences rather than with inherent characteristics. Some of them appear trivial. In any case they would be useful only if more important reasons for subject organization were agreed upon and somebody wanted to show that it could be readily administered and accepted.

The fact, for example, that it is "generally approved by teachers, parents, and students"[24] may signify nothing more than our being used to it and that it would be uncomfortable to change. Similarly the fact that "the colleges have generally approved and perpetuated the subject-centered curriculum through admission requirements"[25] may mean the colleges have been mistaken. To use the subject organization because it "is backed by long tradition and is widely accepted"[26] is a misuse of tradition. We certainly do not want subject organization just because it is old. Moreover, our present version of it is not as old as it looks.

Some of the arguments reported on behalf of subject organization appear not only to be of a surface nature but of a dubious advantage from an educational standpoint. Hopkins reports, for example, an argument based on objectivity of subject organization.

This objectivity is best exemplified in the ease with which the program is authoritatively administered. All subjects are isolated. Subject matter is organized in advance of teaching. Persons in authority control the learning situation. Emphasis is placed upon unchanging facts and information. Fixed habits and skills are developed. All children are uni-

[23] For example, Alberty, *op. cit.*, pp. 127–134; Saylor and Alexander, *op. cit.*, pp. 253–257; Smith, Stanley, and Shores, *op. cit.*, pp. 250–252; Hopkins, *op. cit.*, p. 50.
[24] Reported by Alberty, *op. cit.*, p. 133.
[25] *Ibid.*, p. 132.
[26] Saylor and Alexander, *op. cit.*, p. 255.

formly exposed to the subject matter. Minimum essentials and grade standards are designated. Credits are determined by the number of class hours of exposure to the subject matter to be covered. The whole organization is governed by a central administrative authority.[27]

With such arguments as these reported by Hopkins advanced on its behalf, the subject organization might well pray to be protected not from its enemies, but from its friends. If such unpleasant characteristics are inevitable in subject organization, we might force ourselves to accept them, but we should indeed be reluctant to parade them as assets. But they are not, as we have noted previously, inevitable. For as Hopkins points out in his discussion of the relationship between subjects and learners, "The difference between the subject and experience curriculums on this point is not that one teaches subjects and ignores learners, or that the other teaches learners and ignores subjects. Each curriculum considers subjects and learners, but in a different way, to a different degree, and with a different emphasis."[28]

Among the arguments reported on behalf of subject organization, however, there are also some that deal with its intrinsic features or characteristics. One of these is that "Systematic organization is essential to the effective interpretation of experience"[29] or, in another form, that "The subjects constitute a logical and effective method of organizing learning and of interpreting and systematizing new knowledge and facts."[30]

This argument sounds good, but is it valid? Dewey explores this question through analogy: that of formal organization of material to a map.

Of what use is this formulated statement of experience? Of what use is the map?

Well, we may first tell what the map is not. The map is not a substitute for a personal experience. The map does not take the place of an actual journey. The logically formulated material of a science or branch of learning, of a study, is no substitute for the having of indi-

[27] Hopkins, *op. cit.,* p. 50.
[28] *Ibid.,* p. 21.
[29] Alberty, *op. cit.,* p. 127.
[30] Saylor and Alexander, *op. cit.,* p. 253.

vidual experiences. The mathematical formula for a falling body does not take the place of personal contact and immediate personal experience with the falling thing. But the map, a summary, an arranged and orderly view of previous experiences, serves as a guide to future experience; it gives direction; it facilitates control; it economizes effort, preventing useless wandering, and pointing out the paths which lead most quickly most certainly to a desired result. Through the map every new traveler may get for his own journey the benefits of the results of others' explorations without the waste of energy and loss of time involved in their wanderings—wanderings which he himself would be obliged to repeat were it not for just the assistance of the objective and generalized record of their performances. That which we call a science or study puts the net product of past experience in the form which makes it most available for the future. It represents a capitalization which may at once be turned to interest. It economizes the working of the mind in every way. Memory is less taxed because the facts are grouped together about some common principle, instead of being connected solely with the varying incidents of their original discovery. Observation is assisted; we know what to look for and where to look. It is the difference between looking for a needle in a haystack, and searching for a given paper in a well-arranged cabinet. Reasoning is directed, because there is a certain general path or line laid out along which ideas naturally march, instead of moving from one chance association to another.[31]

Analogies can be dangerous and misleading, even when advanced by Dewey. They can also be suggestive and helpful, as we believe this one is. For one of the functions of organized education is that of economy of time and effort, the provision of short cuts. True, we can and do learn many things outside of schools, often by direct experience. Exceptional individuals with superior intellectual gifts can over many years learn outside of school what most people learn in school. It is also true that the exceptional individuals who create organized subject matter (and it is a creative act) do so without much help from short cuts. Much of what looks simple and obvious to us today is so only because some people went through the sustained intellectual effort of discovery and formulation. Some repetition of these processes has educational value and

[31] Dewey, *op. cit.,* pp. 20–21.

should be included in every curriculum. But why take the time to relearn and reformulate what others have done before us, as far as the bulk of our education is concerned? Why not benefit from these formulations and go on from there? Subject organization is an enormous saver of time and energy, a short cut we can all use. But a short cut to what? The case for subject organization rests not only on its economy and usability, but on the validity of the purposes to which it might be directed. Are there purposes relevant to the economy of time and effort that subject organization seemingly promises?

This brings us to another argument frequently reported: that "the subject curriculum is most appropriate for developing the intellectual powers of the individual."[32] We may assume rather general agreement on the objective of intellectual development. Obviously there is far less agreement on the necessity or appropriateness of subject organization as a means of developing it. The question of formal discipline has thrown the entire matter into a state of overwhelming confusion. Since nineteenth-century advocates of certain subjects used formal discipline as an argument, those who reject formal discipline sometimes tend also to reject subject organization. The nineteenth-century argument ran somewhat as follows. "Certain subjects are said to be introduced into the curriculum in order to cultivate certain specific mental qualities: Mathematics for accuracy and logical order; the Classics for clearness of expression and the cultivation of literary taste; Mental Arithmetic for quickness; History for judgment; Science for observation and initiative. The whole field is marked out into areas of influence."[33] But the modern claims for subjects as means of intellectual development do not rest on formal discipline or the faculty psychology. The contention is rather that each subject worth studying is characterized by a distinctive method or kind of intellectual behavior, some of which are identified in popular speech by such terms as scientific, historical, or philosophical method. It is this uniqueness of method that makes a discipline.

[32] Reported by Saylor and Alexander, *op. cit.*, p. 253.
[33] John Adams, *The Evolution of Educational Theory,* Macmillan and Co., Ltd., St. Martin's Street, London, 1912, pp. 212–213.

The study of such subjects, then, contributes experiences with the important methods of human thought and action and thereby develops intellectual understandings and skills. Furthermore, the method and the organization of a subject are seen as complementary to each other. In this way, the argument from method is fully consistent with the previous argument based on systematic organization.

That each subject possesses methodology appropriate to its subject matter can readily be granted. But that each method is unique to a particular subject is doubtful. Methods of thinking and of advancing knowledge overlap somewhat from one subject to another. Historical method, for example, is used in other subjects besides history; scientific method in other subjects besides science; and philosophical method in other subjects besides philosophy. Furthermore, the study of history need not depend exclusively on historical method, and so on. To the extent that such overlapping of methods and subjects does exist, the argument from method becomes a weapon that could be turned against rather than used for the subject organization. There might conceivably be other and better ways of organizing the classroom studies to foster intellectual development through methods of inquiry. The argument from method is an interesting one and has elements of validity that cannot be brushed aside. Taken by itself, however, it does not make a conclusive case for subject organization.

Another argument puts the case for subject organization on the transmission of culture.[34] But does cultural transmission imply subject organization? This depends on the extent to which our subjects and fields correspond to the historical categories in which culture has been developed and the contemporary ones in which it now exists. Those who see culture as all of one piece and object to its classification into divisions and parts many accept the validity of the transmission function and still reject the subject organiza-

[34] This argument is reported in the following form. "The scholarly disciplines from which the subject content is drawn represent the accumulated reservoir of human experience. The heritage of the race is included in language, mathematics, science, art, literature, history, and other subjects." American Association of School Administrators, Thirty-first Yearbook, *American School Curriculum,* The Association, 1953, p. 60.

tion. The case depends in part on the extent to which culture can be so analyzed and classified.

Suppose we consider culture, as defined in Chapter 2, to be the accumulated knowledge, wisdom, values, and skills needed to advance both the material and non-material aspects of civilized life. Here is one way these human achievements may be stated.

1. Written and spoken language, including the specialized language of quantity and form known as mathematics.

2. Knowledge and skill involved in processing and shaping raw materials to produce objects of use or beauty, or both.

3. The laws, forces, generalizations, and meanings of the natural environment itself, both organic and inorganic.

4. The use and care of the human body.

5. Institutions for the care and nurture of the young, such as the family and the school, and for the governing of human relationships.

6. The consolidation of memory through the use of language for the continuing preservation of relationships between past and present.

7. Religious and/or philosophical systems that explain human destiny and the meaning of life itself.

We have here, then, a series of human achievements, clusters of knowledges and skills that can be organized as those families of subjects called instructional fields. From this standpoint, the subject organization is an appropriate one for transmitting culture, since the culture itself defines the subjects. The subjects are the culture. From the foregoing list we may readily identify the following families of subjects: language, both foreign and the mother tongue; mathematics, industrial arts; agriculture; fine arts, including music; science; physical culture or, as sometimes known, physical education; home economics or family living; education; business and/or economics; political science; sociology; history; and philosophy and/or religion.[35] Some of these achievements, true, are in the realm of physical or material things; but every one of them is from any carefully considered standpoint also an achieve-

---

[35] Not all these, of course, appear as subjects in the high school program.

ment of human intelligence. Wipe out the factor of human intelligence and every single one of these achievements as we know them today disappears. This done, we are back not in "neolithic barbarism," not even in "palaeolithic savagery,"[36] but in the obscure and unrecorded periods before the beginnings of human recorded time.

To the extent, then, that culture may be legitimately expressed in the terms here set forth, the subject organization is an appropriate and necessary way of organizing the classroom studies. Those who do not accept this expression will probably not sympathize with the subject organization, no matter how systematic or logical it may appear. Perhaps the assumptions or contentions set forth in these paragraphs constitute an elaborate rationalization and reflect a desire to save the subject organization at any cost. This is something each student must decide for himself. But it is fundamentally on these contentions that the case for subject organization rests.

Furthermore, it is this case for the subject organization that incorporates and gives meaning and substance to the two arguments previously examined: those based on systematic organization and on intellectual development. If we are to transmit the culture, we shall need system and logic to secure maximum economy of time and effort. These areas of human achievement have been systematized and given logical form. From this it does not follow that they are to be shoved at students without regard for individual concerns, motivations, and the like. Furthermore, the system and the logic of the subjects have grown out of human inquiry and set the directions for future inquiry.[37] This is what makes the subject organization appropriate for intellectual development. It is not necessary to contend that each subject has its unique method as long as each uses some of the methods of intelligent inquiry and

---

[36] See Gordon Childe, *What Happened in History,* Penguin Books, Inc., 1946, chaps. 2 and 3.

[37] "Science has been defined in terms of method of inquiry and testing. At first sight, this definition may seem opposed to the current conception that science is organized or systematized knowledge. The opposition, however, is only seeming, and disappears when the ordinary definition is completed. Not organization but the *kind* of organization effected by adequate methods of tested discovery marks off science." Dewey, *Democracy and Education, op. cit.,* p. 223.

apperception.[88] For what we are transmitting is not a dead culture, but one that is alive with promise for human achievement in the future. Had the generations of our ancestors been concerned merely to transmit, it is doubtful that we today would have even what they achieved at given points, much less the cultural heritage as we now possess it. The negative stereotype of teaching in the subject organization might, it is true, transmit the culture, but it would transmit it as a corpse. For the subject organization has the dual function of developing both content and method. This leads sometimes to dilemmas and difficult choices, some of which are explored in connection with the subjects or instructional fields in Chapters 9 through 20. We must never forget that human beings have the capacity not only to create, but to destroy. In our present age we have inherited cultural elements that could be used for unlimited destruction. One of the surest ways to bring about destruction or stagnation or both is to transmit culture as a finished product. The absorption-regurgitation pattern of teaching is not only unnecessary, but is fundamentally inconsistent with the purposes for which subject organization exists.

SUBJECT ORGANIZATION AND UNIVERSAL SECONDARY SCHOOLING

The subject organization as a vehicle of cultural transmission ties in closely with our ideals of universal secondary schooling. Most societies in the past have provided the majority of their members either with no schooling at all or with schooling at the elementary level. Secondary schooling offers not only additional time for the study of more subjects, but also for the study of some subjects at advanced levels. Universal secondary education makes it possible to transmit more of the essential human achievements

---

[88] Some possibly more than others. But the conjectural differences between one subject and another along these lines do not justify the arbitrary division of subjects into two groups, one with more intellectual potential than another. True, one could concoct a subject from trivial materials, but such a subject could bear no discernible relationship to any substantial area of human achievement. The bases on which we select constants in the school program are not primarily those of difficulty, but of importance in the culture.

at more advanced levels to greater numbers of people than has previously been considered desirable or possible in most societies. It is interesting to note that the extension of secondary schooling to more people in the nineteenth century paralleled to a considerable extent the development and expansion of the subject organization. Prior to that time and as far back as the late Middle ages, secondary schools had transmitted only a portion of the culture, the literary, and had left to the colleges the teaching of a broader range of subjects. The American academy became a "people's college" by taking over these subjects, besides adding others, and the public high school followed along the same lines. Both institutions pursued this idea so zealously that for a time they smothered their students and their curricula with a bewildering variety of subjects. It is, of course, conceivable that universal secondary education in the future may turn to other matters and minimize the cultural transmission function and its achievement through the subject organization. Up to this point, however, the subject organization has been most directly associated with what we hope to achieve through the universalizing of the secondary school.

Another characteristic of the nineteenth century was a great expansion and development of knowledge itself, not only in the sciences, but in practically every field. This may have played some part in the desire to extend common schooling upward to the secondary level. But developments in knowledge and skill have since gone far beyond the levels reached in the nineteenth century. It is clearly impossible for the secondary school to transmit a substantial portion of the culture to any one individual. Neither is it possible for the college or the graduate school to do so. We shall not profit, then, from the nineteenth century example of multiplying indefinitely the number of subjects. Our job today is to recognize clearly the major categories of human knowledge and skill and then, within these categories, to make our selections of materials and resources for teaching, with further selection demanded in making the programs of individual students. Some materials will have to be discarded; but the criteria should be those not of age, but of importance. This is one major reason why the transmission of culture function cannot stand by itself. Selection demands the application of criteria provided by other kinds of educational objectives.

There is possibly one other difference between our attitude toward the heritage and that of the nineteenth century. For better or worse, we do not share the alleged nineteenth-century conviction about inevitable human progress. We are, or at least the interpreters of our age tell us we are, less optimistic that science alone, be it natural or social, will lead to better days ahead. The horrors of world-wide wars have taught us that humanity can go backward as well as forward, or forward in some things and backward in others. Our emphasis on cultural transmission, then, is not that we can learn all our forefathers have learned and inevitably turn out to do them one better. But it would be possible also to react too far in the opposite direction. We need not and should not conclude that humanity is in a hopeless state, that our cultural heritage is of little value, or that science can lead us to nothing but greater destruction. Probably the most direct route to destruction would be an unwise selection from the heritage: to transmit, for example, only the scientific and technological aspects of culture, while neglecting those aspects of culture represented by morality, literature, and the arts. This possibility underlines the need for wisdom and perspective in our selection of cultural materials and resources in the school program. It means that curriculum planning within the subject organization is the most important challenge before the secondary school in our time.

The case for subject organization on grounds of cultural transmission need occasion no conflict between those who favor broader and those who favor narrower categories of subject matter. Culture —that is, the major achievements of humanity—may be defined in terms of the instructional fields or families of subjects. Some courses may represent the various divisions of the fields, others may represent the field taken as a whole, while others may even be crossbreeds between two or more fields. The subject organization is flexible enough to be used in various ways. Choices probably depend on the aspect of culture being transmitted, the educational levels or readiness of the learners, and on the more specific purposes to which cultural transmission may be related. A given high school may contain examples of all three kinds of courses.

Bibliography

Alberty, Harold, *Reorganizing the High School Curriculum,* The Macmillan Company, 1953, chap. 5.

American Association of School Administrators, Thirty-first Yearbook, *American School Curriculum,* The Association, 1953, chap. 3.

Dewey, John, *The Child and the Curriculum,* University of Chicago Press, 1902, reprinted in the Phoenix Books Series, *The Child and the Curriculum and The School and Society,* University of Chicago Press.

Featherstone, William B., *A Functional Curriculum for Youth,* American Book Company, 1950, chaps. 5 and 6.

Hopkins, L. Thomas, *Interaction: The Democratic Process,* D. C. Heath and Company, 1941, chaps. 1 and 2.

Saylor, J. Galen, and Alexander, William M., *Curriculum Planning for Better Teaching and Learning,* Rinehart and Company, Inc., 1954, chap. 8.

Smith, B. Othanel; Stanley, William O.; and Shores, J. Harlan, *Fundamentals of Curriculum Development,* World Book Company, 1950, chaps. 16 and 17.

CHAPTER 8

···

Core Classes

―――――――――――――――――――――――――――――

The case for the subject organization does not rule out other ways of organizing the classroom studies, at least in part. Attempts to identify other patterns have occupied the major attention of many students in the field of secondary-school curriculum. These attempts have produced a variety of special terms and of schemes for classifying these terms. The terminology is often not only complex, but contradictory and confusing. Discussions of such matters occupy a good share of the literature of secondary education. Members of the general public frequently draw the unwarranted conclusion that students of the secondary school curriculum are primarily interested in getting rid of the subject organization. The conclusion is unwarranted, first because practically nobody wants to get rid of subject organization, and second because the amount of space devoted to a topic in a book does not necessarily indicate its importance in the mind of the writer.

In leaving subjects, including the broad fields, we enter curricular organization based not on knowledge and skills, but on problems, activities, needs, and experience. This does not imply the neglect of knowledge and skills. Subject matter is used, but classes are set up around categories that do not depend on divisions of subject matter. These classes are usually known as core classes, although the terms "basic learnings," "common learnings," and "general education" are also used.[1] Such classes do not take up the

---

[1] Course titles do not always tell the whole story. In some schools the term "core" is used for broad fields courses or for any combination of two or more subjects with one teacher.

entire school day, but are used in the general education or required portion of the classroom studies.

The term "core" in its present sense came into popular use during the 1930's. Core classes developed in a number of coöperative experimental studies, such as the Virginia State Curriculum Program, the California Coöperating Schools Study, the Michigan Study of the Secondary School Curriculum, and the Stanford Social Education Investigation. Probably the major impetus to the core movement, however, came from the Eight-Year Study with its thirty "unshackled" schools, a fact that has led to the erroneous identification of core with progressive education. The core movement generated interest, enthusiasm, study, research, and discussion among secondary educators in many parts of the country and in many schools not connected with national projects or experiments.[2] It provided a fresh and invigorating approach to the problems of secondary education, one that avoided and by-passed the older debate about the relative merits of practical and "academic" studies. World War II and its aftermath directed the attention of secondary educators into other interests during the 1940's. The general reaction against what was considered "progressive education" led to the abandonment of core programs in some communities where they had appeared to be well established. But the core did not disappear. In fact it staged a substantial comeback in the 1950's, if not numerically,[3] in terms of the interests of many concerned with secondary education.

It should be kept in mind that the core was developed in everyday school practice and picked up many of its characteristics along the way. Theories about the core for the most part have grown from attempts to explain what the practices were about. Probably one of the forerunners of core was the old-fashioned home room, which provided a time and place for the discussion of problems not included in the subject organization as such. In part at least, the

[2] For example, the development of the core program in the "new school" at Evanston Township High School, Illinois, in coöperation with the School of Education, Northwestern University. See Charles MacConnell, E. O. Melby, C. O. Arndt, and Leslee Bishop, *New Schools for New Cultures* (rev. ed.), Harper & Brothers, 1953.

[3] Statistics on this point are difficult to interpret. Multiple-period arrangements reported as cores do not necessarily represent the core viewpoint or approach.

core represents the home room idea moved into the formal schedule. Another forerunner of core was the attempt to develop larger categories of subjects through correlation and fusion. From this grew the point of view that a problem-centered organization provides a better basis for using materials from many subjects than the attempt to combine the subjects as such. Other elements that entered the core were the desire to extend into the high school some of the features of the elementary-school activity movement and the attempt to reduce the daily teacher-student ratio by combining several periods with one teacher.

CHARACTERISTICS OF CORE CLASSES

One of the clearest statements on the nature of core classes has been provided by Faunce and Bossing.

1. It seeks to establish relationships among areas of living by the study of problems that challenge the pupil to explore and utilize the knowledge and skills of more than one subject.

2. It aims at larger objectives than would characterize any single subject area.

3. It involves the joint planning of those objectives, and of the means of achieving them, by both teachers and pupils. It is directly geared to the goal of increased skill in the processes of coöperative planning.

4. It requires a block of time longer than the traditional period.

5. It involves either a single teacher for two or more periods or a team of teachers who work together.

6. It is dedicated to improved guidance of individuals and groups of pupils.

7. Its basic emphasis in instructional planning is the present psycho-biological and social needs of the pupils themselves.[4]

Some of the foregoing characteristics of core classes are found also in the subject organization, but not in the same ways or for the same purposes. Teacher-student planning, for example, referred to in point three above, may be and often has been used by subject teachers. In some subjects it includes a good deal of student choice of topics or problems within, of course, the framework of the sub-

[4] Roland C. Faunce and Nelson L. Bossing, *Developing the Core Curriculum,* Prentice-Hall, Inc., 1951, pp. 8–9.

ject itself. Teacher-student planning in a core has a wider field of operation. Another feature of core sometimes used in subject organization is the larger time block. Teams of teachers are in some cases brought together in broad fields courses. So far as guidance is concerned, a subject teacher may give considerable attention to the problems and needs of individual students. For the core teacher, however, guidance is not only an opportunity, but an explicit responsibility. The major distinct or unique characteristics nevertheless are expressed in points 1 and 7: the "relationships among areas of living by the study of problems that challenge the pupil to explore and utilize the knowledge and skills of more than one subject," and the "present psychobiological and social needs of the pupils themselves."[5] Again it should be understood that subject classes do not disregard these matters any more than core classes disregard subject matter, but they do not use these as bases for organization.

One of the difficulties with the core idea is its apparent vagueness to anyone who has not worked in it or observed it closely. Teachers and members of the general public in this position are sometimes at a loss to identify what is actually studied in a core class. Common problems? Yes, but what kind, what problems in particular? There is no universal answer to such questions, but there are plenty of examples. Here, as listed by Alberty, are the suggested areas used at one time in the core of the Ohio State University School in Grades 7, 8, and 9.

1. Understanding My Body
2. Beliefs and Superstitions
3. Hobbies
4. Managing My Personal Affairs
5. Sports and Recreation
6. Living in the University School
7. Living in the Home
8. Living in the Neighborhood
9. Personality and Appearance
10. Earning a Living
11. Housing

[5] *Ibid.*

12. Natural Resources
13. Community Agencies and Services
     Recreation
     Protection
     Government
     Education
     Welfare
14. Communication
15. Living in Columbus
16. Living in Ohio
17. Living in Another Country or Other Countries.[6]

At the twelfth-grade level, the suggested areas include such matters as "Implications of Scientific Advancement" and "The American Heritage."[7] These lists are presented here as examples of what might be studied in some core classes and are not to be understood as prescriptive in the Ohio State University School. Outlines for core classes are usually intended to suggest problems for study, rather than to prescribe what shall be taught.

It is obvious that a great deal of subject matter (much of it related to the instructional field of the social studies) will be taught and learned in the study of such problems. The problems include not only those of personal adjustment but also those of the larger civic and economic environment. Furthermore, the students who tackle such problems seriously will get much functional practice of the English skills. There is no need to fear, as some people do, that core programs turn out students who are ignorant or illiterate. "The so-called fundamentals are learned functionally, and there is plenty of evidence to support the conclusion that such learning is more effective."[8] Whether or not such learning is more effective may be open to debate, but it is clear that many students have learned English skills in core classes.

CONTROVERSY ABOUT CORE CLASSES

Nevertheless, the brief history of core has been a stormy one. The enthusiasm of its supporters is well matched by the aversions

---

[6] Harold Alberty, *Reorganizing the High School Curriculum*, The Macmillan Company, 1953 (rev.), p. 185. These are in what Alberty calls a Type-Five Core.
[7] *Ibid.*, p. 186.
[8] *Ibid.*, p. 187.

of its critics. It has been the occasion of numerous controversies in local school systems, leading in some cases to its abandonment. It has been blamed for defects that existed before its inauguration. Nevertheless, core classes have continued to thrive, and core programs are being started in places that have not previously used it. Developing core classes demands strong convictions and a good deal of courage on the part of those who work with them. Timid, cautious, and unenterprising teachers and administrators, even if sympathetically inclined to the idea, are unlikely to move in this direction.

It is easy to see reasons for some of the difficulties of core in practice, none of which can be charged to the theory of the core as an educational idea. For one thing, it is possible that core programs are not always judiciously introduced. Enthusiasts for new ideas sometimes lack charity for the old. Some of the "traditionalists," therefore, are likely to be resentful at the outset and to wait patiently for the day of reckoning. Another problem in the introduction of core is that of making the philosophy of it clear in concrete terms. The general public is used to the familiar subject designations. The fact that core is flexible and fluid does not make it any easier to identify. It should be remembered too that innovations are rarely popular with consumers. This applies to all of us as consumers in every field except our own. New developments in music, architecture, art, food, clothing, and the like are resisted at the outset. And these fields have the advantage of being able to make their ideas more readily tangible. The architect can build a modern house to show people what he is talking about; few people get into a school to stay with a core class in its day-to-day activities. All this means that the introduction of core demands a measure of community study that does not always take place.

Two other human tendencies combine to complicate the picture. One is the feeling that things are worse today than they were yesterday or 10 or 20 years ago. This seems to operate peculiarly in the field of education although it is by no means unique to it. The other is the feeling that it is the new element in the situation that is responsible for the alleged decline. Core classes are often blamed for anything that some people think is wrong with the high school of a given community. If the graduates have difficulty passing the

English placement test in colleges and universities, the core must obviously be the villain of the piece. If employers complain that recent graduates can neither read, write, count, nor spell, it is the core that catches the blame.

Another practical dilemma is that of teacher education. The original core teachers were retreaded subject teachers. Some of these were enthusiasts for the idea and anxious to learn how to carry it into effect; others came in with various degrees of doubts and misgivings. It is not easy to teach a core class, and it is only the enthusiast who is likely to survive the inevitable frustrations attendant on learning the process while trying to do it. One possible solution of this difficulty is to point the preservice education of some teachers specifically toward core. A few teacher-education institutions have developed such programs. This is a promising possibility, but one not without its own problems. School systems delay the introduction of core pending the availability of such teachers; teacher-education institutions postpone the development of such programs until they can see reasonable possibility of placement. It would, after all, be no kindness to prepare teachers for jobs that may not exist. Those teacher-education institutions which have moved along these lines, however, indicate little difficulty in placing their graduates.

The core has also been caught up in the controversy about alleged anti-intellectualism in the schools. Those who feel the schools have abandoned intellectual objectives sometimes think of core as part of life-adjustment education. It should be remembered that life-adjustment advocates have not particularly made a case for one kind of organization over another. Although core classes can be used in the life-adjustment context, the same is true of subject classes. Other critics recognize this distinction, but still insist that core is not and cannot be an appropriate vehicle for intellectual development as such. Here again we encounter a special meaning of intellectual development, one that depends upon identifying the established academic disciplines as unique vehicles for certain kinds of intellectual understandings and skills. If on the other hand intellectual development is synonymous with reflective thinking and problem-solving understandings and skills in general terms, there is nothing in core theory to discourage or disparage this objective. In fact, core advocates usually place much stress on these skills. True, core can be taught in an anti-intellectual context; so can the subjects. Wooden teaching can reduce any classroom study to anti-intellectualism no matter how it is organized. Again we must remind ourselves that core never takes up all the student's time in high school. The larger fraction of the school day can be devoted to the traditional academic disciplines and may be used to achieve the unique intellectual outcomes claimed for and associated with them.

As is true of the subject organization, the case for or against core must be resolved in terms of its intrinsic rather than its surface characteristics. The difficulties noted in the preceding paragraphs are of a surface nature, except for possible loss of unique intellectual methods associated with the traditional disciplines. Many of the arguments urged on behalf of core are similarly based on characteristics by no means limited to core classes.

The most intrinsic characteristic of the core is the direct commitment to the problems and needs of youth. The essential question, then, is whether or not a portion of the classroom studies should be organized along these lines. Those who favor the core put their case in the affirmative. They recognize that common problems and needs may be dealt with in other aspects of the high school program, such as extraclass activities, community-service projects, individual counseling, and school-related work experience. Some of the present-day functions of core were once assumed in home rooms. Classroom studies, therefore, need not bear full responsibility for common problems and needs. But the contention of core advocates is that classroom studies should bear some of the responsibility. They feel it is not enough to use problems and needs as criteria for checking the selection of subject matter in the subject organization. Some part of the classroom studies should be aimed specifically at the meeting of such common needs and should be organized around them. In short, the core has no detours, but goes straight to the point. The subject organization imposes on the learner a devious and roundabout route to goals toward which core classes move directly. Regardless of its values, therefore, subject organization should not have a monopoly on the classroom studies, according to those who advocate the core.

COMBINING CORE AND SUBJECTS IN THE SCHOOL PROGRAM

One way to resolve this dilemma is by assigning part of the classroom studies to the core and part to the subject organization. This solution has been and is acceptable to those who advocate the core. They have never demanded a monopoly for the core organization. Schools with core classes have always used subjects too. Opponents of the core, on the other hand, are less tolerant. It would seem, then, that the core people are more moderate and reasonable. It would also seem that middle-of-the-road students of secondary curriculum could easily accept the idea of combining the two kinds of organization in the school program.

Unfortunately this compromise generates further difficulty, for the core by its very nature cannot be placed in the elective portion of the classroom studies. The whole theory of the core demands that it be among the constants, that is the required courses or classes in every student's program. Usually the core class replaces the existing requirements in social studies and English. A student who takes two periods of required core each of four years in high school has used up eight units. This is half the total program in the 16-unit framework and two fifths of it within that of 20 units. The possible abandonment of the Carnegie unit system entirely would not change this situation, for the core would still demand a substantial share of the student's time in high school.

There is, however, one further possibility of compromise, one which requires some increase in the constants. It depends on the extent to which the core itself serves the purposes of transmitting certain aspects of culture. Or to put it another way, can those aspects of culture represented by English and social studies be transmitted through the core? With regard to English, a number of studies seem to indicate that achievement in reading, writing, and language usage generally does not suffer in a core class as compared with English offered on a separate-subject basis. The core, furthermore, offers many opportunities for the development of literary taste, understanding, appreciations, and interests. Some of this is done through the problems approach, and those teaching or interested in English may object to this apparent subordination of literature to something else. But a great deal can be done directly within core theory on other grounds, namely, the development and enrichment of the individual student. The cultural materials transmitted by English need not suffer from their incorporation in core classes.

What, then, about social studies? Core classes use a good deal of social studies material. There is little difference between the kinds of problems and topics studied in core and those found usually in twelfth-grade problems of democracy courses or ninth-grade community civics. In fact, the cores at those levels could be and often are set in the broad areas represented by those courses.

The big difficulty is with history. Core students of course inevitably learn some historical subject matter in the study of social-civic or social-economic problems. But they do not learn it as history, for the fundamental principle of history is continuity. Those who are not satisfied with historical subject matter divorced from this principle will not be satisfied with the core. They will want history retained as a constant.

Our possible compromise then may be that of requiring two units of history in addition to the core and the other constants. We might then have as requirements eight units of core and two of history, plus those that might be seen desirable in science, mathematics, and physical education. This is not an easy solution, but it is a possible one, particularly if we move in the direction of having many more students take more than the usual 16 units in their four-year high school program. The possibility might be more acceptable if, as has been true in some schools with core programs, the core class were placed on a single-period basis in the twelfth grade. This has been done on the grounds that the need for a large general-education block decreases as students proceed further in school. It would on the other hand require abandoning in the twelfth grade the important feature of one teacher with a group of students for two periods.

Objections to this kind of compromise may be anticipated both from adherents of subject organization and adherents of core. Some English and social studies teachers would certainly object to having their subject matter assimilated or absorbed by the core. Some would object to teaching the core, as would be necessary under such an arrangement. To these objections the answers may be given that while the core would assimilate material from English and social studies, it would not destroy them; and that English and social studies teachers are usually well qualified for core teaching.

Core adherents, particularly those who hold to the most rigorous theory, may object to possibly unwarranted identification of their idea with the subject matter of English and social studies. After all, core is *not* a combination or fusion of English and social studies on a board fields basis. It has no commitment to the objectives of those subjects as such. Its commitment is to common problems and needs that require subject matter from many instructional fields. Nevertheless, core classes in the high schools have in fact used a great deal more material from English and social studies than from science, mathematics, industrial arts, and the like. This has arisen partly from the use of former English and social studies teachers as core teachers. But there is a more intrinsic reason, namely that the *common* problems and needs do make considerable demands on English and social studies material. What need is more universal than that of language? Are not social problems common concerns of all? The heavy use of English and social studies materials in core classes is then not necessarily in conflict with good core theory. It is consistent with it.

There are valid theoretical and practical grounds for the argument that core classes can transmit the cultural materials represented by English and by social studies apart from history, although the cultural transmission function does not demand core organization. In the light of these considerations, a school would be justified in using the core provided it included additional history constants or requirements. Whether or not a school wishes to do so depends on the extent to which setting up a portion of the classroom studies on the basis of common problems and needs is seen as valid and desirable. This again is a point that can be resolved only through study and discussion on the part of teachers and other members of local communities.

USE OF CORE CHARACTERISTICS
IN SUBJECT ORGANIZATION

Some of the characteristics of core classes, furthermore, may be used in a program of classroom studies organized entirely around subjects. These are intrinsic, but not unique to the core. One of these is teacher-student planning of many aspects of classroom work. There is nothing in subject organization that precludes this. True, it is not desirable in many subjects to invite students to select the topics for study, but teacher-student planning applies to many other kinds of classroom decisions. And there are some subjects in which teacher-student planning even of topics and problems is both possible and desirable.

Another core characteristic is that of the larger time block with one teacher. This is brought about by multiple-period scheduling and has the advantage of giving the teacher fewer students to know and work with over the school day. But a multiple-period organization can also be used in the subject organization. A teacher may have the same group of students in English and in social studies. This demands a teacher competent in both fields and requires daily preparation in two fields instead of one. But a teacher with two double-period classes and one single-period class will have only 90 students as contrasted with 150 under a schedule with five single periods, assuming 30 students per section. The periods in the multiple-period class need not be adjacent. One may have a group of students for history the first period and the same group for English the fourth period. Neither is it necessary to fuse or correlate the subjects. They may be taught as separately as desired, although opportunities for unobtrusive correlation will be offered to those who want to use them. Since the subject organization demands a knowledge of individual differences among students on the part of the teacher, this reduction of daily teacher-student ratio becomes just as important a matter in subjects as in core.

The use of multiple-period scheduling opens a third possibility of incorporating core characteristics in the subject organization: namely, that of relating classroom instruction and guidance. This can be done in subject organization just as it can be done in core. The multiple-period teacher may assume designated responsibility for guidance. Of course he does not act alone in this, but neither does the core teacher. Both use the services of guidance specialists if those are available. And other teachers will continue their informal and spontaneous guidance as they should no matter how the classroom studies are organized.

One important contribution of the core movement, then, has been to show how the use of subject organization may be improved. Some of these things had been done in subject organization prior to the core movement. But the vigor and enthusiasm of core teachers unquestionably brought them much wider attention and study in all quarters. It should not be assumed, however, that the incorporation of core practices in the subject organization precludes further development and use of the core itself.

Bibliography

Alberty, Harold, *Reorganizing the High-School Curriculum,* The Macmillan Company, 1953, chap. 6.

Faunce, Roland C., and Bossing, Nelson L., *Developing the Core Curriculum,* Prentice-Hall, Inc., 1951.

Lurry, Lucile L., and Alberty, Elsie J., *Developing a High School Core Program,* The Macmillan Company, 1957.

MacConnell, Charles; Melby, E. O.; Arndt, C. O.; and Bishop, Leslee, *New Schools for New Cultures,* Harper & Brothers, 1953.

Mudd, Dorothy, *A Core Program Grows,* Board of Education, Harford County, Maryland, 1949.

Noar, Gertrude, *Freedom to Live and Learn,* Franklin Publishing and Supply Company, 1948.

Saylor, J. Galen, and Alexander, William M., *Curriculum Planning for Better Teaching and Learning,* Rinehart & Company, Inc., 1954, chap. 10.

Smith, B. Othanel; Stanley, William O.; and Shores, J. Harlan, *Fundamentals of Curriculum Development,* World Book Company, 1950, chaps. 16, 17.

Wright, Grace S., *Block-Time Classes and the Core Program in the Junior High School,* U.S. Department of Health, Education, and Welfare, Bulletin 1958, No. 6.

Zapf, Rosalind M., *Democratic Processes in the Secondary Classroom,* Prentice-Hall, Inc., 1959.

....

CHAPTER 9

English

The subject organization is at the mercy of the subjects and the subject matter they contain. This is obvious, but throughout the history of schools has not been obvious enough. Naming the subjects does not define the curriculum. An impressive list of academic disciplines may serve only to conceal dead wood or trivialities within. Subjects can suffer more from internal deterioration than from outside attack. Deterioration can take place not only from the uncritical tenacity of traditionalists, but from the misguided enthusiasms of innovators. Curricular study of subjects and subject matter, on a continuing basis and in the local system, becomes therefore a matter of absolute necessity in the subject organization and in the life and well-being of the secondary school.

Examination of subjects demands the use of two kinds of objectives. One kind flows from the general function of the subject organization in the transmission of culture. Each subject or instructional field has its body of cultural material to transmit. For each subject it is possible and desirable to develop an inventory of understandings and skills closely related to the nature of the subject itself or the instructional field of which it is a part. These serve as check points or criteria for subject matter to be included. They become bases for strengthening content and for preventing deterioration from uncritical innovation. They help guarantee the integrity of the transmitted culture.

But these kinds of objectives cannot do the whole job. It is necessary also to use the objectives for which the culture is transmitted: those of intellectual development, moral development, citizenship, self realization, and the like. They offset uncritical traditionalism, which clings to materials neither ornamental nor useful. They help guarantee not only the transmission of culture from the past but its enrichment and development for the present and future. But objectives of this kind need not and in many cases should not be used mechanically to determine the form or structure of the subjects or of the instructional units around which subject matter is organized.

It is not the purpose in this and the following chapters to present detailed expositions of content or method in the instructional fields under consideration. Some of the excellent books that do this for each field are listed in the various chapter bibliographies. The intention is rather to identify the development and present situation of each field in the high school program, to consider its relationship to the balance of constants and electives, and to examine current issues pertaining to selection and organization of subject matter. For it is on the way these issues are resolved that the present and future contributions of each field will depend.

Again it must be emphasized that resolution of these issues must of necessity be worked out in the thousands of local school systems throughout the land. There are no national commissions, organizations, or authorities who can or will do this job for the faculties and general publics of local school communities, although points of view of national groups are important considerations in local decisions.

Neither can these issues be resolved once and for all. They will reappear in many forms and will be supplemented by issues that have not yet suggested themselves. Such controversies are signs of vigor and life in a complex, interdependent, and rapidly changing society. They demonstrate the importance of cultural transmission even in the context of rapid cultural change. Without them the culture of the past would become fossilized, and society would go on changing anyway. This would be a tragedy, for such a society would change without direction and purpose. There is little chance of this, however, so long as teachers, students, and the general public take school subjects seriously enough to be aware of need for improvement. Such discontents emerge particularly in creative periods of history. For in such periods culture accumulates too rapidly for easy assimilation into the school subjects. There are far too many decisions that demand attention for any subject or field to rest itself content. Let us then accept our problem thankfully. There is no need for the false assurance that a solution achieved today can and will endure for all time.

THE NATURE AND CONTENT OF ENGLISH AS AN INSTRUCTIONAL FIELD

We turn first to the field of instruction concerned with the understanding and use of the mother tongue. The long name for this field, used by the National Council of Teachers of English in its series of reports issued in the 1950's, is the English language arts. This descriptive term is usually reduced to English as convenient shorthand. Neither term has ideological significance. The term "English" does not suggest narrowness or traditionalism; neither does the term "language arts" link its users with progressive education.

Although English is often referred to as one of the traditional academic disciplines, its place in our subject organization is of recent origin. Even when grammar and rhetoric dominated the curriculum, there was no thought of studying these subjects in the vernacular tongues. English studies broke into the secondary school program in the academies and formed important parts of the curricula of high schools founded in the 1820's and thereafter. The high schools, however, were soon divided into classical and English departments, with English at a lower prestige level. This subordination of English continued until the decline in foreign language enrollments, which took place after 1900.[1]

---

[1] The following protestations about the value of English by the Committee on College Entrance Requirements, 1899, indicate that prestige and status questions survived even at the end of the century. "The committee presents first the proposition that the study of the English language and its literature is inferior in importance to no study in the curriculum. It offers all, or nearly all, the opportunities for mental training afforded by the study of any language, and introduces the pupil to the literature of his own tongue, which must always be the chief source of his own thought,

It is true, of course, that a vernacular tongue will be transmitted in a culture without including it as a study in the school curriculum, or, for that matter, without schools at all. A few years of primary schooling will suffice to transmit the ability to read and write it on a mechanical basis. The need for including vernacular studies in the secondary curriculum, however, develops as (1) the language becomes the medium for a substantial body of literature and (2) it becomes a powerful and flexible tool for the expression of thought. The vernacular language in that case is needed both for the transmission of culture and for cultural extension and growth. When these conditions are reached, vernacular studies can no longer be shut out of the curriculum of secondary and higher schools. There may be a lag of some centuries before the curricular changes are made, but inevitably they come. By the early part of the nineteenth century the changes were long overdue so far as English was concerned.

Another important historical point about English is the time it took to develop in the unified form we know today. It started out in such separate pieces as composition, rhetoric, literature, and grammar. Even in recent years, some high school courses of study divided the year's work into a semester of literature and a semester of composition and grammar. A possible return to this may be detected in the very recent interest in specialized courses or electives at the higher secondary grades. For the most part, however, our English courses represent a high degree of unification of elements once taught separately. One might regard English as a broad field. Even the differences from one grade level to the next are less sharply marked than is true in other subjects, a point that brings about not a little concern or confusion to those who work with the English sequence.

The English curriculum is dedicated in part to the development of language skills in the individual—skills of reading, writing,

---

inspirations, ideals, and aesthetic enjoyment, and must also be the vehicle of his communication with his fellow-men. Hence this study should be placed in a position at least not inferior to that allotted other languages." National Educational Association, *Report of Committee on College Entrance Requirements,* The Association, University of Chicago Press, 1899, pp. 12–13.

speaking, and listening—and the use of these skills both in ordinary communication and in the processes of reflective thought. These skills can, of course, be developed in any subject, a fact that has led to the accurate but dangerous generalization that every teacher is an English teacher. The offsetting generalization or cliché, however, is that everybody's business becomes nobody's business. Important matters demand specific assumptions of responsibility. Although every teacher should assume some responsibility for language skills in his own subject, neither the English teacher nor the subject of English can be dispensed with.

Whether the English curriculum has distinctive subject matter of its own or is merely a collection of miscellaneous subject matters picked up to serve as vehicles for the skills program is a question that often distresses those who work in the field. It arises in its sharpest form in connection with the teaching of reading. In the traditional English program the subject matter for reading was provided by literature. But the use of literature does not exclude other kinds of materials in the teaching of reading skills. Such materials, in fact, become necessary as the English teacher participates in the all-school program of developmental reading. This term implies an acceptance of responsibility for the advanced teaching of reading by the secondary school in contrast with the older view that relegated almost the entire responsibility to the elementary grades.[2] This responsibility is shared by the English teacher. People use reading skills not only to read literature, but to gain information and ideas from many kinds of everyday writings such as newspaper articles, business reports, committee recommendations, political argument, "how-to-do-it" directions, and textbooks. While some of these productions may become literary

[2] This point of view is well expressed in the following statement. "Research has revealed the complex nature of reading and the necessity for adapting skills learned in the early grades to the more mature tasks of the high school. This challenge is being met by recognizing the need for both a developmental and a remedial program— the first to develop more mature powers needed to cope with more complex learning activities in secondary schools and the other to aid those pupils who need further assistance with the skills to which they have already been exposed in elementary school." National Council of Teachers of English, the Commission on the English Curriculum, *The English Language Arts in the Secondary School,* Appleton-Century-Crofts, Inc., 1956, p. 161.

in substance and style, the majority do not, but they must none-theless be read. Such materials, therefore, are not out of order in the English class even when major emphasis is placed on the study of literature.

Just as English teachers use some non-literary materials, other teachers will on occasion use materials classified as literary. The difference is that although every teacher is a teacher of reading, he is not by function a teacher of literary reading. On the other hand, even though the English teacher helps students develop general reading skills, his "special province" is properly that of "developing the essential skills for reading literature."[3] If this can be legitimately regarded as the English teacher's special responsibility, it follows that literature provides the distinctive subject matter of the field called English. This viewpoint can be defended not only on the grounds of the developmental reading program, but also on the function of English in transmitting its portion of the general cultural heritage.

Use of literature as the distinctive subject matter of the English curriculum demands some notion, rough as it may be, of what constitutes literary material. This is not an easy matter, for literature is another word that everyone understands and nobody can define. It includes many kinds of poetry and prose. But not all poetry and prose is thought of as literature. Obviously any two people may disagree as to whether or not a given piece of writing has literary quality. Most are agreed, however, that it demands a combination of style and substance. Neither can stand by itself. Apart from these there are no limits. Literature may deal with the purest fantasy or the most sober reality. Literary writing may include histories, scientific reports, philosophical analyses, plays, poems, novels, short stories, political addresses, prayers, and hymns.

Here surely is subject matter enough for any instructional field!

[3] *Ibid.*, p. 179. This viewpoint of the National Council of Teachers of English is also well expressed in the following. "The developmental program in reading includes many different strands, among them enrichment of vocabulary, adjusting speed to purpose and material, improving basic silent and oral reading skills, promoting habits for reading for personal pleasure and profit, and, in the language arts, promoting special skills for the reading of literature." *Ibid.*, p. 165.

Yet it is the very wealth and diversity of the material that creates the problems facing English teachers today. Even a thirteen-year program provides hardly enough time for an introduction to literature on which the student may build further in his adult life. It is necessary to make selections from this vast body of material and to arrange and organize these selections for teaching purposes. Both of the two kinds of objectives referred to earlier demand attention as bases for the selection and the arrangement. Transmission of cultural heritage objectives, taken by themselves, suggests that certain classics be taught and studied for their own sake, simply so they will not disappear from awareness on the part of coming generations. But literary selections must also pass the test of being good for something outside of themselves, good for the students who read them in the sense of contributing to their moral, social, and personal development. Ideally, there is no conflict between the two; practically, English teachers have gone through several generations of soul-searching on this very point.

APPROACHES TO THE TEACHING AND STUDY OF LITERATURE

English literature in schools first developed as a body of classics selected for intensive study. This approach to the selection and use of literature, it is assumed today, grew out of a desire to imitate the approaches used in the classical literatures of Latin and Greek. In those subjects a few major selections were studied in great detail over long periods of time. English, to prove itself as a worthy subject, must do the same. Just how the English classics themselves were selected is not particularly clear. At any rate the lists were soon standardized, partly in response to patterns developed for college entrance examinations. English teachers quite justifiably wanted to know the selections on which their students would be examined and quite understandably, after finding out, proceeded to put the emphasis on these selections. This did not make these selections college preparatory, but rather college-entrance preparatory in character. Non-college-bound students, who made up the majority, studied them along with the college bound. The lists were revised from time to time in conferences and committees representing both college and high school teachers, but the major works held their places remarkably well.[4]

This approach was not necessarily so bad as present-day observers often contend. There is much to be said for knowing a few things well over against knowing many things superficially. On the whole, however, this approach to literature was probably overdone. Much of the detailed analysis was undoubtedly strained and forced. Some of the materials studied could hardly meet the test of long-range literary criticism on the quality basis taken by itself. Doubtless some if not many students learned to hate literature in the process. Yet there must have been teachers who through this approach and these selections inspired their students to a genuine love of literature and of reading beyond the years of formal schooling.

When the theory of formal discipline declined in popularity and could no longer be used as a practical defense of the classics approach, English teachers turned to other kinds of justifications. Among the objectives invoked were moral or character development and citizenship. It is only a human characteristic to want to continue using those things to which we have become accustomed. All of us as teachers do this to some extent. Many English teachers similarly clung to those classics they had mastered and knew how to teach.

Nevertheless, the domination of literature by the classics was doomed as far back as the turn of the present century. It has slowly

[4] The Committee on College Entrance Requirements in 1899 presented a list of suggestions consisting of 30 titles for each of the four high school years. Special indication was made of those titles recommended by the joint conference on English in April of that year as "college requirements for general reading and composition work" and as "college requirements for careful study." The following were listed as "college requirements for general reading and composition work": *Ivanhoe, Merchant of Venice, Vision of Sir Launfal, Julius Caesar, Last of the Mohicans, Silas Marner, Vicar of Wakefield, Paradise Lost* (Books I and II), *Palamon and Arcite* (Dryden), *Sir Roger de Coverley Papers,* Carlyle's *Essay on Burns,* Tennyson's *Princess,* and *Rime of the Ancient Mariner.* The following were listed as "college requirements for careful study": *Macbeth,* Milton's *Minor Poems,* and Macaulay's essays on *Milton* and *Addison. Op. cit.,* pp. 18–19. Of these titles some survived into the third decade of the twentieth century, such as *Ivanhoe, The Vicar of Wakefield,* and *The Princess,* while the Shakespearean plays plus *Silas Marner* are still major items in English programs.

given ground ever since, although it has by no means disappeared in English programs. Various theories or approaches have grown up to take its place as bases for selecting and arranging literary materials. Among these are literary history, literary types, themes, and problems, plus that of highly individualized free reading on a personal basis. These approaches are not necessarily conflicting in practice and in fact are often used in combinations.

Literary history was an early competitor of the classics approach and tended to replace it to some extent in the eleventh and twelfth grades, even in the nineteenth century. The eleventh-grade course in many places became English literary history, from the Anglo-Saxon period to modern times, while the twelfth-grade course became American literary history. A few classics, however, were intensively studied along with literary history. At its best, in courses organized as historical surveys, literary history included the reading of selections from each of the periods covered. At its worst, it could degenerate into the memorizing of authors, works, and dates with little reading of the materials themselves. Unfortunately, it is the latter connotation that has persisted as a negative stereotype in the minds of many who comment on the English curriculum. Literary history has been condemned as study about literature instead of the study of literature itself. It has, however, claims for consideration that cannot easily be overlooked.

The tendency of literary history to degenerate in some quarters into study about literature led to acceptance of what has been called the types approach, that is, the organization of literature around its various forms of expression, such as epic poetry, narrative poetry, lyrics, novels, short stories, essays, and plays. Within the study of each type a number of selections could be included from various authors and periods. The approach lent itself well to providing room for intensive study of one or two classics in connection with each type. Where the literary history approach was based directly on cultural transmission, the types approach was justified on the grounds of teaching the reading skills needed for the understanding and appreciation of literature. One possible criticism of the approach is that the study and discussion of literature along these lines demands a degree of insight and understanding characteristic of advanced or older students rather than beginners.

All three of the foregoing approaches—classics, history, and types—tended to center in literary materials themselves rather than the needs and interests of learners. The next development was that of themes or centers of interest, based on the needs and interests of students at particular age levels. From these evolved fairly lengthy units with themes such as adventure, hobbies, making friends, pioneer life, animals as pets, travel, and the like. In each unit or theme it was possible to include selections from various literary types, authors, and periods. Such units have proved popular at the early secondary levels, particularly in the junior high school. For older students the theme approach has been adapted in a variety of ways, sometimes along historical, sometimes along regional or geographical lines. It should not be assumed in any case that the themes approach nullifies the direct study of literature, for the unit titles and themes are in many cases only convenient strands for organizing the materials and motivating the students.

The approach through problems is a variation of the theme approach. Where a theme unit, however, deals with general topics in which students presumably are interested, a problems unit deals with an unresolved issue or dilemma in which students presumably are deeply and vitally concerned. A problem may be of the kind usually termed "personal-social," such as "how to get along with others," or it may be a larger "social-civic" problem such as "intergroup relations." The 1930's witnessed considerable advocacy of the problems approach, especially from the social-civic standpoint. Many plays and novels of that and following decades of course are available as means of penetrating the realities of the problems under study. This approach is usually weighted heavily in the direction of contemporary or current literature, although nineteenth-century novels, particularly *Silas Marner,* have been used for comparative purposes.

Two major criticisms have been made of the problems approach. One is that it subordinates literature to other considerations. In the themes approach, the interests of students provide the bases for helping them grow in literary taste, knowledge, and appreciation. But in the problems approach, the center of attention is likely to be the problem itself. It suggests a heavy-handed "life is real, life is earnest" connotation presumably foreign to enjoyment outcomes of literary study. Literature should be serious, but not solemn. Perhaps this controversy is simply a specific case of the long-standing debate about art for art's sake. The other criticism is a practical one, namely, that social problems are also studied in social studies. Lists of units in English programs using the problems approach are sometimes indistinguishable from those in social studies courses, particularly twelfth-grade problems of democracy. This sometimes leads to friction between the English and social studies departments and in addition may bore the students.

Still another approach is that of free reading on a personal and individual basis. This is a flexible approach that may easily be used to supplement some of the others. The teacher has an extremely important role as the guide of individual student explorations. He must obviously have a well-stocked library at his disposal plus a deep and wide knowledge of many kinds of literature from his reading. The usability of this approach will, therefore, vary with these considerations, as well as with the degree of reading interest that exists or may be stimulated among the students.

There is no need to select one approach for use all the way through the secondary English program; neither is it necessary to use one approach exclusively at any one grade level. In Grades 7 through 9, themes have proved to be popular vehicles for the development of tastes and interests. Within the themes, some attention may be paid to literary types, but not to the extent of making complex and sophisticated analyses. The tenth-grade level provides an opportunity to introduce students to world literature in translation, organized along geographical or regional lines within a broad framework of history. A more definitely historical approach is suitable for American literature in Grade 11 and English literature in Grade 12, but this may be tempered in part by further study of literary types. Such courses at the senior high school level obviously cannot be used for all students, but they are both workable and desirable for those of average or above-average abilities in reading.

A sequence of this kind, based largely on the subject matter provided by literature, is open to the possible criticism that it disregards the interests and needs of adolescents or even such objectives as health, citizenship, and family living. The validity of this criticism depends on the extent to which such objectives should determine the form or structure of materials in the subject organization. Mental and emotional health and personality development are important objectives; but it does not follow that units or courses in English, or any other field, need therefore be organized around these headings. Since there is usually more literature available than can be used, such objectives can serve as criteria for selection of materials within the patterns of world, American, or English literary history, not only for groups of students, but for the free reading of individuals. The subject matter of literature is the most varied of any in the school program, for it encompasses the broadest possible range of human interests, topics, problems, and needs. Perhaps this is why the study of Latin classics was considered to be practically self-sufficient in the humanistic secondary school; since these classics dealt with such varied material, no other subject appeared to be necessary. While the use of literature as the basic subject matter helps to give greater shape and coherence to the English program, it by no means reduces it to narrow dimensions or removes it from human concerns.

The nature and extent of literature in the high school curriculum depends in part on the levels of reading ability found in given schools. Some students in high schools read at low levels that seriously limit their study and enjoyment of literary materials. Poor reading also limits student achievements in other subjects. It is possible, however, for the poor reader to gain information in science and social studies, for example, through audio-visual aids and other non-reading media. The literary subject matter of the English teacher, on the other hand, depends to a very large extent on the use of the printed page. In primitive societies literature is of course transmitted orally. This can also be done in school, but for the literature in our culture it must remain an extremely limited possibility. What the English teacher is likely to encounter at any level is a range of reading ability dipping several grades below and reaching several grades above the one he is teaching. A ninth-grade population may include some students whose reading ability runs as low as the fifth-grade national norms and others as high as the average for college students.[5]

There is nothing in this situation to justify the casting of reproaches at the elementary school. Ideally there should be no such thing as remedial reading, but we have no evidence that justifies blaming either elementary teachers or elementary programs. Neither is it helpful to try to resolve this complex dilemma by blaming particular methods of reading instruction. The range in reading levels parallels the range in levels of general academic intelligence, although this relationship does not necessarily hold true in individual cases. It would be possible of course to require a certain level of reading attainment for admission to the senior high school, but this would repudiate our traditional ideal of universal secondary schooling.

Sectioning by reading ability helps to mitigate the problem to some extent. But it mitigates it more for the teacher who gets the fast or average sections than for the one who gets those at lower levels. The work of the English teacher in low-ability sections becomes largely that of remedial reading. Results are usually encouraging enough to justify continuing the effort. Considerable adaptation, however, must be made in the subject matter and in the nature of the reading material. It is necessary to find materials that combine upper-level interest value with lower-level vocabulary and treatment, at least at starting points. This is not easy, and it may be necessary in low-ability sections to modify the sequence of literary studies used with average and above-average students. In addition, the teacher must be familiar with a variety of specialized techniques to overcome poor reading habits and negative attitudes

[5] Bond, for example, presents a distribution of reading levels of 127 ninth-grade students entering a given high school. (Gates Survey Reading Test.) On level of comprehension the group ranged from the 5.0–5.4 grade level to 13 plus, on vocabulary from 4.5–4.9 to 12.0–12.4, and on speed from 3.5–3.9 to 13.0 plus. The "mental grade" level on the Stanford-Binet Intelligence Test for this group runs from 4.5–4.9 to 13.0 plus. Bond comments, "A survey of the reading scores of the lower half of the class indicates the need of a wide range in the difficulty of the reading materials provided and of careful diagnosis and remedial treatment for some students." Guy L. Bond, "Identifying the Reading Attainments and Needs of Students," National Society for the Study of Education, Forty-seventh Yearbook, pt. 2, *Reading in the High School and College,* The Society, 1948, p. 70.

toward reading itself. When possible, it is desirable to add reading specialists to the staff either to help the English teacher or to teach some of the low-ability sections. Since the problems of some poor readers are emotional in part, it is further desirable to have available the services of clinical psychologists.

THE WRITING, SPEAKING, AND LISTENING SKILLS

High school English programs, however, deal not only with reading, but also with the skills of writing, speaking, and listening. The subject matter of literature provides the basis for much of the work in these skills, but as in the case of reading, other kinds of subject matter are not necessarily excluded. Unit organization, used in connection with any of the approaches to literature previously discussed, offers the flexibility and coherence needed for various kinds of writing, speaking, and listening activities.

Unit teaching, therefore, provides a natural setting for well-motivated learning. It places the skills of communication where they belong—in purposeful activity in a social setting. It demands orderly planning and assumption of responsibility for carrying out the plans. It furnishes opportunity for extensive group work and for individualized procedures to meet the needs, the interests, and the capacities of all members of the class. It stimulates curiosity and creativeness, giving those with unusual powers of self-direction a chance to forge ahead on their own. Yet it keeps the entire class working together on a common problem. It permits the use of all types of literature—new and old, prose and poetry, easy and mature—and the development of skill in reading each of them. It recognizes the place of the library in the learning activities of the classroom and teaches economical use of the facilities available. It takes advantage of the natural relationships between speaking and listening and writing and reading in the normal pursuit of well-integrated problems. It gives opportunity for enjoyment of literary selections by the class as a whole and at the same time develops personal standards of literary appreciation and personal habits of reading to suit individual interests. It gives opportunity for careful evaluation of progress by the students themselves and for the planning of next steps in learning.[6]

[6] National Council of Teachers of English, the Commission on the English Curriculum, *The English Language Arts in the Secondary School,* Appleton-Century-Crofts, Inc., 1956, p. 112.

To manage all this with a group of adolescents varying widely in abilities, interests, degrees of enthusiasm, and the like is no simple matter. All aspects of the skills program, including reading, therefore demand lower daily teacher-student ratios for English teachers. This is especially necessary in the development of writing skills, for the most important aspect of the writing program is the specific, detailed criticism of what students write. Consider then the plight of the English teacher with five classes of 30 students each, who must for each assignment read and comment on 150 student compositions.[7]

Reduction of teaching loads by giving English teachers fewer classes or fewer students in each class is practically closed, particularly in the days of rising enrollments ahead. It seems that the only feasible way available is that of multiple-period scheduling in which the teacher has the same students in two or more subjects. This does not necessarily imply fusion, correlation, or core. To maintain the integrity and identity of the subjects, however, requires adequate preparation by the teacher in two or more fields. This is particularly true when one of the subjects is English, for it would be easy to let the subject matter of the associated field dominate the selection and use of materials. While this arrangement

---

[7] The loads of English teachers are rarely appreciated by the general public or even by their own high school colleagues. The California Council of Teachers of English sponsored a study in which the average amounts of time needed for various kinds of manuscript marking were reported as follows.

	Average number of minutes for marking 250 words of manuscript	Average number of hours for marking 150 such papers
I. Marking to assign a grade	3.5	8.8
II. Marking to indicate faults	5.9	14.8
III. Marking to correct	5.9	14.8
IV. Marking to teach writing and thinking	8.6	21.5

Moreover, it was calculated that a teacher who spends 21.5 hours per week marking compositions would spend an additional 25 hours in class and seven hours "checking the corrections or revisions of these compositions." If this teacher had 2.7 hours "Available for correcting during class hours," his net load would come to 50.8 hours per week, *apart from* "hours for lesson planning and preparation for teaching the other skills and knowledge expected of the English program." William J. Dusel, "Determining an Efficient Teaching Load in English," *California English Bulletin,* March 15, 1956, pp. 6–15.

bristles with problems, it is more within the possibilities we face in the future than attempts to reduce class size or number of teaching periods[8] to the extent that would be necessary.

It is also possible to lighten the task of the English teacher by employing lay readers, educated people of the community, to read, grade, and criticize student writing. Experimentation along these lines has been carried on by the Educational Testing Service with the aid of the Fund for the Advancement of Education in selected high schools throughout the country.

Developing the speaking skills poses difficulties for the general English teacher, difficulties that can be resolved neither by library facilities nor lowered daily student-teacher ratios. The subject matter of literature lends itself readily to a variety of writing activities. Although the English teacher will use other kinds of subject matter for this purpose, he does not need to do so at the expense of literature. Furthermore, teachers of subjects other than English tend to teach writing to some extent in relation to their own bodies of subject matter. In speech the situation is different in two ways. The subject matter of literature is more limited with regard to the variety of speaking skills that need to be developed. Teachers of other subjects are less likely to pay specific attention to speech skills. Even if the English teacher has enjoyed adequate training in the teaching of speech, he will be handicapped in this connection unless he is prepared to sacrifice some of the subject matter of literature to make room for large amounts of other kinds.

Consequently, there is need for separate courses in speech, although these do not and should not eliminate speech activities from regular English classes. The required English sequence in Grades 7, 8, and 9 should include one semester devoted to the fundamentals of speech needed by all students, with special sections for corrective speech when needed. But there is also place in larger high schools for specialized advanced electives, such as dramatics. Whether or not speech should be organized as a department separate from English is not intrinsically a matter of curricular im-

---

[8] The Conant report suggests 100 students as the maximum load for English teachers. James Bryant Conant, *The American High School Today*, McGraw-Hill Book Company, Inc., 1959, p. 51.

portance and may be resolved by the administrative circumstances in given school systems.

GRAMMAR AND USAGE

Public concern about English in our schools frequently involves questions of correctness in speech and writing. The term most frequently used in discussions of these matters is "grammar."[9] Many who work in the fields of English and English curriculum, however, introduce a second term, usage, which they distinguish from grammar along the following lines. "The point is that English usage (accepted constructions) is one thing and grammatical theory (descriptions of the word forms and word order which express the relationships among words) is another. *Usage and grammar raise different kinds of teaching problems and should not be confused just because some individuals use these terms synonymously.*"[10]

Usage, then, is a matter of custom and convention. Good usage covers the language customs that have gained widespread approval. What most of us call good grammar implies the study and description of this body of good usage, that is, acceptable English. Writers in the field of English, however, usually prefer not to use the qualifying adjectives.

The best way to learn good usage is to grow up in an environment where good usage prevails. Unfortunately, many of our students do not grow up in such an environment; even though they hear good or standard English in their homes, they will encounter other varieties among their associates and in the community. The school provides still another part of the environment, and its most important responsibility in this connection is to have teachers who themselves speak and write standard English. This applies not only to English teachers, but to all teachers of all subjects.

Most people, however, feel that the school can and should do more than just provide a good example. It should, according to

[9] The term "grammar" has been and is still used with a great variety of meanings. For an overview of the historical development of these meanings see Ferdinand Bernard Gruen, *English Grammar in American High Schools Since 1900*, The Catholic University of America, 1934, pp. 1–65.

[10] National Council of Teachers of English, *op. cit.*, p. 356.

this point of view, develop good usage through the teaching of grammar. The effectiveness of grammar for this purpose has long been debated among English teachers and curriculum leaders in the field of English. Many are frankly skeptical about it, and research appears to support the skeptical position. From this it does not follow that we throw grammar out of the curriculum. Even those who doubt the transfer of grammar to usage support the teaching of grammar for other reasons. Pooley, for example, points out that "the building of sentences and the manipulation of sentence materials for improved style are at the very center of grammar instruction and are the chief reasons for the teaching of grammar."[11]

In spite of the adverse findings in the studies, the issue concerning grammar and usage is not closed. The generalization theory of transfer suggests the possibility of using generalizations or principles that can be applied to specific instances.[12] Such generalizations presumably could be drawn from the scientific descriptions provided by grammar. Just why grammar has not functioned effectively for this purpose is by no means clear. One possible reason was suggested in a report of the National Council of Teachers of English issued two decades ago, namely "that *a study of the real grammar of Present-day English has never been used in the schools* and that the conclusions concerning its effectiveness relate only to the type of 'grammar' that has been tried."[13]

The idea that traditional grammar as used in the schools may not be an accurate description of English is one that has been advanced for some time by a number of linguistic scholars. "In summary,

[11] Robert C. Pooley, *Teaching of English Grammar,* Appleton-Century-Crofts, Inc., 1957, p. 107.

[12] Roberts comments as follows on the use of generalizations. "Native speakers, however, can utilize very simple generalizations when they are trying to change from one dialect to another. For example, the person who habitually says, 'Him and me milked the cows' learns the generalization, 'In Standard English, pronouns used as subject are in the nominative case.' Grammatical generalizations are useful also to those seeking skill in writing, for they give a clearer idea of the resources of the language." Paul Roberts, *Understanding Grammar,* Harper & Brothers, 1956, pp. 3–4. The foregoing is part of what Roberts calls "The Second-Best Reason for Studying Grammar." He also says, "The best reason for studying grammar is that grammar is interesting." *Ibid.,* p. 1. This is a reason which, unfortunately, is often overlooked, not only in grammar, but in other school subjects as well.

[13] Charles C. Fries, *American English Grammar,* National Council of Teachers of English, English Monograph No. 10, D. Appleton-Century Company, 1940, p. 285.

traditional English grammar, which at the present time is the grammar of English that has been adapted for use in secondary schools, has been justly criticized as not a scientific analysis of the English language, not adequately descriptive of the English language, too prescriptive and authoritarian in attitude, and tending to interfere with careful study of the actual structure of English."[14] From this point of view, much of what English teachers have heroically ground into their students for generations has been irrelevant and of little use. It is difficult for anyone but an expert in the field of English to judge the validity of these criticisms. They are, however, advanced by reputable scholars who in addition have engaged in painstaking research to obtain more valid descriptions of our language and how it works. Text materials combining some of these developments with the use of some traditional terms have been prepared for use in schools. As more teachers use these materials, we shall be in a better position to identify the effectiveness of such grammer as a teaching tool. The possibility is one that deserves serious consideration in the study of the English curriculum.

For the most part, efforts to improve the teaching of grammar have taken the form of selecting from traditional grammar itself those elements which seem to pertain most directly to everyday language use. The need for such discrimination was expressed in the 1917 report of the National Joint Committee on English. "A sane attitude toward the teaching of grammar would seem to be to find out what parts and aspects of the subject have actual value to children in enabling them to improve their speaking, writing, and reading, to teach these parts according to modern scientific methods, and to ignore any and all portions of the conventional school grammar that fall outside these categories. In general, the grammar worth teaching is the grammar of use—function in the sentence—and the grammar to be passed over is the grammar of classification—pigeonholing by definition."[15] A good deal of attention was devoted to this matter in the years following 1917, and

[14] National Council of Teachers of English, *op. cit.,* p. 385.

[15] James Fleming Hosic, *Reorganization of English in Secondary Schools,* Report by the National Joint Committee on English representing the Commission on the Reorganization of Secondary Education of the National Education Association and the National Council of Teachers of English, Department of the Interior, Bureau of Education, 1917, p. 37.

the National Council of Teachers of English Commission on Curriculum in 1956 summarized the major agreements that apparently had been reached. "In general, the needs for grammatical knowledge on the part of those capable of applying it to speech and writing will be related to six problems: sentence structure, modification and subordination, agreement, noun and pronoun, verbs, and adjectives and adverbs."[16] Although this selective approach to grammar eliminates a great deal of terminology formerly used, it is still traditional grammar in the sense that the terminology retained is the traditional kind. If it is truly useful, however, it should also be valid from the standpoint of accurate description. It does appear to furnish principles and generalizations that can be used in speech and writing and is probably the most practical approach available for everyday teaching in our schools at the present time.

Such a selective and functional approach obviously does not render full justice to the study of grammar for its own sake. Larger high schools might well consider including a twelfth-grade elective course in English grammar for students who are interested in such instruction, and in smaller high schools there is always the possibility of doing it through independent study.

In conclusion, grammar has neither been eliminated from our schools nor is there any danger that it will be. True, there are differences of opinion about grammar among curriculum workers in the field of English, but these do not suggest the elimination of grammar. They involve rather the reasons for which grammar should be taught and the kinds of grammar that should be used in teaching.

The most specific issue—the functional value of grammar as a guide to usage—probably cannot be resolved in general terms. Those students who manage to grow up hearing and reading standard English and nothing else will use standard English. They obviously do not need grammar as a guide to usage. Students of low-academic ability who grow up with substandard English will probably continue to use substandard English whether they study grammar or not. This leaves, among others, a group of students who are of superior academic ability and who have grown up in an

[16] National Council of Teachers of English, *op. cit.,* pp. 370–371.

environment of substandard English. It is with students in this group that the study of grammar, when properly motivated, can be of greatest help so far as usage is concerned.

GRADUATION CONSTANTS AND COURSE SELECTIONS

Graduation constants in English are by no means easy to determine or to administer. The complexity of the problem reflects the difficulties involved in organizing English as an instructional field. Literature, the basic subject matter of English, includes a range of topics as broad as life itself and is not easily categorized in a series of clearly defined courses. This difficulty is accentuated by the fluid nature of the reading, writing, speaking, and listening skills. English teachers, therefore, find it difficult to be as tangible and specific about what they teach in particular grades as seems to be possible in many other fields. Real gains have been made along these lines, but it is important for the public to appreciate the unique nature of this instructional field and the degree of flexibility necessary in applying it to students of widely varying abilities and interests.

With these cautions in mind, let us assume that three full years of English are required in the junior high school Grades 7, 8, and 9, with one semester in either the eighth or ninth grade devoted to fundamentals of speech. Let us assume further that courses in world, American, and English literature are available in Grades 10, 11, and 12. Of these three bodies of subject matter, the one most immediately and directly important for students in the United States is the literature of their own country. American literature then should be a graduation constant, usually but not necessarily taken in the eleventh grade. For students in low-ability sections, the nature and scope of this American literature will of course be interpreted with considerable flexibility.

But it is also important when possible that students gain some familiarity with the literature of other societies or cultures. Average and above-average readers should take at least one additional year of English chosen either from the tenth-grade course in world literature or the twelfth-grade English literature survey, the choice preferably being made on the grounds of interest and ability rather than on those of preparation for college. Ability becomes a possible factor in this choice to the extent that the English literature survey may demand a high level of reading skill, but it becomes difficult to separate this from the more basic matter of interest. For students of very low ability in reading, it may be necessary to design this second year of required English in Grades 10, 11, and 12 on somewhat different bases from those used in either the world literature course or the English literature survey.

Overall requirements for graduation then should include at least five years of English in the six-year period of secondary schooling. The Conant report, however, recommends four full years of English in Grades 9 through 12 for all students;[17] since this presumably assumes two years of English in Grades 7 and 8, it comes to a six-year requirement, or English every year. Many students should be encouraged to take six years of English, and a few may take even more. The sixth required year for all students is difficult to provide for in relation to other legitimate constants and the need to preserve some flexibility for electives. There are at least two arguments for requiring all students to take six years. One is that all students should take both the world literature and the English literature survey. This is a practical impossibility in schools that include students who read at very low levels. Differences in ability and interest even among good readers make it inadvisable to require the English literature survey of all students. A second argument is that skills once acquired must be kept up not only through continued use, but through development at higher and more advanced levels of performance. This is possibly true, but it does not necessarily demand an additional year in the subject of English. While it would be foolish to ask teachers of other subjects to take over the basic responsibility for teaching English, we may reasonably expect that instruction in these other subjects at the upper years of high school will include both the use of language skills previously acquired and stimulation for their improvement.

Requirements should be administered so that students may choose various patterns or routes. A student planning to take the English literature survey in Grade 12 may omit English in Grade 10. On the other hand he may, by electing to include six years of

[17] Conant, *op. cit.*, p. 47.

English, plan to take both the world literature and the English literature survey. Or he may, if his reading level is high, take American literature in Grade 10, the English literature survey in Grade 11, and then choose some elective such as dramatics, creative writing, or journalism in Grade 12. Still another possibility for students with special interests in English is to take world literature in Grade 10, American literature in Grade 11, and two English courses in Grade 12, one of them being the English literature survey. This is by no means an impossibility, since students in many high schools have room for two or more twelfth-grade electives. For the college-bound student this may lead to advanced standing or placement in college English, but the opportunity to take as much English as possible may be just as important for students who do not continue formal education beyond high school.

Bibliography

Cross, E. A., and Carney, Elizabeth, *Teaching English in High Schools,* rev. ed., The Macmillan Company, 1950.

Fay, Leo C., *Reading in the High School,* What Research Says to the Teacher, No. 11, Department of Classroom Teachers and the American Educational Research Association, National Education Association, September, 1956.

Fries, Charles C., *American English Grammar,* National Council of Teachers of English, Monograph No. 10, D. Appleton-Century Company, 1940.

Fries, Charles C., *The Structure of English,* Harcourt, Brace and Company, 1952.

Fries, Charles C., *The Teaching of English,* The George Wahr Publishing Co., Ann Arbor, Michigan, 1949.

Gruen, Ferdinand Bernard, *English Grammar in American High Schools Since 1900,* The Catholic University of America, 1934.

Hatfield, W. Wilbur (chairman), *An Experience Curriculum in English,* A Report of the Curriculum Commission of the National Council of Teachers of English, D. Appleton-Century Company, 1935.

Hook, J. N., *The Teaching of High School English,* The Ronald Press Company, 1950.

Hosic, James Fleming, *Reorganization of English in Secondary Schools,* Report by the National Joint Committee on English representing the Commission on the Reorganization of Secondary Education of the National Education Association and the National Council of Teachers of English, Department of the Interior, Bureau of Education, 1917.

Jewett, Arno, *English Language Arts in American High Schools,* U.S. Department of Health, Education, and Welfare, Office of Education, Bulletin 1958, No. 13, 1959.

La Brant, Lou, *The Teaching of Literature in the Secondary School,* Harcourt, Brace and Company, 1931.

National Council of Teachers of English, The Commission on the English Curriculum, *The English Language Arts in the Secondary School,* Appleton-Century-Crofts, Inc., 1956.

National Society for the Study of Education, Forty-seventh Yearbook, pt. 2, *Reading in the High School and College,* The Society, 1948.

Pooley, Robert C., *Teaching English Grammar,* Appleton-Century-Crofts, Inc., 1957.

Roberts, Paul, *Patterns of English,* Harcourt, Brace and Company, 1956.

Roberts, Paul, *Understanding Grammar,* Harper & Brothers, 1954.

Rosenblatt, Louise M., *Literature as Exploration* (For the Progressive Education Association Commission on Human Relations), D. Appleton-Century Company, 1938.

....

CHAPTER 10

Foreign Languages: Classical and Modern

The study of classical languages, Latin and Greek, was once not only the main but the whole business of secondary schooling in the western world. Our colonial grammar schools represented and continued this humanistic-classical tradition, devoting almost their entire course of study to Latin and Greek, with Latin occupying the more prominent place. Neither the academies nor the public high schools rejected this tradition, although they included in their programs the study of modern foreign languages,[1] plus other "newer" subjects as well. The Boston high school of 1821 was, it is true, set up originally for English studies only, but as the high school movement developed, provision was made for study of foreign languages, both classical and modern. Most of the students who took foreign languages, moreover, were enrolled in Latin. The nineteenth-century growth of academies and high schools broke the older Latin-and-Greek monopoly of the curriculum, but it brought no repudiation of foreign language study as an important part of secondary schooling.

Foreign language study held up well throughout the nineteenth century. There was in fact a substantial increase during the decade

[1] Modern languages appeared early in the colleges. "As early as 1735 Harvard taught French and continued to do so intermittently for the next half century. . . . William and Mary established a professorship of modern languages in 1779. Other early beginnings are found at Columbia in 1784, Williams in 1792, University of North Carolina in 1795, Transylvania in 1799, Princeton in 1806, Bowdoin in 1820, Yale and University of Virginia in 1825." Robert D. Cole, *Foreign Languages and Their Teaching,* D. Appleton and Company, 1931, pp. 3–4.

from 1890 to 1900. One third of the students in public high schools (34.69 percent) took Latin in 1889–1890, but one half (50.61 percent) did so in 1899–1900. In the same period, French rose from 5.84 percent to 7.78 percent and German from 10.51 to 14.33 percent. The only falling off, from 3.05 to 2.85 percent, occurred in Greek.[2] All this happened, moreover, in a ten-year period during which the public high school population more than doubled, going from 221,522 in 1889–1890 to 519,251 in 1899–1900.[3] Some might ascribe the increase in foreign language enrollments, particularly in Latin, to the pressure of college-entrance requirements. But the portion of public high school students listed as preparing for college actually declined from 14.44 percent to 10.82 percent during this period.[4]

DECLINE OF ENROLLMENTS IN FOREIGN LANGUAGES

The high point of enrollment in the foreign languages was reached in 1910, when the combined totals for Latin and modern languages came to 83.3 percent of the 915,061 students in public high schools. By 1915, combined enrollments in Latin and modern languages had slipped to 77.2 percent of the high school population. The virtual abandonment of German during World War I was largely responsible for bringing the figure down to 54.9 percent by 1922. From then on, however, the decline became catastrophic, amounting by 1955 to a state of collapse. In that year, combined enrollments came to only 20.6 percent of the students in high school.[5] Moreover, 46 percent of the public high schools in the middle 1950's offered no foreign language study whatsoever,

---

[2] *Report of the Commissioner of Education for the Year 1899–1900,* Government Printing Office, 1901, chap. 39, "Statistics of Secondary Schools," p. 2123.

[3] *Ibid.,* p. 2119.

[4] *Ibid.,* p. 2123.

[5] William Riley Parker, *The National Interest and Foreign Languages,* Prepared for Citizen Consultations, sponsored by the U.S. National Commission for Unesco, Department of State, Revised Edition, January, 1957, pp. 52–53.

It is also important to know what percentage of high school graduates have taken foreign language. In Wisconsin, 36.8 percent of the one-sixth sample of seniors of June, 1957, had taken a foreign language at some time in their high school careers. Edward A. Krug, Clifford S. Liddle, Russell C. Mosely, and Daniel Parkinson, *The College-Preparatory Function in Wisconsin High Schools,* School of Education, University of Wisconsin, 1959, table 14, p. 53.

either ancient or modern,[6] while 54.6 percent offered no modern foreign language.[7]

According to many observers, this decline in foreign language enrollments has weakened the position of the United States in world affairs. Our inability or lack of inclination to learn foreign languages is interpreted as smug satisfaction with ourselves and a corresponding contempt for others. "It is becoming increasingly evident that our ignorance of other languages is causing us expense, embarrassment, and loss of prestige the world over."[8] In addition there is substantial loss in communication. "There are now approximately 2,800,000 Americans on active military service, roughly half of them stationed outside the continental United States. Only a handful of them have any foreign language competence whatsoever. To be so heavily dependent upon foreign translators, upon whose accuracy and reliability supervisors are often unable to check, or where sensitive materials are concerned, is obviously undesirable."[9] These are serious matters that should be of concern to every citizen of the United States. Obviously the high school cannot teach all the languages that are important in world relationships. Neither can it always bring the student to the level of competence demanded in the armed forces, the diplomatic services, and in foreign trade. Much of this has to be done at higher levels, particularly in universities, which can afford variety in their course offerings, and in specialized language schools conducted for career purposes. What the high school can do is to provide many students with fundamental instruction in a few languages to serve as a foundation for later career purposes, as well as for direct values in general or liberal education. But relatively few students in our schools are being reached by such fundamental instruction.

Just why the decline has taken place is anybody's guess. The immediate answer is purely mechanical. Neither parents nor teachers

---

[6] "Foreign Language Offerings and Enrollments in Public High Schools," *Publications of the Modern Language Association of America,* vol. 70, no. 4, pt. 2, September, 1955, p. 53.

[7] Parker, *op. cit.,* p. 13.

[8] Jacob Ornstein, "To Win the 'Languages' Race with Russia," *New York Times Magazine,* September 15, 1957, p. 49.

[9] *Ibid.,* p. 52.

for the most part have urged students to elect foreign languages except for college-entrance purposes. As classes dwindled in size, school administrators, particularly in small communities, had to face financial facts. The easiest solution in the small high school was to drop foreign languages entirely. This meant that even the few students who wanted them could no longer enroll. But these are surface explanations only, and the real question still has to do with what lay back of it all. Some have seen in it a reflection of American isolation from world affairs, but we are less isolated now than we were in 1910. Others lay it at the door of life-adjustment education or other alleged anti-intellectual tendencies. But the life-adjustment movement did not appear until the middle 1940's, and its leaders did not exhibit any specific bias against foreign language study. Some have blamed it on alleged shortcomings in foreign language curricula and teaching. Even if such shortcomings exist, there is little reason to believe them more pronounced now than they were a half century ago. Those who are unfriendly to foreign language study have seen the decline as evidence of enlightenment and progress in secondary schooling. The emotions of those who contemplate the decline are perhaps as mixed as reasons set forth to account for it.

VALUES OF FOREIGN LANGUAGE STUDY

Probably the most valuable clues lie in the history of controversial discussion about the values or purposes of foreign language study. True, the demands of the national interest provide a compelling argument for reëxamination of foreign languages in the curriculum. This, however, raises the recurring question as to whether education should serve society or the individual. To put the case for any subject on the grounds of group interest may suggest overtones of the very totalitarianism against which our national efforts are directed. It is necessary, therefore, to consider the contributions of foreign languages to individual development.

The traditional classification of educational values as disciplinary, practical, and cultural[10] is a particularly convenient one for

[10] This has been used in the discussion of various instructional fields. See, for example, the comment on it in mathematics in Progressive Education Association Com-

the study of foreign language objectives. It is in these broad categories that controversy and dispute have centered. Of course the categories overlap. Disciplinary values can be highly practical, but depend on indirect rather than direct application of materials studies. It would be difficult in an era of increased leisure to characterize cultural values as impractical. What is cultural for one person may be practical for another. But the point is not only what may happen, but what kinds of possible happenings should be used as the bases for decisions in the foreign language program.

Contentions both for and against disciplinary values of foreign languages dominated the discussions throughout the nineteenth and the early part of the twentieth centuries. The term "disciplinary" is used here to include not only formal discipline but other theories of transfer of learning as well. Formal discipline, however, is the oldest of these theories. It is important, therefore, to recognize what formal discipline is and what it is not. The term "formal" in this context does not mean what it has come to mean in everyday speech. It connotes an emphasis on form rather than matter. A formal disciplinarian values a school subject more for its process and method than for its subject matter or content. This is an old doctrine, but it was natural for those interested in the classics to turn to it in the nineteenth century. Latin was under attack as a dead language, one not needed to get along in the world as had once been the case. The defense of Latin accordingly shifted from one based on substance to one based on form. What students were to gain from Latin was not a body of information, but training in exactness, precision, and clarity of thought and expression.[11]

---

mission on the Secondary School Curriculum, *Mathematics in General Education,* D. Appleton-Century Company, 1940, p. 4.

[11] "As an instrument of training in the essentials of a working method no modern language and no science is the equal of Latin, either in the number and variety of mental processes which may be stimulated with a minimum expenditure of effort, or in the ease and accuracy with which the results of these processes may be checked up, errors of observation or inference detected, and corrections made. Latin has the further advantage over science that it is a more effectual means of fixing the attention. It is not necessary here to analyze a Latin sentence in order to show how the differences in the forms and relations of words in the simplest exercises require for their mastery concentration as an indispensable condition; then, exactness of observation, accuracy of discrimination, and carefulness in drawing conclusions, the shortcomings of which are obvious the moment that a phrase or sentence is translated from Latin

It was a formidable argument, so formidable that the advocates of other subjects took it up and sought to claim disciplinary values of their own. Teachers of English and modern foreign languages particularly set forth claims along the same lines. For some time the discussion centered not on the validity of formal discipline, but on the claims of Latin to have greater disciplinary value than other subjects and particularly than other languages. Near the end of the nineteenth century, however, the very doctrine itself was questioned by students of psychology. Questions were followed by experimental studies, and the triumphant announcement was made that formal discipline had been disproved. Whether or not these experiments of James, Thorndike, and others really did explode formal discipline is something for each reader of the studies to decide for himself.[12] The more important fact for Latin was that the general public as well as the great body of teachers and administrators accepted the psychologists' conclusions. Latin appeared to be done for. Teachers of other subjects lost very little if at all. Science, history, and other "content" subjects were justified on the basis of their material, while teachers of French, German, and Spanish could claim for their subjects the advantages of knowing not dead languages, but those which were very much alive.

There is, however, a better argument that can be made along the lines of intellectual discipline, one that applies not only to the study of Latin, but to any foreign tongue. Words are not things or ideas in themselves, but symbols of these things or ideas.[13] They

---

into English or from English into Latin. Principals of schools remark that the discipline and spirit of a school are better in which the majority of the pupils are studying Latin. The reason is that no other study, excepting Greek, so well serves the purpose of bringing the boyish mind under control, of helping to gain self-master." Francis W. Kelsey, "The Value of Latin and Greek as Educational Instruments," in *Latin and Greek in American Education* (Francis W. Kelsey, ed.), The Macmillan Company, 1911, pp. 22–23.

[12] James's experiment, for example, had to do with the strengthening of the ability to memorize poetry. This is only one aspect of formal discipline, and probably the most narrow aspect. The doctrine of formal discipline in its entirety is a philosophical proposition and one that will probably not be settled one way or the other by experimental evidence.

[13] This point of view is not that of epistemological or ethical relativism. The relativism of words affects neither the independent existence of objects nor the validity of ethical ideas and principles.

mean, as Humpty-Dumpty said, what the user intends them to mean, no more, no less. Their precise meaning varies with the circumstances in which they are used and with the writers and speakers who use them. This does not mean that communication is impossible, but it does demand freedom from rigidity on the part of those who use words. The argument then runs that a person who knows only his own language will necessarily be the prisoner of his own word system to a much greater extent than one who has learned to receive and express ideas in at least one other language. This is true not only of individual words, but of those combinations of words known as idioms. So far as theories of transfer are concerned, this viewpoint is most consistent with that known as generalization. This is a strong argument for the study of foreign languages, one that deserves full and serious consideration from curriculum-makers today.

It is interesting to note the effective expression of this argument that comes from Thomas Huxley, ordinarily identified not with the promotion of foreign languages, but of science. "The knowledge of some other language than one's own is, in fact, of singular intellectual value. Many of the faults and mistakes of the ancient philosophers are traceable to the fact that they knew no language but their own, and were often led into confusing the symbol with the thought it embodied. I think it is Locke who says that one-half of the mistakes of philosophers have arisen from questions about words; and one of the safest ways of delivering yourself from the bondage of words is, to know how ideas look in words to which you are not accustomed."[14]

After stating several other values for language study, Huxley goes on in the same passage to contend "That if your languages are properly chosen, from the time of learning the additional languages you will know your own language better than you ever did."[15] He recommends particularly Latin and German. This argument is in part an extension of the one with which Huxley's statement begins and in part a different argument based on different

[14] Thomas H. Huxley, "On Science and Art in Relation to Education," (1882) in *Science and Education: Essays,* D. Appleton and Company, 1897, p. 187.
[15] *Ibid.*

assumptions about transfer. It is one thing to argue that foreign language contributes to the understanding of one's own in the sense of generalized understanding of what any language is about and for; it is another to base the case on the similarities between one's own language and the one being studied. The latter aspect of this argument depends neither on the formal discipline nor the generalization theories of transfer, but on that of identical or similar elements.

It was in fact the theory of similar elements that provided support for the continued existence of Latin in the curriculum after formal discipline had fallen into disrepute. The contention was based on the Latin derivations of many English words. It was applied particularly to English vocabulary, although some claims were made for similarities between English and Latin grammar. These do not appear to any extent in more recent controversy, especially since the conclusions of linguistic scholars that the grammars of English and Latin are more different than they are alike. If these conclusions are valid, they raise the possibility of negative transfer from Latin to English. On the other hand, the study of Latin seems likely to force the student to be more aware of grammar and particularly of the terminology of grammar than would be true if he confined his studies to English only. The same argument could be made for the study of French, German, Spanish, or any modern tongue. This would also be true of vocabulary transfer, since many French and Spanish words reflect their Latin origins and since many English words are of Germanic origin. The study of Latin, French, Spanish, or German should, then, contribute something to English vocabulary. An extension of this argument is that the study of Latin has transfer value for simultaneous or later studies in Spanish or French.[16] The argument would not apply par-

---

[16] The transfer of Latin to other languages has also been studied. One major investigation was that of George A. Rice, 1925–1927, concerning which the Modern Language Investigation report states, "This experimental evidence tends to corroborate the widespread and reasonable belief that a second language is learned more readily than the first, but throws doubt upon the frequently made statement that previous study of Latin is more effective an aid in the learning of a modern language than is another modern language." Algernon Coleman, *The Teaching of Modern Foreign Languages in the United States: A Report Prepared for the Modern Language Study,* The Macmillan Company, 1930, pp. 99–100.

ticularly well to transfer from Latin to German since these are not highly similar even though both belong to the loose family of languages known as Indo-European.

The argument for similar elements makes a good deal of common sense. Furthermore, it looks like the kind of argument that could be verified or disproved experimentally with matched groups. Many such studies have been made, usually showing some gain in the learning of various aspects of English by Latin as compared with non-Latin students.[17] The variables are difficult to control and include not only the students themselves but the content and the method of courses studied by both groups. At any rate the interpretations of these studies have been disputed over a long period of years. It is also conceivable that students could learn materials related to English word origins in English classes without studying Latin or German as separate subjects. On the whole, it seems best to regard the argument from similar elements as one that supports rather than establishes the desirability of foreign language study.

The direct practical values claimed for foreign languages are by no means new or modern. Well into the seventeenth century Latin was a vocational subject for most of its students. It is still such for students in certain professional fields, particularly Christian theology, although it is no longer so regarded for the study of law or medicine. But the day of Latin as a vocational study is over, so far as the great majority of students is concerned. French and German are today the practical languages for students contemplating careers in the natural sciences and in history and other social studies, as well as for advanced work in such arts as medicine and engineering. Much has been made also of the value of Spanish for careers in business, but it is doubtful that the cause of this particular language has been well served by this argument. Beyond all this lies a vast area of career opportunities in the armed forces and other government services, which demand competence in one or more foreign tongues.

---

[17] See The American Classical League, *The Classical Investigation: Part One, General Report*, Princeton University Press, 1924, pp. 38–54 for a summary of such studies.

But the practical argument is not exhausted by vocational possibilities. There is also, the argument runs, the need for languages in
foreign travel, with the increase of American foreign travel apparently strengthening claims along these lines. Unfortunately the
results seem to be disappointing, and the frustration of those who
stumble painfully through conversation in a foreign tongue has become a weapon turned against the study of foreign languages on
the grounds that it "isn't practical." It is perhaps a human tendency
to place more stress than is desirable on the ability to speak a foreign language as compared to the ability to read or write it.[18] Speaking ability in a foreign tongue is a colorful and spectacular accomplishment, much like the ability to perform well in dancing, fencing, drawing, or the playing of musical instruments. In all these
important accomplishments, instruction can accomplish much, but
not beyond the limits imposed by individual differences in native
ability. At any rate we have not enjoyed conspicuous success in this
kind of practical objective, perhaps because many of our students
of foreign language have not pursued the subject for more than
two years.

[18] It should be noted that teachers of foreign languages in the United States over a
long period of time did not attach much significance to the practicality of the speaking objective. Note, for example, the following from the report of the Committee of
Twelve of the Modern Language Association of America (1898). "It is next in order to remark briefly upon what is popularly called the 'practical' value of French and
German, that is, their utility as a means of intercourse. The practical command of a
foreign language has a potential value that is at once perceived by everyone. It is felt
to be desirable by multitudes who would probably care but little for the considerations presented in the preceding paragraphs of this section. The committee holds,
however, that in our general scheme of secondary education the ability to converse in
French or German should be regarded as of subordinate importance. We by no means
say that it should be ignored, or that colloquial practice may safely be neglected in
teaching. With this point the report will deal further on. Here we merely express the
opinion that the ability to converse should not be regarded as a thing of primary importance for its own sake, but as auxiliary to the higher ends of linguistic scholarship
and literary culture." From the Report of the Committee of Twelve included in National Education Association, *Report of Committee on College Entrance Requirements,* The Association, University of Chicago Press, 1899, p. 83. Or consider a
more recent expression along the same lines. "In most cases learning to use a language actively, that is, for speaking or writing, is difficult in proportion to age and
to mental maturity. The cost in time and effort is so great that the attempt should
not be made unless clear and direct gains are in sight. To enforce methods aimed at
this goal as a *required* discipline in schools could easily become an abuse from
which all foreign language might ultimately suffer." H. R. Huse, *Reading and
Speaking Foreign Languages,* University of North Carolina Press, 1945, p. 13.

The ability to read a foreign language easily and well is also a practical attainment. In 1930, the Coleman report recommended that emphasis be placed on the reading objective for students who studied a foreign language for only two years. "If, for local reasons, only a two-year course is feasible, or if, in any instance, a considerable percentage of students discontinue the modern language at the end of the fourth semester, it is particularly recommended that the course be organized with ability to read the modern language directly as the central aim, with an acceptable standard of reading ability as the minimum attainment requisite for passing."[19] But the more recent tendency and one that parallels a similar development in English is to regard the reading, speaking, writing, and listening skills as interrelated and interdependent, as pointed out, for example, in the 1956 syllabus of the New York City public schools. "The present course of study emphasized the four communication skills: listening, speaking, reading, and writing. These skills are interrelated and are developed in the same sequence as language power develops in a growing child. The elements of the skills are taught and practiced in relation to each other. Ability developed in any one of the four skills helps to develop ability in the others."[20] Presumably, this point of view would be applied to any number of years a foreign language might be studied. Most authorities in the curriculum of foreign languages today urge, however, the four-year period over the two.

The third group of objectives includes those of cultural significance. Every language is in itself a part of culture, that is, of human achievement. Cultural transmission takes place as one learns his native tongue, both in and out of school. Study of a foreign language reinforces and supplements cultural transmission in this sense, that is, of enabling the individual to receive and to use one of mankind's most significant achievements, namely, language itself. All four of the language arts, reading, speaking, writing, and listening, are involved in this kind of acquisition. As the individual

[19] Coleman, *op. cit.*, p. 232.
[20] New York City Board of Education, *Modern Language and Latin—Grades 8–12,* June, 1956, cited in Mario A. Pei, "The New York City Language Syllabus and the FL Scene," *The Modern Language Journal,* March, 1957, p. 118.

gains skill and power in all these, he acquires more of the cultural heritage that the given foreign language represents.

Language also becomes a means of penetrating the culture of a given society in the broader anthropological sense of understanding its way of life, its customs, values, and beliefs. This may be accomplished in part through the reading of literature, but written literature is only one way of entering the way of life of another culture. Much is transmitted through oral speech, even through the gestures or facial expressions that accompany or sometimes even replace speech itself. Some writers in the field of foreign languages have placed great stress on language as the medium for the understanding of a culture in this broad meaning of the term. "Equally important is the redefinition of the cultural objective in foreign language learning. The term *culture* is no longer used only to mean that which is superior and admirable in a civilization or literature. It is now used to refer to all of the belief and behavior patterns which are shared by a group of people living together. Contemporary foreign language programs attempt to give the student an opportunity to participate actively and with pleasure in a different culture pattern with different habits, modes of behavior, and values."[21]

This point of view obviously supports the use of foreign languages for the social objective of international understanding. "Experience in direct communication through speech or writing, imaginative identification with the people whose language is used, a feeling of personal involvement, induction into a different thought process and cultural medium—these are the ways in which modern foreign language can make a significant and indispensable contribution toward international understanding."[22] Study of foreign languages can without doubt add much to the kinds of international understanding which may be achieved through the social studies. It is necessary, however, to realize that international understand-

[21] Mary P. Thompson, "Longer Sequences of Study," in Marjorie C. Johnston (ed.), *Modern Foreign Languages in the High School,* Bulletin 1958, No. 16, U.S. Department of Health, Education, and Welfare, Office of Education, 1958, p. 80.

[22] Marjorie C. Johnston, "How Can Modern Language Teaching Promote International Understanding," *Bulletin of the National Association of Secondary School Principals,* December, 1956, p. 70.

ing, whether gained through social studies or foreign languages or both, does not necessarily or automatically guarantee international brotherhood or world peace. Even the sharing of a common language has not prevented civil wars. Understanding of one another's cultures nonetheless can help reduce or eliminate irrelevant irritations or tensions between peoples.[23]

The language of a people, however, serves not only as a means of understanding their culture in the broad anthropological sense, but also of sharing their culture in the more selective meaning of the knowledge, wisdom, values, and skills of civilized life, the common storehouse of human achievement. This kind of cultural transmission is served particularly well by literature, although it is by no means confined to literature in writing. The amount and quality of literature in a particular foreign language become criteria for including or not including that language in the school curriculum. It can be argued, of course, that literature in translation also serves the purpose of cultural transmission. This is good as far as it goes. Most of us by necessity will have to limit ourselves to a small number of foreign languages and to depend on translation for the rest. It is desirable to include world literature in translation in the English curriculum. What is not desirable is to be limited to translation in all literatures save our own. The cultural values of literature lie not only in content, but also in style. Translations convey content only. Even a translation that is in itself an excellent example of literature is a piece of literature different from the original.

Transmission of culture through literature depends primarily on reading. If students do not learn to read a foreign language easily and well, little cultural transmission through literature, apart from the drama, can take place. This seems to be a difficulty peculiar to Latin, since not a few students gain the ability to read French, German, and Spanish well after even two years of high school in-

[23] "In this connection, one of the greatest barriers to international understanding is the normal tendency of human nature to react against the unfamiliar, and foreign language learning is probably the quickest and most direct method of making familiar what before was strange, by actually participating in and experiencing a different mode of thought. A person who can speak German, for example, may not like or admire the Germans, but he is no longer disliking them on instinctive grounds just because they sound queer." Johnston, *op. cit.*, p. 74.

struction. Perhaps these languages are easier than Latin. Or it may be that the reading skills need to be reinforced by practice in writing, speaking, and listening, all of which appear more prominently in modern language instruction.[24] We know, however, that many students in the past learned to read Latin well enough to use it as a lifelong source of leisure-time satisfaction and cultural enrichment. Apparently this degree of skill is not beyond the reach of human abilities. This is a matter of particular importance, since Latin has much to commend it for purposes of cultural transmission.

PAST DILEMMAS AND FUTURE POSSIBILITIES

It is in relation to all these claimed values of foreign language study that we may speculate further on why foreign language enrollments have declined and on future possibilities of increasing these enrollments. First of all, the overselling of language study, particularly that of Latin, on the grounds of formal discipline led to what was probably an equally uncritical rejection not only of formal discipline, but of language study itself. The ground lost was never fully recovered, even by the argument that the study of Latin helps the student improve his English. Although the formal-discipline controversy centered on Latin, the repudiation of formal discipline, when combined with other circumstances, has damaging consequences for modern languages as well. The slogans against formal discipline became widespread not only with the general public, but penetrated the teaching profession itself, affecting the points of view of those who counseled and guided students in their selection of subjects.

So far as modern languages were concerned, the vacuum created by the rejection of formal discipline was filled by claims related to practical value and use. Many students, however, cannot fit more than two years of foreign language study into their high school programs, a period considered too short by many people for the attainment of practical competence. This conviction is shared by experts

---

[24] This is implied by the recent tendency to foster student development in the four related skills of reading, writing, speaking, and listening. See Reginald C. Reindrop, "The Reading Aim Reexamined," *The Modern Language Journal*, May, 1957, pp. 239–243 for an examination of the relationship between reading and speech.

and authorities in the foreign languages, as well as by the general public. The Conant report recommends four years of one foreign language for academically talented students generally and those with "ability in the foreign language field."[25] This is undeniably what we should strive to achieve. Skepticism about the values of studying a foreign language for only two years, however, has not helped increase foreign language enrollments. When the choice lies between four years of language or none, many students are likely to choose none. The same is true of the administrator or school board of a small high school when confronted by the same choice.

There has been, however, one kind of practical objective that could be served by two years of language study, namely, that of satisfying a language requirement for college admission. This is not intrinsically practical in the sense of using the foreign language, but it satisfies a practical motive nonetheless. The consequence has been that many parents, students, and teachers think of foreign-language study as pertinent only to the college-preparatory student. Although a revival of language requirements for college entrance coupled with an increase in the percentages of high school students planning on college will bring about some increases in enrollment, we should not and dare not be satisfied with this. To be so would continue the unfortunate identification of foreign language study with college preparation only. Increase in enrollments in foreign languages should be based not on the mechanical relationship to college-entrance requirements, but on sound objectives that apply to all qualified students.

Two years of a foreign language need not be regarded as pointless in the light of the cultural objectives, particularly when these are understood in the broad anthropological sense of gaining understanding of cultures other than our own. If this point of view has any validity whatsoever, two years of such experience with a foreign language should be better than none. The case is admittedly more difficult when the cultural objectives are understood as those related primarily to the reading of literature. But the extent to

[25] James Bryant Conant, *The American High School Today,* McGraw-Hill Book Company, Inc., 1959, pp. 57, 69.

which reading ability can be gained in two years will vary from one student to the next. It is not necessary to reject entirely the conclusion of the Coleman report that progress can be made on the reading objective in a two-year program. The reading objective, moreover, does not necessarily imply devotion to the so-called reading method in the sense of excluding other kinds of language activities. Cultural objectives in the broad anthropological sense may then apply to all students taking a language for two years; in addition, some students may learn to read the language easily and well. In addition, we should remember that cultural and disciplinary values are not without practical significance. Ability to read a foreign language, for example, is important in all three categories. And the understanding of other peoples is daily becoming a matter of practical significance for all. Some disciplinary value, particularly in the modified sense of understanding the power and limitations of language itself, may also be possible in two years of study.

Possibly all the objectives of foreign language study, whether for four years or two, are too abstract or remote to gain popular appeal in our country. We do not know, since little systematic effort has been made to present the case along these lines. It is doubtful that teachers generally, apart from language teachers, are themselves sufficiently convinced to make such a presentation to the students whom they advise on course selection. Furthermore, as we get more and more teachers who themselves have never studied a foreign language (an inevitable state of affairs in the light of past decline in foreign language enrollments), the possibility seems even more remote. But any good teacher, regardless of his own background of language study, is willing to examine the matter without prejudice in the study situations of curriculum planning groups. It becomes the responsibility of curriculum consultants and directors to see that the place of foreign languages in the high school program receives adequate consideration. This obviously does not mean that the curriculum director forces his conclusions on the participating teachers. But it is his job to develop awareness of questions that need study. Unfortunately, the study of the foreign language situation has only rarely appeared on the agenda of secondary curriculum planning groups.

There seems to be little desire to include foreign language study among the constants. Much can be said on both sides of this question, but it is a doubtful place to begin, at least with regard to the national problem. What needs to be done first is to see that high schools offer opportunities to study foreign languages. Nearly half (46 percent) of our high schools provide no such opportunities. Every such high school should reëxamine its reasons for omitting foreign languages from the program of studies. Second, when foreign languages are offered, those who advise on subject selection should raise with every qualified student the question of taking a language even when the student is not college bound.

Beyond this lie the troublesome decisions concerning how many foreign languages to offer, how many years of each should be offered, and which languages should be included in the offerings. The first two of the foregoing obviously depend on the size of a given high school and the numbers of students who seek foreign language study. It is difficult to justify offerings in several languages with very small classes. On the other hand, every effort should be made to maintain instruction in at least one language even when enrollments are low. Schools with several hundred students should aim at offering two years of study in each of two languages, one modern language and Latin. The two-year offerings should be increased to four as rapidly as interest can be developed. Some schools run third-year and fourth-year language study together in one class. A student can get both years, although the sequence of materials may be reversed.

We should recall also that the offering of foreign language in Grades 7 and 8 was one of the early aspirations in the junior high school movement. The ideal sought was that of six years of study in a given foreign language.[26] Foreign language study, however, has not prospered in Grades 7 and 8, although a few schools have maintained such programs. Curriculum study groups might well give attention to the possibility of foreign languages in junior high

[26] The Committee of Twelve of the American Philological Association in its 1899 report provided for four-, five-, and six-year sequences in the study of Latin. Included in the National Education Association, *Report of Committee on College Entrance Requirements,* the Association, 1899, p. 713.

school grades. Otherwise we may find ourselves in the strange situation of promoting foreign language study in the elementary grades and the senior high school with a two-year gap between those levels. If the movement for teaching foreign languages in the elementary school continues to grow, it will be necessary to plan for needed modifications in the sequence of courses at the secondary level. This planning will of necessity include the junior high school grades. A ninth-grade language course in the future may be an advanced rather than a beginning course.

The choice of languages to be offered also depends on such circumstances as the availability of teachers, materials, and the like. But it should also if possible be related to the objectives served by foreign language study. The choice will be affected more by some objectives than by others. Many languages are practically interchangeable so far as disciplinary values are concerned, whether these be thought of as formal discipline or as the contribution that foreign language study can make to the nature and limitation of language itself. One requisite is that the language have sufficient vocabulary and modes of expression to handle philosophical, scientific, and religious thought. Any such language will serve even though its grammar may not present unusual difficulties to the student.

This cannot be said with regard to the practical and cultural values. Here the choice of a language does make a difference. But the practical values do not clarify the matter, since there are many different kinds of practicality that give different answers. If practicality were the only thing to be considered, it would serve in a general way to establish higher priority for modern languages than for Latin or classical Greek. Otherwise it provides little to go on. What is practical for the career diplomat is not necessarily so for the research scholar in science or history. The practical needs of a specialist in foreign trade may not coincide with those of the vacation traveler. Moreover, the dynamic nature of world political relationships is such that a given language or set of languages may be impractical one decade but not the next. Few people in the 1930's would have predicted the practical significance taken on by the modern Arabic tongues in the 1950's. While practical values are important considerations in language study, the practicality criteria are so diversified and complex that an attempt to use them in this connection leads to riding off madly in all directions at once, at least as far as the high school is concerned. It is a different story in the large university or the specialized vocational school where greater variety in offerings can be established.

Cultural values, on the other hand, although not furnishing ready-made answers, may serve to point the directions in which answers may be sought. The broad cultural objective of international understanding does not throw too much light on the choice of languages, but cultural transmission through literature does. A suitable language for the high school curriculum from this point of view is one that offers both quality and breadth in its literature. There are, of course, many languages that meet the tests of literary quality and scope. Fortunately, and in part because these tests have been used to a certain extent, the languages currently offered in our high schools do meet these tests.

It is of course these cultural values that justify the retention of Latin. This is not to say that Latin should be the language offered when only one is possible, but rather that Latin presents strong claims, which cannot be readily ignored. The same is true of classical Greek with the important difference that where Greek ceased to be an important medium in the living culture of western society, Latin continued so well into modern times. It is the most common language factor of European civilization, both ancient and modern. Its literature contains most of the ideas that constitute our western cultural heritage and provides a common base for European culture as a whole. It would be a tragic loss indeed if Latin ever truly became a dead language in the sense of being known only to a few specialists. Modern European languages as well as those of other world regions, however, are also strong in cultural value. Ideally a high school should offer Latin along with one or more modern tongues, with the choice left open to the student. But when only one language is possible, the application of both the practical and cultural objectives points to a modern language as the wiser choice.

Still another difficulty intrudes. The argument may be reasonably advanced that a wider appreciation of humanity's culture demands the study of non-European tongues as well as, or perhaps even instead of, those from the European culture region. Large high schools of course might well provide diversified offerings, which include Oriental and other non-European languages. This lies beyond the means of the great majority of high schools, however, and is better left to the college and the vocational school.

The task of reëstablishing foreign language study is one of the most important and demanding that confronts those concerned with the high school curriculum. Problems will not be met by the tendencies of various groups of educators to blame one another for the situation. But they can be met by taking constructive first steps in the curriculum planning carried on by local school staffs and communities. Every such constructive step brings the high school closer to its functions of transmitting the cultural heritage and equipping young people to live intelligently and effectively in today's and tomorrow's world.

Bibliography

Allerton House Conference on Education, *Foreign Language Teaching in Illinois,* Southern Illinois University, Carbondale, 1957.

American Classical League, *The Classical Investigation: Part One, General Report,* Princeton University Press, 1924.

Bodmer, Frederick, *The Loom of Language,* W. W. Norton & Company, 1944.

Cole, Robert D., *Foreign Languages and Their Teaching,* D. Appleton and Company, 1931.

Coleman, Algernon, *The Teaching of Modern Foreign Languages in the United States: A Report Prepared for the Modern Language Study,* The Macmillan Company, 1930.

Huse, H. R., *Reading and Speaking Foreign Languages,* University of North Carolina Press, 1945.

Johnston, Marjorie C., "How Can Modern Language Teaching Promote International Understanding," *Bulletin of the National Association of Secondary School Principals,* December, 1956, pp. 70–85.

Johnston, Marjorie C. (ed.), *Modern Foreign Languages in the High School,* Bulletin 1958, No. 16, U.S. Department of Health, Education, and Welfare.

Kelsey, Francis W. (ed.), *Latin and Greek in American Education,* The Macmillan Company, 1911.

Parker, William Riley, *The National Interest and Foreign Languages,* Prepared for Citizen Consultations sponsored by The U.S. National Commission for Unesco, Department of State, Revised edition, January, 1957.

Reindrop, Reginald C., "The Reading Aim Reexamined," *The Modern Language Journal,* May, 1957, pp. 239–243.

CHAPTER 11

Mathematics

Mathematics is a language, a more specialized, exact, precise, and refined form of language than any of those to which the term "language" is ordinarily applied.[1] It has become a powerful and indispensable tool in the description, analysis, and control of phenomena that can neither be accurately expressed nor understood in ordinary language alone. It is the most truly international of all languages. It is one of the most remarkable of all human achievements and as such forms part of the cultural heritage that schools seek to transmit and on which they build for the future.

Nevertheless, mathematics did not occupy an important part of the curriculum in the early colonial Latin Grammar Schools.[2] Arithmetic and geometry were offered by the colleges from the outset, but algebra did not appear until the middle of the eighteenth century.[3] The introduction of mathematics at the secondary level was largely an academy-sponsored innovation. It represented the

---

[1] This is not to say, however, that language about mathematics is necessarily more precise or standardized than in other fields. "The desirability of specifying a precise concept of variable is obvious. Unfortunately, such a precise concept does not exist in mathematics today. Different groups of mathematicians use the word in different ways." Bruce R. Meserve, "Implications for the Mathematics Curriculum," National Council of Teachers of Mathematics, Twenty-Third Yearbook, *Insights into Modern Mathematics,* The Council, 1957, p. 409.

[2] It was as late as the period from 1814 to 1828 that mathematics became well established in the program of the Latin Grammar School. Willis Lloyd Pickard, *Evolution of Algebra as a Secondary School Subject,* George Peabody College for Teachers, Nashville, Tenn., 1948, p. 16.

[3] Pickard, *op. cit.,* p. 8.

trend both to popularize culture and to offer practical studies. The free public high schools, taking their lead from the academies, also made mathematics an important part of curricular offerings. Furthermore, the various mathematics branches worked their way down to the lower levels of schooling, with arithmetic establishing itself in the elementary grades and algebra and plane geometry in the first two high school years. By the end of the nineteenth century the program had evolved much as we know it today, and the N. E. A. Committee on College Entrance Requirements in 1899 recommended two years of mathematics as constants for high school graduation.[4] This group suggested algebra and plane geometry in Grades 9 and 10, solid geometry and plane trigonometry in Grade 11, and advanced algebra and mathematical reviews in Grade 12,[5] forming the so-called traditional sequence which, with minor modifications, has survived generations of criticism and attack.

As is true of other language studies, the objectives of mathematics have been often described as disciplinary, practical, and cultural. The disciplinary values of mathematics were considered to be second only to those of Latin. In more recent times, advocates of mathematics have felt little need to draw on disciplinary justifications, except at times in connection with plane and solid geometry as usually taught. Even cultural objectives are rarely mentioned. They are nonetheless important, whether viewed as the preservation and transmission of human achievement or as the enrichment and satisfaction that mathematics study may bring to the individual. But the usual claims for mathematics are practical ones, ranging all the way from the everyday applications of arithmetic to the specialized contributions of the higher branches to every form of scientific and technological advance.

ENROLLMENTS IN MATHEMATICS

Neglect of such a field as this in the high school curriculum would clearly be a cultural and practical disaster. This awareness is so widely shared that decline in mathematics studies and enroll-

[4] National Education Association, *Report of Committee on College Entrance Requirements,* The Association, University of Chicago Press, 1899, p. 32.
[5] *Ibid.,* p. 21.

ments, although not nearly as pronounced as those in foreign languages, has aroused far more apprehension and concern. The field of mathematics is, therefore, one to which critics of high school programs have devoted special attention and on which many citizens feel present-day high schools to be particularly vulnerable to valid criticism.

In 1900, 56.3 percent of the students were enrolled in beginning algebra; by 1952–1953 this figure had declined to 24.6 percent. Algebra enrollments then made a partial recovery, the figure reaching 28.7 percent for the school year 1956–1957. In the case of geometry the figures declined from 27.4 percent of total enrollment in 1900 to 11.4 percent in 1954–1955, rising to 13.6 percent in 1956–1957. On the other hand, the figures for trigonometry increased slightly from 1.9 percent in 1900 to an all-time high in 1956–1957 of 2.9 percent. The upswing in trigonometry was a late development with only 1.7 percent of the students enrolled in this subject just four years before.[6]

Comparisons between more recent figures and those as far back as 1900 are made on the basis of total school enrollments. Another way of looking at enrollments, however, is to compare the enrollment in a given subject with the total enrollment in the grade where the subject is usually taken, such as the ninth grade for beginning algebra and the tenth grade for plane geometry.[7] They stood as follows in 1956.[8]

General mathematics (9th)	43.1 percent
Elementary algebra	67.0
Plane geometry	41.6

[6] Kenneth E. Brown, *Offerings and Enrollments in Science and Mathematics in Public High Schools,* Office of Education Pamphlet No. 120, 1956, U.S. Department of Health, Education, and Welfare, 1957, table 16, p. 29.

[7] The term "usual" is subject to some qualification. Some students take algebra in Grades 10, 11, or 12, while some take geometry in 11 or 12. A survey made in Wisconsin in 1950 showed that 57.6 percent of the students enrolled in beginning algebra were tenth graders while 43.5 percent of those enrolled in plane geometry were eleventh graders. Lawrence F. Wahlstrom, *The Status of the Teaching of High School Mathematics in the State of Wisconsin.* Unpublished doctoral dissertation, University of Wisconsin, 1950, table LII, p. 190.

[8] Brown, *op. cit.,* table 17, p. 31. The combined figures of 110.1 percent for ninth-grade general mathematics and elementary algebra probably reflect the presence of students above ninth grade in both subjects.

Intermediate algebra	32.2 percent
Trigonometry	9.2
Solid geometry	7.6

Few would contend that the plane geometry enrollments represent a satisfactory state of affairs, regardless of how the figures are drawn. On the other hand, the enrollments in algebra and general mathematics seem more encouraging. Although the merits of the general mathematics course are open to debate, high schools cannot be fairly accused of contempt or indifference toward the field as a whole on the basis of the first-year or ninth-grade course. Still another indication of mathematics enrollments is the percentage of students who have taken various courses at some time in their high school careers. A survey made of a sample of seniors in Wisconsin public and private high schools in the spring of 1957 showed that 77.4 percent had taken algebra, 53.6 percent had taken geometry, and 12.7 percent had taken trigonometry.[9]

What seems more alarming is the presence of high schools with limited offerings in mathematics. In the fall of 1956, only 91.9 percent of high schools with ninth-grade students were offering elementary algebra, leaving 8.1 percent which did not. Plane geometry was offered in only 81.2 percent of high schools with tenth-grade students, intermediate algebra in only 63.3 percent of those with eleventh-grade students, and plane trigonometry in only 33.4 percent of those with twelfth-grade students.[10] Regardless of the sizes of these schools and the numbers of students in them, it is tragic that some students are so deprived. This is not an indictment of American high schools in general, nor even of the particular schools concerned, for they are undoubtedly the victims of local circumstances and difficulties. It is a state of affairs that all should seek to correct.

Mathematics is practically a universal constant in the seventh-grade and eighth-grade programs of junior high schools. So far as Grades 9 through 12 go, the tendency has been to require one

[9] Edward A. Krug, Clifford S. Liddle, Russell C. Mosely, and Daniel Parkinson, *The College-Preparatory Function in Wisconsin High Schools,* School of Education, University of Wisconsin, 1959, Table 14, p. 53.

[10] Brown, *op. cit.,* table 12, p. 23.

year of mathematics toward graduation. A 1950 survey made in Wisconsin shows that 52.9 percent of the schools required one year and 18.7 percent two years, with figures of less than 1 percent for one-half year, one and one-half years, and three years, while 26.4 percent of the schools required no mathematics whatsoever.[11] Even the one-year requirement, however, seems meager to many people, especially when compared with the more extensive requirements in social studies and English. Whether it is or not depends on a number of things, particularly on attempts to resolve the question of individual differences and on the nature of the mathematics sequence itself.

MATHEMATICS AND THE INDIVIDUAL STUDENT

Individual differences in such matters as native intelligence, cultural background, motivation, and need are important considerations in all school subjects. Mathematics is affected by all these, plus one other by which it is sharply and peculiarly affected, namely, emotion. For reasons about which we have had many speculations but few conclusions, mathematics is to many people an emotional blind spot. They have learned to hate and fear mathematical symbols, expressions, and activities. Such people may show a considerable range of intellectual ability in other subjects, but no matter how hard they try, mathematics seems beyond them. In the days when grades represented absolute rather than relative achievement, mathematics contributed far more than its share of school failures. This state of affairs, rather than indifference toward the field itself, had much to do with the gradual abandonment of mathematics requirements, particularly in the algebra-geometry sequence.

One widespread attempt to adapt the mathematics program to individual differences has been through courses called general mathematics. The term is a confusing one and has meant several different things. It has been used to refer to courses that include the traditional materials of algebra, geometry, and trigonometry, but with a more integrated or correlated pattern of organization. For the most part, however, a general mathematics course means

[11] Wahlstrom, *op. cit.*, table LIV, p. 195.

one that is designedly both easier and more practical than those in the traditional sequence. The two aspects are not mutually interdependent. Easy mathematics is not necessarily more practical; nor on the other hand is practical mathematics necessarily easy. General mathematics seeks to be both and to resolve two curricular dilemmas at one time.

The practical aspects of the general mathematics course reflect several kinds of assumptions or concerns. One is that a certain minimum level of mathematical literacy is necessary for everyday living. This is the level represented by the four fundamental operations with whole numbers, fractions, decimals, and percentage. This level is presumably reached by the average student at the end of the eighth grade. Students who do not reach it by that time will, it is hoped, get there at the end of the ninth-grade general mathematics. The course is, therefore, partly remedial in much the same sense as remedial reading. Another kind of practicality consists of possible vocational applications, particularly to shop work and routine business operations. This is an older view, reflecting the unwarranted assumption that a poor student academically is good material for learning mechanical trades. But the case for the practicality of general mathematics has been made overwhelmingly on the grounds of applications to such personal-social activities as keeping budgets, handling of checking accounts and other banking procedures, planning insurance and investments, and computing taxes. Such topics as these have supplied the major content areas for general mathematics; they represent matters largely adult in nature and have had little appeal or motivation value for ninth-grade students. Probably no course in the history of the high school curriculum has had to carry so many disadvantages and liabilities as general mathematics. Most teachers in mathematics departments seek to avoid it if at all possible and accept their assignments to it as a contribution to harmonious interdepartment relationships or as an unavoidable chore. None of this means that the objectives or materials of general mathematics are undesirable or wrong. But it does suggest a reëxamination of familiar assumptions and the possible reorganization of the curriculum to achieve better placement of such materials.

The existence of parallel courses at the ninth-grade level (general mathematics and elementary algebra) makes it necessary for the student to choose between them and for the school to provide wise counsel in making the choice. Previous achievement in mathematics is of course one important base, but not always an accurate one. Some students with good mathematics aptitude have poor records for various reasons: laziness, poor motivation, carelessness in computation, and the like. Algebra aptitude tests may, therefore, throw additional light on the chances of the student's success in the traditional sequence. The level and intensity of the student's mathematical interests are also important indications. Finally there is the question of need or future possible use of mathematics. This is, of course, very difficult to determine with a fourteen-year-old boy or girl.

Unfortunately, the tendency has been to fall back on the old dualism between college-preparatory and non-college-preparatory tracks. In some schools this is the only basis used. College-preparatory students are advised to take algebra, non-college-preparatory students to take general mathematics. This dualism is sometimes modified by advising college-bound students with poor records in previous mathematics to take general mathematics in ninth grade as preparation for algebra in the tenth. As has been previously noted, however, it is possible to enter a number of colleges and college programs without algebra and geometry. College-bound students who are weak in mathematics do not, therefore, need to take algebra and geometry for college entrance purposes, if they choose their college accordingly. On the other hand, non-college-bound students who can profit both practically and culturally from the traditional sequence have in many instances not been encouraged to select it. This practice has undoubtedly contributed to the decline of relative enrollments in the algebra-geometry-trigonometry sequence.

A somewhat different approach is indicated in the following statement, one that seeks a classification of students based on interest in mathematics rather than on the distinctions among various high school programs or tracks.

Gradually he (the writer) has arrived at the tentative judgment that there are four categories of secondary school mathematics pupils and that there should be consequently four categories of curricular offerings. These offerings would be for: (a) The pupil who feels no interest in mathematics and would be studying it unwillingly and primarily or solely as a present and future consumer; (b) The pupil who has some interest and is studying it primarily as a part of a liberal education; (c) The pupil who may or may not have interest in mathematics, but who is studying it because he does have interest in applied mechanics and knows his need for it as a machinist, toolmaker, draftsman, or other such trades; (d) The pupil who has high interest in mathematics, and average or superior ability, and who expects to use mathematics as a professional worker in the field of teaching, chemistry, insurance, engineering, or other such professional fields.[12]

In this approach, a student in category (b)—that of liberal education—might take the algebra-geometry sequence regardless of future college plans or career goals that demand mathematics. The one in category (c)—that of interest in mechanical trades—conceivably could choose either general mathematics or algebra. One writer suggests that qualified students with vocational goals of this kind might well make algebra their choice. "If an able boy is planning to enter the trades or industry instead of attending college, he will profit greatly by electing this course usually designated as college preparatory. Such work as that of the pattern maker and machinist—widely expanding fields—are surprisingly mathematical. Recent technical advancements are based upon a foundation of mathematics that makes promotion difficult, even if the worker is equipped with the ever-helpful handbook, unless he is grounded in arithmetic, algebra, geometry, and some trigonometry."[13]

[12] Douglass Brown, "The Mathematics Teacher's Part in Effective Guidance for Optimum Use of Differentiated Curriculums," National Council of Teachers of Mathematics, Twenty-Second Yearbook, *Emerging Practices in Mathematics Education*, The Council, 1954, pp. 95–96.

[13] Mary A. Potter, "Using Homogeneous Grouping to Lead Pupils to Their Own Highest Level of Achievement," National Council of Teachers of Mathematics, Twenty-Second Yearbook, *Emerging Practices in Mathematics Education*, The Council, 1954, pp. 35–36.

Another approach makes the differentiations along the lines of use of or need for mathematics.

First, we must recognize that we cannot have the same goals for all our students. Students arrive in our hands with a wide range of ability, mathematical training, interest, and initiative. Most of us teach in schools where we are required to take the students as they arrive and do what we can for them. What should we do? Let us consider an answer to this question with reference to three groups of students—those needing remedial work in mathematics, those so-called average mathematics students who expect to use little mathematics in their life work or training, and finally those students who expect to enter college curriculums requiring at least college algebra or to enter technical training in which mathematics is used. For the first group, those needing remedial training, our path is clear—we must supply the remedial training. Except for the few students who are mentally incapable of completing the remedial work, we then find ourselves with essentially two groups—those whose life work will require extensive use of mathematics and those who need only enough mathematics to become good citizens in our scientific society.[14]

Each of the foregoing statements takes various kinds of differences into account. The choice before the student is a complex one, since he must reckon with his own ability and previous performance in mathematics, his interests in the field, and his vocational goals. Ability, interest, and future vocational use are to a certain extent interwoven and interdependent. Few students with low mathematics ability develop a high degree of interest; on the other hand, high interest does not necessarily accompany high ability. Vocational choices when realistically made inevitably reflect both interest and ability. Unfortunately such choices are not always realistic, but may include a good deal of romanticizing and vague emotional impulse. What to tell students who wish to make unrealistic choices is one of the most difficult problems of counseling. It seems best, after all the cautions are expressed, not to stand in the way of such students. "Every pupil should have help in his curricular choice from his counselor and his mathematics teacher and, perhaps, from other sources. But, finally, *he must be free to*

[14] Meserve, *op. cit.*, pp. 422–423.

make his own choice. If he chooses wrongly and fails one semester, so be it. What one of us has not failed, at least once, in life outside of academic walls? No counselor and no mathematics teacher is omniscient enough to make important life decisions for some other. Few pupils, if they have the help outlined above, will make grave errors in their own decisions."[15] To permit students to make apparently mistaken choices may appear unpalatable, but it is probably less so than for the counselor arbitrarily to close doors, especially when the counselor may be mistaken.

The school, then, does not ordinarily close doors against the willing student, but the question remains whether or not it should guide the unwilling student through doors he would rather not enter. Should the choice not to take mathematics be open to qualified students? This is not so with regard to English and social studies. As far as general education values are concerned, a good case can be made for stipulating mathematics as a graduation constant. Let us consider first the desirability of such a requirement in the light of curricular offerings as now organized: namely, the algebra-geometry-trigonometry sequence on one hand and the general mathematics on the other.

One of the specific reasons for the existing requirement is to bring up to some minimum level of mathematical literacy those students who have not reached this point at the end of the eighth grade. Such students are usually enrolled in general mathematics. If they are college bound, this is done with the hope that the course will equip them to go on with algebra in tenth grade. In any case, the presence of such students is a handicap to the development of the general mathematics course. This difficulty can be met in part by ability grouping, which is probably advisable as a general policy in setting up general mathematics classes or sectioning. As far as the very low-ability student is concerned, however, it might be better to enroll him in a special non-credit remedial arithmetic class, similar to those that are in some schools set up for remedial reading. He would stay in this class until he reached a minimum level of achievement or until in the judgment of the teacher he had gone as far as seemed possible at a given time. In some cases

[15] Douglass Brown, *op. cit.,* p. 99.

students might be required to join such a class at a point later in their high school work, at which point they would have gained months or years in their mental ages. It would be advisable to administer a test in arithmetic fundamentals to all students at the beginning of the twelfth grade as a final check. In any case, the very low-ability students in mathematics would be exempted from the one-year requirement on a grade-and-credit basis. These students represent only a tiny fraction of the entire student body.

All others would be enrolled in one year of mathematics as a minimum, either in the algebra-geometry sequence or in some alternative course. Perhaps students electing algebra might be held to a two-year requirement, including geometry. In practice this would probably decrease algebra enrollments. The one-year requirement need not necessarily be met in the ninth or tenth grade. As noted previously, a student with a chronological age of 16 or 17 has made some growth in mental ability since the time he was 13 or 14. Since mental ability appears to be closely related to mathematics studies, some students could pursue the algebra-geometry sequence more effectively in the eleventh and twelfth grades than in the earlier high school years. If the school is large enough, separate sections in beginning algebra and plane geometry may be organized for students taking these subjects in the last two high school years.

General mathematics, understood as a program that develops mathematical abilities in relation to personal-social needs, might well be moved into the eleventh and twelfth grades for most students who elect this way of fulfilling the mathematics requirement. Such matters as insurance, investments, social security, and family finance are more appropriate to older than to younger adolescents. Student motivation in and attitudes toward general mathematics would probably be considerably improved if this practice were followed. Under these circumstances, general mathematics would gradually lose its designation as a bonehead subject and become a vehicle for substantial learning, related to objectives some would not accept, but substantial nonetheless. It could be related not only to immediate personal needs, but also to the study of political, social, and economic topics, fulfilling some of the functions of the twelfth-grade American problems course in schools where the latter is not offered.

Students would be counseled to take the algebra-geometry sequence largely on the basis of ability and interest. The college-preparatory versus non-college-preparatory dualism as a basis for counseling should be abandoned. Choice of particular colleges or college programs, however, should remain an important consideration. It is one thing for a student to choose algebra because he intends to enter a particular college, which requires it, or to follow a college program in which it is necessary, but something quite different to choose algebra simply because it is tagged generally as a college-preparatory subject.

Students with outstanding mathematical interests and aptitudes would take four years of mathematics in Grades 9 through 12, either in the traditional algebra-geometry sequence or in a reorganized sequence including the traditional materials. Such students should be encouraged to plan for higher schooling and for careers in mathematics itself or in its various applications. But the full sequence would not be restricted to those with college plans or career objectives specifically related to mathematics. Some students might follow it as preparatory to study in a post-high school vocational school. Others might take it for personal satisfaction and cultural enrichment regardless of their career plans.

Several national reports in the late 1950's urged that superior students take more than the two years of mathematics traditionally identified with college-entrance requirements. The Conant report recommended four years for academically talented students, that is, the top 15 percent.[16] The Commission on Mathematics of the College Entrance Examination Board recommended three years as the minimum amount for students it termed the "college capable," with efforts made to have such students take four years.[17] The NEA Conference on the Academically Talented recommended three years of mathematics for all academically talented students

[16] James Bryant Conant, *The American High School Today*, McGraw-Hill Book Company, Inc., 1959, p. 57.
[17] Commission on Mathematics, College Entrance Examination Board, *Program for College Preparatory Mathematics*, The Board, 1959, p. 11–12.

and four or possibly five years for "pupils with special talents in science and mathematics."[18] Possibly not all these students have the interest in mathematics that would justify their taking it for three or four years even when their aptitudes in mathematics are consistent with their general intelligence. Counselors should, however, raise the question of electing three or four years of mathematics with all such students.

POSSIBLE REORGANIZATION OF THE SEQUENCE IN MATHEMATICS

The conventional mathematics program is not the only possible context in which to examine offerings and requirements. Mathematicians have been critical of the traditional organization of materials in algebra, geometry, and trigonometry, contending, among other things, that the separation between algebra and geometry results in loss of time and in the failure to develop relationships between the two bodies of material. Solid geometry as a separate course has long been under criticism. The suggestion is not, however, that the subject matter of solid geometry be eliminated. "Rather it appears that some solid geometry should be done in conjunction with the study of plane geometry, while other topics from solid geometry, such as mensuration formulas, should be done in conjunction with algebra."[19]

As is true in many fields, some cautions about integration need to be kept in mind. The interrelationships of subject matters that become apparent to the advanced student may not provide the best approaches for beginners. On the other hand, mathematics may be a field where such integration is possible without loss of comprehension to the beginner, since it depends primarily on a sequential development of necessarily interrelated concepts and operations. Comprehension for the beginner may even be facilitated. These points cannot be determined by speculation alone, but need careful checking as new programs are developed and used.

---

[18] Daniel B. Lloyd (chairman), "Education of the Academically-Talented Secondary School Pupil in Mathematics," in *The Identification and Education of the Academically-Talented Student in the American Secondary School,* The Conference Report, National Education Association, February, 1958, pp. 97–98.

[19] Meserve, *op. cit.,* p. 425.

The ideal of a more rational sequence of mathematics studies is not a new one, although it seems nearer to fulfillment today than in the past. Discussions of such possibilities extend back at least to the early 1920's. Renewed interest in mathematics education in the middle 1950's stimulated a number of attempts to reorganize the traditional sequence. Among the groups concerned were the University of Illinois Committee on Secondary School Mathematics, the School and College Study of Admission with Advanced Standing, The Commission on Mathematics of the College Entrance Examination Board, the Science Teaching Improvement Program of the American Association for the Advancement of Science, and the Curriculum Committee of the National Council of Teachers of Mathematics.[20] These groups have sought in the main not only a better organization of mathematics, but the possibility of including new materials and topics.[21]

The following comment, although made with specific reference to the programs in Illinois, indicates some of the general directions of the movement toward curricular reorganization in high school mathematics.

What comes out in the end is more a change in emphasis than in content. Along with that goes a change in the traditional sequence in which high school math is taught. A full four year course used to begin with one year of algebra followed by one year of plane geometry followed by another year of algebra followed by a semester of solid geometry followed by a semester of trigonometry. (A relatively small percentage of American high school pupils go the route. Many of those preparing for college drop out after the first two years, when the math requirement for entrance to most United States colleges is fulfilled.) Under the Illinois system pupils follow threads of arithmetic and alge-

[20] Henry S. Dyer, Robert Kalin, and Frederic M. Lord, *Problems in Mathematical Education*, Educational Testing Service, Princeton, New Jersey, 1956, pp. 23–25.

[21] The Commission on Mathematics of the College Entrance Examination Board has recommended a four-year program for college-capable students that involves some reorganization of and additions to the traditional sequence for the first three years plus possible arrangements and selections of advanced content for the fourth year. Each of the fourth-year possibilities includes one semester of materials termed "elementary functions," with the second semester consisting of "introductory probability with statistical applications" or "introduction to modern algebra" or "elementary functions enlarged to a full year by additional topics." Commission on Mathematics, College Entrance Examination Board, *op. cit.*, pp. 30–33.

bra and geometry all through, and so develop a feeling for the essential unity of all mathematics.

To get an idea of how the subjects are woven together, follow the freshman course. Traditionally called "elementary algebra," it is known in the Illinois system simply as "first course." It is mainly, but not all, algebra. It is also a little arithmetic and a little geometry. And first, last, and always, it is a course in language.[22]

Which students should take such a sequence in mathematics? Some modification of point of view in the Illinois schools using it has apparently developed. "The original thought that the new approach would have to be limited to college preparatory candidates is gradually being revised by experience to include more high school enrolees."[23] This suggests a possible way out of the present dualism between the traditional sequence on one hand and the general mathematics sequence on the other. A single sequence of mathematics ideas may serve for all students except those who need remedial arithmetic or those with mathematical blind spots that cannot be overcome. By means of ability grouping it would be possible for each section in mathematics at any level to begin at the place in the sequence most appropriate for the students in it and to move as far and as fast as the capacities of the students would permit. The sequence might be planned from the seventh grade rather than from the ninth grade upwards. There would be no ceilings on the progress of the high-ability sections. Some of these would be dealing with algebra and plane geometry materials to a considerable extent before the end of the eighth grade. Some students in the eleventh and twelfth grades might not only enter but complete the work of differential and integral calculus as traditionally handled in the introductory college courses. The degree of differentiation would depend on the size of the school and the number of ability sections that could be organized. All but the very smallest high schools, however, would permit some differentiation through ability grouping.

Some of the topics now included in courses called general

[22] Helen Rowan, "The Wonderful World of Why," *The Saturday Review,* November 2, 1957, p. 44.
[23] *Ibid.*

mathematics would be moved to appropriate courses in science, social studies, business education, industrial arts, and the like. The twelfth-grade problems of democracy course is an excellent vehicle for the study of taxation, investments, insurance, public finance, and personal and family finance. This does not mean that the mathematics courses of the unified sequence would be devoid of applications. Such applications are inherent in the mathematics ideas developed and would be used in the mathematics class to the degree needed for making those ideas concrete and meaningful.

The advantages of such a program over most of our present arrangements is that it provides a single sequence of mathematics studies with provisions for individual differences on a flexible basis through the timing and pacing of studies within the various sections. Our present algebra-general mathematics dualism both goes too far and fails to go far enough. It arbitrarily splits the school population into two general groups and then fails to provide sufficient differentiation within those groups unless the algebra sections and the general mathematics sections are set up on ability bases and criteria. With a single and unified sequence accompanied by ability sectioning, high schools could justifiably require two years of mathematics in Grades 9 through 12 as a graduation constant.[24] Each student would be placed in a section appropriate to his achievement and aptitude levels. The present agonizing decision between general mathematics and algebra would be avoided; the college-preparatory versus non-college-preparatory dualism would have no meaning. Each student would move as far as possible in the light of his capacities during the two-year requirement. Those with special mathematics aptitudes and interests would take additional work on an elective basis.

MODERN MATHEMATICS

Much interest in mathematics curricular revision generally as well as in the development of the reorganized sequence has been

---

[24] With provisions for the waiving of these requirements for the weakest students on an individual basis. It would be preferable to place such students in a non-credit remedial arithmetic class as indicated in the preceding consideration of the conventional mathematics program.

stimulated by the rapid development of ideas and materials known as modern mathematics. "Twentieth-century mathematics has a new look. Its form and structure are in many respects quite different from that of previous centuries. Teachers must understand this form, must know what 20th century mathematics is about, if they are to prepare their pupils for living in the 20th century."[25] Those who are interested in penetrating these developments might well turn to the National Council of Teachers of Mathematics, Twenty-Third Yearbook, *Insights into Modern Mathematics,* published by the Council in 1957. The scope of modern mathematics is indicated by the topics treated in the chapter on curricular implications: sets; numbers and operations; variables; functions; coördinates; mathematical systems; proof; statistical thinking and machine computation; terminology; and generalization, abstraction, and arithmetization.[26]

The ideas of modern mathematics are numerous, varied, and range from some that appear very simple to others so complex that only those equipped with considerable mathematical knowledge can comprehend them. Some are highly abstract and at present have no particular applications, while others have proved to be of immense practical value in a number of fields. The term "new" in this connection may be somewhat inaccurate, as is true in various disciplines; these new ideas have been developing over some period of time. Some of the topics listed in the foregoing paragraph are, of course, familiar to those who have studied older mathematics, for example, function and variable. The newness lies not in the topic itself, but in its treatment and interpretation. Conventional mathematics courses usually have not stressed the central importance of these as ideas. "The approach to our work through mathematical operations is typical of many of the changes in *mode of presentation rather than content* that are implied by modern mathematics."[27] Other topics, however, are new in the sense of not appearing to any great extent in our past and present mathematics courses at the high school level.

[25] Meserve, *op. cit.,* p. 404.
[26] *Ibid.,* pp. 404–427.
[27] *Ibid.,* p. 408.

Although the incorporation of modern mathematics does not necessarily require the abandonment of the traditional sequence, experimental programs, such as those in Illinois, have made definite and specific use of modern mathematics ideas and topics.

The most pervading mathematical idea that the Illinois experiment sets out to propagate is the concept of sets. Sets in themselves are old, but their presentation as a point of view is new. A set is any collection of things. The things can be numbers, points, lines, vectors, physical forces, people, or a set can be a philosophical notion such as brotherhood. By thinking in terms of sets, children learn to see apparent relationships, discover hidden patterns, and invent new arrangements to meet new problems. Having evolved this habit of thinking, they forget the details and retain a mental discipline which can be useful in such advanced modern mathematical techniques as public opinion sampling, statistical testing of the validity of drugs, programming of high speed computers, or calculating the orbit of a manmade moon from the position of "beeps" in the sky.[28]

Mathematics promises to be one of the most creative fields for curricular study and improvement. The desire to bring about such improvement is no passing fad, but a serious recognition of the importance of the field not only in science and technology but in the intellectual development of the individual. Such desire is shared by mathematicians, by specialists in mathematics education, by students of the general secondary curriculum, by many teachers in other fields, and by many interested members of the general public. Central to the development of modern mathematics itself as well as to the reorganizing of the mathematics sequence is the stress upon meaning and logic. And this is another way of saying that the mathematics curriculum is moving toward a fuller realization of mathematics not as a body of mechanical manipulations and routines, but as a language of unparalleled beauty, precision, and power.

Bibliography

Beberman, Max, *An Emerging Program of Secondary School Mathematics,* Harvard University Press, 1958.

[28] Rowan, *op. cit.,* p. 44.

Brown, Kenneth E., *Offerings and Enrollments in Science and Mathematics in Public High Schools,* Office of Education Pamphlet No. 118, U.S. Department of Health, Education, and Welfare, 1956.

Commission on Mathematics, College Entrance Examination Board, *Program for College Preparatory Mathematics,* The Board, 1959.

Commission on the Reorganization of Secondary Education of the NEA, *The Problem of Mathematics in Secondary Education,* Department of the Interior, Bureau of Education, Bulletin 1920, No. 1.

Dyer, Henry S.; Kalin, Robert; and Lord, Frederic M., *Problems in Mathematical Education,* Educational Testing Service, 1956.

National Council of Teachers of Mathematics, Fifteenth Yearbook, *The Place of Mathematics in Secondary Education,* The Final Report of the Joint Commission of the Mathematical Association of America and the National Council of Teachers of Mathematics, Bureau of Publications, Teachers College, Columbia University, 1940.

National Council of Teachers of Mathematics, Twenty-Second Yearbook, *Emerging Practices in Mathematics Education,* The Council, 1954.

National Council of Teachers of Mathematics, Twenty-Third Yearbook, *Insights into Modern Mathematics,* The Council, 1957.

National Council of Teachers of Mathematics, Secondary-School Curriculum Committee, "The Secondary Mathematics Curriculum," *The Mathematics Teacher,* May, 1959, pp. 389–417.

Pickard, Willis Lloyd, *Evolution of Algebra as a Secondary School Subject,* George Peabody College for Teachers, 1948.

Progressive Education Association Commission on the Secondary School Curriculum, *Mathematics in General Education,* D. Appleton-Century Company, 1940.

CHAPTER 12

Social Studies

The distinction between content subjects and skill subjects is largely a matter of convenience. All subjects have content, and all subjects demand and teach the use of skills. Nevertheless the distinction persists, with the instructional fields of social studies and natural science usually regarded as being more on the content side. This probably reflects the vast areas of knowledge represented by these fields, the world of human affairs on one hand and that of natural phenomena on the other. Other fields have content, but their content is usually more specialized and clearly limited. The generalized and almost unlimited domains of social studies and science undoubtedly account for the claims as well as the dilemmas of curricula in these fields.

Some critics of the schools interpret the term "social studies" as a departure from the solid content of history, just as they interpret "language arts" as a departure from English. In neither case is such interpretation justified. It is possible, of course, to organize social studies on a fused or correlated basis in which history does not appear as a separate subject. But the term usually means the instructional field representing the separate subjects of history, civics, economics, sociology, and contemporary problems. History has not disappeared from our high schools as a separate subject, nor is it likely to disappear.

The unifying thread in such diversity of courses is the study of human relationships, particularly as these have been expressed in the forms, institutions, customs, and patterns of societies. When we speak of history as one of the social studies, we mean the history of these aspects of human relationships, supplemented by historical materials related to art, mathematics, music, and like fields of endeavor. The history of mathematics alone would not be a social study in the strict sense. This is consistent with long-term usage, for when we pick up a book called the *History of France,* we expect it to deal with the social life of the French people. In such a book the history of French art, philosophy, music, and the like would appear only as these affect and are affected by the broader aspects of French society. History is, then, like English, a unifying subject, one that draws together many strands of human experience in relation to the organizing principle of chronology or continuity. The specific materials of a history course depend to a large extent on arbitrary selection. Other social studies courses define themselves in more intrinsic terms suggested by their titles, although this is probably less true of sociology and geography than of economics or political science. These courses do overlap, however, and there are many interrelationships among them; it is possible, nevertheless, to identify the specific content or emphasis that applies to each one taken by itself.

Various courses in the field we now call social studies (the term itself was not used until after 1900) entered the secondary school program as part of the great nineteenth-century expansion of the school subjects. Of these the most numerous and prominent were courses in history, previously regarded in the secondary schools of the English-speaking world as a by-product of classical languages or as an extracurricular diversion.[1] The American academies and

---

[1] As illustrated by this opinion of a seventeenth-century Anglican bishop, "It is next to be considered what are these subjects he (the teacher) sould entertain his pupill with: they sould be therefore chiefly vertuous documents: but because a boy cannot be much taken with long lectures on morality, history sould be the frequentest subject of his longest discourses, and by this meannes as a boy shall be often released from the drudging pennance of learning a language, which chequer work in his study cannot but much please him, so he shall also learne things, both plain, suitable to his capacities, and usefull. As likewise, since all boyes naturally love talking about histories, he shall be hereby much enamoured of his master's company, and made to preferre it to many of his idle games." *Thoughts on Education: By the Late Bishop Burnet* in John Clarke, *Bishop Gilbert Burnet as Educationist: Being His Thoughts on Education with Notes and Life of the Author,* Aberdeen, printed for the University, 1914, p. 45.

high schools welcomed the study of history and to a lesser extent that of political economy and geography. Even the colleges recognized limited amounts of history as acceptable for meeting entrance requirements.

By 1892, not only history but its related fields had gained sufficient respectability to be included by the Committee of Ten as one of the major fields of high school instruction, under the general heading of history, civil government, and political economy, with some history recommended in each of the four tracks or programs. The Committee on College Entrance Requirements recommended one year of history as a high school graduation constant and "one or two years of history, of which one should always be American history and civics"[2] as the minimum offering in the high school program. From then on, this instructional field gained ever increasing prominence leading to the present requirements of two, three, and in some cases four units for high school graduation. Next to English and physical education, it is today the most solidly established field in the high school program so far as quantitative requirements are concerned.[3]

This is a mixed blessing, and many social studies teachers feel their subjects would be better received on an elective basis. Student antagonism often seems to run high. In addition, members of other high school departments sometimes regard social studies teachers as imperialists who have consciously worked to extend their domain. This domain, if it may be so designated, is at best only insecurely established, and there are in many high schools fre-

---

[2] National Education Association, *Report of Committee on College Entrance Requirements,* July, 1899, The Association, University of Chicago Press, 1899, pp. 32–33.

[3] These requirements account in part for the fairly substantial percentages of total students who are enrolled in various social studies courses. In 1948–1949, 22.8 percent of all high school students were enrolled in the advanced course in U.S. history. "Offerings and Enrollments in High School Subjects," *Biennial Survey of Education in the United States, 1948–1950,* Federal Security Agency Office of Education, 1951, table 5, p. 100. This enrollment reflects the fact that practically all students who stay in high school four years take U.S. history in the eleventh or twelfth grade. World History enrolled 16.2 percent of the total student body and 59 percent of the total number of the tenth grade. *Ibid.,* p. 8. "Community civics, which is usually the ninth-grade subject in the social studies sequence, like American history is taken by one in three pupils in Grades 7, 8, and 9." *Ibid.,* p. 9.

quent rumblings of revolt against the impressive array of quantitative requirements, especially in view of demands for more work in foreign languages, mathematics, and sciences. On the other hand, the recent Conant report recommends that all students take "three or four years of social studies—including two years of history (one of which should be American history) and a senior course in American problems or American government."[4] The nature and extent of social studies requirements, therefore, is one of our most pressing issues in the curriculum. As is true of other issues, it deserves serious examination on the grounds of relevance to important objectives.

SOCIAL STUDIES OBJECTIVES

One of the most relevant objectives, although by no means the only one, is that of citizenship. But the citizenship objective is not the unique responsibility of the social studies field. The exclusive identification of social studies instruction with the citizenship objective has been of benefit to neither. Some of the more obvious examples of ineffective citizenship, such as low voting records, political corruption and apathy, and crime are cited as evidence of ineffective social studies instruction. In part at least these shortcomings might be charged against the entire school program and even against the educative influence of society itself. But the social studies program with its exclusive identification with citizenship and its allegedly inflated requirements offers the most likely target.

Nevertheless the social studies field must assume some responsibility for citizenship education and correspondingly assume some of the blame for any shortcomings in everyday citizenship practices. It is necessary, however, to identify more clearly the nature of good citizenship and the kinds of contributions that the social studies field may be legitimately expected to make. There have been many attempts to define the qualities of a good citizen. Most of these include the familiar categories of understandings, attitudes, and skills, although in some cases these are interwoven in more

[4] James Bryant Conant, *The American High School Today,* McGraw-Hill Book Company, Inc., 1959, p. 47.

direct statements along behavioral lines.[5] The general ideal in these statements is not only the conforming citizen who obeys the laws and performs his civic duties, important as these are, but one who intelligently and constructively takes part in the development of policies and the making of decisions.

This is a difficult and perhaps an unattainable ideal, but it is one we must ever strive to approach. It calls first of all for an informed citizenry, informed, that is, not only on the immediate questions of the hour, but on the pertinent historical background of those questions. This obviously demands historical subject matter plus contemporary materials in the fields of government, sociology, economics, and geography. As is often pointed out, however, information no matter how accurate or comprehensive does not alone make a good citizen. Our schools seek also to develop loyalty to the United States and its ideals and values. There is the need also for a body of intellectual and social skills including those of (1) acquiring new information as needed, (2) reflective thinking, (3) joining with others in the processes of group decision-making and action, and (4) relating decisions and actions to valid and defensible moral principles.

All the foregoing are relevant to the subject matter and activities of the social studies field. But the one most uniquely relevant is informed understanding of history, geography, government, sociology, and economics. The others are shared with other subjects and aspects of the school program beyond the classroom studies. English instruction with its present-day commitment to developmental reading shares the objective of building skills needed in the seeking and acquiring of new information. Units on communication media, such as the press, movies, radio, and the like, including specific study of particular newspapers, magazines, and programs as information sources for current events, can be and often are in-

---

[5] See, for example, "Characteristics of the Good Democratic Citizen," in the National Council for the Social Studies, Twenty-second Yearbook, *Education for Democratic Citizenship,* Ryland W. Crary (ed.), The Council, 1952, pp. 154–160. The committee that worked on this statement included representatives from the National Council and the Armed Forces Information and Education Division, Office of the Secretary of Defense.

cluded in English as well as in social studies. Science, along with other fields, shares the responsibility for developing the reflective thinking skills. The processes of group planning and decision-making may be worked on not only in a number of classroom studies, but also in the extraclass activities including the student-body council. The same can be said for the ability to relate decisions to moral principles. For the learning of civic responsibility, we now place much hope in school-and-community service projects, some of which may originate in the social studies classroom, but many of which can and should be developed through extraclass activities and other aspects of the school program beyond the classroom studies. Loyalty and devotion to the United States are important objectives of the social studies, but they are also relevant to the study of American literature, besides being outcomes we may legitimately expect from the environment of the school as a whole.

In short, all the citizenship objectives can be developed not only in social studies, but in other studies and activities of the school program,[6] with the exception of information in and understanding of the fields of history, geography, government, sociology, and economics. The entire body of social studies requirements could be abolished and all the objectives of citizenship apart from these specific understandings and bodies of knowledge would or could still be taken care of in our secondary schools. It follows then, if the foregoing conclusions are granted, that the determination of social studies requirements as constants, as far as the citizenship function is concerned, depends on the importance of the subject matter that the social studies courses are uniquely developed to transmit.

The immediate relevance of subject matter dealing with government and with contemporary social affairs in general is usually taken for granted. Even though such "mere knowledge about" does not guarantee good citizenship behavior, it is difficult to see

[6] The important question with many of these objectives is not whether they are met in social studies, but whether they are met at all. It is desirable in any high school to check periodically to see that some department or aspect of the school program is really providing for these essential learnings. While it is possible, for example, for either English or social studies departments to help students become familiar with important newspapers and magazines, it is also possible for neither of them to do so.

how one could be a good citizen if ignorant of such matters, except at the lowest level of conformity and docile acceptance. This widespread conviction undoubtedly accounts for the development of courses in civics and contemporary problems, plus the stress on current events in English as well as in social studies courses.

But history is another matter as far as many people are concerned, at least with regard to its formal and systematic study as a school subject. Among those who grant the importance of the past are many who feel that the past can be learned when needed in relation to some present situation. According to this point of view, we can when confronted by a crisis in the Middle East "read up" on the background of the crisis and learn the history we need for that purpose at that time.

Whether or not this is a valid point of view depends on how history is used in the citizenship context. The "reading up" idea depends on three possible uses. One is to detect trends and to predict what will happen in a given situation. A second is to draw analogies from the past as clues for present decisions and actions. A third is to identify cause-and-effect relationships to predict what would happen if certain actions or decisions were taken. These are limited if indeed not incorrect uses and interpretations of historical subject matter. Common sense would be just as valuable a guide to present actions as would history used in this way, and possibly more valuable.

A better use of history in the citizenship context is to gain understanding of what our present problems are. Probably the most important step in the reflective thinking process is that of problem definition and identification. It is difficult in any important problem to do this unless its genesis and development are taken into account. Without such consideration a world crisis is nothing more than a mass of confusion. History then is used not to solve problems, but to help define them. It is precisely this use of history that cannot be readily accomplished by "reading up" on present crises or problems as they occur. True, study on a particular point is usually necessary in such situations in order to fill in detail. But the broader framework of history is needed to make studies of given problems at given times meaningful and significant. Detached from this framework, the facts picked up will be patchwork and fragmentary and more likely to remain at the "mere information" level than the knowledge gained through formal and systematic historical study. Beyond this it may be argued that a person seeking his history in this manner would waste time finding out where to look and probably give it up as a bad job.

History also contributes awareness of moral criteria needed in judging political, social, and economic actions and decisions. The public schools may not use religious doctrines as bases for moral instruction. They are not likely to use an abstract philosophical idea such as the natural law. The remaining basis is that of social agreement, which can become narrow or even dangerous when the areas of agreement are too limited or confined in time and space. History provides the means of extending these areas so as to achieve wider consensus. Moral principles so identified will not conflict with those of the Judaic-Christian tradition. Several cautions must be observed. One is that such teaching supplements the moral teachings of homes and churches. It does not replace them. The other is that moral principles identified in our intellectual and cultural heritage are not to be reduced to formulas and lists. Individuals gain awareness of their meaning only through continued systematic study of history. Obviously we shall not find complete agreement on moral principles or complete consistency in their application. But the meaning and significance of moral truths and principles often appear all the more fresh and startling in contrast to their denials and contradictions.

A reasonable case, then, can be made out for the study of history in relation to the citizenship objective. But there are other considerations that apply to history and the other social studies. One of these is to supply a context for other cultural materials transmitted by the curriculum. The other school subjects—science, mathematics, languages, industrial arts, the fine arts, and the like—take on greater meaning and substance when understood in the light of their historical developments. Specific historical content in these fields should of course be included in the teaching of their own relevant courses and subjects. Science courses should include material on the history of science, music courses on the history of music, and so on. Again, the information so developed is likely to be sketchy and fragmentary unless related to the broader patterns of history as a social study. The history of man's specialized activities, such as art and music, becomes sharper and clearer when considered in relation to man's more generalized activities of human relationships and the development of social institutions. Formal study of history then becomes a vehicle serving the general cultural transmission function of the school and is important to the degree that cultural transmission itself is considered important.

Still another value of history is its contribution to the personal satisfactions of individuals who find it worthwhile for its own sake. Many students have found in history a lifelong source of worthy leisure-time satisfactions. This may not justify history as a graduation constant. After all, every subject has such possibilities. The wide range of human concerns touched by historical study, on the other hand, offers greater possibility of awakening such interests than is true of more specialized fields. Our larger high schools at least should recognize this by offering elective courses in history beyond the usual graduation constants or requirements.

Another claim advanced for history is its value as mental discipline. Historical study does contribute to the development of reflective thinking skills, but so do other studies. As far as the difficulty criterion is concerned, history has not made out very well. The English historian Buckle felt that the ease with which history may be read, studied, and written, at least in superficial terms, tends to attract inferior minds to its pursuit. Obviously this extreme position is a mistaken one, but it illustrates the lack of agreement on history as mental discipline. Fortunately such agreement is not needed. The difficulty of a subject is not always a true index of its other values, and historical study can be defended without recourse to this particular criterion or claim.

Although social studies requirements do on occasion stir up controversy in the high school curriculum, most teachers and other citizens will grant that some requirements in this field are justified. This does not, however, dispose of the matter. The nature and extent of social studies requirements depend also on the kinds of courses available and the possibilities of working out better arrangements if present courses are inadequate. Our present course sequences evoke controversy and disagreement even among those friendly to social studies as an instructional field.

THE DEVELOPMENT OF THE PRESENT SEQUENCE IN THE SOCIAL STUDIES

The present sequence runs as follows in many schools: seventh grade, world geography or geography of one of the hemispheres; eighth grade, United States history; ninth grade, community civics; tenth grade, world history; eleventh grade, United States history; and twelfth grade, problems of democracy or a semester each of sociology and economics. Of these, the seventh-grade geography and the two United States history courses in Grades 8 and 11 appear most frequently as constants. Most high schools require two years of social studies in Grades 9–12, with civics, world history, and the twelfth-grade problems course competing for the year to accompany eleventh-grade United States history. The elementary school program that precedes all this consists of home, school, and community activities in the primary grades, plus the geography of type regions and certain aspects of United States history and state history in Grades 4 and 5 and various possibilities in Grade 6, such as "old world backgrounds" and portions of world geography.

This lineup of courses bears the scars of battles long ago, contains the results of many compromises and adjustments, and in part represents historical accidents for which no logical explanation can be advanced. The first major national recommendations came from the Committee of Ten. Unfortunately, the Committee appointed not one but two conferences to deal with the subjects we now call the social studies. One of these was the conference on History, Civil Government, and Political Economy, the other the Conference on Geography, including Geology and Meteorology. The first of these conferences recommended two years of "biography and mythology" in the elementary school, followed by American history and civil government in Grade 7, Greek and Roman history in Grade 8, French history in Grade 9, English history in Grade 10, American history in Grade 11, and a "special period studied in an intensive manner" plus civil government in

Grade 12.[7] It also recommended a program omitting French history and the "special period studied in an intensive manner" for schools that could not "adopt the longer program."[8]

The Conference on Geography, including Geology and Meteorology, was concerned not only with what we would now call the social studies, but also with the physical sciences. It recommended that "elementary geography, a broad treatment of the earth and its inhabitants and institutions" be pursued in "the primary, intermediate, and lower grammar grades," but made no recommendation for such cultural geography either for the "later grammar grades" or for the high school.[9] Perhaps this accounts for the fact that we have continued to think of cultural geography as an elementary school subject and have never made adequate provision for it at the high school level. It is also possible that the separation of geography from history, civil government, and political economy by the Committee of Ten accounts for the tendency of subsequent curriculum workers to minimize the place of geography when dealing with the social studies field.

In 1899, The Committee of Seven of the American Historical Association recommended a four-year program for Grades 9 through 12 consisting of one year each of ancient history, medieval and modern European history, English history, and American history and civil government.[10] While this committee of historians recognized the importance of geography, they obviously did not feel recommendations for geography courses to be within the scope of their assignment. A condensed version of this report appeared in the general publication of the Committee on College Entrance Requirements, as did also a separate report from a committee on physical geography.

Along with other instructional fields, the social studies came up for critical examination by the Commission on Reorganization of

[7] The conference did not refer to these by grades, but as years of a six-year program. We are assuming they meant this to begin in the seventh grade.
[8] National Educational Association, *Report of the Committee of Ten on Secondary School Studies,* The Association, 1894, pp. 163–164.
[9] *Ibid.,* p. 209.
[10] The Committee of Seven of the American Historical Association, *The Study of History in Schools,* The Macmillan Company, 1899, pp. 34–35.

Secondary Education. The Committee on Social Studies of this Commission issued its report in 1916, two years before the appearance of the summary report on the Cardinal Principles. Its anticipation of the general spirit of the Cardinal Principles is indicated, however, in the statement that, "Whatever their value from the point of view of personal culture, unless they (the social studies) contribute directly to the cultivation of social efficiency on the part of the pupil they fail in their most important function."[11] The recommendations of this committee for Grades 7, 8, and 9 were rather complex: a combination of geography and European history or a full year of European history in Grade 7; a half year each of American history and civics in Grade 8; and Grade 9 either a half year of civics and a half year of economics and vocational civics or a combination of economic and vocational civics with economic history.[12] For Grades 10 through 12, the committee recommended a full year of European history to the end of the seventeenth century, plus either a full year or a half year each of European history since the seventeenth century, American history since the seventeenth century, and a course called by the new term "problems of American democracy."[13] The major innovations of this group were the emphasis on civics in the junior high school, the expansion of the general European history course, and the introduction of the twelfth-grade course in problems of democracy. Ancient history as such was not recommended, and the course in English history was absorbed into the general European history course.

The survey of high school curricula in fifteen major cities made by Counts in the school year 1923–1924 shows some of the impacts of the foregoing recommendations, but does not indicate acceptance of them as a whole. Nearly one fourth of the time in social studies, for example, was being devoted to ancient history, a course that the 1916 committee had not recommended at all.

[11] Commission on the Reorganization of Secondary Education, Committee on Social Studies, *The Social Studies in Secondary Education,* Department of the Interior, Bureau of Education, Bulletin 1916, No. 28, p. 9.

[12] *Ibid.,* p. 15.

[13] *Ibid.,* p. 35.

English history was down to 1.3 percent of the total time, however, while "mediaeval and modern history" and "modern history" were represented to the extent of 10 percent and 11.3 percent respectively. The 16 percent figure for civics probably reflects the influence of the report in that area of study. On the other hand, Counts's table does not even mention "problems of American democracy," although it shows separate courses in economics, sociology, and government and politics.[14]

Most interesting of all in the Counts survey is the appearance of a course called "world history" to the extent of 6.3 percent of the total time as an average figure for all fifteen cities, but running as high as 31 percent in Joliet and 38.9 percent in one "representative high school in Detroit."[15] This course had apparently developed spontaneously with no recommendation whatsoever from any national committee, and it has continued to thrive in the face of much criticism and opposition.

In fact, whatever developed in the years following 1916 had to do so without the blessing of national committee recommendations. There were groups at work on the social studies curriculum, but they recommended no programs and no sequences.[16] Not until the report of the Committee on American History in Schools and Colleges of the American Historical Association, The Mississippi Valley Historical Association, and The National Council for the Social Studies do we get a major recommendation, and this one was made only for the specific area of American history. The social studies program since 1916 has evolved largely through the efforts of local school systems and in some cases through state committees, with the sharing of ideas through national organizations such as the National Council for the Social Studies. In the course of these many local developments, geography and civics recommended by

[14] George S. Counts, *The Senior High School Curriculum,* The University of Chicago Press, 1926, table XXXIV, p. 80.

[15] *Ibid.*

[16] These included the Commission on the Social Studies of the American Historical Association and the Committee on the Function of the Social Studies in General Education of the Commission on Secondary School Curriculum of the Progressive Education Association.

the 1916 committee have survived in the seventh and ninth grades, while American history has survived in the eighth and eleventh. The development of twelfth-grade problems of democracy represents a fulfillment of or a delayed response to the 1916 recommendations. As noted earlier, the world history course has not only prospered, but in doing so has shoved the European history courses recommended by the 1916 committee almost completely out of the program.

Those who seek logical bases for curricular sequence based either on the nature of the subject matter or on the needs and development of adolescents will not find them in the social studies program. Few would defend the program as it now exists. On the other hand, it does exist, while many logical plans for the social studies have stirred up considerable discussion only to pass into oblivion. One of the questions perennially faced is whether to make renewed attempts to identify a logical overall plan or to seek improvements in the sequence as it stands. One approach can be written off as abstract and doctrinnaire, the other as patchwork or piecemeal planning. On the other hand, the first can be praised as dynamic and creative, while the second can be extolled as practical, realistic, and down to earth.

Much effort has been spent on the identification of generalizations or concepts inherent in or pertaining to the social studies field.[17] These materials may be used in either approach to the problems of the social studies curriculum. They provide at least one way of trying to evolve a more logical general or overall sequence or program; but they may be used also in attempts to improve the curriculum through specific modifications in the existing

---

[17] A pioneer effort along these lines was that of Neal Billings, *A Determination of Generalizations Basic to the Social Studies Curriculum,* Warwick & York, 1929. A significant recent statement, organized around 14 themes, is found in The National Council for the Social Studies, *A Guide to Contents in the Social Studies,* The Council, 1957. Among the themes dealt with are "The Intelligent Uses of the Forces of Nature," "Recognition of the Dignity and Worth of the Individual," and "The Effective Development of Moral and Spiritual Values." See also California State Central Committee on Social Studies, *Building Curriculum in Social Studies for the Public Schools of California,* Bulletin of the California State Department of Education, xxvi: 4, Sacramento, May, 1957, for the development and use of concepts in a state program.

organization. In addition, they are useful to those who develop inventories of understandings for curriculum guides and resource units, even in the conventional program.

POSSIBILITIES AND PROBLEMS IN THE PRESENT SEQUENCE

Regardless of the possible advantages to be secured in the creative production of a new overall plan, most curriculum workers in school systems must start with things as they are. This does not mean a commitment to keeping them that way. But it does suggest using the present status as a referent from which improvements and departures might be made. Let us begin, then, with some observations about the present state of affairs.

The courses at Grades 7 and 8 present little difficulty, at least as far as their being generally required is concerned. They provide essential information to extend the student's environment in time and space and to serve as a basis for future study. When the seventh-grade geography course is preceded by some name-and-place geography in the elementary grades and is followed by other social studies courses that give consideration to geographical context, there is little need for additional courses in geography as constants or graduation requirements. Additional geography courses should be offered on an elective basis for students with special interests. The eighth-grade course can give the student the chronology and basic facts of United States history. If this is well done, there is no need to teach the eleventh-grade United States history course in the same way. Both these courses should be as carefully organized and taught as any in the social studies sequence. It would be well to test all students at the end of the eleventh grade and to provide remedial instruction on a non-credit basis for students with marked deficiencies in the facts of world geography and in the history and geography of the United States.

Ninth grade presents less uniformity in practice and less agreement in theory than any other year of the junior and senior high school sequence. Community civics, known sometimes as "citizenship,"[18] offered either for one or two semesters, competes with other offerings such as economic geography, a single year of world

[18] A misnomer. Citizenship is an objective, properly speaking, and not a course.

history, or the first year of a two-year world history sequence. The civics course, however, is found in nearly half the ninth-grade programs throughout the country. It has been the particular object of criticism and controversial discussion.

Study of government was at one time a standard item in the eighth-grade program of 8–4 schools and still appears at this point in rural communities. It was justified on the grounds that many students completed their formal education with eighth-grade graduation and did not go on to high school. As more students began attending high school at least for a year or two, the study of government in eighth-grade United States history was moved into the ninth grade as a separate course.

It is obviously difficult to concentrate on government for an entire year or even one semester with ninth-grade students. Units on government, therefore, form only a portion of such courses. Two approaches may be used as far as the rest of the course is concerned. One is to put community government in the context of the general study of community life, with emphasis on such social functions as health, recreation, protection, and the economic processes of producing and distributing goods and services. Such a course can include content on local history and geography as well. The other approach is to develop the course around orientation to the school, particularly in 8–4 systems, and group guidance, sometimes supplemented by driver or general safety education. The two approaches may be combined by using portions of each.

There are good grounds for the approach based on community functions. For one thing, it provides meaning and substance to the study of government, not only in the local community but in the state and nation as well. Secondly, it offers the only place for the study of the local community apart from the third-grade level in the primary school. It is reasonable to expect social studies instruction to deal both with the extension of time and space and with the realities of the here and now. A third advantage is that of reinforcing and supplementing geographic understandings by applying them to the immediate environment.

Devoting a limited portion of the civics course to school orientation and group guidance is not objectionable. It is not desirable, however, to set up a course consisting of a few units on government supplemented entirely by such materials and activities. A course of this kind tends to be both thin and confusing. If more time is desired on school orientation and group guidance, it would be better to develop these in the home room.

Community civics as the study of government in the context of other social functions and supplemented by local history and geography can be a good course. Since most of our direct social relationships and contacts with social institutions and processes take place in the local community, it can be regarded as a general education course, that is, one which should be a constant or graduation requirement. There is enough potential content in such a course to warrant its being required for the entire year; local circumstances, however, may make it desirable or necessary in some cases to limit it to one semester. Placement of this course in ninth grade is based on practical considerations rather than on any inherent logic in the social studies sequence or on aspects of adolescent growth. The heavy dropout rate in Grade 10 is one of the practical considerations; the other is the desirability of reserving the study of world history, advanced United States history, and contemporary social problems for students intellectually more mature.

The sequence for the three upper years of the senior high school presents difficulties all its own. One year for world history is admittedly inadequate. Yet even this single year for the study of history other than our own is not generally required for graduation. How to make best use of the eleventh-grade opportunity in United States history is a subject of much disagreement. The twelfth-grade course in contemporary problems takes a variety of forms, each the center of enthusiastic controversy.

At first glance, the year of world history looks like an impossibility. Three full years of study were once devoted to ancient, English, and European history; and these comprised only a part of what world history is supposed to cover today. In addition, today's teacher assumes responsibility for including Asia, Africa, Australia, Canada, and Latin America. It is easy to see why many courses labeled world history are in reality the history of western Europe. On the other hand, some teachers have done a surprisingly good job of developing at least the broad outlines of historical development not only in Europe, but in other important centers of world civilization.

Some persons interested in social studies have advocated a two-year world history course. Two years would be better than one, but the proposal raises difficulties about graduation constants. Many schools do not require even one year of world history for graduation; two required years would represent an even more unlikely possibility. Schools that now require one year might be more skeptical about requiring two years and possibly drop the requirement entirely. The only way of resolving this would be to provide two different world history courses, one running for one year, the other for two. Students could meet the graduation requirement with either course. Those who selected the two-year course would have to complete the two years, since the first half taken by itself would not fulfill the purposes. This would require anticipation of other subject choices a year in advance. It would be more practical to require a single one-year course of all students and to supplement this by additional one-year elective courses in modern European history, history of the Far East, and the like. In any case, only the larger high schools would be able either to provide two different world history courses or the supplementary electives.

Eleventh-grade United States history should not be a repetition of the eighth-grade course, but should build on the factual and chronological overview that a good eighth-grade course supplies. Full consideration of difficulties in the United States history sequence was given in the early 1940's by a joint committee representing three scholarly and professional associations. The report of this committee, popularly known as the Wesley report, took into account not only the eighth-grade course in the junior high, but also the usual fifth-grade course, plus a year's additional study in the college. With regard to the secondary school sequence, the report suggested "The Building of the Nation" and "A Democratic Nation in a World Setting" as the junior high and senior high themes. The report recommended that "the period between 1776 and 1876 . . . occupy about two thirds of the time" in a junior high course entitled "The Building of the Nation" and that "the period since 1865 occupy about half the time" in a senior high course entitled "A Democratic Nation in a World Setting."[19] These recommendations provide a basis for the study of this important matter in local high schools. In part at least, the selection of subject matter for the eleventh-grade course will depend on requirements or absence of requirements in other courses of the social studies sequence.

Objections to the development of senior high course in United States history along lines somewhat different from those of the eighth-grade course are sometimes raised on the grounds that students forget much of what they learn in the eighth grade. The rate of forgetting of historical facts is high, but more apparent than real. Even well-informed adults do not show up well on such tests when suddenly confronted with them. The same is true of eleventh-grade high school students. From this it does not necessarily follow that either adults or eleventh graders need to restudy their historical facts the same way they have once or several times before. Most eleventh graders will quickly recapture and reassemble their facts in a brief opening review and in connection with subsequent units of a good eleventh-grade course. Those who have not learned these facts to begin with or who suffer from more deep-seated forgetting can be directed to additional reading without taking up the time of the entire class. When ability grouping is used, the low sections will of course spend more time on review of facts and chronology from the earlier course.

At the twelfth-grade level, the course known variously as problems of democracy, senior problems, social problems, and contemporary problems has in most schools replaced the older separate courses in sociology, economics, and government. The nature and content of these courses vary as widely as the titles, but not always in a manner consistent with the titles. A course known by any one

---

[19] Edgar B. Wesley (director), *American History in Schools and Colleges,* The Report of the Committee on American History in Schools and Colleges of the American Historical Association, The Mississippi Valley Historical Association, and The National Council for the Social Studies, The Macmillan Company, 1944, pp. 70–71.

of the foregoing titles may in practice be any one of the following: (1) a semester of economics and a semester of sociology; (2) a series of social-civic-economic problems cutting across the divisions of sociology, economics, and government, such as housing, public health, international relations, intergroup relations, civic rights, labor and management, and social security; (3) a series of personal-social problems such as job orientation, family relationships, use of leisure time, consumer problems and personal budgeting, and building personal values; (4) combinations of any two or even all three of the foregoing. Most courses are either the sociology-economics combination or a combination of various social-civic-economic and personal-social problems.

A course developed as a series of problems cutting across the subject divisions can be flexible enough to permit a good deal of student initiative in selecting and organizing the materials of study. It can also provide a good deal of student practice in the problem-solving or reflective thinking skills, particularly those having to do with the locating and appraising of ideas, facts, and arguments on controversial issues. This is especially true if the students have reasonably good background in community civics, world history, and American history. Such a course can make an excellent culmination of a good social studies program.

Whether or not such a course is a good one for students with little background in history and other social studies is another question. This is a most practical question, for in many schools students who elect or are required to take the twelfth-grade course have had no history of cultures other than our own and in some cases have not had the factual study of government or the fundamental study of social functions provided by a good ninth-grade course in community civics. It is not the contention here that factual study must in all cases precede the more flexible study of problems and issues. Good teachers make provision for problem solving and reflective thinking activities in the direct study of history and civics and often use issues and problems as approaches to such direct study, especially in the senior high United States history. But in these cases the problems approach is interwoven with direct study over several years of work. The twelfth-grade teacher confronted by students without such backgrounds faces the dual task of dealing with a range of modern social problems and developing their relevant backgrounds within the span of a single year. And the most dangerous possibility in such a situation is not the obvious one that students may fail to learn the factual backgrounds, but the subtle one that students will develop facility in making off-the-cuff generalizations and conclude that historical foundations are irrelevant and unnecessary.

The twelfth-grade course, then, can be intellectually one of the most stimulating in the high school program. To promote this possibility and to guard against negative ones it is necessary for counselors to make their recommendations most carefully in relation to the individual student if the course is elective. If the course is required, there is no choice. It probably should not be required unless the school is prepared to require world history as well. When the course is elective, it should be used mostly for students with special social studies interests and abilities and not to correct previous social studies deficiencies.

Within this traditional or conventional sequence, then, the junior high school program will consist of one year of geography, one year of United States history, and either one semester or one year of community civics. It would be desirable to follow this with three years of constants in senior high: world history, United States history, and contemporary problems, making a total of five and a half years of constants in Grades 7 through 12. Most schools will undoubtedly continue to strive for two years of constants within this three-year period. Since the United States history is a fixed item, the choice resolves itself into one between world history and the problems course. The wiser selection appears to be the world history. This is indicated in part by the considerations discussed in the foregoing paragraphs. In addition we need to consider the kinds of reading matter and other sources most available to the high school graduate in his adult life. Contemporary problems are all around us, and the person with a good historical background will not find it difficult to keep informed on current events and their immediate antecedents, particularly if his English or history courses have helped him to know and use newspapers and magazines with national coverage. On the other hand, the person who has missed world history will find it more difficult to direct his reading and study along historical lines. It is assumed that good courses in world history and United States history will bring the student up to the present. The eleventh-grade United States history in particular will place stress on recent history if preceded by a good eighth-grade course. A student who omits the twelfth-grade problems course then is not necessarily deprived of the study of contemporary affairs and materials.

It may be possible, as previously noted, to redesign the senior high school program both in the interests of better learning and of saving time. The three strands of world backgrounds, recent United States history, and contemporary problems might be woven together in a sequence of units extending over four semesters. When added to the two and one-half years of the junior high school (geography, United States history, and civics) this would provide four and one-half years of social studies constants over the six-year span of secondary schooling. Such a sequence in the senior high school would have to be worked out with care in order not to end as a jumble of unrelated units.

The social studies constants may be based either on the present sequence of courses or on some possibly new sequence. In either case this minimum program should be supplemented by electives, including a full year of civics in ninth grade and a full year of contemporary problems in twelfth grade. Larger schools should offer additional and more specialized electives in history, geography, and government.

Bibliography

Billings, Neal, *A Determination of Generalizations Basic to the Social Studies Curriculum,* Warwick & York, 1929.

Commission on the Reorganization of Secondary Education, Committee on Social Studies, *The Social Studies in Secondary Education,* Department of the Interior, Bureau of Education, Bulletin 1916, No. 28.

The Committee of Seven of the American Historical Association, *The Study of History in Schools,* The Macmillan Company, 1899.

Dimond, Stanley E., *Schools and the Development of Good Citizens,* The Final Report of the Citizenship Education Study, Detroit Public Schools and Wayne University, Wayne University Press, 1953.

Gross, Richard E., and Zeleny, Leslie D. (eds.), *Educating Citizens for Democracy,* Oxford University Press, 1958.

Johns, Eunice (ed.), *Social Studies in the Senior High School: Programs for Grades Ten, Eleven, and Twelve,* Curriculum Series Number 7, National Council for the Social Studies, November, 1953.

National Council for the Social Studies, Twenty-Second Yearbook, *Education for Democratic Citizenship,* The Council, 1952.

Progressive Education Association Commission on Secondary School Curriculum, Committee on the Function of the Social Studies in General Education, *The Social Studies in General Education,* D. Appleton-Century Company, 1940.

Quillen, I. James, and Hanna, Lavone A., *Education for Social Competence: Curriculum and Instruction in Secondary-School Social Studies,* Scott, Foresman and Company, 1948.

Wesley, Edgar, *American History in Schools and Colleges,* The Report of the Committee on American History in Schools and Colleges of the American Historical Association, The Mississippi Valley Historical Association, and The National Council for the Social Studies, The Macmillan Company, 1944.

Wesley, E. B., and Wronski, S. P., *Teaching Social Studies in High Schools,* 4th ed., D. C. Heath and Company, 1958.

CHAPTER 13

··

Natural Sciences

Herbert Spencer asked himself what knowledge is of most worth and came to the following answer.

Thus to the question with which we set out—What knowledge is of most worth?—the uniform reply is—Science. This is the verdict on all counts. For direct self-preservation, or the maintenance of life and health, the all-important knowledge is—Science. For that indirect self-preservation which we call gaining a livelihood, the knowledge of greatest value is—Science. For the due discharge of parental functions, the proper guidance is to be found only in—Science. For that interpretation of national life, past and present, without which the citizen cannot rightly regulate his conduct, the indispensable key is—Science. Alike for the most perfect production and highest enjoyment of art in all its forms, the needful preparation is still—Science. And for purposes of discipline—intellectual, moral, religious—the most efficient study is, once more—Science. The question which at first seemed so perplexed, has become in the course of our inquiry, comparatively simple.[1]

In this compelling essay Spencer voiced the confidence and optimism of many of his nineteenth-century contemporaries. They were thrilled both by the amount and quality of nineteenth-century scientific discovery and by their vision of a human future that they believed would be achieved through scientific knowledge and progress. Although confronted by a secondary school pro-

[1] Herbert Spencer, *Education: Intellectual, Moral, and Physical*, D. Appleton and Company, 1900, pp. 84–85.

gram overwhelmingly literary in character, they had public opinion and the future on their side. The dazzling and tangible achievements of technology convinced the Western world that scientific studies were the most practical, useful, and important offered by the school. This conviction has persisted, even though no longer necessarily associated with optimism about the future. Many people, including scientists themselves, have become more impressed by the destructive uses of science than by its contribution to human happiness and welfare. But these fears have increased rather than diminished the prestige of the scientific studies. The realities of international relationships and the need for maintaining our national safety and defense have combined with other considerations to make science the most compelling single item of public interest in our high school and college programs today.

It may seem strange that a field as tangible as science and as clearly identified with such dramatic symbols as retorts and atom smashers should present questions of definition. But the questions are there. Furthermore, the answers bear considerable relationship to the ways science is organized and taught in schools. At the surface level there seems to be no difficulty. The term "science" as a school subject means first of all the natural sciences as distinguished from what some call the social sciences, more modestly known as the social studies. We can readily identify physics, chemistry, and biology, the usual high school subjects, as well as call to mind others not ordinarily taught in high school, such as geology and astronomy. It is easy to name the sciences, but difficult to identify the nature and meaning of science itself.

As is often the case, the derivation of the word provides little help. It comes from a Latin noun meaning knowledge. But knowledge alone does not define science. "Science cannot simply be defined as exact knowledge. In the first place, as Jeans once remarked, a heap of unorganized facts is no more a science than a heap of bricks is a house. Too, information that is both precise and highly organized need not be scientific. The classical Chinese scholar or the modern English professor knows just what he is talking about, but the subject matter is proudly non-scientific. Music and theology also come to mind. Even exact, systematic knowledge about the physical universe is not necessarily science as we understand it."[2] Definitions of science usually take into account the way scientists work, often called scientific method, a term about as difficult to pin down as science itself. "By science, therefore, we Westerners mean a body of more-or-less organized fact and theory together with a process of discovery (the scientific method) involving hypothetical explanations whose deductive consequences are checked against observed data and which are discarded when they don't work."[3]

Notions of scientific method range from the narrow to the broad, some so broad that the term becomes synonymous with thinking in general and is applied to every conceivable question with which mankind has ever been faced. Natural scientists usually prefer to avoid the broader connotations. Sometimes they prefer not to use the term at all. In a book proposing a college course on "The Tactics and Strategy of Science," Conant writes, "One might call it a course in 'scientific method' as illustrated by examples from history, except that I am reluctant to use this ambiguous phrase."[4]

Ambiguous the term "scientific method" undoubtedly is. Still it is the layman's term for something that scientists agree is part of science; it provides convenient shorthand that may be used provided we understand it as such without the emotional connotations often attached. Scientific method is not spectacular. It moves from established knowledge to more knowledge in the light of explanations (theory) and facts. Inspiration and accident also have much to do with scientific discovery. Nevertheless, it is through the orderly use of scientific method that scientific knowledge is usually advanced, and method is inherent in science as we think of it today.

SCIENTIFIC METHOD AND LABORATORY WORK

The development of scientific method or scientific understanding is a slow process. Those who are learning it must have time to

[2] Poul Anderson, "How Social is Science?" *The Saturday Review,* April 27, 1957, p. 9.

[3] *Ibid.,* pp. 9–10.

[4] James B. Conant, *On Understanding Science: An Historical Approach,* A Mentor Book, published by the New American Library of World Literature, Inc., by arrangement with Yale University Press, 1951, p. 33.

think. At the same time, the science teacher seeks to impart a body of information in the natural sciences, technical information not always easy for the student to assimilate. He must do this for two reasons. One is that the scientific information is necessary in general education. It is part of the scientific culture the school seeks to transmit. The other is that understanding scientific method cannot be developed without information or subject matter. This is true at the elementary school level, where the problems and their related subject matters are relatively simple, just as it is true at the highest and most advanced research levels.

Laboratory work has served as the major approach to the teaching of scientific method. Such work, however, may go in various directions. Ideally, students should discover or rediscover scientific laws or generalizations. This ideal can easily degenerate into a highly artificial process, so much so that the Committee of Ten over 60 years ago recommended, "That in the instruction in Physics and Chemistry it should not be the aim of the student to make a so-called rediscovery of the laws of these sciences."[5] Now, if students do not spend laboratory time rediscovering known laws or principles, the most obvious alternative is to spend it verifying these principles through their own observations and measurements.

Activities of the verification type have obvious values, one being that of making the subject matter real and perhaps more understandable, another that of developing habits of care and precision in making and recording observations. But they are only in part related to scientific reasoning or thinking. There are also some practical difficulties. If the exercises are graded on the accuracy with which the law or principle is demonstrated, students who know how things are supposed to come out are tempted to make them come out that way by fudging the data, thereby developing a lack of respect for the accurate observation they are supposed to be learning. Furthermore, as the laboratory manual or workbook came to be extensively used, students learned to fill in the

[5] National Education Association, *Report of the Committee of Ten on Secondary School Studies,* The Association, 1894, Resolution no. 21 of the conference on physics, chemistry, and astronomy, p. 118.

answer blanks on the basis of what they already knew to be the case rather than on the basis of their laboratory observations.

As a consequence of these and other difficulties, many science teachers and school administrators have questioned the value of some aspects of laboratory work. The traditional arrangement of scheduling science classes for seven periods a week, with four periods definitely scheduled in the laboratory, has been replaced by one of five single periods a week, with laboratory work introduced as needed on a more flexible basis. Science teachers today feel this arrangement makes it possible to do a better job of correlating laboratory work and other activities, such as reading, recitation, and lecture. This practice does, however, reduce the total time available from seven periods to five, compensated for in part by longer class periods, in a subject where time is always a difficult problem. And it does not in itself make clear what the nature of laboratory activities should be.

One attempt to clarify this took the form of lecture-discussion-demonstrations in which the teacher performed the experiments. In this way the teacher could reproduce the original processes of discovery and thinking leading to the conclusions or generalizations. Through discussion stimulated by the teacher's questions, students could participate in the thinking part of the experiment even though they did not handle the apparatus themselves. Student assistants could be used for parts of the experiment, and in some cases the entire demonstration could be handled by student groups, with the teacher supplying supplementary narration and discussion questions. When lecture-discussion-demonstrations were first introduced, science teachers tended to line up for and against them. Much controlled and matched-group experimental research was conducted to determine the value of this approach. It is regarded today as a valuable and timesaving approach, but not one that should be used exclusively for the laboratory parts of a science course.

The present-day science teacher uses a variety of laboratory-type activities and approaches. If he is so fortunate as to meet his class every day in a room furnished with laboratory equipment, he can adjust the amount of laboratory time as needed, spending more on some topics and less on others. He can lead a discussion up to the point where the students understand the questions before them and then turn to laboratory work for data needed in answering the questions. This work can be student conducted, individually or in groups, either on a demonstration basis before the entire class or simultaneously by five or six groups working independently. Or the teacher may conduct it himself. In any case, the gathering of the data can be accompanied or quickly followed by discussions of what the data mean and what conclusions if any may be legitimately drawn from them.

It may be possible, furthermore, to teach some aspects of scientific method or thinking without laboratory work at all, for example, through the use of films that stress questions rather than conclusions. Teachers may use these films as leads into discussion, thereby encouraging thinking and inquiry on the part of the students. Another possibility is that of paper-and-pencil exercises in which the data are supplied to the student and to which the student responds. These exercises are similar to those used in social studies and are particularly well suited both as teaching and as testing activities to the development of such specific skills as application of principles and interpretation of data. In one example of an interpretation-of-data exercise in chemistry, students are given the solubility at $20°$ C., the solubility at boiling point of saturated solution, and the boiling point of saturated solution in degrees C. for a number of chemical compounds, and are then required to check the degrees to which various statements and conclusions are supported by the data presented.[6] Good textbooks in science, which include not only bodies of content and information but also consideration of how knowledge is obtained, also provide material for class discussion along these lines. In addition, historical case studies in the strategy and tactics of science, as suggested by Conant,[7] should be of much help in teaching the understanding of scientific method. Probably no one would recommend that lab-

---

[6] National Society for the Study of Education, Forty-sixth Yearbook, pt. 1, *Science Education in American Schools*, chap. 13, "The Content and Methods of Senior High School Science," The Society, 1947, p. 205.

[7] See James Bryant Conant (ed.), *Harvard Case Studies in Experimental Science*, Harvard University Press, 1957.

oratory work be discontinued, but such non-laboratory approaches may be useful supplements to laboratory activities.

SELECTION OF CONTENT

Modern approaches to the use of the laboratory and the teaching of scientific method have mitigated to some extent the process vs. content dilemma of the science curricula. Still it must be admitted that even the modern approaches take time, more time than would be needed just to teach science information alone. The dilemma is perhaps unresolvable, since the teacher cannot evade his responsibility for transmitting a selected body of material from our cultural heritage in the natural sciences. Selection of content areas for emphasis becomes, then, a major question in science, as it is in the social studies. Both fields suffer from embarrassment of riches in this connection; in neither field is it possible in the high school curriculum to do more than transmit a small fraction of the material available.

There is no formula to determine what content should be selected and taught, but there are bases for selection that may be kept in mind. One is obviously that of the nature of the subject itself. In a course called physics there are key concepts or generalizations without which the title of the course would be a misnomer. These are not necessarily defined by the way physics courses have been traditionally organized and so should be reëxamined from time to time from a critical point of view. A second basis for choice is that of developing some awareness of new ideas and findings in the field, plus a realization of problems not yet solved. Otherwise students may conclude that all the returns came in many years ago. One of the obvious examples is that of nuclear energy in physics, a topic barely touched in many of the older texts and curriculum guides. There are some dangers in these topics since they are usually easier to talk about than to study, and the temptation of superficiality is always with us. In general, however, the science teacher faces much the same problem as the mathematics teacher, that of not only keeping his courses abreast of new developments, but of taking into account those modern ideas which seem to demand a rethinking of what the subject is. There is even a question about the scientific outlook represented in older treatments of various science subjects. The First Annual Report of the Physical Science Study Committee, Massachusetts Institute of Technology, states that "Textbooks in general reflected a scientific outlook that dated back half a century and was no longer representative of the views of the scientific community."[8]

There are in addition the demands made by the criteria implied in such objectives as health, citizenship, family living, use of leisure time, character, and the like. This point of view was invented neither by modern life adjustment educators nor by the 1918 Commission on the Reorganization of Secondary Education. It is directly stated in Spencer's essay referred to at the beginning of this section. He came to the conclusion that science was the knowledge of most worth precisely because in his opinion it made the maximum contribution to those areas of everyday life problems and activities.

Many would disagree with Spencer, some with his conclusions, some with his reasons, or both. Objectives implied in these areas of living, however, may be legitimately used along with other bases in the selection of science content. Physical health, for example, has about the same relationship to science, particularly biological science, that citizenship has to social studies. The parallelism can be developed along several lines. Citizenship is not the only objective of social studies; health is not the only objective of science. Social studies has no monopoly on citizenship education in the school program; neither does science on health education. It would be difficult, however, to imagine a social studies curriculum irrelevant to citizenship; similarly it would be difficult to imagine a science curriculum irrelevant to health. Furthermore, each field has something to do with the objective primarily related to the other. There is social studies content relevant to health, and there is science content relevant to citizenship, particularly on matters such as conservation of natural resources.

It is also true that many students will find science a rewarding field of inquiry and activity for enjoyment. Likewise respect for

[8] Physical Science Study Committee, *First Annual Report,* The Committee, 1957, Massachusetts Institute of Technology, p. 3.

intellectual honesty and truth in the science field should contribute to character development. For many students science will provide the means of livelihood. All these are legitimate and important. Their use as criteria in no way conflicts with standards of scholarship or with the integrity of the natural sciences as bodies of knowledge worthy in themselves. What needs to be avoided is the use of such objectives as the exclusive determiners of content in the science field, or, more particularly, the attempt to show that everything taught in science directly contributes to some such area of living. These approaches have several unfortunate consequences. One is the tendency to make far-fetched and artificial claims about the practical applications of this or that piece of content, especially when the content could stand squarely on its own merits without such claims. The other is excessive overlapping and duplication of content and topics among the fields of instruction. Some overlapping may be desirable, but there is a limit somewhere. High school departments have often been unjustly accused of fostering overlapping; what they have done in some instances is to follow conscientiously the demand that their subjects deal with all possible areas of living. When such a conscientious effort is made, overlapping is bound to be the result.

Another content question confronting curriculum workers in the sciences as well as in the social studies is that of generalizations in relation to specific facts. The emphasis on generalizations developed as a reaction against the apparently hopeless task of trying to make sense of the thousands and thousands of specific facts that have accumulated in both fields. It was encouraged also by the generalization theory of transfer as contrasted with the theory of identical or similar elements. The concern with generalizations (or as sometimes termed, principles and concepts) is then a concern with meaning and understanding. The argument for generalizations is summarized in the following statement.

In and of themselves, however, facts should not be considered as the ultimate objectives. The ultimate objective is an understanding of the generalization which makes clear the relationship of a number of facts to the interpretation of a natural phenomenon. For example, there are many incidents in which one animal may be observed eating some form of plant. There are many incidents in which one specific animal may be observed eating or otherwise using another animal to maintain itself. One may read that green plants use carbon dioxide in manufacturing food. Furthermore, one may read, or observe through indirect means, that human beings give off carbon dioxide as a waste product. Each of these may be considered a fact of science and possibly an interesting fact. But these facts individually have little meaning or significance in understanding the environment, or in solving problems related to use of our biotic resources. On the other hand they can have meaning when, thru guided learning experiences, they are related to an important generalization of biology: Living things are interdependent. This generalization in turn has a significance when it is applied with understanding in making decisions regarding such questions as: Should we kill off the hawks in our community?[9]

Few would contend that facts are ends in themselves. It would be frustrating if they were, for students do have the disconcerting habit of quickly forgetting many of the facts they learn in history and science. The writer of the foregoing quotation cites this as additional argument for the generalization viewpoint. "It has been found that up to 70 per cent of the specific facts learned in a science course are forgotten within one year after the completion of the course. The loss in understanding of generalizations and in ability to apply generalizations is very much less."[10]

There is little doubt that generalizations are more manageable than specific facts in making content inventories in curriculum guides, resource units, and other teaching materials. A body of generalizations can give more coherence to an instructional field than a body of separate or miscellaneous facts. It seems clear also that generalizations, when understood, will give the student a clearer grasp of the essential subject matter of a given course or field. Evidence on transfer also suggests that generalizations, when understood, provide a workable basis for the extension of learning

[9] J. Darrell Barnard, *Teaching High-School Science,* What Research Says to the Teacher Series, No. 10, Department of Classroom Teachers and American Educational Research Association of the National Education Association, April, 1956, pp. 6–7.

[10] *Ibid.,* p. 7.

beyond the immediate situation in which the initial learning takes place.

Certain difficulties in the teaching and use of generalizations must nevertheless be recognized. If they are not recognized, the educational value of generalizations may be lost. In fact, generalizations may educate in wrong directions. One of the difficulties about generalizations, or perhaps one of the realities about generalizations, which must be faced, is that they do not hold up well or in fact even have much meaning when detached from the facts that support them and from which they have been developed. They are therefore better understood when arrived at through the patient study of facts than when announced at the outset. Their place is in the curriculum guide or resource unit inventory, not in the initial development of a topic with students. When taught by themselves and in and of themselves, generalizations may promote the worst forms of rote learning without comprehension.

A second difficulty is that overemphasis on generalizations may conflict with the development of scientific method or the spirit of inquiry. This is a real possibility even when the teacher avoids the difficulty indicated in the foregoing paragraph. The teacher may have a generalization in mind and then may carefully direct students to facts that have been selected because of their value in building an understanding of the generalization. This is all to the good except for one thing. Some generalizations may be wrong, and the stubborn facts that contradict them may be overlooked. Those who long held to the Ptolemaic theory of the universe undoubtedly had a number of facts to support their generalizations. But there were other facts of which they were not aware and possibly some they did not consider relevant. Not all the facts relevant to a particular question or problem necessarily appear so when first turned up. In selecting the facts pertinent to a generalization or in arranging the laboratory exercises that will demonstrate such facts, the science teacher must guard against letting the generalization become his master rather than his servant.

All the foregoing considerations—the nature and development of scientific method, the bases for content selection, and the uses and misuses of generalizations—add up to rather weighty business for the science teacher. It is in no way lightened or diminished by the highly diversified characteristics of his clientele. The science teacher and other curriculum workers in the field of science, like their colleagues in other fields, confront high school students varying both in their capacities for learning and in their present and future relationships to the various subject matters of the high school curriculum. There are those of high general ability and of highly developed special interests in the science field, those who may be quickened to pursue careers in expanding and enriching the body of scientific culture itself. Others will join the engineers, physicians, and other workers who apply the findings of science to the advancement of technology and human welfare. Then there are those average to very superior students whose interests and careers will not run in scientific lines at all, but who presumably need and can achieve an understanding of science as part of general culture and for use in citizenship, health, and leisure time activities. Also in the school are students whose handicaps in reading and mathematics seriously limit their learning of science, but who will also exercise citizenship responsibilities and who will need science understandings for personal health.

OFFERINGS, ENROLLMENTS, AND REQUIREMENTS IN THE SCIENCE SUBJECTS

In the conventional science program, general science appears in Grade 9, biology in Grade 10, chemistry in Grade 11, and physics in Grade 12.[11] School systems organized on the 6–3–3 or 6–2–4 plans usually offer one, two, or three years of general science in the junior high school. One year of junior high school science is almost always required in such school systems. In some cases this may consist of a two-year program with classes meeting only two or three times a week. There is often an additional one-year requirement

[11] Even under the conventional program, large high schools have offered additional science courses, usually as electives. The following offerings occurred in 15 or more states in the 1948–1949 survey of the U.S. Office of Education: botany, physiology, zoology, earth science, aeronautics, advanced general science, physical science, advanced chemistry, fundamentals of electricity, radio including electronics, advanced biology, conservation, and related science. "Offerings and enrollments in High School Subjects," *Biennial Survey of Education in the United States 1948–1949,* Federal Security Agency Office of Education, 1951, table 2, p. 33.

beyond the eighth grade, usually met by taking ninth-grade general science or tenth-grade biology. This one-year requirement in Grades 9 through 12 is a familiar one in 8–4 systems as well, but it is difficult to identify the nature and extent of science instruction in the seventh and eighth grades of such systems for the nation as a whole.

Many people have come to feel that more science should be required of all students, or at least that qualified students should be encouraged to elect additional science courses beyond the requirements. The charge is sometimes made that we have gone soft on the science portion of the curriculum and that enrollments relative to the student population have declined over a period of years. It is true that relative enrollments have declined in physics, from 22.8 percent of the total high school population in 1890 to 4.4 percent in 1956. As far as chemistry is concerned, however, there is no such clear picture of declining enrollments. The figure stood at 10.1 percent in 1890, went down to 7.7 percent by 1900, and was still holding at 7.5 percent in 1956. Biology does not appear in the statistics until 1910, at which time it was just being established, but in 1956 it enrolled 20.5 percent of all high school students.[12]

As is true in mathematics, it is desirable to examine enrollments as percentages of students in the grades where the subject is usually offered. In 1956, biology enrollments came to 75.5 percent of the tenth-grade student population, chemistry to 34.6 percent of the eleventh grade, and physics to 24.3 percent of the twelfth.[13] Note that although students taking physics in 1956 made up less than one twentieth of the high school population, they came to nearly one fourth of the high school seniors. The grade-level percentages are somewhat more reassuring than those based on total student population, but they cannot disguise the overall decline in relative enrollments that has taken place in the field of physics over the past 60 to 70 years.[14]

[12] Foregoing figures from Kenneth E. Brown, *Offerings and Enrollments in Science and Mathematics in Public High Schools,* Office of Education, Pamphlet No. 120, 1956, U.S. Department of Health, Education, and Welfare, 1957, table 3, p. 9.

[13] *Ibid.,* table 4, p. 12.

[14] The survey of public and private high school seniors in Wisconsin in the spring of 1957 showed that 30 percent of the sample had taken physics, 45.4 percent had

Few would disagree with the proposition that competent students should be encouraged to take more science. This should be done not only to identify those with ability for careers in science and to encourage them to consider such careers, but also to enrich and deepen the cultural acquisitions of students who are capable of going beyond the minimum requirements. The Conant report recommends that students in the top 15 percent nationally take three years of science,[15] this to be accomplished through individual counseling rather than blanket prescription.

For the general student, however, the Conant report recommends "at least one year of science, which might well be biology or general physical science."[16] Quantitatively, this does not differ from present practice governing Grades 9 through 12. Combined with one year of science in Grade 7 or 8, this makes an overall two-year requirement in the six-year span of secondary education beginning in the seventh grade. This is certainly not excessive and should receive general approval at least as a minimum figure. Students coming from schools without seventh-grade or eighth-grade science should take two years in Grades 9 through 12, probably one year of general science and one year of biology. This makes a complicated state of affairs in high schools that draw some students with and some without seventh-grade or eighth-grade science work, as is often the case.

Criticisms have been directed not only at the state of enrollments in science, but at the absence of advanced science offerings in some of our high schools. In 1956, 9.7 percent of our high schools were not offering biology, while 18.2 percent offered neither chemistry nor physics.[17] But the 18.2 percent of the schools offering neither chemistry nor physics enrolled only 4.8 percent of all

---

taken chemistry, and 78.9 percent had taken biology at some time during their high school careers. The differing interests of boys and girls is indicated by the fact that 47.3 percent of the boys had taken physics while only 13.5 percent of the girls had done so. Edward A. Krug, Clifford S. Liddle, Russell C. Mosely, and Daniel Parkinson, *The College Preparatory Function in Wisconsin High Schools,* School of Education, University of Wisconsin, 1959, table 14, p. 53.

[15] James Bryant Conant, *The American High School Today,* McGraw-Hill Book Company, Inc., 1959, p. 57.

[16] *Ibid.,* p. 47.

[17] Kenneth E. Brown, *op. cit.,* table 1, p. 6.

twelfth-grade students. Obviously these are small schools. The importance of these figures, however, cannot be dismissed on the grounds that the percentage of students affected is small. The plight of the one senior in twenty who does not have access to either chemistry or physics is serious and important. We should be as concerned about his educational opportunities as we are about the other nineteen. The fault here does not lie with school administrators or school boards. The average twelfth-grade enrollment in schools offering neither chemistry nor physics in 1956 was only 18.6.[18] In terms of the national average of twelfth-grade students taking physics, this represents a potential physics class with five students.

NEW DEVELOPMENTS IN THE SEQUENCE OF STUDIES

Let us turn now to promising new developments which, in spite of discouraging circumstances, are taking place in the science program. One of these is the offering of science work for qualified students at a level beyond that reached by most science programs in the past. This may be done, for example, through high-ability sections in physics that include content and treatment ordinarily not included in the conventional high school physics course. Or the school may offer a second year of physics, chemistry, or biology for students who have completed the conventional program by the end of the eleventh grade. In either case there is the possibility of advanced standing in the college through the testing program of the College Entrance Examination Board.

If the advanced work is offered as a second year of the subject following the usual introductory course, it is advisable to place superior students in biology rather than in general science in the ninth grade. This makes it possible for them to take chemistry in the tenth grade, physics in the eleventh, and the advanced biology, chemistry, or physics in the twelfth. In fact, a good argument can be made for having all students with previous general science work in the junior high school proceed directly to the study of biology without taking the conventional general science course in the

18 *Ibid.*

ninth grade.[19] Students not planning to take four years of science may take biology in either Grade 9 or Grade 10, or possibly later.

Another development is the one-year physical science course, a combination of portions of chemistry and physics plus earth science in a manner analogous to the botany-zoology combination in one year of biology. Many students do not have room in their programs for two years of physical science after the completion of biology. These students must in the conventional program choose between chemistry and physics, thereby getting a somewhat one-sided view of physical science taken as a whole. Science teachers often dislike this physical science course, partly because they feel it does justice neither to chemistry nor physics, partly because it has been used in some schools for low-ability students. Most biology teachers, on the other hand, have come to accept the combined course of botany and zoology as a better means of developing understandings in the life sciences than was done when the subjects were separated. It is possible that the physical science combination may offer similar advantages at the introductory level.[20]

The physical science course, then, may be regarded as an alternative to the two-year program in separate chemistry and physics. If this is done, it is necessary to guard against the identification of

[19] The ninth-grade placement of biology with the accompanying omission of ninth-grade general science is a fairly recent "trend," but by no means a new idea. It was recommended by the Science Committee of the 1918 Commission on the Reorganization of Secondary Education for what it called the junior-senior high school. Commission on the Reorganization of Secondary Education of the National Education Association, *Reorganization of Science in Secondary Schools,* Bureau of Education, Department of the Interior, Bulletin 1920, No. 26, p. 23.

[20] The Physical Science Study Committee, Massachusetts Institute of Technology, considered the possible advantages of combining physics and chemistry, but concluded that a two-year program would be necessary. "One matter that was compromised rather than resolved concerned the scope of the new course. Many members pointed out that the interrelationship between physics and chemistry made it inadvisable to erect an arbitrary division between them. It was generally agreed that this was indeed the case, but it was further agreed that an adequate course combining both subjects would require at least two years, with consequent complications in attempting to fit it into the existing academic structure. In the end, it was decided that the long-term purpose of the Committee might well be the preparation and encouragement of such a course, but that as a practical matter the Committee would be well advised to restrict its efforts to a one-year physics course. As will be seen, however, the Committee has resisted any arbitrary position, and a certain amount of chemistry has been included in the syllabus." Physical Science Study Committee, *First Annual Report,* The Committee, Massachusetts Institute of Technology, 1957, p. 4.

the combined course as non-college-preparatory and the separate courses as college-preparatory in character.[21] Neither should the physical science course be regarded as primarily for low-ability students. The student's choice should be made on the basis of his science interests. Considerable attention has been given to the possibility of varied student programs involving both biology and the physical sciences. One sequence could be designed primarily for students with high ability and marked interests in science and might consist of biology with a cultural emphasis in the ninth grade, chemistry in the tenth, physics in the eleventh, and the possibility of advanced science in the twelfth. Another might consist of human-oriented biology in the ninth grade, physical science in the tenth, and possibly chemistry in the eleventh or twelfth. With ability grouping, this might be used both for low-ability students and for those of average to high ability without marked interest in science.

On the other hand, the physical science course need not be regarded as alternative to physics and chemistry, but as a course preceding them. It could be made the standard introductory course in physical science for all students, just as biology is the standard introductory course for all students in the life sciences. Ability grouping could be used both in biology and in the physical science course. A greater degree of mathematical analysis would be used in those sections of the physical science course designed for high-ability students. Beyond these introductory courses in general biology and general physical science, a school might develop advanced electives in physics, chemistry, biology, and possibly in earth science and astronomy. Advanced biology could be handled either on a combined basis, as is the case now in some college pro-

[21] For example, "The status of integrated physical-science courses in senior high schools was investigated by Ray (36) who queried 100 secondary schools in cities of 5000 or more population in 24 states. Seventy schools responded. Forty of them offered a physical-science course, chiefly in Grades XI and XII, which integrated physics, chemistry, geology, meteorology, and astronomy. Findings showed an increase in such courses and in enrolments in them. The courses were usually substituted for the traditional chemistry or physics courses by students not planning to go to college." Herbert A. Smith and Nathan S. Washton, "Science in the Secondary Schools," *Review of Educational Research,* October, 1957, on the Natural Sciences Mathematics, p. 350.

grams at the freshman level, or as separate courses in zoology and botany. These courses could be used as the basis for advanced standing in college, but should not be restricted to college-bound students.

Such a physical science course in such a sequence might well be made a constant, thereby raising the requirements from two years to three years in the six-year span from Grades 7 through 12. This should be done only in high schools where all or most students have taken science in the seventh or the eighth grade; otherwise students coming without such background would face a three-year requirement in the four upper high school years. Obviously every effort should be made, for this as well as other reasons, to develop science programs in seventh or eighth grade, regardless of the kind of vertical organization in effect.

The courses in biology and physical science in this kind of sequence would be common to all students. Those who anticipate taking advanced science work should take biology in the ninth grade and the physical science course in the tenth. Others might take biology either in ninth or tenth grade and the physical science course either in eleventh or twelfth. All this would require careful counseling, but no more so than does the possibility of advanced science in the upper high school years under the present program.

This sequence makes possible a high level of intensive study on the part of those with marked science abilities and interests, coupled with the advantages of advanced-standing credit to reduce the present overlap between courses at the high school and college levels. The student who takes physics as a separate course in high school would move directly to the second-level college course in that subject. On the other hand, those who take the combined physical science course in high school could take either the usual college physics or college chemistry course without serious overlapping between these and their previous studies. Non-college-bound as well as college-bound students with high abilities and interests in science would have the opportunity of taking four or more years of high school science made up of one year of biology and one of combined physical science, plus one to four of the advanced specialized courses. In these courses some of the non-college-bound students might find the motivation to change their plans and include college in their future, especially if encouraged by sumpathetic teachers and by scholarship provisions in cases of economic need.

Such a program as this gives promise of stimulating and advancing the development of the future science specialist and also of providing for the fundamental education of the general student. Four or even five years of science for the high-ability student with marked science interests do not constitute too large a fraction of the total program for such a student, especially when he takes five subjects at a time. Neither is the three-year requirement in the six-year span of secondary education excessive for the general student in the light of the cultural-transmission function. He should take enough science so that he may have more than just a casual acquaintance with scientific content and method.

The balance of studies, however, is always an important consideration. Knowledge of science cannot stand by itself either in the well-being of society or in the development of the individual. Not even Spencer claimed science to be the only knowledge worthy of transmission. Both the general student and the science specialist need a wider context of studies in which scientific knowledge can be placed. High schools therefore require study in mathematics, literature, social studies, and the arts. The relationship between the natural sciences and the social studies is a peculiarly significant one, for the kind of community in which scientific advance takes place has much to do with the question of how beneficial such advance will be. In one that disregards and suppresses the human individual and closes the avenues of free discussion and study, scientific advance will without question be a destructive force. In a human community that cherishes and respects the dignity and importance of the individual, scientific advance promises to bring about an enrichment of human life beyond the most extravagant dreams of human progress envisioned by the enthusiasts of the nineteenth century.

Bibliography

Anderson, Poul, "How Social is Science?" *The Saturday Review,* April 27, 1957, pp. 9–11, 29.

Barnard, J. Darrell, *Teaching High School Science,* What Research Says to the Teacher Series, No. 10, Department of Classroom Teachers and the American Educational Research Association, 1956.

Brown, Kenneth E., *Offerings and Enrollments in Science and Mathematics in Public High Schools,* U.S. Office of Education, Pamphlet No. 120, 1956, Department of Health, Education, and Welfare, 1957.

Commission on the Reorganization of Secondary Education of the National Education Association, *Reorganization of Science in Secondary Schools,* Bureau of Education, Department of the Interior, Bulletin 1920, No. 26.

Conant, James B. (ed.), *Harvard Case Histories in Experimental Science,* Harvard University Press, 1957.

Conant, James B., *On Understanding Science: An Historical Approach,* A Mentor Book, published by the New American Library of World Literature, Inc., by arrangement with Yale University Press, 1951.

Koelsche, Charles L., *The Academic and Teaching Backgrounds of Secondary Science Teachers in the State of Ohio,* Research Foundation, University of Toledo, 1958.

Martin, W. Edgar, *The Teaching of General Biology in the Public High Schools of the United States,* Office of Education, U.S. Department of Health, Education, and Welfare, Bulletin 1952, No. 9, Reprint 1954.

Merrifield, Charles W., "Science and Society: Intellectual and Social Implications of Science and Technology for Democracy," chap. 9 in National Council for the Social Studies, Twenty-Seventh Yearbook, *Science and the Social Studies,* The Council, 1956–1957, pp. 162–186.

National Society for the Study of Education, Forty-sixth Yearbook, pt. 1, *Science Education in American Schools,* The Society, 1947.

Pella, Milton O., "The Nature of the Academic Preparation in Science of Wisconsin High School Teachers of Physics, Chemistry, Biology, and General Science," *Science Education,* March, 1958, pp. 106–137.

Physical Science Study Committee, *First Annual Report,* The Committee, Massachusetts Institute of Technology, 1957.

....

CHAPTER 14

Visual Fine Arts

Speculation about the nature and meaning of art is both inevitable and desirable. What is worth doing is worth speculating about. Fortunately, we need not attempt a definition of art as a starting point in the study of the arts in the school program. But we do need working boundaries around those parts of the school program considered under the general heading of the arts.

For curricular purposes we shall regard the arts as those creative and aesthetic activities of man that produce something tangible enough to be transmitted or recorded. This excludes activities sometimes considered under the idea that art is synonymous with life itself. It includes some that are not treated in this chapter, such as the arts of literature, music, drama, and dance. In the high school program, literature becomes part of English and foreign languages, music stands by itself as a special case, drama is an integrating art that draws upon and combines other arts, and dance is handled as part of physical education. This leaves those instructional fields related to the fashioning or creating of objects of beauty and use that can be seen and felt, namely the visual fine arts and the practical or industrial arts. Many such objects are both beautiful and useful. While there are some that are useful but ugly and others that are beautiful but useless, there is no sharp line that can serve to put all objects into one category or the other. Similarly, there is no sharp line that can distinguish the fine from the practical arts. But historical circumstances have given us the separate programs and separate departments in the school curriculum. For convenience, then, the visual fine and the industrial arts are treated in separate chapters.

The work of art departments in high schools and of scheduled art periods in elementary schools can be identified as the visual fine arts of drawing, painting, sculpture, and design, carried on today with a variety of materials and techniques. Like science and history, these subjects are new arrivals in the secondary curriculum. They are found in today's high schools under a variety of course names, such as freehand drawing, art appreciation, general art, applied art, commercial art, or simply as Art I, II, III, and IV, further broken down as design, life drawing, figure drawing, costume design, and still life.

Enrollment statistics for art subjects present a mixed state of affairs and have not on the whole attracted much public attention. "Art subjects are pursued much more frequently by junior high school pupils than by pupils in the upper years of the secondary school. Enrollments in art courses amount to 48 percent of all junior high school pupils as compared with 10 percent in regular and senior high schools, and 13 percent in junior-senior and undivided schools."[1] The high figure for junior high schools reflects the tendency either to require art as such or to require students to choose between art and some other subject such as music or speech. On the other hand, art is only rarely listed as a senior high school graduation constant. The high school figures of 10 to 13 percent seem lower than desirable, especially when we bear in mind that these are totals for all the courses in the art field.[2] They should be com-

[1] "Offerings and Enrollments in High-School Subjects," *Biennial Survey of Education in the United States, 1948–1950,* p. 25, Federal Security Agency, Office of Education, 1951.

[2] De Francesco comments on this as follows. "Much lip service is given to the meaning of creative activities in senior high schools, especially by secondary educators. The changing emphases in senior-high-school programs, the popular demand for art at the adult level, and the insistence that education must seek to integrate are signs that raise the hope that what is being accomplished at the elementary-school levels and even at the junior-high-school levels may presently manifest itself in the senior high schools and in the public junior colleges. A survey of art programs today, however, discloses that most small high schools do not offer art. In medium-sized school systems, art is offered on an elective basis. In large schools, the elective system also prevails, although certain high schools have more elaborate offerings that range

pared not with individual courses such as algebra or world history, but with the entire fields of mathematics, social studies, and the like. Whether or not more students should be encouraged to elect art or even required to take it depends on the educational functions that the field can and should assume.

OBJECTIVES OF ART EDUCATION

These functions have been vigorously debated among art teachers and other students of the art curriculum. Surprisingly, they have evoked little discussion on the part of teachers generally or of the public. Most teachers, parents, and administrators would probably find it difficult to identify the issues or dilemmas in the art field. Such apparent acceptance might be a welcome one to teachers in science, social studies, and mathematics, who find themselves constantly in the public spotlight; art teachers might well wonder whether the attitude is one of acceptance or indifference. We have here a field in which discussion of the issues is confined largely to those who work in the field itself.

The following summary of the characteristics of "two main camps of art teachers" serves as a valuable sketch of what might be termed major orientations in the field of art education, at least in terms of generalized responses to specific questions.

To all these questions more than one answer is possible. On most of them, art teachers tend to divide into two main camps: first, the so-called "progressive" wing, favoring comparative freedom for the student, a psychological and sociological approach, and integration rather than the subject curriculum; secondly, the more conservative wing, sometimes called "academic," favoring more discipline, required knowledge and technique, and more intensive, directed systematic study of a limited realm of art. The former camp inclines to be more sympathetic to modern Post-impressionist art and to liberal politics; the latter to conservative politics, realism, and traditional standards in art. But such

---

from the elective system to fully accredited 'major' curriculums. The overall picture, nevertheless, indicates that the vast majority of senior-high-school pupils are denied any appreciable art opportunity beyond the junior-high-school years." Italo L. De Francesco, *Art Education: Its Means and Ends,* Harper & Brothers, 1958, pp. 351–352.

views do not always go together, and most art teachers object to being definitely labeled. They are conscious of the unwise extremes to which both attitudes have been carried: the one to absurd freakishness and pampering of children's whims; the other to stodgy, repressive conventionality. Most art teachers regard themselves as being at a happy medium between the two extremes, and as combining in their approach both sets of values. Nevertheless, vigorous disputes still arise over details of method and content.[3]

As indicated in the foregoing paragraph, the tendency is to find some happy medium between the extremes. This often takes the form of including objectives consistent with the various points of view, as is true in other school subjects besides art. When this happens, it is not a matter of mere concession-swapping between two sets of antagonists, but rather the expression of reasonable people who recognize some validity in viewpoints not necessarily their own, or at least those they would stress. As specific issues in art education arise, each group will naturally seek the bases for decisions in the kinds of objectives about which it is most concerned.

One writer, for example, recognizes both kinds of objectives as follows, "Art education should be concerned primarily with the development of understanding, appreciation, and abilities pertaining to art itself. In addition, it must take into account the personal and social objectives of general education, insofar as these ends are capable of being realized through the experience of art."[4] He goes on, however, to distinguish between primary and secondary objectives, with the primary objectives "related to the development of understanding, appreciation, and skills in art—the nonverbal perceptual and expressional skills essential to understanding."[5] From his point of view, objectives of personal and

---

[3] Thomas Munro, *Art Education: Its Philosophy and Psychology,* The Liberal Arts Press, 1956, pp. 29–30.

[4] Edward Warder Rannells, *Art Education in the Junior High School: A Study of Objectives.* Bulletin of the Bureau of School Service, College of Education, University of Kentucky, vol. 18, June, 1946, No. 4, p. 11.

[5] *Ibid.,* p. 12. He states in this connection, "To this end, the clearest goal and, from the standpoint of general education, probably the most important one is the training of vision. I use the term vision in place of visual perception to suggest art as a visual language; aesthetic perception would be the fullest development of it." *Ibid.*

social development are secondary as far as art education is concerned.[6]

A somewhat different position is stated by the Committee on the Function of Art in General Education in the Eight-Year Study of the Progressive Education Association Commission on Secondary School Curriculum. This group reports its interpretation of developments in art education as follows: "Thus there grew up in art education the increasing conviction that the newest conception of education would advance the ends both of art and of people."[7] Again we see the desire to recognize the value of both points of view. Neither aim presumably can stand alone. But when the committee comes to make its own statement of purpose, the personal-social development aspect seems to predominate. "The aim of art education in the secondary school is to further the growth of individuals in rich enjoyment and effectiveness and to encourage them to create a society where such living is possible for all."[8]

The willingness of people to recognize the validity of other viewpoints does not, then, eliminate preferences for their own. There is no reason why it should. Neither art teachers nor other students of secondary curriculum wish to promote a passive uniformity in which all convictions and distinctions are explained away by formula. Different parts of the art programs may well be governed by more stress on some kinds of aims than on others. Individual differences in students will call for adaptation of general aims to particular circumstances. It is desirable to have statements that promote awareness of the various aims and points of view so that no important consideration is overlooked when specific problems and issues are being studied. On a particular question, some choice of aim will have to be made, but the various aims should be

[6] *Ibid.,* p. 18. He does not deny the primary importance of these in general education as a whole. "Both the personal development and the socialization of individuals are of primary importance in general education. It is only from the standpoint of art education, where art is employed as one of the several educational means to achieve these objectives, that they may be regarded as secondary." *Ibid.*

[7] Progressive Education Association Commission on Secondary School Curriculum, *The Visual Arts in General Education,* A Report of the Committee on the Function of Art in General Education, D. Appleton-Century Company, Inc., 1940, p. 14.

[8] *Ibid.,* pp. 17–18.

kept in mind during the early stages of the study. Some aims may be primary for one kind of decision and secondary for others. In general, we may draw on a principle applicable to all subjects of instruction, namely, that objectives inherent in the discipline itself establish its place in the school program and the broad outlines of its presentation, while other objectives, such as those associated with personal-social development, serve as guidelines for the many everyday decisions of teachers in using the discipline for the educations of individual students.

Comprehensive lists, therefore, serve useful purposes by including the important considerations that identify the role of the arts in the school curriculum.[9] The objectives of cultural transmission and disciplined creativity make the arts a valid instructional field. But they are not detached from the personal, vocational, and civic contexts within which they function. If the arts had no functions in these contexts, they would constitute dead rather than living culture and there would be no point in transmitting them. We expect the arts to contribute to citizenship, but do not seek in citizenship the structure of the art curriculum as far as course offerings are concerned. A course called civic arts would not be called for, but attention to arts in community living might well pervade a number of art courses, as well as various extraclass activities or community-service projects. The Owatonna (Minnesota) Art Education Project of the 1930's provides an example of the possibilities of the arts in personal and community life.[10] Contributions

---

[9] A good comprehensive list of this kind is suggested by Munro. In his first aim, he states that aesthetic education "should *foster the aesthetic and artistic strains* in individual personality through active exercise and application in the observation, production, performance, and discussion of works of art." Munro, *op. cit.,* p. 15. But, "Another aim of aesthetic education is to convey to every student as much of the *cultural heritage of the world's great art* as he can effectively absorb and utilize." *Ibid.,* p. 16. Furthermore, "Aesthetic education should help to prepare the student for *vocational and professional success,* for a career which will gain him a livelihood and at the same time perform a constructive service to society," while "The fourth main aim is the use of the arts for *developing constructive, co-operative* citizenship." *Ibid.,* pp. 16 and 17.

[10] See Edwin Ziegfeld and Mary Elinore Smith, *Art for Daily Living: The Story of the Owatonna Art Education Project,* University of Minnesota Press, 1944. For an expression of the point of view which inspired the program by the man who had the most to do with its initiation see Melvin E. Haggerty, *Art a Way of Life,* University of Minnesota Press, 1935.

of the arts to everyday living permeated the entire sequence of art instruction in the Owatonna schools and extended beyond the classroom program into extraclass activities and community-service projects in which both the art teachers and the students took part.[11] One of the first requests that came to the art teachers themselves was to help plan the redecorating of the boiler room in the municipal power plant.[12] Neither in the objectives as stated nor in the instructional program as carried out was there any disparagement of standards or slighting of disciplined technique. This project demonstrated a number of important truths, but perhaps most important of all it brought home the artificial nature of the distinctions sometimes drawn between art for art's sake and art for the daily round of human life.

ART AND THE ADOLESCENT

Like their fellow staff members in other subjects, high school art teachers regardless of the camps to which they may adhere must carry on their own daily work with adolescents, each of whom is an individual with his or her own particular interests, talents, and drives. It is natural for the literature of art education to show much concern with the nature of adolescence and with individual differences. Two aspects of adolescence in relation to art have particularly attracted the attention of curriculum workers in this field —one, the apparent decline of creativity or interest in the arts during the later adolescent years, the other, the relationship of adolescent motivation to the disciplinary effect of techniques and skills.

The apparent decline of spontaneous creativity in the adolescent

[11] Such services were performed at first by the art teachers, but later on by students also. "During the last three years of work, much of what the staff had done to begin with as art service now began to be worked upon by school groups and even by individual students. From the school flowed dozens of projects, single home-interior redecorations, garden plans, planting schemes for park and school, color schemes for high school and grade schools, redecoration of the high-school auditorium—all of these as well as continued work, this time by students on such projects as window displays, large-scale illustrated albums, ticket booths, drapery designs, and so on." Frederick M. Logan, *Growth of Art in American Schools,* Harper & Brothers, 1956, pp. 188–189.

[12] Ziegfeld and Smith, *op. cit.,* p. 25.

years is a point difficult to pin down. Perhaps it is only folklore, but teachers in all fields testify to its existence.[13] It would be of course an especially difficult matter to cope with in a field such as art. One writer in the art field sees it partly as a reflection of the neglect of arts in American schools and partly as an intrinsic characteristic of adolescence itself.

If the freedom of expression and freshness of observation that the child possesses at the age of six could be preserved and built on as the child grows up, teaching would be a simple matter. But the vision of the six-year-old is not static; it changes and grows with the child. Children who are teeming with ideas at six, tend to become barren at twelve or fourteen. This tendency seems to be true, at least of American children.

If art development were stressed in American schools, our children would probably continue their creative interest through adolescence and continue to grow in artistic prowess to maturity.

It remains a fact, however, that creative power and interest diminish at adolescence. Imagination and expression run low and the teacher often finds himself besieged by children, totally uninspired by the art media before them, asking him what to do.[14]

All of which perhaps testifies to the fact that adolescents are not six-year-olds, in art or in anything else, and perhaps that adolescent creativity is not as directly or naïvely expressed as is that of younger children. At one time it was popular to ascribe this to the allegedly crippling or repressing effects of schooling, especially the stereotype of past authoritarianism and harshness. But schools have according to popular impression become less harsh and less authoritarian without any noticeable outburst of adolescent creativity. More recently the tendency has been to see this as one aspect of a

[13] A somewhat dissenting expression on creativity in adolescence comes to us from the teachers who worked in the Owatonna, Minnesota, art project. "The young adolescent is so vibrantly responsive to the myriads of new experiences which color all his waking hours that he must at all costs make known his feelings about them. He is eager to explore new media, to discover new ways of communicating his ideas graphically and three-dimensionally as well as verbally, to find new challenges for his imagination and his inventiveness. He wants to know how things are made and how things work, and he has not yet acquired the self-consciousness that comes when a maturing mind grows critical of its own achievements." *Ibid.*, p. 137.

[14] Victor D'Amico, *Creative Teaching in Art,* International Textbook Company, 1942, p. 2.

generalized conformity pattern in adolescence. The adolescent seeks approval by doing well what adults and fellow adolescents expect of him. While creativity in the arts is not frowned on in our society, it is usually not a means of gaining approval, a fact that may testify to a lack of enthusiasm for art in our society as a whole. The popular notion of creativity as a characteristic of small children is hardly one to motivate adolescents to display such creativity even when they possess it.

Perhaps the clue to this characteristic lies in the other aspect of adolescence discussed in the literature of art education, namely, the need for disciplined accomplishment through the mastery of skills, techniques, and critical power. According to this point of view, the adolescent is no longer satisfied with creativity at the more naïve level of the child, but is unable to progress beyond this without acquiring definite skills. "The development of skills appears of vital importance in the secondary classroom for it is through them that the adolescent individual gains confidence in his individual art expression."[15] Another writer puts the case in direct terms that adolescent indifference or lack of creativity reflects the carrying of what he terms "child-pedagogy in art" beyond the childhood level. "It is my own observation that the creativeness of childhood does carry over into adolescence, but it is continually being modified by the expanding and changing interests and experiences of adolescence so that soon it is completely transformed. Failure to understand the nature of this transformation has per-

---

[15] Viktor Lowenfeld, *Creative and Mental Growth,* The Macmillan Company, 3d ed., 1957, p. 338. Lowenfeld further develops the importance of this "technical involvement" as follows. "One of the most important factors in promoting freedom of expression during this vital period is the recognition that adolescents are afraid to use any method which *directly* projects their imagery. In countless cases, I have seen adolescent youngsters discouraged by the 'primitivity' of their pencil drawings, but if the identical drawings were used for etchings or embossing, they were well satisfied. The *direct* form of expression apparently was emotionally too close to them and their self-critical attitude could not bear the 'naïveté' which was in contradiction to their grown-up feelings. Etching or embossing introduced a procedure which brought about a somewhat more remote attitude toward the original and direct form of expression. This introduced distance, however, was vital to the acceptance of the work. Now it is no longer the naïveté which counts, but the technical involvement in the art expression of the adolescent. To provide adolescent youth with the opportunity of such technical involvement without losing the initial desire for expression is one of the foremost tasks of the teacher in promoting adolescent art." *Ibid.*

mitted the schools to extend a child-pedagogy in art into the adolescent period. The result is that the young adolescent comes to
associate art with the childhood that he wants to outgrow, and thus
his interest dies."[16] The adolescent, then, "is trying to incorporate
more meanings in his work, to say more and say it more objectively,
and thus the demands of expression are greater, and to meet them
he needs more educational help."[17] Lowenfeld, while endorsing
the need for skill and technique in adolescence, points out the danger of too much teacher imposition, contending that "As long as
technique is separated from individual expression, technique is
only a handicraft which may even restrict the individual instead of
encouraging him."[18] The high school art teacher apparently must
foster creativity within the discipline imposed by technique and
skill, avoiding at the same time the tendency to teach these techniques and skills for themselves. This is indeed a difficult charge on
the teacher's own skill and creativity, for it demands not only a
sensitive appreciation of the general characteristics of aesthetic
development in adolescence, but an adaptation of the program to a
wide range of individual differences.

The dilemmas and challenges of individual differences, therefore, confront the art teacher with peculiar, almost unique force.
In attempting to identify categories or groups of such differences,
the Progressive Education Association Committee in the Eight-
Year Study refers not only to the gifted and the handicapped, but
to five kinds of average students.

One numerous group of students is composed of those who are excellent or average in academic work but definitely retarded in art. They
are accustomed to using their minds, to intellectualization and verbalization, but quite without experience in working out ideas with their
hands. Often in addition they have little consciousness of their own
emotional life and no desires of their own which they wish to express. Usually they feel inferior in the studio; frequently they wish
to avoid it. . . .

In contrast is a second group of students who are noticeably slow in
intellectual work but who use their hands well and who respond read-

---

16 Rannells, *op. cit.*, p. 49.
17 *Ibid.*, pp. 49–50.
18 Lowenfeld, *op. cit.*, p. 340.

ily to art materials when these can be used in practical situations. . . .

A third group comprises students with real aptitude for art, with imagination and originality, but with poor motor coördination. . . .

A fourth group, students with primarily technical interests, are found in every school, more often among boys than girls. . . .

A fifth group are students with ability in plastic arts but little or no interest in two-dimensional expression. . . .[19]

In a similar fashion, the categories of the handicapped and the gifted could be broken down into subgroups, each with problems and possibilities of its own. One might almost draw the conclusion that group or class work in the arts is out of the question, and that the nature of the field demands one teacher for every student. The Progressive Education Association committee, however, contends that the group situation can be handled with most students and is indeed of value in itself. "Though it is essential to recognize the needs of all students and to provide adequate opportunity for each, physical separation is not necessarily indicated, for a number of students may work in one room on different expressions using different media. The social situation here has, in fact, great educational value."[20] On the other hand, when referring to badly handicapped students, the committee feels that "students of this type should, wherever possible, be instructed under special conditions by a person trained to meet their problems."[21] It should be kept in mind, of course, that most art classes can be handled on the basis of individual or small-group activities. There is, however, a limit to the number of such activities a teacher can keep in mind at one time. Art classes, therefore, should be kept small, but this goal will become increasingly difficult to achieve.

Individual differences affect not only the specific teaching procedures within a given class but also the organization of courses within the art program as a whole. They probably become the most important considerations in the setting up of courses, since the art field does not break down readily into a series of topics or bodies of material. Beyond the introductory or general level,

[19] Progressive Education Association Commission on Secondary School Curriculum, *op. cit.,* pp. 53–56.

[20] *Ibid.,* pp. 56–57.

[21] *Ibid.,* p. 53.

courses are organized on the basis of differences in abilities and interests, reflecting in part the uses of the arts in such courses as costume design or commercial art, and in part the various art media or processes in such courses as drawing, design, and sculpture. Only the larger high schools can offer a broad range of such specialized advanced courses; in most cases the teacher still faces the job of providing the diversified activities in a single group.

ART PROGRAMS, REQUIREMENTS, AND ELECTIVES

So far as the sequence of art courses in the high school is concerned, De Francesco suggests two plans, one for large or middle-sized schools, the other for small schools. As initial or introductory general art course is included in both plans, but recommended for the larger schools in Grade 9 and for the smaller schools in Grade 10. In the larger schools, the general art course is followed in Grade 10 by electives open to all students in crafts, drawing and painting, theater arts, and commercial art. The courses in Grades 11 and 12 are identified as an art major curriculum and are developed as design foundation, graphics foundation, modeling and sculpture, and crafts foundation. In this program, according to De Francesco, "The interests of all are served through general art, the further interests of some through the elective area, and those of talented pupils through the art-major curriculum."[22] His recommended program for small schools includes elective courses in drawing and painting, crafts, and commercial design in Grades 11 and 12. "Here, art for daily living is stressed for all in the tenth grade. The elective area should permit all pupils who so choose to develop their gifts and deepen their appreciation through broad areas."[23]

Few administrators, curriculum workers, teachers in fields other than art, and members of the general public would disagree with the suggestion that every high school should provide as great a variety of elective art courses as possible. True, the budget must always be considered, and what might seem to be excessive spending in any one instructional field will inevitably be questioned by those

[22] De Francesco, *op. cit.*, p. 366.
[23] *Ibid.*

not in the field itself. The main controversy about art in the school program, however, is one that occurs in every instructional field, namely, whether study in the field should be required of all students, particularly at the senior high school level or in Grades 9 through 12.

The suggestion for required art work in the senior high school is not a new one. Neither is the practice new. Counts found prescribed art in the high school programs of three of the 15 cities included in his survey of 1923–1924 and commented on the matter as follows. "Whether this prescription of art is wise or not would seem to depend on the character of the materials which can be offered. If the work is dominated by the emphasis on productive technique which is now generally characteristic, it is hardly likely to be successful. If, however, the work is dominated by the purpose of stimulating in the ordinary individual a love for beautiful things and by the desire to raise the level of beauty in the community and in the objects of daily use, it would be justified in claiming general recognition in the high-school curriculum."[24]

In most cases today, the advocates of required art tend to stress the kinds of outcomes accepted by Counts. De Francesco summarizes well the modern arguments set forth on behalf of such a requirement.

A general art course required of all students in the senior high school would result in heightened appreciation, sounder standards of taste, deepened interests, and the possible identification of those who should be guided into professional fields of art. General art would, furthermore, promote the growth of those personal qualities that education desires for all citizens. The home, the community, business, industry, religion, recreation, and the moral and spiritual resources needed by man are spheres of living that touch all youths. Properly organized, those areas could form a basis for general art activities.[25]

Compelling as these arguments are, they seem to be relevant only to school systems in which little or no attention has been paid to the arts prior to the ninth grade. Where this is the case, a general

[24] George S. Counts, *The Senior High School Curriculum,* The University of Chicago, 1926, p. 114.
[25] De Francesco, *op. cit.,* p. 364.

art course should by all means be required. Suppose on the other hand that the school system has provided a good program throughout the elementary grades, followed by at least one year of required art in Grade 7 or 8. Under these circumstances, a required general art course in ninth grade, or any grade of the senior high school, seems difficult to defend. Those high schools which draw students from various systems where the art programs prior to ninth grade may range from zero to excellent should of course offer a general art course and should require it of those students who have previously been without opportunities in the art field.[26]

But, some will say, the general art course is not the only one that might be listed as a graduation constant. It is possible to require even the student with a good general art background to take one of the advanced or specialized courses. Logan comments on the development of such requirements in the Eight-Year Study of the Progressive Education Association. "Variations in the required course consisted of a requirement for having each student do work in at least one fine-arts field, with the fields broadly defined to include shop, music, visual and plastic arts, drama, creative writing, and dance. Schools establishing this type of requirement usually had outlined an arts area as one of the necessary elements of secondary education."[27] While more students should be encouraged to elect such courses than is now the case, it is difficult to see why they should be required. One possible reason is that of awakening the interests of students for even more advanced and specialized study in the arts. By this time, however, students with the abilities and interests for further work in art should be identified, provided, of course, that there has been a good art program preceding the ninth grade.

Why then, art teachers may ask, should requirements exist in other instructional fields? The case for these requirements in most other fields is based on subject matter to be transmitted, not on

---

[26] A more recent variation of the general arts course is one called integrated arts in which the visual arts are included along with other art forms such as music, dance, and drama. This has been vigorously advocated in some schools as a graduation requirement or constant. Here again, the need would seem to depend on provisions for these art experiences in the elementary and junior high programs.

[27] Logan, *op. cit.,* p. 195.

performance skills to be developed. It is true that the advocates of required art do not list the development of performance skills as the primary objective. But the kinds of outcomes stated by Counts in 1926 and by De Francesco in 1958 are precisely those which most art teachers contend cannot be developed except through participation in art activities. For the student who has already had such work in the elementary school and the junior high, this can mean only one thing: advanced development in the performance skills. Of the usual requirements in the secondary school, only English and physical education present demands for continued development in skills. Those who support these requirements in English do so on the basis of general or universal need for the skills involved or on the grounds of the related subject matter in literature. Arguments for the physical education requirement are somewhat more diversified and complex. In mathematics the courses that provide for continued development in specialized performance are elective courses. The requirements present only the fundamental knowledge of the subject. Social studies and science requirements are usually based on the subject matter they transmit.

A possible case might be made for advanced requirements in art on the grounds of subject matter. There is plenty of such subject matter in the field of the visual arts. It includes the history of art, standards of taste and criticism, knowledge of contemporary schools and movements, biographies of artists, familiarity with various types of art media and expression, and understanding of the relationships of the arts to the everyday aspects of personal, family, and community life. To the outsider, a course or a series of courses dealing with such materials might be developed much as any other course in the program of studies without having the students engage in painting, drawing, sculpture, or any art activities at all. To many art teachers, however, the idea of developing such subject matter without concurrent participation by students in art activities is self-contradictory. And it remains self-contradictory to them no matter how much is done through the use of slides, prints, and field trips to museums.

In spite of these objections, many classes along these lines have

been offered in high school programs. Logan summarizes the difficulties encountered in such courses and expresses the doubts felt
by art teachers and art curriculum workers as follows.

Less often, but frequently enough to be noteworthy, schools offered
required courses in appreciation of the arts, or, as some of the more
journalistically slanted course titles put it, 'consumer arts.' When these
appreciation courses are described, there seems to have been a heavy
emphasis on literature, architecture, and painting, particularly in the
historical context of European history from the medieval period to the
present. Art teachers who have labored to do a course in appreciation
of the arts, sometimes with enlarged sections of students numbering
fifty or more, have raised bitter questions as to the value of requiring
such work of all students or indeed of any students, except under very
favorable circumstances with adequate equipment and classes small
enough for extended discussion. The revised art-appreciation class
would seem to be the least desirable method of enlarging the scope of
art in high schools. It is a talking about art at a time in the life of the
individual when he prefers, as much as possible, direct action, real
grappling with the tricks of a trade, skill, or vocation. It is easier for a
high-school student to think about activity and its implications if he is
simultaneously working at it.[28]

One of the difficulties mentioned by Logan need not be accepted
as inevitable. There is no more reason to schedule 50 students in a
class in art history than in one in American history or plane geometry. The other point made, that high school students prefer direct
action to talking, is subject to individual differences both in students and teachers. Reading and discussion in the arts entirely detached from art experience would of course be objectionable. It
would be undesirable to present such a course as this to students
with no background of experience in the arts. Such a course would
be most appropriate in schools with good programs in the elementary grades and junior highs. Whether the doing aspect of the arts
needs to be simultaneous with the study-reading-discussion aspect
is another question.

Such courses also suffer from some of the bad connotations of
the term "art appreciation" itself. Logan suggests the term be

[28] *Ibid.*, pp. 195–196.

junked.[29] "There is too great a limitation in this connotation that has grown up around the word appreciation; we think of polite tea-table chatter when we really hope for strongly held creative convictions upon which people will take action."[30] Appreciation in this sense of admiring the right things is in fact irrelevant to the purposes for which such courses might be established. The purpose is not to develop appreciation, but to cultivate understanding and literacy in the arts through transmitting a body of substantial information in past and contemporary art history. This is not an easy assignment, but it is one that conceivably could justify a senior high school constant in the field of art.

The suggestion for required art in the senior high school does not necessarily come from art teachers. We need not ascribe to art teachers any more than to teachers in other fields the desire to promote their enterprises for the sake of numbers alone. Logan probably expresses the feelings of many art teachers in the following comments on this matter.

Most art teachers, if quizzed sympathetically and not frightened out of their normal missionary spirit, would readily agree that all secondary students should take art.

The next step, if such a situation were to be brought about by administrative fiat, could be chaotic. The fact is that we are not ready or able to teach all high-school students in art classes. In the unlikely event that they were suddenly assigned to a required art period, there would be waged, for some time at least, a heavily unequal contest between doubtful, unconvinced students and teachers by no means sure of their objectives or of their use of the equipment available. We are lacking in practices calculated to create among these general students an interest in the visual and plastic arts. Unfortunately, in the few schools which have had general art-education courses as a requirement, there has seldom been enough time for planning, enough experimentation, enough recognition of the wholly different nature of the job from that of the customary selective senior-high art group.[31]

Perhaps the demand for required art courses in senior high comes more from general curriculum workers who are concerned

[29] *Ibid.*, p. 160.
[30] *Ibid.*
[31] *Ibid.*, p. 226.

about the neglect of aesthetic objectives in the school program as a whole. But responsibility for the aesthetic objectives need not be centered in the department of visual arts. Other fields of instruction, particularly music, industrial arts, physical education, English, and foreign languages deal with subject matter and activities directly related to aesthetics. Some subjects, such as mathematics, usually not thought of as among the arts, are in actuality far from irrelevant to the development of aesthetic insight and understanding. Further opportunities for development of aesthetic creativity may exist in the program beyond the classroom studies, such as the extraclass activities and school-and-community service projects.

It is difficult, then, to make a convincing case for a required art course in the senior high school for students who have enjoyed a good art program in the elementary school and the junior high. But this does not mean we should be satisfied with the present level of art enrollments. We cannot believe that the present enrollees in art classes include all the students who are interested in art and capable of studying it further. As is true in other subjects, art enrollments are undoubtedly affected by the four-subject-at-a-time tradition with the notion that only the exceptional or superior student should be permitted to take five. More flexibility on this matter of student loads would make it possible for some students at least to take the art courses they would like to take, but cannot take now because of specific requirements in their own programs. If some external stimulation is needed, it would probably be better to require 18+ units for graduation than to specify a unit of art as a graduation constant.

Such a resolution of the matter, however, does not render palatable the fact that many students go through high school without acquiring some basic knowledge of art history or the place of the arts in contemporary life. Among these students will be many who have had good art work in elementary school and junior high, for these programs necessarily deal more with individual skill development and experience in a variety of art media than with historical subject matter. One resolution of this dilemma is to include art history and contemporary art movements in social studies courses. But the social studies program has very little room for additional subject matter or responsibilities. This is particularly true of the course in world history, which on the surface at least should be an especially good vehicle for art understanding and information. History teachers, furthermore, are not necessarily well prepared to teach this kind of material, and it is perhaps unreasonable to expect them to add a comprehensive knowledge of art history to the other demands of their field. Some schools have experimented with arrangements under which teachers from the art department come into social studies classes to handle art history materials, sometimes in separate units, sometimes as related subject matter in units on cultures and civilizations. This is a good arrangement, but one difficult to handle administratively in the assigning of teaching schedules and determining of teaching loads. The idea is a laudable one, but it takes a high degree of conviction on the part of all concerned to sustain it in school practice from one year to the next.

In general, then, it appears that the following represent the most likely possibilities for strengthening the secondary curriculum in the arts: (1) to develop as good a program as possible in the junior high school, with at least one year of art required of all students at that level; (2) to require one year of art of students in senior high school who have not had a good program in elementary or junior high; (3) to develop in each high school as extensive a program of electives as the size and resources of the school permit; and (4) to modify the four-subject-at-a-time tradition so that more students may include art in their programs. The last possibility is one that will open up not only more registrations in art, but in a number of other fields like art, which are represented largely or entirely as electives.

It may be true, as some writers have claimed, that the state of the arts in our high schools reflects the state that the arts occupy generally in American life and culture. The fine arts, according to this point of view, are regarded as extras and frills in American life and so will inevitably be regarded as extras and frills in the high school program. Art, therefore, prospers in the elementary school, so this explanation runs, since childhood is regarded as a time for frills and toys, but the high school student is expected to put away childish things. This explanation assumes the survival in American society of the notion that culture, in its superficial sense, is the concern of children, who cannot escape it, and of women, who find some compensation in it for their alleged exclusion from the real affairs of the world. This may once have been the notion held in American society, but it is an obvious caricature of the state of affairs as it exists today. Art is no longer regarded as childish or effeminate. In fact, practically everybody is "for" it. But it is probably true that most of us still think of art as something in museums only and that art and the vital aspects of American culture have still failed somehow to establish effective contact with each other. One of the unfortunate evidences of this lack of contact is the defensive attitude with which many art teachers discuss their field with other teachers in high school curriculum study groups and committees.

All this reinforces the importance of the school and of the art program in the school. Here is one area at least in which the school may justifiably seek to do something about the culture as it exists. This will be a slow process. Important cultural change of this kind does not take place in a single generation.[32] The rate of change will depend on the skills and understandings of those students who have studied art and are in a position to influence others in their families and communities. Students forced unwillingly into art courses at the senior high school level will hardly make good ambassadors for this kind of cultural change. In the long run, more good will be done by students who choose art courses without compulsion and who feel that these courses mean something real and important to them. The quality of art instruction in the elective

[32] In the Owatonna, Minnesota, project, some changes became apparent within a period of several years. The art program in that community had apparently ceased to exist prior to the project (Ziegfeld and Smith, *op. cit.,* p. 62), presumably a victim of depression curtailment as in many communities. At the beginning of the project the junior high program consisted of two elective programs a week. Before 1944, however, art had become a seventh-grade and eighth-grade requirement five days a week. *Ibid.,* p. 137. This furnishes at least one example of the belief that the art program in the school reflects the importance of the arts in community life. Few communities of course have the chance of launching a program with outside financial aid as was the case in Owatonna, but many schools do have sufficiently strong art programs to make some impact on community life if turned in this direction.

courses becomes therefore a matter of particular significance, and the strengthening of the art program must be recognized as a compelling responsibility by all who are concerned with the contribution of the high school to American culture as a whole. Art may remain an elective subject in our senior high school programs, but there is no reason why it should remain an afterthought.

Bibliography

D'Amico, Victor, *Creative Teaching in Art,* International Textbook Company, 1942.

De Francesco, Italo L., *Art Education: Its Means and Ends,* Harper & Brothers, 1958.

Kouwenhoven, John A., *Made in America: The Arts in Modern Civilization,* Doubleday & Company, Inc., 1948.

Logan, Frederick M., *Growth of Art in American Schools,* Harper & Brothers, 1956.

Lowenfeld, Viktor, *Creative and Mental Growth,* The Macmillan Company, 3d ed., 1957.

Lynes, Russell, *The Tastemakers,* Harper & Brothers, 1954.

Munro, Thomas, *Art Education: Its Philosophy and Psychology,* The Liberal Arts Press, 1956.

Progressive Education Association Commission on Secondary School Curriculum, *The Visual Arts in General Education,* A Report of the Committee on the Function of Art in General Education, D. Appleton-Century Company, Inc., 1940.

Rannells, Edward Warder, *Art Education in the Junior High School: A Study of Objectives,* Bulletin of the Bureau of School Service, College of Education, University of Kentucky, 18:4, June, 1946.

Ziegfeld, Edwin, and Smith, Mary Elinore, *Art for Daily Living: The Story of the Owatonna Art Education Project,* University of Minnesota Press, 1944.

CHAPTER 15

Industrial Arts

There is no valid line of separation between the visual fine arts and the industrial arts. Many art programs include craft work, and many industrial arts teachers are sensitive to the form-and-function relationship. Nevertheless we have separate programs of instruction for these two aspects of the same human enterprise. Perhaps this reflects the extent to which machine production and standardization have developed in modern industrial work, although much industrial arts instruction in the schools involves the use of hand tools rather than machines. Also reflected may be some of the historic controversies in the industrial arts field itself, particularly the one centering around the balance between its general and vocational objectives.

The industrial arts may well lay claim to the unhappy distinction of being the most misunderstood field in the school program. It has suffered both from its enemies and from its friends, but probably more from its friends. One of the most serious misunderstandings is that which makes a one-to-one relationship between industrial arts and vocational education. The industrial arts field grew up as part of general or liberal education and is still so regarded by many of its teachers. It is true that some work in the industrial arts is distinctively and specifically vocational training; but this is true of other fields in the school program as well. It is also true that much of the work in the industrial arts may contribute to the individual's occupational success; but this is no more true of the industrial arts than it is of English, mathematics, and a number of other fields. But the identification of industrial arts and vocational education as one and the same thing continues as the popular stereotype. When many school administrators, high school teachers outside of industrial arts, and members of the general public think of vocational education, whether with approval or disapproval, they have in their minds a picture of some shops. And when they think of the industrial arts program of the school, they identify it with "teaching boys a trade."

This might not be bad in itself, except that it ushers in a sequence of other and even more damaging errors. One of these is the tendency to create an artificial distinction between vocational and academic studies and to set something called a vocational curriculum against the stereotype of the college-preparatory curriculum. The next step is even worse. It cannot be denied that many people have regarded industrial arts or vocational education as an inferior substitute for an academic education and one peculiarly fitted to inferior students whose abilities are not equal to other kinds of studies. The industrial arts courses, and in many cases their related vocational programs, have in consequence been used as dumping grounds, a somewhat unhappy term, but a familiar one in high school practice. It must be admitted that some industrial arts educators have contributed to these misunderstandings themselves by claiming for their field a practical value superior to other fields in the high school program and a degree of motivation that conceivably challenges and interests potential dropouts who see little value in these other fields.

These misunderstandings and controversies are all part of the rich and colorful history of industrial arts in the curriculum, a history that includes about every intellectual current and cross current in the history of education itself. Handwork has always fascinated intellectuals who concern themselves with educational reform, particularly with protests against verbalism or excessive preoccupation of the schools with language studies. It was stressed particularly by such eighteenth-century reformers as Rousseau, Basedow, and Pestalozzi as a means of dealing with things as well as words. These men saw handwork as part of liberal or cultural education, and their point of view stressed the development of the whole child or the whole person. Liberal education to them meant the harmonious development of all aspects of human personality. Modern defenders of the industrial arts are fond of citing the writings of those who in the past proclaimed the need for handwork in the development of the all-around or well-rounded human being.

For the most part, the ideas of the eighteenth-century reformers did not change the programs of secondary education, although they did find expression in a number of experimental schools and institutes under private and philanthropic sponsorship. The motives of these founders included both the desire to put certain educational theories into practice and to provide education for the poor. It was this latter motive that recognized the possibilities of hand or manual training for vocational purposes. This was a relatively new idea, since vocational training for industrial and mechanical work had been traditionally handled through apprenticeship and not in school. Perhaps it was felt that the apprenticeship system was closed to the poorest children of the community. And perhaps it was a reflection of what many writers have referred to as the gradual decline or breakdown of the apprenticeship system.

One fact that confronted educational theorists and practical philanthropists in the latter half of the eighteenth century and the first part of the nineteenth was the industrial revolution. More mechanics and technicians were needed. Those who deplored the horrors of the factory system at that time and especially the employment of young children viewed industrial education as a means of helping people prepare themselves for skilled jobs, thereby avoiding the drudgery, long hours, and low pay of most factory workers. Enlightened industrialists regarded industrial education as a means of improving production and their workers' welfare. The early decades of the nineteenth century, therefore, saw the establishment of a number of private adult schools known as mechanics' institutes both in Great Britain and in the United States, such as the Franklin Institute founded in Philadelphia in 1824, the Mechanics' Institute of Boston founded in 1827, and the Ohio Mechanics' Institute founded in Cincinnati in 1828. The founders of the Franklin Institute soon became aware of the lack of general education on the part of those who came to the lecture sessions and established a high school department with a program including the traditional academic studies plus mechanical drawing.

In England, the industrial revolution stimulated the reaction known as the arts-and-crafts movement, which in turn contributed to the development of the manual arts in schools.

While thus in the early decades of the nineteenth century attempts were made, through instruction in the sciences and arts in mechanics' institutes and the like, to counteract the injurious influence upon the laboring classes of the machine and factory system of manufacture, the middle of the century witnessed the rise of a movement for the elevation not only of the so-called working classes, but of society in general, through the study and practice by all of the handicrafts which the Industrial Revolution threatened to destroy. Receiving its initial impulse from Carlyle's panegyrics of the nobility and beneficence of labor, it was developed through Ruskin, Morris, and other disciples.[1]

This was in part a forerunner of the present day "do-it-yourself" arts-and-crafts movement in which the general citizen works with his hands for creative use of leisure time and also to make allegedly better household articles than those made in factories and sold in stores. Ruskin put the case as follows. "It would be part of my scheme of physical training that every youth in the state— from the king's own son downward—should learn to do some thing finely and thoroughly with his hand, so as to let him know what stout craftsmanship meant; and to inform of many things besides. . . . The result would be in after life that among the middle classes a good deal of the house furniture would be made . . . by the master himself and his sons . . . to the extinction of a great deal of vulgar upholstery and other mean handicraft."[2] It was this arts-and-crafts movement that gave early support to the essential unity of the fine and practical arts, a point of view that

[1] Lewis Flint Anderson, *History of Manual and Industrial School Education,* D. Appleton and Company, 1926, pp. 70–71.

[2] John Ruskin, *Time and Tide,* Letter 21, cited in Anderson, *op. cit.,* pp. 71–72.

gained expression both in theory and practice well through the nineteenth century. Many arts-and-crafts societies were founded in Great Britain, both to promote these activities among adults and also to introduce them in schools. The ideas promoted by these societies were picked up by leaders of the industrial arts movement in the United States and contributed in part to the non-vocational emphasis in early industrial arts programs in this country.

Manual or industrial education in the United States then was influenced both by the industrial revolution and by the counter-revolution of the arts-and-crafts movement, one of which put the emphasis on the need for vocational, the other for general education. Industrial training for vocational purposes gained expression both in the mechanics' institutes and in various private experimental schools, usually at the adult or higher education levels. The demands of advancing technology for engineers and specialists led to the passing of the Morrill Land-Grant Act of 1862, which provided for the establishment of state colleges of agricultural and mechanical arts in a setting of general higher education.

THE MANUAL TRAINING MOVEMENT

All this ferment gained little expression in the programs of elementary and secondary schools, either public or private, before the 1870's. The leaders who in that and subsequent decades promoted and sponsored manual training in the general schools, however, had back of their efforts a great deal of historical development, including the vocational emphasis stimulated by the industrial revolution, the arts-and-crafts viewpoint of general education, and the earlier educational theorists and philanthropists who believed handwork to be an essential element of all-around personality development in the individual human being. Much of this background was European in origin, and it is of interest to note that not only our traditional and academic studies, but also many of the newer fields came into our program through European influences.

It was in fact a specifically European stimulus, the exhibit of the Imperial Technical Schools of Moscow and St. Petersburg at the

Philadelphia Centennial Exposition in 1876, which set off the industrial movements in our secondary schools. Two Americans in particular were impressed by this exhibit, John D. Runkle, president of the Massachusetts Institute of Technology, and Professor C. M. Woodward of Washington University, St. Louis. Both men soon established shopwork after the Russian system for engineering students at their respective schools.

Woodward, however, did not stop at the college level. In 1879, he established the Manual Training High School of Washington University, an event accepted by writers in this field as the real beginning of manual training in United States school programs. This school included not only shopwork, but also mathematics, science, and literature, with electives in Latin and French. "The manual training facilities in the school included a blacksmith shop, a machine shop, a turning shop, a carpentry shop, a drawing room, a physical science laboratory, and rooms for academic subjects."[3]

Similar schools were soon established in Chicago, Cincinnati, New Orleans, Toledo, and New York, all of these under private auspices. The movement spread to the public schools, taking the form both of manual training high schools like the one in St. Louis and of manual training departments in the general or academic high schools. The first public manual training high school was established in Baltimore in 1884. Among the first cities to establish manual training departments in academic high schools were Omaha, Minneapolis, Washington, D.C., Eau Claire, Wisconsin, and Peru, Illinois.[4]

Both the objectives and the practices of manual training work in these schools are important in the history of industrial arts education. The objectives were primarily non-vocational in character, although possible applications to vocational life were admitted.

While there was naturally much that was vague and tentative in the reasons given for the introduction of tool instruction into general education, three or four stand out as fairly definite. First, it was held that

[3] Roy W. Roberts, *Vocational and Practical Arts Education,* Harper & Brothers, 1957, p. 72.
[4] *Ibid.,* pp. 75–76.

by gratifying the constructive and creative impulses it supplied what had hitherto been a serious lack in general education. It made it possible, as Woodward expressed it, "to send the whole boy to school." Secondly, it seemed to make general school work more directly contributory to the training of the young for some form of manual industry. While the leaders, Runkle, Woodward, and others vigorously disavowed any intention of substituting vocational for cultural education, they did not fail to point out that the manual training in the arts underlying the various handicrafts constituted a valuable though incomplete preparation for any form of skilled handwork.[5]

The other two objectives referred to in the foregoing quotation are "cultivation of habits of industry"[6] and "respect for manual labor," the latter to "elevate the social status of the working classes."[7] Probably the dominant objective, however, was that of providing a more well-rounded education as implied by Woodward's expression, "to send the whole boy to school." This idea is forcefully expressed in the first catalogue of the school as follows. "The Manual Training School owes its existence to the conviction, on the part of its founders, that the interests of St. Louis demand for young men a system of education which shall fit them for the actual duties of life in a more direct and positive manner than is done in the ordinary American school."[8] The implication in the foregoing statement was one not likely to evoke enthusiasm from teachers of other subjects. As is often the case with those who promote something new and different, the early advocates of manual training sometimes appeared to disparage the old and traditional. But we must remember also that Woodward provided in his school for a rather complete program of academic as well as manual training studies.

Since this was the period of formal discipline, advocates of manual training did not hesitate to claim disciplinary values.

[5] Anderson, *op. cit.*, pp. 164–165.
[6] *Ibid.*, p. 165.
[7] *Ibid.*, p. 166.
[8] Washington University, *Prospectus of the Manual Training School . . .*, November, 1879, cited in Ray Morton Stombaugh, *A Survey of the Movements Culminating in Industrial Arts Education in Secondary Schools,* Bureau of Publications, Teachers College, Columbia University, Contributions to Education No. 670, 1936, p. 31.

Nicholas Murray Butler, founder and first president of Teachers' College, Columbia University, a school originally dedicated to the training of practical-arts teachers, spoke as follows on this point in 1888. "If the term manual training is used in antithesis to mental training, it is wrongly understood. Manual training, as I use the term, is mental training. It is mental training by means of manual training. It is included in the psychologically determined course of study because it reaches important mental faculties which no other studies reach. It is also a most valuable and important stimulus to the receptive faculty of observation. The child can neither draw accurately nor construct correctly unless he observes acutely."[9] Shopwork was in Butler's thinking a "means of manual training" used for "its disciplinary value, not because of its utility."[10] Other leaders in the manual training field did, however, recognize introductory shopwork as providing a base for later specialization. For the most part, though, the vocational applications of industrial arts in this period played a distinctly secondary role to the objectives of well-rounded development and mental discipline. The vocational possibilities were more likely to be stressed by academic educators who probably objected to the tendency of those in the industrial arts to claim the best of all possible worlds.

Instructional practices in most of these first manual training schools were based on the Russian System that had impressed Runkle and Woodward at the Philadelphia Centennial Exposition.

The Russian system of manual training was a formalized system based on the principle of a logical method of procedure in which exercises were assigned in order of increasing difficulty and were undertaken by students in this order. Each course of instruction in manual training under the Russian system consisted of a series of graded exercises without special reference to their application in the construction of useful articles. The teaching of the course involved three stages. The first consisted of a study of tools and materials, the second involved the acquisition of skill in joining together the materials under study and the third stage was the construction stage in which whole or parts

[9] Cited in Roberts, *op. cit.,* p. 74.
[10] *Ibid.*

of the projects were made. Students learned to sharpen, care for and adjust tools and to know the nature of materials. Emphasis was placed on freehand and mechanical drawing throughout the course.[11]

A rival system soon appeared in the form of "sloyd," another European import, this one from Sweden. The term sloyd we are told means "sleight" in the sense of "sleight of hand" or "dexterity." Where the Russian system emphasized a sequence of exercises to develop particular skills, the sloyd system put the student to work on the making of whole objects from models. The sloyd system was introduced in the late 1880's and soon gained immense popularity both at the elementary and the secondary levels. According to one historian of the industrial arts movement, "This new type of handwork proved a distinct improvement over the Russian system."[12] The initial enthusiastic reception subsided, however, and sloyd also drew a good deal of criticism from manual training teachers, largely on the grounds of its formality and the tendency to use the same models that had been developed for school practice in Sweden.

Although most schools followed either the Russian or the Swedish system, the Philadelphia public schools from the beginning were influenced more directly by the arts-and-crafts movement from England. Charles Leland, the founder of handwork in the Philadelphia schools, had been one of William Morris' followers, and his program was characterized by emphasis on aesthetic outcomes and activities. He summarized his point of view as follows. "The universal truth that man develops the ornamental during the infancy of the race before the useful, is illustrated in every individual. The child who cannot as yet make a shoe or file metals or master a trade, can, however, learn to design decorative outside patterns, mould beautiful pottery, set mosaics, carve panels, work sheet leather and repoussé or embossed sheet brass."[13] In keeping with this idea about the development of the arts in history, the leaders of the Philadelphia schools provided for a gradual transition to "constructive work" on the part of the older students. "When pupils have acquired a certain dexterity of hand and

[11] *Ibid.,* p. 79.

[12] Stombaugh, *op. cit.,* p. 98.

[13] Charles Leland, United States Bureau of Education, "Circular of Information," No. 4, 1882, cited in Anderson, *op. cit.,* p. 188.

accuracy of eye and are able to draw, model, and carve reasonably well, then it is of advantage for them to attempt constructive work and mechanical drawing. They should then be about fourteen years of age."[14] Although the objectives of this program were general and cultural rather than specifically vocational, both Leland and Tadd defended its vocational possibilities. Leland "made the claim that any child twelve to fifteen years of age could, after a series of two-hour lessons, take his place as a worker in industry where a knowledge of design or modeling was required. Furthermore, he claimed that the training the pupils received under his system fitted them to be expert buyers and salesmen, or if the pupil preferred, he could make eight dollars a week from the sale of his products."[15]

Two shifts in the name of the general handwork field took place shortly after 1900. One of them was contributed by the arts-and-crafts emphasis. "James P. Haney, in an address at the 1903 meeting of the National Education Association, suggested that the term *manual arts* be used instead of manual training as a means of placing more emphasis on artistic elements of manual activity."[16] A year later, "Charles R. Richards of Teachers College of Columbia University, suggested in an editorial in the October 1904 issue of *Manual Training Magazine* that the term *industrial arts* be used instead of manual training or manual arts. . . ."[17] Back of the change to industrial arts lay the point of view that the field should develop not only manual skills and creativity, but also knowledge "of the industrial processes that operate in transforming raw materials into usable products."[18]

THE ERA OF VOCATIONAL INDUSTRIAL EDUCATION

It was in this period of name changing that a powerful and on the whole successful movement developed to promote the specifically vocational emphasis so clearly disclaimed by the

[14] J. Liberty Tadd, *New Methods in Education,* 1899, p. 305, cited in Anderson, *op. cit.,* p. 189. Tadd was Leland's successor as director of the Philadelphia school.
[15] Stombaugh, *op. cit.,* p. 116.
[16] Roberts, *op. cit.,* p. 82.
[17] *Ibid.,* p. 84.
[18] *Ibid.*

earlier leaders. The non-vocational point of view came to be regarded as traditional and somewhat out of date by the leaders of
the new vocationalism. As has happened frequently in American
education, the new emphasis was triggered by a commission report, in this case the report of the Massachusetts Commission on
Industrial and Technical Education in 1906. The commission expressed sharp criticism of the prevailing general education viewpoint in the manual training—manual arts—industrial arts field.
"The wide indifference to manual training as a school subject may
be due to the narrow view which has prevailed among its chief
advocates. It has been urged as a cultural subject mainly useful as
a stimulus to other forms of intellectual effort,—a sort of mustard
relish, an appetizer,—to be conducted without reference to any
industrial end. It has been severed from real life as completely as
have the other school activities."[19] Often in educational history,
what is narrow to men of one period is broad to those of another.
To the commissioners of 1905, industrial arts as a cultural subject
reflected "the narrow view." But to their predecessors of the
1880's and 1890's as well as to many industrial arts educators
today, it is the vocational emphasis that appears narrow and the
cultural emphasis that appears broad and comprehensive.

The Massachusetts commission did not confine itself to
criticism, but went on to recommend vocational industrial training
in existing high schools and separate and specialized vocational
schools. Widespread discussion of the report followed, not only
in Massachusetts, but across the country. "During the next two
years, the topic of industrial education engaged the attention of
educational conventions more frequently than any other single
topic."[20] The National Education Association responded almost
immediately by appointing a committee on "The Place of Industries in Public Education," which reported in 1910 and expressed caustic views on the manual training movement. This
committee followed the recommendations of the Massachusetts

---

[19] "Report of Massachusetts Commission on Industrial and Technical Education,"
Columbia University, Teachers College Educational Reprints, No. 1, p. 14. Cited in
Anderson, *op. cit.,* p. 200.
[20] Stombaugh, *op. cit.,* p. 117.

commission with respect to the establishment of vocational courses in high schools and the creation of specialized vocational schools It cited the Technical High School of Cleveland as an example of what it had in mind and dismissed the other technical high schools established in the late 1890's and early 1900's as those which "do not radically differ from the ordinary manual training schools."[21]

Industrial arts educators in the general public high schools made strenuous efforts to adapt their programs to vocational objectives. Commissions similar to the one in Massachusetts were appointed in a number of states and made the usual recommendations. "During the six-year period from 1906 to 1911 the following five states established state systems of vocational education: Massachusetts, New York, Connecticut, New Jersey, and Wisconsin."[22] This period also saw the intensive development of various kinds of part-time vocational schools, such as apprenticeship schools, continuation schools, and coöperative schools, the features of which foreshadowed school-related work experience for vocational purposes in general high schools.

Proponents of industrial vocational education looked to the national government for financial aids to encourage local school systems to move in the approved directions. An organization called "The National Society for the Promotion of Industrial Education," established in 1906 "To unite the many forces making towards industrial education the country over,"[23] took the lead in this campaign for federal aid. Their hope was to achieve something for technical education in high schools comparable to what had been achieved under the Morrill Act of 1862 for colleges. Bills to carry out this purpose were introduced in Congress between 1906 and 1914, but without success. When the widely discussed and vigorously promoted Page bill failed of passage, however, Congress passed a joint resolution early in 1914 estab-

[21] Report of Committee on the Place of Industries in Public Education, 1910, p. 104, cited in Anderson, *op. cit.,* p. 204.

[22] Roberts, *op. cit.,* p. 132.

[23] National Society for the Promotion of Industrial Education, Bulletin No. 1, Proceedings of the Organization Meeting, January, 1907, cited in Stombaugh, *op. cit.,* p. 118.

lishing a Commission on National Aid to Vocational Education to give further study to the matter. This Commission moved swiftly and brought out its recommendations by June of that year. The first Smith-Hughes bill was introduced a year later, but a long series of amendments and discussions delayed its progress. Finally the leaders of the vocational education movement saw their hopes realized with the signing of the revised Smith-Hughes bill in February, 1917.

The Smith-Hughes Act established a Federal Board for Vocational Education and appropriated funds both for teacher training and for teachers' salaries in the fields of agriculture, trade and industrial training, and home economics. Since 1917, additional laws have been passed providing for greater funds and extending the fields covered to include distributive education as well. One important effect of the Smith-Hughes and succeeding acts has been to establish state systems of vocational education, since the funds must be administered by state boards following criteria set in the national legislation. The State Boards of Vocational Education are identical with the State Boards of Education in forty of the forty-eight states. In all states but one local vocational schools have remained part of the local public school systems.

It was in this period of intensive persuasion for vocational industrial education that the linking together of vocational education and industrial arts became firmly established.[24] This identification

---

[24] This point of view persists well into our own times. The following statement, from an art educator, indicates the closeness of the identification: "So it would seem that the industrial arts in the junior high school are no longer meant for vocational training. This must be confusing to the pupils who elect them, expecting jobs. I am not prepared to say precisely what needs of the learners are served by these courses. I only know that they have very little relation to art. And I would question the relation to industry, also especially when the learning experiences constitute handwork in the construction of objects normally machine-made." Edward Warder Rannells, *Art Education in the Junior High School: A Study of Objectives,* Bulletin of the Bureau of School Service, College of Education, University of Kentucky, Vol. XVIII, June, 1946, Number 4, p. 32. In the subsequent paragraph, the same writer goes on to say, "As for the qualifications for employment in industry (quite apart from the abnormal situation that prevailed in time of war) the development of highly integrated industrial machinery has so simplified the operation of factory workers that special training in schools as preparation for specific trades is no longer practical. Industry trains them itself." *Ibid.,* pp. 32–33. This would presumably leave industrial arts with no function at all.

has never been accepted by teachers and curriculum workers in the general industrial arts; neither has it been accepted by nor been acceptable to the enthusiastic proponents of vocational industrial education. We must remember, however, that the years of emphasis on vocational education coincided with years of great increase in high school enrollments. Administrators and teachers in general high schools acutely aware of larger numbers, although not necessarily larger proportions of indifferent students, turned naturally and eagerly to the artificial distinctions between academic subjects and vocational subjects and between college-preparatory and non-college-preparatory programs that have confused and plagued us ever since. Students indifferent to the appeals of or incapable of mastering the difficulties of traditional subjects were judged to be fit candidates for the non-academic subjects and hence for vocational programs. This was different indeed from the ideals of the early manual training advocates such as Woodward, who had held that handwork was good education for all students and who included in their schools a full program of the traditional studies.

One is tempted to wonder how the general industrial educators fared during the period from 1905 to 1917. Some of them undoubtedly sought to prove that their kinds of industrial arts courses had vocational possibilities. Others stoutly defended what they considered to be the cultural or liberal functions of their fields. Some developed the contention that vocational education is also liberal and cultural, the possibilities of which are certainly difficult to deny. In school practice, general industrial arts courses moved in the direction implied by their new name, that is in the direction of stressing the learning not only of skills, but also of information about industrial life and processes.

The movement to develop industrial arts as a content subject gained more success at the elementary school level than in high schools and owed much to the point of view set forth by Dewey in *The School and Society*.[26] Dewey's idea of industrial arts was largely non-vocational. After commenting on the importance of man's natural environment, Dewey goes on as follows.

[25] See citations in Stombaugh, *op. cit.,* p. 127.

It is through occupations determined by this environment that mankind has made its historical and political progress. It is through these occupations that the intellectual and emotional interpretation of nature has been developed. It is through what we do in and with the world that we read its meaning and measure its value.

In educational terms, this means that these occupations in the school shall not be mere practical devices or modes of routine employment, the gaining of better technical skill as cooks, seamstresses, or carpenters, but active centers of scientific insight into natural materials and processes, points of departure whence children shall be led out into a realization of the historic development of man.[26]

This should not be taken to mean opposition to education for one's life work. In his later *Democracy and Education,* Dewey devotes an entire chapter and much of the rest of the book to an examination of vocation and vocational education. But his contention is that vocational education in its broad sense affects all students and that it is unnecessary and undesirable to view some subjects as vocational and others non-vocational in character. "But an education which acknowledges the full intellectual and social meaning of a vocation would include instruction in the historic background of present conditions; training in science to give intelligence and initiative in dealing with materials and agencies of production; and study of economics, civics, and politics, to bring the future worker into touch with the problems of the day and the various methods proposed for its improvement."[27] In the same connection he expresses doubts about the kinds of vocational education being widely advocated at the time. Bear in mind that he wrote this in 1916, at the height of the vocational education movement.

But, at the present juncture, there is a movement in behalf of something called vocational training which, if carried into effect, would harden these ideas into a form adapted to the existing industrial regime. This movement would continue the traditional liberal or cul-

[26] John Dewey, *The School and Society,* University of Chicago Press, 1900, pp. 16–17.
[27] John Dewey, *Democracy and Education,* The Macmillan Company, 1916, p. 372.

tural education for the few economically able to enjoy it, and would give to the masses a narrow technical trade education for specialized callings, carried on under the control of others. This scheme denotes, of course, simply a perpetuation of the older social division, with its counterpart intellectual and moral dualisms.[28]

The recent tendency to put vocational training on a post-high school basis would be more consistent with Dewey's position than the 1905–1917 movement to put the specific vocational courses in the high school itself. On this basis, industrial arts would be free to develop as a general education subject, with such vocational implications and outcomes as are normally derived from other subjects such as English, mathematics, social studies, and science. To be fair to the proponents of vocational education in the 1905–1917 period, however, we must remember that four years of general high school education followed by several years of specific vocational training constituted a program beyond the economic reach of many high school students and their families. It was difficult for many to afford even the four years of high school, a circumstance that the vocational leaders recognized and took into account. The motivation of being prepared for a job at high school graduation undoubtedly brought many students into the high schools who otherwise might never have gone at all.

There is no doubt, however, that the zeal of the vocationalists carried them to extremes, especially in their criticism of general industrial arts. Meanwhile a new force was developing in secondary education that tended to offset the vocational emphasis and to strengthen the position of those who saw industrial arts as a general subject. This was the junior high school. It was clear from the beginning that junior high school courses in the industrial arts could not be of a specifically vocational training character. True, much was said in the early days of their values in vocational exploration and guidance, but this is different from specific job training as such. Of course there had been industrial arts work in seventh and eighth grades prior to the establishment of junior high schools, but this was regarded as elementary education. The junior high school movement put the work of these grades by

[28] *Ibid.*, p. 373.

definition into secondary education and helped carry general industrial arts into the ninth grade as well. This probably helped to maintain general industrial arts to some extent at the secondary level despite the onslaught of the vocational industrial educators.

Apparently industrial arts did not prosper during the first part of the 1920's as far as enrollments were concerned. The following observation was made by Counts in his survey of high school programs in 15 cities for the school year 1923–24.

As the movement toward vocational education got under way, it manifested such strength that many expected the industrial arts rapidly to assume a position of dominance in the high-school curriculum.

This expectation has not been fulfilled. Although the high schools included in the investigation are, in most instances, located in cities of considerable size, where the need for industrial training is the greatest and where progressive tendencies are most likely to exhibit themselves, the industrial arts were shown in Table IX to play a relatively humble role in the curriculum. These subjects have experienced little of the popularity which has been enjoyed by the commercial branches. The Smith-Hughes Act of 1917, which placed federal subsidies back of industrial training, has apparently had little influence in the high schools of these cities. More units of work are offered in this field than in any other, but the pupils are not found in these courses in large numbers.[29]

Counts's survey showed that an average of 7.5 per cent of the total number of pupil recitation hours was devoted to industrial arts in the schools he studied, with a range from 1.0 percent in Rochester in 11.7 percent in Cleveland.[30] He suggested the following possible reasons for this state of affairs. "The reasons for this relative failure of the industrial arts to gain favorable recognition in the high school will not be considered here. It is probably due to the strong academic tradition of secondary education, to an overestimate on the part of the advocates of vocational training of the demand for skilled artisans of native parentage in the United States, and to ineffective organization and administration of the program of training."[31]

[29] George S. Counts, *The Senior High School Curriculum,* The University of Chicago, 1926, p. 98.
[30] *Ibid.,* table IX, p. 24.
[31] *Ibid.,* p. 98.

Counts did not indicate the relative distribution of general industrial arts enrollments as against those in vocational industrial courses. His list of subjects, however, showed a high degree of specialization.[32] Courses called manual training, which we may infer were of the general education variety, occupied on the average only 20 percent of the total time devoted to industrial arts in these schools. Apparently high school industrial arts was closely identified with the specialized courses as contrasted with those of the general education type. It is possible that we have here another clue to the low state of industrial arts enrollments. Students potentially interested in electing industrial arts courses may have been deterred by their unwillingness to enroll in specifically vocational courses of study. Intensive concentration on vocational industrial education may then have had some negative effect on enrollments in the industrial arts field taken as a whole.

INDUSTRIAL ARTS AS VOCATIONAL AND GENERAL EDUCATION

After the middle 1920's, the emphasis in industrial arts education began to swing slowly away from vocationalism. In 1940, a committee on secondary curriculum of the American Youth Commission of the American Council on Education commented as follows. "The history of vocational education since 1917 shows, quite apart from the steady reduction of jobs for young people, that the organization of shop courses is by no means a solution of the problems of public secondary schools. Much of the work provided in vocational classes fails to meet the needs of pupils because it is quite as specialized as were the traditional preprofessional courses."[33] The members of this committee were general educators, not specialists in the industrial arts field or even in the field of vocational education as a whole. Specialists in the industrial arts, while not disparaging vocational education, also tended increasingly to put the case for their field in general educa-

[32] Mechanical drawing, manual training, machine shop, printing, architectural drawing, forging, auto repair, electricity, pattern-making, carpentry, sheet metal, welding, shop mathematics, and miscellaneous. Counts, *op. cit.,* table XLVI, p. 100.

[33] American Youth Commission and Other Cooperating Organizations, *What the High Schools Ought to Teach,* American Council on Education, 1940, p. 10.

tion terms. By 1946, a committee of the Industrial-Arts Division of the American Vocational Association could write of their field in the following terms.

Industrial-arts courses are part of general education and do not have a distinctly bread-and-butter justification. They are assumed to generate sympathetic interest in the whole of industry, as compared or contrasted with agriculture, homemaking, commerce, and certain technical professions. Instructors in this field aim at broad, rather unspecialized, and often remote values. They consider their subjects and their associations with pupils to be largely informational and inspirational.[34]

The objectives of industrial-arts teachers are not essentially different from those of teachers in other subjects or areas. The place of industrial arts in the school curriculum is justified and assured because this field, with its distinctive physical setting and pupil activities, provides a highly effective means of reaching worthy ends. The legitimate purposes of academic subjects are the legitimate purposes of industrial-arts subjects. The valid aims of general education are the valid aims of industrial-arts work, because the latter is merely a phase of the former. Industrial arts should always be conceived and practiced as general education, for youth and for adults, in day and evening hours.[35]

The last sentence in the above quotation seems to complete the swing of the circle and is far removed from the tone and emphasis of the 1905–1917 period.

The swing back to general objectives does not mean the abandonment of specialized courses. But even these specialized courses are not always regarded as trade or vocational training. Among the non-vocational industrial arts courses listed in the Biennial Survey of Education 1948–1950 were general shop, woodworking, mechanical drawing, metal work, printing, electrical work, handcrafts, automobile mechanics, home mechanics, photography, and ceramics. In the trade and industrial education section were listed general industrial shop, machine shop, automobile mechanics, mechanical drafting, carpentry, cabinet making, radio, electrical work, printing, sheet metal, aviation, welding, and cosmetology. Some of the specialized courses such as automobile

[34] American Vocational Association, Inc., Industrial-Arts Division, *Improving Instruction in Industrial Arts,* the Association, June 15, 1946, p. 12.
[35] *Ibid.,* p. 50.

mechanics, electrical work, and printing were offered both in the non-vocational and in the vocational divisions.

The non-vocational industrial arts courses claimed a much larger percentage of total student enrollments in 1948–1949 than did those listed as trade and industrial. But the differences may be exaggerated by difficulties in organizing and presenting statistics in the two categories. The biennial survey stated that "Nonvocational industrial arts enrolls 25 per cent of all pupils in all types of schools."[36] This figure includes the seventh and eighth grades of junior high schools. On the other hand, the figure of 6.8 percent of enrollments given for trade and industrial courses is based on Grades 9 through 12 only.[37] The total number of students enrolled in preparatory trades and industries courses after making corrections for enrollments in related subjects was estimated at 250,000.[38] "Generally speaking, there are approximately 46 pupils in every thousand in the last 4 high-school years who are studying a trade."[39]

For the most part, industrial arts educators have clarified their position with regard to vocational education, even though confusion on this point still persists among many high school teachers of other subjects and among members of the general public. There is general agreement that industrial education for vocational purposes is more appropriate after than before high school graduation. This calls for post-high school vocational schools and junior colleges, with close relationships between these and the training and apprenticeship programs of industries and unions. But it does not mean the complete exclusion of vocational industrial education from all high schools. The need for and desirability of specific job training varies from community to community. There is no formula on this matter applicable to secondary schools in the country as a whole.

In stressing the general education character of their field, industrial arts educators have fallen to the temptation of claiming too many broad and comprehensive outcomes. This is not, of course, unique to industrial arts. Specialists in all fields show the tendency to become intoxicated by the apparently unlimited vistas opened by such statements as the Cardinal Principles and the Imperative Needs of Youth. There is no need for this, in the industrial arts or any other field. It weakens rather than strengthens the positions of those who seek to advance the claims of a particular instructional field in the curriculum as a whole.

The case for the industrial arts in the school program is substantially the same as that for any instructional field worthy of inclusion, namely that it represents a distinctive organization of an important part of culture to be transmitted. It was this point of view that led to the growth of the term "industrial arts" rather than manual arts or manual training. The shaping of the earth's resources into objects of beauty and use has always been one of mankind's major activities; the advances of technique in this activity have been among mankind's major achievements. A curriculum that omits this part of human culture is an incomplete curriculum.

As is true of the visual fine arts, this culture cannot be transmitted even to the limited extent possible in schools solely by studying about it, although reading and study are important and necessary elements. Some work and some experience with the processes themselves are in order, but need not be carried to a high level of skill in the required courses. Beyond this, there are some immediate and practical reasons for including handwork or manual training. Many jobs today, even those classified under the heading of service rather than production, demand a minimum degree of acquaintanceship with and understanding of tools. And even if the do-it-yourself movement turns out to be another fad, many students will find in their industrial arts courses the opportunity to build useful and worthy leisure-time interests for the future. Where do-it-yourself skills are not used to pursue leisure-time interests, they are often of practical value in the everyday management of modern family life. Neither should the vocational guidance possibilities of handwork be overlooked. Some students at least will find in their industrial arts courses clues to vocational futures in the various industrial or mechanical trades. These immediate and practical benefits of handwork should be obvious even though they do not affect all students to the same degree or in the same ways. Most important of all, however, is the sense of personal satisfaction necessary to the well-being of the human individual. Ours is a mechanical and industrial age, and it is important that no individual be cut off from the spirit of his times because he lacks the basic terminology and understanding that can be gained from a good general introductory course in the industrial arts. For young people growing up in our society today, gaining this basic understanding may well be regarded as an aspect of the developmental tasks of adolescence.

We suggest, therefore, some industrial arts for all students at the junior high school level, preferably in a one-year course combined with homemaking. Such a course has much to commend it in light of the interrelated general education values of both fields. If such a course is not available, the requirement might consist of one year of industrial arts for boys and one year of homemaking for girls, with considerable attention paid in each course to some of the skills and processes of the other.

It is desirable also to consider the possibility of combining industrial arts with courses in the visual fine arts at the junior high school level. Perhaps the split between these two aspects of the arts has gone so far that it must be recognized and accepted as a continuing reality in our school program. The high degree of interrelatedness and unity among the three fields of industrial arts, homemaking, and the visual fine arts should, however, stimulate continued experimentation among those curriculum workers who are interested in the correlation of subjects. Here are three fields where such correlations may take on significance beyond those claimed for other parts of the curriculum.

The range and variety of industrial arts offerings will always depend on the populations and resources of given local schools. Industrial arts shops are expensive, and many schools have put too much money into facilities for advanced and specialized courses elected by relatively few students. At the senior high school level, however, possibilities are numerous and varied even though the courses are not aimed specifically at vocational training. The list of advanced industrial arts courses given in the biennial survey of 1948–1950 provides one basis for discussion and study in local staffs and communities. Few schools could or perhaps should include all these advanced offerings. Generally, on this question of what the senior high school should offer, even the experts in the industrial arts field will conclude that it is up to the local school.

One further difficulty persists in this field as well as in art, science, and some others. Many seventh-grade and eighth-grade students have no opportunity to take industrial arts. This is particularly true in small elementary schools of 8–4 systems. It is possible, of course, to require industrial arts of such students in the ninth grade, a requirement similar to that of ninth-grade general science for students who have had little science instruction up to that time. This restricts the ninth-grade program and in some cases even affects students' programs in the upper senior high school years. In addition it introduces an element of confusion in those high schools which draw partly from their own related junior high schools and partly from other districts that are on an 8–4 basis. Such difficulties must be handled as well as possible, as long as present conditions exist. There are two possible ways to correct them, one by placing all seventh-grade through twelfth-grade work in the secondary system, the other by making the administrative reorganizations to provide for industrial arts work in the seventh or eighth grades of the 8–4 system itself.

Bibliography

American Vocational Association, Inc., Industrial-Arts Division, *Improving Instruction in Industrial Arts,* The Association, June 15, 1946.

Anderson, Lewis Flint, *History of Manual and Industrial School Education,* D. Appleton and Company, 1926.

Bennett, Charles Alpheus, *History of Manual and Industrial Education up to 1870,* The Manual Arts Press, 1926.

Hawkins, Layton S.; Prosser, Charles A.; and Wright, John C., *Development of Vocational Education,* American Technical Society, 1951.

Roberts, Roy W., *Vocational and Practical Arts Education,* Harper & Brothers, 1957.

Schweickhard, Dean M., *Industrial Arts in Education,* The Manual Arts Press, 1929.

Stombaugh, Ray Merton, *A Survey of the Movements Culminating in Industrial Arts Education in Secondary Schools,* Bureau of Publications, Teachers College, Columbia University, Contributions to Education No. 670, 1936.

Wilber, Gordon O., *Industrial Arts in General Education,* International Textbook Co., 1948.

CHAPTER 16

....

Physical Education

The fields of physical education and music have much in common. Both are highly dynamic arts characterized by rhythm and movement. Both are and have long been popular arts that can be enjoyed by most of us without a high degree of special training, but are capable of intricate and advanced development as well. In the classical Greek world, physical education and music were regarded as the fundamental subjects in the rearing of the young.

Physical education is an established fact in American schools. State laws and local regulations make it the most universally required of all high school fields and the most passively accepted of all high school requirements. It is, on the surface at least, a field easy to identify. Everybody knows what physical education is. No explanations seem to be required. Merely to pronounce the term is enough to set up images of gymnasiums, athletic fields, calisthenics, apparatus, sports, games, and drills.

Yet it is not a field exempt from public criticism. The public has in two world wars severely charged physical education with failure to carry out its job, or at least what the public thinks its job should be. Neither is the field one that school administrators and teachers in general have found easy to absorb into the everyday operations of a school. Many high schools persist in a state of confusion and uncertainty on such matters as physical education credits, physical education marks, class size in physical education, and the scheduling of physical education activities.

Within the field itself there have been and are controversies on a number of points. Physical educators are by no means agreed on what the field is, what its objectives should be, and what materials and activities should be used in its programs. In fact, some writings in the field leave the reader with the impression that physical education is not an instructional field at all, but rather an entire way of education or a way of life.

DEVELOPMENT OF PHYSICAL EDUCATION IN AMERICAN SCHOOLS

Like most of our school subjects, physical education owes much to European influences. German immigrants brought an enthusiasm for physical culture in the *Turnverein* (exercise club) movement and established such clubs in a number of American communities. "In the *Turnverein,* German-American youth developed a keen interest and skill in physical activity. These young men and young women formed the backlog of physical-education teachers in America for a generation, and the *Turnverein* set the pattern for special normal schools that were opened to prepare teachers in this field."[1] But immigrants had no monopoly on enthusiasm for physical culture; there were native American enthusiasts as well. To all who shared this enthusiasm, progress in the schools must have seemed disappointingly slow. Although gymnastic classes and exercises were occasionally established in United States colleges and high schools, little development of physical education as a school subject took place until after the Civil War.[2] "Formal gymnastics found a place in the secondary

---

[1] Clifford Lee Brownell and E. Patricia Hagman, *Physical Education—Foundations and Principles,* McGraw-Hill Book Company, Inc., 1951, p. 86.

[2] There was a tendency to identify or perhaps to confuse physical education with military drill, as indicated by the following remarks made by a speaker at the NEA convention of 1891. "With reference to physical culture we have this only to suggest: That all boys in high schools, belonging to military companies, have been observed to show larger intellectual growth in a given time than those who were not so drilled, age and other unfavorable conditions being duly considered; and that from the closest observation in high schools, with and without the practice of physical culture, the general health and energy shown by pupils in the former would strongly recommend some system of physical exercises. Military drill is practised in both public and private schools now, and as a means of cultivating habits of mental and physical alertness, ready and instant obedience, proper carriage of body, and a courteous recogni-

school of the second quarter of the nineteenth century for a short time and were prominent periodically until they secured a firm position in the schools in the last quarter of the nineteenth century."[3]

National interest in these matters led to the Physical Training Conference held at Boston in 1889, a meeting that set the pattern followed in physical education up to the time of the first world war. The point of view represented in this conference is not one always regarded highly by present-day writers on the physical education curriculum. One of these, Jesse Feiring Williams, seems to regard it as having set physical education off in the wrong direction. He points out that much of the discussion of physical education prior to the 1889 conference had emphasized "the physical weakness and physical defects of American boys and girls" and that the conference was dominated by the ideal of physical education as corrective.[4]

But the Conference was not a meeting of specialists in physical education alone; it was also attended by educators, and these school people set up a number of conditions that reflected the ideas they had concerning the function of education. In effect, the schoolmen proposed that any physical training that was to be taken into the school must require very little time, must be inexpensive and not demand specially trained teachers, must conduct its activities in the classroom (activity carried on outside the school building could not be educative), and must not require apparatus.

Unfortunately, the experts in physical training of the time came forward and said in effect: We have just what you want. We propose systematic exercises that can be taught by the regular teacher in the class-

tion of superiors, to say nothing of military advantages to the country in case of war, and the reverence it provokes for a more loyal citizenship, its advantages are indispensable to thorough mental discipline. Therefore we shall add to the province of the Western high school as an essential in the important work it has to do—both for boys and girls—a system of light military drill or gymnastics." L. H. Austin, Lincoln, Nebraska, "The Province of the Western High School," National Education Association *Journal of Proceedings and Addresses,* Session of the Year 1891, held at Toronto, Ontario, Canada, The Association, 1891, pp. 683–684.

[3] Alexander Inglis, *Principles of Secondary Education,* Houghton Mifflin Company, 1918, p. 652.

[4] Jesse Feiring Williams, *The Principles of Physical Education,* 6th ed., W. B. Saunders Company, 1954, p. 211.

room. No apparatus will be required, and the expense is very moderate. These exercises will correct the schoolroom stoop, provide relief for the mind, and bring health and vigor to the body. The antiseptic request of the schoolmen was accorded a sterilized program, vestiges of which remain today as "ten minutes a day for calisthenics."[5]

This resulted, according to Williams, in "two types of physical education in the schools," a condition persisting "for more than three decades after 1889."[6] One of these consisted of "artificial exercises," with the other "represented by the extreme development of competitive athletics which arose as a natural activity of youth, stimulated by the commercial and advertising values of games, and without the educational leadership which such an activity should attract."[7]

In spite of the interest symbolized and stimulated by the national conference, many high schools apparently did little or nothing about physical education in the period which followed. A survey of physical education in 2,392 public high schools in 1910 showed that only 104 or 4.3 percent had a teacher in charge of a physical education department, in fact, that only 109 or 4.6 percent even had such a department. Only 183 or 7.6 percent of these schools gave instruction in gymnastics, while only 175 or 7.3 percent had gymnasiums. Work in gymnastics was prescribed in 114 or 6.0 percent of these schools. Swimming pools were practically nonexistent, being found in only nine of the 2,392 schools, or to the extent of 0.3 percent. On the other hand, 469 or 19.6 percent of these schools had athletic fields, while 339 or 14.2 percent has tennis courts.[8] These figures indicate that the spontaneous athletic program fostered by students was developing to a greater extent than the formal instruction directly sponsored in the school program.

Neither did the situation improve rapidly during the following decade. Inglis wrote as follows in 1918.

[5] *Ibid.*
[6] *Ibid.*, p. 212.
[7] *Ibid.*
[8] All figures from *Proceedings of the Fourth Congress of the American School Hygiene Association* in *American Physical Education Review,* vol. xv, pp. 174–175, cited in Inglis, *op. cit.,* p. 641.

While conditions have improved noticeably since 1910, it remains true that woefully inadequate provisions are made for physical education in the public secondary schools at the present day. In the great majority of public secondary schools little or no provision is made for gymnasiums, no qualified teacher is employed for physical training or even for the teaching of hygiene, athletics are supervised and directed by teachers with few or no qualifications, no adequate machinery is provided for physical examination or even for medical inspection, and what little physical training is given is of a formal and perfunctory character. The common provision, even in some of our best schools, of two periods a week for gymnasium exercises, is little more than a pretense of education.[9]

EXPANSION AFTER 1918

But the day of expansion was at hand. It came with the draft statistics of World War I. "It is difficult to say how long it would have taken physical education to achieve its present status in the school had it not been for the general interest aroused by the findings of the Selective Service Act of 1917."[10] State after state enacted laws that required or encouraged the offering of physical education in the local schools. "By 1921 twenty-eight states had passed legislation on physical education, most of them making it mandatory."[11] The movement closely resembled other waves of enthusiasm in the history of American schools, particularly the drive toward vocational education of the period between 1905 and 1917. It was pushed not only by professional physical educators, but by many other groups as well. "The feeble opposition never had a chance!"[12] Physical educators have expressed mixed reactions toward this phase of our educational history. Brownell and Hagman, for example, cite the evident and tangible results in programs, equipment, and the like.

[9] Inglis, *op. cit.*, pp. 641–642.
[10] Laurentine B. Collins and Rosalind Cassidy with the collaboration of Charles C. Cowell, Hilda C. Kozman, Herbert R. Stolz, and Participants in Summer Workshops of the Progressive Education Association, *Physical Education in the Secondary Schools,* Progressive Education Association Committee on Workshops, 1940, p. 15.
[11] Leonard V. Koos, *The American Secondary School,* Ginn and Company, 1927, p. 504.
[12] Brownell and Hagman, *op. cit.*, p. 121.

In the main, the results of state legislation have proved beneficial. Observed benefits include more and better programs in public schools; improved professional preparation of teachers; higher standards of certification; increased facilities and equipment; credit toward promotion, graduation, and for college entrance; and general public approval. Much remains to be done in all of the areas listed above, especially in getting physical education out of hallways and dark basements, building more swimming pools and larger playgrounds, reducing the teacher load, and convincing some educational administrators that the time allotment contained in state laws represents a *minimum*—not a maximum.[13]

Collins and Cassidy, on the other hand, feel that such legislation, based as it was on the draft statistics, placed physical educators in the untenable position of trying to meet a demand that could not be met.

Misinterpretation and inadequate analysis of the real facts impelled physical educators to make, again, unsubstantiated claims for the program. The Draft found men to be unfit largely on the basis of infected teeth, infected tonsils, tuberculosis, venereal disease, eye defects, heart lesions. No physical education program could have altered these conditions materially. It was a dis-service to physical education to gain recognition as part of a school program on a platform that demanded that physical education improve the health of boys and girls in areas where the contributing factors were entirely beyond its province.[14]

There was little tendency in the 1920's to hesitate on the basis of such considerations as the above. Counts found in 1923–1924 that 13 of the 15 city systems included in his curriculum survey were listing physical education as a required subject. "Among the high-school constants physical education holds second place, ranking next to English. In the fifteen cities combined it receives almost one-half as many semester hours of prescribed work as does English."[15] The extent of the requirement ranged from "two periods a week for one semester in Pueblo to five periods a week

[13] *Ibid.,* pp. 121–122.
[14] Collins and Cassidy, *op. cit.,* p. 15.
[15] George S. Counts, *The Senior High School Curriculum,* University of Chicago, 1926, p. 115.

for eight semesters in Berkeley and Los Angeles."[16] It is surprising, however, in the light of Counts's survey and the general development of physical education in the 1920's, to note that the percentage of all students in Grades 9 through 12 enrolled in physical education increased only from 5.7 to 15.0 between 1922 and 1928.[17] Still this represented an increase from 123,568 students enrolled in physical education in 1922 to 435,383 so enrolled in 1928, a considerable degree of expansion although perhaps less than has been assumed.

Expansion in physical education offerings was accompanied by a shift in the curriculum. In the 15 cities of Counts's study, organized play activities comprised 39 percent of the total amount of time devoted to boys' physical education in the ninth grade, while formal gymnastics and light and heavy apparatus work occupied only 31 percent of the total time. In the girls' ninth-grade programs, organized play comprised 33 percent of the program from the time standpoint, with only 26 percent devoted to formal gymnastics and apparatus work. Eighteen percent of the time in the girls' program was devoted to dance. Swimming had come forward as an important part of physical education, occupying 8 percent of the boys' and 10 percent of the girls' programs respectively.[18] Counts's approval of these shifts is evident in his comment, "The movement away from formal gymnastics toward greater emphasis on organized play, dancing, and swimming is fundamentally sound."[19] That physical education still functioned under disadvantages is also evident from his further comment that "The great lack is in the realm of physical-education facilities and teaching personnel. In many instances the work is so handicapped at this point that it is carried on in a perfunctory manner."[20] So matters stood in the middle 1920's, and there they remained up to the eve of World War II. The field continued to make gains in

16 *Ibid.*

17 "Offerings and Enrollments in High-School Subjects," *Biennial Survey of Education in the United States, 1948–1950,* Federal Security Agency, Office of Education, 1951, table 7, p. 108.

18 *Ibid.,* tables LIII and LIV, pp. 116–117.

19 *Ibid.,* p. 117.

20 *Ibid.,* pp. 116–117.

percentages of students enrolled (50.7 percent in 1934),[21] but things still were not what they should have been in terms of facilities, at least from the point of view of physical educators and those general educators who shared in the enthusiasm for physical education.

The draft statistics of World War II practically repeated those of World War I, although this time the condition was one that had been preceded by about two decades of required physical education. The public responded with alarm as it had done earlier. Where the blame in World War I had been fixed on the lack of physical education, it was now fixed on its shortcomings. The outcry about quality in physical education almost matched that about science and mathematics in the fall and winter of 1957–1958. Physical educators responded to the storm of criticism partly by stressing the lack of time, personnel, and facilities from which their programs had suffered and partly by engaging in controversy among themselves about what did or did not constitute valid objectives of the physical education field. The situation evoked additional legislative and regulatory activities as shown by the following summary written shortly after the end of World War II. "As a result of this interest in health and physical education, practically every state has been engaged in reorganizing its policies with respect to these subjects to provide (1) increased time allotment for physical education, and (2) improved programs for physical fitness and health. State laws are being revised and progressive school systems are initiating programs for supplementing minimum essentials in physical education and health."[22]

Again enrollments increased. A comprehensive survey of the U.S. Office of Education showed that 91 percent of all junior high school pupils and 69 percent of all pupils in regular or senior high schools were taking physical education in 1948–1949. The 31 percent of the pupils not enrolled in physical education in regular or senior high schools may be accounted for in two ways, one the presence of extremely small high schools offering little

[21] *Ibid.*
[22] Bess A. Specht in William T. Gruhn and Harl R. Douglass, *The Modern Junior High School,* The Ronald Press Company, 1947, p. 179.

or no physical education, the other the tendency to require somewhat less than full four years of the subject from students, leaving
a certain number each year who have already fulfilled or are
deferring the fulfillment of the requirement. In the overall secondary program including both junior high schools and those
classified as regular or senior highs, three fourths of all pupils were
enrolled in physical education classes. "Physical education, next
to regular English, has the largest registration of any single subject
throughout the high-school years. . . ."[23] The combined percentages of enrollments in physical education classes and in health
classes in 1948–1949 came to more than 100, indicating concurrent registration in the two subjects on the part of many students.
At least as far as quantity is concerned, the dreams of those who
enthusiastically promoted physical education in the first years of
this century have been more than realized.

THE NATURE OF PHYSICAL EDUCATION AS AN INSTRUCTIONAL FIELD

What, then, is the nature of this field that has become almost as
widely required as the study of our mother tongue itself? What are
its functions, and on what bases have these extensive requirements
been developed? These are questions to which writers on the
physical education curriculum have devoted much inquiry and
thought. The resolution of these questions is by no means easy or
obvious in any field. It is an especially difficult task in physical education, where writers have sought in part to derive objectives from
the nature of the field and in part to define the field in terms of its
objectives.

There is to begin with the difficulty presented by the name of
the field itself. Physical educators have made much of the alleged
breakdown of body-mind dualism and emphasize their commitment to a theory of personality as unified rather than fragmented
or divided. But according to one writer, Seward C. Staley, the acceptance of personality as unified contradicts the idea implied by
the term "physical education."

[23] "Offerings and Enrollments in High-School Subjects," *Biennial Survey, op. cit.,*
p. 24. Figures in above paragraph from same source.

If the human organism and life are considered unitary and indivisible, then education must be conceived as unitary and indivisible. There cannot be (except by arbitrary choice) a distinctive education of the body (or education in physical attributes, or education in physical activities) nor a distinctive education of the mind, nor a distinctive education of the soul, nor a distinctive education of the spirit. There cannot be (except by arbitrary choice) a distinctive physical education, nor a distinctive mental education, nor a distinctive social education, nor a distinctive spiritual education.[24]

One way of getting around this difficulty is to regard the physical in physical education not as an aspect of personality to be developed, but as a method used to develop the whole personality. For example, "Physical education is a fundamental method of education—a method that proceeds by means of or through predominantly physical activities."[25] As Staley points out, this leads to further difficulties. "A system of education that deals with mental activities, by the same line of reasoning, would be a second method —the mental method. And finally a system of education that deals with social activities, by the same line of reasoning, would be a third method—the social method."[26] A variant of this method theory is one which contends that the field if defined by the nature of its activities—namely, physical activities. Staley objects to this also, stating, "The thesis that human conduct may be divided into physical, mental, and social categories is so manifestly unsound that the entire proposition falls down."[27] From these and other considerations, he comes to the conclusion that the idea of physical education is untenable and that the term should be abandoned.[28] He suggests instead that the field be named sports education, which he defines as "the division of the school curriculum that is concerned with directing individuals in learning socially and hygienically approved sports according to social and hygienic standards."[29]

[24] Seward C. Staley, *The Curriculum in Sports (Physical Education)*, Stipes Publishing Company, Champaign, Illinois, 1940, p. 80.
[25] Frederick Rand Rogers, *Educational Objectives of Physical Activity*, A. S. Barnes, 1930, p. 12 cited *Ibid.*, p. 102.
[26] Staley, *op. cit.*, p. 104.
[27] *Ibid.*, p. 105.
[28] *Ibid.*, p. 108.
[29] *Ibid.*, p. 125.

We should remember, of course, that some other instructional fields in the curriculum also call themselves by terms which suggest kinds of education rather than bodies of content. Teachers in what were once known as commercial subjects have successfully renamed their field "business education." Some in home economics have tried to put across the term "family life education." At one time there were curriculum workers in the social studies who veered close to calling their field "social education." Perhaps the difficulties in which physical educators find themselves should serve as a warning to these other fields. On the other hand, one might contend that the difficulties implied in the term "physical education" have been exaggerated, or even that they do not exist except in the minds of theorists straining their minds to achieve a precision in nomenclature that is neither possible nor desirable. After all, even such an allegedly clear-cut term as history presents difficulties. It can, then, be argued that the program in physical education is a fact, not a theory. Classes in sports, dance, gymnastics, swimming, and the like are concrete realities. As a generic term, physical education serves as well as any. What may be needed, then, is to get on with the job of identifying what the field is for and the contributions it can make, namely, its objectives.

OBJECTIVES IN PHYSICAL EDUCATION

Discussions of objectives, however, in many cases lead back to the question of what physical education is. Consider, for example, the following clear and definite statement of objectives. "The chief purpose of physical education is to develop strength, endurance, stamina, coördination, and agility in each child through a well-rounded program of activities based on his physical condition, his size, and his maturity."[30] This statement of purpose would probably impress most of the general public and most high school teachers outside physical education departments as reasonable and complete. But it would not be completely acceptable to many physical educators, partly because they would regard it as too limited and partly because it would suggest to them a wrong notion of what physical education ought to be. Those who feel that physical education should be aimed at a broader range of objectives or out-

[30] Bess A. Specht in Gruhn and Douglass, *op. cit.,* p. 179.

comes contend that physical education does not mean education of the physical, but rather education through the physical.

This point of view has been developed by a number of writers, but is most closely associated with Jesse Feiring Williams, who introduced the phrase, "through the physical," several decades ago. It is expressed by him as follows in the 1954 edition of his book, *The Principles of Physical Education.*

> It has been the unfortunate heritage of physical education to conceive of its programs in physical terms alone because its activities were so obviously physical. When mind and body were thought of as two separate entities, physical education was obviously an education *of* the physical; in similar fashion mental education made its own exclusive demands. But with new understanding of the nature of the human organism in which wholeness of the individual is the outstanding fact, physical education becomes education *through* the physical. With this view operative, physical education has concern for and with emotional responses, personal relationships, group behaviors, mental learnings, and other intellectual, social, emotional, and esthetic outcomes. Although important and not to be neglected, it is quite insufficient to develop strength of muscles, bones, and ligaments, to acquire motor skills, and to secure physical endurance.[31]

The question, then, is not merely one of choice of objectives, but of definition of the field. Brownell and Hagman call this question "one of the significant controversial issues of the profession."[32] As they put it, "Shall physical education be regarded as a program to develop and strengthen the organs and systems of the body, or shall physical education use large-muscle activities as a medium for obtaining the best kind of complete education that the schools and colleges have to offer?"[33] Note that both Staley and Williams refer to the unity of human personality and reject body-mind dualism. To Staley this position implies an abandonment of the term physical education itself in favor of a somewhat more restricted title, while to Williams it calls for a distinctive and

[31] Williams, *op. cit.,* p. 2.
[32] Brownell and Hagman, *op. cit.,* p. 20.
[33] *Ibid.*

broadened interpretation of what the present title means. Staley, however, would probably agree with Williams in accepting a broad range of objectives to which the field that he calls sports education would apply.

The question of physical education objectives involves the definition of the field in another connection also, that of the health objective and the relationship between physical education and what is referred to as "health education," a term sometimes used as synonymous with physical education itself. Today in a number of schools the department is known as the department of physical education and health education. The field of physical education cannot, of course, escape its connection with health objectives. It was this very connection that stimulated the passing of state requirements in physical education as a response to the draft statistics of the first World War. But to accept health as an objective is one thing; to identify physical education as one and the same with health education is another. Such identification appears unnecessarily to limit the range of physical education objectives.[34] and also to preclude the concern of other departments or instructional fields with health objectives. On the latter point, Blanchard comments as follows. "It is both fortunate and unfortunate that health has been bracketed with physical education, fortunate in that it has some recognition in an over-departmentalized school curriculum and unfortunate in that such bracketing has given rise to the erroneous impression among school administrators that it is a *subject* to be taught in one particular department. It should no more be compartmentalized or departmentalized than should character or safety education."[35] It is the same kind of mistake as that which identifies social studies exclusively with citizenship. There are some objectives that are the particular concerns of some fields, while others are more appropriately objects of attention in others. It is legitimate to regard health as an objective of particular concern in the field of physical education. But it cannot be used to

[34] Delbert Oberteuffer, *Physical Education,* Harper & Brothers, 1951, pp. 326–327.

[35] Vaughn S. Blanchard, *Curriculum Problems in Health and Physical Education,* A. S. Barnes and Company, 1942, pp. 14–15.

define what physical education is any more than citizenship can be used to define social studies.

The confusion between physical education and health education symbolizes the difficulty of defining the nature of a field through its characteristic objectives, or through objectives at all. To do so is to adopt a form of organization for the classroom studies different from that of the subject organization. This is legitimate in the consideration of core classes, since the point of view implied does not define these classes as subjects. But it cannot be done when the classroom studies are organized as subjects. Physical education is a subject, not an aspect of the core curriculum, and it must seek its definition and characteristics in subject terms. Subjects are defined by their content, that is, by the portion of the culture they transmit; objectives are used as criteria in the selection of content within the subject, since no subject as organized in schools can transmit all the possible content it represents.

As a subject, physical education transmits a portion of our human heritage of culture. The portion it transmits is that which has to do with the use of the body as an instrument of power, precision, and grace. Human beings have been accumulating and building this aspect of culture for thousands of years. Sports, games, gymnastics, and dance are as much aspects of this human culture as are language, mathematics, science, the visual fine arts, the industrial arts, and the like. Without the transmission effected through education, all these aspects of culture would die out in a single generation. Without the formal education provided in schools, most of them would probably die out within several generations, perhaps to be revived in other times by retracing their original growth.

The acceptance of physical education as a school subject depends on the degree of importance attached to this portion of human culture taken on its own terms and the extent to which we think it might survive without school instruction. It is true, of course, that the subject matter of physical education overlaps somewhat that of other fields. Such overlapping is found between or among various subjects and is especially noticeable between the fine and the industrial arts. Physical education and music overlap in the dance. This does not prevent our recognizing physical education and music as separate subjects. They might be combined and treated as one subject, just as the fine and industrial arts might be so treated, since there is always an element of arbitrary choice in defining an instructional field for school purposes. The names too are arbitrary. Physical education is not necessarily a good descriptive term for the culture it transmits, but it can serve if we understand what we intend it to mean.

If physical education then is taken as a subject defined by its characteristic subject matter, the use of the human body as an instrument in various art media and forms, it may be related to the various aspects of individual development represented by our objectives. The objectives will have much to do with the kinds of activities used in the physical education curriculum. By general acceptance, one of the important objectives related to physical education is that of health, but this does not define the field as health education. It would be difficult to conceive a physical education program in our society not closely related to the objective of leisure time use and enjoyment of living, but this does not make physical education one and the same with leisure-time education or with recreation.

It is possible, then, in the context of physical education defined through its subject matter, that is, its distinctive portion of the human heritage of culture, to examine the relationship it bears to various objectives. One of these is physical fitness, which is presumably one aspect of the larger and broader objective of health. Much of the criticism of physical education in the second world war period tended to center on this point. It is true, as Collins and Cassidy as well as numerous other writers have pointed out, that physical education programs cannot do much about the defects for which men were rejected on the Armed Forces medical examinations. No amount or kind of physical education can do anything about most cardiovascular defects, vision defects, and the like. It is possible, however, for a person to be healthy in the sense of freedom from disqualifying physical defects and still not be what is known as physically fit. Popular criticism, therefore, centered not only on the large percentage of draft rejections, but on the alleged softness, lack of vigor and stamina, and lack of muscular strength in those who were accepted. The contention was advanced both by sections of the public and by some professional physical educators that the program had swung too far in the direction of recreational, social, and personal outcomes and had neglected the development of strength, agility, and endurance.

Those who speak for the broader point of view have responded that they do not neglect the fitness objectives. They object, however, to the fixing of arbitrary standards of performance and make much of the need for varying standards to fit particular individuals. Oberteuffer puts their case as follows.

Whichever way one looks at it, fitness is "neither a fixed standard nor an average, but rather an objective." There has been a great interest among physical education personnel to test a lot of people on a "fitness" test, establish norms, and then measure others to see if they are above or below this standard. Status on such scales, or measured by such standards, is probably meaningless, in terms of informing the student of the state of his health. Surely deviations from the norm do not mean the person is "substandard," nor should the effect of knowing one is different from the norm produce either the inflated ego of the "super-fit" or the frustration and other psychological repercussions likely in those who fail to measure up.

There can be no standard of fitness for all—for firemen, teachers, bankers, students, housewives, laborers, or merchants. Persons will vary by sex, by occupation, by heredity, by many factors, and thus a measure of fitness for one will be wholly inadequate for another. What we are after is not a status but a functional fitness—an ability to do one's work, live one's life effectively and without fatigue or preventable illness. To be fit is to be able to function on the job, in the home, in school, and on the field of play. Each function may require not only a different degree of fitness but a different way of arriving at it. All of the functions involve a total fitness and not merely a muscular or physical one.[36]

In the light of Oberteuffer's statement, which appears to be a sound one, it is unfair to demand that physical education programs bring every student up to arbitrarily defined levels of strength, agility, and endurance. What might be legitimately expected is that each student attain his own maximum levels on the various

[36] Oberteuffer, *op. cit.*, pp. 146–147.

fitness criteria. This recognition of individual differences, however, is not in conflict with specific provisions for the fitness objective in the physical education program.

Closely related to the fitness objective, although not exactly the same, is what some call physical literacy, that is, specific motor skills. This objective is an inherent characteristic of the subject, much as the learning of history is inherently related to the subject of history. According to one critic, however, it is an objective often neglected.

Almost fifty years ago, the writer read a fine exposition of how to teach the dance of that period, a work by a German writer by the name of Zorn, entitled (English translation), "The Grammar of the Dance." The writer has wondered ever since if physical educators did not need to give much more attention to the "grammar of motor skills." For example, some public school physical education recently observed showed almost no evidence of successful training in skills. The writer is sure that, in a class of English, if the pupils were to use such expressions as "He ain't got no time for talking to she," the teacher would immediately take steps to correct such incorrect speech. Or if, in a class in arithmetic, a pupil stated that "seven times nine equalled fifty-eight," the teacher would immediately correct the statement—and probably prescribe considerable drill in the use of the multiplication tables. But— when a number of seventeen-year-old girls, who had had practice in physical education classes for eleven years, were still unable to throw a ball to or at another pupil, using correct form, with the correct foot forward, etc.,—the teacher stood stolidly on the sideline and said nothing.

The writer recently observed numerous gymnasium classes of both boys and girls where poor form in performance was the rule rather than the exception—and observed not a single attempt to correct such poor performance. In other words, in the classroom the teacher strives constantly for academic literacy; in the gymnasium and on the athletic field, all too frequently, motor illiteracy almost seems to be encouraged. The writer believes that such states of affairs in physical education should not exist.[37]

The foregoing kind of criticism is familiar in the fields of English, mathematics, and the like, where writers often deplore

[37] C. H. McCloy, "Towards a Greater Degree of Physical Literacy," *The Physical Educator,* 14:3, October, 1957, pt. 1, p. 83.

the lack of achievement in the fundamentals. Again, as in the case of fitness, differences in native capacity will account for differences in performance. The important thing again is whether students are being helped to make progress toward their own performance limits. Certainly the objectives represented by the fundamentals in any subject are fully consistent with the broader objectives of social development, mental health, and enjoyment of living. It is difficult to see how a student can gain self-realization and the like in physical education without some feeling of assurance and security in the motor skills.

Those who call attention to the importance of physical fitness and motor skills do not insist on these as the only objectives of physical education. Neither do those who write a good deal about other kinds of objectives deny the importance of physical fitness and the motor skills. They do, however, direct specific attention to the importance of such objectives as leisure-time use, personality development, social development, and citizenship. According to Collins and Cassidy, "The program in physical education, resting upon an understanding of the innate capacity of the organism to maintain physical balance and integrity, is directly concerned with those activities which promote organic power and neuro-muscular skill together with social understandings and appreciations appropriate for democratic living."[38] Cowell lists five specific social functions of physical education, the first of which is providing "in the gymnasium and on the playing fields, the social intercourse and coöperation—the 'give-and-take'—of common experiences that promote social efficiency and social appreciation."[39] The acceptance of such broad objectives does not necessarily imply defining the physical education field as a physical method or approach to education in general. It is possible to define the field in terms of its content and also to insist on a broad range of criteria for the selection of particular content and the making of specific decisions.

There is some danger, nevertheless, to any instructional field in the tendency to list a great range of possible objectives. One possi-

[38] Collins and Cassidy, *op. cit.*, pp. 23–24.
[39] Charles C. Cowell, *Scientific Foundations of Physical Education*, Harper & Brothers, 1953, p. 33.

bility is that the listing will be interpreted as a sales or promotion device to further the expansion of the field in the school program. Another is that the objectives will be used deductively: "Now that we have this objective, what shall we put in the program to achieve it?" This use of the Cardinal Principles in a number of subjects has led both to much artificiality in unit designations and to unwarranted duplications and overlappings in content among the various instructional fields. There are occasions, however, when some of the general objectives are needed to arrive at judgments or decisions in particular instructional fields, even though they are not ordinarily given stress as objectives of those fields. For example, physical education practices consistent with a totalitarian or authoritarian notion of citizenship would not be desirable in a society such as ours which stresses democratic citizenship. As Williams has pointed out, "In these crucial days physical education, a field that will be used early by any authoritarian group that might attain power, must assay anew the democratic philosophy, and, if convinced, must hearken to democratic ideals. The contrasts are sharp indeed in the authoritarian and democratic views of national organization. The marching groups, the regimented discipline, the external controls mark both the Fascist and Communist ideologies."[40] No instructional field should engage in practices that contradict our general objectives; some explicit awareness of these objectives is, therefore, necessary in each instructional field to keep this from taking place. Such awareness is particularly important in physical education, for, as Williams has pointed out, it is a field peculiarly attractive to authoritarian ideologies and one that may easily be distorted to promote the ends of authoritarian societies or groups.

One broad and general objective closely related to physical education that may legitimately be used in a deductive sense is that of leisure-time use or enjoyment of living. This implies providing opportunities for youth to explore and become acquainted with a variety of sports and games, particularly those used in adult life, and to gain as much proficiency as possible in at least one or two of them. But even this objective should not

[40] Williams, *op. cit.*, p. 48.

become exclusively identified with physical education, for there are many avenues to enjoyment besides sports and games. Some people, including at least a few who are fairly proficient in sports, prefer to fine their enjoyment and to spend their leisure time in non-athletic activities. It may become necessary, therefore, to insist at times that physical education has no monopoly on the recreation objective, even while granting that recreation is an objective that should be kept in mind in the physical education program.

The major objectives toward which the content of physical education should be directed are those of health, including physical fitness, motor literacy or skills, and the enjoyment of living. Other objectives that physical educators do well to keep in mind as supplementary criteria for decisions are those of citizenship, personality development, and effectiveness in group relations. There should be nothing in the physical education program that contradicts or nullifies these general objectives of the school.

CHOICE OF CONTENT AND ACTIVITIES

The scope of the physical education curriculum will, as in all subjects, necessarily represent a selection from the total range of content available in the field. It will be a selection made in the light of the objectives deemed relevant and important. Williams outlines six major areas of content as follows: (1) games, sports, athletics; (2) aquatics; (3) dance; (4) self-testing activities; (5) camping and outdoor activities; and (6) body-guiding activities and adaptive physical education.[41] The term "self-testing activities" is defined by Williams as including "boxing, wrestling, and hand-to-hand for boys, and fencing for boys and girls" as well as "exercises on apparatus, tumbling, and stunts of various kinds" and he adds the warning that "Great care is to be used in the choice of particular activities in these groups especially with respect to age, sex, and general contribution to the activities of the program."[42]

[41] Jesse Feiring Williams, "Physical Education in the Curriculum," in Harl R. Douglass, *The High School Curriculum,* The Ronald Press Company, 1956, pp. 566–568.
[42] *Ibid.,* p. 567.

Some physical educators while recognizing the value of some of these self-testing activities would specifically exclude boxing from the school program. This has become a matter of some disagreement, not only in the physical education curriculum, but in the program of interscholastic athletics. According to Oberteuffer, "The question is raised as to whether boxing has a place *anywhere* in the program because of the rather clear evidence that injuries are frequent and serious."[43] This is a good example of the exclusion of certain content on the grounds that it conflicts with an important objective, in this case that of physical health and safety. Obviously there are some hazards in all physical education activities. In this case, however, many physical educators feel that the hazards outweigh any possible advantages. Neither is it possible to justify the instruction on the grounds of protection against hazards, since people are not placed in the position where these kinds of hazards are part of normal living. If the desire is to equip people with defense against assault, it would be more to the point to provide instruction in rough-and tumble fighting or possibly judo. There is also some danger in swimming. The exposure of people to water hazards, however, makes it more dangerous to be ignorant of swimming than to engage correctly in swimming activities. In addition, swimming has social and recreational values that it would be difficult to ascribe to boxing in any form.

Another item of disagreement is that of gymnastics or calisthenics. Opposition to these activities is based on contentions that they are unnecessary even for the fitness objective and that they contradict or conflict with other school objectives. "Surely stereotyped calisthenic drills were not conducive either to good emotional health or good social health. Formal marching falls in the same category. Neither was there much mental stimulus in regimented exercises or heavy apparatus. Such programs . . . were adapted from countries basically different in their emotional and social backgrounds from those of the United States."[44] Of course much depends here on what is meant by stereotyped or regimented. Proponents of calisthenics and gymnastics would contend that

[43] Oberteuffer, *op. cit.*, p. 165.
[44] Blanchard, *op. cit.*, p. 29

such activities need not necessarily be developed along those lines. Even Williams, who is opposed to "the old formal exercises done to response-commands" grants that "there will always be a place for gymnastic practice of a natural kind because all of the preceding activities have a technic that must be learned in relation to the whole activity that goes on."[45] The controversy centers then not on gymnastics, but on the kinds of gymnastics and the setting in which they are carried on. Here again there is much which reminds us of similar controversies about drill in grammar, arithmetic, and spelling.

Dance presents some specific curriculum problems, although few would deny that it has an important place somewhere in the school program. As one writer has pointed out, "the dance remains delicately poised between physical education and the fine arts."[46] In which field does it belong? It may belong in either or both. The same logic that would place dance in a department of fine arts would require that music be placed there also. Unless this is done, the fine arts department remains what it is in most schools, a department of painting, sculpture, and the like. This is not necessarily a bad arrangement. When such an arrangement is chosen, however, a somewhat better case can be made for including dance in the physical education curriculum.

Another characteristic of the dance has been its almost exclusive identification with physical education for women. Counts's survey of 15 city school systems in 1923–1924 showed that 18 percent of the time in girls' physical education was devoted to dance, whereas dance did not even appear in the boys' programs.[47] Except for the introduction of some coeducational social dancing, the situation is very little different today. This situation probably reflects certain stereotypes in our society. Certainly the history of the dance does not indicate that it has been exclusively or predominantly a part of the cultural heritage for women only. The dance has been, however, a most creative force in women's physical education in this country, and it may be somewhat unfortunate

---

[45] Williams, *The Principles of Physical Education, op. cit.,* pp. 248–249.
[46] Brownell and Hagman, *op. cit.,* p. 143.
[47] Counts, *op. cit.,* pp. 116–117.

that men's physical education programs have been remote from its general impact and influence. Physical educators sometimes observe that women's physical education in general has shown more imagination, creativity, and flexibility than men's physical education. Perhaps the dance has had much to do with this.

Those who are not in the physical education field need to remind themselves from time to time that the physical education curriculum is by no means confined to the gymnasium, the athletic field, the swimming pool, and the like. Some of it is carried on in classrooms and by the same processes of lectures, readings, discussions, and use of audio-visual materials that characterize other subjects. At least part of this classroom work may legitimately be devoted to the understanding of such popular sports as football, basketball, baseball, and hockey for consumer or spectator purposes. This can be an important part of developing resources and materials for leisure-time use. With regard to the frequently expressed dangers of spectatoritis, Williams comments as follows.

It is rather remarkable that the role of the spectator at music recitals, dance recitals and art exhibitions is socially approved, but that watching such intensely dramatic and human art as football and baseball contests is called 'spectatoritis' and frowned upon. It may be granted that participation is desirable, and surely the pages of this book argue for that. It may also be observed that participation in music, dance, painting, drawing, and sculpturing is also admirable. But all cannot play football, nor baseball, nor compete in the Olympic games. There is a place for the dramatic festivals of sport and the modern American culture gives them a welcome. The role of the understanding spectator is not to be despised.[48]

The same discussion of participation versus appreciation goes on in music and the visual fine arts as well. It is a hardy perennial, which will probably survive for many generations to come. But at least we might admit the desirability of spending some of the time in physical education on the history, rules, strategy, and fine points of our major spectator sports.

In some schools, part of the time in physical education is devoted to classroom work on health or hygiene topics and first aid,

[48] Williams, *op. cit.*, p. 214.

with some material on anatomy and physiology. There is nothing specifically against this practice. The important thing is that such materials be taught. But they are not part of the subject matter of physical education, and their presence in the physical education curriculum symbolizes the long-standing confusion between physical and health education. A better case can be made for treating most of these topics in general science or biology. Of course if physical education is required and biology is not, the matter becomes one of practical reality, at least pending the establishment of a biology requirement. Some schools have tried to remove the discrepancy by requiring a separate semester of hygiene. The fact that this usually replaces one semester of physical education and that the course is often taught by a staff member in physical education serves to continue the confusion rather than to clarify it.

The sequence in physical education can be and often is flexible and diversified from one grade to the next in the six years of the junior and senior high school. One criticism sometimes expressed is that it is difficult to tell the difference between twelfth-grade and ninth-grade physical education, since the same activities appear at both levels. There are, however, relatively few criteria that can be used to determine grade placement in this field.

A large number of the activities offered at the high school level are the same as those in the intermediate grades and in the junior high school. To the inexperienced observer, it would seem that there is no progression in physical education because such a large number of the activities are offered year after year throughout the elementary and secondary school program. Those experienced in the field, however, known that because of the need of teaching a wide variety of different activities the progression is largely within the activities. Teachers in physical education are faced with the double duty of teaching the activity and then actually developing skill in performing the activity.[49]

One possible basis for sequence is the physiological, but even here it is difficult to get agreement among experts on such points as tackle football for junior high and senior high boys. Another possible basis is that of social development, especially with re-

[49] Leslie W. Irwin, *The Curriculum in Health and Physical Education*, The C. V. Mosby Company, 1951, p. 155.

gard to coeducational dancing or other coeducational activities such as swimming and tennis. It appeared at one time that golf should be introduced late in the senior high program since this was largely an adult activity. The avidity with which junior high school boys have taken up golf entirely on their own in some communities does not tend to bear this out. Flexibility in sequence is, therefore, inescapable in physical education, a fact that should encourage the use of pupil participation in the choice and development of activities.

CLASS ORGANIZATION AND GROUPING

A closely related matter is that of grouping students. Individual differences probably stand out more sharply in physical education than in any other subject. Students with poor motor coördination need special help and instruction; they should not be placed in situations where their lack of physical ability is accentuated by the presence of students with average or superior abilities. When students of varying abilities are thrown together in the same class, the teacher must recognize the dangers to individual mental health and self confidence that such a situation represents.

As for the individual, there should be ample opportunity for a wide enough variety of activities to meet many individual needs. The fat boy should have opportunity to participate in something that he can do and in which he can feel the joy and satisfaction of accomplishment. He should not be subjected to situations where he can be ridiculed. The overgrown, awkward eighth-grade girl should not be required to do stunts that may embarrass her. The shy bashful boy should not be forced into social dancing but encouraged and guided sympathetically into this activity. The new boy in the class, inept at skills, should not be made to attempt unknown and untried activities when failure heaps ridicule on him.[50]

To provide for individual differences in a large class is no easy matter, and physical education classes unfortunately tend to run larger than most others in the school program. If administratively feasible, some kind of ability grouping seems to be desirable. "It is always a handicap to try to teach a group with a wide range of

[50] Blanchard, *op. cit.,* p. 31.

interests and abilities. When the grade plan is followed, this is likely to be the situation during the years of adolescence; marked differences in the rate of maturation will pose the most trying problems to a teacher with a group organized by grade."[51]

Other writers, however, recommend grade-level grouping as the most generally desirable, partly on the grounds that it provides for social interests and similarities. If the school is large enough to permit several sections per grade, it is possible to use grade-level groupings combined with ability sections. Otherwise the choice must be made between ability sectioning that cuts across several grades and grade-level groups that include students with a wide range of abilities. Preference should then be given to ability sectioning cutting across probably not more than two or three grades, since this promises the best provision for individual differences. As is true in other subjects, it is the general ability or proficiency of the student in the subject that should determine his placement, rather than his performance on any one test or kind of test.

In any subject, the size of the class will have much to do with the teacher's opportunity to provide for individual differences. Even under a system of ability grouping individual differences are minimized, but not eliminated. Unfortunately the practice has developed in many schools of scheduling large numbers of students in physical education sections. "By far the most perplexing problem of class size belongs to the secondary school where youths are often crowded into physical education like a swarm of bees in a hive."[52] Specht reports classes as large as 40 to 60 pupils at the junior high school level.[53] Irwin says, "In some of the larger high schools and colleges it is not uncommon to find classes ranging in numbers from 150 to over 200 students with only one instructor."[54] It is true, of course, that a section should include enough students for certain team sports, but this would not need to run over the class size of 30 or so deemed desirable in the classroom subjects.

The individual differences under consideration here are not

---

[51] Williams, *op. cit.*, p. 304.
[52] Brownell and Hagman, *op. cit.*, p. 317.
[53] Gruhn and Douglass, *op. cit.*, p. 183.
[54] Irwin, *op. cit.*, p. 345.

those of physical or medical handicaps that prevent participation in normal physical education activities. They are largely differences in motor coördination, strength, agility, and the like. Students with medical handicaps present further challenges to the physical education curriculum. In some cases these students can be helped through what were once known as corrective but have come to be known as adapted physical education activities. Others must necessarily be excused from physical education altogether; administrative policies on this point are frequently objects of criticism, but it is not an easy matter to administer. It is probably better to make mistakes in the direction of granting excuses where they are not justified than it is to withhold them where they are.

Physical educators usually testify that unwarranted excuse-seeking reflects an unsatisfactory program or unsatisfactory facilities. Few students probably would seek unjustified excuses from an ideal program of physical education conducted under ideal circumstances by ideal teachers. Not only the physical education staff, but all teachers in a high school, plus the administrative officers, should accept the obligation of approaching such ideal programs and facilities as nearly as possible. Weak programs and poor facilities not only motivate students to seek excuses, but deny adequate learning opportunities to those students who do not wish to be excused.

PHYSICAL EDUCATION AS A REQUIRED SUBJECT

Whether or not physical education should be required of all students all the way from the seventh through the twelfth grade is another question. Physical education is the most heavily and universally required of all our high school fields with the exception of English. This extensive development has in part been motivated by legislative enactment and state department regulations. In part at least it has been based on the idea of providing students with regular physical exercise for the sake of health and fitness. Most physical educators, however, reject this point of view and contend that physical education is primarily a field of instruction to be examined on the basis of its contributions to what the students learn.

If physical education is regarded from the latter point of view, the question becomes one of the common understandings and skills that all students should have the opportunity to learn. Some physical education should be required, partly to transmit the common elements of the culture it represents, partly to enable every student to explore physical activities as a source of personal interest to which he might wish to devote further and more extended study. In this sense, the field is comparable to the visual fine arts and the industrial arts. All students should have an initial common experience in these fields; some students will pursue them further. Much of the advanced work consists of a refinement and further development of the basic skills and understandings that justify the requirement. Perhaps then required physical education should be confined to the junior high school grades and not extended beyond Grade 9. As is true in the arts, this might mean requiring physical education in the senior high school of those students who have not had previous physical education experiences and opportunities.

This would not mean the abandonment of physical education programs in the senior high school. The programs and facilities should be made so attractive that many students will continue physical education on an elective basis. Under such circumstances the program in large schools should develop more specialized offerings, such as separate sections for golf, tennis, swimming, and the like, much the same as is true in the visual fine arts and the industrial arts. This can be done to some extent in the required program also, but it is limited by the idea that requirements imply continued common participation in a broader range of activities.

On the whole, physical education in our schools has functioned under peculiar advantages and disabilities. Even the advantages, such as those of practically universal requirements, may turn out under scrutiny to be no advantages at all. For the most part the public, the school administrators, and the other members of high school staffs have accepted the requirements as desirable, or at least inevitable. But on the other hand, the public has not made it possible for administrators to develop policies to carry out the program. Oversized classes, shortages of staff, crowded facilities, and the like can in the final reckoning be traced to school budgets and public financial support. We are referring here to the physical education program as an instructional field, not to the extraclass activities of interscholastic athletics. These are an extension of the basic physical education class. Often the extension has enjoyed better support than the classwork it is supposed to extend.

Administrators and teachers in other departments have in addition never completely accepted physical education as an instructional field on the same level with others in the curriculum. What is needed is full recognition by all concerned that this is an instructional field that transmits an important and essential aspect of our cultural heritage. It teaches important, needed, and desirable understandings and skills. Once this is accepted, we can all perhaps approach the problems of the physical education curriculum without the stereotypes, conflicts, and prejudices that have characterized the thinking of teachers both inside and outside the physical education field itself.

Bibliography

Blanchard, Vaughn S., *Curriculum Problems in Health and Physical Education,* A. S. Barnes and Company, 1942.

Brownell, Clifford Lee, and Hagman, E. Patricia, *Physical Education —Foundations and Principles,* McGraw-Hill Book Company, Inc., 1951.

Collins, Laurentine, and Cassidy, Rosalind, with the collaboration of Cowell, Charles C.; Kozman, Hilda C.; Stolz, Herbert R.; and Participants in Summer Workshops of the Progressive Education Association, *Physical Education in the Secondary Schools,* Progressive Education Association Committee on Workshops, 1940.

Commission on the Reorganization of Secondary Education of the National Education Association, *Physical Education in Secondary Schools,* Department of the Interior, Bureau of Education, Bulletin 1917, No. 50.

Cowell, Charles C., *Scientific Foundations of Physical Education,* Harper & Brothers, 1953.

Irwin, Leslie W., *The Curriculum in Health and Physical Education,* The C. V. Mosby Company, 1951.

McCloy, C. H., *Philosophical Bases for Physical Education,* F. S. Crofts and Company, 1940.

Oberteuffer, Delbert, *Physical Education,* Harper & Brothers, 1951.

Schwendener, Norma, *A History of Physical Education in the United States,* A. S. Barnes and Company, 1942.

Staley, Seward C., *The Curriculum in Sports (Physical Education),* Stipes Publishing Company, Champaign, Illinois, 1940.

Storey, Thomas A.; Small, Willard S.; and Salisbury, Elon G., *Recent State Legislation for Physical Education,* Department of the Interior, Bureau of Education, Bulletin 1922, No. 1.

Williams, Jesse Feiring, *The Principles of Physical Education,* 6th ed., W. B. Saunders Company, 1954.

CHAPTER 17

::

Music

Music is an art valued not for its practical utility, but for its contribution to human enjoyment and satisfaction through intellectual and emotional appeals. This makes it what some people would call a frill. Yet it is a frill that has enjoyed solid popularity and support as a school subject. It is a feature of our culture that has been assimilated and embraced in thousands of American communities, and the school music program has done much to bring this about. Few instructional fields as completely symbolize and identify the essential unity of school and community life.

In the history of American schooling, music holds a somewhat distinctive position. It developed without an overwhelming stimulus from Europe. True, European influences did play a large part in the way school music developed, but it did not arise initially by way of response to European intellectual or cultural movements, as did, for example, physical education and the industrial arts. It is one of the most distinctively American features of our school curriculum.

The beginnings of school music in our country took place in private and very informal singing schools conducted by part-time teachers for those who wished to improve their singing in church. "A singing school existed in Boston as early as 1717, and about this time we find a number of psalm-books published, which were in fact primitive vocal methods."[1] The movement spread rapidly,

[1] Louis C. Elson, *The History of American Music*, The Macmillan Company, 1904, p. 9.

and numbers of such schools were established not only in New England, but in other colonies as well. "It (the singing school) was truly educational in that both of its major aims, the study of choral music and acquiring the art of music reading, laid the national foundations for musical culture and appreciation, the full strength of which did not become evident until the next period."[2]

Singing schools grew into singing societies and stimulated a further public interest in music, especially through contests. Church choirs became large and ambitious. In 1815, the choir of the Park Street Church in Boston organized the Handel and Haydn Society for the giving of public performances.[3] Music was beginning to assume an important place in the cultural life of New England and other American regions. A number of the leading music enthusiasts in Boston came together in 1833 to organize the Boston Academy of Music.[4] One of these was a young banker named Lowell Mason, who had a large and comprehensive vision of future possibilities. He took the lead in developing a nine-point program for the academy, including instruction for both children and adults, the education of teachers, the giving of concerts, and the publication of tracts and books.[5] Point 8 called for the introduction of vocal music in the public schools.[6]

Efforts to put music in the public schools had already been started by another organizer of the Boston Academy, William C. Woodbridge, who had visited Europe and had been impressed by the music instruction in the schools of the Pestalozzian movement. Woodbridge converted Mason to the Pestalozzian teaching methods.[7] This is one of the instances of European influence in music education in our country, but the groundwork for music in the schools had already been well laid by the singing schools and the music societies. Whether or not this particular reliance on Euro-

---

[2] Edward Bailey Birge, *History of Public School Music in the United States,* Oliver Ditson Company, 1928, pp. 10–11.

[3] Elson, *op. cit.,* p. 30.

[4] *Ibid.,* p. 79.

[5] Frank Damrosch, "Music in the Public Schools," in the *History of American Music* (W. L. Hubbard, ed.), published by Irving Squire, London, 1908, pp. 19–20.

[6] *Ibid.,* p. 20.

[7] Elson, *op. cit.,* p. 78.

pean influence was a happy one is apparently a point of some disagreement, one recent music educator writing that "Perhaps the
most-to-be-regretted endeavor of the first teachers of music in our
public schools was their uninformed attempt to introduce Pestalozzian method."[8]

In 1837, the Boston school board voted to put music in the
schools and accepted Mason's services as a teacher without pay. A
year later they put Mason on the payroll with the impressive title
of Superintendent of Music. Public school music was under way.
As in many other school movements, Boston had taken the lead,
but many other school systems soon followed its example and made
music part of the public school curriculum. The continuity of this
instruction with the early beginnings of music study in our country
is brought out by Birge as follows. "The first teachers of public
school music as well as the methods of teaching came directly from
the singing-school. The public school music class was, in fact, a
transplanted singing-school. Even the books were in many cases
the same, though juvenile song collections prepared for children's
classes were soon plentiful."[9] So extensive was the development of
public school music that a historian writing in 1904 could declare,
"There is possibly no country on the globe where the rudiments of
music are so widely diffused among the masses as in America."[10]

MUSIC IN THE HIGH SCHOOL

All this was at the elementary school level. The movement to
place music in the high school program was much slower in developing. Prior to 1900, high school music, where it existed at all,
consisted almost entirely of informal assembly singing or scattered
instances of school choruses. A few instrumental organizations began to make their appearance just at the end of the century.

With the increasing number of private teachers trained in numerous
colleges and conservatories in this country and abroad it was inevitable
that sooner or later young instrumentalists would become interested in

[8] Allen P. Britton, "Music in Early American Public Education: A Historical
Critique," National Society for the Study of Education, Fifty-seventh Yearbook,
p. 1, *Basic Concepts in Music Education,* The Society, 1958, p. 206.

[9] Birge, *op. cit.,* p. 72.

[10] Elson, *op. cit.,* p. 339.

musical activities other than solo playing. Just before 1900, small student orchestral groups were formed here and there, generally under the
leadership of some enterprising music lover who sought out his fellow
students and urged them to join the group. The personnel of these organizations was solely a matter of chance, depending upon the instruments various families had selected for their children. Any miscellaneous assortment of instruments was dignified by the term "high school
orchestra." Occasional public performances were given, and not infrequently the orchestra became a community, as well as a school organization, playing at church socials, civic celebrations, and various school
functions.[11]

At this point the development of music as a high school field
was stimulated by one of the phenomena so frequently encountered
in our educational history—namely, a conference, this one sum-
moned by the New England Education League to meet in Boston
in 1902. It was this Conference on the Secondary-School Music
Curriculum which delivered the blast calling for a greatly expanded set of offerings at the high school level. The proposal was
to inaugurate four full years of music study besides choral work.
"In addition to the courses in applied music it provided for elementary and advanced harmony, counterpoint and form, and musical biography and history. . . . This was the first constructive
attempt to organize high school music as a major study and on
a regular credit basis. It received the endorsement of the Music
Teachers National Association and the Music Section of the N.E.A.
in 1904."[12] And as has been true in other fields, schools were not
slow to act on these recommendations, at least in part, "so that by
1910 the framework of the present secondary school program, including chorus, orchestra, harmony and appreciation became
plainly visible over the country at large, the most striking feature
of this advance being the rapid spread of instrumental work."[13]

The rapid acceptance of music in the high school is indicated in
a survey reported by the United States Bureau of Education in 1914.
Of the 631 high schools surveyed, 442 or 70 percent had "some

[11] Theodore F. Normann, *Instrumental Music in the Public Schools,* Oliver Ditson
Company, 1941, pp. 10–11.
[12] Birge, *op. cit.,* p. 164.
[13] *Ibid.,* p. 168.

music other than assembly singing."[14] There were 238 orchestras,[15] and 49 of the schools indicated specific attention to music history, appreciation, and harmony, 39 of these through regular courses or classes.[16] The writer of the report, however, was not enthusiastic about the vocal work, particularly since he suspected that some of the reported choruses were nothing more than singing practice in school assemblies. "On the other hand, many who reported chorus singing, as required, evidently had in mind nothing more than assembly singing, even when this involved but the singing of hymns or patriotic songs as incidental to a chapel service, and, it is safe to assume, without classification as to the parts sung."[17] In fact, the high school chorus continues to be an object of general suspicion in the literature throughout this entire period, even when not identified with assembly singing. Inglis, for example, characterized the "one or two periods of chorus work" as "frequently of a useless or worse than useless character—worse than useless in many instances because it arouses a positive distaste for the study of music and an opposition to the ineffective work which is attempted."[18] Despite some of these adverse comments, however, it is evident that the recommendations of the 1902 conference had registered a marked effect and that music had by the World War I period become an established part of the high school program.

The portion of total recitation time devoted to music was reported by Counts as 2.5 percent in his survey of high school programs in fifteen cities for 1923–1924. Only art had a smaller overall percentage allotment.[19] This may suggest that the spread of music while extensive was somewhat thin, but Counts did not accept that conclusion. He called attention to the fact that much of the music work was done without credit and on an extraclass activity basis. "As a consequence, the emphasis given to music in the

[14] Will Earhart, *Music in the Public Schools,* United States Bureau of Education Bulletin 1914, No. 33, p. 26.
[15] *Ibid.,* p. 31.
[16] *Ibid.,* pp. 33–34.
[17] *Ibid.,* p. 26.
[18] Alexander Inglis, *Principles of Secondary Education,* Houghton Mifflin Company, 1918, p. 628.
[19] George S. Counts, *The Senior High School Curriculum,* The University of Chicago, 1926, p. 108.

schools is markedly greater than is indicated by the percentages which have been quoted."[20] Moreover, the music teachers in all the cities reported "that the attitude of the principal toward the work is distinctly favorable."[21] The special attention drawn to this comment in the Counts report suggests some lingering feeling that high school administrators were not in all cases enthusiastic about the rapid development of music in their schools. On the other hand, in only nine of the 15 cities was the "general attitude of the teachers" (that is, of teachers other than those in music) reported as favorable.[22]

Whether the attitudes of other teachers were favorable or not, music had arrived to stay. The percentage of the total high school enrollment, Grades 9 through 12, found in music classes declined from 31.5 to 25.3 between 1915 and 1922, but held firm after that time. By the time of the 1949 survey of high school enrollments, the figure had risen again to 30.1 percent.[23] In spite of the percentage decline in enrollments in the 1920's, there was evidently a phenomenal increase in instrumental activity. "A generally accepted estimate claims that by 1930 there were 30,000 orchestras (high school and grade), many of them including in their programs symphonies and other advanced works."[24] Besides orchestras, there were the always popular high school bands. "In the fifteen years from 1924 to 1939, bands increased at a remarkable rate, some estimates maintaining that there were 100 bands at the latter date for every one at the former."[25]

The high school music story has been most impressive, evoking the following expression from the Director of the Royal Conservatory of Music in Toronto.

So the nineteenth century witnessed the rise of vocal teaching in schools. Since 1900, instrumental music and appreciation (or listening) lessons were added to the school music programme: with the as-

---

[20] *Ibid.*, p. 109.

[21] *Ibid.*, p. 110.

[22] *Ibid.*

[23] "Offerings and Enrollments in High-School Subjects," *Biennial Survey of Education in the United States, 1948–1950,* Federal Security Agency, Office of Education, 1951, table 7, p. 108.

[24] Peter W. Dykema and Karl W. Gehrkens, *The Teaching and Administration of High School Music,* C. C. Birchard and Company, Boston, 1941, p. 9.

[25] *Ibid.*

tonishing result that nearly every American high school (think of it: nearly every American high school—there are thousands of them) has boys' and girls' glee clubs, mixed choruses, instrumental classes, bands and orchestras; to which sometimes *a capella* choruses are added, courses in theory, history and appreciation of music. The most advanced students form intercollegiate orchestras and choruses whose technical proficiency is simply astounding.[26]

This quantitative growth presumably has not been achieved at the expense of quality and is therefore all the more impressive. There can be little doubt that the music program constitutes one of the most substantial achievements of our free, popular, and universal high schools.

CURRICULAR OBJECTIVES OF MUSIC

What is it all for? Such a question as this seems both irreverent and irrelevant in the face of the striking achievements already noted. One might also ask whether music has to be for anything, except for music. The question of objectives, however, is one that has exercised a good deal of fascination, particularly on music educators themselves. One music educator, James L. Mursell, approaches this question with the following hint of skepticism about the reasons behind the expansion of the music curriculum.

New subjects were introduced gradually, not in accordance with any general plan or well-considered theory, but largely under the pressure of specially interested groups who resorted to various forms of propaganda and pressure. This, for instance, was the case with the natural sciences, which came in during the latter half of the nineteenth century, and whose claims were very eloquently defended by Herbert Spencer and Thomas Henry Huxley. The same is more or less true of music. It has reached its present enormous, and indeed astonishing proportions in the schools, not in response to an intelligible educational philosophy which clearly demanded its introduction and extension, but as a result of extremely effective and plausible promotion.[27]

[26] Arnold Walter, "Music Education on the American Continent," *Music in Education,* International Conference on the Role and Place of Music in the Education of Youth and Adults, UNESCO, 1955, p. 69.

[27] James L. Mursell, *Human Values in Music Education,* Silver, Burdett and Company, 1934, p. 252.

In his own treatment of objectives, Mursell develops the relationships of music to transmission of the cultural heritage, to "mental growth and personal development," and to leisure time and pleasure.[28]

The attempt to identify valid curricular purposes for music is just about as old in this country as the introduction of music in the public schools. The Boston committee that recommended public-school music in 1837 wrote as follows.

Let music be examined by the following standards:—

1. Intellectually. Music had its place among the seven liberal arts, which scholastic ages regarded as pertaining to all humanity. Arithmetic, Geometry, Astronomy, and Music—these formed the quadrivium. Memory, comparison, attention, intellectual faculties—all of them are quickened by a study of its disciplines. It may be made to some extent a mental discipline.

2. Morally. It is unphilosophical to say that exercises in vocal music may not be so directed and arranged as to produce those habits of feeling of which these sounds are the type. Happiness, contentment, cheerfulness, tranquility—these are the natural effects of music.

3. Physically. It appears self evident that exercise in vocal music, when not carried to an unreasonable excess, must expand the chest and thereby strengthen the lungs and vital organs. Judging then by this triple standard, intellectually, morally, and physically, vocal music seems to have a natural place in every system of instruction which aspires, as should every system, to develop man's whole nature.[29]

Although this committee claimed intellectual values for music, it proceeded further in the report almost to expose itself to charges of anti-intellectualism. "Now the defect of our present system, admirable as that system is, is this, that it aims to develop the intellectual part of man's nature solely when, for all the true purposes of life, it is of more importance, a hundredfold, to feel rightly than to think profoundly."[30]

By claiming intellectual, moral, and physical values for music, this report illustrates the tendency to claim the whole range and scope of educational values for every school subject. This approach

[28] *Ibid.,* pp. 255–257.
[29] Cited in Birge, *op. cit.,* p. 41.
[30] Cited *ibid.,* p. 47.

became pronounced in practically every subject after the statement of the Cardinal Principles in 1918, but it is foreshadowed here by the Boston School committee nearly a century before. The characterization of physical education, for example, as education through the physical symbolizes the attempt to define a particular subject as the means of achieving a wide range of purposes. It is paralleled by a similar characterization in the field of music. "So it is not merely *public school music* that we are advocating, not even—to adopt the broader terms—*school music* or *music education*. It is *education through music*—to borrow the title of Charles Hubert Farnsworth's epoch-making book. . . ."[31] The literature of music education accordingly tends to include a wide variety of desirable outcomes to which the study of music may be applicable. As is true in other fields, the consequences of this tendency may be beneficial or otherwise, depending on the ways in which objectives are used. If a broad range of objectives is used inductively as criteria to check decisions and practices, the consequences are more likely to be beneficial than if used deductively to set up units, courses, or activities and the like aimed directly and specifically at such objectives.

Music as a field of study is defined by the culture it transmits. Its role in the curriculum is to transmit those portions or aspects of culture. A previously quoted music educator, James L. Mursell, who questioned some of the motivation behind the expansion of the music field, characterizes this transmission role as follows.

First of all, we shall point out, as a matter of historical and sociological fact, that music is a very important element in our common culture. It is a pursuit to which a considerable number of men of the highest genius, and multitudes of others less supremely endowed, have devoted their most serious efforts. From the earliest times it has played a notable and imposing part in the common life of western civilization. Now clearly this is a very strong argument for its inclusion, to some degree at any rate, in a school curriculum which undertakes to reflect our common cultural heritage.[32]

As is true in other fields, cultural transmission is dedicated to the intellectual, personal, social, and moral development of indi-

[31] Dykema and Gehrkens, *op. cit.,* p. xxiv.
[32] Mursell, *op. cit.,* p. 255.

viduals. Mursell and other music educators quite properly identify the potential contributions of music to these aspects of human development. It is obvious that one of the most important of these will be the creative and constructive use of leisure time or the enjoyment of living. It is also obvious that it can be for some of our students a field of highly specialized interest even to the extent of making it their life's work. These points were clearly brought out by Counts in his report for 1923–1924. "The head of the music department in a school where the instruction is most successful stated that the chief purposes of music instruction are 'to awaken an interest in, and a liking for, music in the general mass of pupils and to stimulate a desire for advanced study among the talented.' "[33]

To go beyond this by listing claims for a host of other outcomes weakens rather than strengthens the position of a field of study, and this is just as true in music as in other fields. The tendency to claim a broad range of values for a particular subject may in some cases even reflect a defensive or protective attitude toward the subject itself. No subject needs to be or can be defended on such grounds. And as the writer of the following quotation points out, the proponents of music in the curriculum have no reason for feeling uncertain about their subject in the first place.

Music, as one of the seven liberal arts, has formed an integral part of the educational systems of Western civilization from Hellenic times to the present. Thus, the position of music in education, historically speaking, is one of great strength. Unfortunately, this fact seems to be one of which most educators, including most music educators, remain unaware. As a result, the defense of music in the curriculum is often approached as if something new were being dealt with. Lacking the assurance which a knowledge of history could provide, many who seek to justify the present place of music in American schools tend to place too heavy a reliance upon ancillary values which music may certainly serve but which cannot, in the end, constitute its justification. Plato, of course, is the original offender in this regard, and his general view that the essential value of music lies in its social usefulness seems to be as alive today as ever.[34]

[33] Counts, *op. cit.*, p. 110.
[34] Britton, *op. cit.*, p. 195.

Even if we take music on its own terms, as we should, there are specific purposes that have much to do with decisions made on a number of points in the music program. One of these is the development of musical taste and discrimination. The second is the development of technical knowledge in the field of music, particularly with regard to the reading of music symbols and notations and to the use of technical vocabulary. The third is the stimulation of desire to take some part in musical activity, especially in adult life. Neither music educators nor general educators are agreed on the importance these purposes should assume, the ways in which they might be carried out, or the degree to which they are being effectively attained.

The first of these, development of musical taste and discrimination, will inevitably be a controversial point in a culture where people encounter and respond to a great deal of music in their daily lives, especially with the increase of musical transmission through radio, television, recordings, and films. People like music, but they do not always like the music approved by professional musicians and music educators. This is a complex matter and goes far beyond the conventional or stereotyped distinctions between music called classical and popular. Is it then a legitimate purpose to wean the student away from music he likes to music he should like? Are some types or styles of music inherently superior to others? In the early days of high school music, writers on the curriculum tended to favor types of music labeled as "good," such as oratorios, cantatas, choral selections from operas, and the like. The U.S. Bureau of Education 1914 bulletin on music classified high school choral music as strong, good, and weak on the following bases.

Under "strong" is included only material that is worthy of the attention of the average small choral society, such as cantatas by the best composers, short oratorios or oratorio selections, choral ballads, excerpts from operas, and some of the lesser and easier operas. These are used in larger schools for concert purposes, their preparation often constituting the greater part of the season's work.

Under "good" are included all the better supplementary octavo publications arranged for high-school use, and consisting of oratorios and opera choruses, as well as part songs of varying degrees of length and difficulty, but of unquestioned musical value, and also of several of the better song books for high schools that cover much the same ground as the octavos mentioned.

Under "weak" are included principally song books that are hardly beyond the standards recognized for assembly singing. These books are characterized by part writing that is rudimentary and implies no organized chorus drill, by subjects and texts that are commonplace, by editing that betrays lack of artistic conscience and musical knowledge, and by the inclusion of much material that has no value beyond the fact that it is familiar or popular and can be sung in any style without detriment to it.

Measured by these standards the table shows gratifying accomplishments in high-school chorus singing, over two-thirds of all schools reporting being aligned on the side of music that must be of value to those studying it.[35]

Well-meaning teachers following along these lines established the notion of "good" music as genteel music and undoubtedly converted many high school students to the cause, although they may also have prejudiced other students against any future consideration of music other than the popular or familiar.

Fortunately, these matters of individual preference are no longer what music educators and critics regard as the sole bases for development of taste and discrimination. They have moved away from classifying music as good and bad by types or styles. A symphony is not good just because it is a symphony; it must be judged by standards of excellence applied to the particular form or type it represents. Jazz is not bad because it is jazz; individual jazz compositions may be good, bad, or somewhere in between. Even on this point many critics in the fine arts are not convinced that standards of taste can be made absolute in nature, but think of them as exploratory and tentative. The history of the fine arts certainly shows many shifts and changes in the criteria of excellence. This has been true even in church music, where we might expect to find more fixed adherence to particular styles and forms. In attempting to develop taste and discrimination, therefore, the modern teacher uses many kinds of music and helps students to familiarize them-

[35] Earhart, *op. cit.*, p. 30.

selves with a broad range of qualities or characteristics by which music may be judged. Our high school music curriculum today includes not only the compositions loosely called the classics, but a wide variety of other musical expressions, including musical comedy, light opera or operetta, folk songs, current hit tunes, and jazz. Britton, for example, points out that "American school children may now sing 'Wayfaring Stranger' and 'On the Erie Canal,' forbidden items one hundred years ago."[36] The sales of recordings of symphonies, concertos, and chamber music do not indicate that the cause of so-called classical music has suffered in any way from this more comprehensive approach.

Attempts to develop ability to read music and to impart technical vocabulary have been controversial among music educators themselves. Birge reports that the reading objective was a predominant one in the latter years of the nineteenth century. "Success in school-music meant success in teaching music reading, and the best energy and thought of music teachers went into a study of this problem. Rote singing was largely taboo, and general song singing in the grades was given rather scant attention for its own sake."[37] There was a subsequent reaction against this, many music educators contending that music was designed to be heard, with reading as an artificial aid necessary only to the professional musician. According to the Counts report for 1923–1924, "The technique and the grammar of music are being subordinated to actual participation in musical activity, whether by listening, by singing, or by playing."[38] Nevertheless, Mursell wrote in 1943 that "The development of power and capacity in the reading of music is consistent with the basic purpose of promoting the use and enjoyment of music as widely as possible, which of course is an essential component in authentic musical development."[39]

There are, however, degrees of ability in music reading. Skilled readers can pick up written music they have never seen before and proceed to sing it directly from the notes. To force most of our stu-

---

[36] Britton, *op. cit.*, p. 211, note 37.

[37] Birge, *op. cit.*, pp. 138–139.

[38] Counts, *op. cit.*, pp. 110–111.

[39] James L. Mursell, *Music in American Schools*, Silver Burdett Company, 1943, p. 234.

dents into exercises and drills designed to achieve this kind of skill is probably futile and unnecessary. This does not mean, on the other hand, that the general student should be ignorant of the symbols and notations by which music is recorded in written form. These symbols form a language system comparable to that of mathematics. They have developed slowly over some period of time, and they can undoubtedly be improved. They are also part of the culture that the school transmits. With some knowledge of these symbols, a person can better understand the music he enjoys. He can also read books on music with better understanding and can more readily follow articles on music and music criticism that appear in newspapers and magazines. In fact, he can read with greater insight the essays that are today included in packages of phonograph records and are designed to help him enjoy the music he purchases in such recorded form. There are good reasons, therefore, why our music curriculum should help students acquire some knowledge of music symbols and notations, plus appropriate technical vocabulary as well.

The third specific purpose, that of stimulating participation in music activities in adult life, is a desirable one and parallels comparable purposes in a number of other instructional fields. Some of our students will play in community orchestras or other instrumental groups or will sing in choral organizations. Some will just listen to music and read about it. Between these extremes are many variations. There are in all our lives, however, some occasions for participation of a more direct sort, and it is here, to the casual observer at least, that it seems our school music programs have borne the least fruit. The half-hearted mumbling of a crowd supposedly singing the national anthem at public gatherings would not lead one to believe that the majority of the crowd had spent at least several years in some kind of school music.

Much the same phenomenon may be observed in most of our churches, where the congregations seem well content to let the choir do the singing for them. In no church are the clergy happy about this state of affairs; many have made heroic efforts to overcome it. Year by year, however, our people have become more inarticulate and withdrawn in church singing. Perhaps a return to the singing schools of the early eighteenth century is called for! It may be that we tend to romanticize the past and that church congregations have always been like this. Why this state of affairs should have persisted, or perhaps developed, in the face of our intensive efforts in public school music is a mystery that so far no one has been able to resolve. Perhaps we have put too much stress on technical excellence in performance with the result that the average citizen prefers to remain silent rather than to risk making a mistake.

REQUIREMENTS AND ELECTIVES IN HIGH SCHOOL MUSIC

Or it may simply be that we have not had enough of our students take enough music to give them any sense of ease or confidence in the handling of it. Perhaps we should require more music. As in every instructional field, we are confronted here by the question of constants. Should all students take music? How much? How long? What kind? The question of constants or requirements in music, however, differs somewhat from that in many of the other fields. For one thing, almost all elementary schools provide some music instruction. There are very few students who come to high school without previous experience in the field. This is not the case in such fields as physical education, industrial arts, science, or even the visual fine arts. A second difference is that music teachers are by no means unanimous on requirements in their field. There are some who favor requirements, but others who share with some teachers in the industrial and the fine arts the feeling that a better job can be done on a completely elective basis.

This lack of unanimity is reflected in the history of music requirements. The 1914 survey by the Bureau of Education showed that only 37.5 percent of the high schools with choruses made this activity a requirement.[40] Counts in 1923–1924 found music a senior high requirement in only 7 of the 15 cities studied.[41] The state of affairs on this matter, however, was somewhat different in the junior high school, especially in the seventh and eighth grades, with the National Survey of Secondary Education reporting in

[40] Earhart, *op. cit.*, p. 27.
[41] Counts, *op. cit.*, p. 109.

1934 that "the majority of schools now require all pupils in the first two junior high school grades to take general music—a course in which is implicit training in singing, music reading, theory and appreciation."[42] This tendency to require music in seventh and eighth grade has continued, but there has been little in the way of requirements in Grade 9 and above.

Required music in the junior high school has been advocated on the grounds of exploration. "Although not always required, it seems highly desirable that all pupils in the junior high should participate in general music classes. The reasons for this are fairly obvious. The junior high school is exploratory in nature; it offers pupils a wide variety of courses in an effort to acquaint them with their own abilities, interests, and talents."[43] This is probably a valid argument even though music programs are found in the elementary grades, for there are sometimes pronounced shifts of interests in this period of early adolescence. It might appear that the junior high is the worst time for required music because of voice changes, especially in boys. This contention has validity only to the extent that we assume the junior high program to be exclusively one in vocal music. Since the student's previous music work in the grades has been almost entirely vocal, there is good reason from the standpoint of exploring future interests why the junior high school course should be one in general music, with vocal work as only part of the total activity. The nature of such a course in the junior high school is indicated by the following suggested objectives.

1. Helping each child find some musical activity in which he can participate with satisfaction and some degree of mastery.

2. Building a repertoire of songs the class can sing with musical enjoyment.

3. Building a listening repertoire that is both immediately satisfactory and of lasting musical significance.

4. Developing musical learnings, including reading skills and familiarity with the materials of music-making (instruments of the or-

[42] National Survey of Secondary Education, Leonard V. Koos and Staff, *Summary,* Bulletin 1932, No. 17, Office of Education, United States Department of the Interior, 1934, p. 204.

[43] Frances M. Andrews and Joseph A. Leeder, *Guiding Junior-High-School Pupils in Music Experiences,* Prentice-Hall, Inc., 1953, p. 68.

chestra, voice types, technical information) through singing, rhythmic, and listening activities.

5. Correlating music with other areas of school activity, and with the child's out of school world.

While such objectives as these may be clear in the teacher's mind, in this form they are beyond the child's grasp and interest because they are objectives in the long-term view. . . . In clarifying objectives in the child's mind, pupil-teacher planning is an important aid.[44]

General music in the junior high school, then, can be and usually is a course with a variety of activities, characterized by flexibility and adaptation to the circumstances and talents of students. As such it parallels the junior high required course in general art. Few would question this requirement for one year at least. Whether or not it should include two years depends on the overall junior high school program and the extent of other requirements.

The requirement of general chorus has been a more controversial matter, particularly when it has been applied to the senior high school years. But general chorus is a controversial point whether required or not. It has long been out of favor with some music educators and has at various periods of our history declined in comparison with other music activities. But it has not been without its adherents, as indicated in the following quotations, the first one calling for general chorus as a requirement, the second favoring it but permitting substitution of other music courses.

The value of choral music is not at first apparent to high school students. The best way to make this value apparent is to have all the pupils take it. The very fact that choral music has sufficient value to make it required for all, stamps it at once as something worth while. When the pupils have worked in the chorus for a time, its value will speak for itself.[45]

Selective musical organizations will not bring about Walt Whitman's dream of "I Hear America Singing." With the limited possibilities for developed part-singing in the general assemblies, we should like to make a plea for the return of the general chorus. We would even go so far as to say that it should be required for the first year in

[44] *Ibid.,* p. 69.

[45] T. P. Giddings and Earl L. Baker, *High School Music Teaching,* published by Earl L. Baker, 1922, pp. 21–22.

the senior high school. If it is a four-year high school, we should expect students to participate during the first two years. The student might substitute some other form of musical activity, such as orchestra or band, a special choral organization, or one of the music classes.[46]

General chorus, however, has been far from extinct in high school music. In 1949 it enrolled nearly 700,000 students, or approximately 10 percent of all students in Grades 7 through 12.[47]

One argument in favor of requiring general chorus is that it makes possible widespread participation in a common activity. Practically any student regardless of his ability or training can take part in choral singing. Instrumental music demands specialized training and ability, as do the more selective vocal organizations such as glee clubs and *a capella* choirs. This argument commends itself to those who believe that participation is the only valid road to understanding and appreciation. It is similar to contentions in the visual fine arts.

As is true in the visual fine arts, much depends here on what is meant by participation. One writer suggests that music experience may consist of singing, playing, listening, and composing.[48] This approach resembles the definition of language arts as reading, writing, speaking, and listening. From this point of view, participation in music need not be regarded only as singing and playing. Listening can be a form of participation, perhaps to a greater extent than simply looking at pictures would be in the visual fine arts. Those who object to the passive participation of listening, however, could accept composing. An offhand reaction might be that composing is the most difficult and unattainable of all the musical arts, but one writer suggests that such is not the case.

Small children show a natural aptitude for singing their own tunes in order to give musical meaning to their daily experiences. The school must nurture this natural aptitude and make it a normal means of expression. It has been killed all too often by the time the pupil has reached the senior high school. A definite effort must be made to arouse

[46] Harry Robert Wilson, *Music in the High School,* Silver Burdett Company, 1941, pp. 134–135.

[47] "Offerings and Enrollments in High-School Subjects," Biennial Survey, *op. cit.,* table 2, p. 40.

[48] Wilson, *op. cit.,* pp. 39–42.

again the desire to express one's experiences in musical design. We *expect creative expression* in literature and in the visual arts of high school students. *Why not in music?* It is granted that the technical difficulties are not exactly comparable. But are they insurmountable? If composition is taught directly and not through a maze of harmonic and contrapuntal rules, we will nurture the creative process which is stressed in modern educational thought and provide opportunity for many students to develop natural aptitudes.[49]

At any rate, we may draw from this the conclusion that singing and playing are not the only possible kinds of participation in music. Consequently, required music in the senior high school need not, even if we accept completely the necessity of participation, be confined to vocal and instrumental performance.

Another possibility at the senior high school level, either required or elective, is an integrated or general music course as an upward extension of the general music course found in junior high schools, but with a somewhat different purpose. The junior high school general music course is exploratory in character, designed largely to sample a variety of activities in which interests might be awakened and abilities identified. As one advocate of general music at the senior high level puts it, "The primary aim of this general music course is to acquaint students with the wide and rich heritage of music literature."[50] Such a course would probably include singing, but would not be confined to it, any more than would its counterpart at the junior high school level.

Also available in many high schools are courses in music appreciation or history of music. These overlap to some extent the senior high school course in general music, but are more specialized and include less of the singing or playing type of direct participation. The term "music appreciation" has been somewhat disparaged, just as has art appreciation in the visual fine arts. Birge, for example, refers to the supervisors who "cling tenaciously to the idea that true appreciation comes from actual participation in the music, through singing or playing from the printed notation."[51] The

[49] *Ibid.,* p. 42.
[50] *Ibid.,* p. 59.
[51] Birge, *op. cit.,* p. 210.

idea of music appreciation through listening was advanced after the development of the phonograph; in fact, it was hardly possible before that invention. In 1913 the music committee of the Commission on the Reorganization of Secondary Education in its preliminary report gave music appreciation courses their endorsement, but one that was highly qualified.

Musical appreciation as a high-school study is particularly appropriate for third and fourth year students, as the mature quality of thought and feeling with which great music is invested is largely incomprehensible prior to these years to any but the exceptional boy or girl. A musical experience and a technical foundation that can be gained only in the first two years are also necessary; and two years of chorus practice, such as was outlined, or two years of harmony or orchestra ensemble are therefore recommended prior to taking this course. This recommendation is made notwithstanding the fact that classes of first and second year students in this branch have been known to members of the committee to make excellent progress.[52]

Viewed in these terms, the course in music appreciation would be more suitable for the student specializing in music throughout his high school career, rather than as a requirement, or even as an elective, for the general student. A different approach is suggested in the 1934 National Survey statement on the matter. "Also of vital importance in the musical training of the youth of the country are courses directed toward the large body of consumers of music, or classes in music appreciation, which train in discriminating listening."[53] Here the course is viewed as one for "the large body of consumers of music" rather than for the specialist. It is from this point of view that the music appreciation course has been developed in recent years. Since music appreciation courses are often organized chronologically or by epochs, there is no clear distinction between them and courses often called history of music.

If we are to have required music in the senior high school, the courses in music appreciation or history of music seem better for

---

[52] United States Bureau of Education Bulletin 1913, No. 41, *Preliminary Statements of Chairmen of Committees of the Commission of the National Education Association on the Reorganization of Secondary Education,* p. 71.

[53] National Survey of Secondary Education, *Ibid.*

the general student than do additional courses in singing or playing. The former provide the student with additional content and are thereby consistent with the general function of cultural transmission, the latter serve primarily for advanced development of skills. The performance-type courses should of course be included for students with particular music interests and abilities.

The best resolution of the senior high school situation would appear then to be one in which students might choose from a number of different kinds of courses to meet their music requirements. If music is to be required in the senior high school, however, the junior high school requirement should be one year rather than two years as it is now in many schools. The main question, however, is whether or not two years should be required in the sequence from Grade 7 through 12. It is difficult to make a case for requiring more music than art, especially in view of the fact that music usually gets more attention than art in the elementary school program. One argument might be that music is a more popular art than those in the visual fine arts field and is closer to the everyday life of the student in our communities. If this is the case, we might well expect more students to elect music anyway, thereby making the requirement less necessary.

A desirable high school program in music will include a variety of courses designed to stimulate interest on the part of the general student and to provide advanced or specialized study for those with more specialized talents and interests. Such a program is beyond the reach of very small high schools, but those with several hundred students or more should provide at least two years of general music, including some history and appreciation, plus orchestra, band, and chorus or choral organizations. Large high schools may provide what is practically a music major or a vocational music program. Here the problem is one of avoiding excessive specialization, which interferes with choices of subjects in other fields.

ADMINISTERING THE MUSIC CURRICULUM

The development of music in the high school has been accompanied by administrative dilemmas that perplex not only the music teacher but other teachers as well and are sometimes the source of minor or even major irritations. One of these is the scheduling dilemma. Scheduling is always a dilemma, but it seems to be an especially severe one in the case of music. Part of the reason for this is the diversification of the music program into specialized courses and activities, no one of which can usually be offered more than one period in the day. A student who wishes to be in *a capella* choir or in a special string organization finds, for example, that what he wants is offered in the fourth period. But the fourth period may be the only one into which he can fit some other course he must or would like to take. No matter in which period the harassed administrator places a specialized music course, he will encounter conflicts. These difficulties are, of course, particularly acute in small high schools, but they do not disappear even in very large ones.

Wilson has suggested several ways of mitigating these difficulties.[54] One is to have more periods in the school day. "Some administrators have experimented with a larger number of shorter periods per day to facilitate the programming of musical activities during school hours."[55] This permits more flexible scheduling, but is in conflict with a well-established trend toward longer periods, particularly to class periods 55 minutes or more in length and toward a school day with not more than six periods. The future, however, may bring a return to the eight-period day in many schools; recent discussion has favored at least a reconsideration of this question.

Another possibility suggested by Wilson is that of clearing certain periods entirely for music. "If the music director works in close harmony with the administrator, the latter is often willing to clear at least two periods each day to be devoted, for the most part, to selective musical organizations."[56] This device requires more periods in the school day. To clear two periods out of six for music leaves an impossible situation to be dealt with in the scheduling of classes in other subjects.

Wilson's third possibility is the staggered system. "In this system the class meets at a different hour each day of the week. In case of

[54] Wilson, *op. cit.*, pp. 290–291.
[55] *Ibid.*, p. 290.
[56] *Ibid.*

conflict the student attends the music class. In this way he misses his regular class only once in every five weeks."[57] Wilson recognizes that this is not a popular solution with other teachers, "who fail to see why their subjects should be interrupted by the music program."[58] We may take for granted that no teacher who values his subject will welcome interruptions by any program, whether it is music or something else. It is one thing to lose a class period entirely. This is undesirable, but endurable. But it is something else to have some of the students taken from a class while others remain. This both interrupts and disorganizes the continuity of instruction. Wilson concludes that the situation can be resolved only by agreements based on the welfare of students. "There is only one solution. When all teachers, both music and others, set themselves to study the needs of youth and are able to estimate the value of various activities, in reference to these needs, an agreement should be possible. Then teachers will not insist that their particular subjects be taught five days per week for the entire year with never an interruption. Music teachers may have to be satisfied with two or three rehearsals a week for the choir or band."[59]

In recent years high schools have developed the activity period, a scheduling device that can be used to incorporate various aspects of the foregoing suggestions. If an activity period at least as long as a regular class period is scheduled every day, it can be used by students for a variety of purposes, including band, orchestra, or singing groups. Some of the activity time is used for assemblies, home room activities, and the like, but this arrangement usually leaves three days a week for participation in other activities, such as music organizations. In this way no interruptions of other classes need take place. If it is considered undesirable to add an entire activity period to the school day, one might be set up on the staggered basis Wilson has proposed for music classes. This would interrupt every class at infrequent intervals, but as a scheduled interruption involving all the students in the class. In schools that do not face the problem of bus transportation, specialized music organizations

[57] *Ibid.*
[58] *Ibid.*
[59] *Ibid.,* p. 291.

might meet after school along with school clubs, interscholastic athletics, and the like. This makes it impossible for students to be in a music organization and in interscholastic athletics at the same time, and it cuts out of activities entirely those who must work after school. The activity period is a preferable arrangement in most cases. Music educators, however, may object to the use of the activity period on the grounds that their organizations should meet as regular classes rather than as extraclass activities.

A second dilemma in the music program has been that of credit. It is this problem that undoubtedly makes some music educators wary of having their activities regarded as extraclass. Birge has summarized the prejudices against granting credit for music as they stood around 1900. "The early stages of secondary school-music development were complicated with the question of crediting the work, especially of applied music. The long hallowed tradition that music is an accomplishment rather than a serious study made the principals of high schools cautious in dealing with the question at a time when the disciplinary value of the old curriculum was still the deciding factor in estimating credit values. During this period applied music was on trial, so to speak, and had to prove its worth."[60] Over the years a series of compromises have been worked out under which courses in music history or theory are granted full credit, but with band, orchestra, chorus, and the like usually carrying only minor or partial credits, such as one half or one fourth of full Carnegie units for a year's work. The rationalization of this practice has been that applied music organizations do not demand outside preparation or homework. This assumption is a difficult one to maintain, particularly for instrumental work. Even though the usual practice is not entirely satisfactory, it is from the music teacher's point of view better than no credit at all. There is no reason, however, why present credit arrangements cannot be used even though music organizations meet during an activity period. Some schools have done this, as well as granting credit for music organizations that meet before and after school. Credit, however, should not be mandatory as far as the individual student is concerned, since "frequently the limitations of the institution re-

[60] Birge, *op. cit.,* p. 163.

garding the number of credits which may be earned in a given period disqualify a student with a full program from adding a credit-bearing course, although he might have the time, energy, and desire to take an extracurricular non-credit course."[61]

One aspect of the general credit question is the more particularized one of granting school credit for outside music study with private teachers. The granting of such credit was inaugurated by the Chelsea, Massachusetts, High School in 1906 in relation to the comprehensive program recommended by the New England Conference on Secondary School Music. This question was widely debated in the following years, and in 1913, the music committee of the Commission on Reorganization of Secondary Education in its preliminary report made the following recommendation. "It is recommended that study of voice, piano, organ, violin, or any orchestral instrument, under special teachers outside of the school, when seriously undertaken and properly examined and certified, shall receive equal credit with any academic, five-hour study regularly pursued in high school, and shall be accepted in substitution for any regular school work that could command the same amount of credit."[62] Some schools still make this opportunity available to students, but difficulties in administering the plan have tended to restrict its use. It is always administratively difficult to grant school credit for work not under the direct supervision of the school. This may, however, be a way of introducing desirable flexibility in the school program and of providing students with educational opportunities the school itself cannot give. Perhaps the whole question should be studied again, not only in music but also in other fields.

In some school systems, further difficulties have been occasioned by public performances. Festivals, concerts, operettas, and the like demand intensive rehearsals that often exhaust both the student participants and the faculty members of the music department. Students may neglect their studies and lay the blame on the music rehearsals. In some cases extra rehearsals may be scheduled on school time, thereby taking students from other classes. Contests

---

[61] Dykema and Gehrkens, *op. cit.,* p. 24.
[62] United States Bureau of Education, *op. cit.,* pp. 73–74.

held away from the school may lead to more loss of school time. Music educators point out that such things do not need to happen and do not always happen. They may further contend that similar difficulties appear in programs of interscholastic athletics. Such disturbances of normal school life, however, are undesirable no matter which program is responsible for them, and we should reduce them whenever possible.

Public performance in music is usually defended on two grounds: (1) that it serves as desirable motivation for the students in music organizations; and (2) that it brings good music to the community. The first of these may be served by simpler and more informal performances given in the school itself, while the second seems superfluous in these days of recordings, television, and radio. Although public performances need not be the occasion for some of the irritations mentioned above, it is possible that some of the energy that goes into them might be better expended on other phases of the school music program. There will always be a place for festivals, contests, and the like, although on a somewhat less extensive and intensive basis, but they should not excessively disturb other parts of the school program.

CORRELATION OF MUSIC WITH OTHER SUBJECTS

The importance of music and its obvious relationships to many aspects of everyday living suggest the correlation of music with other subjects. Particular interest was centered on this matter in the 1930's, paralleling a similar development in the visual fine arts. There are points of obvious and valid correlation between music and such fields as history, English, foreign languages, speech and drama, and physical education. Music educators themselves have suggested that general history include the history of music. "The solution of the music history question is to incorporate it with general history. In this way students would get an idea of the history of music in its proper setting as a part of the development of the human race."[63] Similarly, the objective of music appreciation might be handled in history, foreign languages, and other appropriate fields. One difficulty is that teachers of these fields do not

[63] Giddings and Baker, *op. cit.,* p. 190.

always know music, or do not know it well enough to do the correlating themselves. This suggests the use of the music teacher as a consultant, either in the planning of units or in the classroom teaching or both, a practice long followed in many elementary schools. Although such arrangements are less easy to carry out in the conventional high school schedule, they need not be regarded as impossible.

Some schools have experimented with integrated fine arts courses, including music, painting, speech, drama, dance, and the like. If such courses can be worked out, they may resolve in part the difficulties involved in establishing general requirements in the fine arts taken as a whole. A one-year requirement of an integrated fine arts course could be more easily absorbed than a series of one-year requirements in a number of fine arts subjects. Under such an arrangement, however, none of the fine arts would have as much time as might be desirable. Some teachers might feel that a little time is less desirable than no time at all. This would not be true, however, if students had previously studied some of the fields in the elementary grades and in the junior high school.

Any attempt to bring the fine arts to a stronger position in our curricula is a laudable one for the individual development of the student. Not all proposals are feasible in view of our present circumstances. Some may be undesirable in the light of desirable balance between these and other parts of our high school programs. But all should receive careful study and consideration. The danger of neglect is less in the case of music than in the other arts. Music has long been an essential part of the culture of our American communities. Our school publics will see that it maintains its established place in the curriculum. Music educators, however, have the responsibility of seeking and welcoming all legitimate means of relating their fields to the other arts. Through this, they will be helping all the arts make fuller and richer contributions to our high school students, both now and in their lives as adults.

Bibliography

Andrews, Frances M., and Leeder, Joseph A., *Guiding Junior-High-School Pupils in Music Experiences,* Prentice-Hall, Inc., 1953.

Birge, Edward Bailey, *History of Public School Music in the United States,* Oliver Ditson Company, 1928.

Dykema, Peter W., and Gehrkens, Karl W., *The Teaching and Administration of High School Music,* C. C. Birchard and Company, 1941.

Earhart, Will, *Music in the Public Schools,* U.S. Bureau of Education Bulletin 1914, No. 33.

Giddings, T. P., and Baker, Earl L., *High School Music Teaching,* Earl L. Baker, 1922.

International Conference on the Role and Place of Music in the Education of Youth and Adults, Brussels, 29 June to 9 July, 1953, *Music in Education,* UNESCO, 1955.

Mursell, James L., *Human Values in Music Education,* Silver, Burdett and Company, 1934.

Mursell, James L., *Music in American Schools,* Silver Burdett Company, 1943.

National Society for the Study of Education, Fifty-seventh Yearbook, pt. 1, *Basic Concepts in Music Education,* The Society, 1958.

Normann, Theodore F., *Instrumental Music in the Public Schools,* Oliver Ditson Company, 1941.

Sur, William Raymond, and Schuller, Charles Francis, *Music Education for Teen-Agers,* Harper & Brothers, 1958.

Wilson, Harry Robert, *Music in the High School,* Silver Burdett Company, 1941.

CHAPTER 18

••

Business Education

In 1902 a writer on secondary schooling reported the following observations on the instructional field then called commercial, but now known as business education.

For several generations, book-keeping and other subjects of this class have found a place, rather uncertain and variable, to be sure, in the courses of study of secondary schools. In the high schools and in many private schools, regular commercial courses have been organized. For the most part, however, such courses have been less exacting than the main courses of the schools in which they have been offered, and too often they have been the last resort of lazy or incompetent students. Not infrequently, too, they have been short courses, only one or two years in length. There have been honorable exceptions, but on the whole these commercial courses have proved unsatisfactory.[1]

A half century later, this field had moved from its "uncertain and variable" position to become from the standpoint of enrollments one of the most thriving and commanding in the high school program. Both the diversity and the popularity of business education are shown in the following percentages of all high school students in Grades 9 through 12 who were enrolled in the various business subjects in 1948–1949.[2]

[1] Elmer Ellsworth Brown, *The Making of Our Middle Schools,* Longmans, Green, and Company, 1902, p. 404.

[2] "Offerings and Enrollments in High-School Subjects," *Biennial Survey of Education in the United States, 1948–1950,* Federal Security Agency, Office of Education, 1951, table 7, p. 108.

	Percentage
General business training	5.2
Business arithmetic	4.6
Bookkeeping	8.7
Typewriting	22.5
Shorthand	7.8
Business law	2.4
Business English	1.0
Economic geography	1.7
Office practice	2.0
Retailing	0.5
Salesmanship and advertising	1.0
Coöperative store training	0.4
Coöperative office training	0.3

Although these percentage figures total 58.1, this does not mean that 58.1 percent of all high school students were taking business subjects; some students undoubtedly were enrolled in two or more business subjects at a time.

Such enrollments do not necessarily imply that the business subjects hold special attractions for lazy and incompetent students. While some schools in the past have used business education as a haven of refuge for the incompetent, this has not reflected the desires of business education teachers. Fortunately such practices are not as prevalent as was once the case. The popularity of business subjects reflects rather their usefulness both for vocational and other activities of everyday life.

DEVELOPMENT OF THE BUSINESS SUBJECTS

Although business education had its greatest expansion in public high schools after 1900, it was by no means a newcomer to the curriculum at that time. Bookkeeping had been introduced in the early academies. The Massachusetts high school law of 1827 stipulated that bookkeeping be one of the subjects offered. In spite of this early and promising beginning, bookkeeping did not come forward rapidly or to any great extent in most nineteenth-century high schools. One possible reason for its slow development was the rise of private business or commercial schools. "The 'business-college' age in American education began about 1827, at which time 'Benjamin F. Foster's Commercial School' was opened in

Boston."[3] Private commercial schools offered direct routes to job competence and success and became highly popular institutions. The subjects taught were bookkeeping, penmanship, commercial arithmetic, and business law.[4]

The Civil War brought in a period of business expansion opening up thousands of jobs for those who had some business skills. It was in the early 1870's that the typewriter was developed as a practical office tool, although it did not gain wide acceptance until the 1890's.

Business education in the schools developed with the perfection of the typewriter in the early 1870's. Typewriting mechanisms had been planned in England as early as 1714 but had not been successful. In the nineteenth century many persons invented typewriting devices, some of which enabled the typist to write almost as rapidly as he could in longhand. The machines were gradually improved, but remained cumbersome until Christopher Sholes and two associates became interested in the possibilities of the typewriter. They completed their first model in 1867 and by 1873 had further improved it, so that it was a proficient aid in business offices.[5]

This opened a whole new field of training, that of stenography, combining typing and the previously invented device of shorthand writing. These developments encouraged many women to enter business employment and created a new and greatly expanded demand for business training.

This new demand was at first absorbed largely by the existing private business schools. By the 1880's, however, business subjects began to pick up in public schools as well. At first this was represented by short programs or curriculums, one or two years in length, but these began to disappear in the following decade. "The establishment of higher commercial schools in colleges and universities,

[3] Jessie Graham, *The Evolution of Business Education in the United States and Its Implications for Business-Teacher Education.* Southern California Education Monographs, 1933–1934 series, No. 2, University of Southern California Press, 1933, p. 24.

[4] *Ibid.*

[5] Herbert A. Tonne, *Principles of Business Education,* Gregg Publishing Division, McGraw-Hill Book Company, Inc., 1957, p. 22.

and the influence of commercial schools of a more liberal scholastic character in European countries led, in the late nineties, to a reorganization of secondary commercial curriculums. From that time forward new curriculums were established, equal in extent to other secondary-school curriculums, and offering an educational content not possible in the earlier schemes. Many of the earlier short curriculums were lengthened."[6] In some cities, however, two-year programs survived well into the middle 1920's.

Those who favored business education interpreted this expansion as response to public demand. Such contentions have been advanced for various school subjects and activities, but it is not always clear that the demands come from the public. In the case of commercial education, the public demand was probably real enough. People who wanted this kind of training for their children were bound to ask why they had to pay for it in a private school when they were already paying taxes for public schools.

The period between 1905 and 1920 was one of intensive emphasis on the need for vocational education. It was the favorite theme of convention orators, national committees, and others who made public pronouncements. True, most of the orations and pronouncements centered on industrial education, but the business education field gained some support as well, even though it did not get a direct share of the federal funds made available through the Smith-Hughes Act.[7] A survey reported in 1915 showed astonishingly high percentages of students enrolled in commercial courses of 16 city school systems. In Boston, the home of the classical tradition, half the students were so enrolled, with correspond-

[6] Commission on the Reorganization of Secondary Education of the National Education Association, Committee on Business Education, *Business Education in Secondary Schools,* Department of the Interior, Bureau of Education, 1919, p. 12.

[7] "The Smith-Hughes Act provided funds for all kinds of office training on a part-time basis in continuation schools. These funds are allocated through the vocational educational services of the various state departments of education. Practically, however, very little of this money was ever made available for commercial education, as the demands from the other fields of vocational education were so great that usually nothing was left for part-time commercial education. The passage of the George-Deen Act in 1937 gave a special allotment of $1,200,000 to distributive education. The George-Barden Bill of 1946 doubled this sum." Tonne, *op. cit.,* p. 34.

ing fractions of approximately one third in San Francisco and Philadelphia and one fourth in Pittsburgh and Detroit.[8] Special high schools of commerce had been established in New York, Boston, Cleveland, San Francisco, and Springfield, Massachusetts.[9] The investigator who reported these findings commented on them as reflections of the spirit of the times. "In the present order of society, the career motive is bound to be a dominant incentive to boys and girls in high schools. Our new environment compels this situation. The influence of the press, the hum of the streets, the multiplication of inventions, the increase of machinery, the stir and bustle of life in the city and in the country, all serve to turn the thoughts of our boys and girls toward the practical activities which are the genius of our age. The academic quietness of school halls cannot and should not resist these influences."[10] Four years later, in 1919, the Committee on Business Education of the N.E.A. Commission on Reorganization of Secondary Education enthusiastically reported figures not just on 16 cities, but for the country as a whole. "From the most reliable data available it appears that about half a million young people at present are pursuing secondary commercial studies in the United States. From the same sources, it appears that more than one-fourth of all pupils attending the secondary schools are taking such studies. Moreover, during the past 15 years the number of pupils pursuing secondary commercial education has grown out of all proportion to the increase of population or to the total increase in attendance in secondary schools."[11]

The fact that a committee on business education had been established as part of the Commission on the Reorganization of Secondary Education symbolized the increasing status and importance of the field. It was not, however, the first national committee on the matter, two previous ones sponsored by the N.E.A. having served briefly in 1903 and 1915. The 1903 committee had recommended

---

[8] F. V. Thompson, *Commercial Education in Public Secondary Schools,* World Book Company, 1915, table on pp. 4–6.

[9] *Ibid.,* p. 7.

[10] *Ibid.,* p. 38.

[11] Commission on the Reorganization of Secondary Education of the N.E.A., Committee on Business Education, *op. cit.,* p. 11.

business subjects as electives, while the one in 1915 had proposed curricula or tracks for stenography and bookkeeping.[12]

By 1919, further development in the field was apparently viewed in part at least in terms of these two tracks, plus a third one in "retail selling and store service."[13] In setting the stage for this three-track recommendation, the 1919 committee advanced the idea that business education was becoming too complex and diversified for containment within the bookkeeping and stenography curricula alone.

Commercial education should have a much wider purpose than the training of stenographers and bookkeepers. Already the broadened commercial education has addressed itself to the task of training for service in the community, for participation in social life, and for knowledge of, and ability to adapt one's self to, business as a whole. Such subjects as economics, business organization, advertising, salesmanship, and store practice are relatively new, and yet in their entirety they make a new purpose of business education comparable with, if not more important than, stenography or bookkeeping.[14]

The committee here established a theme that has repeatedly appeared in the literature of business education ever since: that of the growing complexity and diversification of business itself and the accompanying demand for change and expansion in the programs of the schools.

Observers of high school programs in the 1920's continued to note with astonishment and usually with approval the further expansion of the business field, both in terms of course offerings and percentages of students enrolled. Counts reported, "During the history of secondary education few subjects have risen to a position of prominence in the curriculum as rapidly as have the commercial branches."[15] He also pointed out, "The commercial curriculum is the only one of the many different vocational curricula in-

[12] Graham, *op. cit.*, p. 27.

[13] Commission on the Reorganization of Secondary Education of the N.E.A., Committee on Business Education, *op. cit.*, pp. 16–18.

[14] *Ibid.*, p. 15.

[15] George S. Counts, *The Senior High School Curriculum,* The University of Chicago, 1926, p. 92.

troduced into the high school which may be said to have thrived."[16] It should be noted again that business education expanded and developed without the help of the federal funds available to other vocational fields.

Counts attributed the increase in the business field to "the growth of a complex commercial civilization" and to "the changing status of woman, which has cut many bonds holding her in the home."[17] While these are important factors, they do not necessarily explain the phenomenon of business education. Our country also sustained much growth as a complex industrial civilization, and for some time now women have been taking jobs in factories. But there has been no corresponding development of vocational schooling for industrial jobs. One difference is that business provides many jobs for which the school can offer some specific training, whereas many industrial jobs require little training in advance of the job itself. Moreover, students who follow business programs in the schools proceed directly to jobs without having to meet formal apprenticeship requirements.

Counts found that 12.4 percent of the total recitation time in the 15 cities he surveyed in 1923–1924 was devoted to the business subjects, a figure second only to that for English.[18] He noted also the "tendency to differentiate the commercial program into several curriculums."[19] This was perhaps a response to the recommendations made by national committees both in 1915 and in 1919. The third track recommended by the 1919 committee was beginning to appear under various titles, such as salesmanship, retail distribution, and the like. Six subjects, bookkeeping, typewriting, stenography, commercial law, commercial arithmetic, and commercial geography, accounted for 90 percent of the total recitation time in the business field, with salesmanship, accounting, office practice, spelling, and penmanship taking up most of the remaining 10 percent.[20]

At the end of the 1920's, a bulletin of the U.S. Bureau of Education reported that an increase of 72 percent in business enroll-

16 *Ibid.*
17 *Ibid.*
18 *Ibid.*
19 *Ibid.*, p. 93.
20 *Ibid.*

ment had taken place between 1922 and 1928. It stated also that 17 percent of all public high school students were in the designated commercial tracks or curriculums.[21] This meant that nearly one student in five was not only taking an occasional business subject, but was taking a sequence of such subjects and presumably for vocational purposes. The Bureau of Education report further called attention to the development of general business training at the expense of bookkeeping, shorthand, spelling, penmanship, and commercial arithmetic in the junior high school grades.[22]

In spite of the depression, business enrollments continued to increase between 1928 and 1934. The 1928 survey showed combined enrollments in business subjects coming to 54.3 percent of all high school students in grades 9 through 12. By 1934, the last survey made prior to that of 1949, the corresponding figure was 57.3 percent. This was only a small increase in contrast with those of earlier periods, but it was a significant one in the face of adverse business conditions and an almost catastrophic decline in opportunities for high school graduates to secure business jobs. There was, of course, corresponding unemployment in other fields as well; many high school students probably still considered business training as their best chance.

Having survived the depression, the business education field held its own during World War II and subsequent years, with enrollments in the business subjects accounting (see p. 444) for 58.1 percent of all high school students in Grades 9 through 12 in the 1948–1949 survey. By that year, three business subjects appeared not included in the previous surveys, namely coöperative office training, coöperative store training, and retailing. Combined enrollments in these three new categories, however, came to only 65,638 students, or 1.2 percent of all enrolled in the high schools.[23] The appearance of retailing as a new subject is somewhat confusing, since its presence had been noted in studies going back to the 1920's, but the U.S. Office of Education survey statistics had ap-

---

[21] J. O. Malott, *Commercial Education 1926–1928,* Department of the Interior, Bureau of Education Bulletin 1929, No. 26, p. 2.

[22] *Ibid.,* p. 17.

[23] "Offerings and Enrollments in High-School Subjects," *Biennial Survey, op. cit.,* table 7, p. 108.

parently included it under the category of salesmanship and advertising.

NATURE AND OBJECTIVES OF BUSINESS EDUCATION

It may be said, then, that the business education field reached a point of stability as far as enrollments were concerned by the end of the 1920's. Much of the curricular effort since that time has been directed not to the matter of increasing enrollments but to a continued analysis of what the field is, what it should accomplish, and what its relationships should be to the rest of the high school program. Business educators themselves have taken the lead in the identification and study of these issues, with relatively little participation by high school teachers generally or by general workers in the secondary school curriculum.

In spite of the strong response that some business educators today make against the term "commercial education," terminology has never been a serious issue. The older term, "commercial education," was gradually and almost imperceptibly replaced by the one in favor today. In 1919 both terms apparently were accepted. The committee of the Reorganization of Secondary Education was called the committee on business education, the title of its report was *Business Education,* but the writers of the report used the term "commercial education" throughout. Those who work in the field regard "business education" as a broader term that symbolizes the movement away from earlier and more restricted ideas of what the field includes.

The major issue of what the field is, however, centers on its specifically vocational as compared and contrasted with its more general education functions. This is somewhat analogous to the controversy in physical education between those in favor of education of the physical and those who contend for education through the physical, although the controversy in business education has not been nearly as pronounced as in physical education. It has nonetheless been widely discussed. One writer in 1957 commented on it as follows. "These diverse and often contradictory objectives tended, as already indicated, to obscure the very meaning of business education. So complete was the confusion that leaders in the field were often not aware that they had diverse meanings in mind when they spoke of business education."[24]

Graham's survey of aims of business education in the published literature of the period before 1919 indicates that both kinds of objectives, specific and general, had been prevalent for a long period of time. Specific vocational objectives, however, did appear to a greater extent than those of a more general character, such as mental discipline, citizenship, and the like.[25] According to the assistant superintendent of schools in Boston, writing in 1915, the commercial field had displayed more restraint than the manual arts field along these lines, a tendency he notes with evident approval.

In justice it ought to be said that commercial education has never lapsed into the dissociated-from-life attitude that has been so generally characteristic of manual training. Commercial education has never made the extravagant claims of general culture or of psychological influence in the way of mental discipline, by which the adherents of manual training have endeavored to maintain their cause. Commercial education, within the limits of a restricted vision, has always sought to keep to its objective field. It has aimed to prepare for a job, to enable the individual pursuing the work to fit into economic society and to benefit himself by meeting an evident demand for his talent.[26]

The same writer went on, however, to chide the business education field for its narrowness even in light of its professed objective. "Commercial education, however, must be criticised for seeing its field narrowly, for failing to recognize the newer demands which a rapidly expanding business world is forced to make, and for ignoring the complexities of modern commerce, which have created a whole new array of commercial functions."[27]

[24] Tonne, *op. cit.,* p. 13.
[25] Graham, *op. cit.,* table I, pp. 42–43. Some of the objectives in the list are not classifiable in the categories of specific and general, for example, that of keeping pupils in school. The specific expressions came to 52.4 percent of the total. These included preparing pupils for specific office positions, providing general education to prepare young people to enter business pursuits, to prepare for university work in commerce and the like. The more general expressions came to 27.4 percent of the total. These included adapting business education to social and civic life, mental discipline, fulfilling the general objectives of all secondary education, and providing for citizenship in a democratic society.
[26] Thompson, *op. cit.,* pp. 12–13.
[27] *Ibid.*

Although the statement of the Cardinal Principles in 1918 by the Commission on Reorganization of Secondary Education might have served as an invitation to break loose from the vocational function, the 1919 business education committee refused to be tempted. In the major section of its report devoted to purposes, the committee dealt with four needs: (1) the training of stenographers; (2) the training of bookkeepers and clerks; (3) "training for secretarial work of those who have had a broader fundamental education and who wish to take more responsible positions than to be merely stenographers;" and (4) "the demand for salesmen."[28] Perhaps the committee's report came too close to the one on the Cardinal Principles to be much influenced by it. It seems reasonable to assume the committee would have been more influenced by long-term viewpoints and expressions in the business field itself.

Throughout the 1920's, however, the idea represented by the Cardinal Principles began to make itself felt. Business educators did not attempt as did those in some other fields to claim applications of their field to all seven objectives, but they did begin to put more emphasis on the matter of citizenship, particularly those aspects related to economics. The U.S. Bureau of Education report in 1929 characterized this tendency as follows. "Another objective that has been emphasized during the biennium pertains to the fact that business education is fundamentally a program of economic education. Junior business education in the junior high schools and courses in economics, commercial geography, other marginal social sciences and business subjects in the high schools and colleges represent an endeavor to provide general business education. This objective pertains to the broad social and economic values that are coextensive with all human endeavor."[29] Since that time, much of the literature in business education has called attention to these broader social and economic objectives, including those of consumer education. They have been, of course, particularly emphasized in connection with courses in general business and by those who seek to make general business a constant or graduation

[28] Commission on the Reorganization of Secondary Education of the National Education Association, Committee on Business Education, *op. cit.*, p. 14.

[29] Malott, *op. cit.*, p. 5.

requirement. There has also been some tendency to point out objectives or values related to personality development, although these may be interpreted as part of the vocational function, especially in connection with sales and distributive programs.

Some business educators, on the other hand, have tried to hold to more specific or unique objectives for their field.

Before any satisfactory business curriculum can be organized, possible specific objectives of such a curriculum must be carefully canvassed and those chosen defined in terms which clearly differentiate them from the common objectives of the whole program of which the business curriculum is a part. While every curriculum offered in a secondary school should take cognizance of the common aims of that school, the maker of a business curriculum must have in mind a unique objective which is in itself at least a partial justification for such a curriculum. Too many business educators are prone to rest the case for their curricula on the contention that they may be relied upon to achieve the general objectives of secondary education, and thus put their offerings on a purely competitive basis instead of on a functional basis which is peculiarly their own. Thus no end of difficulty is encountered by those who would appraise the results of teaching commercial subjects in terms of established objectives peculiar to those subjects. No curriculum can possess all the virtues of a sound secondary education. Each should function in such manner as to entitle it to special consideration of some group of pupils whose proper vocational objectives are in harmony with the distinguishing aims.[30]

This is for the most part a commendable position, especially as it may serve to counteract tendencies in other fields to serve all the possible objectives of secondary schools. Those business educators who have sought to go beyond strictly vocational objectives, however, have not sought to claim all possible objectives, but have centered their attention largely on economic understanding. Whether or not this is a legitimate extension depends on the extent to which the business field has substantial content to offer in relation to it.

The question again becomes one of defining an instructional

[30] Frederick C. Nichols, "A Philosophy of the Business Curriculum," National Commercial Teachers Federation, Sixth Yearbook, *The Business Curriculum,* The Federation, 1940, pp. 15–16.

field as an essential aspect of the human heritage of knowledge and skills. There is little doubt about this in business education as far as skills are concerned. In addition, however, the business field represents a body of knowledge, both historical and contemporary, related to the organization and conduct of economic affairs. Money, banking, credit, corporate organization, international trade, government finance, insurance, investment—these are items of substantial knowledge that have played large and important roles in the historical past and in current affairs. "There is abundant evidence that our citizens lack understandings in practical economics. One has only to talk to friends or to observe them daily to discover their woeful lack of knowledge of simple everyday business procedures and understandings. These people, it should be remembered, are products of our educational system."[31] Such materials as these are of practical import and in addition possess considerable interest value for the general student. They are usually taught in such courses as general business, economic geography, and the like, which are referred to in the literature as social-business subjects. We may well agree that "Social-business subjects, of course, have a place in the secondary school; although these subjects have, in some measure, been hampered by a confusion of purposes."[32]

Much of this content, however, overlaps potential content in social studies. Some of it undoubtedly can be and is taught in general history. Other parts of it appear in twelfth-grade problems-of-democracy courses, and a great deal appears in economics. Since no field represents a completely sealed-off compartment, there will necessarily be some instances of subject matter common to two or more fields. The resolution of this is a matter of practical adjustment to the circumstances of particular schools. Economic content in history courses should reinforce business courses by providing historical orientation in relation to other aspects of life. Most schools do not offer separate economics courses in social studies de-

[31] William M. Polishook and Herbert A. Tonne, "General Business Education for Secondary Schools," The American Business Education Yearbook, vol. 6, *General Business Education,* published jointly by The National Business Teachers' Association and The Eastern Business Teachers' Association, 1949, Paul Salsgiver (ed.), pp. 12–13.

[32] Tonne, *op. cit.,* p. 15.

partments, and the amount of economics material in twelfth-grade problems courses does not overlap substantially with those in general business. Whether economic geography should be in the social studies or in the business department is more a matter of administrative arrangements than of fundamental curricular considerations. In general, overlapping between social studies and business courses does not present serious problems.

There has been and still is some undesirable overlapping between business education and other fields besides social studies. General mathematics often includes topics such as taxation, investments, insurance, and the like. This overlapping will undoubtedly be reduced as the nature and function of general mathematics become clarified. Some administrative confusion develops in connection with courses called business English, but there is a good deal of doubt about having business English in the first place. The same doubt applies to the desirability of business arithmetic, a course that enrolled 249,690 students, or 4.6 percent of all high school students in Grades 9 through 12, in the 1948–1949 survey.

Another fact that makes it difficult to regard business education as purely vocational is the presence of students who take courses in business skills for general purposes. This has long been the case, and it is a practice that has much to justify it. The large increase in enrollments in typewriting, from 16.7 percent of all students in 1934 to 22.5 percent in 1948–1949, reflected the desire of students to learn typing for personal use. Typewriting is a practical course for all students and especially for those who plan to go to college. The same can be said of shorthand, although the need there is not so great. A good deal has been said about the application of bookkeeping to personal and family finance. It is doubtful that a year's work in bookkeeping for the general student can be justified on this basis. The case for typing and shorthand is so clear, however, that business departments will undoubtedly continue to serve many non-vocational students in these two subjects.

Although the functions of business education are vocational to a large extent, some provision can legitimately be made for general education functions as well, particularly in economic understanding and in some personal-use skills. This suggests the possibility of including some business subjects among the constants. Business educators, on the whole, have displayed reticence and restraint on this matter, but arguments for required general business have appeared in the literature.

The course which has been developed in the last decade, called elementary business training, everyday business, or introduction to business, is an admirable example of the possibilities in this field. Its purpose is to give an understanding of what business is, how it functions, and how it serves both the individual and the society as a whole. This course may readily be made a unit in the core-curriculum. Certainly business is at least as important a phase of present life as science. The problems of business are possibly even more important as far as human progress is concerned. Why not then give every pupil a non-technical understanding of the place of business in contemporary life, even as we give a course in general science to develop a realization of the contribution of science in our civilization.[33]

The amount of time suggested for required business, however, is usually moderate. "Realism dictates that the maximum amount of time available for general business education for *all* pupils in the secondary school cannot exceed one year. Under our present curricular organization, therefore, general business education for all must be telescoped into one full-year course or two single-semester courses. The best time to teach general business education for all is during the junior-high-school period, preferably in the ninth grade."[34] It does not seem desirable, however, to require the ninth-grade general business course of all students. As noted before, the general business course is not the only one in the high school program that provides material in economics. So far as the general student is concerned, we can depend on the economic understandings developed in social studies. The student preparing for a business career should have the more intensive study provided by

[33] Herbert A. Tonne, "The Senior High School Business Curriculum," National Commercial Teachers Federation, Sixth Yearbook, *The Business Curriculum,* The Federation, 1940, p. 77.

[34] James Gemmell, "Contributions of General Business Education to Occupational Business Education," The American Business Education Yearbook, vol. 6, *General Business Education,* published jointly by The National Business Teachers' Association and The Eastern Business Teachers' Association, 1949, Paul Salsgiver (ed.), p. 30.

business education courses, including the one in general business.

Another possibility is the eighth-grade course called general business. Some have advocated this course for its exploratory or guidance character, a point of view consistent with the older exploratory function of the junior high school program as a whole. Since it is manifestly impossible to require one-semester courses in all the possible areas that students should explore, it is difficult to justify a requirement for all students in this area.

THE VOCATIONAL FUNCTION OF BUSINESS EDUCATION

The major function of business courses remains accordingly that of preparing students for business careers. This is a vocational function, but it is a broad one. Students who take business courses are not limited to a narrow range of possible occupations. The general field of business is highly diversified and provides opportunities for many kinds of talents. Neither should the vocational function be regarded as unworthy or inferior. It is in fact a most important function of schooling, and one not always easy to put into practice. Flexibility of entrance into business occupations combined with the amount of substantial content and skill instruction that can be given in preparation for them makes business education a field almost uniquely suited to the vocational function at the high school level.

How to discharge this vocational function effectively is a question, therefore, that has evoked a good deal of writing and discussion in the business field. This general question breaks down into a series of related issues, such as the desirability of special high schools of commerce, curricular patterns in high schools of various sizes, the kinds of business jobs toward which high school training should be directed, and the number and kinds of specific business courses that should be required of students in business curriculums or tracks.

The desirability of high schools of commerce is part of the larger and long-standing debate about comprehensive and specialized high schools. High schools of commerce developed between 1905 and 1920, a period of intensive advocacy of schools for specialized vocational purposes. Advocates of such schools recognized that only large cities could maintain them, but this was about the limit of their concession to schools of the comprehensive type. One writer, for example, accepted the inevitability of comprehensive high schools, but sought to make the business program almost a separate school within a school. He suggested that each general high school have four subschools, one for college preparation, one for technical and industrial training for boys, one for practical and household arts for girls, and one or two for commercial training, depending on whether the latter program was coeducational or not.[35] Even the non-business subjects were to be taught with reference to the business objectives. "Whenever the size of the school permits, the sub-school should be allowed and encouraged to concentrate upon the appropriate function assigned. The subjects in each program of study, while often designated by the same name, such as English, mathematics, foreign languages, should be taught from the special points of view; or, more familiarly stated, the English, mathematics, and foreign languages should be the kind most useful and fitting to the specific end sought. In this way the career motive will be a continuous incentive."[36] This desire for such a high degree of separation as this within the general high school never really took hold. And the desire for special high schools of commerce did not maintain itself during the 1920's. By the end of the 1930's there were "fewer than twenty such schools."[37] Opinion in secondary schooling had shifted to favor the comprehensive school. Even schools that retained their names as high schools of commerce no longer had their original specialized character. "As far as could be determined all commercial high schools offer college preparatory work. Indeed, an examination of the curricula of ten such high schools reveals in certain instances no differences in the curricula of commercial high schools and general cosmopolitan high schools."[38] The more recent tendency in some metropolitan centers to favor specialized high schools may bring about a dif-

[35] Thompson, *op. cit.,* p. 41.
[36] *Ibid.*
[37] T. Anne Cochran, "Curricula of High Schools of Commerce," National Commercial Teachers Federation, Sixth Yearbook, *The Business Curriculum,* The Federation, 1940, p. 247.
[38] *Ibid.*

ferent state of affairs in the future. Up to this point, however, interest in specialized high schools has emphasized those for vocational industrial training, and there is little indication of a revival of the high school of commerce.

Vocational business training accordingly has been organized around curriculums or tracks in general high schools, but this does not mean subschools such as were advocated by Thompson in 1915. It does mean a definite set of courses for the student enrolled in the track. Business educators generally prefer several such tracks, each leading to a particular set or group of business jobs, but recognize this can be done only in larger high schools, just as the advocates of high schools of commerce had earlier granted the impracticability of such schools in any but the largest cities.

Smaller high schools therefore usually offer business subjects as electives, an arrangement known as the elective-sequence curriculum pattern. "The 'elective-sequence curriculum' is simply the business curriculum offered in a majority of the American high schools: there is no specific curriculum, only a good selection of business subjects, selected by the students through the guidance of the business teachers and the home room advisers."[39] Such schools usually offer general business, typewriting, and bookkeeping.[40] According to one observer, however, even a school with one business teacher might diversify this program by offering one instead of two years of typewriting and adding work in clerical practice and salesmanship.[41] Whether or not shorthand should be offered in small schools depends on the nature of the job market in the community and region.[42]

As more teachers are added to the business education staff, a school may begin to offer diversified or specialized curriculums. Large high schools may have as many as four such curricula, labeled accounting and bookkeeping, stenographic, clerical train-

---

[39] Reed Davis, "The Elective-sequence Curriculum Pattern," American Business Education, Yearbook, vol. 13, *Curriculum Patterns in Business Education*, The Eastern Business Teachers' Association and The National Business Teachers' Association, 1956, p. 166.

[40] *Ibid.*

[41] *Ibid.*, p. 169.

[42] *Ibid.*, p. 170.

ing or practice, and distributive education. The first two are the more traditional, the latter two the more recent or modern.

Of the two traditional curriculums the one in stenography has been well accepted and has a secure place in most large high schools. Stenography tracks usually include two years of shorthand, two years of typewriting, and a year of secretarial practice, with some schools combining the second years of shorthand and typing with secretarial practice in the twelfth grade. In addition students in this track often take general business and business law and sometimes include a year of bookkeeping.

Bookkeeping, on the other hand, has been criticized as unrealistic in relation to actual job opportunities in the business world. This line of criticism goes back at least as far as the 1919 report of the committee on business education. "The young man who enters business as a bookkeeper is more likely to find himself in a 'blind alley' than most educators realize. In a survey of the needs in commercial education made in one of the larger cities a majority of the large concerns canvassed stated that 'bookkeepers do not even need to know double-entry bookkeeping,' as modern record systems are so highly sectionalized. This brings the trained 'bookkeeper' into competition with the untrained workman and the salaries paid for such work show the result of this competition."[43] Nevertheless the committee advocated the retention of bookkeeping on the grounds of its contribution to general business knowledge and to certain desirable character traits.[44] Nearly four decades later, in 1957, Tonne drew attention to the bookkeeping situation along lines similar to those used by the committee. "Today, however, the general bookkeeper has disappeared from most business offices. His place has been taken by the auditor and accountant, who are required to have professional knowledge; by numerous ledger clerks, who need specialized instruction based on duties performed; and by bookkeeping-machine operators, whose numbers have increased rapidly. It must be realized that many small businesses never did, and do not now, keep complete sets of books."[45] He con-

---

[43] Commission on the Reorganization of Secondary Education of the N.E.A., Committee on Business Education, *op. cit.*, pp. 41–42.

[44] *Ibid.*, p. 42.

[45] Herbert A. Tonne, *Principles of Business Education, op. cit.*, p. 283.

cluded that "only a small proportion of the boys and girls receiving bookkeeping instruction will ever be able to use their knowledge vocationally as bookkeepers."[46] The realization of this has undoubtedly played considerable part in the directing of bookkeeping instruction toward general education objectives, such as personal finance, budgeting, and the like. Such objectives could be related to a year's study of bookkeeping, but hardly to a whole track or curriculum. Nevertheless such tracks have persisted in our school programs. They usually include two years of bookkeeping, supplemented by a number of other business subjects, such as typing, office practice, business law, and the like. Actually, the bookkeeping curriculum is in most cases a general business curriculum with an additional year of bookkeeping.

Most of the enthusiasm in the literature of business education over a considerable period of time has been devoted to the relatively modern programs or curriculums in salesmanship and in clerical practice. Salesmanship courses were introduced in the Boston High School of Commerce in 1906.[47] The 1919 committee recommended the widespread development of curriculums in retail selling and store service.[48] Counts found such curriculums or tracks in several of the 15 cities he surveyed in 1926.[49] Demand for further expansion was voiced in the U.S. Bureau of Education report in 1929.

No phase of commercial education has greater opportunity for expansion and has been retarded more than retail selling. As a result of certain difficulties, prejudices, insistence upon the traditional curriculum, and the dearth of qualified teachers of salesmanship in secondary schools, fewer than 100 cities in the United States have coöperative part-time courses in this subject. Initiative for the organization of these courses has frequently come from local merchants. During the past two years researches and courses of study that should facilitate the development of these courses have been made. Nine large cities recently prepared courses of study for this subject. Instructional material

[46] *Ibid.*, p. 284.
[47] Thompson, *op. cit.*, p. 11.
[48] Commission on the Reorganization of Secondary Education of the National Education Association, Committee on Business Education, *op. cit.*, pp. 16–18.
[49] Counts, *op. cit.*, p. 93.

has been prepared specifically for clerks in meat markets and grocery stores.[50]

Federal funds were voted in 1937 and 1946 for more intensive development of what by then had come to be called distributive education, a term with broader connotations than the older one of salesmanship, although salesmanship courses are included. The amounts were small, and distributive education has not grown to the extent some writers in business education would like to see.

Curriculums in distributive education are also heavy in specific business requirements and are unusually time-consuming since they usually include school-related and school-supervised work experience in the upper high school years. The specific courses in distributive education as such include a wide variety of topics and materials, such as salesmanship, advertising, human relations, product information, store organization, store operation, and channels of distribution.[51]

The clerical practice curriculum is advocated on the grounds of being more suitable for entrance into a variety of jobs than is made possible by the more restricted curriculum in bookkeeping. Office practice courses began to appear increasingly in the program of studies during the middle and late 1920's. In larger high schools these have been combined with other business subjects to form clerical practice (non-shorthand) curriculums.

DEGREE OF SPECIALIZATION IN BUSINESS CURRICULUMS

The major question in any business curriculum is that of specialization. Some run as high as eight required units in the four-year program. A student who fulfills these requirements plus the usual ones in English and social studies has practically no room left for electives unless he carries more than four subjects in some semesters. The business student, therefore, finds it difficult if not impossible to take foreign languages, mathematics in the algebra-geometry sequence, or the physical sciences. A school with a large

[50] Malott, *op. cit.*, pp. 18–19.

[51] Louise Bernard and Natalie Kneeland, "The Distributive Education Curriculum Pattern," American Business Education Yearbook, vol. 13, *Curriculum Patterns in Business Education,* published jointly by The Eastern Business Teachers' Association and The National Business Teachers' Association, 1956, p. 223.

number of students in business curriculums will necessarily have relatively low enrollments in these subjects. We are not concerned here with the record of the school, but with the welfare of the student. The business student may suffer from this in one or more of three different ways: (1) by lack of opportunity to participate in some important parts of human culture; (2) by difficulties in meeting college entrance requirements if he should change his mind and decide to go to college; and (3) by missing subjects that could make practical contributions to his business career.

This heavy emphasis on specialized courses in business curriculums has developed largely since the time of the first World War. Graham analyzed 29 curriculums in existence between 1889 and 1918, finding "that the college-preparatory subjects—mathematics, the physical sciences, and foreign languages—were required for 25.84 per cent of the total time of the four years of high-school education—analyzed on the basis of hours required per week for one year—while the technical-business subjects were required for 20.61 per cent of the total time; English, for 15.06 per cent; the social sciences, for 10.41 per cent; and the social-business subjects, for 7.88 per cent of total time."[52]

She also analyzed 52 curriculums for the period 1919 to 1928 and 44 for that of 1929 to 1933. In these the percentage of time required for business subjects had risen to 37 percent, 25 percent for technical-business, and 12 percent for social-business subjects.[53] Where foreign languages had been required in some curriculums in the 1919–1928 period, by the 1929–1933 period, "Of forty-four curricula analyzed, not one included the requirement of foreign languages for business students."[54]

The tendency has been to interpret the presence of academic subjects in business curriculums of the earlier period as a reflection of college-preparatory influence. Again, such an interpretation depends on the widespread idea that such subjects are of value for college-preparatory purposes only. Foreign language study reflects college-preparatory influences only if one arbitrarily defines

[52] Graham, *op. cit.*, p. 50.
[53] *Ibid.*, p. 69.
[54] *Ibid.*, p. 61.

such study as college preparatory. We do not advocate a foreign language requirement, but rather the election of foreign languages and other academic subjects by more students, including those in business curricula.

Foreign languages in particular can represent for the business student not only an important body of cultural values, but practical values as well. True, this was oversold at one point, particularly with respect to Spanish and alleged commercial opportunities in Latin America. Since then, however, our trade relations have become increasingly international in scope; the muteness of our commercial representatives in languages of their customers in many foreign countries is definitely harmful not only to our trade prospects, but to the international relations of our country in general. For the individual student, the working knowledge of a foreign language can be an important asset in his future business career. Opportunities for students with such training exist not only in private enterprise, but in many civil service jobs in the national government.

What we are suggesting is not the abolition of business education or business curriculums, but rather some reduction in specialized requirements. Business education is needed. Reduction of business requirements in business curriculums may in actuality facilitate carrying out the functions for which business curriculums are designed. At least it is a possibility well worth exploring in the planning of curriculums in our secondary schools.

How much reduction should take place and the nature of such reduction would of course vary from one kind of business curriculum to the next. Stenography curriculums may offer the least opportunity, since future secretaries presumably face intensive requirements that cannot be learned easily apart from specific course work. The same would be true of bookkeeping curriculums, if there were still a demand for intensive specialization in this field. Much of the literature in business education, however, assures us that such is not the case. Some reduction accordingly might be achieved in bookkeeping.

To the untutored outside observer, the curriculums in distributive education and in clerical training seem to provide the greatest opportunities for reduction. Some of the activities in these curriculums might be taught on the jobs themselves, for they are highly specialized in particular kinds of businesses. The teaching of office machines may be questioned on the same grounds. In addition, some aspects of the technological revolution in business procedures may make many of the present kinds of office machines obsolete. Whether the term "automation" is justified or not, there are evidences of much present and future development of automatic processes that will not require machine operators. These automatic processes may even reduce the demand for non-machine clerical operations.

It would be highly desirable, then, in all business curriculums, with the possible exception of the one in stenography, to explore the possibility of demanding not more than four units of the 16 taken by most high school students. These might include one year of general business, one year of social-business subjects such as economic geography, one semester of typewriting, and three semesters in the particular specialty, such as bookkeeping, clerical training, or sales. The bookkeeping and clerical training specialties might be combined to form a single pattern. If some such reduction could be accomplished, it would in addition provide relief for our overworked business education staffs by making possible some reduction in class size and in numbers of classes assigned to teachers.

If further technical training is needed, such as specialized machine operation, the supervision of automatic processes, stenotyping, merchandising, advertising, and the like, we could well have further work in thirteenth-year programs in vocational schools or junior colleges. A survey made in 1952 showed that 46.4 percent of 560 junior colleges studied were offering secretarial business curriculums, 41.4 percent were offering general business, and 17.3 percent were offering salesmanship.[55] Of course not all communities provide such opportunities, but indications point to a continued development of the junior college movement. Communities

[55] Jesse P. Bogue, *American Junior Colleges,* American Council on Education, 1952, table 1, reproduced in Lawrence L. Bethel, "Vocational Education," *The Public Junior College,* National Society for the Study of Education, Fifty-fifth Yearbook, pt. 1, The Society, p. 100.

large enough to maintain highly specialized business curriculums in high schools are usually large enough to establish and maintain junior colleges as well. Smaller schools are not plagued by the problems of overspecialization, but must contend with the opposite difficulty of providing a sufficient range of business offerings for vocational purposes.

The strength of the business education field lies in part in its important dual function of providing vocational preparation for some students and useful general education for large numbers of others. Its position in vocational preparation is solid and assured. There is and will continue to be a demand for high school graduates in jobs for which valid preparation can be given in school, valid because there is substantial subject matter and instruction specifically related to these jobs. The other aspect of business education is equally important. Practically all students can profit from instruction in typewriting, and many could gain much from shorthand as well. Other general students can develop better economic understanding from courses in general business and economic geography, particularly where there are limited offerings in social studies.

Finally, the business field meets the test that must be met by any field in the high school curriculum. It represents and transmits a significant portion of human achievement in knowledge and skill, significant not only in its intellectual content, but in its indispensable part in human affairs. For the production of goods and services would be of little value indeed if we lacked the means of marketing them effectively for human use.

Bibliography

American Business Education, Yearbook, vol. 6, *General Business Education,* Paul Salsgiver (ed.), The National Business Teachers' Association and The Eastern Business Teachers' Association, 1949.

American Business Education, Yearbook, vol. 13, *Curriculum Patterns in Business Education,* The Eastern Business Teachers' Association and The National Business Teachers' Association, 1956.

Commission on the Reorganization of Secondary Education of the National Education Association, Committee on Business Education, *Business Education in Secondary Schools,* Department of the Interior, Bureau of Education, 1919.

Douglas, Lloyd V.; Blanford, James T.; and Anderson, Ruth I., *Teaching Business Subjects,* Prentice-Hall, Inc., 1958.

Graham, Jessie, *The Evolution of Business Education in the United States and Its Implications for Business-Teacher Education,* Southern California Education Monographs, 1933–1934 series, No. 2, University of Southern California Press, 1933.

Haas, Kenneth B., *Distributive Education,* The Gregg Publishing Company, 1941.

Malott, J. O., *Commercial Education 1926–1928,* Department of the Interior, Bureau of Education Bulletin 1929, No. 26.

National Commercial Teachers' Federation, Sixth Yearbook, *The Business Curriculum,* The Federation, 1940.

Nichols, Frederick G., *Commercial Education in the High School,* D. Appleton-Century Company, 1933.

Thompson, F. V., *Commercial Education in Public Secondary Schools,* World Book Company, 1915.

Tonne, Herbert A., *Principles of Business Education,* 2d ed., Gregg Publishing Division, McGraw-Hill Book Company, Inc., 1957.

Walters, R. G., and Nolan, C. A., *Principles and Problems of Business Education,* South-Western Publishing Company, 1950.

CHAPTER 19

··

Homemaking

Homemaking is the most immediately practical field in the high school program of studies. The understandings, skills, and attitudes taught in homemaking are not only demonstrably applicable in adult life but can be put to direct use by students while they are still in school. No complicated arrangements for school-related work experience are needed, as is usually the case in business or industrial education, for work experience is readily available to adolescents in the normal everyday activities of the families in which they live. Homemaking is, therefore, an ideal subject for those who extol practical values in schooling, and is probably the most complete and logical expression of the strong drive toward practicality that characterized curriculum planning in the first half of the present century.

Everyone grants, furthermore, that homemaking is important. Not even the most ardent defender of so-called traditional or liberal subjects would enjoy life in a family with the understandings, skills, and attitudes of homemaking conspicuously not in evidence. Of course he might decide to live by himself, but he would still depend either on his own skills or on those of others to supply immediate wants and needs. Nobody can escape the problems of food, shelter, and clothing, even though it may be theoretically possible to avoid the intangibles of family relationships with which modern home-making instruction is also concerned. While these problems, then, may be of greater interest to some people than to others, it would be difficult to write them off as being of trivial or casual nature.

HOMEMAKING AS A SCHOOL SUBJECT

Whether or not homemaking should be taught in schools is another question. Opponents of homemaking as a school subject contend that the understandings, skills, and attitudes of homemaking should and can be learned in the home itself. Those who argue for homemaking in schools do not, however, propose a school monopoly on this matter. Much is made, in fact, of school-home coöperation. They do contend that parents vary in their ability to teach homemaking, just as they vary in their ability to teach history, algebra, foreign languages, or other subjects. School instruction helps more nearly to equalize opportunities for children to learn what is important. Therefore, according to this argument, homemaking is no more alien to the school program than are the materials and concerns of the so-called traditional disciplines. In addition, the proponents of homemaking as a school subject usually marshal arguments based on the alleged change in the nature of home activities from the past to the present. Children, so the argument runs, learned these things at home in some golden age of the past, but do not, at least to such a great extent, in the modern, urbanized, and technology-ridden home of the present. This argument assumes more about the past than we really know. Children in the past probably did take more part in certain household activities. Whether or not parents of the past were more capable than those of the present of teaching these skills is another matter.

For the most part, however, parents do not object to homemaking instruction in the schools; in fact they welcome it. There have been few, if any, community upheavals over the homemaking curriculum. We may assume then a continuing role for schools, including high schools, in the development of homemaking understandings, attitudes, and skills, all of this done, of course, in close coöperation with the homes from which students come.

Does it follow then that instruction in homemaking justifies an entire instructional field? This depends on the bases chosen for organizing the classroom studies. One writer, Ivol Spafford, says that the nature of homemaking, or home economics, is different from that of other fields.

The confusion as to what home economics is arises, partly at least, through a desire to fit home economics into the pattern of other fields which have developed quite differently. The social studies, the natural sciences, mathematics, and the humanities have grown up as logically organized bodies of knowledge, and it is only recently that anyone has thought of teaching them differently. Home economics, on the other hand, has always focused its attention on home-life activities. Applying materials from many fields to home-life situations, it made a new body of educational experiences.[1]

One school of opinion in curriculum has long advocated the organization of classroom studies directly around important areas of needs. To the adherents of this school, most classroom studies are bodies of subject matter separated from the needs to which they presumably should apply. Homemaking somewhat resembles the core in its direct application to needs, but differs from it in concentrating more specifically on one area of needs than it does on others, although others are not excluded. Advocates of core should be and usually are sympathetic to the field of homemaking even though it symbolizes adherence to the subject organization.

What is a virtue to some will be accounted a defect by others. Here is an instructional field that appears not to "have grown up as one of the logically organized bodies of knowledge," one that gains its substance by "applying materials from many fields to home-life situations."[2] Purists in the subject organization demand from candidates for admission that they be exactly what home economics or homemaking does not appear to be, at least to some observers. Instead it looks like a synthetic field, a parasite that draws its materials from other fields or areas. Why not then, according to some critics, dismantle such a field as this and return its appropriated properties to the rightful owners? Let the student, so the argument runs, apply for himself the materials of the social

[1] Ivol Spafford, *A Functioning Program of Home Economics,* John Wiley & Sons, Inc., 1940, p. 3.
[2] *Ibid.*

studies, the physical sciences, mathematics, and the like to the activities and problems of homemaking, just as he does to the activities and problems of citizenship, of leisure-time use, and the like. The same kinds of comments, it may be noted, are expressed about the field of education at the college and university level, since education admittedly draws upon history, political science, psychology, sociology, and biology for much of its material.

The difficulty here lies in the interpretation of criteria for defining a field or subject. It is neither necessary nor possible to demand that a field be a self-contained body of knowledge, free from all overlapping with other fields. All fields and subjects are defined by using some bases for selection and discarding others. The older a field gets, however, the more we are inclined to forget that such a process has taken place. What is the field of history but a classification determined by chronology? As was pointed out in the chapter on social studies, history could also be dismantled and its materials distributed among a number of other fields. History draws its subject matter from politics, military science and tactics, art, literature, and many other lines of human endeavor. There was a long period in which history was not regarded as a proper subject at all, but as an incidental adjunct of literature.

What may be legitimately demanded, however, is that a school subject transmit some important and comprehensive aspect of human achievement. The portion of the achievement transmitted may be organized in various ways and put up in various kinds of packages. These are practical questions of feasibility and convenience. But to begin with there must be something worth organizing and packaging for transmission. The family is an institution of worth and importance, and mankind has long been about the task of developing the arts related to its maintenance and well-being. When these arts are brought together, they include a substantial body of content. The field of homemaking, then, is not merely a subheading under the larger headings of other fields. It becomes an instructional field in its own right. The fact that it draws on certain materials from natural science, social studies, the visual arts, the industrial arts, and other fields does not change its character as an instructional field.[3] None of the aforementioned fields could include much specific material bearing on homemaking without in itself being distorted. A biology course, for example, includes some material on nutrition, but it would be a rather warped biology course that would spend as much time on nutrition as is spent in homemaking.

The plain fact is that other fields paid very little attention to worthy home membership prior to the 1920's. This is said not in criticism—it was perhaps better so—but to underline the reason for the appearance of the subject or field of homemaking. It took care of something important that was not being taken care of otherwise and probably could not have been taken care of as well had it been parceled out among a number of teaching fields.

DEVELOPMENT OF THE HOMEMAKING FIELD

It is possible to speculate on forces in American history that may have contributed something to the development of homemaking education, or at least ran parallel to it. One writer indicates some of the early motivation related both to the helping of the poor and to the impact of industrialism and the employment of women outside the home. "Stimulated by the interest of social-minded women, as an industrial society began to be developed, a few elementary schools, soon after the middle of the nineteenth century, began offering training to young girls from poor and needy homes. Women in the lower economic levels were working increasingly outside the home and either knew no longer how to cook and sew

[3] Dean Frances Zuill of the School of Home Economics of the University of Wisconsin presents the following definition of the homemaking field, one that recognizes the contributions of other disciplines, but also expresses the intrinsic character of homemaking as an instructional field in itself. "Home economics represents a body of knowledge, principles, and understandings that have been brought together, which have been derived from the physical, biological, and behavioral sciences as well as from the arts and the home economics field itself, which have special significance for family living. In other words, it is a synthesis of subject matter drawn from the basic sciences, social sciences, humanities and arts and from research, learnings, and experiences of students of home and family life. Through this body of materials home economics contributes to the development of individuals for family and citizenship responsibilities and in many cases to preparation for productive careers identified with this field of learning." Mimeographed statement, *Present Day Concept of Home Economics.*

or no longer had the necessary time to teach their daughters. Housewifely skills and the simple techniques of cookery and sewing were stressed in the instruction."[4] Similar humanitarian tendencies appeared also in the program of the Industrial Education Association in the 1880's, which "endeavored to teach the poor of the city how to sew."[5]

Another possible influence was the woman's rights movement. While the more militantly feminist members of this movement sought to emancipate women from household duties by putting them to work in offices, factories, and stores, others strove to dignify and raise to a higher level of appreciation what they considered to be the distinctive and ennobling role of women in society at that time. This took the form of regarding homemaking as a vocation or calling fully as worthy as other careers. "The permanency of Domestic Art as a feature in the education of women is assured. It is so vital an expression of her nature that any curriculum which does not include training for the home sphere ignores the very center about which her life revolves. Many of the home talents are innate and develop naturally, but many lie dormant because untrained. When woman begins to preside over her own home, she soon discovers her limitation if she has not had the advantages of training along the lines of household arts and economics."[6] Still a third possible contributing element was the preoccupation of Americans with foods and diets, especially in relation to health. Cooking schools, for example, sprang into existence and into almost instant popularity in the late 1870's. At one extreme this concern about food expressed itself in the numerous diet cults and food fads that form a distinctive chapter in United States history by themselves. On the positive side, it took the form of a constructive interest in the applications of biological science to nutrition. What might be called the more "academic" side of homemaking education really grew out of research and study in nutritional health and science.

[4] Spafford, *op. cit.*, p. 18.
[5] Hazel T. Craig, *The History of Home Economics,* edited by Blanche Stover, published by *Practical Home Economics Magazine,* 1945, p. 7.
[6] Anna M. Cooley, *Domestic Art in Woman's Education,* Charles Scribner's Sons, 1911, p. vii.

At any rate it is clear that homemaking education, like music, developed in our schools under native auspices without much European stimulation or influence. Instruction in the more tangible aspects of homemaking appeared first in elementary schools and colleges, particularly in the land-grant colleges, following the Morrill Act of 1862. Quietly and without fanfare, homemaking, under a variety of names, began to gain strength in the high schools as well, particularly in the 1880's and 1890's. Development on all three levels of schooling took place in various parts of the country, but special historical attention has been centered on the Kitchen Garden Association of New York City, known after 1884 as the Industrial Education Association. This group not only promoted homemaking in the schools, but also brought about the creation of a college for the specific preparation of teachers of homemaking and industrial arts in 1888, an institution called the New York College for Training Teachers, which eventually grew into Teachers College of Columbia University.[7]

As has often been the case in school movements, a few strong-minded leaders took the initiative to bring together informal groups and later to form a national association in the field of homemaking. One of these was Mrs. Ellen Richards, identified as "a crusader in the problems of the home,"[8] who visited Mr. and Mrs. Melvil Dewey at their summer home in Lake Placid, New York, to discuss the setting up of examinations in "household science" for college entrance. Dewey is known primarily for his classification system for libraries, but it was in his role as Secretary of the New York State Board of Regents that he stepped briefly into the history of homemaking education. In the summer of 1899, the Deweys invited not only Mrs. Richards but several others interested in homemaking to confer at their Lake Placid summer home.[9] These conferences became annual events, and the ten Lake Placid conferences are considered milestones in the history of homemaking education. At the last of these in 1908, the conference members decided to form a national organization and did so on Decem-

---

[7] Craig, *op. cit.,* pp. 6–7.
[8] *Ibid.,* p. 9.
[9] *Ibid.,* pp. 8–9.

ber 31, 1908 and January 1, 1909 under the name of the American Home Economics Association, which became and has remained the major organization in the field.

One of the points taken up early in the Lake Placid conferences was that of terminology. The field then was variously known as domestic economy, domestic science, housewifery, and household economics.[10] Instead of selecting one term for the field as a whole, the members of the conference preferred to use terms descriptive of each school level and suggested domestic economy, domestic science, and home economics for the elementary, secondary, and college levels respectively.[11] These suggestions apparently did not gain general adoption, for Anna Cooley, writing in 1911, noted regional variations, with domestic science prevailing in the West and household arts in the Middle West.[12] The term "home economics" eventually prevailed for all levels and in all regions and is still in use today, although people in the field prefer homemaking education for the high school, thereby returning to the earlier suggestions of using different terms for different levels.

Although homemaking education had been introduced before 1900 in many schools throughout the country, enrollments relative to the numbers of students in schools remained fairly small throughout the first decade of the present century. In 1910, for example, only 3.8 percent of all students in Grades 9 through 12 were enrolled in homemaking courses. Since few boys have taken homemaking in any period, it is necessary to multiply percentage figures by two to get a fair approximation of relative enrollments. For 1910, therefore, it is safe to assume that slightly less than 8 percent of the girls took homemaking. This was, however, still a relatively small enrollment. Between 1910 and 1915, a substantial increase was registered, and in the latter year 12.9 percent of all students[13] and presumably about one fourth of all the girls were in homemaking classes. It is difficult to tell why one girl in four took home-

---

[10] *Ibid.*, p. 9.
[11] *Ibid.*
[12] Cooley, *op. cit.*, p. 3.
[13] Percentage figures for 1910 and 1915 drawn from "Offerings and Enrollments in High-School Subjects," *Biennial Survey of Education in the United States, 1948–1950,* Federal Security Agency, Office of Education, table 7, p. 108.

making in 1915 when only one in 12 had done so just five years earlier. Perhaps the general enthusiasm for practical and vocational education that had gotten under way in 1905 was beginning to find applications in the homemaking area, as well as in those aimed directly at employment for pay.

The Smith-Hughes Act of 1917 was definitely stimulated by the strong drive toward vocational education of the preceding decade. It provided federal funds not only for agricultural and industrial education, but for homemaking as well. This provision officially symbolized acceptance of homemaking as a vocation or calling in its own right and on the same level with paid employment outside the home. True, there were some who saw an opportunity to promote homemaking education for outside-the-home employment in restaurants, institutions, and the like. Over the years, however, very little homemaking education in high schools has gone in this direction, although such careers are undoubtedly among the goals of those who major in home economics at the college level.

Smith-Hughes funds, as well as those in subsequent acts, have been made freely available to homemaking programs aimed entirely or primarily at careers as housewives without outside employment at all. Vocational home economics or homemaking therefore has meant almost entirely instruction in the vocation of homemaking. Since so-called non-vocational home economics or homemaking is aimed at the same thing, a certain amount of curricular and administrative confusion has been generated by the terminology. It should be kept in mind that the distinction between vocational and non-vocational homemaking programs is solely an administrative one, the former term referring to those programs which qualify for federal support under the various acts. There are in addition some external characteristics of vocational programs, particularly those under the Smith-Hughes Act, with regard to scheduling, parallel related courses, and the like, but these do not affect the curricular purposes for which the programs are organized.

In spite of the Smith-Hughes Act, home economics enrollments relative to school enrollments as a whole did not increase nearly as rapidly in the period from 1915 to 1928 as they had between 1910 and 1915. The percentage of students enrolled in home economics rose from 12.9 percent in 1915 to only 14.3 percent in 1922 and 16.5 percent in 1928.[14] Again, if we double these percentage figures, they go from approximately 25 percent in 1915 to 28 percent in 1922 to 33 percent in 1928. That is to say, one girl in three was taking homemaking in 1928 as compared with one in four in 1915.

Counts was so astonished by the low percentage of total recitation time (4.7 percent) devoted to home economics in his survey for 1923–1924 that he sought to explain it in the light of changing social and economic conditions in society. After reviewing the conditions favorable to the development of home economics, he goes on as follows.

The expected, however, has not happened. The courses have not been crowded. The girls who were supposed to rejoice at the opportunity of being equipped for the responsibilities of the home and of motherhood have been interested in other things. They have chosen the college-preparatory courses because they desired to continue their education, or the commercial courses because they wished to earn money. They realized fully that to get into college the one was necessary and that to earn money the other was highly desirable but that to register initial success in the field of matrimony the courses in home economics would avail but little. In fact, they probably reasoned, and reasoned wisely, that the college-preparatory and commercial courses would render larger immediate service in the matrimonial venture than the acquisition of the most expert skills in cooking and sewing. In other words, the status of woman has changed, and the girl is allowed a certain measure of freedom in ordering her own life. Today she may even look forward to a career in a large number of fields which were closed to her mother or grandmother. It is not surprising, therefore, that she has not given undivided loyalty to home-economics courses.[15]

This is possibly another way of saying that the advocates of emancipating women by getting them out of homemaking had prevailed in the woman's rights movement over those who sought to ennoble and dignify women by raising the status and dignity of homemak-

[14] *Ibid.*, table 7, p. 108.
[15] George S. Counts, *The Senior High School Curriculum,* The University of Chicago, 1926, pp. 103–104.

ing itself. It is also true that homemaking suffered for some time and probably throughout the 1920's from the same kinds of negative stereotypes as those attached to the industrial arts, namely that it was a field for the inferior student and therefore unacceptable as an elective in so-called college-preparatory programs.

Leaders in home economics, however, were not discouraged by the declining increases in percentages of total enrollments. They pointed rather to improvements in the home economics field itself, such as are indicated in a 1929 Bureau of Education Bulletin.

Home-economics education during the biennium has made notable progress. Among the achievements are the formation of the Organization of Supervisors and Teachers of Home Economics, further curriculum revision, better integration of home-economics instruction with health education, larger opportunities for child development and parental education, organized courses for social and family relationships, increased interest in business opportunities for women trained in home economics, courses for boys and men, greater Federal appropriations, and more research or fact-finding studies in the various fields of home economics.[16]

In spite of these promising developments, high school enrollments in homemaking relative to total enrollments practically stood still between 1928 and 1934, going from 16.5 percent to 16.7 percent.[17] These were depression years, with prospects of early marriage so dubious that to many girls homemaking education may have seemed as remote as the study of Greek.

Between 1934 and 1949, however, the percentage of total students enrolled in home economics rose from 16.7 percent to 24.2 percent,[18] the largest relative increase since the period between 1910 and 1915. By 1949, half of all the girls in the last four years of high school were to be found in homemaking classes, which would mean an even higher percentage of graduates who had taken some homemaking during their high school careers. Two possible reasons might account for this increase. One is the popularity of

---

[16] Emeline S. Whitcomb, *Trends in Home-Economics Education 1926–1928,* Department of the Interior, Bureau of Education, Bulletin 1929, No. 25, p. 1.

[17] "Offerings and Enrollments in High-School Subjects," *Biennial Survey, op. cit.,* table 7, p. 108.

[18] *Ibid.*

early marriages, which was stimulated by a combination of wartime conditions and general economic improvement after 1940. This was accompanied by a greatly increased national interest in many aspects of homemaking, particularly the rearing of children. The other possible reason is that the George-Deen Act passed in 1936 liberalized the criteria under which schools could qualify for federal aid, although the Smith-Hughes Act remained in effect. After 1936, then, schools could choose the particular act under which to qualify. By 1949, about 47 percent of all students in homemaking were in reimbursed programs.[19] In that year homemaking courses were available to about nine tenths of all high school pupils in Grades 7 through 12.[20]

Over this extended period of time since 1910, during which home economics enrollments have had two periods of rapid increase separated by one period of leveling off, the home economics curriculum has moved from exclusive concentration on the tangible aspects of homemaking, such as nutrition, clothing, and child care to include instruction in the intangibles of family relationships and personal adjustment. These supplementary features, although now well established, have taken years to come about. As far back as 1911, Cooley protested against the narrow use of the term "domestic art" as sewing, in which "The ethical, social, and aesthetic values are often lost sight of and the material or utilitarian side made the main issue,"[21] and added, "If properly taught, domestic art should have a highly moral effect. It makes for perfect sanity and mental health, it develops the will and power of inhibition which is the root of self-control in orals; it makes for firmness and force of character."[22] Nevertheless, Counts concluded in 1926 that "The home-economics program is composed almost exclusively of two subjects—cooking and sewing"[23] and that these two subjects accounted for 85 percent of the total time devoted to the field. He recognized, however, that home management was sometimes

[19] *Ibid.,* pp. 22–23.
[20] Hazel M. Hatcher and Mildred E. Andrews, *The Teaching of Homemaking,* Houghton Mifflin Company, 1945, p. 417.
[21] Cooley, *op. cit.,* pp. 6–7.
[22] *Ibid.,* p. 18.
[23] Counts, *op. cit.,* pp. 104–105.

taught as part of cooking. On the other hand, Dyer in her 1927 study said, "The old-time cooking and sewing courses are fast disappearing in the outlines,"[24] although she found the largest amount of content devoted to food, clothing, and the house and its care.[25]

By 1940 the nature of homemaking courses had apparently changed sufficiently to evoke the following comment from Spafford. "People who have not kept informed often think of the home economics laboratory as a place where girls cook and sew. . . . This was the home economics they knew when they were in school or first began teaching. Even then, it had values for the academic student; it was much more than food and clothing study. If these people were to drop into almost any department today and talk with students and teachers about their work, they would find home economics little like the notion they have built up."[26] She goes on to say that "Personal and family relationships, child growth and development, consumption as a primary function of the home, and the intangibles of home life are being stressed."[27] Even with these changes, however, she contends, "Home economics as a medium for personality development and education in personal living has received too little attention,"[28] and concludes much as Cooley had in 1911 that the field "has much to offer in developing and maintaining sane, wholesome physical and mental health, fine human relationships, a well-balanced personality, and a satisfying philosophy of life."[29]

From then on the intangibles assumed larger and larger roles in homemaking education, as indicated by the following summary statement made in 1954. "Formerly one found meal preparation, clothing construction, home care of the sick, home furnishings, and home management as the main content of all homemaking programs. Today family relationships, use of human resources, buying problems of the home, housing, and child development have as-

[24] Annie Robertson Dyer, *The Placement of Home Economics Content in Junior and Senior High Schools,* Bureau of Publications, Teachers College, Columbia University, 1927, p. 99.
[25] *Ibid.,* p. 96.
[26] Spafford, *op. cit.,* p. 1.
[27] *Ibid.,* p. 19.
[28] *Ibid.,* p. 14.
[29] *Ibid.*

sumed a prominent place in a large number of homemaking programs. This does not mean that the abilities included in the earlier
courses have been omitted, but it does mean that less time and effort are devoted to them, and that the personal and social relations
of family groups are emphasized."[30] The advocates of the intangibles have made their case and apparently won their point. Homemaking teachers today are usually anxious to disclaim the cooking-
sewing stereotype and are quick to point out the extent to which
their field has been broadened to include many other aspects of
family living, or living in general.

This point of view, however, raises several difficult questions.
One is that of the privacy and integrity of the home as an institution in its own right. Homemaking instruction may run counter to
the ideals, practices, and values held and used at least in some
families. This is less likely to happen in the tangibles of cooking
and sewing than it is in the intangibles of family relationships.
Homemaking teachers respond that they do not seek to impose
ideals and values on students, but rather to discuss possible approaches to these important matters. Furthermore, it may be argued
that homemaking instruction confines itself to points of view that
are matters of general agreement in our society. These correspond
to what some regard as the middle-class way of life in the United
States to which most of us aspire. Homemaking instruction viewed
in these terms does not, then, conflict with general agreements on
what is right or wrong, good or bad. When there is no fundamental conflict between these agreements on one hand and absolute
moral principles on the other, there is no reason, according to this
argument, why the school should not teach them. This is probably
a good practical resolution of the dilemma, but homemaking teachers must constantly remind themselves of the sensitive and personal nature of family relationships. Theirs is probably the most
immediately sensitive and personal of all areas dealt with in the
school curriculum.

A second question here is the tendency of homemaking instruction to move into broad areas of curricular objectives. Homemak-

---

[30] Maude Williamson and Mary Stewart Lyle, *Homemaking Education in the
High School,* Appleton-Century-Crofts, Inc., 3d ed., 1954, p. 44.

ing occupies a somewhat unique position in the curriculum in that its definition as a field corresponds directly with one broad objective of schooling, namely, that of worthy home membership as stated in the Cardinal Principles. Fields of instruction, however, need not necessarily have this correspondence. The field of homemaking was not so organized. It was set up as a body of content related to the arts of home living. The correspondence to an objective stated in the Cardinal Principles, which incidentally were formulated several decades after the introduction of the field, was a matter of coincidence, not design. Homemaking would exist as a field even though the Commission on the Reorganization of Secondary Education had never stated worthy home membership as an objective of secondary schooling.

It may well be argued, then, that homemaking need not confine itself to the single objective of worthy home membership. Furthermore, since worthy home membership is a comprehensive objective, it probably overlaps to a considerable extent many if not all of the other six. The home, for example, does include the development of ethical character and is one of the settings for the worthy use of leisure time. The wisdom of pointing homemaking instruction toward a wide range of other possible objectives is another matter. As long as a field uses a wide range of possible objectives as supplementary criteria for decision making, the effect is likely to be good. When it sets out to incorporate content specifically aimed at many objectives, the result is likely to be confusion and overlapping in the curriculum. This, in fact, is what has happened, not only as homemaking courses have included content relevant to many objectives, but as fields other than homemaking, particularly since 1918, have done the same relevant to the objective of worthy home membership.

Some of the other broad objectives of schooling are obviously and directly related to homemaking, even in the sense of providing bodies of content. It would be impossible and patently ridiculous to disclaim the health objective or health content in nutrition, clothing, and child care. Since there are paid occupations in food, shelter, and clothing, it would be unrealistic to exclude occupational objectives even when these are restricted to paid employment. Consumer understandings and skills form another group of objectives immediately pertinent to home economics. The increasing role of the family in recreation suggests the possibility at least of directing some homemaking instruction toward the worthy use of leisure time. Other objectives, such as citizenship and personality development, are probably better regarded as supplementary checks on classroom practices rather than as direct guides to content.

ORGANIZATION OF THE HOMEMAKING STUDIES

The movement toward the intangibles has increased the number and variety of topics and problems in homemaking education, raising thereby the question of allocating and organizing these topics in a year-to-year sequence. The 1949 survey found considerable diversity in course titles and sequence designations. On one hand there were separate courses in such areas as food, clothing, home management, health and home nursing, family relationships, child development, the house, and consumer buying. Along with these, however, and accounting for 59.4 percent of the total homemaking enrollment were courses simply called Homemaking I, II, III and IV.[31] The tendency in these programs is to include some study of a number of topics at each level, with the differences from one year to the next reflecting levels of difficulty and application. This, of course, has been the tendency in other fields, notably English and physical education, and it has been advocated and promoted by some in the social studies.

Those who advocate the general course from one level to the next base their case on the high degree of interrelatedness among various topics and problems in the homemaking field. They point out that home management, family relationships, child care, health, and similar topics cannot be separated, for example, from foods, or from one another. The best arrangement, according to this point of view, is one in which these aspects of homemaking are brought together in problem-type units. This provides a flexible pattern that makes possible a good deal of teacher-student planning on the selection and organization of problems and related

[31] "Offerings and Enrollments in High-School Subjects," *Biennial Survey, op. cit.,* p. 23.

materials. Such an organization as this, however, presents difficulties as well as advantages. Dyer, noting this tendency as far back as 1926, wrote, "The repetition of content is a distinct difficulty."[32] Even when the sequence is well planned so that the materials on foods in the fourth-year course are different from those in the first-year course, it is difficult to avoid giving both to students and to outside observers the impression of undesirable repetition. It also leaves an impression of formlessness and chaos in the curriculum which, unjustified though it may be, is not easy to dispel. Students furthermore may have some difficulty deciding how many years of home economics to take in elective programs when the emphases of the various years are not clearly indicated.

Obviously it is not necessary to make a choice entirely for one kind of organization over another. Introductory courses clearly should be general in nature and deal with a variety of topics, partly to provide some instruction in certain important areas for students who will not study further in the field and partly to serve as exploration for those who may be interested in further study. This pattern would have a good deal of justification in the seventh, eighth, and ninth grades. On the other hand the courses in Grades 10 through 12 might well be more specialized and clearly designated by title, organized for students who want to follow a sequence in homemaking all the way through. Such a diversified and extended program is not possible in all schools. Those which can offer only one or two years of homemaking in Grades 9 through 12 will necessarily have to make the courses more inclusive and general.

REQUIREMENTS AND ELECTIVES
IN THE HOMEMAKING FIELD

Required home economics, especially if limited to one year as is usually the case, seems to imply the need for introductory general courses. As is true of other fields, the question of requirements or constants in homemaking generates a good deal of disagreement and controversy, even among homemaking teachers. The universal importance of family living does seem to justify it as a constant,

[32] Dyer, *op. cit.,* p. 105.

particularly for girls and possibly, depending on the course arrangements and content, for boys as well. Homemaking teachers even when agreed on the desirability of a constant are not always in agreement on where it should be placed. Some feel the present practice of requiring it at the junior high school level to be unjustified from the standpoint of interest and motivation. This point of view is in part a reaction against the tendency in some schools to schedule homemaking classes on a two-day or three-day a week basis, with too many students per class, and with inadequate facilities.

Such conditions, however, can be corrected, and there is much to justify the requirement of homemaking in Grade 7 or 8. Homemaking courses have a dual function, one with students as family members while they are in school, the other with the roles of students in homes they will establish after leaving school. The first function meets the criterion of universal application more than the second. Not all our students will establish homes, but practically all are in homes and families while in school. The junior high school homemaking course can be effectively directed toward daily participation in homemaking activities. This is not to say that all work in high school must have immediate application, but rather that the criterion of immediacy is relevant to determining required work in a field that lays stress on practical outcomes.

Another advantage of the junior high school requirement is the opportunity it affords all students of identifying possible interests for future work in the homemaking field. If the required course is deferred until the upper high school years, many students may discover interests in the homemaking field too late to take any more work in the field, at least at the high school level. To capitalize on the alleged motivation provided by approaching marriage would mean placing the requirement in the twelfth grade. If the requirement were placed in the ninth or tenth grade, students could still elect further homemaking study, but it is doubtful that these grades are superior to Grades 7 and 8 for purposes of motivation.

One important consideration in the placement of homemaking requirements is that of including boys. Current practice includes an industrial arts requirement for boys and one in homemaking for girls, both in the junior high school. Modern homemaking, however, includes understandings and some skills that are learned in industrial arts, while conversely much of what is learned in general industrial arts can be applied to homemaking. The sharing of many household responsibilities by husbands and wives seems therefore to justify a requirement of one year of industrial arts and one year of homemaking for all students. When schools do not feel justified in requiring two units in these fields for all students, they might provide a one-unit course combining the two fields. The same criterion of immediate reference to the students' lives in their homes while in school applies to boys as well as to girls. Also, the possibility of electing further work in homemaking, especially from the standpoint of preparation for future paid employment, applies equally to boys. The number of men employed as chefs, fashion designers, interior decorators, and the like should dispel any notion that home economics is purely a feminine field, although the stereotype is admittedly difficult to overcome. Finally, any resentment that boys might feel toward a requirement in homemaking would probably be more intense in the upper high school levels than in the seventh and eighth grades. One possible difficulty at the junior high school level is that presented by differences in social maturity of boys and girls of the same chronological ages. This could be resolved by providing separate sections for boys and girls in the required homemaking and industrial arts courses.

There is considerable feeling that a course in marriage and adult family relationships should be provided and possibly even required in the twelfth grade. This course differs from others in homemaking in the omission of technical instruction in foods, clothing, and child care. It includes topics such as family responsibilities, outside employment for wives, child development, financial management, housing, and the like. Whether or not such a course includes sex education depends on the convictions and attitudes of particular communities. It does not have to include sex education, for there are many other important aspects of marriage relationships.

Such courses as these have long been offered in some high schools. They are usually well received by both parents and students. Even more than in other fields, the effectiveness of this kind of course depends on the skill, perceptions, and sensitivity of the teacher who offers it. But such teachers are to be found. There are many good reasons why the course should be offered and why it should be open to boys and girls whether they have had previous work in homemaking or not. There are also some reasons why it is best left on an elective basis. The prospect of marriage may be a remote one, even for high school seniors. In addition, even when sex topics are omitted, the matters discussed in this course do have emotional connotations. The rights of students who prefer not to take part in open discussions of these matters should be respected.

In general, homemaking electives in the senior high school, including those courses dealing with specialized and technical aspects of foods and clothing, have much to offer to many kinds of students of various intellectual levels and in various tracks or curricula. Fortunately, some ancient prejudices and stereotypes are giving way. Homemaking has been more successful than some other fields in getting away from the notion that it is for inferior students. There is sufficient content to challenge even those of the highest abilities. We have also moved away from the idea that advanced work in homemaking is somehow more relevant to non-college-preparatory students than to those who are college bound. Most college-preparatory tracks have enough flexibility to permit interested students to elect one or two years of senior high school homemaking. The important considerations beyond the initial requirements or constants are the interests, goals, and aspirations of individual students, both boys and girls. A good elective program in homemaking, when understood and supported by the entire school staff, will never lack students.

Bibliography

Calvin, Henrietta W., and Lyford, Carrie Alberta, *Home Economics,* Department of the Interior, Bureau of Education, Bulletin 1918, No. 50.

Cooley, Anna M., *Domestic Art in Women's Education,* Charles Scribner's Sons, 1911.

Craig, Hazel T., *The History of Home Economics* (Blanche Stover, ed.), published by *Practical Home Economics Magazine,* 1945.

Dyer, Annie Robertson, *The Administration of Home Economics in City Schools,* Teachers College, Columbia University, Contributions to Education No. 318, 1928.

Dyer, Annie Robertson, *The Placement of Home Economics Content in Junior and Senior High Schools,* Bureau of Publications, Teachers College, Columbia University, 1927.

Hatcher, Hazel M., and Andrews, Mildred E., *The Teaching of Homemaking,* Houghton Mifflin Company, 1945.

Lawson, Dorothy S., and Creighton, Martha (eds.), "Fifty Years of Progress in Home Economics Education," *American Vocational Journal,* December, 1956, pp. 67–74, 104.

Spafford, Ivol, *A Functioning Program of Home Economics,* John Wiley & Sons, Inc., 1940.

Whitcomb, Emeline S., *Trends in Home-Economics Education 1926–1928,* Department of the Interior, Bureau of Education, Bulletin 1929, No. 25.

Williamson, Maude, and Lyle, Mary Stewart, *Homemaking Education in the High School,* Appleton-Century-Crofts, Inc., 3d ed., 1954.

::

Agriculture

As far as controversy is concerned, agriculture is the most anonymous and least obtrusive of all the fields of secondary schooling and is often overlooked or forgotten by groups making lists of the instructional fields in the high school. One reason for this is the tendency of newspaper and magazine discussion of secondary schooling to reflect the concerns of cities, and agriculture is rarely offered in city schools. Also, the extensive literature existing on agricultural education tends to be somewhat technical and specialized and is addressed to and read largely by those teaching in the field. This general lack of awareness has been unfortunate, for agriculture is not only a major field of secondary schooling, but for all of us, rural and urban alike, a field of national importance.

With its major development taking place after 1900, agriculture was the last of the instructional fields to become established in public high schools. This development represented in part one phase of the rural protest in the late nineteenth century and involved a number of complex social and economic circumstances. It was also part of the drive for secondary vocational education begun in 1905 and culminated in the passage of the Smith-Hughes Act in 1917. Since that time vocational agriculture has been practically synonymous with the field of agricultural education as a whole.

Behind these two forces lay a century or more of preparation in the various social and intellectual currents of American and European life. Major changes in agricultural technology had taken place throughout the eighteenth century. Agriculture was one of the favorite concerns of the philosophers and scientists in the enlightenment movement, and societies for promoting scientific farming were formed in a number of European countries. The Philadelphia Society for Promoting Agriculture, organized in 1785, initiated a similar movement in the United States, and numerous groups, both statewide and in local communities, paralleled the efforts of their European counterparts. The interest of these societies in disseminating scientific knowledge pertaining to agriculture suggested the incorporation of the subject in formal schooling. This had been anticipated both by the founders of King's College, who included agriculture in their prospectus,[1] and by Franklin in his plan for the Philadelphia academy. Neither of these proposals took hold, in spite of Franklin's comment about "The Improvement of Agriculture being useful to all, and Skill in it no Disparagement to any."[2] In 1792, however, Columbia College (earlier King's College) did appoint a professor to work in the three fields of natural history, chemistry, and agriculture.

On the whole, the agricultural societies did more to stir up interest in agriculture than to establish it in school programs. A number of colleges followed Columbia's example and included the field among their offerings. Except for scattered offerings in the academies and the establishment of a few academies specifically devoted to agriculture, the movement had little impact at the secondary level.

There were practically no trained teachers of agriculture to be had and the limited literature of this subject was ill adapted for use in schools. Public attention was more and more directed toward efforts to establish agricultural colleges. It seemed to be dimly understood that these higher institutions would be needed before agriculture could be successfully taught in the lower schools and many people thought that

---

[1] Alfred Charles True, *A History of Agricultural Education in the United States 1785–1925*, United States Department of Agriculture Miscellaneous Publication No. 36, Washington, 1929, p. 9.

[2] Quoted in Willis L. Uhl, *Secondary School Curricula*, The Macmillan Company, 1927, p. 159.

such colleges could supply all the agricultural instruction which it was worth while to give.

The movement for the teaching of agriculture in secondary schools therefore waned, and by the time of the outbreak of the Civil War such instruction had almost entirely disappeared in this country.[3]

Neither did agriculture prosper as a high school subject during the years immediately following the Civil War. Some have seen this as an example of the academic preoccupations of high schools in this period.[4] More likely it reflected the fact that high schools large enough to afford a special teacher were located in cities and that city boards of education were no more concerned about agricultural education at that time than they are today.[5] This possibility is supported by the appearance of manual arts and the development of commercial subjects in the same high schools that neglected or disregarded agriculture.

The appearance of the movement that has come to be known as the agrarian or rural protest brought the social, political, and economic problems of farmers to a nation-wide level of awareness. This movement, on the whole, was an exceedingly complex one and not susceptible to easy generalizations. It is not clear, for example, that farmers wanted agricultural education in the local schools, at least in the early period. Journalists and other spokesmen for farm organizations and groups did from time to time advocate a kind of schooling that they felt was more suited to farm life and conditions. Leaders in the field of education generally began to express like sentiments. One matter of concern both to rural leaders and to others was the migration of farm youth to cities, a tendency that could possibly be offset by agricultural education. Expressions

---

[3] True, *op. cit.,* p. 39.

[4] "After the Civil War the public high schools increased rapidly in number and attendance, but their courses of study were literary and scientific and were very largely determined by the requirements for entrance to colleges, though very many of their students did not take or complete such preparatory courses. Such academies as survived competition with the high schools made their courses conform closely with those of the public high schools." *Ibid.,* p. 322.

[5] As late as 1904 there were 2,175 one-teacher high schools out of a total of 7,174 high schools in the United States. Cited in Clarence Hall Robison, *Agricultural Instruction in the Public High Schools of the United States,* Teachers College, Columbia University, Contributions to Education, No. 39, 1911, p. 14.

along these lines appear in writing well into the first two decades of the twentieth century. One writer, for example, put the case as follows in 1909. "How can a child born and reared in the country respect the life of the farmer when the community in which he lives does not regard the farmer's occupation worthy of study? How can he be expected to look with ambition toward agriculture as a vocation when he finds that training for it is regarded as less important than preparation for a clerkship? How can he think of village and rural life as anything more than a makeshift when he finds that in the schools he attends there is not a word taught concerning crops or cattle or roads?"[6] A writer in the field of agricultural education in 1911 commented as follows on the lack of high schools in rural areas and the consequent sending of rural youth to the nearest village or city schools. "This policy has been followed at the sacrifice to farm and country life of thousands of the strongest and most intelligent youth of the land. The town and city schools included little or nothing designed to stimulate the art of agriculture or to encourage the choice of farming as a life work. Pursuits other than farming have been entered by these young people to the detriment of the agricultural interests of the young people themselves."[7] He follows this by pointing out that the partial introduction of agricultural education in high schools had already served "to turn the tide of sentiment, especially among the young people of the country, back toward the advantages of country life."[8]

Evidently, the first motivation for agriculture in the local high schools came not as much from the desire to improve farming in its technical aspects as from that of strengthening all aspects of rural life and generally extolling the rural way of life itself.[9] In spite of this powerful sentiment, however, agriculture did not immediately appear as a field of instruction in local high schools. Even through

[6] Editorial, "The Martian and the Farm," *Outlook,* XXIX (1909), pp. 433–434, quoted in Benjamin Marshall Davis, *Agricultural Education in the Public Schools,* The University of Chicago Press, 1912, p. 81.

[7] Garland Armor Bricker, *The Teaching of Agriculture in the High School,* The Macmillan Company, 1911, p. 13.

[8] *Ibid.,* p. 14.

[9] These ideas culminated in the calling of the Country Life Commission by President Theodore Roosevelt in 1908. See L. H. Bailey, *The Country-Life Movement in the United States,* The Macmillan Company, 1911.

the 1890's, most large high schools were still located in cities, with administrative provisions for consolidated high school districts in rural areas only slowly taking form.

DEVELOPMENT OF AGRICULTURAL EDUCATION IN HIGH SCHOOLS

The first high schools to teach agriculture were special agricultural high schools under administrative auspices other than those of local districts. State universities led the way. In 1888 the regents of the University of Minnesota established an agricultural high school with a two-year course. This has been called "the first distinctly secondary school in the United States in which agricultural instruction was given."[10] In some states action was taken directly by state legislatures to establish agricultural high schools in various kinds of geographical units, such as congressional districts, judicial districts, or counties. By 1913, there were 80 or so special agricultural high schools throughout the country.[11]

Possibly the rapid development of these special schools led to a more serious consideration of agriculture in local high school districts. Many writers deplored and feared the tendency to establish special kinds of high schools for special purposes, not only in agriculture, but in the manual arts and commercial fields as well. Local high schools may also have been encouraged by the rapid development of agriculture as a subject in the elementary grades,[12] a movement that both inspired and reflected legislation in a number of states on the matter, some of it permissive and some mandatory in character.[13] By 1900 local high schools were confronted by three

[10] *Ibid.,* p. 15.

[11] William Granville Hummel and Bertha Royce Hummel, *Materials and Methods in High School Agriculture,* The Macmillan Company, 1913, p. 5.

[12] As late as 1909, Liberty Hyde Bailey wrote, "It is significant that the popular agitation for agriculture teaching has considered chiefly the children 'in the grades,' and that books and leaflets have been written for this range." L. H. Bailey, *The Training of Farmers,* The Century Co., 1909, p. 157.

[13] By 1915 there were 22 states requiring agriculture in public rural elementary schools. True, *op. cit.,* p. 392. One writer, however, contends that the movement to teach agriculture in the elementary grades tended to retard its introduction in high schools. "It is a significant fact that the states requiring agriculture to be taught in the rural schools have shown the slowest voluntary development of this subject in the high schools." Robinson, *op. cit.,* p. 167.

sets of facts: (1) the long-standing establishment of agriculture at the college and university level; (2) the recent movement to organize special high schools of agricultural studies; and (3) the development of agriculture in the elementary grades.

At any rate it was just about the year 1900 that some local general high schools began to include agriculture in their programs of studies. These must have been village high schools with sufficient increase in enrollment to employ the needed special teachers or larger rural high schools formed by various kinds of consolidation. Once under way, the movement developed rapidly,[14] but it is difficult at any point to specify how many schools were offering what kinds of instruction in the field.[15] By 1910, however, agricultural subjects enrolled 34,418 students in public high schools, or 4.7

[14] "The demand for popular education in agriculture came suddenly. Its rise and triumph have been accomplished almost in one decade. After half a century of propagandism in favor of popular education in this subject by the land-grant colleges, the United States Department of Agriculture, the agricultural experiment stations, and other agricultural organizations, the public mind has been placed in a receptive attitude. When small beginnings in public school agriculture were made in various localities over the country, the people took kindly to the new undertaking, or, at least, did not actively oppose it. In some communities a genuine enthusiasm was engendered by its introduction into the school courses. From these small beginnings, the enthusiasm for the study and teaching of elementary agriculture began to spread, gaining rapidly in force as time went on. From 1900 to 1905, the tide rose very rapidly, and during the following half-dozen years a veritable flood of public sentiment for the teaching of this branch in the schools swept the country." Garland Armor Bricker, *Agricultural Education for Teachers,* American Book Company, 1914, p. 8.

[15] The difficulties involved in statistics of agricultural studies in the period between 1900 and 1910 are indicated in the following quotation. "When any considerable number of schools are said to teach agriculture, either in the published reports, or in private correspondence, the number usually shrinks materially when subjected to an impartial examination of each case on its own merits. Thus one optimistic state superintendent in 1906 reported 200 high schools as teaching agriculture in his state. The report of his successor made the following year, containing the returns from a newly appointed high-school inspector, showed only 60 schools. Personal correspondence with the school principals of this state justifies the conclusion that not over 30 schools taught agriculture that was more than mere book work, without even window-sill or tomato-can experiments. Many of them reported that the subject was not taught at all. Recent estimates running into four figures do not seem at all warranted by the known facts. It must be said, however, that the number of public high schools, both general and special, teaching agriculture is increasing with marvelous rapidity." Robison, *op. cit.,* p. 23.

One historian who presents great detail on other matters in agricultural education cuts through all this with the following statement, "About the beginning of the twentieth century local high schools began to introduce instruction in agriculture, and by 1915 the number of such schools was large." True, *op. cit.,* pp. 350–351.

percent of all students in Grades 9 through 12, figures which increased respectively to 83,573 and 7.2 percent by 1915,[16] representing offerings in 4,390 schools.[17]

After 1905, the study of agriculture was caught up in the second national movement that influenced its development, that of enthusiasm for vocational education in a number of fields. The Smith-Hughes Act of 1917 included agriculture among the fields for which federal funds could be made available. One writer on secondary education, Alexander Inglis, predicted the year following that "Favorable legislation granting State and National aid to agricultural education will in all probability greatly extend its scope within the next few years, giving greater and greater importance to the agricultural subjects in the secondary-school program of studies."[18]

As was the case in home economics and in the industrial fields, the Smith-Hughes Act did not produce any substantial increase in numbers of students enrolled in agriculture. Where the numbers had increased from 34,418 to 83,573 between 1910 and 1915, they increased only from 83,573 to 110,242 between 1915 and 1922. Furthermore, enrollments relative to the total number of students in high school actually declined between 1915 and 1922 from 7.2 to 5.1 percent.[19] This was not necessarily considered a misfortune by the proponents of federally aided vocational agriculture. In fact, some of them felt that true vocational agriculture could not readily be provided at the high school level. "They have complained that the vocational education in agriculture commonly offered in our secondary schools has both weakened and changed from the program originally intended."[20] Nevertheless, high

[16] "Offerings and Enrollments in High-School Subjects," *Biennial Survey of Education in the United States, 1948–1950*, Federal Security Agency, Office of Education, 1951, table 7, p. 108.

[17] *Report of the United States Commissioner of Education* (1916), vol. 2, p. 497, cited in Alexander Inglis, *Principles of Secondary Education*, Houghton Mifflin Company, 1918, p. 606.

[18] Inglis, *op. cit.*, p. 606.

[19] "Offerings and Enrollments in High-School Subjects," *Biennial Survey, op. cit.*, table 7, p. 108.

[20] Herbert McNee Hamlin and Charles Wilson Sanford, *The Place of Agriculture in the Secondary School Program*, University of Illinois Bulletin, vol. 41, No. 12, November 9, 1943, pp. 5–6.

schools sought and managed to get a good deal of federal aid. The difficulties involved in meeting the Smith-Hughes criteria may have discouraged some schools from seeking to qualify for the funds. Furthermore, the criteria when rigorously applied tended to exclude some students who might otherwise have been interested in taking agriculture as a school subject.

Between 1922 and 1928 enrollments in agriculture declined both in actual numbers and in percentages of total enrollments, from 110,242 to 106,086 and from 5.1 to 3.7 percent.[21] This was a period of economic prosperity for city people, but a period of economic recession or depression for farmers. Many rural youth consequently may have felt pessimistic about farming as a career. The onset of general economic depression in 1929 induced pessimism about city careers as well, which may account for an increase in agriculture enrollments to 159,763 by 1934. High school enrollments, however, increased all along the line in those years, and those in agriculture still came to only 3.6 percent of the total, or about the same as had been true in 1928. But the downward trend in percentages of total enrollments that had been operating between 1915 and 1928 was at least checked. From this point on there was no further decline in enrollments in agricultural subjects, but rather a substantial increase particularly after World War II. By 1949, 364,185 students or 6.7 percent of all students in Grades 9 through 12 were taking agriculture,[22] and nine tenths of these were in federally reimbursed programs.[23] In 1956 there were 460,300 day students enrolled in vocational agriculture alone.[24]

THE NEED FOR VOCATIONAL AGRICULTURE

In spite of these increasing enrollments, there is more speculation about the place of vocational agriculture at the high school

[21] "Offerings and Enrollments in High-School Subjects," *Biennial Survey, op. cit.,* table 7, p. 108.

[22] *Ibid.*

[23] *Ibid.,* p. 24.

[24] Division of Vocational Education, Office of Education, *Digest of Annual Reports of State Boards for Vocational Education to the Office of Education, Division of Vocational Education, Summary of Statistical and Financial Information,* Fiscal Year Ended June 30, 1956, the U.S. Department of Health, Education, and Welfare, 1957, table 2, p. 8.

level today than there was three and four decades ago. The old questions about the adequacy of high school instruction for vocational purposes have remained, and to them have been added a host of new ones. And the new questions are much more difficult to resolve. They have arisen primarily from the changing nature of farm technology and economics. They have to do not with how well the high school boy can be vocationally educated for farming, but with his future and destiny after he has received such education.

The ideal of traditional vocational agriculture is the education of farm boys to run their own farms, even presumably to run their family farms as older generations retire. Non-farm boys have not been encouraged to enroll in programs of vocational agriculture, and when they do enroll find it difficult to carry out the required projects. This has been vocational education of a distinctly different kind from that in the industrial fields, where most students know they have to seek employment offered by others. It has contemplated a rural way of life based on small family units manned largely by their own independent proprietors.

We are told, however, that the possibilities of such a rural way of life have been greatly reduced and in fact may virtually disappear over the next several generations. By 1945, for example, although large-scale farms (defined as those with annual production over $20,000) made up only 1.7 percent of all farming units, they accounted for 25.8 percent of all farm acreage and 21.9 percent of gross value of farm production.[25] Furthermore, the number of farms had declined from 6,289,000 in 1930 to 5,379,000 in 1950, and the number of people on farms from 30,157,000 to an estimated 24,000,000 over the same period.[26] It also costs more money to enter or to stay in farming than was once the case. "Young persons looking forward to becoming farm operators will . . . need more capital than did their fathers and will find themselves operating an enterprise (in the medium- to large-scale fam-

[25] Lowry Nelson, "Education in a Changing Rural Life," in National Society for the Study of Education, Fifty-first Yearbook, pt. 2, *Education in Rural Communities,* the Society, 1952, table 1, p. 14.
[26] *Ibid.,* p. 17.

ily farm areas) valued at $40,000 to $50,000. This represents a barrier to farm ownership which young people lacking aid from relatives may not be able to surmount."[27]

There is, of course, another side to the story. Farm ownership in relation to tenancy has been on the increase, the percentage of tenant-operated farms declining from 42.4 percent in 1930 to 31.7 percent in 1945.[28] Contrary to popular impression, the number and percentage of manager-operated farms has not been increasing; it actually declined slightly between 1930 and 1945, although the total acreage in manager-operated farms did increase from 61,500,000 to 106,500,000 in the same period.[29]

The pattern therefore is a mixed one, with tendencies working in both directions. Unfortunately, there seem to be fewer plus than minus signs, from the point of view of those who favor the traditional rural way of life, with its family-owned and family-operated farms. At least this was the conclusion reached in the 1957 digest of annual reports of state boards for vocational education. "The trend continues toward fewer but larger farms and fewer persons in farming. Because of this trend and the amount of capital required it is becoming increasingly difficult for young men to become established in farming."[30]

Likewise, there are two or rather many sides to the story of the place and future of vocational agriculture in our high schools. At first glance, one might think the field has little or no future, at least on the secondary school level. Fewer and fewer farm youth will have the opportunity to own and run their own farms. It is true, of course, that large manager-operated farms require skilled professional managers and directors. Whether or not high school graduates, even if fitted for such positions, could compete effectively with professional graduates of university schools of agriculture is another question. Vocational agriculture then may be dead-end vocational education, with no place to go for those who have completed the work.

---

[27] *Ibid.,* p. 18.
[28] *Ibid.,* p. 26.
[29] *Ibid.,* pp. 27–28.
[30] Division of Vocational Education, *op. cit.,* p. 4.

On the other hand, there will always be some owner-operators, and these will need more competence and skill than those of the present and the past. Will there be enough to maintain an adequate high school program? Bjoraker suggests there will be, even assuming that the farm population drops from 13 percent to 5 percent of the 250,000,000 population predicted for 1980. A further assumption is made that the present one-in-five ratio of farm operators to total rural population will persist, indicating an approximate figure of 2,500,000 farm operators. There would be a need then for 60,000 replacements a year. If graduating seniors made up one fifth of the total number of students in the field, the situation would justify having 300,000 high school students in vocational agriculture at any one time. Since half the graduates of a vocational field may enter other lines of work, there would need to be 600,-000 students. This is a higher figure than the 460,000 so enrolled in 1955–1956.[31] In the light of this analysis, we shall need more rather than fewer vocational agriculture students. The 600,000 figure would probably represent a smaller percentage of total high school enrollments than has been true in recent years, but this in itself does not imply any diminishing of the present program. Skeptics may contend that Bjoraker's analysis contains a number of assumptions and conditions, but so, it may be replied, do the arguments of the skeptics themselves.

Furthermore, Bjoraker contends that "With the greater complexity of our farm business, the larger investment, the greater mechanization, and the greater need to apply the latest scientific 'know how,' we need better trained, not less trained farm operators and prospective operators."[32] There can be little doubt on this point. Economic penalties for incompetent farming have always been severe, but will become more so as farmers make heavier capital investments. This is important not only for the individual farmer, but in our highly interdependent economy for the nation

[31] Walter T. Bjoraker, *Vocational Education in Agriculture to Meet the Needs of Today's Youth,* a talk given before the vocational agriculture section of the Wisconsin Education Association, Milwaukee, November 7, 1957, pp. 4–5, mimeographed. Even if we assume that all vocational agriculture graduates will enter farming, the 300,000 figure is only 60,000 or so fewer than the numbers enrolled in 1948–1949.
[32] *Ibid.,* p. 6.

as a whole, with declines in rural prosperity soon making themselves felt in our urban industrial centers.

Graduates of vocational agriculture programs, furthermore, are not restricted to farming, but may enter or take preliminary steps toward a number of non-farming agricultural occupations. "Many young people from the farms, villages, and small cities are more interested in some of these newer agricultural occupations than in farming; consequently, the range of persons interested in the study of agriculture is extended. Workers in non-farming agricultural occupations include hatcherymen, nurserymen, veterinarians, agricultural teachers and extension workers, farm-organization specialists, farm journalists, dairy manufacturers, rural electricians, salesmen of feeds and fertilizers, farm credit specialists, and soil conservation workers."[33] Many of the occupations listed above demand continued education at the college or university level rather than specific vocational schooling in the high school. Still, a good background in vocational agriculture should be valuable to the prospective veterinarian, farm journalist, and the like. Bjoraker warns, however, that vocational agriculture "should not attempt to train for related occupations at the expense of its principal responsibility."[34]

NON-VOCATIONAL OR GENERAL AGRICULTURE

In spite of changes in rural economy and population characteristics, vocational agriculture still has and should continue to have an important place in our high school programs. On the other hand, not all instruction in agriculture at the high school level need be strictly vocational, although non-vocational agriculture has never quite taken hold. Hamlin and Sanford wrote in 1943, "There has been no development in agriculture paralleling the development of industrial arts, household arts, and general business training as subjects of general education."[35] In 1949, less than 10 percent of all agriculture students were enrolled in general or non-vocational courses.[36]

[33] Hamlin and Sanford, *op. cit.,* pp. 8–9.
[34] Bjoraker, *op. cit.,* p. 7.
[35] Hamlin and Sanford, *op. cit.,* p. 7.
[36] "Offerings and Enrollments in High-School Subjects," *Biennial Survey, op. cit.,* p. 24.

The future of non-vocational agriculture as a high school offering depends on several considerations. One is the extent to which agriculture deals with matters sufficiently important to constitute it as an instructional field apart from purely vocational ends. Here we have another field which, like homemaking, applies materials from a number of areas to a broad human activity. The same considerations apply here as in homemaking. Although the content of agriculture could be taken apart and distributed among a number of other fields, the activity of agriculture represents a comprehensive portion of civilized human achievement and can accordingly stand on its own merits. Few human activities have played so large a part in human destiny and in the establishment and maintenance of civilized communities. In the early days, the advocates of agriculture in the schools sought to justify it not only on vocational but also on disciplinary grounds. While not necessarily erroneous, these arguments were in fact unnecessary, for as Robison pointed out in 1911, "Not that it does not possess as much value in this direction as other studies, but agriculture as a study may justly claim to have a content of its own that is worthwhile."[37]

Other considerations affecting the future of agriculture as a general study are practical in nature, for example, adherence to a long-established and unfortunate stereotype that agriculture belongs in rural high schools only. Its restriction to schools where the vocational implications are direct and obvious has given the field an almost purely vocational character. This need not in the future close the door to the development of general agriculture in rural high schools. It might, for example, be more practical to make the first two years of agriculture studies in rural high schools general and exploratory rather than strictly vocational in character. This would provide a better basis for vocational guidance than is now the case. "Many school officials have found it difficult to believe that their pupils are ready for the serious and definite preparations for farming provided by the Smith-Hughes Act. They have believed that a thorough and comprehensive guidance program should precede any such specialized vocational training. The common practice, however, has been to enroll boys in these federally

[37] Robison, *op. cit.,* pp. 173–174.

aided classes at the beginning of their high school careers and before preliminary guidance has been furnished."[38] The wisdom of delaying vocational agriculture until the third high school year depends on the extent to which adequate training would be possible under such an arrangement. A four-year program made up of two years of general introductory and two years of vocational agriculture obviously could not include as much technical material or field practice as a straight four-year vocational program. But it may not be necessary. Not even the four-year vocational program turns out finished farm operators, and adult education has always been an important part of the total program under the Smith-Hughes Act.[39] Continued study at the junior college level or through the four years of agricultural colleges is another possibility, although a less practical one for many farmers and prospective farmers than adult in-service education in the local community. Vocational education in agriculture need not and in fact does not stop at high school graduation. Some reduction in the amount of vocational content covered up to graduation time might not be too high a price to pay for the better guidance opportunities that could be developed by placing the first two years of study on a general basis for more students.

Neither do we need to rest content with the assumption that agriculture is for rural schools only. If the field is worth studying for non-vocational puposes, it belongs in urban schools as well. But it is easy to see why city school boards hesitate to spend money for a program attracting a conjectural number of students on an elective basis. Development of agriculture in a city high school necessarily takes time, and the board meanwhile faces the task of justifying its action in relation to needs in other fields. It is difficult also to develop vocational programs in city schools under the Smith-Hughes Act. Unless the board is prepared to maintain a school farm, city boys cannot easily carry out the projects required

[38] Hamlin and Sanford, *op. cit.,* p. 5.

[39] In Illinois, for example, "adult farmers have been highly responsive. About 500 classes are provided annually for them. About 10 per cent of the farm operators of the state are enrolled each year." Allerton House Conference on Education, Report of Study Group X (Agriculture), *Replanning Agricultural Education in Illinois Schools,* November, 1958, p. 12.

in federally reimbursed programs, although it is now possible for them to do so if their school enters into agreements with farm owners of the vicinity under the program of placement for farm experience. A few city systems have offered general and vocational agriculture, but the field on the whole has remained one identified almost entirely with rural[40] or village high schools and seems likely so to continue for some time to come. This is too bad, for the value of the field extends far beyond its present restricted scope. As things stand now, agricultural education is about in the position business education would be if confined to city schools and limited to the sons and daughters of small business proprietors.

CURRICULAR ISSUES IN AGRICULTURAL EDUCATION

Even within its present restricted scope, the field of agriculture is important and necessary, and its curricular questions deserve study and consideration by all concerned with secondary schooling. One of the questions is that of sequence in the four-year program, the difficulties here being similar to those in English, physical education, and home economics. Prior to 1920, most programs followed what has since become known as the conventional or traditional organization, within which the instruction for each of the four years centered on a particular aspect of agriculture, such as farm animals, farm mechanics, and the like. A study of programs in 17 states made in 1917 indicated a tendency as follows: first year, soils and vegetable gardening; second year, farm crops and fruit growing; third year, animal husbandry, dairying, and poultry; and fourth year, farm management and farm mechanics.[41]

This kind of organization was gradually supplanted by one known as the integrated or cross-sectional in which some topics from each of the major areas are included at each level, the various year courses being called simply Agriculture I, II, III, and IV.[42] The justification for this is the difficulty of confining actual farm

[40] Rural high schools include those of fairly large enrollments under township, joint, or union districts. Township high schools serving urban communities rarely offer agriculture.

[41] Theodore Hildreth Eaton, *A Study of Organization and Method of the Course of Study in Agriculture in Secondary Schools,* Teachers College, Columbia University, Contributions to Education, No. 86, 1917, p. 70.

[42] Hamlin and Sanford, *op. cit.,* p. 7.

problems to particular bodies of material. "Farming involves the integration and skills from all the specialized agricultural fields. Training for farming must provide much practice in solving problems of the types farmers encounter. If such problems are to be solved, the pupil cannot be restricted in solving them to facts from a particular area. Most of them relate somehow to all of the recognized areas."[43]

The question of sequence is tied to the question of method, particularly the handling of practical field projects and activities. At one time it was considered desirable for schools offering agricultural education to own and operate their own practice farms. Schools in Massachusetts and New York, however, were using home projects "as early as 1908."[44] The Smith-Hughes Act of 1917 made a definite requirement of "directed or supervised practice in agriculture, either on a farm provided for by the school or other farm, for at least six months per year."[45] After this time, most schools shifted from the school-farm project to the home project. There were and still are today many practical and administrative reasons why schools prefer not to own and operate their own farms. Regardless of the reasons, "Heavy outlays for school farms have been largely avoided since the passage of the Smith-Hughes Act in 1917. School farms and school farm equipment and livestock in notable cases have been disposed of and, generally speaking, students now carry on projects and other supervised farm practice on home farms rather than on school-owned farms."[46] Some schools still maintain small farms, usually called land laboratories,[47] but these do not lend themselves to the individual projects required under the Smith-Hughes Act.

Shifting from the school-farm to the home-farm activity meant

[43] *Ibid.*, p. 15.

[44] E. W. Garris, *Teaching Vocational Agriculture,* McGraw-Hill Book Company, Inc., 1954, p. 7.

[45] The National Vocational Education Act, Public Law 347, Sixty-Fourth Congress, Senate Bill 703, Appendix I in Garris, *op. cit.,* p. 350.

[46] Rufus W. Stimson, "Home Project Teaching and Related Educational Developments," chap. 11 in Rufus W. Stimson and Frank W. Lathrop (compilers), *History of Agricultural Education of Less than College Grade in the United States: A Cooperative Project of Workers in Vocational Education in Agriculture and in Related Fields,* Federal Security Agency, U.S. Office of Education, Vocational Division Bulletin No. 217, Agricultural Series No. 55, 1942, p. 605.

[47] Garris, *op. cit.,* pp. 84–88.

a shift from group to individual projects. Moreover, it meant a good deal of diversification in the kinds of projects used, since students might come from different kinds of farms. Unless the teacher saw fit to detach the individual projects entirely from the class work, he had to find curricular patterns more flexible than those of the older or conventional organization. The cross-sectional organization appears to fit this best and will probably persist so long as the individual-project method remains dominant. Feeling on behalf of the individual-project method has been and remains very strong among educators in vocational agriculture and to some extent among those in other fields as well. Back in the days when the project method commanded almost universal enthusiasm among writers in general method, the field of vocational agriculture was applauded as an example of its successful application. The method has now become the traditional one in the field of agriculture and is not likely to be displaced.

Another practice that demands flexible curricular organization is the individual project extending over the four years of the student's program. "When continuation projects and long-time programs of supervised farm practice became common, increasing difficulty was experienced in maintaining a close relationship between supervised farm practice and class instruction; for example, a student with a dairy project extending over 4 years would get dairy instruction during only 1 year, under the vertical organization, whereas he should have such instruction over the entire 4-year period at the times when he needs it to help him make decisions and solve specific problems arising in connection with his supervised farm practice."[48] This practice both promotes and reflects an intensive degree of specialization that probably cannot be avoided if the field purports to train students for particular kinds of farm work. "Students in the same class are often training to enter quite different types of farming and farming situations. The teacher may have one student who is preparing to be primarily a dairy farmer, one a hog farmer, one a vegetable farmer, one a fruit farmer, one a nurseryman, and one a florist. Each boy in the class faces problems in his supervised farming program which must receive careful study at the right time. Under such conditions, the teachers must use individualized instruction in order to meet the differences in the need of each student."[49] Other aspects of agriculture, however, are not neglected, but are related to the major center of interest.

The danger in any flexible sequence that tends to repeat different aspects of the same materials at different levels is that of formlessness or even chaos. Vocational agriculture has avoided this by making very definite allocations of particular units of study at various points in the four-year program. Nevertheless there seems to be sentiment in favor of modifying the extreme cross-sectional kind of organization, one writer reporting that "Reference was made in several replies to modified cross-section arrangements, carrying inferences that a fully-integrated sequence may lead to a hodge-podge of unrelated units with insufficient emphasis on each unit to secure best results."[50] He reports variations in course organization in some states ranging "from the conventional to a strong cross-sectional approach,"[51] including one state where "an integrated content of fundamentals is recommended on the class basis for freshmen, followed in succeeding years with group work in which application is stressed and finally by an individual type of instruction where working plans are developed."[52] This latter arrangement is consistent with the placing of the first year or two of agriculture on a general or non-vocational basis, followed by intensive vocational training in the upper high school years, although this is not the only basis on which such an arrangement can be developed.

Leaders in the field of vocational agriculture have insisted on the need for good general education. "The underlying thought of agriculture in the high school is that of a vocational course corre-

[49] Garris, *op. cit.*, p. 153.
[50] George F. Ekstrom, "Course of Study and Curriculum," The Agricultural Education Magazine, *What Do Studies Show? Summaries and Interpretations of Research in Selected Areas of Agricultural Education,* The Interstate Printers and Publishers, Inc., 1952, p. 6.
[51] *Ibid.*
[52] *Ibid.*

lated with a strong general high school course. . . . The general course should provide a broad training and culture adapted to the needs of any good citizen. Such a course should include work along all the fundamental lines, such as language, history, literature, mathematics, science and the arts, but it is especially important that the general course should include strong work in the fundamental sciences."[53] The vocational agriculture sequence does not demand more than four of the 16 units in the usual high school program. The wisdom of this has been reaffirmed by Hamlin and Sanford. "Probably no high school pupil should be allowed to complete in agriculture more than one-fourth of the units required for high school graduation. Whether or not he goes to college, every pupil needs a balanced education."[54] Administrative provisions make it possible for pupils to get this balanced education; whether they get it or not depends on what they elect and the counseling help received in making these elections. It also depends on what is available in the school offerings. Students of vocational agriculture enjoy few opportunities, for example, of taking foreign languages, since that field has disappeared from many rural high schools. For the most part, however, the ideal of a moderate degree of specialization within the setting of other kinds of studies has been well maintained in vocational agriculture programs.

Bibliography

Bailey, L. H., *The Country-Life Movement in the United States,* The Macmillan Company, 1911.

Bailey, L. H., *The Training of Farmers,* The Century Company, 1909.

Bricker, Garland Armor, *Agricultural Education for Teachers,* American Book Company, 1914.

Davis, Benjamin Marshall, *Agricultural Education in the Public Schools,* The University of Chicago Press, 1912.

Eaton, Theodore Hildreth, *A Study of Organization and Method of the Course of Study in Agriculture in Secondary Schools,* Teachers Col-

[53] Wisconsin Department of Public Instruction, *Agriculture in the High School,* prepared by Henry N. Goddard, assisted by John A. James, The Department, 1917, pp. 17–18.

[54] Hamlin and Sanford, *op. cit.,* p. 29.

lege, Columbia University, Contributions to Education, No. 86, 1917.

Garris, E. W., *Teaching Vocational Agriculture,* McGraw-Hill Book Company, Inc., 1954.

Hamlin, Herbert McNee, and Sanford, Charles Wilson, *The Place of Agriculture in the Secondary School Program,* University of Illinois Bulletin, vol. 41, No. 12, November 9, 1943.

Hummel, William Granville, and Hummel, Bertha Royce, *Materials and Methods in High School Agriculture,* The Macmillan Company, 1913.

Nelson, Lowry, "Education in a Changing Rural Life," in National Society for the Study of Education, Fifty-first Yearbook, pt. 2, *Education in Rural Communities,* The Society, 1952.

Robison, Clarence Hall, *Agricultural Instruction in the Public High Schools of the United States,* Teachers College, Columbia University, Contributions to Education, No. 39, 1911.

Stimson, Rufus W., and Lathrop, Frank W. (compilers), *History of Agricultural Education of Less than College Grade in the United States: A Coöperative Project of Workers in Vocational Education in Agriculture and in Related Fields,* Federal Security Agency, U.S. Office of Education, Vocational Division Bulletin No. 217, Agricultural Series No. 55, 1942.

True, Alfred, *A History of Agricultural Education in the United States 1785–1925,* United States Department of Agriculture Miscellaneous Publication No. 36, 1929.

CHAPTER 21

....

The Curriculum Beyond the Classroom Studies

Few schools in history have so given the appearance of cultivating the informal or non-classroom portions of their curricula as has the United States high school of the twentieth century. This cultivation has proceeded to the point where, in the opinion of many observers, the informal program appears to be pushing classroom studies out of the school altogether, or at least relegating them to a position of subordination or inferiority. Such an unwarranted conclusion is one which the public, confronted as it is by football games, basketball tournaments, music contests, school plays, and school parties and dances, often finds difficult to avoid.

Unfortunately, we tend to center too much attention on the spectacular features of our schools, which, commendable as many of them may be, are hardly representative of either the classroom studies or the non-classroom aspects of the curriculum. All this is probably inevitable, given the natural human tendency to special awareness of those things which are colorful and concrete. It has, however, in the specific instance of school programs led to misunderstanding and sometimes to condemnation of their non-classroom aspects. For we do not always approve of the colorful and concrete things that command our attention. Sometimes, too, we condemn today what we embraced with enthusiasm yesterday. Such has often been the fate of spectacular movements, while the more unobtrusive aspects of the daily task go on with neither special approval nor special rejection.

The truth is that the greater portion of the non-classroom program consists of the ordinary tasks of everyday school life. Many observers might find them hopelessly dull, but this would be indeed a superficial conclusion, for they are by no means dull to the students who take part in them. But they do not command headlines or start many verbal wars. Consider, for example, a counselor helping a student make his program of studies, a meeting of the student council to consider noon-hour activities, the reporting of this meeting by council representatives to their own home rooms, an after-school session of the chess club, a student's working two hours in a drugstore under school supervision, or an intramural volley ball game between two teams of enthusiastic but relatively undistinguished athletes. There are also the more colorful items that gain public attention. We should not, however, conclude that such activities are wrong, for they also play an important part in the curriculum.

Here a further note of disapproval sometimes enters. Even those who do not consider the non-classroom program dangerous or harmful sometimes doubt that it is worth time, money, and effort. This skepticism is sometimes shared by teachers themselves, especially when overburdened by unduly heavy if not impossible assignments.

The non-classroom program is good for a number of things we are concerned about in schooling. An oversimplified allocation of school purposes to this or that part of the curriculum is neither possible nor desirable. Some of the desirable outcomes of the non-classroom program are the same as those of the classroom studies, namely the learning of the instructional fields. Science is taught and learned in the science club as well as in the science classroom. The science classroom, however, carries the major share of the science instruction and we could, as far as the learning of science is concerned, get along without the science club if necessary.

On the other hand, the work of high schools does not stop with the transmission of culture, important and all-pervasive as this function is and should be, or with the use of this culture for intellectual, moral, civic, or occupational development. It includes helping young people develop along other personal-social lines as well.[1] Some of this can be and is done through classroom instruction, but it is best done through the learning activities and the instructional procedures. It is not primarily the job of the classroom studies, at least in the subject organization, to organize instruction around personal-social problems.

Something must, nonetheless, be specifically provided for personal-social development, and that something is the portion of the school curriculum that goes beyond the classroom studies. This does not imply a rigid separation of functions. In fact, it is not always possible even to make a neat distinction between the classroom and the non-classroom program. Guidance, for example, is largely part of the non-classroom program, but group guidance is often carried on in scheduled classroom time. Many teachers have duties in both parts of the program and would find it difficult sometimes to say when they are doing one to the exclusion of the other. Such overlapping is inevitable and desirable, but it does not make classroom instruction identical with the non-classroom program. Neither does it reduce the necessity for the non-classroom program in relation to personal-social development. Under the subject organization, subtraction of the non-classroom program means possible neglect of the personal-social objectives or the weakening and distortion of the classroom studies.

GUIDANCE

Guidance services are indispensable in any high school program based on a recognition of and provision for differences among students. No two students are alike, and no two students pursue identical curriculums. Students therefore are repeatedly confronted by the need to make the choices that determine the nature and direction of their schooling. They deserve the thoughtful guidance of adults in the making of these choices. Some of this is provided by parents, some by the guidance services of the school. But this is not all there is to guidance. It has a teaching function as

---

[1] As stated in chap. 4, this term is used in this book to include such objectives as physical health, mental or emotional health, enjoyment of living, and family living as well as other aspects of immediate or everyday human relationships. Family living, of course, is a direct objective in the field of homemaking or home economics.

well. The notion of guidance is made somewhat complicated by the existence of two kinds of guidance activities: individual counseling and those activities frequently, and perhaps erroneously, named group guidance. Some people in the field do not approve of group guidance, contending that it is a contradiction in terms. Notwithstanding this disapproval, attempts are made in many high schools to practice it in a variety of settings, including home rooms, core classes where these exist, extraclass activities, and even in some classrooms of the subject organization.

Whether or not group guidance is a legitimate aspect of guidance depends on how the term "guidance" is defined. Some definitions make guidance virtually synonymous with the entire enterprise of schooling, in fact with education no matter where or how conducted. The term "curriculum" has also suffered from this breadth of definition, sometimes becoming synonymous not only with all of education, but with all of life. Students of curriculum have found it advantageous to withdraw to more sharply pointed and restrictive definitions. Guidance workers also have been looking for a tighter notion of what their field is. A composite definition summarizing a number of expressions in many guidance books would run as follows: guidance is whatever is done for the explicit purpose of helping individuals (1) understand themselves and (2) develop the capacity to make intelligent decisions and plans.[2]

Guidance thereby gains identity through the purposes it serves and through the focus of its attentions. This focus is the individual, never the group. Purists, consequently, like to insist on individual counseling as the only legitimate kind of guidance activity. The emphasis on the individual in most definitions, however, is on what the individual learns, not how he learns it. Information on the uses and limitations of aptitude tests, for example, is of sufficient general applicability that it may be offered to a number of

[2] For example, "Simply stated, a guidance program is an organized effort on the part of the school to help students understand themselves so that they may become increasingly more capable of wise decisions in making and carrying out educational and vocational plans." Leonard W. Cox, "What Is an Effective Guidance Program in the Senior High School," *The Bulletin of the National Association of Secondary-School Principals,* vol. 42, no. 237, April, 1958, p. 173.

students at one time. Specific interpretations and applications of the test scores of a given individual should, on the other hand, be handled solely with the individual concerned. There are, in addition, some personal matters that ought never to be discussed in a group, even on a general basis. Group guidance, therefore, should be used sparingly and should assume a role distinctly subordinate to that of individual counseling. Indeed, it seems likely that group guidance without individual counseling should not be attempted.

It is customary to refer to various kinds of guidance, such as vocational, educational, and personal-social, the latter term including many diverse aspects of living. The oldest of these, as far as historical identification is concerned, is vocational guidance, the formalized version of which has been with us for at least a half-century. It developed as an aspect of social work in the activities of Frank Parsons, who helped organize the Boston Vocation Bureau in 1908.[3] This agency stimulated the early introduction of vocational guidance in the Boston public schools, and the movement spread into a number of other school systems, partly as a natural and inevitable consequence of the strong movement for vocational education operating in the same period.[4] Vocational guidance necessarily included helping individuals choose training programs both in and out of schools, resulting in the identification of educational guidance as such. The latter term came to include

[3] John M. Brewer, *The Vocational-Guidance Movement: Its Problems and Possibilities,* The Macmillan Company, 1918, pp. 22–24. See the entire book for much interesting detail on the early vocational guidance movement.

[4] Vocational guidance was also motivated by the humanitarian ideals of individual and social welfare that formed part of the background for the vocational education movement itself. In the following quotation from Frank Parsons' pioneer book, *Choosing a Vocation,* the concern shown is not only with efficient production, but with human happiness. "An occupation out of harmony with the worker's aptitudes and capacities means inefficiency, unenthusiastic and perhaps distasteful labor, and low pay; while an occupation in harmony with the nature of the man means enthusiasm, love of work, and high economic values,—superior product, efficient service, and good pay. If a young man chooses his vocation so that his best abilities and enthusiasms will be united with his daily work, he has laid the foundations of success and happiness. But if his best abilities and enthusiasms are separated from his daily work, or do not find in it fair scope and opportunity for exercise and development; if his occupation is merely a means of making a living, and the work he loves to do is side-tracked into the evening hours, or pushed out of his life altogether, he will be only a fraction of the man he ought to be." Frank Parsons, *Choosing a Vocation,* Houghton Mifflin Company, 1909, p. 3.

all educational choices, whether specifically related to vocations or not. Concern about personal-social needs and objectives in the late 1920's and early 1930's led to a large, somewhat undifferentiated third category appearing under a variety of names, but dedicated to helping students along personal-social lines.

All these are important and are obviously interrelated. They do not fit into administrative compartments. A single interview may deal with all three. The central concern of guidance in schools, however, is with educational choices, which are sometimes, but not always, related to vocational and personal-social concerns. These choices determine the curriculum of the individual student. In making them, the student presumably develops increased understanding of himself and increased capacity for dealing with future choices. This kind of guidance is to a certain extent directive, not in the sense of the counselor's making the decisions for the student, but in his presenting information and raising questions that the student should take into consideration.

Educational guidance first of all deals with choices of subjects for study. This is far too complex a matter to be resolved by placing students in programs or tracks, such as college-preparatory, general, and the like. Such tracks serve only as guidance short cuts. What they do is to absorb a number of choices into one choice, that of the track itself. In the absence of effective guidance, the track system is an alternative to chaos, but, unfortunately, a poor alternative. In the presence of effective guidance, it is unnecessary. In the absence of tracks, the only alternative to chaos is effective guidance, but this is, when realizable, a good one.

The effectiveness of this educational guidance depends on the counselor. He must, of course, know a great deal about adolescent development, college requirements, job requirements, and tests. This is usually acknowledged. In addition, however, the counselor must know the classroom studies, as many of them as possible through his own experience with them as a student and the others through a systematic study of their nature, objectives, and content. He must know them sympathetically and be free from the conventional notions with which some subjects are associated: for example, that industrial arts and homemaking are particularly good choices for low-ability students or that a foreign language is an appropriate choice only for a student planning on college. It is this second aspect of the counselor's effectiveness that has not received the attention it deserves, although many counselors are highly competent along these lines.

Choices of subjects will, of course, be affected by and will affect vocational plans. This is not the only reason for vocational guidance in the high school, but it would be a sufficient one even if none other existed. It would be futile to provide four years of vocational agriculture, for example, if the means were not available for helping students decide on agricultural careers. Vocational guidance, moreover, deals not only with choices of high school subjects, but anticipates the need for continued schooling beyond high school. This includes attention to college requirements in general, to the extent at least that such exist, to the requirements of particular colleges and college programs, and to the requirements of vocational schools and apprenticeship programs.

Most personal-social problems and concerns of students are not directly related to choices of subjects. There is, however, one important exception to this, namely the area of personal interests. In the long run this is just as important in subject choices as are vocational goals and plans. A student may wish to take industrial arts, geometry, or Latin for no other reason than that of pure enjoyment. Here is where the counselor must be unusually perceptive and sensitive, especially when it is a non-college-bound student who wants to take Latin and the college-bound student who wants to take industrial arts. To fall back on the accustomed stereotypes about college-preparatory and non-college-preparatory students in cases like this can be disastrous. It is the counselor's duty not only to respect such interests, but to help students become aware of them as bases for subject selections.

In schools that use flexible definitions of minimum and maximum student loads, the counselor will help students decide the number of subjects to take in a given year. It was indicated earlier that more students than is now the case might take five subjects and that some might even take six. Similarly, some low-ability students might do better taking two or three subjects rather than the customary four. These decisions cannot be made by formula, but are unique to each student and as such become matters of concern in guidance.

Just as there is more to schooling than classroom studies, there is more to educational guidance than the selection of subjects. One critical matter is the nature and extent of individual participation in extraclass activities. Again, many schools have tried to deal with this through formal legislation applicable on a blanket basis to all students, but individual counseling is the better approach. The same applies to participation in school-related work experience.

Although educational guidance is central in the responsibility of the school, vocational guidance and personal-social guidance are no mere appendages. They follow as natural consequences the acceptance of vocational and personal-social objectives. Vocational guidance is the one aspect of vocational education that the school cannot avoid. Through it the individual may be helped to realize satisfaction to himself and contribution to society. To the adolescent, vocational guidance is an important means of meeting one of the developmental tasks, namely that of achieving adult social and economic status. This does not mean that all adolescents must make their vocational choices while in high school. It does mean that all adolescents should receive help in understanding their vocational interests and capacities. The best decisions for some adolescents at given times may be to postpone their career choices. It is through the help guidance should provide that students may assess the wisdom or lack of wisdom in such postponement.

There is little controversy about the desirability and the necessity of both educational and vocational guidance. Personal-social guidance is another matter, for this suggests to many the invasion of the private affairs and lives of individuals. Controversy about personal-social guidance is often based on a misunderstanding of guidance itself. Guidance is not snooping; neither does it consist of gratuitous advice. It is not amateur psychiatry; in fact it is not psychiatry at all, for counselors neither diagnose nor treat mental or emotional disturbance.[5] It is never directive in the sense of telling people what to do; on vocational and educational matters it is somewhat directive in the sense of raising questions for discussion. Personal-social guidance is the most non-directive of all. Counselors do not force discussion on students and ought not to propose questions on personal-social matters, with the single exception, previously noted, of those dealing with course selections in relation to personal interests. What personal-social guidance provides is the opportunity for students to discuss with an understanding adult the matters they choose to discuss.[6] If such matters are to be discussed in schools at all, it is better to do so in the privacy of the counseling interview than in the publicity of general classroom activities. Obviously, any counselor who deals with personal-social matters should be a person of wisdom, understanding, sensitivity, and judgment. If a school is so unfortunate as not to have such persons on their staffs, it should avoid the area of personal-social guidance.

Much of the disagreement about guidance in school practice involves the organization of guidance services and the identification of participants in the guidance process. Desirably, these participants include full-time classroom teachers as well as guidance specialists. Yet some easy assumptions in this connection need to be scrutinized. One of our most unsatisfactory truisms is that every

[5] Some school systems employ specialists who are qualified in psychotherapy and who work with emotionally disturbed children referred to them by teachers and other staff members. Although these specialists use counseling as well as other approaches, they are not counselors in the sense that term is used in this chapter.

Every school system has its own pattern or lack of pattern of procedures and facilities for referral. Some have coöperative arrangements or relationships with other community agencies, both public and private. Rural and village schools usually make their arrangements through the county superintendent's office. There are many school systems, however, in which no arrangements for referral exist, or in which they are so casual as to be ineffective.

A teacher new in a school system should make it his business to get exact information from the administrator on these matters. Under no circumstances should he succumb to the temptation to engage in diagnosis or psychotherapy himself. This applies also to those who are designated as counselors and to the director of guidance himself.

[6] As one high school student has put it, although not with special reference to personal-social guidance, "I certainly appreciated the counseling I received. I love to talk to people and not have them *half interested* in me or laugh at my ideas but be *genuinely interested* in my future." Quoted in John W. M. Rothney, *Guidance Practices and Results,* Harper & Brothers, 1958, p. 24.

teacher is a guidance worker. A parallel expression is that guidance is an all-pervasive phenomenon that enters every nook and cranny of school activities. Both of these overlook the necessity of identifying people who have specific guidance responsibilities and of providing specific times and places for guidance to function.

The fact is that not all teachers are interested in performing specific guidance functions or assuming guidance responsibilities. There is no reason why they should be. Teachers are individuals with individual differences and will make differing kinds of contributions to the life and work of the school. Of course any teacher may at times deal with certain guidance matters, such as the election of further work in a given instructional field or the relationship of the field to vocational plans. Practically every teacher has in his lifetime helped some students understand themselves and to gain wisdom and insight into the making of decisions. This incidental guidance, however, is something quite different from specific provisions for guidance services.

At the other extreme is the idea that guidance is something to be carried on only by those designated as specialists. This point of view is usually based on two arguments, one that of efficiency, the other an alleged lack of technical competence on the part of the general teaching staff. But what does it mean to be a guidance specialist? It should of course mean a person who has received specialized training in guidance. Administratively, it means a person who devotes full time or a major portion of his time to specific guidance services. A part-time guidance specialist or counselor is usually also a part-time classroom teacher, but presumably one who has received adequate training in guidance. It is difficult, therefore, to distinguish administratively between a part-time guidance specialist and a general classroom teacher who has an extra period or so for counseling.

Entirely apart from the merits or lack of merits in these arguments, it is impossible under current and foreseeable future school practice for the designated guidance specialists to assume the entire responsibility for guidance. Individual counseling takes a lot of time. Each student should have conference time for the important matter of choosing subjects and extraclass activities, and this not

once but several times each year. And this is only one part of
guidance. Most schools with guidance specialists attempt to provide
one full-time counselor or the equivalent to every 300 students.
Many schools run as high as 500 or more students per counselor.
The fact is, however, that even 300 students per counselor is far too
high to permit the kinds of individual counseling that should take
place.

Some assignment of specific guidance responsibilities to some
members of the general teaching staff becomes, therefore, a matter of practical necessity. The usual approach to the use of classroom teachers as counselors is through the home room, an institution with a most interesting if confusing history. Some home
rooms meet every day, others less frequently, with great variations
in length of periods, some running as little as five minutes, others
extending over an hour or more. Sometimes home room periods
are merged with activity periods. Practically all home rooms are
attendance-checking stations and serve as convenient times and
places for the clearing of a number of routine operations in the
daily life of the school. In schools with student councils, the home
room usually defines the constituency of a council member or representative.

The home room teacher can assume some guidance responsibilities, including those of individual counseling, provided, of course,
that he is interested in counseling and has some competence in it.
It is desirable for a teacher to keep one group of students in a
home room over a period of at least two years. When possible he
should keep them three or four. There are, however, some mechanical flaws in the home room arrangement. It is difficult
administratively to provide the home room teacher with counselees
whom he also has in class.[7] It is also difficult to provide places for

---

[7] Obviously, a teacher who has a student both in home room and in class has a
better chance to get to know that student. Some guidance authorities, however, feel
it is better to separate counseling from classroom teaching, contending that the role
of the teacher is inconsistent with the acceptance role they feel should characterize
the work of the counselor. There are many variations of opinion and belief on these
matters. Ira Gordon points out how this may be affected by the characteristics of the
individual teacher. "A good deal of this depends upon the teacher's understanding of
his own self system. If the teacher does not clearly know how he feels about himself,
it will be difficult for him to provide a fairly consistent framework upon which the

the desirable privacy of individual counseling, especially if the counseling must be done in the home room period itself. After-school sessions are possible only with students who do not have to catch a school bus and who do not have after-school jobs. In addition, they suggest the traditional disciplinary connotations of detention periods. Appointments during the day are limited by the fact that free periods for counselees and teachers do not always coincide.

Additional difficulties intrude themselves, however, because of the long association of home rooms not only with individual counseling, but with group guidance. In fact, it was the desire for group guidance that motivated the initial growth of the home room movement. The idea was to devote home room sessions to teacher-student discussions of topics that could not ordinarily be included in the scheduled classroom studies. As long as these sessions were confined to such matters as information on job trends and requirements, opportunities for participation in extra-class activities, and the nature of school subjects and curricula, they were both manageable and desirable. Enthusiasts for home room group guidance, however, went beyond such matters to urge sessions devoted to topics more or less in the personal-social area, such as good citizenship, character development, use of leisure time, getting along with people, loyalty, reliability, courage, cheerfulness, friendship, and the like. Worthy as such topics are, most of them are either too abstract or too immediately personal to serve as good vehicles for half-hour lessons or discussions in a home room setting, especially when we consider that most home room teachers do not know their home room students as well as they do students in their classes and that the groups rarely overlap. Many home room teachers, with considerable justification, considered these sessions irritating distractions that interfered with preparation for teaching their classes.

---

students can build their concepts of his role. If when he is 'teacher' he does not 'tolerate any nonsense,' he cannot as 'counselor' suddenly be 'permissive' without confusing the students and cutting off opportunities for them to establish counseling relationships with him." *The Teacher as a Guidance Worker,* Harper & Brothers, 1956, p. 268.

Few schools today use home rooms for this kind of personal-social group guidance. The past association of home rooms with such practices, however, has given the home room a bad name. Some schools have abandoned them entirely; some have reduced them to short daily meetings largely for attendance checking or other routine administrative activities.

In the absence of the usual home room arrangements, schools have tried other ways of involving classroom teachers more definitely in guidance responsibilities. One way is to merge the home room with a given class period, usually the opening period of the school day. The period may be lengthened to provide additional time for home room business and possible activities related to guidance. It there is no home room business, the teacher may go directly into the classroom work of his subject, thereby avoiding the awkward lulls that sometimes take place in the conventional home room arrangement.[8] It is difficult, however, to work out a schedule in which every student is in a class during the first period, or any other given period. If such a schedule can be worked out, it is usually necessary to see that practically every teacher has a class during that period. This has the disadvantage of requiring most or all teachers to assume specific guidance responsibilities, regardless of qualifications or interests.

Another device is to designate all teachers of required classes in a given field, such as English or social studies, as counselors for the students in these classes. Usually this is accompanied by a reduction of one class in the teaching load. A ninth-grade English teacher, for example, may have four sections with a total of 120 students or so, all of whom are his counselees. He has one period a day, theoretically at least, for counseling 120 students, a ratio that

---

[8] This kind of home room arrangement goes back at least a quarter of a century in high school practice. Referring to it as a "First-period recitation group," Fretwell commented as follows in 1931. "This plan makes for flexibility; the home-room or the recitation period can be lengthened or shortened according to the demands of the particular day. One principal says, 'We formerly had a fifteen-minute period—just long enough really to do little and too long to waste, so we combined with the first period, making the first period fifteen minutes longer than other periods and all home-room groups have their first recitation in their home-rooms." Elbert K. Fretwell, *Extra-Curricular Activities in Secondary Schools,* Houghton Mifflin Company, 1931, p. 39.

does not compare unfavorably with a full-time counselor who has five periods for counseling 600. The English teacher, however, who is relieved of one class for this function is to some extent a part-time guidance specialist himself, a fact which illustrates the difficulty of trying to distinguish between specialists and non-specialists in administrative terms. It may be argued that the money used to relieve English teachers of one class could also be used to hire more full-time counselors, thereby reducing the ratios in that direction. Another difficulty with this arrangement is that not all English teachers are interested in, temperamentally suited for, or competent to assume specific guidance responsibilities.

One modification of this device is the use of multiple-period classes as guidance centers. A teacher who has two double-period classes in English and social studies will have four teaching periods but only 60 students. This offers more scope for the performance of guidance functions than the arrangement under which the teacher has 120 students in four separate sections, provided, of course, that he has time, competence, and facilities for individual counseling. Of course this arrangement also involves the cost of reducing teaching loads from five classes to four, but with more likelihood of providing better guidance services. Whether or not it would be better to use the same funds for the employment of additional full-time counselors can be debated. It should be remembered, however, that a teacher who has one period for counseling 60 students is about in the same position as a full-time counselor who has five periods for counseling 300, the ratio held up as a fairly workable one by some writers. Obviously it would be better if all teachers had their loads reduced, entirely apart from guidance responsibilities, but the five-class load has been and unfortunately will probably continue to be the prevailing pattern.

While multiple-period classes in the subject organization may serve as guidance centers or stations, they do not exist primarily for this purpose. There are good reasons for multiple-period scheduling even though the teachers of such classes have no specific guidance responsibilities whatsoever. By reducing the daily teacher-student ratio, the multiple-period schedule gives teachers the opportunity of working with fewer students and of doing better teaching in the instructional fields involved. It is a mistake therefore to assume that the need for multiple-period scheduling and the need for guidance are interdependent.

Core classes, on the other hand, are by definition of those who advocate them centers for organized guidance services, and the core teacher is by the same kind of definition a counselor. The core, according to its advocates, represents a merger of guidance and classroom instruction. A substantial portion of the classroom instruction in the core is group guidance, but the teacher carries on individual counseling as well. The merit or lack of merit of this arrangement depends, of course, on the suitability of the core approach to the organization of classroom studies, as well as on points of view regarding the nature of guidance.

No matter what arrangements are made, however, for the involvement of classroom teachers in specific guidance responsibilities, there is always a need for one or more guidance specialists on the high school staff, preferably on a full-time or nearly full-time basis. The guidance specialist is responsible for viewing the program as a whole, for assuming leadership in faculty study and appraisal of the program, for providing needed in-service education of the participating teachers, and for maintaining the testing and records services used by teachers. In addition, he will on referral from the classroom teachers do some individual counseling himself, although his time and opportunities for this under a combined system will necessarily be limited.

In very small high schools (those of 200 or fewer students), the services of full-time guidance specialists are usually not available, at least under our present financial policies, although several small schools sometimes combine resources to employ a guidance specialist. Usually the principal attempts to organize and develop the guidance program and in many cases does a great deal of individual counseling himself. He may or may not have the necessary training to assume such responsibilities. It is almost certain that he does not have the time to assume them. He often functions not only as a building principal, but as a district superintendent as well, and may in addition teach one or two classes. Some guidance responsibilities may be delegated to classroom teachers even in such small high schools, but there is no one with the time to see the program as a whole. Guidance services can be and have been provided in small high schools, but always under severe handicaps. We have here one of the most compelling arguments for district reorganization and high school consolidation.

For systematic and organized guidance services are not luxuries, but absolute necessities in our kinds of high schools. Although they exist in part to help the school exercise its functions in the area of personal-social objectives, they would still be necessary even if the school completely disclaimed such objectives. The only kind of high school that can even pretend to operate without guidance is one with a uniform program for all students, which assumes no responsibility for helping students grow in self-understanding and self-direction. Presumably no such high school exists in the United States, and it may be seriously doubted that such a high school exists anywhere. Much research has been done and needs to be done on the effectiveness of various approaches to guidance,[9] but no research can add to or subtract from the necessity of guidance. This is established beyond question in any society such as ours, which places its highest values on the dignity and importance of the human individual. Obviously, something that looks like guidance on the surface could be used to repress individuals and to mold them into patterns of conformity in a totalitarian group. But this would be a caricature of guidance, not guidance as it has been developed both in theory and practice in American secondary schools.

EXTRACLASS ACTIVITIES

The major function of extraclass activities is to provide opportunities for students to learn and to practice a variety of personal-social understandings and skills. As noted previously, extraclass activities include the spectacular events that attract public attention and sometimes public criticism, but they also include many aspects of school life to which public attention is rarely directed.

Controversy about extraclass activities usually centers on the

---

[9] An unusual body of research and one packed with illuminating details on many aspects of guidance is presented in Rothney, *op. cit.*, the report of a long-term, follow-up study of 690 students in four Wisconsin school systems.

question of emphasis or, as put by the critics, of overemphasis. There is no doubt that overemphasis is undesirable, since extraclass activities are only part of the curriculum and should never be regarded as all, or even most of it. The mistake usually made is to judge the degree of emphasis by the number of different kinds of activities in a given high school program. A fairly broad range is necessary to recognize and provide for differences in interests and abilities among students. Some groups may be very small and specialized. A school may have 50 different kinds of extraclass activities without overemphasis. On the other hand, it may have overemphasis with only three or four. The overemphasis takes place not in the total program of activities, but in the participation of students as individuals. A school with three or four kinds of activities may have 90 percent of the student body in no activities at all, but the other 10 percent may be taking more active part than is good for them. This is overemphasis.

Schools have often tried to handle individual student participation by means of general administrative regulations or formulas. In some cases these set a maximum figure of so many different activities in a given year or semester; in others some variation in the number of activities is introduced through a point system with greater weight for some activities than for others. Such arrangements may or may not be combined with the stipulation of a minimum grade-point-average in classroom studies. The latter provision is based on the idea that a student with low grades will do better work in classroom studies if he is not spending time on activities. This is true for some students, but certainly not with all, for the amount of time spent in study is only one element in classroom achievement. Except in the case of interscholastic athletics, which is usually regulated by regional or state associations, local schools may do as they see fit about this matter of individual student participation. Many have seen fit to dispense with general administrative formulas and to handle the matter through individual counseling. When the counseling is well done, this is by all means the better approach. The amount and nature of participation in extraclass activities should be considered for and with each student at the time classroom studies are selected for the semester or year. In some cases, additional counseling interviews should be scheduled to review and possibly modify the initial choices.

The same considerations apply to the question of minimum participation. Excessive enthusiasm for extraclass activities sometimes leads to statements that every student should take part in them. The sincerity behind such expressions may be commendable, but the idea itself is a mistake. It is a further mistake to carry out such an idea by making extraclass activity participation a graduation requirement. The choice of participation or no participation is one to be made by the individual student. While counselors and others may point out to students the advantages of such participation, they should not become excessively directive in urging reluctant students to get into things. Reluctant participation may sometimes be harmful to the student, and in any case it takes the edge off the spontaneity that should characterize the activities themselves.

One widely used device that sometimes threatens spontaneity in extraclass activities is the activity period scheduled in the school day. Nevertheless, the activity period should not be written off as a liability, for it serves in some cases as the only effective solution of still another problem, that of providing the time for activities to take place. At one time practically all activities took place after school, and some schools still do it this way. But this is out of the question for most schools that transport students by school bus. Neither can it be used in communities where many students have after-school jobs. Most high schools, therefore, have fallen back on the activity period for practically all activities except those of interscholastic athletics.

The activity period is often combined with the home room and is used some days for home room business, other days for activities, with certain days designated for clubs, student council meetings, assemblies, and the like. On club days, the students who do not belong to clubs stay in the home room to study or go to the library. Since adolescents rarely enjoy being left behind, many will go to the clubs whether they have any great interest in them or not. This has its good side in that it introduces some students to the advantages of participation who might otherwise never have gone at all. It has a bad side in that it often tends to fill the clubs with passive students who are content to leave the initiative and direction to the club sponsor. Many teachers have complained about the difficulty of motivating club members to assume some initiative in running their own club. This is a contradictory state of affairs, for no club ought even to exist unless the members of it are sufficiently interested to take responsibility for its direction.

Another aspect of the activity period that takes the edge off spontaneity is the practice of taking roll. In a given period, a student is supposed to be either in the home room or library, or at the meeting of his designated club. Unless the school wants to run the risk of letting students wander from the home room unchecked and possibly never get to the club meetings at all, roll taking becomes a necessity. It wastes a good deal of time, especially in large clubs, and most activity periods are too short to begin with.

On the whole, the activity period has not been a happy solution, and school staffs have continued to search for other ways of providing activity time during the school day. The extended lunch period represents a modification of the activity period with some distinct advantages, provided that a number of favorable circumstances exist for its application. A period of one hour and fifteen minutes, for example, will leave 45 minutes for activities, which is more time than is often scheduled for morning or afternoon activity periods. Students who do not take part in activities may go to the library, study in the home room, or simply sit down and talk in rooms designated for this purpose. There is no particular need to check attendance in the activity groups, since the lunch period is regarded as free time anyway. Of course students could be allowed to go visiting during the more conventional activity period, but the lunch hour with its traditional associations of social freedom and relaxation seems more suitable for this kind of flexibility.

Two conditions are necessary for this use of the lunch period. One is a cafeteria large enough to accommodate at least half the student body at one time. If the division is made on a grade-level basis, there will not be too much interference with activities, since ninth and tenth graders are usually not in the same groups as the upper-division students. Greater flexibility could be secured by having all the students eat at one time, but this is rarely possible.

The other condition is a closed campus, with no students permitted to leave during the noon period except those with permits to have lunch at home. This prevents the wandering on the streets and standing about on corners that might otherwise take place. Some object to this as authoritarian control, but it is no more so than compulsory school attendance itself, or compulsory attendance at classes and assembly programs. Schools with very short lunch periods, of course, do not need to close their campuses, since students have practically no free time after eating lunch anyway. This feature of the short lunch period is a negative virtue at best and does not offer the positive advantages of the extended period with proper controls.

The extended lunch period appears, then, to provide both a way of scheduling activities during the school day and of preserving a reasonable amount of spontaneity. An activity program without spontaneity is nothing but an irritation to teachers and students alike and is practically without value so far as personal-social objectives are concerned. For it is in the give-and-take of working together on jobs that students organize and develop by themselves, with only a minimum amount of adult guidance and direction, that much personal-social growth will take place. Some teacher-student and student-student planning can take place in classrooms, but it is limited both in amount and kind. When an extraclass activity is only a poor imitation of the least favorable characteristics of the classroom, it is probably less effective along these lines than the classroom itself, for it lacks the substance and subject matter of an organized body of material to hold it together.

Even though activities depend to a large extent on the spontaneity of student initiative and control, there is still a need for faculty sponsorship. The purpose of faculty sponsorship is not to annoy the students with adult supervision and control, but rather to provide adult teaching, without which it would be difficult to regard extraclass activities as part of the curriculum. Faculty sponsorship, however, means faculty assignments. This becomes the third major administrative problem in extraclass activities, joining the first two of determining the limits of student participation and the finding of time in the daily schedule.

Obviously, the sponsorship of an activity means work. It is usually as much work as teaching a class. Not all good classroom teachers are good sponsors of activities, and it follows that they should not be required to assume such responsibilities. Teachers who sponsor activities, then, will have more work than those who do not. There are three possible ways of resolving this awkward state of affairs: (1) to assign other extra duties of some kind to teachers who do not sponsor activities; (2) to provide extra pay for the activity sponsors; and (3) to reduce the classroom teaching loads of the activity sponsors. The first approach is limited by the number of extra duties that make sense; it is obvious nonsense to invent duties simply for this purpose. The second approach is based on the long-standing practice in many schools of paying extra for interscholastic athletic coaching. If this is done, there is no reason why extra pay should be withheld from those who sponsor school plays, newspapers, clubs, and the like. Usually the amount of extra pay, even for coaches, is so small as to have no more than token meaning. Some coaches, for example, have found their $400 or so extra annual pay coming down to something like 35 or 40 cents an hour. In addition this opens the door to the possibility of extra pay for a variety of teaching tasks, such as staying overtime for student makeup work and the like. What this would do in the long run to the basic teaching salary schedule may be left to the imagination. The third approach, that of reducing classroom teaching loads for activity sponsors, is the only sound one. It is sound because activity sponsorship for some teachers is a legitimate and important part of their work, not an extra item tacked on. Of course it would cost money, since additional teachers would be hired to teach the classes subtracted from loads of activity sponsors. Whether or not this is worth the cost depends on the value of extraclass activities in the teaching-learning program of the school.

Most of the other administrative policies governing extraclass activities should be developed by the student council and carried into effect by the student body organization. These groups are, of course, part of the total program of extraclass activities, and their main purpose is to help students learn the understandings and skills of managing their own affairs.[10] It is not to have the students run the school or to handle individual cases of student misconduct.[11] That is the responsibility of the teachers and administrators, acting in these capacities for the school board. Most of the students' own affairs, however, lie precisely in the general area of extraclass activities, and the students, through their legislative and administrative bodies, can and should assume responsibility for them. These will include the formation of new activities and activity groups, the undertaking of all-school projects, the management of student assemblies, the determination of student eligibility for various activities and activity groups, some financial policies, and other such matters. The matter of determining eligibility refers to such items as specific competence for a particular kind of activity, age or grade level requirements, and subject prerequisites, and

[10] As noted previously, the home room has for many years provided a simple and effective unit for student council representation. "The school that elects its student council at large from the whole school can expect a quick growth and a quicker failure. The life of the whole is determined first of all by the soundness of its parts. The home-room organization is the core of the idea of pupil participation in government. It is here, so far as the school is effective, that the ability to be self-directive, in whatever degree it is attained, is first developed. This development in self-direction in the home room can come as a result of managing its own affairs and in sending representatives from this small group to the larger group, or groups, and these representatives bringing back for discussion and decision the recommendations of the larger groups." Fretwell, *op. cit.,* p. 32.

[11] Having students administer penalties to other students is one of the most unfortunate practices ever to grow up in connection with extraclass activities. It is unfortunate even when it appears to work in the sense of keeping things under control, for the handling of individual disciplinary cases should be a responsibility of the adult staff. "Although a few writers in the field of school activities and some high-school principals and sponsors claim that the so-called 'student court' provides an effective instrumentality for pupil participation in government, the consensus of opinion is unfavorable. The term *court* itself is unfortunate because it carries an implication of retribution. The offending pupil needs the skillful guidance and sympathetic understanding of a teacher, and should not be irritated by penalties often unwisely imposed by his immature peers. The agency for pupil participation in government should not be permitted to degenerate into a police department. The trend is definitely away from the policy whereby a large portion of the activities of the council is related to disciplinary matters. Police powers do not contribute to the state of mind which should be developed in pupils who participate in the government of the school; they can devote their time, attention, and efforts more profitably to a multitude of other activities." Louis R. Kilzer, Harold H. Stephenson, and H. Orville Nordberg, *Allied Activities in the Secondary School,* Harper & Brothers, 1956, p. 164.

does not include the determination of general eligibility requirements, which is the province of the faculty.

While the major purpose of extraclass activities is to foster personal-social development, it is by no means the only purpose. Many activities contribute to the further learning of academic understandings and skills. In some cases, an extraclass activity provides the means of stimulating unusual achievement on the part of academically gifted students, especially in English, science, and mathematics. Clubs in these and other fields draw for adult leadership not only on the teaching staff, but on talented members of the general public. Extraclass activities also offer another means of vocational exploration and guidance. Although working on the school paper does not usually come under the heading of vocational training for journalism, it can and does help some adolescents consider the possibility of journalism as a career. This possibility is implicit in practically all the activities offered in a school. Since lifelong interests may be formed in activities as well as in classroom studies, the area of leisure-time use is served as well. Extraclass activities, therefore, may have many purposes, some of which are also served by the classroom studies.

This overlapping of purposes has led some writers to deplore the line drawn between classroom studies and extraclass activities and to seek ways of merging these two portions of the curriculum. One of the mechanical devices for accomplishing this is to give credit for activities, thereby erasing one of the distinctions. Unless this credit counts toward the credits required for graduation, the gesture is rather meaningless. If it does count toward graduation, it may serve as a bookkeeping device to keep track of the progress of those students, usually those of low academic ability, who may not be taking full programs of classroom studies. Such bookkeeping, however, is unnecessary. It is simpler to modify the classroom-unit requirements for such students as individuals on the basis of agreements reached among counselors, parents, and the students themselves. On the whole, the granting of activity credits accomplishes little in the way of merging classroom instruction and the activity program, while adding a great deal of unnecessary record keeping.

Another way of breaking down the distinction is to take some activities and offer them as classroom studies. Those who work on the school paper, for example, enroll in a journalism class and receive grades and credits, which count the same as those of any other subject. This creates difficulties, however, for students who want to work on the school paper, but who want to take four or five other classes for credit. It is possible, of course, to accept on the staff of the school paper some students enrolled in journalism and others who are not. This becomes confusing for the faculty sponsor, especially if he is also the journalism teacher and if he tries to get part of the work on the school paper done in class. About the only way of avoiding this confusion is to separate the production of the school paper from the studies of the journalism classroom. Members of the class would still be eligible for the school paper staff, but would like others on the staff come in after school or during the activity period. Such a separation of functions defeats the purpose of breaking down the distinction between classroom studies and extraclass activities.

Not all advocates of merging the classroom studies and the extraclass activities attempt to do so through mechanical devices. They contend rather for the incorporation into the classroom studies of the kinds of procedures and teacher-student relationships that seem to characterize a good extraclass activity program. If the classroom studies were characterized by flexibility and informality, made greater use of teacher-student planning, and provided more specifically for personal-social development, there would be, according to this argument, little or no need for extraclass activities at all.

This approach is a more fundamental one than the various mechanical devices, such as granting credit for activities or the deliberate scheduling of a traditional activity on a classroom basis. It also raises the more fundamental question about the validity of trying to break down the present distinctions. There is no more reason for bringing about a general merger of all parts of the curriculum than there is for trying to integrate all the instructional fields. Obviously, classroom studies can and do accomplish some of the purposes of extraclass activities, and the latter in turn make supplementary contributions to the purposes of the classroom studies. Nevertheless, each has its major purpose to fulfill and its own distinctive approach to that purpose. What we need in the curriculum are more, not fewer, means of instruction that can fulfill distinctive purposes in distinctive ways and will make the school program as a whole more flexible in its services to students as individual human beings.

SCHOOL-RELATED WORK EXPERIENCE

Many high school students have part-time jobs for pay. These do not become school-related work experience, as the term is usually defined, unless the school definitely relates the work to the attainment of instructional purposes. Such purposes include specific job training, vocational exploration, the development of personal-social qualities important in jobs generally, and the application and further learning of the instructional fields; the specific purposes will vary from one student to the next. Work experience with or without pay, therefore, is a curricular means that may be used with students on all levels of ability and with widely varying personal and vocational goals.

Work experience for specific job training has long been a feature of high school vocational programs under the various acts providing federal funds. The broadening of work experience to include more general objectives demands administrative arrangements beyond those that have served for the more specific vocational programs. Supervisors are needed to deal with the program on an all-school basis. Since work experience is usually not part of the required program for non-vocational students, additional responsibilities must be assumed by guidance departments. The amount and kind of work experience for any student in a given semester or year must necessarily be related to the classroom studies and other activities that make up the rest of that student's program. All of this may and often does involve conferences in which the student, the counselor, and the work-experience supervisor come together to weigh the various possibilities.

The general values of work experience are applicable to many students, but this does not justify required work experience, which is sometimes advocated by enthusiasts, although not practiced in the schools. Whether or not it is advisable for a given student to engage in work experience at a given time depends on circumstances unique to himself. In addition, required work experience obviously would not be feasible in many communities.

On the other hand, the values of work experience are not necessarily confined to students of any given level of academic intelligence. For the academically gifted student, the right kind of job may provide not only general values in human relationships and the like, but also curricular enrichment in the instructional fields. Gifted students have worked in editorial offices, in hospitals, in science and engineering laboratories, and in other situations that provide applications of academic learning and demand high-level academic intelligence. The Santa Barbara County, California, schools have provided one example of work experience programs making specific provisions for gifted students, as well as for those on other levels.[12]

Those who are low or below average in academic ability may also profit from the general vocational values of work experience. Many of these students will enter jobs that neither demand nor justify technical job training in the high school program of studies, but do demand good human relationships, character traits, and the like. In many of the jobs available to a low-ability student, these personal qualities will constitute his most important assets. If such students take reduced loads in the classroom, they can profitably devote part of their remaining school time to the work-experience part of the curriculum. Again, this does not mean that work experience is necessarily indicated for all students low in academic ability, for every one of these students is unique and cannot be put into a single all-inclusive category.

The development and supervision of work-experience programs involve policies on a number of specific issues and questions. One of these is the matter of credit. This is an operational question,

[12] For a description of the Santa Barbara program in its various aspects see DeWitt Hunt, *Work Experience Education Programs in American Secondary Schools,* U.S. Department of Health, Education, and Welfare, Office of Education, Bulletin 1957, No. 5, pp. 20–22.

which although of considerable practical importance in some schools does not fundamentally affect the value of the program one way or the other. Granting credit does not automatically make work experience part of the curriculum; nor does absence of formal credit keep it from being curricular. Work experience is made part of the curriculum by the kinds of provisions made by the school for the attainment of instructional objectives through its use. Some students, of course, will have reduced programs in the classroom studies during the semesters in which they are engaged in work experience. This matter can be adjusted either by keeping the 16-unit graduation requirement (or whatever it may be in a given school) and granting work-experience credit, or by reducing the number of units for graduation for these students. In either case it is a matter of academic record-keeping. On the whole it seems simpler to reduce the number of required units; this clearly eliminates the question of giving marks in work experience and the related frustrations of trying to incorporate or avoid incorporating these marks in the student's grade point average.

Another policy question, one of greater importance, is that of trying to find jobs for students. Some work-experience supervisors prefer not to undertake this responsibility, contending that the finding of the job is one of the valuable learning activities for the student himself. In most cases, of course, finding jobs for students is unnecessary, and there would be little justification for an elaborate placement apparatus. On the other hand, the policy should permit job finding for those students who in the judgment of all concerned would profit from work experience, but who for one reason or another cannot find their own jobs. In any case, whether students find their own jobs or not, the work-experience supervisor always checks the job under consideration for an individual student, not only in terms of the actual job conditions, but in relation to the student's abilities and other circumstances. In some school systems, work-experience supervisors categorically exclude certain kinds of jobs from consideration, either because they promise little in the way of educational value or for other reasons.

Whether or not the work should always be paid work is another issue on which there has been a good deal of debate. As far as terminology goes, the term "school-related work experience" is sometimes restricted to paid work, sometimes made more inclusive to cover work done without pay. A school may use either or both. Common sense suggests that many of the claimed values of work experience are unique neither to the paid nor the unpaid variety. Still, for many students, paid work makes a potential contribution to the attainment of developmental tasks such as the achievement of adult socioeconomic status. This varies from one student to the next and should be considered by the student and his counselor in making the work-experience decision.

Opportunities for paid work experience will be severely limited in some communities all the time and in other communities some of the time. When times are bad, available jobs obviously should and will go to adults. Under such circumstances, placing students even in unpaid jobs in private employment will as a matter of general policy gain little community support. It becomes necessary, then, to seek work-experience opportunities in service projects and activities that do not usually require or use paid services of adults.

SCHOOL-AND-COMMUNITY SERVICE PROJECTS

These school-and-community service projects provide many of the same values as does private employment, either on a paid or unpaid basis, and are obviously closely related to work experience as a general category in the curriculum. Sometimes they are identified as a separate category, but this is merely a matter of classification. They should not, however, be regarded merely as something we turn to when other kinds of work experience are not available. Such projects have alleged objectives of their own and may be legitimately included in the school program at all times, either with or without the other kinds of work experience.

The major objective claimed for school-and-community service projects is that of civic responsibility. This includes not only the disposition to participate in civic matters, but the necessary understandings and skills to do so effectively. Again, this depends on a number of assumptions that cannot be easily verified, but seem reasonable and valid in the light of general observation and experience. Among possible projects along these lines are school cleanup campaigns, paper and scrap drives, preparation of vacant and available land for playgrounds or athletic fields, conservation projects, community beautification, and fact-gathering surveys on such community matters as occupational trends and traffic conditions. Such projects may evolve from classroom studies or extraclass activities and in some cases may develop independently of other aspects of the curriculum. The activities of the Owatonna, Minnesota, art project presented in the chapter on the visual arts serve as an example of the initiative that may be taken in a given instructional field. In such cases it is difficult to draw a precise line between this portion of the curriculum and the classroom studies; they become valid instances of the integration of various aspects of the school program desired by some students of curriculum. Fortunately it is not necessary either to achieve such overall integration of the school program or, on the other hand, to be universally successful in keeping differing parts of the school program distinct and separate from one another.

Some high schools have identified such projects as distinctive features of their curricula. One of these high schools, widely known as a community school,[13] is that of Pulaski, Wisconsin. The curriculum of the Pulaski High School includes a full program of classroom studies, plus guidance and extraclass activities, but special attention has been devoted to this matter of community service. Projects have originated in and been closely related to the classroom studies and other parts of the curriculum. One outgrowth of fact-finding surveys carried on by social studies classes was the development of new industries that have contributed substantially to strengthening the economic base of community life. Citizens of the community, including many of the high school students, built a factory that was leased to an outside company for the manufacture of shoes. This factory has provided not only full-time and all-year jobs, but also part-time and short-term jobs during slack sea-

---

[13] This term is extensively used in the literature, but in many different ways. Most schools that consider themselves in this category or are so considered emphasize community service projects both for community improvement and as learning. See National Society for the Study of Education, Fifty-second Yearbook, pt. 2, *The Community School,* The Society, 1953.

sons on the farms; for the Pulaski community includes both the central village and the surrounding countryside. Other new industries have been developed along similar lines. One of the unique features of the Pulaski program has been the use of the school paper as a newspaper for the entire community. It contains the usual items of school news, but in addition includes other matters of community-wide interest and concern. This paper serves an important function for a community too small to support one on a private-enterprise basis. So the possibilities of community-service projects are many and varied, limited only by the imagination and energies of the school staff and of the community members themselves.

Such a distinctive emphasis on school-and-community service projects is more feasible and more desirable in some high schools than in others. Furthermore, no high school, not even the one at Pulaski, has or needs to have some identifiable project going on at all times. Community projects, however, are rich in possibilities for general education in citizenship and may, in addition, contribute to some of the values of other kinds of work experience. Every community, accordingly, should explore the possibilities of such projects and carefully consider the desirability of incorporating them in the high school curriculum.

All the non-classroom aspects of the curriculum considered in this chapter have important potential contributions to the objectives of secondary schooling. No two schools will have identical programs in the non-classroom curriculum. Community circumstances will govern both the selection of particular kinds of activities and the degree of attention or identification accorded those selected. As far as the broad categories are concerned, no high school that professes the concern for the individual implied in our general objectives of secondary schooling can neglect or omit making provisions for counseling or guidance. Classroom instruction plus guidance, therefore, are essential components of every high school program. The others are matters of choice. A high school may omit extraclass activities and school-related work experience and still be a good high school in terms of most or all of the criteria implied in our objectives. It is difficult to imagine an American high school without extraclass activities, but the existence of such a high school is at least a theoretical possibility. On the other hand, many high schools have no programs for work experience whatsoever. These are matters on which high schools properly have considerable local autonomy, since the choices obviously depend on those circumstances and characteristics that make every local community different from all others.

Bibliography

Brewer, John M., *The Vocational Guidance Movement: Its Problems and Possibilities,* The Macmillan Company, 1918.

Fretwell, Elbert K., *Extra-Curricular Activities in Secondary Schools,* Houghton Mifflin Company, 1931.

Gordon, Ira, *The Teacher as a Guidance Worker,* Harper & Brothers, 1956.

Hunt, DeWitt, *Work Experience Education Programs in American Secondary Schools,* U.S. Department of Health, Education, and Welfare, Office of Education Bulletin 1957, No. 5.

Johnston, Edgar C., and Faunce, Roland C., *Student Activities in Secondary Schools,* The Ronald Press Company, 1952.

Kilzer, Louis R.; Stephenson, Harold H.; and Nordberg, H. Orville, *Allied Activities in the Secondary School,* Harper & Brothers, 1956.

Kirkendall, Lester A., and Zeran, Franklin R., *Student Councils in Action,* Chartwell House, Inc., 1953.

National Society for the Study of Education, Fifty-second Yearbook, pt. 2, *The Community School,* The Society, 1953.

Parsons, Frank, *Choosing a Vocation,* Houghton Mifflin Company, 1909.

Rothney, John W. M., *Guidance Practices and Results,* Harper & Brothers, 1958.

Tompkins, Ellsworth, *The Activity Period in Public High Schools,* Federal Security Agency, Office of Education, Bulletin 1951, No. 19.

CHAPTER 22

Present and Future Possibilities: A Summary

It is necessary in any enterprise to identify what matters a great deal, what matters less, and what matters not at all. This necessity applies to questions concerning the high school curriculum, especially in periods of analysis and appraisal such as the present. The materials for this sorting are at hand in the extensive and diversified body of writing and thinking about high schools in the past several decades. This literature expresses our enduring convictions, our doubts, our apparent achievements and failures, and it affords some insight into where we seem to be going. Much of this has been reviewed in numerous proposals for improving or correcting our high school programs from various points of view.

The preceding chapters of this book have been devoted to examination of many of these materials in relation to specific questions of high school practice, extending to details of selecting and organizing content in our instructional fields. This chapter consists of an attempt to identify in broad outline those fundamental considerations which appear to matter most in the development of high school programs. Obviously there is room for disagreement on points such as these, and they are accordingly presented not as final pronouncements, but as theses for discussion, study, and debate.

First, we need to recognize and to take pride in our convictions about the universalizing of secondary schooling. This means continued effort in the direction of guaranteeing to all normal youth the opportunity to enter high school and to remain through the period usually designated as the twelfth grade, either in public or private schools. By normal youth are meant all whose general intelligence level is above the point identified with the need for special or institutional care and who are prepared to live and work with teachers and fellow students on the basis of everyday, decent human relationships. Our American convictions along these lines are based on what the high schools can and should do both for the individual development of students and for the benefit of society as a whole. They are implicit in our ideals of individual opportunity and responsibility in a free, open, and competitive society. True, these motives are sometimes mixed with others of a less desirable character, but our highest ideals are those in which we can take pride, the kind of pride that includes some humility as well. And we do usually take pride in our ideals of universal secondary schooling, except for those periods of frustration and dismay when we turn angrily on ourselves and what we cherish most. The first fundamental consideration in the high school curriculum is to remember that we do as a people believe in universal secondary schooling, even in periods of population increase when additional facilities, staffs, and the like must be provided.

A second fundamental consideration is that the free, popular, and universal high school exists both to transmit culture and to foster individual development along the lines represented by the aspects-of-living objectives such as intellectual development, moral development, citizenship, and the like. Accordingly, there is no conflict between subject matter and students. Neither is complete without the other. Subject matter divorced from human beings is pointless; individual development without participation in the intellectual and moral traditions of our common humanity is incomprehensible. This is not to say that the energy that went into the long-sustained controversy about curriculums based on subject matter versus curriculums based on needs was wasted. In fact, it was necessary to make a thorough exploration of all possible aspects of the matter, for the impression of apparent conflict is not always easy to avoid. Some attention will always need to be paid to this matter, for without it we may easily relapse into the old debate about teaching subjects or teaching students.

The high school is not unique in being concerned both with subject matter and with students. Schools at other levels have the same concerns as well. The function of the high school in relation to each of these concerns is, however, distinctive to the high school itself. With regard to cultural transmission, the high school transmits more of the culture than is possible in the years of elementary schooling and it does so on a less specialized basis than is done in the college or university. It does so through the general studies, some of which are common studies, that is, required of all students, while others are elective. Schooling, however, is always continuous from one level to the next; no one level of schooling is divorced from those adjacent to it. High schools continue the teaching of the skills of literacy, although the fundamentals of literacy are the responsibility of the elementary school. Some work in high school is directed toward specialized preparation for jobs, although highly specialized education for this purpose is primarily the responsibility of the college, university, or vocational school. Similarly, elementary schools begin teaching some of the general studies. Colleges and universities, in addition to providing specialized professional education, also include some general studies on an advanced basis, particularly during the first two undergraduate years. Each level of schooling, however, still has its own distinctive function in cultural transmission, and it is this distinctive role that provides the bases on which practices at each level may be studied.

The high school also has an obviously distinctive function with regard to individual development in the various aspects-of-living objectives. It is to foster such individual development during the adolescent years. The elementary school does so during the years of childhood, while the college does so with adults. Adolescents are neither young children nor adults; therein lies one of the unique characteristics of secondary schooling. Continuity of schooling must be recognized on this point as well as in relation to cultural transmission, for adolescents were young children yesterday and will be adults tomorrow. There are no sharp breaks between one level and the next; growth is continuous. Nevertheless, adolescence is a distinctive period in human development, and adolescents have their own distinctive needs and tasks.

Third, the function of cultural transmission defines the scope and nature of the classroom studies in the curriculum. The subject organization is the major vehicle for this cultural transmission. There are many ways of naming subjects, and the categories may range from the very specific to the very comprehensive. But no formulation of categories for the high school that starts with the idea of human cultural achievement will wander far from the 12 or 13 families of subjects that make up our major general fields of instruction. The commitment of our high schools to these fields and to the subject organization including them is demonstrated by the fact that other approaches to organizing the classroom studies, such as core, have not prospered in spite of the intensive study and experimentation devoted to them. The subject organization by no means precludes some valid use of core classes, but enthusiasm for core has apparently never been strong enough in most quarters to establish it even as a partial modification of the general pattern.

Our instructional fields and the various courses within them provide, then, a working definition of the transmitted culture both in broad outline and in specific detail. In this connection, it is important to recognize that the great majority of high schools have not departed from this definition. Popular articles have spread a mistaken notion that many high schools offer courses in dating, personality development, and the like. This has never been the case in the history of the United States high school. It is true that some high schools have offered units on such matters under the traditional or conventional course designations. This is unfortunate, not only for the amount of time subtracted from the courses in which they are included, but because such units are dubious and possibly dangerous approaches to the objectives of personal-social development. Subject matter learned in the classroom has many potential contributions to personal-social development, but it does not follow that personal-social problems provide useful categories for unit organization. Besides, we must not forget that extraclass activities and the life of the school as a whole provide direct experience in human relationships and in general social development.

It is equally important for those who consider themselves educational liberals to realize that subject organization and cultural transmission do not imply rigid, authoritarian teaching centered on the absorption and regurgitation of meaningless facts. True, such teaching has sometimes been carried on, but not by virtue of the subject organization. Cultural transmission means not only passing on the culture of the past, but developing in students the intellectual qualities for advancing and enriching the culture of the future. Subject organization not only permits but demands the fostering of creativity and inquiry through a variety of teaching practices and procedures. In every subject, however, creativity and inquiry depend on knowledge and effort, and it remains part of the teacher's job to clarify and explain, even at times to insist that materials and techniques be correctly learned to the limit of students' abilities at various growth levels. But this is a far cry indeed from the straw-man image of subject-matter teaching as the meaningless memorizing of words.

Retention of the subject organization, furthermore, does not imply a static curriculum. Every instructional field in the high school curriculum is today undergoing rigorous scrutiny and study. Many things accepted in the past are being questioned by the specialists in these fields. New points of view are being applied to the examination not only of traditional content, but of traditional sequences and forms of organization. New content is accumulating and demanding to be included. It appears in fact that the subject organization instead of being the preserver of rigid custom is today the most powerful stimulus to the study and improvement of the high school program.

Fourth, every high school student deserves an individualized curriculum shaped to his own abilities, interests, and goals. The function of cultural transmission does not mean that identical subject matter is transmitted to every student. True, there is an overall or general curriculum that applies to a high school as a whole and contains all the means available for the fostering of individual student development. But no student ever uses this whole curriculum. He makes his selections from it, preferably on the basis of adult advice for parents, teachers, and counselors. A portion of every student's curriculum is normally set by the common requirements or constants, but even these should be flexible enough to permit exceptions in individual cases. Beyond these constants, the widest possible provisions for individualization should be established and maintained. Some students may take five or even more academic subjects; for others at given times it may be advisable to take fewer than the standard program of four. This means that the quantity of subjects defined for graduation should not be rigidly fixed. In addition to selecting subjects, students also make choices in the non-classroom means of instruction, such as extraclass activities, school-related work experience, and school-and-community service projects. There are no general formulas adequate to determine the individual participation of students in these portions of the curriculum. In all of this, individual counseling is indispensable. Counseling is in itself part of the curriculum, for it is a means of teaching, but it is also the means by which students are helped to make selections from the curriculum as a whole.

Track plans are never a substitute for counseling and may in fact interfere with adequate selection of subjects by the students. Particularly unfortunate has been the dualism implied by the so-called college-preparatory track on one hand and all the other tracks—business, general, vocational, agricultural—on the other. From this has flowed the disastrous notion that foreign languages, mathematics in the algebra-geometry-trigonometry sequence, and the physical sciences are appropriate only for college-bound students. The long identification of these subjects with the college-preparatory track as such will require that counselors make special efforts to call the attention of all competent students, college-bound or otherwise, to their educational values. Apart from this, college-bound students should be advised on the basis of the specific requirements of colleges they might enter and of the specific programs they may pursue at the college level.

The importance of viewing every student's curriculum as one unique to himself applies also to provisions for those who are among the academically gifted. A gifted student might, for example, satisfy a portion of his required courses through attainment examinations, thereby leaving time for independent study under faculty direction or for desirable kinds of school-related work experience or community-service projects. Other provisions for gifted students, such as college-level courses and ability grouping in regular courses, also require flexibility and individualized counseling for their most effective application.

Fifth, the maintaining of academic standards depends on accurate recording of student achievement, not on punitive measures or symbols. As long as the conventional report card is used, the marks should represent student achievement as defined by teachers in the various school departments and in terms independent of class average, student attitude, student growth in relation to ability, or student placement in ability sections. It is not necessary, however, to regard low marks as automatic failure in the sense of depriving the student of credit toward graduation. Whether or not a given student with a low mark should repeat a course or be deprived of credit depends again on the characteristics and circumstances of that student as an individual, and the decision should be one arrived at in a counseling situation involving the teacher, the counselor, the student, and, if possible, the parents. Under such a policy, it would be unnecessary to introduce extraneous considerations into the marking system itself. Student records would provide accurate information on achievement and could be used as such by colleges, prospective employers, or others concerned.

Sixth, it is necessary to recognize but not to misinterpret the importance of good teachers and of good teaching conditions. Without these, even the best possible curriculum could not be effectively applied. We need teachers who know and are interested in their subjects, who possess and are adding to broad and rich general or liberal educations, who understand and are interested in adolescents as people, who understand the history of schooling and the relationship of school to society, and who are reasonably proficient in the procedures of teaching. Obviously, the preservice education of teachers should provide the beginning stages of all these qualities. In addition, the work schedules of such teachers should permit ample leisure time, not only for continued formal education, but for personal and private study and reading. This requires reassessment of demands made on teachers in community activities and in the busy-work chores that run rampant even in the best school systems.

On the other hand, good teachers do not in and of themselves define a good curriculum and in fact are seriously hampered when a good curriculum is not in effect. A good curriculum is one consistent with valid and defensible purposes, which in turn depend on the identification of values related not only to schooling, but to many other aspects of the human enterprise. But a good curriculum does not remain good without constant attention from all who are engaged in its application. Changes must and will take place, but the process of making change should be one of orderly and reflective study and decision making in the light of relevant and valid purposes. This means continuous curriculum planning in every school and community. Such a process necessarily involves teachers, but it does not require every teacher to serve at all times on curriculum committees. It does require that every teacher take some part in faculty study and discussion of important school decisions. School administrators, whether superintendents or principals, obviously have general and specific responsibilities in establishing and maintaining the conditions under which effective curriculum planning can take place.

While such curriculum planning is centered in local school communities, it reflects and takes into account the guidelines established by state policy, as well as those concerns which from time to time occupy the country as a whole. Nation-wide controversies and discussions in the public press will of course suggest matters worthy of examination and study in local schools. But local schools and communities must at all times guard against the temptation to be caught up in national bandwagon movements. Our miracles of mass communication through television, radio, magazines, and newspapers do make it possible for wisdom to be widely dispersed in the shortest possible time. They also make it possible for snap judgments and slogans to be so dispersed as well. The responsibility for discriminating between wisdom and the lack of it rests finally with teachers and other citizens in local communities, and this responsibility must never be surrendered, either overtly or by default.

In addition to evaluating the spontaneous national enthusiasms or frustrations that spring up from time to time, local communities have the additional responsibility of critically studying the more carefully considered reports of national conferences or commissions. These have long been a feature of American educational history, and from time to time major assessments of secondary schooling have not only pointed new directions, but have supplied materials for intelligent study, discussion, and criticism for many years after they appeared. Some of them deserve study today, particularly the 1894 report of the Committee of Ten on Secondary School Studies and the 1918 report of the Commission on the Reorganization of Secondary Education. These two reports did not reach identical or even similar conclusions; one may disagree with either or both. But they shared some important and praiseworthy characteristics: (1) they were not doctrinaire schemes, but appraisals of historical realities, designed as responses to specific conditions and problems; (2) although rooted in the realities of their own times, they were not mere expedients to contend with uproars of the moment; and (3) the writers of these documents used historical perspective to relate the issues of their own day to more enduring questions of educational policy and value. They proposed for the future, but they also summarized and incorporated the past.

We are today apparently heading toward another major attempt to reconstruct the theory and practice of secondary schooling in terms appropriate to our own times and to what we can discern of future conditions and circumstances. The middle decades of the twentieth century have produced not only many deeply felt if somewhat contradictory criticisms of secondary schooling but a great variety of plans to put our high schools right from this or that point of view. As the criticisms are assessed and as the proposed plans are put to the test of criticism in publications and in conferences both national and local, certain lines of conviction and commitment will probably appear. At some favored time, they will come together in a new platform for our secondary schools, new in the sense of creativity, but yet old in its incorporation of past experience and wisdom.

In the meantime we shall in our local communities be devoting our attention to the resolution of immediate dilemmas and to the achievement of specific improvements in high school theory and practice, all of which will find their way into the future casting of accounts. It is difficult in a period such as ours to avoid confusion and frustration, especially in dealing with the complicated issues of the high school curriculum. Nevertheless healthy criticism and innovation will go on. The only thing that can stop it and can head off the anticipated future summary of our current efforts will be loss of interest in the whole matter on the part of the people of the United States themselves. This and this alone would be the final catastrophe for our high schools. If, on the other hand, we continue to take our high schools seriously enough to engage in criticism and study, we shall be moving closer to the time when the words of John Dewey, "What the best and wisest parent wants for his own child, that must the community want for all its children," will apply not only to elementary schools, but to high schools as well.

INDEX